Travel with
Kids

William Gray

For my wife, Sally, and children, Joseph and Eleanor

D1372380

Take your kids travelling! Take them now! Children grow up fast and you'll never find a better, more rewarding opportunity to enrich their lives, minds and souls – or yours – than during a family holiday. It doesn't matter whether you skive off work and take them for a day trip to the seaside or rent out the house and embark on a three-month expedition across Asia. From bucket-and-spade to epic escapade, family holidays create memories that will live with you long after your children have grown up. They provide quality time away from the rush and stress of everyday life; they are precious, hard-earned and over all too quickly. Yes, they can also be pricey and hard work – and occasionally they might not go to plan. But they are always money well spent, and even the bad bits inspire priceless family jokes in years to come. So, ignore all those miserable types who pour scorn on this indispensable part of life – whose blinkered, joyless view of family holidays never sees beyond travel sickness, stroppy teenagers or how parents could possibly enjoy themselves without banishing the children to a crèche or kids' club 12 hours a day. Travelling with kids is about making compromises to meet everyone's needs. It's about sharing and bonding as a family unit. It's the immeasurable pleasure and satisfaction of showing your children just how amazing the world is; of seeing their faces light up at things you might otherwise have taken for granted. Family holidays allow you to take stock of life and appreciate what's really important. So seize them. Travel with your kids. Do it this year and every year you can.

> 66 *There have been fraught moments when it hasn't been so much a holiday, as a 'hell-a-day'. But I can honestly say I don't regret a thing. Family holidays are often hard work, but the rewards are rich. Travelling with Joe and Ellie is like exploring the world afresh. I wouldn't want to leave home without them.*
>
> *Will*

INTRODUCTION

3

Contents

Greece & Turkey 199

Scandinavia 223

Africa 245

Asia 273

Australia & New Zealand 303

North America 329

Latin America 359

About the book

Structure

Travel with Kids is unique. No other guidebook provides such detailed coverage of worldwide family travel. Over the following pages you will find inspiration, advice and ideas for taking your children on holiday pretty much anywhere. The book is split into three main sections. The first is a *10 best holidays* guide to everything from world wonders to hard-to-please teenagers. The second, *Essentials*, deals with basics, like what to pack, how to get around and how to stay safe and healthy. The bulk of *Travel with Kids*, however, is dedicated to destinations. Each country or regional chapter is divided into five parts. An introduction sets the scene with a map and several family-friendly highlights. Next is *Kids' stuff* – packed with ideas, resources and activities to get children interested in each destination, whether it's books to read, games to play or traditional meals to try at home – while *Tots to teens* provides a holiday planner for various age groups. This is followed by the main part of each chapter – a detailed look at the family-holiday potential of key locations. *Grown-ups' stuff* rounds things off with essential information on travel nitty-gritty. Throughout *Travel with Kids*, look out for special features, such as *Telling tales* ... (where some well-known families reveal their holiday hotspots) and *Kids' top 10* – cool highlights seen from a youngster's perspective.

Coverage

Travel with Kids is designed to be both inspirational and informative. You will find plenty of advice, encouragement and reassurance to plan a lifetime of family holidays throughout Europe and beyond. You won't find exhaustive directories of family-friendly hotels and restaurants or laborious lists of post offices and tourist information centres. Nor will you find every country in the world featured. Those that have been selected, however, reflect a mixture of the most popular, unusual and exciting destinations to take your kids.

Environment

Some might argue that the best way parents can do their bit for the environment is to stay firmly grounded on holiday, rather than flying with their kids halfway around the world. There is no doubt that the environmental impact of aircraft emissions is a serious issue that needs tackling, but a stay-at-home policy is neither a practical nor desirable solution. Not only does just about every national park and numerous eco- and cultural-tourism projects rely on international travellers for their survival, but there is also a fundamental need for our children to see and experience the world's last wild places if they are to develop a real and profound appreciation and empathy for nature. *Travel with*

Kids is full of suggestions for supporting environmentally friendly organizations, activities and accommodation, including price indicators for offsetting the CO_2 emissions generated by your flights. You will also find details on how to travel to numerous destinations without flying.

Ages

Individual development varies greatly from child to child, but as a guide the following age categories are used throughout *Travel with Kids*:

Babies (0-18 months) Wonderfully portable, either in a stroller, papoose or backpack; may still be breastfed or require baby food; unable to communicate when things are wrong except through the obvious medium of bawling.

Toddlers/pre-school (18 months-4 years) Terrifyingly mobile, with issues of balance and fearlessness demanding constant surveillance; able to communicate more articulately when unwell or unsure about something.

Kids/school age (4-12 years) Insatiable thirst for just about everything; able to interact with other children and respond with sensitivity to certain issues; game for most activities but many may require adult supervision.

Teenagers (13 years+) Keen to be independent; prone to moody moments when everything seems boring, but can also be great 'adult' travel companions.

Above: Portrait of the author by a young artist (daughter, Ellie).

Key to symbols

Each of the main entries in this book is accompanied by a series of symbols. These are designed to give readers a quick summary of what each destination has to offer and for what age group.

- ◐ walking/trekking
- ◑ horseriding
- ◉ cycling
- ◎ swimming
- ◉ snorkelling/scuba diving
- ◉ canoeing/white-water rafting/kayaking
- ◉ sailing
- ◉ snowshoeing/cross-country skiing
- ◉ elephant/camel riding
- ◉ wildlife-watching/whale-watching/birdwatching
- ◉ Hot-air ballooning
- ◉ fishing
- ◉ extreme/adrenaline sports
- ◉ risk of malaria
- ◉ baby/toddler friendly
- ◉ ideal for short breaks
- ◉ ideal for teenagers
- ⅲ museums
- ◉ theme park
- ◉ ruins

About the author

It's hard to say which was the more pivotal moment of William Gray's travelling career – surviving his first long-haul flight with toddler twins or clinching the coveted Travel Writer of the Year award in 2002. One thing is certain, however. Few people are more qualified than the 38-year-old writer, photographer and father to compile the ultimate reference book on family travel. Not only did William present several family travel pieces for the 2006 series of the BBC's *Holiday* programme, but he is also the family travel columnist for *Wanderlust* magazine and regularly contributes features to *The Sunday Times* and numerous other national and international publications. A member of the British Guild of Travel Writers, William wrote and illustrated his first book at the age of 23. *Coral Reefs & Islands: The Natural History of a Threatened Paradise* was highly commended in the Conservation Book Prize, and acclaimed by Jonathan Porritt as "A truly impressive piece of work, as hard-hitting in its text as it is beautiful in its photographs." A sought-after photographer, William supplies images to several leading agencies including Photolibrary, Travel Ink and John Warburton-Lee. In 1995 William accompanied Patrick Lichfield as guest lecturer on the *Oriana*'s maiden Atlantic crossing and he now gives slide talks throughout the UK. William is married to Sally, an educational editor and author. Their seven-year-old twins, Joseph and Eleanor, have totted up over 350 hours' flying time, investigated the electrical hazards of countless hotel rooms, destroyed the ambience of several dozen restaurants, thrown up in six different car seats, trekked through the Atlas Mountains, kayaked in New Zealand and made fire with Bushmen. For more information, check out william-gray.co.uk.

Photography

Most of the images in *Travel with Kids* are by the author, William Gray. See Photography Credits on page 391 for a full list of other photographic contributors.

Acknowledgements

Travel with Kids has been very much a family effort. It wouldn't have been possible without the tremendous support of my wife, Sally, who is not only a brilliant mother to our twins, Joseph and Eleanor, but has also been the calming, super-efficient mastermind behind the extensive family trips we've undertaken for this book. As for Joe and Ellie, now seven, they have both responded superbly to every weird and wonderful travel experience their parents have hauled them off on. They are fantastic little travellers, always happy to confront new challenges, whether it's learning to surf or coping with jetlag. I feel privileged and immensely proud to have shared so many wonderful experiences with them around the world – and I hope this book will be the inspiration for many more to come.

I must also say a huge thank you to family and friends for their help, advice, constant encouragement and for putting up with my antisocial behaviour during the writing of this book; particular thanks to my parents, parents-in-law, Simon Gray, Sue Dayus, Adam Gray and Gill Gray.

I owe a huge debt of gratitude to the many people who have taken the time to share their family travel experiences and supply quotes for the book. My apologies to those whose quotes could not be squeezed in: Matt Berna, Chris Breen, Maxine Browning, Emma Bunce, Simon Calder, Katie Derham, Judith Escribano & Steen Eriksson, Emily Gage, Judith & John Gage, Sarah & Philip Gale, Lottie Gale, Tina Gandy, David Gower, David Gray, Kerrina Gray, Robert Gray, Sanka Guha, Martin Henderson, Sarah & Duncan Hetherington, Charlotte Hindle, Jason Hobbins, Rachel Hosier, Charlotte & Huw Jenkins, Samuel Jenkins, Dan Linstead, Celia & Alan Littlefield, The Mason family, Caroline & Robin Mewes, Chris McIntyre, Lori & John Oestreich, Charlie Panton, Victoria & Mark Pougatch, Sir Steve Redgrave, Alison & Alex Rippon, Ben Roseveare, Sharon Ryan, India Seely, David Shepherd, Magdalena Slawecka-Williams, Jennifer Stevens, The Stockwell family, Sally & Chris Sugg, Su & Carl Taylor, Olivia Titmuss, Sarah Tucker, Mike Unwin, Antonia Vaquero, Sara Wheeler, David Wickers, The Williams Family, Alison & David Williams, Emma Woollacott, Hannah Wright, Mark Wright, Mike Wynne.

I am particularly grateful to Dr Jane Wilson-Howarth for checking the main health and safety section of the book and I strongly recommend that all readers get hold of a copy of her excellent book, *Your Child Abroad* (Bradt). It's the only comprehensive English language health manual for kids.

Far too numerous to list, but grateful thanks must go to the hundreds of tour operators, tourist boards, travel PR companies, airlines etc who have supplied invaluable information and practical support for the research of this book. Thanks, also, to *Wanderlust* magazine and *The Sunday Times* Travel section for supporting my obsession with family travel.

Finally, I am immensely grateful to the team at Footprint for sharing my vision for *Travel with Kids* and for their support and patience as I effortlessly managed to sail past every deadline they gently imposed. They are without doubt the friendliest and most dedicated team I've had the pleasure of working with. Very special thanks to Alan Murphy and Patrick Dawson for their calming influence.

10 best holidays

Seeing endangered wildlife
The 10 wildlife holidays you simply have to take before it's too late

Grey Whale Migrations
Where? British Columbia.
Why? Play real-life Crusoes on this teenage family expedition, staying in wooden huts on an uninhabited island while learning how to identify grey whales and gather information that's crucial to their conservation. There's also plenty of time for kayaking, fishing and toasting marshmallows around the campfire.
How much? From £795 per person, including accommodation, meals and training.
Contact Earthwatch (earthwatch.org).

Andasibe-Mantadia
Where? Madagascar.
Why? Because that's where you will find the indri. First, you'll hear their haunting siren call, then it's off on guided walks through the rainforest to spot this enigmatic and endangered lemur. At Vakôna Forest Lodge, you can explore on horseback or by canoe, rounding off your adventure with beach time at Nosy Be.
How much? From £1800 per person for 14 days half board, including UK return flights.
Contact Cedarberg African Travel (cedarbergtravel.com).

Nature's Trail
Where? Costa Rica.
Why? Paddle a canoe through the jungle canals of Tortuguero National Park searching for sloths and poison-dart frogs. Watch turtles laying their eggs on wild Atlantic beaches and hike through the cloudforest of Monteverde Reserve on a quest for the elusive quetzal.
How much? From £5942 for a family of four (minimum age six) sharing a family room, including accommodation, local flights, excursions and most meals.
Contact Journey Latin America (journeylatinamerica.co.uk).

Elsa's Kopje
Where? Meru National Park, Kenya.
Why? The Private House at Elsa's Kopje has its own swimming pool and family room. Children of all ages are welcome and under fives stay free. Activities range from game drives to fishing, but the highlight is a visit to the Rhino Sanctuary – home to 21 black rhino and 35 white rhino.
How much? From US$1600 per day for four people on a full board basis.
Contact Cheli & Peacock (chelipeacock.com).

Pandas & Pagodas
Where? China.
Why? This Chinese odyssey not only takes in the country's cultural highlights, but also includes a visit to the giant panda breeding and research centre at Chengdu. Families will be able to learn about the project and – the big plus for kids – help feed baby giant pandas.
How much? From £2315 per adult and £2115 per child under 12 for a 13-day guided tour, including UK return flights, tours, transfers and some meals.
Contact Cox & Kings (coxandkings.co.uk).

Polar Bear Weekend
Where? Churchill, Canada.
Why? Churchill is transformed into the world's polar bear capital every October and November when these magnificent 'ice bears' gather on the tundra, waiting for the sea in Hudson Bay to freeze before they set off to hunt seals. Giant-wheeled tundra buggies provide the perfect (and safe) vantage for watching the polar bears in their natural habitat (and they're great fun to ride in too).
How much? From £1640 for a four-night package (child prices available on request).
Contact Discover the World (discover-the-world.co.uk).

Temples & Wildlife
Where? Northern India.
Why? The highlight of this nine-day family tour is a visit to Panna Tiger Reserve which supports a healthy population of Bengal tigers. Keoladeo Ghana National Park provides a chance to tick off dozens of bird species, while a visit to the Taj Mahal adds a slice of exotic culture.
How much? From £1495 per adult and £1325 per child under 12, including return UK flights, hotel and lodge accommodation and some meals.
Contact Naturetrek (naturetrek.co.uk).

Thonga Beach Lodge
Where? Maputaland, South Africa
Why? Join nocturnal walks along the shores of Mabibi Bay to record the nests of endangered leatherback and loggerhead turtles, snorkel on the stunning offshore coral reef, canoe on Lake Sibaya and spot monkeys and birds in the lush coastal forest.
How much? From £430 per adult and £215 per child sharing with parents for three nights full-board accommodation.
Contact Cedarberg Travel (cedarbergtravel.com).

Bears & Wolves
Where? Romania.
Why? The Carpathian Mountains are home to some of Europe's rarest wildlife, including bears, wolves and lynxes. Suitable for children aged seven and over, this four-day adventure provides an exciting opportunity to observe them in their forest stronghold – either by staking out a hide or tracking them with an experienced guide.
How much? From £929 per adult and £599 per child, including UK return flights, guesthouse accommodation and most meals.
Contact Families Worldwide (familiesworldwide.co.uk).

Headhunters of Borneo
Where? Sabah, Malaysia.
Why? The Kabili-Sepilok Forest Reserve in Sabah provides a lifeline to orang-utans that have been orphaned through deforestation or hunting. Boardwalks thread through the sanctuary to special feeding stations that provide intimate views of these endearing primates – just one of the highlights on this 13-day family adventure.
How much? From £1699 per adult and £1499 per child (aged 5-12), including UK return flights, all ground arrangements and some meals.
Contact The Adventure Company (adventurecompany.co.uk).

Above: Grey Whale migrations, British Colombia; **Above right:** Elsa's Kopje, Kenya.
Right: Polar Bear Weekend. **Top:** Nature's Trail, Costa Rica.

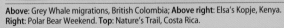

World wonders

The 10 family holidays that you have to take to see the best of the world's natural and cultural wonders

Rome Cavalieri Hilton
Where? Rome, Italy.
Why? For children, merely seeing the famous sights of Rome (one of the New World Wonders) instantly energizes all those dull history lessons at school, but the Cavalieri Hilton goes one step further with activities ranging from gladiator lessons (for children aged seven and over) to pizza making.
How much? From €325 per double room per night.
Contact Rome Cavalieri Hilton (www.cavalieri–hilton.it).

Reef and Rainforest
Where? Port Douglas, Queensland, Australia.
Why? With easy access to the Great Barrier Reef and Daintree Rainforest, Port Douglas offers a host of activities, from croc-spotting cruises and whitewater rafting to snorkelling trips and a dramatic Skyrail train journey to Kuranda in the Atherton Tablelands.
How much? From £4934 for a family of two adults and two children, including UK return flights, 10 nights accommodation and car hire.
Contact Bridge & Wickers (bridgeandwickers.co.uk).

The Land of the Incas
Where? Peru.
Why? Machu Picchu is the focus of this Peruvian family adventure which includes an exciting (but manageable) mixture of river rafting, mountain biking and sightseeing, before embarking on the classic day-hike to the impressive Lost City of the Incas. Then it's off to the Amazon for three days of jungle wildlife spotting.
How much? From £1395 per adult and children over 10 years for a 13-night tour, excluding international flights.
Contact KE Adventure Travel (keadventure.com).

Pharaohs and Feluccas
Where? Egypt.
Why? The wonders of ancient Egypt never fail to impress, but kids appreciate a bit of action too. On this trip, they'll view the Pyramids on camelback, glide down the Nile on a sailing felucca, ride a donkey to the Valley of the Kings and set out in a horse-drawn carriage to the amazing Karnak Temple complex.
How much? From £520 per person (minimum age six; no child reductions), including 12 nights accommodation and private air-conditioned transport.
Contact Imaginative Traveller (imaginative-traveller.com).

Beyond the Arctic Circle
Where? Finland.
Why? The mesmerizing Northern Lights will almost seem like a bonus on this six-day, action-packed Lapland break, where children (aged five and over) can get to grips with snowshoeing, cross-country skiing, ice-fishing and husky sledging.
How much? From £829 per adult and £769 per child, including UK return flights, hotel accommodation, most meals and activities.
Contact The Adventure Company (adventurecompany.co.uk).

The Mighty Himalaya
Where? Nepal.
Why? This 15-day family adventure seeks high and low for natural and cultural wonders, ranging from the wildlife of Chitwan National Park and the temples of Kathmandu to the magnificent peaks of the Annapurnas. There's even an option for a sightseeing flight over Mount Everest.
How much? From £1699 per adult and £1469 per child (minimum age six), including UK return flights, accommodation and some meals.
Contact Exodus (exodus.co.uk).

Essential Jordan
Where? Jordan.
Why? Epic and adventurous, yet small enough to keep long journeys to a minimum, Jordan has cultural and natural wonders that are perfect for budding Indiana Joneses. On this eight-day trip, they can float in the Dead Sea, explore the temples of Petra and venture into the desert landscape of Wadi Rum for two days of camel trekking and stargazing.

How much? From £799 per adult and £689 per child (under 12 years), including UK return flights, accommodation and some meals.
Contact Families Worldwide (familiesworldwide.co.uk).

Wild West Fun
Where? Arizona and Utah, USA.
Why? The red-rock national parks of southwest USA boast some of the world's most magnificent landscapes, from Monument Valley to the one-and-only Grand Canyon. This 11-night Wild West tour includes easy hiking, a rafting trip on the Colorado River and horse riding at a high country ranch.
How much? From £1045 for adults and children over eight, excluding international flights.
Contact KE Adventure Travel (keadventure.com).

Waterfall and Wildlife
Where? Zambia.
Why? Staying in spectacular private safari houses with personal guides, vehicles and chefs, families can set their own pace and plan their own activities on this ultimate Zambian safari which combines Victoria Falls and South Luangwa National Park.
How much? From £2733 per adult and £2572 per child (aged 2-12), based on a family of four for a seven-night fly-in safari, including UK return flights, transfers, meals and activities.
Contact Expert Africa (expertafrica.com).

Brazil for Pioneers
Where? Brazil.
Why? Eyeball a caiman (South American alligator) in the Pantanal, feel the thunder of Iguaçu Falls and relish the views of Rio de Janeiro from the Sugar Loaf cable car or Corcovado's Christ statue (one of the New World Wonders).
How much? From £3904 for two adults and a child (age 6-12) sharing a family room, including 12 nights accommodation, most meals and guided excursions.
Contact Journey Latin America (journeylatinamerica.co.uk).

66 99

The wonders of ancient Egypt never fail to impress, but kids appreciate a bit of action too …

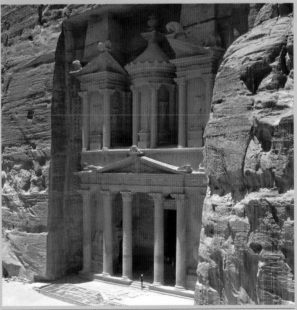

Top left: Iguaçu Falls, Brazil. **Top right:** Making a pizza in Rome.
Above and left: Essential Jordan.

Hard-to-please teenagers
The 10 family holidays guaranteed to be a hit with even the stroppiest of teenagers

Salsa de Cuba!
Where? Cuba.
Why? Explore offers special departures for children aged 11 and over on this guided family adventure – a big plus for teenagers who are happiest on holiday with fellow teens. Cuba is also a seriously cool destination. Highlights on this trip include the classic cars of Old Havana, camping in Topes de Collantes National Park and chilling out on the beaches of Cayo Levisa.
How much? From £1455 per adult and £1245 per child, including UK return flights, transfers, 12 nights accommodation and some meals.
Contact Explore (explore.co.uk).

Surf Scene
Where? Newquay, Cornwall.
Why? Sleeping six and boasting excellent facilities, including an indoor swimming pool and communal roof garden, the contemporary 1 Horizons apartment is the perfect base for a surfing holiday in Newquay.
How much? From £820 for one week's rental, including gas and electricity.
Contact Blue Chip Vacations (bluechipvacations.com).

Wilderness Christmas
Where? Nellim, Finnish Lapland.
Why? You won't hear even the slightest whimper of boredom on this six-night Lapland adventure, where activities include snowmobiling, cross-country skiing, snowshoeing and a husky safari. Competitive teens will love the snow games, featuring ice fishing, ice sculpting, snowshoe racing and reindeer lassoing.
How much? From £1245 per adult (twin share) and £1015 per child (under 14 years), including UK return flights, transfers, full-board accommodation and activities.
Contact Activities Abroad (activitiesabroad.com).

Active Turkey
Where? Turquoise Coast, Turkey.
Why? Specially designed for teenagers, this family trip combines a three-day cruise on a traditional sailing gulet (plenty of time for snorkelling, swimming or just lazing on deck) with optional extras like sea kayaking and a Discover Scuba course.
How much? From £599 per person (minimum age 12), including UK return flights, accommodation and some meals.
Contact The Adventure Company (adventurecompany.co.uk).

Kraków and the Tatras
Where? Poland and Slovakia.
Why? Combine the buzz of one of Europe's finest cities with the thrill of a mountain adventure and you should meet with the approval of most teenagers. Just to be certain, this 11-day tour includes a visit to Poprad's Aqua City with its daredevil water slides.
How much? From £699 per person, including UK return flights, accommodation and some meals.
Contact Exodus (exodus.co.uk).

Rocky Mountain High
Where? Canada.
Why? Horse riding, hiking and mountain biking are just the warm-up for the main event on this epic 13-night journey – a four-day canoeing trip down the Athabasca River, traversing uninhabited territory and camping, pioneer-style, on the riverbanks. Just keep an eye out for elks and bears.
How much? From £1295 for adults and children over 11 years, excluding international flights.
Contact KE Adventure Travel (keadventure.com).

Duinrell Parc
Where? Wasssenaar, Netherlands.
Why? Free rides at the Duinrell Theme Park and free entry for two hours every morning to the Tiki Water Park with its splash-happy array of whirlpools, wave machines and water slides. Bored? No chance.
How much? From £349 for a family of five (up to two adults and three children under 18 years) for seven nights accommodation in a two-bedroom Comfort mobile home with decking, including return Dover to Calais ferry crossings.
Contact Eurocamp (eurocamp.co.uk).

A Two Week Winter Warmer
Where? New South Wales and Queensland, Australia.
Why? South Stradbroke Island has loads to do, from bush walks to softball – and it's within easy reach of the Gold Coast's mega theme parks. Lamington National Park has forest frolics, like night walks and an aerial slide; Hamilton Island is the perfect place to chill, while Sydney boasts the Harbour Bridge climb and surfing at Bondi Beach. Put it all together and you have the ultimate Aussie tour for teens.
How much? From around £1117 per person, based on a family of four sharing on a room-only basis, including domestic flights and transfers.
Contact Bridge & Wickers (bridgeandwickers.co.uk).

Forte Village
Where? Sardinia.
Why? Forte Village is particularly appealing to teenagers who love the freedom to experience its huge range of social and sporting activities, from karaoke to go-karting. They also have their very own, very cool Crecheto Teens club, while the luxury resort's sandy beach is just the place for watersports and hanging out with friends.
How much? From £3605 for two adults and two children under 12 sharing a family bungalow at Il Villaggio for seven nights on a half board basis, including UK return flights and private transfers.
Contact Original Travel (originaltravel.co.uk).

Pyrenean Adventure
Where? France.
Why? There's so much packed into this eight-day multi-activity break that teenagers will barely find time to text their mates back home. It's complete mountain madness with a frenzy of horse riding, canyoning, caving, whitewater rafting, mountain biking, abseiling, *via ferrata* and paragliding.
How much? From £1049 per person (minimum age 11), excluding flights.
Contact Families Worldwide (familiesworldwide.co.uk).

Above: Wilderness Christmas, Finnish Lapland. **Left**: Surf Scene, Newquay. Below: Duinrell Parc, Netherlands.

You won't hear even the slightest whimper of boredom …

Tiny tearways
The 10 family holidays guaranteed to keep even the most demanding and active kids happy – and their parents sane

Devon Family Active holiday
Where? Barton Hall, near Torquay, Devon.
Why? Set in 19 ha of grounds, this family-friendly activity centre is ideal for younger kids. Qualified instructors provide a weeklong programme of sporty pursuits for children and their parents, including archery, snorkelling and a high ropes course. Parents can opt in or out as they like.
How much? From £306 per adult and £150 per child aged 2-5 for a seven-night holiday, including all meals and activities.
Contact PGL (pgl.co.uk).

Beau Rivage
Where? Mauritius.
Why? A deluxe resort-style hotel with an informal atmosphere, the Beau Rivage has a wide sandy beach lapped by calm waters. Should the kids tire of sandcastles and swimming, the Mini Club (for three- to 11-year-olds) organises glass-bottom rides, mini football, fish feeding and a weekly disco.
How much? From £1359 per adult and £477 per child (sharing with two adults) for seven nights' half board accommodation, including UK return flights.
Contact Kuoni (kuoni.co.uk).

Pyramids & Mummies
Where? Egypt.
Why? With a minimum age of just one, this weeklong infant adventure is appropriately paced to allow young families the opportunity to see Egypt's wonders. Although temperatures can be very hot, all hotels used in Cairo and Luxor have that all-important swimming pool.
How much? From £849 per adult, £789 per child (aged 2-12) and £629 per infant (under two), including UK return flights, accommodation and some meals.
Contact The Adventure Company (adventurecompany.co.uk).

La Casella
Where? Umbria, Italy.
Why? Consisting of four farmhouses that have been converted into 32 guest rooms, this idyllic Umbrian bolthole promises a relaxing Italian break for parents, while kids are kept busy with swimming, tennis and pony riding (minimum age four).
How much? From £518 full board per adult per week and £306 per child under 13 sharing their parent's room.
Contact Real Holidays (realholidays.co.uk).

Country Kids & Country Tots
Where? Herault, near Montpelier, France.
Why? With its complimentary crèche, splash-pool, play area, petting farm and two free nights babysitting, this stylish self-catering accommodation appeals particularly to parents with babies and toddlers. There's also a huge range of nursery and play equipment on hand, so you can even revert to the days of packing lightly. The grounds include a tennis court, heated swimming pool and a farm shop fully stocked with homemade ready-meals.
How much? From €2450 per week for a family of four.
Contact Baby Friendly Boltholes (babyfriendlyboltholes.co.uk).

Chalet Mara and Chalet Sonnenalp
Where? Kaprun, Austria.
Why? Esprit caters for all ages, whether you have nursery-age tots or independent-minded teens. There's a Snow Club and ski classes for children as young as three, while Esprit staff take the older ones to ski-school, collect them, give them lunch, run activities to keep them happy and then take them back to their chalets for high tea.
How much? From £995 for two adults and two children under 11 sharing a room, excluding childcare or ski pack hire.
Contact Esprit Holidays (esprit-holidays.co.uk).

The Sani Resort
Where? Halkidikí, Greece.
Why? Managed by childcare specialist Powder Byrne, the Sani's children's club ensures that kids have the time of their lives. Tots as young as six months are catered for in the crèche, while a Babe Watch service allows adults to enjoy an occasional swim in total peace.
How much? From €156 per night per room in a Marina Junior Suite on a bed and breakfast basis.
Contact Sani Resort (saniresort.gr).

High Atlas Adventure
Where? Morocco.
Why? A surprisingly accessible mountain adventure for children as young as two, this Atlas trek is mule-supported, which means kids can opt to ride when they tire of walking. Two day-walks are combined with a longer trek, staying overnight in a Berber village.
How much? From £699 per adult and £589 per child (under 18), including UK return flights, accommodation and most meals.
Contact Families Worldwide (familiesworldwide.co.uk).

Cycling in the Loire Valley
Where? France.
Why? With trailer-bikes provided for four- to six-year-olds and kids' bikes for older children, this eight-day cycling trip makes light work of the rural (mostly flat) backroads of the Loire Valley. Luggage is transferred for you and there's no shortage of perfect picnic spots.
How much? From £699 per adult and £649 per child (aged 4-11), including train travel from the UK, accommodation and some meals. Bike hire is extra.
Contact Exodus (exodus.co.uk).

St James's Club
Where? Mamora Bay, Antigua.
Why? As if this stunning property, overlooking a sheltered, palm-fringed bay, wasn't tempting enough, the Just Kids Club keeps children as young as two busy with activities like treasure hunts, face-painting and beach games. Paradise-found for toddlers.
How much? From £949 per adult and £399 per child (aged 2-11) room-only, including UK return flights.
Contact Hayes & Jarvis (hayesandjarvis.co.uk).

" "

Paradise found for
toddlers …

Top: Mini mutiny at the Sani
Resort.
Far left: La Casella, Umbria.
Left: Espirit ski classes in
Kaprun.

Keeping teacher happy

The 10 family holidays that are so steeped in educational value that even the meanest headteacher wouldn't think twice about letting your holiday over-run into term time by a day or two

Galápagos on Land and Sea

Where? The Galápagos Islands, Ecuador.

Why? This is the ideal way to introduce children to the evolutionary treasure chest of the Galápagos Islands. Your mini-Darwins will be captivated by close encounters with seals, seabirds and iguanas during a four-day voyage on the *MV Santa Cruz* (with its family cabins, glass-bottomed boat and children's meals), while three days at Finch Bay Hotel on Santa Cruz island provides beach time and activities like kayaking and mountain biking.

How much? From £4808 for two adults and a child (aged under six), sharing a family cabin/room, including accommodation, all meals, excursions, and land transport.

Contact Journey Latin America (journeylatinamerica.co.uk).

The Icelandic Way

Where? Iceland.

Why? A fascinating realm of brooding volcanoes, smouldering lava flows, bubbling mud pits, crashing waterfalls, vast ice caps (and even the odd troll if you look hard), Iceland provides the ultimate lesson in geology. Kids will be blown away by the amazing landscapes (not to mention the occasional whiff of sulphur) as they explore by horseback, superjeep, snowmobile and whitewater raft.

How much? From £723 per adult and £274 per child (under 17) for 11 or 12 nights' self-catering, with departures May to September.

Contact Discover the World (discover-the-world.co.uk).

Nile Explorer

Where? Egypt.

Why? This is one history lesson they'll never forget: pyramids, mummies, tombs, the Sphinx, Tutankhamen and the thrill of discovering Ancient Egypt's treasures on a three-day cruise down the Nile.

How much? From £1415 per adult and £1115 per child for a seven-night tour, including UK return flights, local transport, accommodation and most meals.

Contact Cox and Kings (coxandkings.co.uk).

Great Wall & Warriors

Where? China.

Why? From Great Wall hiking to Kung Fu fighting, this comprehensive 16-day family odyssey provides an unforgettable insight into one of the world's most fascinating countries. Kids will stand in awe of the stony-faced Terracotta Army at Xian and the towering rice terraces of the Dragon's Backbone near Longji.

How much? From £1799 per adult and £1599 per child, including UK return flights, local transport, accommodation and some meals.

Contact Explore (explore.co.uk).

Beyond Paddington

Where? Peru.

Why? Visit the lost city of Machu Picchu, cycle through the Sacred Valley, discover the legacy of the conquistadores in Cusco and explore the Amazon by canoe or canopy walkway to learn about rainforest conservation and local communities. A superb 12-day introduction to Latin America.

How much? From £3263 for two adults and a child (under 10) sharing a family room, including local flights, accommodation, excursions and some meals.

Contact Journey Latin America (journeylatinamerica.co.uk).

Bush Bonanza

Where? Namibia.

Why? This 15-day self-drive safari takes in a varied slice of Africa, including the rugged mountains and deserts of Damaraland, the wildlife hotspot of Etosha and the fascinating culture and traditions of Bushmanland.

How much? From £1775 per adult and £1279 per child (aged 6-11) for a family of four, including UK return flights, car hire, some meals and activities.

Contact Expert Africa (expertafrica.com).

Kenai Peninsula Family Adventure

Where? Alaska.

Why? Cruise the magnificent Kenai Fjords learning about humpback whale migration; hike to the top of Exit Glacier to witness the impact of global warming and cycle the Seward Scenic Byway for a vivid insight into the gold rush days.

How much? From US$2798 per adult and US$2238 per child (aged 7-15) for a six-day tour.

Contact Austin Lehman (austinlehman.com).

Kenyan Family Adventure

Where? Kenya.

Why? Staying in family-friendly lodges and using a private vehicle so you can take things at your own pace, this 17-day safari includes visits to the giraffe and elephant sanctuaries in Nairobi, as well as excellent children's activity programmes in the Masai Mara and Samburu National Park.

How much? From £1995 per person, including flights, transfers, meals and activities.

Contact Wildlife Worldwide (wildlifeworldwide.com).

Jungle Book

Where? India.

Why? Children will feel like they're stepping into the pages of Kipling's classic as they explore Kanha National Park – the inspiration for Mowgli's home – on this nine-day Indian journey which includes an overnight train ride to Agra and the Taj Mahal.

How much? From £1299 per adult and £1049 per child, including UK return flights, accommodation and some meals.

Contact Families Worldwide (familiesworldwide.co.uk).

Good Morning Vietnam!

Where? Vietnam.

Why? This easy-going 15-day family adventure (minimum age five) provides an eye-opener to one of Southeast Asia's most fascinating countries. As well as venturing by boat into Halong Bay and the Mekong Delta, there are markets to explore and (for those with more time) an optional excursion to Cambodia's Angkor Wat.

How much? From £1549 per adult and £1369 per child, including UK return flights, accommodation and some meals.

Contact The Adventure Company (adventurecompany.co.uk).

" "

This is one history lesson
they'll never forget …

Clockwise from left: Nile Explorer; Maasai meeting; Icelandic way; Galápagos Islands.

Single-parent families
10 family holidays that make life easier for single parents

Yellowstone & Tetons Multisport
Where? Wyoming, USA.
Why? Yellowstone and Grand Teton National Parks showcase some of America's most awe-inspiring and uplifting natural wonders. Everything's taken of on this six-day family tour where you'll cycle past steaming hot springs to Old Faithful, kayak on Yellowstone Lake, hike in the Tetons and round things of with a group-bonding whitewater rafting trip on the Snake River.
How much? From US$1798 per adult, US$1618 for 11- to 16-year-olds, US$1438 for seven- to 10-year-olds and US$1079 for three- to six-year-olds.
Contact Backroads (backroads.com).

France Family Active Holiday
Where? Chateau de Grande Romaine, near Paris.
Why? This PGL adventure centre offers single-parent families a fun, sociable and cost-effective holiday, combining activities from tennis to abseiling with a day at Disneyland and a day sightseeing in Paris (Seine cruise included).
How much? From £469 per adult, £439 for six- to 18-year-olds and £249 for two- to five-year-olds for a seven-night holiday, including coach travel from the UK.
Contact PGL (pgl.co.uk).

Lukimbi Game Lodge
Where? Kruger National Park, South Africa.
Why? A 15,000-ha private reserve, Lukimbi promises a hassle-free, child-friendly safari thanks to a special programme of activities, including the Basic Tracker programme for seven- to 12-year-olds. Professional child supervision frees single parents to enjoy bushwalks or simply relax by the pool.
How much? From £595 per adult and £455 per child under 12 for three nights full board accommodation and all activities.
Contact Cedarberg African Travel (cedarbergtravel.com).

Into the Wild West
Where? USA.
Why? Small group trips led by tour leaders,

Explore's family adventures are ideal for single parent families. This 14-day trip to Arizona, Nevada and Utah takes in the razzamatazz of Las Vegas before cruising Route 66 to the Grand Canyon and beyond to Monument Valley's Navajo Reservation and the spectacular Bryce Canyon and Zion National Parks.
How much? From £1715 per adult and £1439 per child, including UK return flights and accommodation (with four nights in a teepee and two nights camping).
Contact Explore (explore.co.uk).

Tamboti Safari
Where? Namibia.
Why? A professional guide leads this 15-day family camping safari, with an assistant taking care of day-to-day chores. Everything is organised for you, from wildlife-viewing in Etosha National Park to climbing the dunes at Sossusvlei.
How much? From £1700 per adult, £1620 for 12- to 18-year-olds and £1500 for five- to 11-year-olds, including UK return flights, accommodation and most meals.
Contact Wild about Africa (wildaboutafrica.com).

Chile Multi-Activity
Where? Chile.
Why? Stay three nights at a remote riverside lodge (cosy atmosphere, communal meals and home cooking) in the Lake District's stunning Cochamó Valley, joining other guests for kayaking and hiking. Then strike out on horseback along the Pioneer Trail, suitable for novice or experienced riders.
How much? From £778 for an adult and child (over six) sharing a room, including land transport from Puerto Montt and seven nights full board accommodation.
Contact Journey Latin America (journeylatinamerica.co.uk).

Jolly Beach Resort
Where? Antigua.
Why? Savvy single parents can take advantage of an impressive range of children's facilities, including the Jolly Beach Kidz Club (for three- to 12-year-olds) which

organises everything from beach games to dance lessons.
How much? From £1080 per adult and £974 per child for an all-inclusive seven-night single parent package with UK return flights and transfers.
Contact Kuoni (kuoni.co.uk).

Tanque Verde Ranch
Where? Arizona, USA.
Why? An excellent option for single-parent families, ranching in the United States is all about communal adventure and sharing an authentic Western experience. In addition to horseriding, cycling, swimming, art classes and a spa, Tanque Verde Ranch has children's clubs for four- to 11-year-olds.
How much? From £1089 per person for a five-night package, including full board accommodation and all ranch activities.
Contact Hayes & Jarvis (hayesandjarvis.co.uk).

Elephant Paradise
Where? Sri Lanka.
Why? Take advantage of The Adventure Company's dedicated Single Parent Departures on this 16-day tour combining Sri Lanka's coastal and cultural highlights with a visit to the Uda Walawe elephant orphanage.
How much? From £1199 per adult and £1079 per child (minimum age five), including UK return flights, accommodation and some meals.
Contact The Adventure Company (adventurecompany.co.uk).

Camping Cabopino
Where? Costa del Sol, Spain.
Why? Eurocamp not only offers discounts to single parent families, but its easy-going camping holidays are the ideal place for both children and adults to meet new people, whether popping to the shop for baguettes in the morning or lazing around the pool. Children, meanwhile, will also enjoy making friends at the free kids' clubs.
How much? From £436 for one adult and up to four children under 18 years for seven nights in a mobile home, including return Dover to Calais ferry crossings.
Contact Eurocamp (eurocamp.co.uk).

66 99

Savvy single parents
can take advantage of
an impressive range of
children's facilities …

Clockwise from top left: Elephant encounter in South Africa; PGL Family Active Holiday; climbing dunes in Namibia; Into the Wild West.

Pampering parents
Yes, it's your holiday too – the 10 holidays that care for grown-ups as much as kids

Mardavall Hotel & Spa
Where? Mallorca.
Why? Located just a short walk from the Marina Puerto Portals, this luxurious resort has a children's club to keep three- to 12-year-olds busy, while parents enjoy the AltiraSPA and two golf courses.
How much? From £1155 per adult and £862 per child under 12 for seven nights bed and breakfast accommodation, including UK return flights and transfers.
Contact Abercrombie & Kent (abercrombiekent.co.uk).

Aphrodite Hills Resort
Where? Cyprus.
Why? Parent pampering is available at The Retreat, a blissful Greco-Roman spa overlooking the Mediterranean Sea, while the resort also boasts an 18-hole golf course and tennis academy. Kids needn't feel left out – they get indulged with just about every activity going, from horseriding and dance lessons to mini football and golf tuition.
How much? From £619 per adult and £295 per child under 12 (sharing with parents) for seven nights bed and breakfast accommodation, including UK return flights.
Contact Olympic Holidays (olympicholidays.com).

The Elms
Where? Worcestershire, UK.
Why? Close to Cadbury World, West Midlands Safari Park and the Severn Valley Railway, this member of the Luxury Family Hotels collection has a spa designed for indulging the whole family, from pre and post-natal mothers to new fathers.
How much? Room rates from £300.
Contact Luxury Family Hotels (luxuryfamilyhotels.com).

Sandy Lane
Where? Barbados.
Why? Synonymous with glamour and luxury, Sandy Lane is also excellent for families. There's a superb Treehouse Club for three- to 12-year-olds and a Den Teen Centre for older children. Parents, meanwhile, can indulge themselves at the beautiful spa or the trio of championship golf courses.
How much? From £7215 for two adults and two children for seven nights bed and breakfast, including UK return flights.
Contact ITC Classics (itcclassics.co.uk).

Explora en Atacama
Where? Chile.
Why? A stunning 50-room contemporary hotel in the Atacama desert, Explora smoothes the edges of one of Chile's harshest environments with high quality (yet unpretentious and family-friendly) accommodation, fine dining and a sauna. Guided excursions include hiking, mountain biking and horse riding.
How much? From £5579 for a family of four sharing two rooms for seven nights full board, including ground transport and excursions. Suitable for children aged 12 plus.
Contact Journey Latin America (journeylatinamerica.co.uk).

Porto Elounda
Where? Crete.
Why? With a ratio of three children to one adult in the crèche and never more than seven children to one adult in the various kids' clubs, parents can take full advantage of Port Elounda's Six Senses Spa, safe in the knowledge that the kids are being well cared for and entertained.
How much? From £1292 per adult and £288 for children aged 2-11 sharing parents' room for seven nights half-board, including return flights and transfers.
Contact Powder Byrne (powderbyrne.com).

Le Sérignan Plage Parc
Where? Languedoc, France.
Why? With direct access to the beach this parc has something for everyone. For children there is a giant lagoon pool, water slides, bike hire, disco and on-parc entertainer, while parents can enjoy the free, adult only, water spa fitness centre which boasts a hydro-massage whirlpool.
How much? From £510 for seven nights accommodation in a Comfort mobile home for a family of five (two adults and three children under 18), including return Dover to Calais ferry crossings.
Contact Eurocamp (eurocamp.co.uk)

Jumeirah Beach Hotel
Where? Dubai.
Why? Superbly located on a white sandy beach overlooking the Gulf, the Jumeirah has 22 restaurants, cafés and bars, a plethora of watersports, as well as sauna, jacuzzi and massage facilities. The Sinbad's Kids Club organises visits to the Wild Wadi water park and various activities for two- to 12-year-olds. Needless to say, there is also plenty to keep teenagers occupied.
How much? From £3630 for two adults (with two children under 12 staying free on a room-only basis) for eight nights in a junior suite with private terrace and full access to the Premium Leisure Club, including breakfast and UK return flights.
Contact Kuoni (kuoni.co.uk).

Scenery, Sea Life and Snowy Peaks
Where? South Island, New Zealand.
Why? You fly all that way, so the very least you can do is treat yourself to some special accommodation. Easily combined with a tour of North Island, this ten-day itinerary features two-bedroom apartments, suites or cottages in Marlborough Sounds, Kaikoura, Christchurch and Queenstown.
How much? From £692 per person, including accommodation and car hire.
Contact Bridge & Wickers (bridgeandwickers.co.uk).

Pure Lapland
Where? Finland.
Why? Combining relaxation at its trendy spa with exciting activities like cross-country skiing, husky sledging and snowmobiling, the Jeris Village hotel is the perfect place for families to chill out in the Arctic.
How much? From £653 per adult, £450 for five- to 14-year-olds and £398 for two- to four-year-olds for three nights accommodation with departures November to April.
Contact Discover the World (discover-the-world.co.uk).

Left: Six Senses Spa, Porto Elanda, Crete. Below: Sandy Lane, Barbados.
Bottom: Explora en Atacama.

66 99
… a spa designed
for indulging the
whole family …

Essentials

The author's children, Joseph and Eleanor, in Sydney.

Have baby, won't travel

Go on, admit it. You'd much rather not have one sitting near you on a flight. You board the plane, shuffle down the cramped aisle, coerce your hand luggage into the overhead locker, glance down and there it is – all cute and innocent on its mother's lap. But she's bound to be a hopeless parent, completely incapable of stopping it from howling, vomiting and shredding the newspaper that you try to hide behind for the 15-hour, non-stop flight.

It's hardly surprising that more parents shun holidays when their children are aged between one and four than at any other time. Not only do practicalities, like flying, become fraught with stress and logistical nightmares (for new parents, the journey of a thousand miles does not begin with a single step – it usually starts with trying to change a nappy in a cramped toilet before take-off), but you are constantly striving to reduce the impact of your little darlings on other, often unsympathetic, travellers. That, combined with the general fatigue that stalks new parents, does little to set the wheels of family travel in motion.

We've all been there: sleep deprived, irritable, barely capable of summoning the energy (or baby paraphernalia) for a trip to the shops, let alone a holiday. However, there are at least six good reasons why it's never too early to start travelling with kids:

➔ Babies are easy to transport in pushchairs, backpacks or papooses.

➔ They can't dictate where you go or what you do (so make the most of it while it lasts).

➔ In most countries locals will make a big fuss of them which is a great morale boost for weary new parents.

➔ Babies often go free. The older children get, the more expensive they become, and travel is no exception.

➔ There are plenty of innovative baby travel products designed to make life easier.

➔ Choose the right hotel or resort and you get some well-deserved pampering.

Onwards, upwards and falling over

With toddlerdom comes new challenges. In fact, many parents claim this to be the most demanding time to travel with children. If only toddlers had an on-off switch or some way of containing all that energy and frustration pent up in a body that won't always do what it's meant to – or, worse still, is prevented from doing so by ever-watchful parents. With this age group, you have to be especially careful over your choice of accommodation. Toddlers have an alarming tendency to wander off when something interesting catches their eye. Health and safety is not exactly foremost in the minds of these mini-explorers and you need to be particularly wary of unfenced swimming pools and balconies with squeeze-through railings. Toddlers also tend to shove a lot of

❷ Should we book a group trip?
Pros ...

✔ You're with like-minded families who share similar interests in travel.

✔ Children have instant holiday pals.

✔ Trips usually have a good balance of activities and time out.

✔ Everything is organized for you, from transport to activities – and you know it's all going to be child-friendly.

✔ You can explore countries that you wouldn't consider visiting independently.

✔ Children in a group are more likely to feel motivated to try adventurous things.

✔ There are trips to suit all ages, from tots to teenagers.

... and cons

✘ Perfect families with angelic children make you feel inadequate and tense.

✘ Personality clashes lead to awkward situations in the confines of a group.

✘ You feel under pressure to adapt your routines to fit into other families' rules for bedtime, meals etc.

✘ Schedules can be restricting; no time to linger in a place you like or lie low for a day or two if children are ill.

✘ You may well spend more than by travelling independently.

✘ Some guides pitch talks and briefings way above children's heads.

✘ You might still feel out of your comfort zone.

✘ Frustrations may arise if some children can't keep up with the others.

✘ Some groups may have an uneven balance of ages, such as a lone teenager with half a dozen five- and six-year-olds.

unsavoury stuff into their mouths. Usually this is nothing more harmless than a bit of sand, although the author's son used to be fond of those large, irresistibly crunchy beetles that frequent Mediterranean climes.

If there's one thing that makes travel with toddlers easier it's their increasing ability to talk – even if it's just to tell you they are about to be sick or that they object to another child walking off with their bucket and spade. In the latter case, of course, actions often speak louder than words – why struggle with newfangled speech when a tried-and-tested thump

❝ ❞ It's important for your children to see you having a good time. Our everyday lives can be quite fraught and often a child's impression of dad is someone who comes home stressed every evening. On holiday you get to show them the fun side of their parents.

Jennifer Stevens

usually does the trick? Nevertheless, communication does take a large chunk of paranoia out of family travel.

The 'why, what, when, how' years

By the time they reach school age (four or five), kids are a real pleasure to travel with. There is something wonderfully refreshing about their innocent and undisguised joy over experiencing even the most mundane aspects of travel. For example, no other age group is particularly bothered about watching the laborious task of weighing and labelling luggage at an airport check-in desk – but to a six-year-old boy it is an utterly transfixing event, punctuated by inconceivable weights, whirring sticker-producing machines and mysterious conveyor belts that whisk suitcases through trapdoors. Even airline food trays instigate goggle-eyed wonder and at least five minutes of vocal hyperactivity.

Whether it's building a dam on the beach to hold back the tide or embarking on a trek in the Andes, school-age children have seemingly limitless enthusiasm and energy. They are also at an age when they can tell you what they like and dislike, which can either be a blessing or a curse when it comes to holiday planning. Be prepared, too, for endless questions as their minds grapple to comprehend new experiences, places, cultures and issues.

Call it educational

A whole generation of globetrotting backpackers from the 1980s and 1990s now have young families. Rather than shred their passports and settle for the odd week with the grandparents, they also want adventure and unusual places – everything, in fact, that they had before, except with youngsters in tow. Eagerly meeting this demand are several adventure-tour operators with dedicated family programmes offering everything from a fortnight in Borneo travelling by longboat to visit Iban headhunters to a week in Egypt sailing down the Nile. Relaxed in the knowledge that a reputable tour operator has taken care of all technical and safety issues, you can take your tribe whitewater rafting in Nepal, horse riding in Iceland, canyoning in Croatia or sea kayaking in New Zealand. The world has become an enormous adventure playground where kids can sample tamed-down versions of all the things that got their parents whooping it up 20 years earlier.

The thrills and spills may be the lure of these trips, but school-age children will also absorb a huge amount of educational value from them. They'll interact with children from other cultures and learn at first hand about efforts to save endangered wildlife. They'll expand their palettes as well as their minds and they will probably pick up a new skill or

66 99 It was one of those moments, no matter how incredible the spectacle, that you simply had to look away and watch your children instead. The sheer, wide-eyed amazement that bloomed across our children's faces when they saw their first whale was so captivating that I barely registered the procession of pilot whales off Tenerife's west coast. As toddlers they didn't have the words to spoil the moment with crass exclamations. Instead, for just a few seconds, they were quietly spellbound. Admittedly, they then returned to ransacking the brochure stand in the lounge of our tour boat…

Will

Reality check #1: The city break

66 99 For a moment I thought the *maître d'* might actually bar us from the restaurant. He glanced at our toddler twins, Joe and Ellie, then fixed me with an abhorrent look as if I was trying to bring a pair of rabid, mange-ridden dogs to dinner. We'd booked an early table, the restaurant was empty and there was nothing to say that young children weren't allowed. Earlier, we'd narrowly escaped eviction from the cathedral cloisters when Joe discovered its potential for echoes.

I admit that there are certain things in the world of family travel that simply don't mix. There's little point, for example, in taking toddlers to an antique-riddled boutique hotel, or six-year-olds to anywhere with a low occurrence of swimming pools. But I don't see why young children and city breaks should be considered so incompatible.

I suppose, more than anything, the city break embodies those heady days of pre-parenthood when, as a carefree couple, you could nip off to Paris or Rome with nothing more than an overnight bag and a pair of theatre tickets. You could dawdle over lunch, go shopping and take in an art gallery or two. With youngsters in tow it can become more like a city breakdown as you haul your bored offspring from one museum to another, desperately trying to do the sights between tantrums. The mistake new parents make (and I am as guilty as any) is to try to recapture the essence of a city break as it was before they had children. It rarely works.

The key to remaining sane in the city is to re-prioritize. Don't scour the city map for galleries and museums until you've pinpointed the parks, public toilets, family-friendly restaurants and nearest toy shop. As tempting as that new Picasso exhibition may be, begin your city escapade with something for the kids, whether it's a hands-on exhibition, boat ride or trip to the zoo. With a bit of forward planning you can also pick out sites that have child-friendly activities, such as quiz sheets, craft areas, interactive exhibits and, joy of joys, a crèche.

One city that went down well with our kids was Naples – though not for obvious reasons. Pushing a double buggy around the cobbled backstreets was pure hell. For some reason, though, Neapolitans have a soft spot for twin babies. "*Gemelli, belissimo!*" people would cry as they spontaneously grabbed Joe and Ellie by the cheeks before delving into the nearest paticceria to emerge with fistfuls of cakes. My wife, Sally, and I would then watch, bemused, as our children were force-fed chunks of *sfogliatelle* and other traditional pastries. I'm not sure whether Joe and Ellie absorbed anything of particular artistic or historical value during that city break – but they certainly never went hungry.

Will

That all-essential swimming pool – even in the Namib Desert.

two, whether it's how to speak a few words of Spanish or haggle in a Turkish bazaar.

Usually, the minimum age for family adventure trips is around five or six, but you can also find tours suitable for children as young as two. Others, meanwhile, are reserved exclusively for teenagers.

The main advantage of booking an organized trip instead of going independent is peace of mind – all travel arrangements are made for you, while the itinerary is intrinsically family friendly. You will also be with like-minded parents, many of whom are facing the same challenges of raising children as you are. The kids in the group will quickly bond and find new playmates, while the guide will provide added 'family value'. This last point, however, is worth researching carefully. Find out if the guide on your trip is a parent or has experience of communicating with children (as a teacher for example). A good guide will not only make the effort to gain the children's confidence, but will also ensure that mealtimes, talks and activities are tailored to meet their ages. If kids are happy and engaged, their parents will be happy and relaxed. It could be something as simple as turning a traditional city tour (fractious children, fretting parents) into a treasure hunt (focused children, stress-free parents).

Tuning in to teenagers

It's easy to tarnish all teenagers as moody, sullen, bored and generally peeved that you've dragged them away on holiday with you. But this hackneyed image is perhaps a little unfair. Teenagers not only make stimulating travel companions (able to tackle physical and intellectual challenges on a par with adults), but they also simplify travel logistics by being able to stay up late or be flexible with meals. Just remember to cater for their specific needs, whether it's a few shopping trips, some extreme adrenaline abuse or somewhere to meet

> 💬 As teenagers, Matthew and I had been dragged along to the Everglades for the day. It sounded like a long boring walk around a national park, and we would have much rather been at the theme parks or on the beach, but it turned out to be one of the best days of our holiday – especially when a huge alligator walked across the path right in front of us. Later on our boat broke down and we were left floating in alligator-infested waters for an hour, which was also really cool.
>
> *Emily Gage*

socially with youngsters of their own age. Teenagers also like some personal space, so try to take this into account when planning accommodation. Getting up early, on the other hand, is something teenagers don't always appreciate, so trips like safaris (which involve lots of dawn game drives) may well elicit a good moan.

Something for everyone

So, is there a magic formula for travelling with kids? No doubt you've met parents with infuriatingly well-behaved children who will tell you (*ad nauseam*) that family holidays are a piece of cake; that their little angel sleeps through flights, never whinges on long car journeys, always eats foreign food and never cries when, each morning, she's dispatched to the crèche so mummy and daddy can go skiing or relax in the spa. For most normal families, however, getting holidays right is about making compromises. You won't necessarily please everyone all the time, but you can ensure that all ages have at least something going for them.

Ten things that should definitely go into the equation are:
Water Whether it's the sea, a lake or a swimming pool, most children (and plenty of adults) consider swimming an intrinsic part of every holiday.
Food Don't skip the local flavours entirely, but always ensure there's something on the menu that kids know and like.
Friends Opportunities for interacting with other children of their own age is particularly important for teenagers and, whatever your views, organized kids' clubs are usually a big hit with children and allow parents some adult time.
Gear Plan and pack with military precision to ensure you've got everything you need, especially if travelling with a baby.
Versatility Research your destination, accommodation and activities carefully to make sure they meet the needs and ages of everyone in the family.
Challenges Banish boredom by ensuring there are plenty of new experiences and adventures available for both you and your children.
Money Don't feel you have to spend a fortune to have a memorable family holiday.
Attitude Children quickly pick up on stress or anxiety, so try to stay relaxed, particularly during long journeys.
Expectations Keep them realistic; remember that what you might find interesting might bore your children senseless. Don't chastise them for ignoring the architecture in Venice's Piazza San Marco in favour of feeding the pigeons.
Fun What it's all about. Travelling with kids might not always be easy, but try to keep the stressful (or just downright miserable) moments in perspective. You'll laugh about them in years to come.

Five ways to save money

Let's face it, kids aren't cheap – particularly when it comes to holidays. As soon as you start multiplying airline fares and hotel rates by a factor of three or four your budget can quickly spiral out of control. So, how do you travel more for less with the tribe in tow?

1 Mousework Perhaps the most obvious thing is to trawl the internet for bargains. Look out for special online deals, which can range from free child places to extra days. You will also find that it's cheaper to book direct on an airline's website, rather than through a travel agent. While you're online, don't forget to hunt down the best family travel insurance deal. Try cover-all.co.uk for starters.

2 DIY-style For total flexibility and independence, you can't beat the self-drive, self-catering option for a great-value family holiday. Simply throw some camping and cooking gear into the back of your car and mainland Europe is yours for a fraction of the cost of a package deal. If that sounds too much like hard work, why not rent a villa or farmhouse? Sharing the cost of a bigger property with another family may well be cheaper than booking something smaller just for yourselves.

3 Timing With pre-school children you can dodge the high-season premiums and take them on holiday whenever you choose. But even when you're confined to school holidays it is still worth being selective about when you travel. For example, the last week in August is usually cheaper than the first and you may also find that midweek flights offer better value than weekend ones.

4 Pound-stretching Choose countries where the cost of living is comparatively low. Turkey and Tunisia, for example, are relatively cheap compared to more traditional Mediterranean destinations like Greece and Spain. For long haul, consider Brazil and Mexico – both represent excellent value and have plenty to offer families. If it's warm winter beaches you're after, think Goa rather than the Caribbean. And if you're set on a safari, opt for countries like Namibia or South Africa where it's easier and cheaper to do it yourself, compared to pricier, all-inclusive options in Botswana and Zambia.

5 Cost-cutting It's the little things on holiday that often give your bank balance the biggest bashing. Take drinks, for example. You'd probably be amazed at how much you could save by buying a bottle of squash and mixing your own drinks rather than shelling out for cans of Coke and Fanta several times a day. Other ways to cut costs on holiday include booking a family room instead of two separate ones, hiring a car rather than arranging organized tours, and making your own picnics instead of eating out.

🌴 Tips for teen bliss
Give them some local currency Retail therapy is obligatory on holiday.

Give them some cyber space Take them to an internet café so they can catch up on gossip with their mates back home (emails are cheaper than using a mobile phone).

Give them a break Don't nag them about food or if they want a lie-in every morning.

Everyone needs a holiday
The Family Holiday Association (fhaonline.org.uk) is the only charity in the UK that specializes in helping provide holidays for families and children in need. According to Professor Richard Layard, author of *Happiness: Lessons of a New Science*, "Holidays are a vital event in personal well-being. It is tragic that so many people still have no holidays away from home." You can make a donation online.

When to go

Hot stuff – the pyramids.

Europe

Activity	J	F	M	A	M	J	J	A	S	O	N	D
Go dog sledging in Lapland	★	★	★	★								★
Spot bears in Romania				★	★	★	★					
Take a hike in the Alps				★	★	★	★	★				
Explore the coast of Turkey			★	★	★	☆	☆	★				
Go whale watching in Iceland				★	★	★	★	★	★	★		
Cycle through the Loire Valley				★	★	★	☆	★				
Kayak along the coast of Croatia				★	★	☆	☆	★				
Explore Pompeii in Italy			★	★	★	★	★	★	★			

Australia and New Zealand

Activity	J	F	M	A	M	J	J	A	S	O	N	D
Tour New Zealand in a motor home	★	★	★	★	★				★	★	★	★
Snorkel on the Great Barrier Reef			★	★	★	★	★	★	★			
Hike through the Blue Mountains	☆	☆	★	★	★				★	★	★	☆
See whale sharks on Ningaloo Reef				★	★	★	★					
Visit Uluru (Ayers Rock)	☆	☆	★	★	★	★	★	★	★	★	★	☆
Spot whales off Queensland									★	★	★	★
Explore Kakadu National Park						★	★	★	★	★		
Paddle a kayak in South Island	★	★	★								★	★

North America

Activity	J	F	M	A	M	J	J	A	S	O	N	D
Go horse riding in Arizona				★	★	★	★	★	★	★		
Ice skate in Central Park, New York	★	★	★								★	★
Visit Alaska's Denali National Park						★	★	★	★			
Go skiing in the Rockies	★	★	★	★							★	★
Gaze at the Grand Canyon	★	★	★	★	★	★	★	★	★	★	★	★
Paddle a canoe in the Everglades	★	★	★	★								★
Take a hike in Yosemite						★	★	★	★	★	★	
Watch orcas off Vancouver Island						★	★	★	★	★		

Africa

Activity	J	F	M	A	M	J	J	A	S	O	N	D
Sail down the Nile on a felucca	★	★	★	★	★	★	☆	☆	★	★	★	★
Hike in Morocco's Atlas Mountains		★	★	★	★	★			★	★		
Watch the wildebeest migration					★	★	★	★	★			
Ride a camel in the Sahara Desert	★	★	★	★	★	★			★	★	★	★
Scuba dive in the Red Sea	★	★	★	★	★	★	☆	☆	★	★	★	★
Tour South Africa's Garden Route	★	★	★	★						★	★	★
Spot lions in the Luangwa Valley							★	★	★	★	★	
Look for lemurs in Madagascar						★	★	★	★	★	★	

Asia

Activity	J	F	M	A	M	J	J	A	S	O	N	D
Trek in the Himalaya of Nepal		★	★	★					★	★	★	
Camp out in Wadi Rum, Jordan	★	★	★	★	★	★			★	★	★	★
Spot tigers on safari in India		★	★	★	★							
Meet orang-utans in Borneo	★	★	★	★	★	★	★	★	★	★	★	★
Ride an elephant in Thailand	★	★	★	★	★	★	★	★	★	★	★	★
Avoid being fried in Dubai	★	★	★						★	★		
Walk on the Great Wall of China			★	★	★				★	★	★	
Relax on Sri Lanka's tropical coast	★	★	★	★								

Latin America

Activity	J	F	M	A	M	J	J	A	S	O	N	D
See turtles in Costa Rica							★	★	★	★		
Trek the Inca Trail to Machu Picchu						★	★	★	★	★	★	
Cruise the Galápagos Islands	★	★	★	★	★	★	★	★	★	★	★	★
Spot whales in Baja California	★	★	★	★								
Trek in Patagonia	★	★	★	★						★	★	★
Explore the Amazon					★	★	★	★	★	★		
Perfect sandcastles in the Caribbean	★	★	★	★								★
Chill out on the Yucatán Peninsula	★	★										★

Festivals and events

January
Sydney Festival, Australia (sydneyfestival.org.au) Sydney's big culture-fest sees Darling Harbour full of tall ships.
Venice Carnival, Italy (carnivalofvenice.com) St Mark's Square attracts thousands of masked revellers.
February
Rio Carnival, Brazil (rioconventionbureau.com.br) Rio is reduced to a gridlock of gyrating bodies as the Samba Parade struts its stuff from dusk to dawn.
Abu Simbel Festival, Egypt (touregypt.net) On 22 February and 22 October (Ramses II's rise to the throne and his birthday) early morning sunlight illuminates the temple's inner sanctum.
March
Chichén Itzá, Mexico (visitmexico.com) During the spring equinox, afternoon sun creates a play of light and shadow on the Maya pyramid's steps, symbolizing the arrival of the feathered serpent god, Kukulcán.
St Patrick's Festival, Ireland (stpatricksday.ie) Dublin throws its biggest celebration of the year with parades, fireworks, dance and music.

April
Greek Orthodox Easter (gnto.gr) Holy Week is Greece's most important religious festival with processions and outdoor feasts of roast lamb.
May
Feria del Caballo, Jerez, Spain (turismojerez.com) The famous white horses demonstrate the art of dressage.
Hamamatsu Kite Festival, Japan (jnto.go.jp) Measuring up to 4 m across and taking 10 men to fly, some 150 Hamamatsu kites fill the sky amid chanting and drumming.
June
Inti Raymi, Cuzco, Peru (peru.info) The fortress ruins of Sacsayhuamán host this sacred Inca festival which culminates in a re-enactment of the traditional blessing offered to Wiracocha, God of the Sun.

July
Calgary Stampede, Alberta, Canada (calgarystampede.com) Watch the dust rise as the top cowboys take on anything with four hooves.
Macy's 4th July Fireworks Spectacular, USA (nyctourist.com) New York's famous department store makes a song and dance over 14,000 fireworks.
August
Henley on Todd Regatta, Alice Springs, Australia (henleyontodd.com.au) Imagination flows freely during Australia's bizarre boat race day when competitors carry bottomless boats along the dry riverbed of the Todd.

Reality check #2: The school holidays

School holidays might come as something of a shock. Suddenly you're faced with the challenge of planning child-friendly trips that fit, as neatly as possible, around school term dates. Here is a wonderfully impractical wish list.

First up is **February half-term**. Skiing in the Alps would be fun, but not nearly as exciting as a winter adventure in the Arctic. It would be a close call between Iceland and Lapland. Both offer four-to five-day family itineraries, including activities like reindeer sledging, snowmobiling and ice fishing. A full two weeks off beckons during the **first half of April** – the perfect time to take children to North Africa or the Middle East before the sweltering heat of summer kicks in. The ancient sites of Egypt certainly have educational value, but if your children have yet to begin learning about pharaohs and pyramids take them instead to Morocco, which offers a good balance of relaxing beach retreats and mountain escapades. **Half-term in late May/early June** is prime time for a multi-activity break in Europe – perfect if you need to cater to the needs of children of various ages. Then it's headlong into the **summer holidays** – the best opportunity for a long-haul trip if you want to give your kids time to recover from jet lag before term starts. However, it's also high season, so look for somewhere where you can travel independently and save money on accommodation and eating out. In a perfect world **October half-term** really ought to be spent in the Seychelles. The flight from London is long (10 hours), but it's direct and the archipelago is only GMT+4 – very tempting for a few days exploring Mahé in a mini-moke and a spot of snorkelling off Praslin's wonderful beaches. That just leaves the **Christmas holidays**. You can't beat a traditional family Christmas at home, but having said that, India's Ranthambore National Park does promise excellent tiger viewing during December.

September
Hermanus Whale Festival, South Africa (whalefestival.co.za) Fun-filled focus of the Cape's whale-watching season (July-December).

October
Festival du Vent, Calvi, Corsica (lefestivalduvent.com) Homage to the wind, where everything from kites to hang-gliders receive a breath of fresh air.
Chonburi Buffalo Races, Thailand (tourismthailand.org) Parades, music and beauty contests, rounded off with a frenzied bovine derby.
November
Pushkar Camel Fair, India (incredibleindia.org) Thar Desert camel drivers (and up to 50,000 camels) converge on Pushkar to do business and race camels.
Christkindlesmarkt, Nuremburg, Germany (christkindlesmarkt.de) Peruse stalls crammed with decorations, toys and cakes; breathe in the spicy aroma of freshly baked gingerbread and sing along to Christmas carols.
December
Junkanoo, Nassau, The Bahamas (bahamas.com) It's party time as Nassau's Bay Street becomes a seething mass of shimmying and shaking to the infectious beat of goatskin drums, trumpets and whistles.

Easter options

Egypt Combine visits to the Giza pyramids and Abu Simbel with a Nile felucca trip to Luxor, a donkey trek into the Valley of the Kings and some time on the Red Sea coast at Hurghada for relaxing and snorkelling.

Finland Embark on a wilderness experience with activities ranging from ice-fishing to dog sledging.

Kenya Have two full days on safari in the Masai Mara and visit Lake Nakuru, famed for its flamingos.

Activity holidays

PGL pgl.co.uk
Summer camps, adventure holidays and activity breaks in the UK and Europe.
Pick of the trips Domaine de Segries, France – raft the rapids during a dramatic two-day descent of the Ardèche River and enjoy other activities, such as rock climbing, mountain biking and archery; a perfect holiday for a family with teenagers.

Crystal Active Holidays crystal-active.co.uk
Hotel- or mobile home-based holidays in Austria, France, Greece, Italy, Slovenia and Turkey. Choose from a bewildering array of activities, including biking, canyoning, climbing, diving, hiking, horse riding, kayaking, paragliding, sailing, surfing, waterskiing, whitewater rafting, windsurfing and yoga.
What the brochure says "Active holidays are perfect for families, giving you the chance to take part in loads of different activities together. With a fantastic range of kids' clubs you'll also get the freedom to go and do something a little more challenging in the knowledge that your children are with professional childcare staff."

Also consider: Freewheel Holidays freewheelholidays.com; Headwater headwater.com; Inntravel inntravel.co.uk; Neilson Active Holidays neilson.co.uk.

African safaris

Aardvark Safaris aardvarksafaris.com
Bespoke African safaris and family holidays to the Indian Ocean.
What the brochure says "More and more top safari camps are now catering for families and have introduced specialist guides, private vehicles, interconnecting rooms, early meal times and baby sitters."

Bushbaby Travel bushbabytravel.com
Malaria-free family holidays and safaris to South Africa, Mauritius, Dubai and Oman.

Expert Africa expertafrica.co.uk
The UK's leading Africa specialist with extensive knowledge of southern and East Africa, and competitive prices for family safaris and fly-drives.
What the brochure says "Africa can be an amazing and inspiring place, but it's important to visit places that actively welcome children, rather than simply accept them."

Also consider: CC Africa ccafrica.com; Safari Drive safaridrive.com.

All-inclusive resorts

Club Med clubmed.com
Worldwide collection of all-inclusive holiday villages. Packages include return flights, transfers, accommodation, full board (including drinks with lunch and dinner), open bar and snacks, sports activities with equipment and tuition, Club Med Baby Welcome for babies up to 23 months, Mini Club Med for children aged four to 10, Juniors' Club Med or Club Med Passworld for teenagers.

Mark Warner markwarner.co.uk
Long-established ski and beach resort operator with comprehensive kids' facilities. Flights, transfers, meals, sailing, tennis, childcare for two- to 13-year-olds and an Indy Club for teenagers are all part of the package.

Esprit Holidays esprit-holidays.co.uk
Family specialist in skiing and alpine summer holidays. Renowned childcare programme includes nurseries, babysitting, children's ski classes and activity clubs. Also arranges visits to Santa in Lapland.
What the brochure says "It's the age-old family dilemma: there are lots of things to do where the whole family can have fun together, but there are activities and pleasures that parents can only really enjoy if their children are safe and happy elsewhere. With Esprit you can have the best of both worlds. Our Esprit Nurseries, with friendly, qualified nannies, are available five days a week in four resorts. Our Alpies Club brings adventure, fun and friends to three- to 11-year-olds, and 12- to 15-year-olds will love our exciting Teen Rangers in Chamonix and Saas Fee."

Also consider: Beaches beaches.com

The Arctic

Discover the World discover-the-world.co.uk
Specialist travel programmes to Iceland, Lapland and Polar regions with several family offerings.
Pick of the trips A 14-day 'Alaska Family Adventure' offering everything from whitewater rafting and a safari in Denali National Park to a ride on the Alaska Railroad. Land-only prices start from around £2160 per adult (based on two sharing) and £785 per child (under 11 and sharing parent's room).

Australia and New Zealand

Bridge & Wickers bridgeandwickers.co.uk
Experts in tailor-made holidays to Australia and New Zealand.
What the brochure says "For toddlers there are miles of safe and sandy beaches, as well as resorts that warmly welcome little guests and cater specifically to their needs. Older children, including restless teens, can weave in lots of adrenaline-pumping activities – with New Zealand, of course, having that added *Lord of the Rings* location-spotting appeal!"
Pick of the trips A July or August three-weeker: fly direct to Cairns and spend the first week exploring the Great Barrier Reef

> 66 99 The joy on a child's face when they first see a herd of elephants is priceless, but spending a few days in a rural African village – that's really life-changing stuff!
>
> *Chris McIntyre, Expert Africa*

THE HOLIDAY THAT
CHANGED MY FAMILY'S LIFE

An Explore Family
Adventure offers a
unique and rewarding
chance for families to get
to know each other again.

explore.co.uk
0844 499 0901

Ref: Footfam

Explore – fun, safe travel in small groups, or as one family
in deserts or snow, jungle or savannah. An Explore Family
Adventure is more than just another holiday. It can provide
a unique family event with memories to match, letting both
kids and parents see each other in a different light as you
encounter new experiences together.

EXPLORE!
FAMILY ADVENTURES

and Queensland rainforest from family apartments in Port Douglas and on Dunk Island. Then take a four-day safari in Kakadu National Park and a two-day Discovery Eco Tour at Uluru before rounding the trip off with five nights in Sydney. From £1795 per person, including accommodation, domestic flights and tours.

Conservation holidays

Earthwatch earthwatch.org
Research and conservation expeditions for the whole family. No special skills are necessary, but your children need to be at least 10. Seven-day projects, such as a mammoth graveyard dig in South Dakota and a study of coastal ecology in the Bahamas, cost from around £1000 per person, including accommodation with a swimming pool, meals, training and special activities for children.

Holiday villages

Center Parcs centerparcs.com
A selection of 20 holiday villages in the UK, Netherlands, Belgium, Germany and France renowned for their extensive range of sports and leisure activities, plus numerous restaurants, bars, retail outlets and spa facilities.

Eurocamp eurocamp.com
Over 150 *parcs* in 12 European countries, including France, Spain, Italy, Germany, Switzerland, Austria and Croatia.
What the brochure says "Besides the swimming pools and waterslides that many *parcs* offer, you can also play tennis, football and many other games and sports, and often play golf, canoe or mountain bike nearby too. Most popular of all are our free, organized Fun Station clubs where children always meet new friends."
Pick of the trips Self-drive to Le Grande Métairie, Carnac, Brittany – a superbly equipped *parc* close to Carnac's famous standing stones. Starting price for one week in a Monaco Deluxe mobile home from around £230.

Keycamp keycamp.com
Mobile-home holidays in around 100 of the best campsites in France, Spain, Italy, Austria, Switzerland, Croatia, Sardinia and the Netherlands.
What the brochure says "Introducing new levels of luxury, the Prestige mobile home has all the comfort expected from a villa, including dishwasher, flat-screen TV and DVD player,

American-style fridge-freezer and an outdoor deck."
Pick of the trips Seven nights at Paris International staying in a Villanova mobile home with decking costs from around £470 for a family of four during August.

Also consider: Canvas Holidays canvasholidays.co.uk; Siblu siblu.com.

Latin America

Journey Latin America journeylatinamerica.co.uk
Leading Latin America specialist with extensive family programme offering tailor-made trips, escorted group tours and one-stop holidays (see also page 383).
What the brochure says "While you delight in places you have dreamed of visiting, your children will benefit from an incredible educational and horizon-expanding opportunity."

North America

Footloose footloose.com
Adventures in the United States and Canada for families with children aged eight and above.
Pick of the trips The 10-day 'Yellowstone Discovery' tour explores America's most famous national park on the look-out for bison, elk and wolves. Children have a chance to take part in the National Parks Service Junior Ranger Program. From around £530, departing Salt Lake City (10% discount for children).

Overland adventure

Dragoman dragoman.com
Claims to have developed the ultimate people carrier for adventure-seeking families. Its customized Mercedes Benz trucks carry adventurous families on overland trips in India, Morocco, East Africa, Botswana and Namibia.

Also consider: Guerba guerba.co.uk

Worldwide adventure

The Adventure Company adventurecompany.co.uk
Leading specialist in worldwide family adventures with over 60 holidays on offer, including special departures for single-parent families, as well as those with infants and teenagers. Some adventures offer a more stylish and comfortable level of accommodation. Centre-based adventures and school trips are also available.

phil&teds®

www.philandteds.com

Gidday Guys!
Remember when travelling with the kids was a complete nightmare? NO MORE! We've discovered phil&teds & now we're organised & mobile!
The in line buggy (perfect for taking 2 kids) goes anywhere.
The traveller ensures they sleep anywhere.
And with the lobster (the high chair that clamps onto any table) plus the shakeaway laté (that allows us to mix & feed on demand) they feed anywhere! So now we go EVERYWHERE! See ya, Sharon.

adapt&survive!™

" " There are a growing number of families who want more from their holidays than a standard, stay-put package, or a sterile world of crèches and kiddies' clubs. Our trips are designed to be an adventure for all members of the family.
Matt Berna, The Adventure Company

Five of the best family travel websites
1 family-travel.co.uk
2 takethefamily.com
3 travellingwith children.co.uk
4 kidsintow.co.uk
5 babygoes2.com

What the brochure says "The best school in the world *is* the world!"
Pick of the trips The two-week 'Headhunters of Borneo' itinerary includes travelling by longboat to stay with Iban villagers, visiting an orang-utan rehabilitation centre and turtle watching. It costs from around £1520 per adult and £1400 per child. 'Beyond the Arctic Circle' (£700/adult, £660/child) is a four-day trip to Finnish Lapland with lots of snowy activities, from dog sledging to igloo building.

Cox & Kings coxandkings.co.uk
Dedicated Family Explorer programme offering tailor-made journeys to India, China, Sri Lanka, Nepal, Bhutan, Egypt, Jordan, Morocco, Kenya, Namibia, South Africa, Tanzania, Zambia, Laos, Cambodia, Thailand, Malaysia, Mongolia, Costa Rica, Belize, Guatemala, Brazil, Argentina, Ecuador and Peru.

Pick of the trips A 10-day adventure combining Ecuador's highlands with the Galápagos Islands from around £2195 per adult and £1795 per child, including flights, accommodation and excursions.

Explore Worldwide explore.co.uk
Pioneers of small-group adventure holidays with around 50 trips for families, including special departures for teenagers.
What the brochure says "Our philosophy is simple: we travel in small, informal groups of four or five like-minded families, headed by a trained Explore tour leader. Most tours are designed for ages five upwards. The formula is tried and tested; our experience second to none."
Pick of the trips 'Go Independent' trips are for families who prefer to create a group of their own choosing, or find themselves unable to fit into scheduled departure dates. Choose from 19 trips, including Borneo, Cambodia, India, Jordan, Peru, South Africa, Sri Lanka and Vietnam. Many have no minimum age, making them even more appealing to busy families in search of flexibility.

Exodus exodus.co.uk
A wide range of family adventure holidays, including small group departures, individual family trips and centre-based activity holidays.
What the brochure says "The key to our family holidays is flexibility and choice. After all, families come in all shapes and sizes, so whether you're a single parent or a large extended family, we think you'll find a holiday that ticks all your boxes."
Pick of the trips A 15-day trip in Nepal combining an Annapurna trek with whitewater rafting and a jungle safari from around £1590 per adult, £1370 per child).

Families Worldwide familiesworldwide.co.uk

Experts in family adventures, with trips suitable for children as young as two.

What the brochure says "Learn to paint animals with a wildlife artist while on safari in Africa; find out about star constellations from a desert sky in Jordan; cook a curry in India; discover bush skills in a wilderness environment; learn photography in a rainforest; dress up as a Masaai warrior in Tanzania…"

Pick of the trips Eight action-packed days in Jordan, visiting Petra, exploring Wadi Rum and visiting Crusader castles, from around £800 per adult and £660 per child.

Virgin Holidays virginholidays.co.uk

According to a poll by Virgin Holidays, a third of families find holiday planning so stressful that they would rather stay at home. And of the 600 families surveyed, one in four graded the experience more stressful than moving house. Virgin's answer is 'Taste of Adventure' – a selection of 35 holidays that sandwich mini-adventures between beach or city breaks in an attempt to accommodate the needs of all family members

Also consider: Hayes & Jarvis hayesandjarvis.co.uk; The Imaginative Traveller imaginative-traveller.com; KE Adventure Travel keadventure.com; Kumuka kumuka.com; Peregrine Adventures peregrineadventures.com; Reef and Rainforest Tours familytours.co.uk; Walks Worldwide walksworldwide.com.

Worldwide luxury

Abercrombie & Kent abercrombiekent.com

Long-established luxury holiday operator with family programme.

What the brochure says "We've searched the world for family-friendly destinations, then featured them in special itineraries with sightseeing everyone can enjoy and activities interesting for all generations. Add the support of our 47 offices around the world and you have simply the best way to travel."

Powder Byrne powderbyrne.co.uk

A selection of the best hotels and resorts around the Mediterranean, Caribbean and the Indian Ocean, plus top ski resorts in the Alps. Free Scallywags Kids' Clubs.

What the brochure says "Our aim is to ensure that both parents and children enjoy the perfect holiday by combining some of the world's finest luxury resorts with our personal service that is second to none."

Pick of the trips Porto Elounda, Crete, where in addition to sailing and PADI-recognized scuba-diving, teenagers also have their very own boatman for snorkelling trips and barbecues on the beach.

Also consider: ITC Classics itcclassics.co.uk; Kuoni kuoni.co.uk; Scott Dunn scottdunn.com.

> **❝❞** Where a mass-market package holiday may leave you feeling like you're on a conveyor belt, or living in a sterile, plastic bubble, you'll be proud of the trip you've taken with us. You'll explore new landscapes, discover new cultures, experience new activities and, perhaps most importantly, you'll have learned a little more about life.
>
> *Mark Wright,*
> *Families Worldwide*

Travel light? Yeah, right!

It's a wonderful concept isn't it? Pack everything you think you're going to need for your holiday, then reduce it by half. The 'travel light' mantra of globetrotting gurus might suit backpackers with their handkerchief-sized super-absorbent towels and erratic rotation of underwear, but it's not always an easy, or necessarily desirable, option for families. Obviously, excessive luggage is a stress you can do without. However, depending on whether you skimp on things or take enough in the way of clothes, equipment, toys and supplies can be the difference between making travel with kids enjoyable or just bearable. See pages 40 to 43 for 30 best buys.

Documents

Many countries, including the UK, USA and Australia, require children to have their own passport (for the UK Passport Service visit ukpa.gov.uk). Apply for these at least two months in advance of your departure date – longer if you also need visas. Brace yourself for some fun and games when trying to get a legal passport photograph of your fidgety baby or toddler. Babies under one are allowed to have their eyes closed, children under five do not need to have a neutral expression or look directly at the camera, and photos of children under 11 can show a head size of between 21 and 34 mm instead of the adult minimum requirement of 29 mm. Otherwise, it must be a sharp, shadowless photograph – no grins, no dummies, no fingers up noses and no evidence that mum is supporting baby's head. Forget photo booths – you'll spend a fortune trying to get an acceptable image and the experience might put you off family travel for life. A professional photographer at a studio, on the other hand, will have lots of tricks for getting the perfect shot.

In addition to passports and visas, make sure you have adequate family travel insurance, certificates of any medical prescriptions or vaccinations (like yellow fever) that may need to be shown at immigration or customs controls, a print-out of your itinerary and e-tickets (more likely nowadays than flight, rail or ferry tickets) and contact details while away. Take two copies of everything, stash one set in your hand luggage and leave the other with a friend or relative at home.

Packing

What you take will depend on several factors, such as the age of your children, the type of trip (city break, trek, beach holiday etc), the likely climate (hot, cold or wet) and whether you're going to fly somewhere or pile everything into the car and drive.

The amount of gear you take is adversely proportional to the size of your child. Essentials for travelling with babies can include nappies, umpteen changes of clothes, feeding equipment, pushchair, favourite toys, travel cot, bedding, portable high chair and car seat. For toddlers you'll still need a

pushchair, car seat, toys and travel potty. Once kids reach four or five, they will probably want to pack their own small daypack with a few games, some activity pads and colouring pencils, a soft toy and some sweets. Teenagers meanwhile are often content with a book or magazine, an MP3 player or games console, a supply of spare batteries and a 'do not disturb' sign.

When children (especially girls) reach a certain age, they take a determined – though not always realistic – interest in what clothes to pack. Diplomacy and supreme negotiating skills are required by parents to ensure that half your luggage isn't filled with a dozen varieties of sandals and a summer dress for each day you're away. Generally, though, clothes need to be lightweight, casual, durable, compatible with each other and easy to wash and dry. See opposite for a suggested clothing checklist.

Once you've finished deliberating over what to take you need to decide how you're going to carry it. A suitcase or holdall is fine – you can find things quickly and easily – but make sure it has wheels for those inevitable airport situations when you need to simultaneously carry a tired child and shift heavy luggage. A medium-sized case for each member of the family can be more practical than one or two colossal ones. It gives children independence, they can find their own things without turning out everyone else's and, if you're not sharing the same room in a hotel, it saves a lot of running back and forth along the corridors.

Hand luggage

Pack spare clothes and other essentials (such as wet wipes, nappies and favourite toys) in your hand luggage in case your suitcases get lost, the flight is delayed or cancelled, or you discover that your child is airsick. Following increased security measures at airports there are now restrictions on the quantities of liquids (including all drinks, syrups, creams, lotions, oils, sprays and pastes) that can be carried in cabin baggage. You can carry small quantities of liquids, but only in separate containers that must not exceed 100 ml and are clearly visible in a single, transparent, resealable plastic bag (about the size of a small freezer bag) ready for inspection by airport security staff. Medical equipment, such as inhalers for asthma sufferers, are permitted. Prescribed medicines, accompanied by relevant documentation, may also be allowed in quantities over the 100-ml limit, but you should check with your airline beforehand. Although liquid baby food and sterilized water, sufficient for the journey, can be taken through airport security, the accompanying adult will be required to verify by tasting.

Boredom busters

Whether it's a rainy day, a long car journey or a delayed flight, there will be occasions during every family holiday when

? Can Rover come too?

Check out dogsaway.co.uk for details of how to get your pooch a passport and plan a doggy-friendly break in Europe.

Reality check #3: Best-laid plans

Lists. Where would we be without them? To travel listless, so to speak, is to miss out on one of the great rituals of holidaymaking. Bedtime toys, high-factor sunblock, travel cot, nappies, Calpol, a change of clothes if they're sick on the plane, ditto for the airport taxi, ditto for the rental car, ditto for yourself… forget any one of these (and a hundred other essentials) at your peril. You might think you're a hardened traveller because you've trekked to Everest and haggled in Marrakech, but try sitting on a plane for a few hours with a toddler drenched in regurgitated milk and cauliflower cheese.

Sometimes things you have intentionally omitted from the all-important list can prove your downfall. You might suppose, for example, that having prebooked a child seat with your rental car that something vaguely resembling a child seat might actually have been installed in your vehicle. But it's amazing how often rental companies instead substitute a polystyrene contraption with a harness that looks like it's been pillaged from My Little Pony.

Perhaps the most foolproof option for family holidays is to buy a bigger car, disgorge most of your house contents into it and then drive to your destination. We tried that once. I seem to remember a spectacular mobilization of colour-coded Tupperware, copious toys (general, bath, cot and car), several dozen jars of assorted baby food, a double buggy, two high chairs, two travel cots, a bottle sterilizer, milk powder, sleepsuits, cot linen, at least a thousand bibs and enough nappies to plug a hole in a sinking battleship.

Will

---

children simply need to have some time out and occupy themselves quietly. You can encourage these all-too-ephemeral moments by packing a few books, games, toys and activities. See pages 40-43 for a selection of best buys.

Babies and toddlers need familiar, comforting playthings which smell and feel like home. But, given the chance, they will also find endless fascination with new and exciting objects like telephones, sugar sachets and minibars in hotel rooms or brochure stands, fire extinguishers and waste bins with revolving lids at airports. It doesn't always work, but try diverting their attention with a surprise toy or two.

Left to their own devices, school-age children will stuff a fairly random array of their favourite knick-knacks into their hand luggage and, while Barbie, a few Hot Wheels cars, a Tamagotchi and a tube of Smarties could well be in there, you might want to make a few additional suggestions. For girls, a Polly Pocket doll set takes up little space and can be totally absorbing. Boys can play Top Trumps card games with each other or simply study the statistics on their own. Activity books with quizzes, stickers and colouring pages are a must, as are pads (with a mixture of ruled and plain paper) and plenty of colouring pens and pencils. Sometimes the simplest, most traditional games, such as Shut the Box or magnetic travel versions of Ludo or draughts, can become utterly addictive. Inevitably, though, pride of place in any kid's personal travel kit is going to go to an electronic games console. Whatever your views on them, these high-tech gizmos are a great way of getting hyperactive or overtired children to sit quietly for an hour or so. With all the exciting things happening on holiday, fanatical obsession is unlikely – and don't forget that some brands, like Leapfrog's Leapster, have a strong educational element.

One of the best ways to keep boredom at bay is to

encourage children to keep a journal of their travels. Make it as fun and interactive as possible. Pack scissors and glue stick so they can cut and paste postcards, tickets and other souvenirs into their literary masterpiece. An envelope stuck to the inside back cover can be used to store other treasures. You may need to help younger children with cues, such as "The journey was…", "I like the beach because…" or "The food was disgusting because…" The playback function on digital cameras is also a great prompter when kids complain that they can't think of anything to write.

Top tips for travelling with babies or toddlers

▸ Reusable cloth nappies are easy to pack and can double up as towels. If taking disposables, note that your preferred brand may not be available. One option is to stuff a holdall full of nappies and check it in.

▸ Consider taking your own travel cot for extra familiarity. Many models are lightweight and fold away neatly and compactly. They also make excellent 'holding pens' while you check out a new room for potential hazards.

▸ Pack a raincover, sunshade and insect net for your buggy, a non-slip bath mat for the hotel tub, sun protectors for car windows, a waterproof undersheet for small children and a stair gate if staying in two-storey accommodation.

▸ If renting a car, consider taking your own child seat. The ones provided by the rental company may not meet required safety standards. Use a luggage-wrapping service at the airport to protect the seat in transit.

▸ With check-in times of up to three hours before long-haul flights be sure to take plenty of toys and books to keep you and your toddler sane.

What to pack

▸ Cotton short-sleeve shirts
▸ T-shirts
▸ Blouses
▸ Long-sleeved shirts
▸ Long trousers
▸ Cotton skirt
▸ Shorts
▸ Cotton wrap
▸ Lightweight dress
▸ Lightweight fleece jacket
▸ Tracksuit
▸ Pyjamas/nightwear
▸ Underwear
▸ Socks
▸ Lightweight cagoule
▸ Sweater/sweatshirt
▸ Sunhat
▸ Sunglasses
▸ Shirt with built-in sun protection
▸ Comfortable walking shoes
▸ Sandals
▸ Swimwear
▸ Jelly shoes
▸ Gloves/scarf/thermals
▸ Torch
▸ Spare batteries/charger
▸ Washkit
▸ Towels
▸ Universal bath plug
▸ Detergent
▸ Clothes line
▸ Sewing kit
▸ Travel plug adaptor
▸ Travel alarm clock
▸ Wet wipes
▸ Moisturizing cream
▸ First aid kit (page 56)
▸ Camera
▸ Memory cards/film
▸ Toilet paper
▸ Sun cream
▸ Lip salve

Athens Crocs

Healthy, hip summer footwear for kids, these lightweight shoes have a supportive, shock-absorbing construction that moulds to your child's feet. Bacteria and odour resistant, the Athens has non-marking, slip-resistant soles and can be easily wiped clean or sterilized in water and bleach. Available in six colours and from children's size 6-7 to size 3.

£17, lookatmycrazyshoes.com

Beach Cosy

Just the job for wrapping up warm after a swim in the sea, this super-soft cotton towelling robe has a roomy hood for hair-drying and protection from the sun, plus a big kangaroo pouch that's ideal for collecting stuff. Available in pink or blue for children aged one to eight.

£18, muddypuddles.com

Beach Heads

Give sandcastles a facelift with these wacky face packs. Each one contains sand moulds to make two heads and bodies that you can then decorate with weird and wonderful face parts.

£9.95, kit2fit.com

Car Seat Activity Centre

Get creative in the car with this fold-out desk that attaches firmly to the front seats and has plenty of space for storing colouring books, pencils and crayons.

£22.99, gltc.co.uk

Escape Carrier

Phil & Teds have thought of everything with this superb child carrier for ages three months to four years. You'd expect the seat to be adjustable, but the foot stirrups for increased circulation are a nice touch. You'll also find loads of other useful extras, such as a rear-vision mirror, sun cover with rain flaps, storage for drinks and toys, stowaway changing mat and detachable dribble cloth. Folds flat and weighs just 2 kg.

NZ$249.95, philandteds.com

Expedition Natural Insect Repellent

Kinder to your children's skin than chemical-based sprays, this repellent uses an extract of eucalyptus oil to deter nippers like mosquitoes, midges, horseflies and sandflies for up to six hours. Recommended for children over two years of age.

£6.50 for a 100-ml bottle, lifesystems.co.uk

Harry Potter and the Deathly Hallows

Audio CD book narrated by Stephen Fry, in which Harry discovers what fate has in store for him at his final meeting with Voldemort. A thrilling climax to JK Rowling's epic series – and gripping stuff for long car journeys.

Bloomsbury.com

8. Horrible Geography

Find out about the Intrepid Explorers, Bloomin' Rainforests and other geographical gems in this amusing series of paperbacks for children aged seven and above.

£7.99, scholastic.com

9. Ladybird Daysack

Cute little 'bugpack' for one- to four-year-olds with clip-on rein and nifty top pocket containing a water resistant, colour-coordinated hood.

£14.99, littlelife.co.uk

10. Leapster

Help children aged four to 10 grasp essential maths, reading, spelling, writing and logic skills with this interactive, hand-held games gizmo. Additional cartridges feature Disney Princess, *Finding Nemo*, *The Incredibles* and *Cars*. The more expensive L-Max unit interacts with your TV.

£59.99, leapfroguk.com

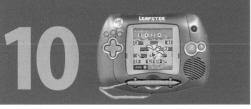

11. Little Shield Travel Cot

One of the more sturdy travel cots available on the market, with a fold-flat frame, wipe-clean padded trim and four mesh sides for good air-circulation and visibility.

£39.99, littleshield.com

12. Mini MULE

Getting active kids to drink enough fluids isn't always easy. But with the Camelbak Mini MULE they've got constant access to up to 1½ litres of water in a smart and practical backpack fitted with a flexible drinking tube. Suitable for children aged five and over.

£39.99, camelbak.com

13. Movie Traveller

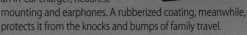

Boasting an 18-cm widescreen TFT display, integrated stereo speakers and a lithium-ion battery providing up to 2½ hours playback, this ultra-compact portable DVD player comes with an in-car charger, headrest mounting and earphones. A rubberized coating, meanwhile, protects it from the knocks and bumps of family travel.

£199.99, powertraveller.com

14. Olympus Mju 725SW

Not only is this stylish seven-megapixel compact camera shockproof from drops of up to 150 cm, but you can also take it underwater to depths of 5 m, making it a great family all-rounder, whether you're hitting the beach or the pistes. Other features include a bright 6.4-cm-wide LCD screen, 3x optical zoom and 25 scene modes for trouble-free shooting.

£300, olympus.com.

15. Outdoor Explorer

A great kit for nature detectives aged five to nine. Make a bug catcher for mini-beasts, design a snail park, take bark rubbings, cast tracks, age trees and more.

£8.99, letterbox.co.uk

16. Pocket Scrabble

Word fun on the run, this travel version of Scrabble has a magnetic playing surface that locks tiles firmly in place. Suitable for ages 10 and over.

£9.99, mattelscrabble.com

17. Pocket Scribbler

A handy magnetic scribbler that's just the right size for quick sketches or a game of noughts and crosses.

£3, elc.co.uk

18. Queasy Pops

Lollipops that are good for you! Drug-free and recommended by healthcare professionals, Queasy Pops use all-natural ingredients to combat motion sickness, drowsiness and nausea. Available in seven flavours: natural cola, sour raspberry, cinnamon, sour lemon, peppermint, papaya and green apple.

US$3.95 for a pack of seven, threelollies.com

Rash shirt

19

Ideal for surfing or for just playing and swimming at the beach. Made from loose-fitting polyester which is breathable, cool and comfortable to wear. Built-in sun protection (SPF50+).

£17.95, sun-togs.co.uk

SolarSafe

20

A waterproof wristband that lets you monitor your family's exposure to harmful UV radiation. Once coated with suncream the band turns blue when exposed to sunlight, brown when it's time to reapply and yellow when it's time to seek shade. Also acts as an identification band in case you and your child become separated.

£4.99 for a box of seven, solarsafe.com

Sony PSP

21

Play games and access videos, photos, music and internet on a Sony PlayStation Portable – quite possibly the most desirable travel gadget of them all. And it comes in pink too.

£129.99 for base unit console, playstation.com

Swimsafe floatsuit

22

A small price to pay for added piece of mind in the sun and in the water, these swimsuits have SPF50+ sun protection and built-in neck float and flexible buoyancy panels to keep your child's head above water.

£29.95, jakabel.com

TomTom GO 910

23

In-car navigation system offering door-to-door route-finding across Europe, USA and Canada. Boasts a 10-cm-wide LCD touch screen and clear spoken instructions, including street and place names in no less than 36 languages and 50 different voices.

£349.99, tomtom.com

Top Trumps

24

From *Pirates of the Caribbean* and *Star Wars* to *Chelsea FC* and *Wonders of the World*, these boxed card sets are not only addictive to play with, but you can also boost your brain power at the same time. Other titles include *Disney Heroes*, *Power Rangers*, *Thomas the Tank Engine* and *Dogs* – where you can see how your favourite pooch scores on categories such as weight, guard-dog skill, rarity and lovability.

From £2.49, toptrumps.com

Totseat

25

If you've ever been frustrated by the lack of high chairs in restaurants and cafés while travelling abroad, help has arrived in the form of this washable, squashable travel high chair that simply slips over a chair back, then can be wiped clean and stuffed in a pocket after use.

£22, totseat.com

Trunki Towgo

26

Keep kids in tow with their very own ride-on, pull-along, pack-it-yourself hand luggage. Made from durable plastic and suitable for children aged three and above, Towgo packs a generous 18 litres of space and features locking catches, teddy bear seatbelts (or internal straps to grown-ups) and a secret compartment for storing goodies. The perfect stress-reliever for parents struggling with luggage and children at airports or train stations.

£29.99, trunki.co.uk

Window Sox

Developed in Perth, Australia, these fine-mesh sunblinds slip over the frame of the rear doors of your car and block 80% of the sun's harmful UV rays. Unlike conventional car window blinds, they shade the entire window, inquisitive children can't pull them off and you can still open the window and let in fresh air.

£23 for a pack of two, windowsox.co.uk

27

The Great World Search

From a crowded Moroccan souk and an East African safari to a cruise ship and an Antarctic expedition, this large-format book takes you on a puzzle-solving grand tour through 18 travel scenarios –each one beautifully illustrated with enough detail to keep kids absorbed for hours.

£4.99, usborne.com

28

Zoobug

Trendy sunglasses for active kids aged three to 15. Interchangeable lenses offer 100% UV protection. The infant range features flexible, hypo-allergenic silicone arms and adjustable nosepieces, while the junior ranges have sporty or designer looks.

From £30, zoobug.co.uk

29

Vibe Inline Buggy

A tough, versatile buggy to keep pace with a growing family, the Vibe has a cleverly designed multi-positional seat (upright, heads-up, sleepy and lie flat), five-point harness and central brake. Simply click on the double kit to carry a baby and a toddler. With an ultralight aluminium frame, lockable swivel front wheel and washable fabric, this 9 kg stroller is suitable for newborns up to kids aged four.

philandteds.com

30

How to get there

Are we there yet?

Experienced globetrotters will often tell you that it's the 'journey' not the 'getting there' that really matters; that travel is enriched by taking your time on the road, meeting people and having chance encounters. Suggest this to most parents, however, and they will either stare at you blankly, laugh out loud or start twitching uncontrollably. Whether it's the memory of dealing with a screaming baby on a flight, bickering siblings on an interminable car journey or a moping teenager who didn't want to come in the first place, every parent has good reason for treating family journeys with some trepidation.

Of course, just because you're travelling with kids doesn't automatically guarantee it's going to be a journey from hell. However, when you consider what you are putting yourselves (and them) through it's only to be expected that things occasionally go awry. Planning and packing for a family holiday requires a lot of effort and you will naturally be anxious about taking your brood to unfamiliar places. Then there's all the queuing at airports, the confinement of children to cramped aircraft cabins (or cars) and the constant expectation for them to behave. It can all add up to tension, short tempers and tears. Just remember these three saving graces: even the longest long-haul flight eventually ends; you'll probably never see the people who were sitting near you again; and the worse the experience, the better the dinner-party story in years to come. And don't forget that most journeys with kids also have their fair share of relaxed moments and laughs – whether it's a sing-along in the car or the bumpy landing that, for some reason, young children always find hysterically amusing.

34-point plan for air travel
Think green

▸▸ Consider carefully whether there is a viable, more environmentally friendly alternative to flying.

At the time of booking

▸▸ Budget for children under two paying 10% of the adult fare, but remember that they have to sit on your lap and are not usually given a food or baggage allowance.

▸▸ Reserve seats so you can all sit together. If you are travelling with a baby, request bulkhead seats where bassinets can be fitted. Remember to obtain approval from the airline if you want to use your child's car seat on the flight.

▸▸ Pre-order children's meals.

▸▸ Check whether you can take your pushchair to the boarding gate or the aircraft door and find out where it will be available again after landing.

▸▸ Find out what other special children's facilities may be available, such as goody bags, seat-back entertainment systems etc.

▸▸ If possible, choose a daytime flight to minimize disturbance to sleeping routines.

▸▸ Arrange a meet-and-greet service with an airport parking operator such as Purple Parking (purpleparking.com). You simply drop your car off at departures, someone parks it for you and then has it waiting at arrivals when you return.

Packing for the journey

▸▸ Take all baby essentials in your hand luggage.

▸▸ Pack a supply of healthy snacks.

▸▸ Don't forget to take a few sachets of Calpol (infants' paracetamol).

▸▸ Remember trainer cups with non-spill lids for toddlers.

▸▸ Have a few boiled sweets handy to help ears pop during the final descent.

▸▸ Pack a familiar pillow or soft toy to comfort and help children sleep.

▸▸ Help children to pack their own small in-flight backpack (see page 38).

The day before flying

▸▸ Try to keep things calm and normal.

▸▸ Eat light, bland meals so as not to risk upset stomachs.

▸▸ Sort out comfortable, loose-fitting clothes for the flight.

At the airport

▸▸ Get there in plenty of time so you're not stressed out or stuck at the back of a huge check-in queue.

▸▸ Fit reins on toddlers to give them freedom – safely.

▸▸ Find out if there's a children's play area.

▸▸ Before boarding, always check the floor where you've been sitting – a favourite teddy or toy is bound to have been dropped there.

▸▸ Make use of priority boarding for families with young children.

During the flight

▸▸ Feed your baby on take-off and landing to reduce discomfort caused by changes in cabin pressure.

▸▸ Don't be afraid to ask flight attendants for help, warming baby food etc.

▸▸ Ensure your children drink little and often to ward off dehydration.

▸▸ Don't drug your child with medicines, such as Piriton, unless you've tried them before flying. Although they can help some children sleep, other side effects include irritability or

66 99 If there's a long stopover of a few hours or more, leave the airport and try to find a hotel nearby with a pool. We found this worked really well in Bangkok.

Charlie Panton

10 of the most family-friendly airlines

	General child-friendly facilities	Pre-book seats	Nappies	Milk formula	Baby food	Seat-back entertainment
Gulf Air ★★★★★	Dedicated Sky Nannies available to assist with boarding and disembarkation, arranging children's meals and drinks and helping to keep kids comfortable and entertained. Skycots and activity packs.	✓	✓	✓	✓	Kids' movies and Disney channel.
Virgin Atlantic ★★★★★	Skycots for infants up to 12 months, baby-changing facilities, Care Chairs for children aged 6-36 months, children's meals and aviator snack boxes, K-iD backpack, *First News* newspaper for children aged 9-12.	✓	✓	✓	✓	Family movies, dedicated V Kids' channel for pre-school, 5-11-year-olds and teens, computer games.
Singapore Airlines ★★★★	Bassinets, disposable bibs, feeding bottles and baby wipes available on board, children's meals.	✓	✓	✓	✓	Kids' movies, games, cartoons, and language-learning programme.
Air New Zealand ★★★★	Bassinets for children up to 8 months, children's meals, bottle-warming service, activity packs.	✓	✓	✓	✓	Kids' movies, cartoons and games.
British Airways ★★★★	Family check-in on ba.com from 24 hours before departure, Britax seats on first-come-first-served basis, skycots for babies, feed kids first policy, 5 portions of fruit or vegetables guaranteed in every meal for young flyers, Skyflyers activity packs, hand-held games consoles in World Traveller Plus and Club World.	✓				Disney and Cartoon Network channels, family movies on long-haul flights.
Qantas ★★★★	Dedicated Wiggles website, bassinets, baby bottles, cereals and rusks, activity kits, children's meals.	✓	✓		✓	On-demand movies and games on Boeing 747s and Airbus A330s.
Emirates ★★★	Skycots, children's meals, surprise cakes for kids flying on their birthdays, activity packs.				✓	Skysurfers channel with movies, games and cartoons on Boeing 777s and Airbus A340s.
Thai Airways ★★★	Skycots for children up to six months, children's meals, gifts.				✓	On-demand movies on Boeing 777s and Airbus A340s.
KLM ★★★	Junior Jet Service offering extra attention for young children and their parents, Skycots on intercontinental flights, children's meals, activity packs.					On-demand movies and games on Boeing 777s and Airbus A330s
American Airlines ★★	Changing tables available on wide-bodied aircraft, bottle-warming service, pre-bookable skycots, no children's meals or activity packs.	✓				Audio headsets available for US$2, 10-channel screens on Boeing 777s.

Note: Rating airlines on how family-friendly they are is very subjective. Even the best goody bag, for example, is no substitute for a particularly attentive and sympathetic flight attendant – and getting one of those is often pot luck. Also bear in mind that the facilities listed above are subject to availability and type of aircraft.

Airlines

Aer Lingus aerlingus.com
Aeroflot aeroflot.ru
Aerolineas Argentinas aerolineas.com.ar
Air Canada aircanada.ca
Air China air-china.co.uk
Air France airfrance.com
Air India airindia.com
Air Mauritius airmauritius.com
Air Namibia airnamibia.com.na
Air New Zealand airnewzealand.com
Air Seychelles airseychelles.net
Air Tanzania airtanzania.com
Alitalia alitalia.com
All Nippon Airways anaskyweb.com
American Airlines aa.com
British Midland flybmi.com
British Airways britishairways.com
Cathay Pacific cathaypacific.com
Continental Airlines continental.com
Croatia Airlines croatiaairlines.hr
Czech Airlines czechairlines.com
Delta Airlines delta.com
easyJet easyjet.com
Egyptair egyptair.com
Emirates emirates.com
Finnair finnair.com
Flybe flybe.com
Garuda garuda-indonesia.com
Gulf Air gulfair.com
Iberia Airlines iberia.com
Icelandair icelandair.net
Kenya Airways kenya-airways.com
KLM klm.com
LOT Polish Airlines lot.com
Lufthansa lufthansa.com
Malaysia Airlines malaysiaairlines.com
Mexicana Airlines mexicana.com
Qantas qantas.com.au
Royal Air Maroc royalairmaroc.com
Ryanair ryanair.com
Scandinavian Airlines flysas.com
Singapore Airlines singaporeair.com
South African Airways flysaa.com
Sri Lankan Airlines srilankan.aero
Swiss Air swiss.com
Thai Airways thaiairways.com
Turkish Airlines thy.com
United Airlines united.com
Varig Brazilian Airlines varig.com
Virgin Atlantic virginatlantic.com

66 99 Helping Ellie with her breakfast tray, I innocently peeled the lid off her yoghurt pot. She snapped. Big time. Sleep deprivation, the rush of time zones, the endless queues… all the tension and tiredness of the whole long-haul flight experience suddenly triggered a 9.5 on the temper scale. She wanted to peel that lid off and nothing I could say or do would put it right. Globules of strawberry yoghurt began to fly as the screams of an irate four-year-old bludgeoned the other passengers. Some spontaneously adopted the brace position.

Will

Please fasten your seatbelts and prepare for mayhem.

Reality check #4: The flight

There is a lot to be said for flying with babies when they are still small enough not to have discovered the liberating joys of crawling or walking. Joe and Ellie were fully mobile at 13 months when we took them to Tenerife on their first flight. The potential for some quality parent-to-child bonding while sitting quietly on our laps during a three-hour plane ride was completely lost on them. Wriggling aside, however, what really threw us was how systematically the twins managed to destroy our carefully conceived stress-busting strategy.

The first of our clever tricks (intended to take their minds off the flight) involved surprise toys. Verdict: waste of money. Joe and Ellie were more thrilled with the detachable headrest covers which they insisted on flapping in the faces of the people sitting behind. Trick number two: give them a drink at take-off to ease pressure in their ears. Flawed again. At the last minute, three planes jumped the runway queue and Ellie drained her bottle. When we finally got airborne, Joe threw his bottle on the floor; it slid out of reach as the plane climbed, and his head cracked on the fold-up tray as I tried to grab it.

All of this wouldn't have seemed so bad if the people sitting next to us were a little more sympathetic. One was a businessman who insisted on ordering red wine with his meal – a disaster waiting to happen with fidgety toddlers about. Joe, meanwhile, was trying to make friends with our other neighbour who was hiding behind a copy of *The Times*. Frustrated by this man's inability to grasp even the basics of 'pee-po', Joe proceeded to shred the newspaper with his toy digger.

Will

short-lived deep sleep followed by hyperactivity.

▸▸ Do try natural relaxants, like lavender oil or camomile tea.
▸▸ If the cabin's dry air causes discomfort to your child's nose, lips or sinuses, try getting them to breathe through a handkerchief soaked in a little water.
▸▸ Don't expect a toddler to be absorbed with one activity for the duration of the flight – bring lots of toys, books and snacks to distract and amuse them.
▸▸ Take kids to the toilet well before the seat-belt signs come on for the final descent.
▸▸ Respect the comfort of other passengers by dealing firmly with unacceptable behaviour (such as children kicking the

What is the best airport to get stuck in?

Let's face it, an airport is a means to an end. Few families would actually choose to spend more time in one than was absolutely essential. But if your flight is delayed or you miss a connection, certain airports make the waiting considerably easier than others. Singapore's **Changi** airport, for example, has a swimming pool, five themed indoor gardens, six Xbox stations, an Explorer's Lounge with Discovery and National Geographic channels and free two-hour city sightseeing tours for stopovers of five hours or more. **Narita** airport in Tokyo has several children's play areas and nurseries; Florida's **Orlando** airport is packed with shops (Disney, Sea World etc) and offers occasional views of space shuttle launches from the top of the terminal car park; Copenhagen's **Kastrup** airport has a large family play area with a pirate ship sailing in a sea of plastic balls, while Amsterdam's **Schipol** airport has an annex of the famous Rijksmuseum and even has its own children's website with airport information and games.

seat in front), but be prepared for some people to give you the 'raised eyebrow' treatment merely at the sight of your little darlings.
▸▸ Remember, the more you tell kids not to press the hostess call button the more they will do it.

Coping with jet lag

▸▸ Trans-continental, overnight flights will leave your children flagging, but try to keep them going during your first day. Help their body clocks readjust by getting outside, doing some moderate exercise and drinking plenty of water. A few gentle hours in a local park is ideal. There's nothing wrong with them grabbing a short nap, but try to get them to bed at the same time as they would back home. Then just pray that they sleep through.

Four good reasons to stay put in the UK

With today's global spread of family-adventure destinations it's easy to become seduced by the exotic and far-flung. But spare a thought for the UK. By staying grounded, Brits can do their bit to reduce CO_2 emissions by avoiding air travel, while overseas visitors may well be surprised at the range of holidays available.

1 Self-catering in Cornwall Renting a property is definitely the way to go if you're looking for independence and flexibility. Located in a quiet lane above Sennen Cove with its superb sandy beach and surfing, Atlantic House costs around £525 per

66 99 Low-cost airlines that don't allocate seats are great because most people don't want to be anywhere near children. We often get six seats between the four of us!

Alison Williams

week from Classic Cottages (classic.co.uk). The bright and uncluttered New England-style interior includes a bespoke kitchen and accommodation for up to seven people.

2 All-inclusive in Suffolk If your idea of a perfect family holiday is minimal effort and stress, it's hard to beat Center Parcs (centerparcs.co.uk). Their Elveden Forest village in Suffolk, for example, boasts everything from a Balinese-themed water centre and nine-hole golf course to a luxury spa and revolving restaurant. Midweek rates (for four nights in July) staying in a two-bedroom villa start from around £555.

3 Multi-activity in Scotland You can try a little bit of everything at Cape Adventure International (capeventure.co.uk), an outdoor activity centre in the Scottish North West Highlands. A six-day family holiday (suitable for children aged eight and over) promises non-stop excitement with hiking, sea kayaking, abseiling, land-yachting, surfing and even a survival course on a remote island. From £440 for adults and £340 for under-16s.

4 Dolphin-watching in Wales Around 140 bottlenose dolphins live year-round in Cardigan Bay, and you have an excellent chance of spotting them during a guided holiday with The Whale and Dolphin Conservation Society (wdcs.org/outoftheblue). Four-day trips cost from around £400 for adults and £325 for children under 14, including accommodation and most meals.

The long and whining road

It's not surprising that so many families opt for self-drive holidays, either renting a car or taking their own. With the freedom of the open road you can travel when you want and for as long as you want (although the latter is often dictated by the capacity of your children's bladders). You can schedule regular breaks at parks, beaches and other recreational areas to let children burn off energy. You can tweak your itinerary as you go along, there's more space for luggage and you can even time drives to coincide with when your baby or toddler normally has a daytime nap. Sounds like a piece of cake. So what's the catch?

Boredom. Close confinement. Sibling squabbles. Stress from coping with traffic. Stress from getting lost. Stress from rushing to catch the ferry. These and a dozen other factors conspire to drive you to distraction. In order to endure long car journeys with the kids you need a few good tactics and plenty in the way of ICE (In-Car-Entertainment).

Tactics fall into three main categories. The first is piece of mind. Make absolutely certain, especially when renting a car, that your children will be safe. Engage child locks on the rear doors and windows, fit blinds to windows if you are travelling in a hot and sunny country and give rented child seats a thorough going-over to make sure that harnesses, buckles and head supports are not damaged in any way. It's impossible to predict the condition of child seats provided by

Reality check #5: The car journey

When they were 10 months old, we took our twins, Joe and Ellie to the Shetland Islands. Nothing particularly epic about that you might think. We didn't even fly there. But I look back on that journey to Britain's far-flung northern outpost with a kind of weary nostalgia. Several long-haul adventures later, it still stands as our greatest, most stressful moment of parental endeavour – the turning point at which we realized that nothing could ever get worse.

On the day of departure, my wife, Sally, and I were feeling relaxed and organized. We'd booked an overnight stop in Hexham to break the long drive to the ferry port in Aberdeen. All we had to do was get going reasonably early and we'd be there by bath time. A doddle. But at 0700 Ellie returned her breakfast with a vengeance. By the time we'd collected antibiotics from the doctor it was already noon. We made a dash for the motorway and an hour later pulled into a service station – more for the sake of sanity than anything else. You see, baby twins, when restrained in a car for long periods, can not only drown out the sound of your engine with their screaming, but also that of every other vehicle within a three-mile stretch of the M1.

We arrived at Hexham feeling bludgeoned. Our hotel room was on the third floor in the furthest corner of the building – far enough away, I hoped, to cause as little disturbance to other guests as possible. Joe immediately felled a standard lamp and ate two sachets of complimentary Nescafé, while Ellie helpfully scattered jars of baby food across the floor. I managed to sidestep three jars of spaghetti hoops, but the Moroccan chicken that was lurking under a fold of the bedspread sent me cartwheeling into the en suite.

The good news was that Ellie seemed to be perking up on the antibiotics. Even Joe, a notoriously lazy feeder, had downed his bedtime milk. But it's amazing how babies can lull you into a false sense of security. The enthusiasm with which Joe proceeded to vomit across the room was unprecedented. If you had detonated a bomb inside a bucket of milk you still wouldn't have matched the range and coverage that he achieved.

Sally and I moved swiftly into organized panic mode: put sick-drenched Joe in bath; Joe grabs shower hose; shower head falls off wall and hits Joe on head; Joe screams; put Ellie down to comfort Joe; Ellie slips in sick; Ellie screams . . .

It sounds horrendous and, in fact, it was. The following morning we stubbornly continued to Aberdeen. The ferry car deck was so tightly packed that Sally, laden with travel cots and changing bags, became wedged in an aisle. She might have been there for the entire 14-hour voyage, trapped like a fly in a spider's web, had a kindly gentleman not offered to hold the twins while I went to free her.

Will

🎮 Travel games

In the car…

Car bingo Give players a sheet of paper and ask them to write down 25 different numbers between one and 99. The person in the front passenger seat calls out the last one or two digits from the licence plates of passing cars. The winner is the first to cross off all their numbers.

Licence to thrill Make up phrases based on the letters of licence plates. For example, 234 IFS 00 could be "Ice-cream for Sally" or "I feel sick!"

Buzz words Pick a word, then turn on the radio or play a story tape and try to be the first to shout "buzz" when the word is mentioned.

Anywhere…

Alphabet animals Starting with 'A', take it in turns to name an animal beginning with each letter of the alphabet. For an added challenge, you must repeat all the animals that have been named prior to your go.

Word association Say a word; the person sitting to your left must respond with the first word that comes into their head.

What am I? One player thinks of an object, animal, profession etc and can only answer "yes" or "no" to simple questions, such as "Are you alive?", "Are you small?" or "Can I eat you?"

Power to the pedal

Not for the faint-hearted, bicycle touring with children in tow (sometimes literally) requires fitness, stamina, detailed planning and serious equipment. As well as sturdy adult bikes, you will need a child seat or trailer for young children. Child seats should fit securely on to a bike rack and have extra padding in case of a fall. Trailers are heavier, but have the advantages of accommodating two small children and even some luggage, as well as providing protection from rain and sun. Trailer bikes that attach to an adult cycle are an option for older children. With all ages, however, be realistic about daily distances and try to pick routes that are largely traffic-free.

❓ How much greener is train travel?

According to independent research commissioned by Eurostar, passengers on its trains generate 10 times less of the greenhouse gas, carbon dioxide (CO_2), than travellers who fly the same route. For example, a return flight between London and Paris generates 122 kg of CO_2 per passenger trip, compared to 11 kg on Eurostar.

car rental companies, so if in doubt take your own.

The second tactic involves planning. If your children are old enough get them to help you research the route, compile a schedule and pick a few options for rest breaks and side trips. Giving kids joint ownership of the drive plan offers them an incentive to look forward to journey highlights rather than lapsing into 'moan mode'. And, thirdly, try to stay upbeat and positive. You're stuck together in the car for another two hours, so make the most of it: play travel games (see above), sing songs or just chat.

Of course, there's no point having tactics without backing them up with some 'armour' – tangible stuff that will appeal to children either through their minds or their stomachs. Make sure you've packed a good supply of snacks and drinks (see page 52). Car seats with fold-out cup holders help to minimize spillages, while drop-down trays that attach to the back of the front seats can be used as dinner tables, writing desks or play surfaces. Bring along colouring pads, crayons and pencils, magnetic board games, reading books, activity books, card games, dressing-up dolls, construction models… anything really that doesn't involve tiny pieces that are constantly going to end up dropped, out of reach, on the floor. A map or mini-atlas is a great idea for children who want to trace the route.

Upping the technology stakes slightly, story tapes or CDs played through the car stereo are often a good means of calming a back-seat fracas or eking out another quiet hour on the road. If your kids are widely different ages or simply don't like listening to the same music or talking books, invest in some personal CD or tape players. Hand-held games systems, from the likes of Nintendo and Sony PSP, are guaranteed to absorb most kids, although you may find they pass the entire journey with barely a glance at the passing scenery. When it comes to in-car entertainment, however, few things receive such universal approval from children and adults alike than a DVD player. High-spec cars often come with them ready-fitted in a ceiling-mounted unit or in the back of the front-seat headrests. Alternatively, you can buy portable DVD players that strap on to the headrests or can simply be held in your lap. See pages 40-43 for a selection of 'best buy' boredom-busters.

Coaching pros and cons

The idea of travelling by coach might initially appeal to children. They love buses. You only have to think back to their last school trip to see how much fun they can have in them. But before you get carried away and commit your family to a trans-American jaunt by Greyhound, spare a moment to consider the realities of a long-distance coach trip with the kids.

Logistically, you need to treat coach travel rather like flying – you're stuck in a confined cabin with limited legroom and your luggage is stowed out of reach in the hold. Luxury services will have an on-board toilet, TV screen and hostess service, but rarely approaching the standards you find on many airlines. Rest stops may be sporadic and too short-lived and unlike flying, of course, coach travel is slower and prone to traffic jams.

Any advantages? Well, there's no doubt that coach travel is better for both your bank balance and the environment compared to flying. You also get to see more than just clouds out of the windows. And you can often step off a coach right into the heart of your destination, rather than going through the rigmarole of baggage claim and airport transfers following a flight.

Coach travel also gives your itinerary huge flexibility. For example, Eurolines (eurolines.com) covers over 30 independent coach companies serving some 500 destinations across Europe, Russia and Morocco. A few specialist operators actively welcome families. Try UK-based Gemmaway Coach Tours (gemmaway.com) which offers guided itineraries throughout Britain and continental Europe.

On track with trains

There's no denying it: rail travel is definitely more family-friendly than going by coach. Not only do you get more legroom and often a table where kids can spread out their scribble pads and pens, but you can also get up and stretch your legs and visit the buffet car for a snack or meal. Trains are faster, more frequent and basically just a lot more exciting than coaches – particularly overnight sleeper services where kids love the idea of nesting in a couchette.

That's not to say train operators exactly go off the rails to make families welcome. Eurostar and French TGV trains have 'family-friendly' coaches (usually numbers 1 and 18) with baby-changing facilities – but that's about it. And don't forget that train travel with kids is not without its fair share of stressful 'crunch points' – the most notorious, of course, being the short stop at your final station when you have approximately 13 seconds to disgorge luggage, infants, buggy and other belongings on to the platform before the train leaves again. Then there are the tight connections where you have to cajole recalcitrant toddlers and unruly suitcases from one platform to another, negotiating crowds of commuters and several flights of steps. And, yes, there are plenty of trains serving Paris (and even Disneyland Paris), but what about your holiday park in Provence or Brittany? To reach that you'll need to pile everyone and everything into a taxi at the train station.

Undeterred? Then check out The Man in Seat 61 (seat61.com), a superb online resource with detailed information, schedules, fares and advice for rail travel anywhere in the world.

Making waves

Ferries pop up in a lot of holiday itineraries whether it's nipping across the Channel from England to France, getting from North to South Island in New Zealand or island hopping in the Bahamas. Not surprisingly, kids love them. There's space to move around, different decks to explore, horizons to scan and shops to peruse… some ferries even have soft-play areas and games rooms.

But what about family cruises of a week or more? Are these also plain sailing? There used to be a time when cruising was considered rather dull and old-fashioned – fine for granny and the blue-rinse brigade, but anathema for parents contemplating endless days at sea with mutinous children. But now cruising is cool for kids!

Several cruise lines have children's clubs for different age groups. Carnival, for example, caters for toddlers (face painting, crafts etc), 'junior cruisers' (cookie decorating, T-shirt painting, puppet shows), nine- to 11-year-olds (dance classes, scavenger hunts, talent shows) and teenagers (games tournaments, discos, late-night movies and a special shore-excursion programme).

Most cruise liners also have dedicated kids' areas, whether it's somewhere cool for teenagers to hang out or a ball pit for five-year-olds to rampage through. The Fun Factory on Celebrity's cruise liners is packed with craft activities, toys and arcade games. Of course, every ship also has a pool or three, but some operators really push the boat out when it comes to family entertainment. Royal Caribbean's on-board activities range from ice-skating and minigolf to rock climbing and surfing on a wave simulator. On Disney cruises, of course, you get to 'feel the magic' afloat with live shows, cinema screenings and character meetings.

Childcare, accommodation and meals are pretty much as you would expect from a good land-based family resort. On P&O's *Aurora*, *Oceana*, *Oriana* and *Ventura* ships, for example, you will find a well-qualified Youth Crew, a night nursery and an in-cabin listening service. Accommodation ranges from inter-connecting cabins to staterooms with extra beds or sofa beds, while children's dining arrangements usually feature a special tea, as well as a choice of meals.

For something more adventurous, try Windjammer. Kids will be blown away by its fleet of graceful tallships, especially if they are fans of the *Pirates of the Caribbean* movies. Teenagers get to learn about sailing and navigation (even taking the helm if they feel up to it), while children as young as six can learn to scuba-dive.

Cruise lines

Carnival Cruise Lines
carnival.com

Celebrity Cruise Lines
celebrity.com

Costa Cruises
costacruise.com

Crystal Family Cruises
crystalcruises.com

Disney Cruises disney cruise.disney.go.com

Holland Cruise Lines
hollandamerica.com

Imperial Majesty Cruise Lines
majestycruise.com

Norwegian Cruise Lines ncl.com

P&O Cruises
pocruises.com

Princess Cruises
princess.com

Royal Caribbean Cruise Lines
royalcaribbean.com

Star Cruises Lines
starcruises.com

Windjammer Barefoot Cruises
windjammer.com

Check it out before you check in

Family-friendly. Just rolls off the tongue, doesn't it? But it's a phrase that's used all to glibly by hotels, resorts and campsites keen to tap into this lucrative market. Just because they've plonked a plastic slide in the garden and scribbled chicken nuggets on the menu doesn't mean they're going to go out of their way to welcome kids or make your stay as comfortable as possible. Look beyond the superficial stuff and ask which of the following are available:

» Family rooms, interconnecting rooms or suites
» Children's menus and meal times
» Supervised childcare
» Babysitting or baby listening
» Family activities or kids' clubs
» Dedicated play areas for children
» Cots, high chairs and other baby gear
» Family pricing or discounts for children.

In addition, you should assess safety issues, such as proximity to busy roads and whether swimming pools are fenced off.

Hotel heaven and havoc

Remember those halcyon holidays before you had kids when you would casually check into your hotel room, test how bouncy the beds were, fling open the balcony doors and treat yourself to a welcome bottle of wine from the minibar? Well, with kids yapping excitedly at your heels you will be trying, mostly in vain, to stop them doing all those things. That wonderful moment of arrival, when the holiday really starts, is a super-exuberant time when kids find joy and wonder in even the smallest things. "Wow, look mum, you've got a chocolate on your pillow – and have you seen the cool view of the building site!"

Another difference you will notice is that hotel rooms shrink once you have children. Squeeze a travel cot and a child's bed into your average double room and the floor space is reduced to roughly the area of a bath mat. Getting from one side of the room to the other is like negotiating a soft-play area – and that, of course, is exactly how your kids treat it. Then there's the en suite where the hotel staff have thoughtfully gift-wrapped all sorts of goodies for children to open – from shower caps and sewing kits to little tubes of toothpaste. And when they tire of ransacking the mini milk pots on the complimentary coffee/tea-making tray, there are always the long hotel corridors – ideal for running relay races.

Perhaps it's not surprising that a lot of families tend to use their hotel room as a kind of base camp – a technical necessity where you sleep, wash and store your clothes, but spend as little time as possible. Of course, budget permitting, you can find sensational apartments, suites and even family chalets within the grounds of a large resort. It's probably safe to say that your hotel room is unlikely to feature in your holiday snaps, but at least you've got everything you need onsite – from

restaurants, room service and babysitting to swimming pool, games room and someone making your beds.

Villas, houses and apartments

With space to spread out, villas and other self-catering accommodation offer a home-from-home atmosphere where you have flexibility and independence to maintain mealtime and bedtime routines, do the cooking, load the dishwasher, lay the table … A big advantage over hotels and resorts is that you don't need to worry about disturbing other guests. Villas can also offer better value than hotels or resorts, particularly if you upsize to a bigger property and share with another family.

Camping

There are two types of family camping – the DIY version where parents spend most of day one grappling with multi-jointed tent poles and fiddling with an obstinate gas stove, and organized camping where you simply drive up to a ready-pitched family tent, usually on a site that has excellent facilities, such as a swimming pool and supermarket. Both are essential experiences for all families – you need to try one to appreciate the other. If you are planning on going it alone, make sure you are properly kitted out (see checklist opposite) and try a dummy run in the back garden before setting off on something more epic. As a general rule of thumb, buy a tent that's one size up from the one you think you'll need – the extra space will always come in handy for storage and wet

> 66 99 We decided to take 15-month-old Abi to Tuscany with friends of ours who had an eight-month-old. This meant we could afford a better villa, we were with other parents that were sympathetic to things like sleep times, there were four pairs of eyes on the kids around the pool and we could babysit for each other.
>
> *Jason Hobbins*

Organized sites take the *pain* out of camping.

❓ What about farmstays?

You should check whether any age restrictions apply, but in general most farmstays are ideal for families. Children will love feeding the animals, collecting eggs or even helping out in the kitchen. Needless to say, on a working farm, you must be aware of your children's safety at all times – including any potential allergic reactions they may have in response to contact with animals. You usually sleep in a self-contained cottage or in the farmhouse itself. As you'd expect, most meals are based on fresh produce and include home-made breads, cakes and soups, as well as home-grown fruit and veg. It's up to you if you want to help out on the farm. Nobody is going to drag you out of bed at dawn to muck out the cowshed or round up the sheep. If you simply want to relax and restrict your farm activities to occasionally patting the border collie then that's fine. Farm tours are often available, while some farmstays offer activities like fishing, hiking, mountain biking or horse riding. Top countries for farmstays include New Zealand, Iceland, Argentina and the USA.

Camping checklist

- Tent
- Sleeping bags
- Extra blankets
- Pillows
- Air beds and pump
- Dust pan/brush
- Large water jug
- Oven mitts
- Cooler boxes
- Pots and frying pans
- Thermos
- Stove with fuel
- Cooking utensils
- Matches/lighter
- Charcoal/firewood
- Can opener
- Bottle opener
- Barbecue grill
- Folding table and chairs
- Fire starters/ newspaper
- Plates and bowls
- Mugs
- Cutlery
- Mixing bowl
- Measuring jug
- Cutting board
- Aluminum foil
- Ziplock bags
- Paper towels
- Trash bags
- Washing-up liquid
- Scrubbing pad
- Cooking oil
- Seasonings and sugar
- Food storage containers
- Potato peeler

days. Organized 'ready-made' campsites are particularly popular in Europe where you also have the option of staying in well-furnished mobile homes or chalets. These typically have a galley kitchen and lounge area with mod cons such as LCD television, DVD player, microwave and fridge-freezer.

Again, it's worth upgrading if you can – a double bed might sound fine until you discover that it's in a room the size of a double bed. Of course, these mobile homes aren't actually mobile, but motorhomes certainly are and make an excellent roving base for family holidays (see below).

Reality check #6: The motorhome

There's no better way to roam than in a motorhome. Not only do they offer flexibility and self-sufficiency, but most models offer levels of comfort undreamt of in the days of the old VW camper van. Whereas your typical VW, with its pop-up roof and flatulent exhaust, might have had little more than two coffin-sized berths and a lethal camping stove, modern motorhomes boast two or three double beds, fridge-freezer, microwave, four-ring cooker, DVD player, flat-screen TV, shower and toilet. If you've got kids, motorhome touring is definitely the way to go. The idea that you can have bedroom, kitchen, playroom and car rolled into one is almost too much for them to comprehend. But motorhomes also have lots of practical advantages. For example, you can stick your children in seats 6 m away from the driver's cab, so that you don't have to hear them whingeing on long journeys. And when it rains, you can keep warm and dry inside the van while you rustle up a meal. Best of all, you can explore large swathes of country without having to lug suitcases in and out of hotels all the time. You only have to unpack once. And you only have to get used to one bed. Don't forget, though, that you have to make that bed. Literally. Your motorhome may have had the latest in TV technology, but when it came to beds, it might not be cutting edge. More like "cut your bleedin' fingers off", in fact, as you struggle each evening with sliding plywood shelves, hinged legs and stow-away tables to build your beds. Once the bases are constructed, the real fun starts when you attempt to piece together 17 random-sized seat cushions into something vaguely resembling a mattress.

Will

What to eat and drink

Culinary culture shock

It's a perfectly natural reaction. You arrive at your holiday destination, dump the luggage, check out the pool and then enter the intriguing, but slightly disconcerting, world of local restaurant menus and foreign supermarkets. Is that spicy? Does it come with chips? Which one is skimmed milk? Will that cheese be too strong? Will I be handed a packet of frozen fish fingers when what I thought I'd asked for was a box of ice lollies? Some things look perfectly familiar, while others leave you flummoxed. But don't worry – culinary culture shock isn't terminal. No matter where you are there is always something to eat, no matter how fussy you or your children are.

Breastfeeding

Breastfed babies, of course, have no qualms about coping with foreign food. They have a familiar, convenient, safe and nutritious source of nourishment wherever they go. Breastfeeding mothers, however, do need to ensure that they drink lots of fluid, eat well and keep relaxed. If you are discreet, breastfeeding is acceptable in most countries. Consider packing a nursing shawl for modesty.

Bottle-feeding

Don't assume that your preferred brand of milk formula will be available in the country you are visiting. If possible take enough with you from home. Remember that you will need to use purified, bottled or boiled water to make up the formula and that it needs to be kept refrigerated if not used within 24 hours. Sterilization is also crucial. Either invest in a compact travel sterilizer (which usually holds one or two bottles, plus teats) or use boiling water or sterilizing tablets.

In-flight food and drink

It's a good idea to feed babies on take-off and landing to reduce the discomfort caused by changes in cabin pressure. Make sure toddlers have non-spill cups to sip on and give older children boiled sweets to suck. Remember that most flight attendants seem to be programmed to fill cups (even for children) right up to the rim – and they rarely supply lids. To avoid inevitable spills, bring your own bottles or cups to decant drinks into. Don't assume baby food will be available – again, the best strategy is to bring your own. Plastic bibs with scooped rims along the bottom are useful for minimizing mess – particularly if your baby is sick.

Most airlines offer children's meals if you book them in

> **" "** Even with an exclusively breastfed baby, it's advisable to take half a dozen pre-sterilized disposable bottles and small cartons of ready-made milk, in case you fall ill and cannot feed the baby yourself.
> *Emma Woollacott*

The one that got away – trying new food (and new ways of eating) is all part of the travel experience

advance, although you should also bring plenty of snacks in case they turn their noses up at what lurks beneath the (often extremely hot) foil cover. Children's meals are usually served first which means you can help them negotiate all those fiddly pots and plastic bags of utensils (which invariably explode like Christmas crackers) before relaxing later with your own haute cuisine.

Travel snacks

Having a stash of goodies to nibble on is all part of the fun of travel if you're a child – and they can be a godsend if you're delayed. Leave it to them, however, and they'll stuff their hand luggage with nothing but crisps, chocolate bars, chewing gum and lurid-coloured chews encrusted with sherbet. You don't want to be a complete killjoy (the odd packet of crisps and a chocolate bar is fine), but nor do you want your children going barmy on a 'sugar high' while you're stuck in a car or queuing at customs. Healthy travel snacks that you can buy straight off the supermarket shelf include cereal bars, string cheese, small boxes of raisins and individual (low sugar) boxes of cereal. And, of course, nothing beats a fresh apple or orange for healthy food on the go. With a little more time and effort you can help children prepare their own tasty, unprocessed travel snacks (see box opposite).

Clash of the cereal bars

When it comes to the crunch which cereal bar is best for your kids?

	Weight per bar (g)	What's inside	Energy per bar (KJ)	Carbohydrate (g)	Sugar (g)	Fat (g)	Protein (g)
Nestlé Cheerios	23.5	Each bar has as much calcium as ⅓ pint of milk.	417	15.5	7.9	3.3	1.8
Alpen Fruit and Nut with Chocolate	29	Made with natural wholegrains, plus 24% milk chocolate and 9.5% raisins.	514	19.8	n/a	3.9	1.9
Nature Valley Crunchy Granola	21	52% wholegrain rolled oats, 5% almond pieces, 3% banana flakes.	402	14.1	5.4	3.9	1.7
Jordans Fruit Frusli Toppers	29	25% wholegrain oat flakes, 13% dried and concentrated fruit.	492	20	7.7	3.5	1.3
Kellogg's Chocolate Caramel Krispie Squares	36	26% toasted rice cereal, 13% chocolate-flavoured coating, 10% milk chocolate pieces.	650	27	15	4.5	1.5
Traidcraft Geobar Chocolate and Raisin	n/a	19.8% raisins, 3.9% honey, 3.4% plain chocolate chips.	584	28.6	18.6	1.9	1.6
Organix Apple and Orange	30	44% organic oats, 34% organic raisins, 6% organic apple juice concentrate.	493	18.6	9.3	4.9	1.9
Kellogg's Nutrigrain Raspberry	37	34% cereals, 11% raspberry purée from concentrate.	556	26	12	3	1.5

Fussy feeders

Although some kids have more adventurous palates abroad than at home, others can be frustratingly inflexible when it comes to food. They'll love Marmite, but hate Vegemite. They'll consume Cheddar cheese by the wagonload, but run a mile from a French fondue. The tomato sauce won't be the same as it is back home and the milk will taste funny. So, how do you deal with a fussy feeder on holiday? Try this list for starters:

▸▸ Self-catering gives you the flexibility to prepare food you like, when you like.

▸▸ International resorts, hotels and restaurants offer a wide selection of meals, including several that your children are bound to be familiar with.

▸▸ Fine for an occasional treat, fast-food outlets can be found everywhere nowadays.

▸▸ Take staples with you, such as soup powders, pasta and cereals – but remember that you won't be allowed to take fresh produce across some international borders.

▸▸ Make mealtimes enjoyable and relaxed by picking restaurants with stunning views, play areas or aquariums. The novelty of room service may also get kids in the mood for eating.

▸▸ Don't fill children up on juice, milk, fizzy drinks or even water just before a meal.

▸▸ Ask for smaller portions in restaurants and let children take their time over eating.

▸▸ Keep mealtime routines as regular as possible.

▸▸ Get them involved – kids tend to eat up if they can serve themselves at buffets or help prepare the meal.

▸▸ Seeing other children eating well on a group trip might be an incentive for your picky feeder to tuck in.

▸▸ Do not force your child to eat. Be sensitive to the fact that travel can naturally affect appetites and unsettle stomachs.

▸▸ Take some children's multi-vitamins.

🥜 DIY snacks

Trail mix Combine raisins, Cheerios, dried apricot, cranberries and pineapple, banana chips and yoghurt-coated raisins in a mixing bowl. A handful of Smarties or M&Ms isn't going to harm anyone, but only add nuts if your children are over five. Give everything a good stir, then make up individual portions in small freezer bags.

Dippers Add a scoop of peanut butter, hummus or whatever savoury dip appeals to your children to a small plastic food container. Clean and slice small pieces of celery, carrot, apple and cucumber and plant them in the dip. Add a lid and keep refrigerated until you are ready to go.

Cheese and crackers Use a cookie cutter to stamp out fun-shaped slices of cheese. Pop them in a food storage container along with a few crackers and some grapes sliced lengthways. Kids will love crafting their own cracker creations.

What age is best?

Many families do not even entertain the idea of travelling with small babies, but in reality, the first six months of infancy are generally healthy, especially if the child is exclusively breastfed. From six months, babies are more likely to suffer from colds, ear infections and upset stomachs, so you need to travel prepared.

Things start to get more challenging at the crawling baby and wobbly toddler stages. Being more susceptible to accidents and infections than any other age group they require constant supervision. Certain vaccinations and medicines are not available to very young children, while toddlers may take exception to your efforts to keep them covered up from the sun or mosquitoes.

By the age of five or six, children are more able to shake off infections and are generally more resilient. This is the age of reason (if you are lucky) and greater communication and understanding are great aids to the travelling family. If a child can describe their symptoms and can understand why they need to wear a sun hat or long trousers then it makes your job a whole lot easier.

Safety issues change across the years – from toddlers climbing on balcony railings to teenagers taking their first bungee jumps. Coping with the invincible attitude of a rebellious adolescent is every bit as challenging as baby-proofing your hotel room.

Immunizations

Plan well ahead for immunizations, taking advice from a travel clinic or your GP at least three months before you travel. Some vaccinations are part of a course, spread over several weeks, and other immunizations are not recommended to be taken together. Specialist travel clinics will have the latest information on disease outbreaks and changing immunization requirements.

Many of the vaccinations that children need for travelling are part of their routine childhood immunization programme. Between 0-18 months your child will have been offered vaccinations for diptheria, tetanus, whooping cough, Hib, polio, Meningococcus C and MMR (measles, mumps and rubella). Between three and five years they will receive boosters for some of these, and at 10-14 years they may have a BCG, as well as boosters for other vaccinations.

Safety first

The moment you arrive at your hotel, divert your baby's attention with a surprise toy while you quickly assess the room for potential hazards. Tape over plug sockets, tuck away trailing flexes, remove plastic bags from bins, place any coffee/tea-making facilities on a high shelf and ask staff to remove standard lamps, trouser presses or any other easily toppled objects.

🔎 How to avoid being bitten

➤ Cover up before dusk with long sleeves and long trousers (preferably in light colours). Apply insect repellent to any exposed skin and remember to reapply after washing hands.
➤ Tuck trousers into socks and spray clothing with repellent. Malaria mosquitoes tend to attack at ankle level.
➤ Aim to be inside an air-conditioned or mosquito-screened room between dusk and dawn. To help reduce the chances of being bitten, use mosquito coils or mats if the room hasn't been sprayed with insecticide on a daily basis.

Additional inoculations that may be required if travelling to developing countries include typhoid (requires a booster every three years), hepatitis A (available after the age of one; a single dose gives 12 months' protection, while a booster six to 12 months later gives 10 years' protection) and rabies (a course of three injections over 28 days, with boosters every three years). For certain geographical areas and in certain situations you may also need to have the following vaccinations: Yellow fever (from age of nine months, lasts 10 years – may be a statutory requirement when entering countries in tropical Africa, Central and South America); Japanese Encephalitis and Hepatitis B. Cholera is not required anywhere nowadays, but a new vaccine, Dukoral, gives some protection against travellers' diarrhoea.

The crucial thing to remember is to seek professional medical advice on what vaccinations you may or may not need.

Malaria

The old adage 'prevention is better than cure' is never more pertinent than when dealing with the prevention of malaria. Young children are particularly vulnerable to this potentially fatal disease and preventative measures must be vigorously observed if you are travelling to malarious areas, particularly in sub-Saharan Africa. The most effective prevention, of course, is to choose a holiday in a malaria-free region or to time your visit when the risk is at its lowest (although unstable weather patterns make this increasingly hard to predict). Otherwise, remember the three As:

1 Awareness both before and after travelling – know when you and your children are at risk and inform any doctor that you have been to a malarious region if, at any time up to a year after travelling, you become ill.

2 Avoidance of mosquito bites, particularly between dusk and dawn. DEET is the most effective form of insect repellent, although it should not be used on pregnant women or on children under one year. For young children use less concentrated formulas. Premetherin-impregnated clothing can help to prevent bites but make sure you also use repellent

> 💬 Getting malaria medication into a toddler often takes some doing. Lily thought you were supposed to throw the pills at the mosquitoes rather than eat them. Yoghurt and mashed fruit somehow managed to slide freely down her throat, leaving the pill sitting on her tongue undiminished. We tried the liquid version of Chloroquine, which you can squirt in with a syringe, and your child can squirt straight out again. The one reliable method we found was to hide the tablet in a spoonful of chocolate spread.
>
> *Emma Woollacott*

on exposed areas of skin.

3 Antimalarial medicines – have a strict routine for taking them and continue to take them, as directed, after leaving the area. Remember that malaria prophylactics do not give complete protection.

Other nasties

Spiders Australian funnel webs, South American banana spiders and the widow spiders of North America all have deservedly bad reputations. In the rare event of being bitten, however, antivenom treatments are readily available.

Hairy caterpillars Children need to know that these intriguing fluff-balls deserve respect. The hairs can penetrate the skin and cause pain and irritation. Pluck the hairs out with fine-pointed tweezers and administer antihistamine if necessary.

Ticks Tick bites occasionally spread disease, although the risk is low. To remove a tick, grasp it firmly between finger and thumb, as close as possible to where it is attached and pull steadily away from the skin (never jerk or twist the tick). Flood the bite site with diluted iodine or alcohol.

Aedes mosquitoes These day-active stripy-legged mosquitoes are responsible for spreading dengue and yellow fever. Keep covered up in light-coloured clothing and avoid areas where they breed.

Snakes Fear of snakes is often out of proportion to the risk they pose. They very rarely strike unprovoked; stay still if cornered and the chances are you'll be safe. In the event of a bite, however, keep the affected region below heart level, cover the wound with a dressing (do not use a tourniquet), keep the victim calm (death by snakebite is very rare) and seek antivenom treatment. It helps if you can identify the snake so that the right serum can be administered.

Rabies Statistically, dogs are the most dangerous animals after mosquitoes. Not only can they inflict serious bites, but they may also transmit rabies. Enforce on children the importance of never approaching an unknown dog.

Weaver fish Found in the UK and other parts of Europe, weaver fish bury themselves in the sand and, if trodden on, can inject a seriously painful dose of venom (rarely fatal) through their dorsal spines. The key is to immerse the injured foot in water as hot as can be tolerated in order to break down the poison. If you feel dizzy or unwell, seek immediate attention (preferably from a lifeguard) in case an allergic reaction has set in.

Jellyfish Most jellyfish stings are painful but not

Useful contacts

➤ fco.gov.uk
➤ malariahotspots.co.uk
➤ masta.org

Reality check #8: The jungle

Are you kidding? If the snakes don't get 'em, then some deadly disease certainly will. They'll spend the whole time whingeing about the heat and, in the process, scare away every bird and monkey within a 10-mile radius. And then there are the creepy-crawlies. Tropical rainforests and young children don't mix. End of story. Or is it?

It's odd that jungles are considered such no-go zones for young families. By the time they're two or three, most children have followed the exploits of numerous fictitious jungle heroes. Not once does Mowgli or Elmer the Patchwork Elephant get stricken by dengue fever or bitten by a rabid vampire bat. To kids, jungles are magical, gentle places, teeming with exotic wildlife.

The trick to finding a really family-friendly jungle is to widen your search to include subtropical rainforests which, compared to the full-blown tropical varieties, are usually easier to reach, have more comfortable climates and a minimal risk of malaria. Brazil's Iguassú Falls National Park, for example, is an ideal first-timer's choice. If the whole rainforest thing doesn't work out, there's still the added attraction of the waterfall. If only the Amazon will do, however, head for Manaus from where you can take a boat to various lodges offering jungle treks, canoe trips, fishing expeditions and alligator-spotting by night.

An important point to remember about taking kids into a jungle is that the wildlife is not always easy to see. Bug-viewing boxes with built-in magnifying glasses will help them focus on small wonders, like ants and spiders, while binoculars will allow them to zoom in on colourful birds. You can't expect children to feel the same sense of awe or humility that adults might feel upon entering a rainforest, but there is every chance that a tiny seed of awareness and respect for these special places will be planted in their minds.

» Anti-bacterial hand wash
» Anti-malarial medicines
» Antihistamine syrup
» Antiseptic wipes
» Child ibuprofen syrup
» Clear plastic bags for storage
» Cotton wool and cotton buds in resealable bag
» Crêpe bandage
» Drying antiseptic, such as iodine
» Ear drops (antibiotic, or for trapped water)
» Eye drops (antibiotic)
» Insect bite relief cream/calamine lotion
» Insect repellent (natural, or low DEET concentration for children)
» Nappy rash cream
» Non-stick dressings and micropore tape
» Oral rehydration salts
» Paracetamol syrup or dispersible tablets
» Pointed tweezers
» Scissors
» Sore-throat pastilles
» Steristrips
» Sticking plasters
» Teething gel
» Thermometer
» Thermos flask
» Travel sickness pills (or herbal alternatives)
» Water bottle with measure indicators
» Water-purifying tablets or filter
» Water-resistant suncream SPF 15+

life-threatening. Very rarely a sting can lead to collapse, in which case emergency resuscitation is required. Particularly nasty is the box jellyfish, found in some coastal regions of the Indo-Pacific. Avoid swimming in susceptible areas unless they are fenced off during the months of November to March – or wear an all-in-one stinger suit with hood and mitts.

Safe water
Boiling is the most effective way of sterilizing water. Travel with a thermos flask and regularly fill it with boiling water. Bottled water is usually safe, although you should always check that the seal is intact. Some brands may have a high mineral content that is not suitable for very young children. Chemical sterilization is another option – iodine kills most bugs. An alternative, but expensive, method is to use a special travel water filter, which usually contains an iodine matrix.

Diarrhoea
Severe diarrhoea can be life-threatening, particularly to children under three who find it harder to recover from bouts of gastrointestinal illness. The biggest risk is dehydration – knowing how to prevent this and how to treat it is crucial. The risk of contracting severe diarrhoea is greater in certain parts of the world, such as the Indian subcontinent and Latin America (especially Peru). However, there are several ways to minimize the risk:

» Avoid ice cream or ice from unreliable sources; avoid food that has been cooked and left to go cold; don't eat raw food unless it is fruit or vegetables that you have peeled, and steer clear of shellfish if you are in areas a long way from the sea or where the effectiveness of refrigeration is suspect.

» Follow strict hand hygiene rules, washing or using anti-bacterial handwipes before eating or preparing food.

» Only eat food that has been cooked thoroughly and is still piping hot when served.

» Only drink water that you have boiled or sterilized, or bottled drinks from reputable sources.

If your child has a bout of diarrhoea and/or vomiting there are several steps to follow. First, keep clear fluid intake up, offering water, juices and oral rehydration drinks frequently (an alternative to rehydration drinks is Coca Cola with a pinch of salt added). Keep checking for signs of dehydration. If your child wants to eat, then offer bland carbohydrates such as crackers.

Sunburn
Children are very susceptible to getting sunburned. It is important to keep young children and babies out of direct sunlight during the middle of the day (between 1100 and 1500). This is especially important when they are still getting used to hot temperatures. As with most dangerous illnesses, prevention is better than cure. Here are some tips for keeping your children sun-safe:

Natural remedies
Local people and tour guides will often enthuse about natural remedies used to treat various ailments. In South Africa for example, the aloe plant is referred to as a 'pharmacy on a stick'. However, even purely natural ingredients must be treated with caution, as they may cause a reaction or may not be suitable for children. Here are some tried and tested alternatives to over-the-counter medicines:

Motion sickness Ginger biscuits, crystallized ginger and peppermints.

Constipation Camomile tea and liquorice.

Indigestion, nausea and stomach aches Peppermint or camomile tea, ginger biscuits and crystallized ginger.

Fever Lemons and limes.

Decongestant properties Honey.

Settling the stomach Live yoghurt and probiotic yoghurt drinks.

Essential oils have many healing properties and can be bought in pre-diluted blends for children. Never use them neat and always follow the guidelines carefully. Useful travelling remedies (for external application only) include:

Antiseptic properties Tea tree oil and lavender oil.

Repelling insects Lavender oil, tea tree oil, citronella oil.

Soothing burns Aloe vera cream or oil and calendula cream.

Treating bites and stings Lavender oil, aloe vera cream or oil and arnica cream.

» Stay out of the sun during the middle part of the day.

» Cover up with loose, comfortable 100% cotton clothes.

» Wear sun-protection suits for playing on the beach and swimming.

» Wear a wide-brimmed sun hat.

» Drink lots.

» Have a siesta.

» Do not run around in the middle of the day.

» Use water-resistant suncream of SPF 15 or more and reapply regularly.

» Come straight out of the sun if any reddening of the skin occurs; more cream will not stop the child burning.

Heatstroke
Heatstroke is life-threatening and can occur when children push themselves too far during sport and play when they are unacclimatized. In severe cases, collapse due to dehydration and overheating can occur and urgent medical attention is required. As with avoiding sunburn the best precaution is to stay out of the heat during the hottest part of the day, avoid rigorous exercise until acclimatized and drink plenty. Signs of

What are the signs of dehydration?

⧭ Mouth and tongue are dry; thirstier than normal – early warning signs.
⧭ Passing less (and darker) urine than normal; sunken eyes – serious dehydration.
⧭ Skin has lost elasticity; listlessness, drowsiness and unable to drink – severe dehydration, requiring hospitalization.

overheating include lethargy, flushed skin and excessive sweating. It is at a more serious stage if the child has stopped sweating and they show signs of dehydration (see above). Tips for cooling down include:
⧭ Pour cool water over the child's head.
⧭ Soak a light-coloured cotton hat in water and allow it to dry slowly on the child's head.
⧭ Cool them in tepid bath or with towels soaked in cold water.
⧭ Remove clothes and sponge down the body.
⧭ Give plenty of clear fluid drinks.

Staying safe

Insurance Make sure your insurance covers the whole family, is valid for all the activities you may want to try and lasts the duration of your trip.

Sleep walking Make sure doors to balconies and low windows are securely fastened at night.

Dangerous countries Check the FCO website, fco.gov.uk/travel, for advice before travelling to any volatile regions.

EHIC for European travellers This free European Health Insurance Card (EHIC) will provide members of the EU with free or reduced-cost emergency medical treatment in the European Economic Area. Details from ehic.org.uk.

Pools and beaches Always familiarize yourself with local conditions before taking the plunge. Look out for obstacles such as rocks and ledges and take note of any flag warnings. Find out the depths of a pool and never dive in water less than 150 cm. Swim parallel to the shore within your depth and be aware of any motorsport zones.

Roads and transport Children will need reminders that traffic may not come from the direction they are expecting. Some public transport in developing countries can be unreliable or dangerous.

Health clinic Q&A

Is it safe to fly with babies? Ideally you should wait until your baby is two or three months old and has had its routine vaccinations, as germs tend to circulate in aircraft. However, providing your baby was full-term with no complications and has a clean bill of health, flying is usually permitted after one or two weeks (though this may vary between airlines).

What if my child has asthma? Understand your child's symptoms and be prepared with spare inhalers, emergency steroids (if you have used them in the past) and a peak-flow meter if your child is old enough to use one. Be aware of the triggers for your child's asthma and take any necessary preventative measures.

Can I take my child to high altitudes? Children are probably no more likely to suffer altitude sickness than adults, but the difficulty is in diagnosing the condition in very young children, as the symptoms of fractiousness and sleepiness may be attributed to travelling in general. Other symptoms such as headache and nausea are not visible and a child under the age of three may have trouble communicating this. As with adults it is safest to ascend slowly and have a plan for how to go down quickly if necessary (a rapid descent of at least 500 m is the best cure for mountain sickness). It would be inadvisable to plan a first trek above 3000 m with your child. Flying, driving or going by rail into areas of high altitude (such as in La Paz, Mexico City and Colorado) may cause altitude problems for adults and children alike. Avoid taking your child to high altitude if they are suffering from a cough or a cold as they may be more susceptible to high-altitude pulmonary oedema.

What if my child is travel sick? Children between the ages of three and 12 are more susceptible to travel sickness (and girls are more likely to suffer from it than boys). Try to sit in the middle of buses or trains (where movement is less) and, if possible, get out on the open deck of a ship and focus your child on the horizon. There are various medicines available (ask a pharmacist or your GP for one that is appropriate to your child's age), wrist bands (that press on acupuncture points) or natural remedies, such as ginger or peppermint (see box above left).

Can I travel when I'm pregnant? The safest time to travel when pregnant is during the second trimester, between three and six months. It is strongly advised not to travel to malarious areas or places where stomach upsets are likely. Some anti-malarial prophylactics are not safe to take during pregnancy. Airlines have different policies on when it is safe to travel – generally you may not fly after the 36th week of pregnancy (or earlier if carrying twins or more). Pregnant women are more susceptible to blood clots, so wearing flight socks on long-haul flights is advisable.

The health and safety section in this guide has been ratified by leading family travel health expert, Dr Jane Wilson-Howarth, co-author of *Your Child Abroad – A Travel Health Guide* (Bradt Travel Guides, 2005). This highly recommended book contains: advice on diagnosis and treatment; who is fit to fly; travelling with allergies; new antimalarials and bite-prevention gizmos; first-aid guidance and suggested kits; basic medical questions in five languages, plus a region-by-region analysis of risk.

Holding back the tide, East Devon.

Britain and Ireland

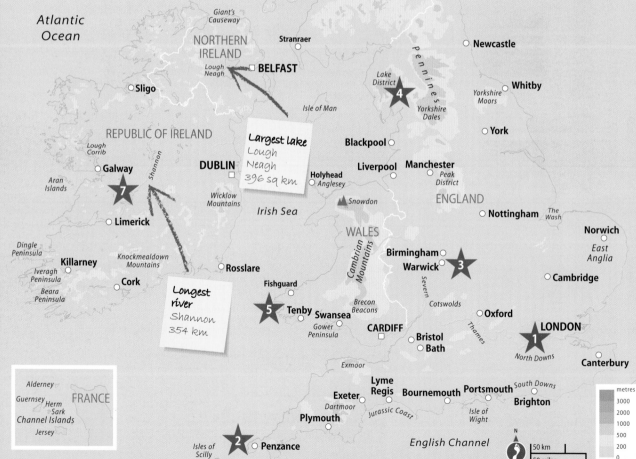

Did you know?

- More than 250 million portions of fish and chips are eaten in Britain every year.
- World record roller-coaster rider, Richard Rodriguez, rode the Big Dipper at Blackpool Pleasure Beach for 2000 hours, day and night.
- Wales has more castles per square kilometre than any country in Western Europe.
- JK Rowling wrote her first novel, *Harry Potter and the Philosopher's Stone*, in a café in Edinburgh.
- The 24,000 people who live on the Shetland Islands are outnumbered by 30,000 gannets, 250,000 puffins and at least 330,000 sheep.
- In the catacombs under Christ Church Cathedral, Dublin, are the remains of a medieval cat and mouse which died when they got stuck in the organ pipes.

Highest mountain
Ben Nevis
1343 m

Orkney Islands

John O'Groats

Shetland Islands

Lerwick

Orkney Islands

Kirkwall

John O'Groats

Lewis

Harris

North Uist

South Uist

Skye

Rum

Mull

Jura

Islay

Arran

Inverness

Loch Ness

Cairngorms

Aberdeen

Fort William

Ben Nevis

Grampian Mountains

Dundee

Perth

Oban

EDINBURGH

Glasgow

SCOTLAND

North Sea

Atlantic Ocean

Giant's Causeway

Stranraer

NORTHERN IRELAND

BELFAST

Lough Neagh

Sligo

Isle of Man

Largest lake
Lough Neagh
396 sq km

REPUBLIC OF IRELAND

Lough Corrib

Galway

Shannon

DUBLIN

Wicklow Mountains

Irish Sea

Newcastle

Pennines

Lake District

Whitby

Yorkshire Moors

Yorkshire Dales

York

Blackpool

Liverpool

Manchester

Peak District

Holyhead

Anglesey

Snowdon

ENGLAND

Nottingham

The Wash

Norwich

East Anglia

Aran Islands

Limerick

Dingle Peninsula

Killarney

Iveragh Peninsula

Beara Peninsula

Knockmealdown Mountains

Cork

Rosslare

Longest river
Shannon
354 km

Fishguard

Tenby

Swansea

Gower Peninsula

Brecon Beacons

CARDIFF

WALES

Cambrian Mountains

Severn

Birmingham

Warwick

Cotswolds

Cambridge

Oxford

Thames

LONDON

North Downs

Canterbury

Bristol

Bath

Exmoor

Lyme Regis

Bournemouth

Portsmouth

South Downs

Brighton

Exeter

Dartmoor

Jurassic Coast

Isle of Wight

Plymouth

Isles of Scilly

Penzance

English Channel

Alderney

Guernsey

Herm

Sark

Jersey

Channel Islands

FRANCE

metres
3000
2000
1000
500
200
0

50 km
50 miles

N

★ **Take a spin on the London Eye**
▸▸ London, page 66

★ **Find the perfect surfing beach**
▸▸ Cornwall, page 70

★ **Explore a medieval castle**
▸▸ Throughout Britain and Ireland

★ **Go in search of Peter Rabbit**
▸▸ Lake District, page 74

★ **Spot seabirds, seals and whales**
▸▸ Pembrokeshire, page 76

★ **Tour the Highlands and Islands**
▸▸ Scotland, page 78

★ **Cruise the River Shannon**
▸▸ Ireland, page 80

Introduction

Many visitors to Britain and Ireland (and quite a few of its residents) love to have a good moan about the weather and how expensive everything is. The fact remains, though, that these islands are not only incredibly beautiful, but they also squeeze more child-friendly beaches, cities and family attractions into one small, accessible region than anywhere in the world. Admittedly, the weather can be temperamental (or downright frustrating) at times, and there's no denying that a British family holiday sometimes requires a fair degree of stoicism – but it doesn't rain constantly. In any case, Britain and Ireland are great family holiday destinations whatever the weather. Kids can have just as much fun exploring rock pools and building sandcastles on a wind-strafed Cornish beach during winter as they can surfing on one during a summer heatwave. As for the cost issue, some of the best family holiday highlights in Britain and Ireland don't cost a penny – cycling in Pembrokeshire or the Isle of Wight, visiting London's Science or Natural History Museum, and finding the perfect picnic spot in the Lake District or Cotswolds to name just a few.

❝❞ *When I asked our seven-year-old twins what they'd like to do on holiday if they could go anywhere in the world or do anything they wanted, they barely hesitated before replying: "Go surfing, build big sandcastles, catch shrimps in rock pools and eat fish and chips by the sea." So, Cornwall it is then.*
Will

Britain and Ireland rating

Wow factor
★★★

Worry factor
★

Value for money
★★

Keeping teacher happy
★★★★★

Family accommodation
★★★★★

Babies & toddlers
★★★★★

Teenagers
★★★

Kids' stuff

🔍 How to be a Harry Spotter

You don't need a broomstick or magic wand to visit several of the places featured in the Harry Potter movies. Platform 9¾, the mystifying departure point for the Hogwarts Express steam train, was filmed at Platform 4 of London's King's Cross station. Harry and his fellow wannabe-wizards disembark at Hogsmeade station which is none other than Goathland, a village in the Yorkshire Moors, while Glenfinnan Viaduct in the Scottish Highlands featured in a spectacular action sequence in the *Chamber of Secrets*. The interior of the Hogwarts School of Witchcraft and Wizardry is based on several locations, including Lacock Abbey in Wiltshire, Gloucester Cathedral, Oxford University's Bodleian Library and the Great Hall at Christ Church, Oxford. Alnwick Castle in Northumberland, meanwhile, will always be remembered as the setting for broomstick lessons and Quidditch matches.

10 reasons to love the seaside
1 Fish and chips Bridlington, Yorkshire.
2 Punch and Judy Codman's, Llandudno.
3 Ice cream Morelli's, Broadstairs, Kent.
4 Donkey ride Weymouth, Dorset.
5 Sea kayaking Beara Peninsula, Co. Cork.
6 Rock pools Wembury, South Devon.
7 Shells Rhossili, Gower Peninsula.
8 Crabbing Southwold, Suffolk.

Top: Alnwick Castle. **Above left:** Great Hall, Oxford.
Above right: Lacock Abbey cloisters.

Books to read

Katie Morag's Island Stories, Red Fox, 2003
A small Hebridean community seen through the eyes of a child. Katie Morag always seems to be in some sort of bother, but her family and the friendly islanders manage to keep her out of serious trouble. Ages 4-8

The Mousehole Cat, Walker Books, 1993
A brave fisherman and his cat battle through a storm to bring food to the children of a Cornish village. Written by Antonia Barber with award-winning illustrations from Nicola Bayley. Ages 4+

Five on a Treasure Island, Hodder Children's Books, 2001
Meet Julian, Dick, Anne, George and Timmy the dog in their first adventure. There's a shipwreck off Kirrin Island, but where is the treasure? The five go on the trail, but they're not alone. Ages 6+

Ireland, Horrible Histories, Scholastic, 2000
Find out the terrible truth about Ireland's foul famines, savage sieges and wretched rebellions, and the formidable Irish people who lived and died in them. Plus the top 20 Irish curses. Ages 8+

Friend or Foe, Mammoth, 2001
Set during the Second World War, London is under the Blitz and two friends, David and Tucky, have been evacuated to the countryside where they are faced with a terrible dilemma when they witness a German plane crash on the moors. Ages 10+

Plus 8 classics
Beatrix Potter – The Complete Tales, by Beatrix Potter
Winnie the Pooh, by AA Milne
A Bear Called Paddington, by Michael Bond
The Wind in the Willows, by Kenneth Grahame
Peter Pan, by JM Barrie
Oliver Twist, by Charles Dickens
Pride and Prejudice, by Jane Austen
Macbeth, by William Shakespeare

How to pick the best theme park

Park	Ride	Thrills and spills	Wow factor	Min height (age)
Thorpe Park	Tidal Wave	Climb to 26 m then get soaked as you splash down to earth	●●●●	120
	Detonator	Get fired to ground level from a height of 30 m at 75 kph	●●●●●	130
	Stealth	0-130 kph in less than 2 seconds, and heights of 62 m	●●●●●	140
	Colossus	Swirl and corkscrew around a thundering steel track	●●●●	140
Chessington World of adventures	Dragon's Fury	A fiery, family spinning roller coaster	●●●	120
	Tomb Blaster	Battle with mummies to beat the curse of the tomb	●●●	110
	Vampire	Fly over Transylvanian treetops on a blood-curdling coaster	●●●	110
Alton Towers	Nemesis	Experience G-forces greater than a space shuttle take-off	●●●●●	140
	Oblivion	More bonkers than a bungee – plunge 61 m into the abyss	●●●●	140
	Air	Float, swoop, soar, dive and feel like you're flying	●●●●	140
	Charlie and the Chocolate Factory	Explore Willy Wonka's fantabulous world on foot and by boat and jaw-dropping glass elevator ride	●●	100
Drayton Manor	Apocalypse	The world's first stand-up tower drop (drop 54 m at 4 Gs)	●●●●●	140
	Shockwave	Europe's only stand-up roller coaster	●●●●●	140
	Stormforce10	Plunge backwards down a 9 m water drop	●●●●	120
Blackpool Pleasure Beach	Pepsi Max Big One	World's tallest (72 m) and fastest (140 kph) coaster	●●●●●	132
	Infusion	Suspended coaster, 5 loops, water features	●●●●●	132
	Grand National	Twin track racing wooden roller coaster	●●●	117
	Ice blast	Get catapulted at 129 kph up a vertical 64-m tower	●●●●	132
Legoland	Viking's River Splash	Surge downstream in a fantasy Viking world	●●●	90
	Jungle Coaster	Legoland's fastest (60 kph) with a hair-raising 16-m drop	●●●	110
	Driving school	Drive an electric car around roads and roundabouts	●●	6-13
	Miniland	35 million pieces of LEGO recreate scenes from Europe	●	–

A taste of Wales: Bara Brith

What you need
➤➤ 110 g sultanas
➤➤ 110 g raisins soaked overnight in 150 ml cold tea
➤➤ 110 g demerara sugar
➤➤ 1 tbsp coarse cut marmalade
➤➤ 1 beaten egg
➤➤ 1 tsp mixed spice
➤➤ 220 g self-raising flour

What to do
➤➤ Mix all the ingredients together in a large bowl.
➤➤ Put the mixture into a greased loaf tin.
➤➤ Bake at 160-170°C for about one hour.
➤➤ Leave to cool in the tin for 20 minutes before turning out on to a wire tray.
➤➤ Cut into slices and butter before serving.

Castles

Windsor Castle (royal.gov.uk) Follow a family activity trail around the world's largest occupied castle, one that has been a royal home and fortress for over 900 years.

Castle Urquhart (historic-scotland.gov.uk) More sightings of Nessie have been made from this ruined fort than from any other point around Loch Ness.

Tower of London (hrp.org.uk) London's ancient fortress is home to the Crown Jewels, weapons, armour, ravens, the Yeoman Warders and numerous ghosts.

Windsor Castle

One to watch
The Railway Children, Based on the book by E Nesbit, this classic film, rooted in the early 1900s, follows the lives of three children and their mother when they move from London to a simple country cottage by a railway.

Family travel in Britain and Ireland is pure child's play. Nothing could be simpler. There are activities and attractions to suit every age; getting around is generally straightforward, and accommodation covers the whole gamut from campsites to luxury hotels.

Babies (0-18 months)

The climate is gentle, baby supplies are easily found, many places are buggy-friendly and, no matter where you go, you'll usually find at least one café with highchairs or a hotel that provides cots. Seaside holidays are the natural choice – you can plonk tiny tots on the beach, swoosh them through the shallows and wheel them to sleep along the prom. The Marine Conservation Society publishes the *Good Beach Guide* (goodbeachguide.co.uk), an online database of 1200 beaches in the UK and Ireland.

Toddlers/pre-school (18 months-4 years)

More fun, but also more fraught, beach holidays with toddlers demand eagle-eyed surveillance by parents to ensure safety. City breaks can also work well with this age range – parks usually have excellent playgrounds, while zoos and aquariums are always a hit. They are still too young to get much out of the major theme parks, although Legoland (legoland.co.uk) in Windsor will appeal, as will the countless farm parks where they can feed lambs and cuddle rabbits.

Kids/school age (4-12 years)

Beach safety is even more paramount with this fearless age group (rnli.org.uk). However, with expert tuition at surf schools, activity centres and riding stables, kids can safely start learning all kinds of new skills. They are also at an age when camping, hiking and cycling holidays start to sound feasible. As for exercising their minds, Britain and Ireland are chock-a-block with interactive science museums, mysterious castles and well-interpreted nature reserves. Organizations like the National Trust (nationaltrust.org.uk), the RSPB (rspb.org.uk) and the Wildlife Trusts (wildlifetrusts.org) arrange numerous child-friendly events throughout the year. For thrills, over 90% of the rides and attractions at Chessington World of Adventures (chessignton.com) are for under-12s.

Teenagers (13 years+)

You really need a surf school, sailing club or some other kind of extra incentive to keep teens keen on the beach. Sandcastles and rock pools just won't do it for them. Try giving them a taste of freedom at summer camps operated by Camp Beaumont (campbeaumont.co.uk) and PGL (pgl.co.uk) where they'll not only try out cool new activities but also meet lots of people their own age. City breaks will also strike a chord with teenagers, particularly in places like London, Glasgow and Manchester where you can combine

Above right: Splash down at Chessington World of Adventures; roly-poly at Legoland.

🦆 Buggy-friendly walks

Totnes to Dartington riverside path, Devon This level 4-km walk follows the River Dart from Totnes Bridge to the Cider Press Centre in Dartington where you'll find a toy shop and child-friendly café. The walk also links to the Dart Valley Steam Railway station at Littlehempston.

Cotswold Water Park, Gloucestershire A 4-km walk encircles two lakes, taking in a visitor centre, lakeside café, wood sculpture trail and two adventure playgrounds en route. You can also hire bikes with kiddie trailers.

Durham city and riverbanks Durham's impressive cathedral and castle dominate the first part of this 2-km walk as you stroll down South Bailey towards Prebend's Bridge, from where a peaceful woodland path follows the river all the way back towards the city centre.

sightseeing with great shopping and popular culture. For adventure and adrenaline, hit the theme-park trail, challenge them to climb a Munro in the Scottish Highlands or paddle a sea kayak off the west coast of Ireland.

Special needs

Holiday Care (holidaycare.org.uk) has information on transport, accommodation, visitor attractions and activity holidays for people with all kinds of disability, while Door to Door (dptac.gov.uk) offers advice about travelling using various forms of transport. Disability Now (disabilitynow.org.uk/directory) lists accessible hotels,

❝❞ We love going to London. Don't underestimate the pleasures of simply travelling around – double-decker buses, tubes and taxis were all a rich source of entertainment for our three- and five-year-old. The highlight was a boat trip down the Thames from Westminster Pier to Greenwich. You can sit inside or out, there's plenty of space to move about and it's a great way to see lots of famous landmarks. The Science Museum was also a big hit. Archie and Esther still talk about the Bubble Show which reaches a finale when a bubble filled with methane rises flaming to the ceiling.
Alison Rippon

What about the Channel Islands?

Nestled in the bay of St Malo off the French coast and over 110 km from mainland Britain, the two largest Channel Islands, Jersey and Guernsey, are prime family-holiday territory. Their wide, sandy beaches and crystal-clear seas are legendary, but there are also plenty of other attractions to inspire kids of all ages. The best family beaches on **Jersey** (jersey.com) include Green Island (a south-facing suntrap), La Rocque (with its Rock Pool Discovery Club), St Brelades Bay (where children age six and above can learn to windsurf or canoe) and St Ouen's Bay (a paradise for surfers). Away from the beach, be sure to visit Jersey's famous animal sanctuary, Durrell Wildlife (durrellwildlife.org) and the hands-on Maritime Museum in St Helier. There's also a medieval castle and Neolithic burial mound to be explored, not to mention a couple of action-packed adventure parks – aMaizing Maze (jerseyleisure.com) and Living Legend (jerseylivinglegend.co.je), where kids can get stuck into everything from go-karting to golf.

On **Guernsey** (visitguernsey.com), two of the best beaches for families are Pembroke Bay, a golden arc of sand that gently shelves into the sea, and Vazon, a hot spot for all

St Ouen's Bay, Jersey.

kinds of watersports. Guarding the entrance to St Peter Port, Castle Hornet is a must-see, while cycling on Guernsey is a real delight for families, thanks to the six 'Gentle and Rolling' routes around the island. Perhaps most exciting of all, however, is how easy it is to visit the nearby islands of **Herm**, **Sark** and **Alderney** – all linked by ferry for carefree island hopping in the English Channel.

cottages and B&Bs in the UK. Vitalise (vitalise.org.uk) has five centres where disabled or visually impaired people and their carers can enjoy themed weeks, activities and excursions.

Single parents

Single Parents UK (singleparents.org.uk) lists organizations offering holidays for single parents and families on low income, as well as companies that provide good deals for one-parent families. Single Parent Fun (singleparentfun.com) is an excellent community site where free membership enables you to meet other single parents and join organized trips and days out. Popular with single-parent families, Acorn Adventure (acornadventure.co.uk) operates activity holidays in the Lake District and Brecon Beacons.

Telling tales …

How much you spend on a family holiday has very little to do with what makes it a success. I've interviewed thousands of parents and children about their best holidays, and they've usually been the cheapest and simplest – the windy days in Cornwall on the beach as opposed to the five-star luxury break in St Lucia. The most important things you need to take with you on holiday are imagination, creativity, confidence and a relaxed attitude towards travel. You have a stressed-out parent, you get a stressed-out kid. You have a chilled-out parent, you get a chilled-out kid. And don't dump them on someone else when you have the benefit of their company. Children want to be with their parents – even teenagers believe it or not. It's the time you spend with your children they will remember – not the stuff that you buy them. And it's usually the holidays that will stick out in their mind as the best bits of their childhood.

Sarah Tucker (yogibabe.com)
Author of The Playground Mafia and
The Battle for Big School (Arrow Books)

City slickers

It's big, busy and bewildering (not to mention being one of the world's most expensive cities), but there's no denying the fact that kids love London. Just being there, in the thick of it, crawling along congested streets in a double-decker bus or rising above it all on the London Eye, gives children a huge thrill. And that's before you've hit any of the attractions. You can tailor a day out in London to suit all ages, whether it's a London Zoo/Hamleys double whammy for six-year-olds or a teenage pilgrimage to the shops along Oxford Street. Whatever you decide to do, resist the temptation to cram too much into a single day. London with kids is best in small, bite-size chunks. You can always come back for more.

Above: Spin and cruise – combine the London Eye with a Thames river trip to see the city sights. **Left top:** badges. **Left bottom:** Natural History Museum.

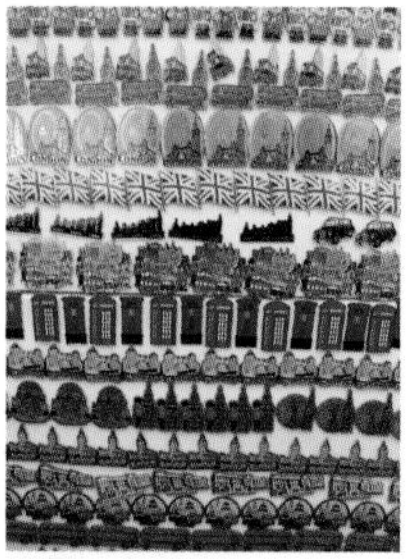

City highlights

- Children up to 11 travel free on buses, trams and London Underground (tfl.gov.uk).
- National museums and galleries are free (but do consider giving a donation).
- The London Pass (londonpass.com) offers free entry to more than 55 attractions.
- For novel sightseeing try London Duck Tours (londonducktours.co.uk).
- For further information, log on to visitlondon.com, kidslovelondon.com and whatson4kids.com.

Two-day action plan

Day 1: the South Bank The London Eye (ba-londoneye.com) is not only a fun (30-minute) ride, but it's also the best way for kids to grasp the scale of London and pinpoint a few landmarks. As the big wheel spins them 135 m above the Thames, they'll be able to see everything from the Houses of Parliament to Wembley Stadium. Back at ground level, take a river cruise for a different perspective of capital attractions like St Paul's Cathedral (stpauls.co.uk), HMS Belfast (hmsbelfast.iwm.org.uk), the Tower of London (hrp.org.uk) and Tower Bridge. However, if that sounds like too much sightseeing for one day, focus instead on other South Bank highlights. The London Aquarium (londonaquarium.co.uk) recreates a watery world of rushing streams, coral reefs, mangrove swamps and teeming rock pools. You can stroke rays in the touch pool and watch a piranha feeding-frenzy, but it's the sharks in the huge Pacific tank that are the show-stealers. The National Theatre (nationaltheatre.org.uk) hosts a free outdoor summer festival between July and September called 'Watch this Space', featuring all kinds of live performances, from circus acts to music and dance. The Tate Modern (tate.org.uk) has weekend and holiday activities for families, while the Unicorn Theatre (unicorntheatre.com) presents acts specifically for children. Altogether less refined, the London Dungeon (thedungeons.com) 'gorifies' the capital's less salubrious past with vivid portrayals of torture, plague and the Great Fire of London. There are even thrill rides like Extremis – Drop Ride to Doom, a simulated hanging for anyone over 120 cm tall. Located on Lambeth Road, the Imperial War Museum (iwm.org.uk) takes a more dignified approach to history with its impressive displays of weaponry and sobering insights into the world wars. Steer younger children towards the Home Front exhibit where they'll be intrigued by concepts like rationing.

Day 2: Classic sights Start at Trafalgar Square where Nelson's Column rises above a swirling torrent of taxis and buses. Flanking the famous plaza are three arty attractions. The National Gallery (nationalgallery.org.uk) offers talks and workshops for families, as well as a choice of two paper trails – one on a Chinese Zodiac theme, the other in pursuit of 'winged things'. The National Portrait Gallery (npg.org.uk) provides activity rucksacks containing jigsaws, dressing-up gear and other goodies to stimulate four- to 12-year-olds in the Tudor, Victorian and 20th Century galleries. However, if it's good old-fashioned brass rubbing that gets your creative juices flowing, head to St Martin-in-the Fields (stmartin-in-the-fields.org). Grab a snack lunch at the café in the crypt, before strolling down The Mall, nipping into St James's Park (royalparks.org.uk) to see wildlife officers feeding the pelicans (daily at 1430). Continue to Buckingham Palace (royal.gov.uk) to wave at the queen, and then take a bus to Knightsbridge where the food halls of Harrods (harrods.com) should distract kids for at least a few minutes before they drag you to the toys on the fourth floor.

🔍 How to do the zoo

Most visitors make straight for Gorilla Kingdom near the entrance of **London Zoo** (londonzoo.co.uk), so skip the crowds by walking in the opposite direction towards the wild dogs, giraffes, zebras and okapis. Next, visit the Clore Rainforest Lookout – a little piece of South American jungle which you can explore both at canopy and ground level. The adjacent Night Zone takes you into a twilight world of bats, rats and other nocturnal critters. If they're out and about, the nearby meerkats and otters are always entertaining – but walk on past the penguins to the flamingo pool and big cat enclosures. Check out the activities at BUGS! (Biodiversity Underpinning Global Survival) before backtracking to the Oasis Café for lunch. You'll then be in prime position for the penguin feeding at 1400, followed by Animals in Action, a wildlife encounter held daily in the Amphitheatre. Next, visit the Children's Zoo, the walk-through African Bird Safari, and the Komodo dragon enclosure – by which time the zoo should be less busy, leaving you to enjoy Gorilla Kingdom with the minimum of territorial posturing.

Best of the rest

British Museum (thebritishmuseum.ac.uk) Don't drift aimlessly through this vast cultural and historical treasure house as your kids will wilt. Instead, make use of the excellent children's programme – six museum trails, family activity backpacks, workshops, storytelling, plus an audio tour. If you see just one thing, make sure it's the Egyptian mummies in rooms 62-63.

Covent Garden (covent-garden.co.uk) Cool cafés, street performers and plenty of shops make Covent Garden a guaranteed hit with teenagers. The London Transport Museum (ltmuseum.co.uk) has a new learning zone, 'driver's-eye' simulators and a play area for under-fives.

Greenwich Take a boat trip from central London with Thames Cruises (thamescruises.com) to reach this World Heritage Site, dominated by Sir Christopher Wren's Old Royal Naval College (greenwichfoundation.org.uk). Damaged by fire in 2007, the glorious 19th-century tea clipper, *Cutty Sark* (cuttysark.org.uk), is scheduled to re-open in late 2008. In the meantime, set a course for the National Maritime Museum (nmm.ac.uk) for a hefty horde of seafaring treasures or, if time is of the essence, head to the Royal Observatory (rog.nmm.ac.uk) which has a spectacular new planetarium.

Natural History Museum (nhm.ac.uk) A skeleton of Diplodocus has long reigned supreme in the Central Hall of this magnificent museum but kids get more of a buzz from the animatronic T Rex in the dinosaur gallery. Other highlights include Creepy Crawlies, Ecology, the Mammal Hall and The Power Within, with its earthquake simulator. Explorer backpacks, complete with pith helmets, binoculars and drawing materials, are available for under-sevens, while Discovery guides containing activities linked to the national curriculum can be purchased

British Museum.

for children aged four to 16. The 45-minute Explore Tour (minimum age eight) takes you behind the scenes of the museum's 22 million-piece collection stored on 27 km of shelving. To get your hands on fossils, crystals and other museum specimens visit the interactive science centre for kids aged 7 to 14.

Science Museum (sciencemuseum.org.uk) London's best museum for hands-on fiddling and twiddling, the Science Museum has play zones targeting different age groups. The Garden helps three- to six-year-olds experiment with water, light and sound, the Pattern Pod engages five- to eight-year-olds, while the Launch Pad is the museum's largest and most popular interactive gallery for school-age kids. Teenagers will find the latest science news at Antenna, while Energy challenges seven- to 14-year-olds to investigate energy demands for the future. There are also motion simulators, daily science shows and an IMAX cinema.

Victoria and Albert Museum (vam.ac.uk) The V&A has excellent family facilities, including a treasure trail which takes you through exhibits on Asia and the Middle East in search of objects for the perfect picnic party. Activity backpacks on themes such as Chinese treasures, glass and fancy furnishings are also available for children aged five to 12. Don't miss the Activity Cart (Sundays and holidays) – a roving art and craft trolley, suitable for children aged three and over. There are also hundreds of hands-on exhibits throughout the museum.

Seven floors to heaven

Take them one step at a time at *Hamleys* (hamleys.com), the UK's biggest toy store, on Regent Street.
Basement Lego, K'nex and other construction toys.
Ground floor Teddy bears and soft toys.
First floor Board games and ride-on toys.
Second floor Baby and toddler toys.
Third floor Barbie, Bratz and other girls' dolls and toys.
Fourth floor Hornby, Corgi, Hot Wheels and Scalextric.
Fifth floor Power Rangers, Transformers and other heroes.

🌍 Local favourites

Battersea Park Children's Zoo (batterseaparkzoo.co.uk) Pat a pot- bellied pig and mingle with meerkats.
The Diana, Princess of Wales Memorial Playground Let their imaginations run wild in this magical playground with its huge pirate ship, sandy beach, sensory trail and mermaids' fountain.
London Wetland Centre (wwt.org.uk) Explore nature trails, stake out bird hides and discover what lurks in the ponds and reedbeds in this wild corner of Barnes.

The Wight stuff

Family attractions in Southeast England include everything from theme parks and castles to traditional seaside resorts like Brighton, Eastbourne and Hastings. However, if you have to pick just one place to take the kids, it has to be the Isle of Wight with its beaches, coastal walks, cycling tracks and watersports. Another great option for active families, the New Forest has miles of cycle tracks and several riding stables, while the North and South Downs offer plenty in the way of gentle walks.

Bottom left: The Needles, Isle of Wight. **Above:** Bodiam Castle. **Below:** Colossus coaster at Thorpe Park.

Regional highlights

▸▸ Brighton Pier (brightonpier.co.uk) is famous for its thrill rides and arcades.
▸▸ Green Island Tourism (greenislandtourism. org) lists eco-friendly accommodation and activities on the Isle of Wight.
▸▸ For further information, log on to visitsoutheastengland.com, Isle of Wight Tourism (islandbreaks.co.uk) and New Forest Tourism (thenewforest.co.uk).

Isle of Wight About half of the 380-sq-km Isle of Wight is an Area of Outstanding Natural Beauty. Although there are over 800 km of footpaths, you'll probably have more luck getting kids to sample the 320 km of cycle trails. Wight Ventures (wight-ventures.co.uk) will deliver rental bikes to your hotel, kit you out with helmets, water bottles and maps, and even accompany you if desired. An easy route to start with follows the disused railway line from Yarmouth to Freshwater Bay, a good spot for swimming. Leaflets describing a dozen or so other cycling trails are available from tourist information centres. A mecca for 'yachties', the Isle of Wight is the perfect place to hone your sailing skills or have a go at learning a new one. Based in Bembridge on the eastern side of the island, X-Isle Sports (x-is.co.uk) offers courses in sailing, surfing, kitesurfing, windsurfing, wakeboarding and waterskiing. There are also several excellent locations for kayaking, including the sheltered beaches of Ryde and Puckpool. For swimming, the best beach is Shanklin. To any dinosaur fanatics in the family,

the Isle of Wight will seem more like a pilgrimage than a holiday: nowhere else in Europe is more important for dinosaur remains. At the Dinosaur Isle museum (dinosaurisle.com) you're whisked back in time to the Cretaceous Period when the island was populated by the likes of the giant lumbering sauropods and armour-plated ankylosaurs. Try your luck by joining one of their fossil walks.

New Forest Once a popular hunting ground for Norman kings, William the Conqueror's 'new' forest is home to peacefully grazing herds of fallow deer and New Forest ponies. For your best chance of spotting wildlife, explore the forest (one of the few ancient oak woods left in England) on foot, bicycle or horseback. Try Country Lanes Cycle Centre (countrylanes.co.uk) and New Park Manor Equestrian Centre (newparkmanorhotel.co.uk) – both in Brockenhurst. Nestled on the banks of the Beaulieu River, Buckler's Hard (bucklershard.co.uk) provides a fascinating glimpse into the past, when the New Forest supplied mighty oaks for Nelson's fleet. To explore the river by canoe, contact New Forest Activities (newforestactivities.co.uk).

Best beaches In Kent, Walpole Bay has a tidal swimming pool, while West Wittering on the Sussex coast has a Blue Flag sandy beach. With babies or toddlers in tow, follow the 2-km, buggy-friendly path alongside the meandering River Cuckmere in Seven Sisters Country Park (sevensisters.org.uk) which leads to a shingle beach with spectacular views of Seaford Head.

Best historical sights Bristling with

turrets and surrounded by a wide moat, Bodiam Castle (nationaltrust.org.uk) in Sussex is a medieval masterpiece with cue cards and play items to help evoke the atmosphere. Leeds Castle (leeds-castle.com) is equally impressive, while Canterbury Cathedral (canterbury-cathedral.org) is famed for its stained-glass windows, the Shrine of St Thomas à Becket and the Tomb of the Black Prince.

Kids' top 10: days out

1 **Legoland** (legoland.co.uk) Windsor, Berks.
2 **Chessington World of Adventures** (chessington.com) Surrey.
3 **Thorpe Park** (thorpepark.com) Chertsey, Surrey.
4 **Marwell Zoo** (marwell.org) Winchester, Hants.
5 **Portsmouth Historic Dockyard** (historicdockyard.co.uk) Hants.
6 **Dickens World** (dickensworld. co.uk) Chatham, Kent.
7 **Brighton Sea Life Centre** (sealifeeeurope.com/uk) East Sussex.
8 **Roald Dahl Museum** (roalddahl museum.org) Great Missenden, Bucks.
9 **River and Rowing Museum** (rrm.co.uk) Henley-on-Thames, Oxon.
10 **Historic Dockyard Chatham** (chdt.org.uk) Kent.

Exploring a wild and windy shore

Bulging out between the Thames Estuary and the Wash, East Anglia may be flat, but it's far from featureless. You can hire a boat to explore the 200 km of reed-fringed waterways of the Norfolk Broads or punt along the River Cam beneath the Bridge of Sighs in the magnificent university town of Cambridge. You can kick through drifts of autumn beech leaves in Epping Forest, a favourite hunting ground of Henry VIII, or stroll beside the River Stour where 18th-century landscape artist, John Constable, sought inspiration. From bustling resorts, like Great Yarmouth and Southwold, to the medieval city of Norwich, this underrated corner of Britain has lots to offer families. Pick of the crop, however, has to be Norfolk's north coast with its beaches, wildlife and traditional seaside towns. This is where your kids will rediscover the pure and simple joys of kite flying, beachcombing and crabbing.

North Norfolk Coast

⚜ ☀ ♨ ⚓ ♿ 🎠 ⛵ ⚱ ⊗ ⊙

» For events listings, pick up a Fri edition of the *Eastern Daily Press*.
» Purchase a tide table; on some beaches sirens warn of fast incoming tides.
» The Coasthopper Bus (norfolk.gov.uk) operates between King's Lynn and Sheringham, connecting with the Bittern Line (bitternline.com) train to Norwich.
» The North Norfolk Railway (nnrailway.co.uk) runs 9 km from Sheringham to Holt – it's usually pulled by steam engines, sometimes by Thomas himself.
» For further information, log on to visiteastofengland.com.

East to West along the coast

Before setting off, make sure you have three essentials – binoculars (Norfolk is a birdwatcher's paradise), a kite and a crab line. Driving north from King's Lynn, you pass Snettisham Park (snettishampark.co.uk) which has a deer safari, adventure playgrounds and children's farm, and Caley Mill (norfolk-lavender.co.uk) which is perfectly purple during July and August when the lavender fields are in bloom. Soon after, you reach Hunstanton, a traditional Victorian seaside resort with compulsory pier, amusement arcades and pony rides on the beach. Kids will love the seal-watching trips operated by Searles Sea Tours (seatours.co.uk) in the amphibious *Wash Monster* which is equally at home trundling across the sand flats as it is bobbing in the sea beneath Hunstanton's striped cliffs. If it's raining, seek refuge at the Sea Life Sanctuary (sealsanctuary.co.uk) which

rescues and rehabilitates sick or injured marine mammals found along the coast and also has permanent displays featuring penguins and otters.

Follow the coastal A149 road to Holme-next-the-Sea where a boardwalk through the dunes provides easy buggy access to the beach. Nearby is Titchwell Marsh Nature Reserve (rspb.org.uk) where top summer ticks include avocets and marsh harriers. Three pushchair-friendly nature trails explore fen and meadow habitats where, if you're lucky, you may glimpse bearded tits, water voles or the ever-elusive, reedbed-skulking bittern. Continuing east to Brancaster, you may well find a long stretch of beach to yourself. It's a great spot to launch your kite, but not so good for swimming due to the strong tidal currents.

Beyond Burnham lies Holkham Hall (holkham.co.uk) set in a magnificent landscaped park and with access to both a nature reserve and a beautiful 6-km swathe of golden sands. Just east of Holkham, Wells-next-the-Sea is an old fishing port with a quay that's just the job for crabbing. All you need is a weighted line with some bacon tied to the end and a large bucket to store your spoils. Wait until high tide, find a gap between the moored boats and dangle away. Keep young children well away from the edge and remember to set your crabs free afterwards. Wells also has a sandy beach that can be reached by narrow-gauge railway.

A thriving port in the 13th century, Blakeney Marshes is now all silt and seals

Grey seal mother and pup on the north Norfolk coast.

– you can see both in abundance with Bean's Boats (beanboattrips.co.uk). Nearby, Cley Windmill (where you can stay the night) overlooks the Cley Marshes where you have another chance to bag a bittern. Continue on towards Salthouse for sublime seafood at Cookie's Crab Shop before reaching Sheringham and Cromer – both of which have sand at low tide, pebbles at high tide, crazy golf and fish 'n' chips.

Best of the rest

1 Woburn Safari Park (woburnsafari.co.uk) Bedfordshire.
2 Wimpole Hall and Home Farm (wimpole.org) Hertfordshire.
3 Colchester Zoo (colchester-zoo.com) Essex.
4 Dinosaur Adventure Park (dinosaurpark.co.uk) Norwich, Norfolk.
5 Pleasurewood Hills (pleasurewoodhills.co.uk) Lowestoft, Suffolk.

❓ Where can I do this?

Aimed at four- to 14-year-olds, *BeWILDerwood* (bewilderwood.co.uk) near Wroxham is an arboreal fantasy adventure where kids can not only explore tree houses, zip wires and bridges, but also meet magical creatures like Swampy the marsh boggle and Mildred, a 4-m-long vegetarian crocklebog.

Striking gold on England's treasured coasts

Brace yourself Brixham; look out Lyme Regis! When the summer holidays arrive, the Southwest receives a flood of families in search of quintessential British seaside. You can almost smell the factor 40 and hear the rattle of spades against buckets. Cornwall, Devon and Dorset are fringed by some of the world's most child-friendly beaches, offering everything from surf, rock pools and unrivalled sandcastle potential to great-value resorts and copious rainy-day attractions.

Regional highlights

>> Avoid travelling on Sat mornings during the height of the holiday season.
>> Beware the weaver fish, a spiny rascal that burrows in sand between high and low tide – wear jelly shoes or wetsuit booties.
>> The weather is notoriously fickle – misty on the north coast, sunny on the south and vice versa - so be prepared to follow the sun.
>> For further information, visit westcountrynow.com.

South Devon Linking the resort towns of Torquay, Paignton and Brixham, the English Riviera (englishriviera.co.uk) is packed with family appeal, from sandy beaches and steam-train rides to days out at Paignton Zoo (paigntonzoo.org.uk) and Quaywest Water Park (quaywest.co.uk). Head south along the coast and you reach the South Hams (somewhere-special.co.uk), an irresistible blend of glorious beaches, intriguing inlets and rolling countryside. Lying at its heart, Kingsbridge and Salcombe offer traditional seaside treats like crabbing and boat trips, while Dartmouth has its superb castle (english-heritage.org.uk) jutting out into the Dart estuary. The beaches of the South Hams, meanwhile, are heaven on earth for kids. From east to west, take your pick from Blackpool Sands (sheltered, safe and simply idyllic), Slapton Sands (good for skimming stones), Millbay (across the estuary from Salcombe, fine sand, good for paddling), Soar Mill Cove (golden sands, streams to dam, caves to explore), Hope Cove (calm waters, small harbour at one end), Thurlestone (great rock pools, plus sand), Bantham (vast swathes of sand, shallow tidal lagoons, good surf) and Bigbury-on-Sea (natural paddling pools, rock pools, views of Burgh Island).

Dartmoor If you can tear the kids away from the beach, Dartmoor (discoverdartmoor.co.uk) makes a fun day out. Hike to one of the famous granite tors, picnic beside rushing streams at Dartmeet, ride the South Devon Railway (southdevonrailway.org) from Buckfastleigh to Totnes, feed lambs at Pennywell Farm (pennywellfarm. co.uk) or cuddle a pony at the Miniature Pony Centre (miniatureponycentre.com).

North Devon Just when you've set your mind on the South Hams, North Devon drops a bucket-load of golden sand and surf potential on your best-laid plans. Woolacombe Bay is the region's undisputed beach beauty, while other top surf spots include Saunton Sands and Croyde. Cutesy, car-free Clovelly (clovelly.co.uk), with its steep cobbled lanes and 14th-century harbour, is almost too picturesque to be true, while the North Devon Biosphere Reserve (encompassing part of the Taw and Torridge Estuary) includes Braunton Burrows, a huge, wildlife-rich dune system. Just inland, you can saddle up at the Exmoor Pony Centre (exmoorponies.co.uk) or, if the weather turns nasty, bolt for The Milky Way (themilkyway.co.uk) – a farm and space-themed adventure park rolled into one.

Bristol Head for the harbour where the vast propeller and rudder of the dry-docked SS *Great Britain* (ssgreatbritain.org) will astound kids and grown-ups alike. Explore-at-Bristol (at-bristol.org.uk) is a hands-on science museum, while highlights at Bristol Zoo (bristolzoo.org.uk) include the Monkey Jungle and Seal and Penguin Coasts.

Somerset The pleasures of Bath range from boating on the River Avon (bathboating.co.uk) to exploring the magnificent Roman Baths (romanbaths.co.uk) where kids can 'meet the Romans' courtesy of a special audio tour. At Wookey Hole Caves (wookey.co.uk) children can search for a witch that was turned to stone. Just make sure little ones aren't petrified themselves.

Follow the Famous Five

The Isle of Purbeck was a favoured holiday haunt of Enid Blyton, whose *Famous Five* adventures were inspired by the region's coves, islands and ruined castles. Kirrin Island was based on Brownsea Island (brownseaisland ferries.com), while the island's fictitious ruin was modelled on Corfe Castle (national trust.org.uk). While you're at Corfe don't forget to call into the Ginger Pop Shop (gingerpop.co.uk) for all-things-Blyton – including, of course, lashings of ginger beer. Three cheers for Julian, Dick, Anne, George and Timmy!

Above: Corfe Castle.

How to be a fossil hunter

Lyme Regis is an official gateway to the Jurassic Coast (jurassiccoast.com), a World Heritage Site that places a 150-km stretch of shoreline between Swanage and Exmouth alongside the Grand Canyon in terms of natural importance. Few places can rival the outstanding geology and coastal formations of Dorset and east Devon.

Lyme Fossil Shop, an archaic Aladdin's cave at the bottom of the high street, is a good place to begin your fossil foray. Its shelves and walls are festooned with prehistoric paraphernalia, from plate-sized ammonites at £500 a throw to fossilized dinosaur poo at £4 a dollop. At the Philpot Museum (lymeregis museum.co.uk) you can find out about Lyme's most famous fossil hunter, Mary Anning, who, in 1823, was the first to discover a plesiosaur skeleton. Both the museum and the nearby Charmouth Heritage Coast Centre (charmouth.org) organize guided fossil-hunting tours where experts transform pebbly beaches into prehistoric graveyards.

Try to time fossil hunts to follow stormy weather when rain and heavy seas expose fossils and wash them on to the beach where they are easier and safer to find. Stay well clear of the cliffs which are extremely unstable and susceptible to landslides, and only go collecting on a falling tide.

Fossil hot spots include Monmouth Beach (west of the harbour at Lyme Regis) for giant ammonites; Black Ven and Church Cliffs (between Lyme Regis and Charmouth) for ammonites, ichthyosaurs and plesiosaurs; Lulworth and Portland for fragments of fossil forest; and Purbeck for dinosaur footprints.

Nearby child-friendly highlights include the Abbotsbury Swannery (abbotsbury-tourism.co.uk) where hundreds of cygnets hatch mid-May to late June.

Kids' top 10: Cornwall

1 Dig the beach, any beach – make a miniature St Michael's Mount, scoop out a network of canals, build a sandy dam to hold back the tide, excavate a paddling pool.

2 Venture into the tropics at the Eden Project (edenproject.com), Cornwall's essential day out. Find out where sugar, chocolate and vanilla come from, play drums and make crafts in the Jungle Town and operate the biggest nutcracker you've ever seen. If you thought plants were boring, think again.

3 Discover how a marine rescue centre works at Gweek's National Seal Sanctuary (sealsanctuary.co.uk), home to seals, otters and sea lions.

4 Explore the sandy snugs, rocky islets and turquoise waters of Kynance Cove (nationaltrust.org.uk) – a real smugglers' haunt if ever there was one.

5 Learn to surf at Whitesands Bay, a golden crescent at Sennen with a surf school (sennensurfingcentre.com), rock pools near the lifeboat ramp, acres of sand at low tide and great fish and chips from the café on the waterfront.

6 Dangle your legs over a harbour wall, a crab line in one hand, a Cornish ice cream in the other.

7 Plan an adventure to St Michael's Mount (stmichaelsmount.co.uk), the legendary home of the giant, Cormoran; walk across at low tide or take the boat.

8 Cycle the 9-km stretch of the Camel

Top: Tropical biome, Eden project.
Above: Kynance Cove.

Trail between Wadebridge and Padstow alongside the estuary; it's flat, easy and there's lots to see.

9 Catch mackerel on a fishing trip from Padstow harbour (padstowboattrips.com).

10 Play beach games, from hopscotch to stony kickers.

How to get a taste of the tropics

Despite being just 45 km southwest of Land's End, the Isles of Scilly seem to have a toehold in the tropics. Abbey Gardens on Tresco, one of the archipelago's five inhabited islands, runs rampant with exotic plants, while the surrounding seas are brilliant turquoise – teeming with corals, sponges and sea fans. All this is nurtured by the Gulf Stream and one of the UK's mildest and sunniest climates. Get there from Penzance or Newquay by boat, helicopter or aircraft (ios-travel.co.uk).

Above: Abbey Gardens, Tresco. **Below:** Jurassic Coast, East Devon.

Beaches

For rock pools Kimmeridge Bay (Dorset), Thurlestone (Devon), Wembury (Devon).
For surfing Newquay (Cornwall), Polzeath (Cornwall), Woolacombe (Devon).
For swimming Blackpool Sands (Devon), Studland Bay (Dorset),Porthminster, St Ives (Cornwall).

➤ *The Good Beach Guide* (goodbeach guide.co.uk) has an online search facility.

The historic heartlands

With its honey-stone market towns and rolling hills peppered with sheep, nowhere does traditional England better than the Cotswolds, the region that inspired a million jigsaw puzzles. Elsewhere, you will find a veritable encyclopaedia of historical sites, from ancient Stonehenge and medieval Warwick Castle to the birthplaces of Shakespeare, the Industrial Revolution and, most significantly to children, the Cadbury Creme Egg.

Regional highlights

⚪🐾🏛️🅾️Ⓜ️❄️✳️

» Rutland, the UK's smallest county, is home to the largest man-made lake in Western Europe where you can windsurf, canoe and sail.
» One of the region's best cycle tracks, the 21-km Tissington Trail follows the old Buxton-to-Ashbourne railway line in the heart of the Peak District.
» For further information, log on to visitheartofengland.com, enjoyenglandseastmidlands.com.

Riding through Sherwood Forest.

Wiltshire The strange stone circle of Stonehenge (english-heritage.org.uk) has been luring visitors for over 5000 years. To protect this ancient wonder, a roped-off walkway keeps visitors 15 m from the giant Sarsen stones (each weighing up to 45 tons), so you'll have to rely on some thought-provoking questions to keep kids interested. How were those mega blocks shifted? How were the lintels placed on top? And why was it built in the first place? For light relief, Longleat (longleat.co.uk) is renowned for its drive-through safari park, but also boasts the perplexing Hedge Maze with nearly 3 km of passageways to get lost in.

Gloucestershire In the Forest of Dean (visitforestofdean.co.uk) you can cycle and canoe, or take to the trees at Go Ape! (goape.co.uk), a high-wire adventure with a minimum age of 10. For more sedate forest rambles, try the Dean Forest Railway (deanforest railway.co.uk) or the Dean Heritage Centre (deanheritagemuseum.com) which has a forester's cottage and woodland trails. At Slimbridge Wetland Centre (wwt.org.uk) in the Severn Vale,

you can hand-feed geese, take a 4WD safari through a nature reserve and spot kingfishers from a hide.

Oxfordshire Let slip to your kids that the Great Hall of Christ Church College doubles as Hogwarts School in the *Harry Potter* movies and they'll be dragging you to Oxford (oxfordcity.co.uk) quicker than a Golden Snitch in a game of Quidditch. Add fact to fiction at the The Oxford Story (oxfordstory.co.uk) where children ride desks (not broomsticks) through 900 years of Oxford University's history, and then visit the anthropological Pitt Rivers Museum (prm.ox.ac.uk) or the interactive Science Oxford Hands-On (oxtrust.org.uk/handson).

Warwickshire The Shakespeare Birthplace Trust (shakespeare.org.uk) manages five properties in Stratford upon Avon, all linked to the life of the great bard. Two of the most interesting for children are Shakespeare's Birthplace in Henley Street and Mary Arden's where you can experience what life was like in a 16th-century farmhouse. For a history lesson with more oomph, Warwick Castle (warwick-castle.co.uk) delivers with a passion. Kids can lay siege to haunted towers, torture chambers and medieval banqueting halls, but it's the legendary activities they'll remember most. Jousting, archery, falconry and combat shows are held daily throughout summer, while winter sees a skating rink and ice slide installed at the 11th-century fort.

Worcestershire Chuffing 26 km between Kidderminster and Bridgnorth, the Severn Valley Railway (svr.co.uk) is a must for all Thomas and Hornby fans,

Top: Stonehenge. **Above**: Only one of these is a waxwork model at Warwick Castle.

while the West Midland Safari Park (wmsp.co.uk) will appeal to the wild at heart with its drive-through safari (spot the white lions) and daredevil amusement park.

Birmingham Hands up who likes chocolate? Cadbury World (cadburyworld.co.uk) takes you on a mouth-watering journey through the origins and production of the sweet sensation and even goes interactive with Purple Planet where you can chase a Cadbury Creme Egg, grow your own cocoa beans and experience chocolate rain.

Staffordshire Taking kids to The Wedgwood Visitor Centre (wedgwood.com) might seem like, well, taking a bull into a china shop, but not only will they be fascinated by the factory tour, they'll also get a shot at the potter's wheel. For a different kind of spin, Drayton Manor

Kids' top 10: Cotswolds

1 Fill a long weekend or more at the Cotswold Water Park (waterpark.org) with everything from sailing, canoeing, raft-building and aerial adventures to birdwatching, angling, horse riding and waterskiing.

2 Burn off some energy in the 850-ha park and pleasure gardens of Blenheim Palace (blenheimpalace.com) which has a maze, butterfly house and adventure playground.

3 Spot wolves, rhinos, zebras, lions and other animals at the Cotswold Wildlife Park (cotswoldwildlifepark.co.uk) – and don't miss the meerkats, penguins and otters in the walled garden.

4 Discover the ultimate setting for a game of hide-and-seek at Hidcote Manor Gardens (nationaltrust.org.uk) where neatly clipped yew hedges partition the estate into countless outdoor rooms.

5 Feed the trout at Bibury (biburytroutfarm.co.uk).

6 Explore the weird and wonderful collection of artefacts (from musical instruments and bicycles to Samurai armour and a decorative elephant's bladder) at Snowshill Manor (nationaltrust.org.uk).

7 Cycle between historic, chocolate-box villages like the Slaughters, Winchcombe, Northleach, Bibury and Burford on a self-guided tour with Cotswold Country Cycles (cotswoldcountrycycles.com).

8 Hike at least part of the Cotswold Way (nationaltrail.co.uk/cotswold), a 160-km walking trail between Chipping Campden and Bath.

Above: Hidcote Manor Gardens. **Below:** Penguin at the Cotswold Wildlife Park.

9 Spend all your pocket money at the toyshop in Bourton-on-the-Water, and then beg to be taken to Birdland (birdland.co.uk) or the Cotswold Motoring Museum (cotswold-motor-museum.com) – home to none other than Brum.

10 Sample freshly baked scones with strawberry jam and clotted cream at Badgers Hall Tearoom (badgershall.com) in Chipping Campden.

(draytonmanor.co.uk) and Alton Towers (altontowers.com) are two of Britain's most popular theme parks (see page 63 to see how their rides compare with the likes of Blackpool Pleasure Beach and Thorpe Park).

Shropshire With no fewer than 10 museums and an iron bridge (albeit the world's first) as its star attraction, you might be put off taking kids to the Ironbridge Gorge Museums (ironbridge.org.uk). Don't be. There's nothing remotely rusty about this World Heritage Site commemorating the Industrial Revolution. At Blists Hill Victorian Town costumed actors evoke a bygone era when steam engines and horses powered industry, while at the Enginuity centre children can scheme away at their own technological innovations.

Leicestershire Famous for its primate collection, Twycross Zoo (twycrosszoo.com) has everything from chimps and bonobos to gibbons and gorillas, while the National Space Centre (spacecentre.co.uk) challenges visitors to undertake a simulated 3D mission in Human Spaceflight: Lunar Base 2025.

Nottinghamshire With its family nature trails, cycling and horse-riding opportunities, the historic royal hunting patch of Sherwood Forest (sherwoodforest.org.uk) is a great place to set free your inner Robin Hood. Designed for under-10s, Sundown Adventure Park (sundownadventureland.co.uk) has gentle rides and story-book-themed attractions.

Derbyshire Designated Britain's first national park in 1951, the heather-clad moors and wooded valleys of the Peak District are ideal stomping territory for active families. Two of the most popular attractions include riding the cable cars at the Heights of Abraham (heights-of-abraham.co.uk) and the trams at Crich Tramway Village (tramway.co.uk) – both near Matlock. For a forest-themed free-for-all, kids can go nuts at Conkers (visitconkers.com) with its assault course, nature trails and playgrounds.

North England

Land of pleasure, whatever the weather

If you feel your warm-weather instincts tugging you southwards, dig your heels in and spare a thought for North England. The Great British family holiday was practically invented in the Lancashire seaside resort of Blackpool, but the region's appeal goes way beyond donkey rides and pleasure parks. Let your kids' imaginations run riot through Roman ruins, Norman castles and cutting-edge science centres; free their spirits in wild places like the Lake District and Yorkshire Moors, and fill their days (even the rainy ones) with attractions ranging from Beatrix Potter to The Beatles.

The Northwest

😎 🏖 🎢 🎡 🏛 🎭

» Most of Manchester's 90-plus galleries and museums are free to enter.
» For further information on the region's cities, log on to englandsnorthwest.com, visitmanchester.com, visitliverpool.com and blackpooltourism.com.

Manchester Footie fans will want to make straight for Old Trafford where the Manchester United Museum and Stadium Tour (manutd.com) takes you into the hallowed heart of the world's most popular football team (controversial, but true). You can strut down the player's tunnel, admire the trophy cabinet and sit at the dressing-room peg of your favourite player. For fancy footwork on the high street, Manchester's shops will satisfy all fashion fans, while the city's mighty industrial heritage is celebrated at the Museum of Science and Industry (msim.org.uk). For family-friendly culture in Manchester, you can't beat the galleries and theatres of The Lowry (thelowry.com).

Liverpool Not to be outdone by its Mancunian rivals, Liverpool FC has the Anfield Experience (www.liverpoolfc.tv), but there's another attraction in Merseyside's great city that overshadows even football. Your kids may never have heard of The Beatles, but that's no reason why you shouldn't at least attempt to improve their music tastes. Think of it as part of their education. Of the many 'Fab Four' tours and attractions, your best bet with kids is The Beatles Story (beatlesstory.com) at Albert Dock. From rocking the world to exploring new ones, Spaceport (spaceport.org.uk) at Seacombe on the Wirral (ride the Mersey ferry to get there) takes you on a virtual journey through space. The nearby Blue Planet Aquarium (blueplanetaquarium.com) offers Bubblemaker diving courses for children aged eight to 15 – but you need to be at least 18 before they let you into the shark tank. If you continue south on the M53, you'll reach Chester Zoo (chesterzoo.org.uk). Family highlights north of Liverpool include the beaches, dunes and red squirrel reserve at Formby Point and a new waterpark near Southport called Splash World (splashworldsouthport.com).

Blackpool Dating from the 18th century, Britain's archetypal seaside resort is still a big crowd-puller, thanks in no small part to Blackpool Pleasure Beach (blackpoolpleasurebeach.com). England's thrill-city-central has over 125 rides and attractions, ranging from the 140-kph Pepsi Max Big One roller coaster (see page 63) to ice-skating, bingo and dodgems. As you'd expect there's also a waterpark (sandcastle-waterworld.co.uk), aquarium (sealifeeurope.com) and waxworks (louistussaudswaxworks.co.uk). For nostalgia mixed with fun, you can't miss the iconic, 158-m tall Blackpool Tower (blackpooltower.co.uk) where views, ballroom dancing, circus shows and one of Europe's largest indoor adventure playgrounds will further conspire to keep you off the beach.

Above: Blackpool beach.
Top right: York Minster.
Above right: Sycamore Gap, Hadrian's Wall.

Yorkshire and the Northeast

🌊 🚣 ⛰ 🏰 🏛 🏕 🚂 🏞 ☢ ✈

▸▸ The York Pass (yorkpass.com) provides entry to 28 attractions.

▸▸ Hadrian's Wall bus leaves Newcastle at 0940, arriving at Housesteads at 1106; you can take bicycles on the bus and pedal sections of Hadrian's Cycleway.

▸▸ For further information, log on to northeastengland.co.uk, visityork.org and newcastlegateshead.com.

From Vikings to Romans

York There's plenty to interest kids in York, and parents will appreciate its largely pedestrianized centre and compact size. Start with York Minster (yorkminster.org), England's largest medieval cathedral. Check out the Great East Window (a tennis-court-sized stained-glass marvel) before climbing the Central Tower for some gargoyle spotting. Back at street level, take your pick of four superb museums. The Yorkshire Museum (yorkshiremuseum. org.uk) has the full works, from Roman statues to meteorites; York Castle Museum (yorkcastlemuseum.org.uk) recreates Victorian life in gritty detail; the National Railway Museum (nrm.org.uk) boasts the world's finest collection of trains, including a replica of Stephenson's *Rocket*; and the Jorvik Viking Centre (jorvik-viking-centre.co.uk) stages battles, marches and warrior training during the summer. Other York highlights include boat trips on the Ouse and nightly ghost tours (ghostdetective. com) through the city's narrow, spooky passageways.

National parks The Yorkshire Dales National Park (yorkshiredales.org.uk) and North York Moors National Park (moors.uk.net) offer no end of walking opportunities, although much will depend on the ages and stamina of your children. For a classic lesson in geography, hike to the impressive natural amphitheatre of Malham Cove where a waterfall once plunged over 76-m high limestone cliffs.

Kids' top 10: The Lake District

1 Learn how to rock climb and abseil with Climb365 (climb365.net).

2 Sail a yacht on Lake Windermere with Outrun Sailing (outrunsailing.co.uk).

3 Visit Peter Rabbit et al at the World of Beatrix Potter (hop-skip-jump.com).

4 Cruise the lakes with Windermere Lake Cruises (windermere-lakecruises. co.uk).

5 Ride a steam train on the Haverthwaite Railway (lakesiderailway.co.uk).

6 Wander around Grasmere before visiting William Wordsworth's house, Dove Cottage (wordsworth.org.uk).

7 Lose yourself in the maze and see the owls at Muncaster Castle (muncaster.co.uk).

8 Find the perfect skimming stone at Buttermere or Coniston.

9 Picnic at Tarn Hows and then walk around the lake.

10 Conquer Scafell Pike, the highest mountain in England at 978 m, or take on the challenge of a wilderness bushcraft course with Woodsmoke (woodsmoke.uk.com).

The coast Hornsea is good for swimming, South Landing at Flamborough is renowned for rock pools, while the spectacular Bempton Cliffs (rspb.org.uk) provide unforgettable encounters with thousands of gannets, guillemots, kittiwakes and puffins (best seen from April to August). Don't miss The Deep (thedeep.co.uk), an impressive aquarium near Hull.

Other attractions The region has more than its fair share of interactive science museums. Get hands-on at Eureka! (eureka.org.uk) in Halifax, Magna (visitmagna.co.uk) in Rotherham and the Thackray Museum (thackraymuseum. org) in Leeds. North Yorkshire's Eden Camp (edencamp.co.uk) transports you back to Second World War Britain using sounds, smells and other special effects.

Newcastle You won't see teenagers for dust once they get a whiff of Newcastle's shops. Younger children will enjoy Seven Stories (sevenstories. org.uk), the Centre for Children's Books, while the high-tech Centre for Life (life.org.uk) should appeal to most ages. The best day out from Newcastle is to explore Hadrian's Wall (hadrians-wall. org) – a 117-km-long Roman fortification snaking across Northern England, from the Tyne at Wallsend to Bowness on the Solway Firth. Easily reached by metro from Newcastle, Segedunum Roman Fort (twmuseums.org.uk) once guarded the

eastern end of the Wall. Reconstructions and an interactive museum reveal what life was like for the garrison of 600 soldiers. Touring Hadrian's Wall west of Newcastle is straightforward – just follow the B6318 which signposts all the major sites, such as Vindolanda (vindolanda.com) and Housesteads Fort and Museum (english-heritage.org.uk).

The coast The best spots on Tyneside are Sandhaven Beach, Longsands South and St Mary's Island on the north side of Whitley Bay. Further north, the spectacular Northumberland coast has long sandy beaches and a string of castles, including Bamburgh Castle (bamburghcastle.com) and Holy Island's Lindisfarne Castle (nationaltrust.org.uk). Slightly inland, Alnwick Castle (alnwickcastle.com) starred in the first two Harry Potter films, while the Farne Islands (accessible by boat from Seahouses) are teeming with seabirds and seals. You can land on Inner Farne, but wear a hat in June when nesting terns dive-bomb visitors.

Other attractions Dominated by its fine Norman cathedral and castle, Durham (durhamtourism.co.uk) has gentle woodland paths and rowing boats to hire on the River Wear. The open-air museum at Beamish (beamish.org.uk) recreates life in the northeast prior to the First World War, complete with a farm, railway, high street and coal mine.

Above: The calm before the stone-skimming begins at Buttermere. **Below:** Out and about in Yorkshire.

❝❞ The best place for a picnic in West Yorkshire is Harcastle Craggs, just outside Hebden Bridge. You can walk along the river, playing skimmers and paddling all the way to Gibson Mill, where you can revive weary children with drinks and biscuits. The Mill itself is good to explore with lots of interactive ideas on how to go green.
Sarah Hetherington

The green heart of a red dragon

Wales is a little beauty – squat, rugged, full of character and brilliant round the edges, just like a Welsh rugby scrum half. 'An area the size of Wales' is often banded around when comparing anything from US national parks to rainforest deforestation, but take a closer look at this 20,779-sq-km country and you will find plenty to shout about in its own right. Not only is Wales king of Britain's castles, but it also has some of the finest and cleanest beaches, great surf, wildlife-rich islands and rugged mountains – all in an area roughly the size of Massachusetts.

Top: Caerphilly castle.
Above: Snowdonia National Park.

Country highlights

◐ ◔ ◑ ▲ ☺ ⚑ ⛵ 🚂 ☺ ☺ ⓜ ✿

» The Freedom of Wales Flexi Pass (walesflexipass.co.uk) provides unlimited access to mainline train services and most buses.
» There are no fewer than 14 steam and narrow-gauge railways in Wales (greatlittletrainsofwales.co.uk).
» For further information log on to visitwales.co.uk.

Cardiff Acres of parkland and a stone's throw from the beach make Cardiff a great city-break destination for families. Kids will be impressed by the roof garden and elaborate banqueting hall in quirky Cardiff Castle (cardiffcastle.com), but it's Cardiff Bay (cardiffbay.co.uk) where they'll have most fun. Just a couple of kilometres from the city centre, there's plenty to see and do here, from delving into the cafés and shops at Mermaid Quay to exploring the science centre, Techniquest (techniquest.org) and Doctor Who Up Close (doctorwhoexhibitions.com). About 6 km west of the city, the open-air museum of St Fagans (museumwales.ac.uk) evokes 500 years of Welsh heritage with historic buildings and craft demonstrations.

Gower Peninsula Like the more westerly peninsulas of Pembrokeshire (see opposite), the 30-km-long Gower is a magnet to beach lovers. Surf GSD (surfgsd.com) runs an excellent Junior Surfing Academy on Caswell Beach, while Gower Coast Adventures (gowercoastadventures.co.uk) operates boat trips in search of seals and dolphins.

Brecon Beacons Covering an area of 1345 sq km of rugged moorland, limestone crags and glacial lakes, Brecon Beacons National Park (breconbeacons.org) runs a programme of children's activities including bug hunts and wilderness survival days.

Elan Valley On average it rains 235 days a year in the Elan Valley of central Wales, but this 180 sq km of moors, woodland and reservoirs is still a wonderful location for walking and cycling. Gigrin Farm (gigrin.co.uk) is famous for its red-kite feeding station where it's not uncommon to witness over 300 of these raptors pirouetting overhead in a spectacular aerial ballet.

Snowdonia It's a five-hour slog up and down Snowdon, the 1085-m highpoint of Snowdonia National Park (snowdonia-npa.gov.uk), but families with younger children can still get spectacular views by taking the rack-and-pinion Snowdon Mountain Railway (snowdonrailway.co.uk) from Llanberis. Located in the south of the park, the Mawddach Trail is an excellent choice for families. Starting at Dolgellau, the 14-km traffic-free route follows the beautiful Mawddach Estuary to Barmouth and can either be walked or cycled. For a shorter walk try the Penmaenpool to Bont y Wern Du route. The pretty riverside town of Betws-y-coed is another popular walking base, while the narrow-gauge Ffestiniog Railway (festrail.co.uk) takes you on a 22-km steam train journey from the slate-quarrying town of Blaenau Ffestiniog to the harbour at Porthmadog.

Other attractions You're never far from a great castle in Wales – and they're all just as castles should be, with rounded towers, arrow slits, drawbridges and moats. One of the most formidable is Beaumaris Castle on the island of Anglesey, although kids will be just as happy to storm the ramparts of Caernarfon, Conwy and Harlech in North Wales, and Caerphilly, Kidwelly and Pembroke in South and mid-Wales.

❝❞ Dad broke my bucket, but it was great fun running into the sea with my clothes on so that he had to come in and get me.
Samuel Jenkins (age 5)

🌀 Watersports

Paddle kayaks or Canadian canoes along a gentle stretch of the River Wye; Wye Valley Canoes (wyevalleycanoes.co.uk).
Learn to surf on the Gower Peninsula's 5-km Llangennith beach; Welsh Surfing Federation (wsfsurfschool.co.uk).
Shoot the rapids on the Tryweryn in North Wales (minimum age 12); Canolfan Tryweryn (ukrafting.co.uk).

❝❞ Whistling Sands on the Llyn Peninsula was a great discovery. A perfectly sized cove maintained by the National Trust. It has all you need within walking distance – wet sand, dry sand, rock pools and a shop that sells everything you forgot to take.
Sarah Hetherington

Best of Pembrokeshire

Best beaches Choose from over 50 sandy beaches, including Blue Flag beauties like Whitesands. The best all-round family beaches (with lifeguards, lots to do and no dogs allowed) are Amroth, Saundersfoot, all of Tenby's beaches, Dale, Broad Haven and Whitesands. Dale, Broad Haven and Tenby North have canoes and boats for hire, while Barfundle and Aber Mawr are idyllic beaches for picnics. For surf, head to Whitesands, Marloes, Manorbier, Broad Haven, Caerfai, Newgale and, for strong swimmers only, Freshwater West. Hire boards from Haven Sports (havensports.co.uk) and West Wales Wind Surf and Sailing (surfdale.co.uk).

Best boat trips Operators include Aquaphobia (aquaphobia-ramseyisland.co.uk), Dale Sea Safari (sail-sailing.co.uk), Porthgain Boat Trips (porthgainboats.ndo.co.uk), Ramsey Island Cruises (ramseyislandcruises.co.uk), Shearwater Safaris (boatrides.co.uk) and Venture Jet (venturejet.co.uk).

Best seal spotting Take a boat trip to Ramsey, Skomer, Skockholm or Caldey Island. The southwest tip of St David's Peninsula, Cemaes Head near Cardigan and the Marloes Peninsula are also good spots. The best time to see grey seals is September to November when they give birth to pups.

Best dolphin spotting Cardigan Bay has a resident population of bottlenose dolphins, while summer witnesses the arrival of common dolphins (sometimes in pods a thousand-strong), as well as humpback, fin, minke and orca whales. Join a boat trip with an operator adhering to the Marine Code (pembrokeshiremarinecode.org.uk). Sea Trust (seatrust.org.uk) operates a lookout from Stumble Head.

Best bird islands Reached by daily boats from Martin's Haven, Skomer is renowned for puffins, guillemots, razorbills and kittiwakes. You can also stay overnight to experience the Manx shearwaters returning to their burrows under cover of darkness. Skokholm's petrels and puffins are best viewed from a boat trip from Dale, while Ramsey can be visited from St David's. Further offshore, Grassholm is smothered with 65,000 gannets during the summer months.

Best cycle trails Cardigan's Cycle Break Centre (cyclebreakswales.co.uk) has set up several easy cycling routes alongside the River Teifi. Other options include St Govan's Head (one of the few sections of the Coast Path that's open to cyclists), the Brunel cycle trail from Neyland to Johnston and the 11-km circuit around Llys-y-Fran reservoir.

Best walks Buggy-friendly paths include the 4-km jaunt from Wiseman's Bridge to Saundersfoot Harbour and the 800-m circuit of Pembroke Castle's moat. For a short walk with a convenient café, try the 10-km trail from Nolton Haven to Broad Haven. For something more ambitious, stride out on the 17-km circuit of the Dale Peninsula. The Walkers Coastal Bus Service (pembrokeshire.gov.uk/coastbus) simplifies access to trails, while the Pembrokeshire Coast National Park's website (pembrokeshirecoast.org/walking) offers numerous ideas for circular walks and easy-access paths.

Best attractions Feel the adrenaline rush on the water coaster and 30 other rides at Oakwood Theme Park (oakwoodthemepark.co.uk), cheer on the knights as they battle it out at medieval Pembroke Castle (pembrokecastle.co.uk) and feed the animals at Folly Farm (folly-farm.co.uk).

Best activities A mixture of climbing, swimming, scrambling along rocky shores and flinging yourself off cliff faces, coasteering is the latest wet-and-wild craze to hit Pembrokeshire. Other more orthodox pursuits include scuba-diving, sea kayaking, and horse riding. Several dedicated centres, such as the Pembrokeshire Activity Centre (pembrokeshire-activity-centre.co.uk), provides courses.

Activities in Pembrokeshire: coasteering and surfing (**top left**); Saundersfoot beach (**top right**); cycling and splashing in the waves (**above**).

From Royal Miles to Shetland Isles

Chances are you won't spot the Loch Ness Monster, but that won't stop your children from staring long and hard at every patch of water they come across in Scotland - and what better way for them to fall under the spell of this beautiful and diverse country. From Edinburgh's historic Royal Mile to the wild and remote Shetlands, kids will find castles to explore, Munros to conquer and deserted beaches to lay claim to. And if Nessie proves elusive, they'll be more than satisfied with sightings of whales, eagles and otters during boat trips in the Hebrides.

Edinburgh and Glasgow

😊 🛈 ⚘ 🏛

›› The Edinburgh Pass (edinburgh.org/pass) provides free entry to over 30 attractions, plus free return airport and city centre bus transport.
›› The Daytripper ticket (spt.co.uk) is a cost-effective way for families to travel by rail, subway, buses and some ferries throughout Glasgow and Strathclyde.
›› Although Edinburgh's famous arts festival (edinburghfestivals.co.uk) takes place in Aug, there's also a Children's International Theatre Festival in May.
›› For further information, log on to edinburgh.org and seeglasgow.com.

Above: Is there anybody out there? Shetland pony seeks hair stylist. **Top right**: Edinburgh Castle. **Above right**: Kelvingrove Museum.

Edinburgh essentials
City highlights Plenty of cities have castles, but not many have a castle perched on an extinct volcano – a double whammy for kid-friendly Edinburgh. A fun way to get an overview of this bonny World-Heritage-listed city is to take a ride through the medieval Old Town and Georgian New Town with Edinburgh Bus Tours (edinburghtour.com). Next, visit Edinburgh Castle (historic-scotland.gov.uk) to see Scotland's Crown Jewels and the Stone of Destiny. Listen out for the One O'Clock Gun and visit the dungeons to see the Prisoners of War exhibition. Just below the castle, West Princes Street Gardens is ideal for letting youngsters burn off energy, while teenagers will prefer to exercise their wallets along adjacent Princes Street. Alternatively, head east from Castle Hill along the Royal Mile – once the main thoroughfare of medieval Edinburgh,

linking the castle to the Palace of Holyroodhouse (royal.gov.uk). Flanked by impressive buildings like St Giles Cathedral and Parliament House, it's the toy-crammed Museum of Childhood (cac.org.uk) that will appeal most to kids. On nearby Holyrood Road, Our Dynamic Earth (dynamicearth.co.uk) has an earthquake simulator, a time machine that will whisk you back 15 billion years and a FutureDome where you decide the fate of the planet. Rearing behind this ultra-modern science centre, you can explore the ancient lava flows of Arthur's Seat, a volcano that blew its top between 350 and 400 million years ago. Rainy-day favourites for younger children include the Brass Rubbing Centre (cac.org.uk) and The Ceramic Experience (theceramicexperience.com), while the excellent Edinburgh Zoo (edinburghzoo.org.uk) is a long-established favourite, whatever the weather. Edinburgh's notorious City of the Dead Ghost Tour is hosted nightly by Black Hart Entertainment (blackhart.uk.com) – but be warned: a possible encounter with the Mackenzie Poltergeist is not for the faint-hearted. The Secret City Tour, meanwhile, is suitable for all ages and features stories as diverse as Harry Potter, the invention of Christmas and the origin of Frankenstein's monster.
Best beaches There are several fine beaches close to Edinburgh, including the popular surf spot of Gullane Bents, the wildlife-rich Longniddry Bents and Cramond, where you can walk and cycle on beachside paths.

Best day out Head east towards North Berwick, taking in the 12th-century Dirleton Castle, the long sandy beach of Yellowcraig and the Scottish Seabird Centre (seabird.org), where you can watch footage beamed live from Bass Rock, 5 km offshore and teeming with over 100,000 gannets between January and October.

Glasgow greats
City highlights Unlike Edinburgh, there are no iconic landmarks in Glasgow, but what this stylish, modern-thinking city lacks in the way of castles and volcanoes it more than compensates for with a buzzing cultural scene and several superb museums. By far the best for kids, the Kelvingrove Art Gallery and Museum (glasgowmuseums.com) has everything from Egyptian mummies to a Second World War Spitfire. Children under five have their own hands-on Mini Museum, while older kids can learn about wildlife, history and art at three discovery centres. Don't miss the webcam link to the Loch Ness Monster, the 4-m Ceratosaur skeleton and the impressive collection of paintings which includes Salvador Dali's *Christ*. Highlights at the nearby Museum of Transport include locomotives from the Caledonian and

Highland Railways. Nip down to the north bank of the River Clyde and you'll find the 19th-century, three-masted *SS Glenlee*, otherwise known as The Tall Ship at Glasgow Harbour (thetallship.com). On the opposite bank, Pacific Quay is the embarkation point for cruises aboard Paddle Steamer *Waverley* (pswaverley.org.uk), as well as the location of the excellent Glasgow Science Centre (gsc.org.uk) – a technological treasure house where kids can tinker with hundreds of interactive exhibits and go goggle-eyed in the planetarium and IMAX cinema. East of the city centre, but still on the Clyde, People's Palace and Winter Gardens reveals Glasgow's social history.

Best days out Less than an hour's drive southeast of Glasgow, New Lanark World Heritage Site (newlanark.org) is a beautifully restored 18th-century village where kids can discover what life was like in a Victorian cotton mill. North of Glasgow, Loch Lomond and the Trossachs National Park (lochlomondtrossachs.org) makes a superb city escape with activities ranging from hiking, cycling and pony trekking to abseiling, windsurfing and lake cruises.

66 99 Get the weather right, and beaches don't come more glorious than those around Gairloch on the northwest coast, with the Hebrides on the horizon and the mountains at your back. My five-year-old, Florence, had a ball, scrawling her name across the sand in tree-sized letters, tiptoeing through warm rock pools and watching porpoises break the glassy surface of the bay. One night she even helped strip the willow at the local ceilidh as the fiddlers did their frenetic stuff. But nothing, not even a jellyfish, crowned the excitement of her own bijou bunk bed on the sleeper train to Inverness.

Mike Unwin

Kids' top 10: Highlands and Islands

1 Find out what the real story in Balamory is by taking a ferry from Oban to Mull, where the multicoloured houses along Tobermory's waterfront provided the setting for the children's television programme.

2 Spot the Loch Ness Monster – and if that fails, have a go at finding a minke whale on a boat trip from Mull with Sea Life Surveys (sealifesurveys.com) and tick off otters and sea eagles during a safari with Island Encounter (mullwildlife.co.uk).

3 Peer into the spectacular kelp forests around Skye from the *Seaprobe Atlantis* (seaprobeatlantis.com), Scotland's only semi-submersible glass-bottomed boat.

4 Play king or queen of the castle on the Aberdeenshire Castle Trail (Aberdeen-grampian.com) which links 13 forts – some rugged ruins, others posh palaces.

5 Walk with a ranger through the native pinewoods of Cairngorms National Park (cairngorms.co.uk) – the largest in Britain.

6 Discover what it's like to climb on ice at the Glen Coe Visitor Centre (nts.org.uk), then stride outside to explore some of Scotland's most dramatic scenery – and perhaps even 'bag a Munro' (a mountain over 914 m or 3000 ft in height).

7 Go wild on the tree-top trail, adventure playground and waterslides of the Landmark Forest Heritage Park (landmark-centre.co.uk) near Aviemore before watching ospreys at Loch Garten's RSPB Osprey Centre (rspb.org.uk).

8 Practise skiing or snowboarding in the winter wonderland of the Nevis Range (nevisrange.co.uk), Scotland's highest ski area.

9 Pinch yourself to make sure you're not dreaming when you discover the golden sands and turquoise seas of Harris and the Uists in the Outer Hebrides. Other fine beaches include Sandwood Bay and Oldshoremore on the northwest coast of mainland Scotland and the irresistible tombolo of sand linking Shetland to St Ninian's Isle.

10 Glimpse shipwrecks and marine life through an underwater camera on a Roving Eye Boat Tour (rovingeye.co.uk), experience life in the 19th century at Corrigal Farm Museum (orkney.gov.uk/heritage) and visit Skara Brae (historic-scotland.gov.uk) – just three of the highlights on Orkney.

➤ Further information: visithighlands.com, visitthebrides.com, visitshetland.com, visitorkney.com.

Balamory (aka Tobermory).

❓ Where can I see lots of these?
Shetland's bird life is some of Europe's finest. Twitchers flock to the islands each spring and autumn to glimpse rare, gale-blown migrants. But for a real pummelling of the senses, few experiences can rival a close encounter with one of Shetland's seabird cities. One of the most spectacular is Noss National Nature Reserve, an imposing rampart of 180-m-tall sea cliffs reached by boat from Lerwick with Seabirds and Seals (seabirds-and-seals.com). For a cliff-top perspective of equally impressive colonies visit Hermaness at the northern tip of Unst which also provides views of Muckle Flugga and Out Stack – the end of Britain.

Easy does it in the Emerald Isle

Slowly – that's the best way to experience Ireland with kids. Take time to roam its beautiful countryside and wild, remote coasts. It's a place to share simple and spontaneous pleasures with your children – pulling off the road to explore a strange ruin or whiling away a day on a beach that was too irresistible to pass by. And whenever you feel like upping the tempo slightly, take the kids sea kayaking, horse riding or introduce them to a spot of local Irish music and dancing.

Trinity College, Dublin.

Dublin

>> The Dublin Pass (dublinpass.ie) provides entry to over 30 attractions, including Dublin Castle and Dublin Zoo.
>> Irish Cycling Safaris (cyclingsafari.com) offers guided tours of the South Dublin coastline, while Sea Safari (seasafari.ie) operates boat trips to Lambay Island and Killiney Bay (minimum age eight).
>> For further information, log on to visitdublin.com.

City highlights An enjoyable way to become acquainted with the Irish capital, Viking Splash Tours (vikingsplash.ie) uses Second World War amphibious vehicles to cruise the city's streets and docks. Horned helmets are standard issue to all passengers, and you are encouraged by the driver (dressed, of course, as a Norseman) to utter lusty Viking war cries at every opportunity. Continuing the Viking theme (after all, Dublin was one of their strongholds), Dublinia (dublinia.ie) uses reconstructions and interactive displays to bring the city's early history to life. The National Museum of Ireland (museum.ie) not only delves into the past but also boasts a treasure trove of archaeological finds, including a fine collection of prehistoric gold artefacts. However, even these pale beside the 9th-century *Book of Kells*, a meticulously crafted illuminated manuscript of the four Gospels on display in Trinity College Library (tcd.ie/library).

A Wild West action plan

Coach tours cajole the Ring of Kerry (corkkerry.ie) into a single day, but you'll see more – and stand a chance of escaping the summer crowds – if you spend at least three days probing this 179-km circuit of the Iveragh Peninsula in western Ireland. Killarney is the most popular, and somewhat touristy, gateway to the region, so consider basing yourself in Kenmare and travelling clockwise around the Ring – the opposite direction to which most tourist buses take.

On day one, get off the road altogether by joining a two-hour seal-watching cruise with Kenmare's Seafari (seafariireland.com), followed by sea kayaking, windsurfing, pony trekking or any of the other activities offered by the Star Sailing and Adventure Centre (staroutdoors.ie) – also based in Kenmare. Next day, head west on the N70, passing the colourful village of Sneem to reach Staigue Fort, an austere 2000-year-old ring fort measuring over 27 m across and with walls up to 4 m thick. You should reach Derrynane by lunchtime – the perfect excuse for a picnic and some surfing on one of Ireland's finest beaches. Spend the night at nearby Waterville, a traditional seaside resort with a variety of B&Bs.

Set off early the following day to reach the Skellig Experience (skelligexperience.com) on Valentia Island before the tour groups arrive. This excellent visitor centre has displays based on the early Christian monastery, lighthouse, seabirds and marine life of the Skellig Rocks – two offshore islands that you can visit with Casey's Boat Trips (skelligislands.com) and a variety of other operators from Portmagee. Back on the N70 later that afternoon, you should have time to visit Kells Beach overlooking Dingle Bay before checking into a guesthouse in Killorglin.

The next morning, backtrack slightly to visit the Kerry Bog Village (kerrybogvillage.ie), a cluster of thatched cottages revealing what life was like in the region during the early 1800s, before continuing north to the Dingle Peninsula (dingle-peninsula.ie). You could easily spend a week on this equally beautiful finger of land, sampling activities ranging from sailing and pony trekking to watching sharks at Dingle Oceanworld (dingle-oceanworld.ie) and swimming in Dingle Bay with Fungi, a wild bottlenose dolphin that first began interacting with humans in 1984.

Go with the flow

The Shannon flows 344 km through the heart of Ireland, nuzzling into a gentle landscape of floodplains and rolling hills. Travelling all or part of this waterway by river cruiser is not only great fun with children of school age but is also one of the best ways to experience rural Ireland. Carrick Craft (cruise-ireland.com) offers an extensive fleet of two- to eight-berth, fully fitted cruisers. Rates include full tuition, a detailed captain's handbook and charts, plus free mooring at quays and marinas. Banagher makes a good starting base for a week-long cruise. About five hours north, you reach the 6th-century monastic ruins of Clonmacnoise (heritageireland.ie), home of the famous Cross of the Scriptures, a 4-m-tall stone cross etched with Biblical scenes. Backtracking past Banagher, navigational skills are put to the test as you negotiate Meelick Lock. Then it's plain sailing on the vast expanse of Lough Derg, stopping at small marinas and villages like Castle Harbour and Terryglass. Killaloe, an attractive town with a 13-arch bridge, marks the southern limit of Shannon pleasure cruising.

Where can I see this?

Over 40,000 basalt columns extending 5 km along the Antrim coast, the Giants Causeway (giantscausewayofficialguide.com) was created by rapidly cooling lava from volcanic eruptions 60 million years ago. Kids will prefer the legend of the two giants (one in Ireland, the other in Scotland) who built a rocky causeway across the sea so they could meet and settle their squabbles.

Top: Cruising on the Shannon. **Above:** Giant's Causeway. **Left:** Bunratty Castle, Co Clare.

County Clare highlights

Bunratty Castle and Folk Park (shannonheritage.com) Medieval castle and 'living' 19th-century folk park with authentic village houses and costumed actors.

Cliffs of Moher (county-clare.com) Sheer 213-m sea cliffs plummeting into the Atlantic – best viewed from the paved cliff-top path.

Inis Mór (visitaranislands.com) One of the three Aran Islands, famous for its spectacular 4000-year-old stone fort, Dún Aonghasa, squatting on the edge of 90-m cliffs.

66 99 Lough Derg was laced with dainty reflections of patchwork hills embroidered with yellow gorse and squares of emerald woodland. In our wake, the tannin-rich water frothed like freshly poured Guinness, while every boater we passed waved and smiled. Squeezing into the narrow Scarrif River, barely two cruisers wide, we burbled happily through a pressing tangle of rural Ireland – willows sweeping our decks, reed warblers filling the air with their ratchet-songs and the meadows blushed with swathes of ragged robin.

Will

When to go

Britain has a mild climate with summer temperatures ranging from 14 to 30°C. The high season runs from April until October, when most attractions are open. School holidays (most of July and August) are very busy, especially at the most popular tourist destinations such as the Lakes, Devon and Cornwall, the Scottish Highlands, Cotswolds and Pembroke Coast. London and the major cities don't really have a tourist season as such, which makes them an excellent alternative in the autumn and winter months (September-March).

Getting there

One of the busiest airports in the world, London Heathrow (heathrowairport.com) is served by most major international airlines. London has three other main airports (Gatwick, Stansted and Luton), while regional airports include Edinburgh, Glasgow, Cardiff and Manchester. With British Airways (britishairways.com) expect to pay from around €130 for a Paris-London return flight; US$800 for a Los Angeles return and from A$2130 for a Sydney return. Try low-cost airlines such as easyJet (easyjet.com) and Flybe (flybe.com) for cheap flights to and from European destinations. For low-cost flights between Ireland and the UK, contact Aer Lingus (aerlingus.com) or Ryanair (ryanair.com). Ferries operate along 33 routes to England and Wales, arriving at ports on the south, east and west coasts, including Dover, Newhaven, Portsmouth, Bournemouth, Plymouth, Harwich, Hull, Liverpool, Fishguard and Holyhead. Prices vary enormously according to season: check cheapferry.com, ferrycrossings-uk.co.uk, or ferrysavers.com, or contact major route operators such as Brittany Ferries (brittanyferries.com). Smyril Line (smyril-line.com) operates a service to Lerwick (Shetland) from Norway and Iceland. Stena Line (stenaline.co.uk) operates an express service from Fishguard to Rosslare,

whisking you across to Ireland in just two hours. There are also services from Holyhead to Dublin, Cairnryan to Larne and Stanraer to Belfast. The only option that doesn't involve travel by air or sea is to use the Channel Tunnel (eurotunnel.com) from mainland Europe.

Getting around

Its compact size and excellent infrastructure make Britain and Ireland easy to get around. Self-drive is a flexible option; roads and motorways are well maintained, but bear in mind that major tourist routes can become heavily congested in peak periods and fuel is expensive. All the major car-hire companies can be found at airports. For coach travel in Britain try National Express (nationalexpress.com) and Scottish Citylink (citylink.co.uk). In the Republic of Ireland, Bus Eireann (buseireann.ie) offers a range of Explorer passes. For rail travel, Britrail (britrail.net) provides a comprehensive online booking service for overseas visitors.

Accommodation

There is no shortage of places to stay in Britain and Ireland: everything from hiring your own private castle to pitching a tent is on offer. Hotels can often be expensive or shabby (or both) and more salubrious ones cost upwards of £150 for a family room for a night. Popular family choices include self-catering cottages (see page 85 for a list of rental companies), farmstays (farmstayuk.co.uk) and family-friendly hotels and guesthouses. Holiday villages have been popular in Britain for decades, ranging from traditional favourites like Butlins (butlinsonline.co.uk) to climate-controlled Center Parcs (centerparcs.co.uk). Another great British institution, B&Bs, can be found everywhere – try Bed & Breakfast Nationwide (bedandbreakfastnationwide.com), Bed and Breakfasts UK (bedandbreakfasts-uk.co.uk) and B&B Britain (bandbbritainuk.co.uk) for online directories. The Youth Hostel Association (yha.org.uk) provides excellent value accommodation at over 250 locations throughout England and Wales, while Bridge Street Worldwide (bridgestreet.co.uk) offers serviced apartments in all major UK cities.

Food and drink

If you're travelling with babies and/or toddlers you may find eating out a frustrating experience, though the days of families being banished to some grubby room at the back, well out of the way of other diners, are, thankfully, a thing of the past in most places. Smoking is banned in all restaurants and pubs. Foreign visitors may find eating times in pubs and hotels limiting (usually 1230-1400 for lunch and 1700-1900 for dinner). In hotels, guesthouses and B&Bs the full English/Scottish/Welsh/Irish breakfast (fried egg, bacon, sausages, tomatoes, mushrooms, beans and black pudding) still reigns supreme. Other breakfast fortes are kippers (the

---

CO₂ How much to offset your emissions?

From London to:

Bristol £0.52
Cardiff £0.59
Manchester £0.65
Dublin £0.95
Edinburgh £1.08

From New York to:

London US$23
Edinburgh US$22

How much for a Big Mac?

USA US$3.22
UK US$3.90

Go green: three ways to skip the flight

▶▶ Get on your bike. Over 16,000 km of the National Cycle Network (sustrans.co.uk) are now open. A third is traffic-free, following disused railway lines, canal towpaths and forest tracks, while the rest of the network uses quiet minor roads and traffic-calmed streets in towns and cities.
▶▶ Island hop along Scotland's west coast with an Island Hopscotch ticket from Caledonian MacBrayne (calmac.co.uk).
▶▶ Take the ferry to the Isles of Scilly with the Scillonian (ios-travel.co.uk); to the Isle of Man with Steam-Packet Ferries (steam-packet.com); to the Shetland and Orkney islands with Northlink Ferries (northlinkferries.co.uk); to the Channel Islands with Condor Ferries (condorferries.co.uk); and to the Isle of Wight with WightLink (wightlink.co.uk).

... And now for something completely different

Canal boating Meander through the peaceful Staffordshire countryside in your own canal boat with Canal Cruising (canal-cruising.co.uk).

Riding holidays Take your horse on holiday to a West Country retreat offered by Farm and Cottage Holidays (holidaycottages.co.uk) where stabling and grazing (and a horse if you haven't brought your own) are all provided.

Woodland hideaways More trendy than you might be expecting from a log cabin, Forest Holidays (forestholidays.co.uk) offers two-storey pine chalets with large picture windows and a well-equipped kitchen overlooking Loch Lubniag in the Trossachs.

Sleepy tipis Stay in an authentic native American-style tipi on the north Norfolk coast with Deepdale Tipis (deepdalefarm.co.uk). Alternatively, try Cornish Tipi Holidays (cornish-tipi-holidays.co.uk) or Tipi West (tipiwest.co.uk), overlooking Cardigan Bay.

best are from Scotland), scrambled eggs and boiled eggs with toasted soldiers. At lunchtime the sandwich is king and comes in all shapes and sizes: from fashionable breads and exotic cured meats in the major cities to sliced white and reconstituted ham in pubs. That said, pub food has been transformed in recent years, and now many so-called 'gastropubs' offer ambitious lunchtime and supper menus. Don't miss the diet-busting cream tea, which achieves its apotheosis in Wales and the southwest of England. For a cheap lunch or supper try the nation's favourite, fish 'n' chips. Fish'n'Chip shops can be found in most small towns, especially in the north and on the coast.

Health and safety

No vaccinations are required for entry. Citizens of EU countries are entitled to free medical treatment at National Health Service hospitals on production of a European Health Insurance Card (EHIC). For details see dh.gov.uk/travellers. Australia, New Zealand and several other non-EU European countries have reciprocal health-care arrangements with Britain. Citizens of other countries will have to pay for all medical services, except accident and emergency care given at Accident and Emergency (A&E) Units at most (but not all) National Health hospitals. Health insurance is therefore strongly advised for citizens of non-EU countries.

Tour operators

In the UK and Republic of Ireland

Adventure Company,
adventurecompany.co.uk

Blakes Holidays
blakes.co.uk

Camping and Caravanning Club
campingandcaravanningclub.co.uk

Channel Islands Direct
channelislandsdirect.co.uk

Forestlidays
forestholidays.co.uk

Hoseasons
hoseasons.co.uk

Kate Boats
kateboats.co.uk

Luxury Family Hotels
luxuryfamilyhotels.co.uk

Premier Holidays
premierholidays.co.uk

River Deep Mountain High
riverdeepmountainhigh.co.uk

Scotsell Holidays
visitislands.co.uk

The Venture Centre
adventure-centre.co.uk

Youth Hostel Association
yha.org.uk

In the USA

The Backroads
backroads.com

Classic Journeys
classicjourneys.com

Luxury Vacations UK
luxuryvacationsuk.com

The Real Britain Company
realbritaincompany.com

Fact file

	Time	*Language*	*Money*	*Code*	*Tourist info*
UK	GMT	English, Welsh, Irish and Scottish Gaelic	GB pound (sterling) £ £1 = US$2	+44	visitbritain.com enjoyengland.com discovernorthernireland.com visitscotland.com visitwales.com
Ireland	GMT	English, Gaelic	Euro € £1 = €1.50	+353	discoverireland.ie tourismireland.com

10 family favourites

Knoll House Hotel
Where? Studland Bay, Dorset.
Why? Set in 40 ha of gardens, Knoll House has an adventure playground, children's dining room and baby-listening service. Studland Bay's glorious beach is just five minutes' walk away, while local attractions include Monkey World, Marwell Zoo and Weymouth SeaLife Centre.
How much? From around £108 per adult per night, full board (children's prices vary).
Contact knollhouse.co.uk.

Woolley Grange
Where? Bradford-on-Avon, Wiltshire.
Why? Luxury family hotel with excellent children's facilities, including a nanny-supervised Woolley Bears Club for children up to eight and a den for older kids. Outside there's a heated pool, adventure playground and croquet lawn.
How much? From around £350 per night (including dinner and breakfast) for a de luxe double room for up to four people, based on midweek rates in high season.
Contact woolleygrangehotel.co.uk.

Gleneagles
Where? Perthshire, Scotland.
Why? Children's activities don't get any better than this. As well as junior lessons in falconry, archery, horse riding and golf, five- to 11-year-olds get to drive off-road Junior Cats, while Agro Cats (all-terrain, semi-amphibious vehicles) are available for children aged 12 and above. Inside, there's a fabulous pool, plus a teenagers-only games room with jukeboxes, PlayStations and juice bar.
How much? From £455 for two people, per night including breakfast and one special interest activity each, with reduced rates for children.
Contact gleneagles.com.

Bedruthan Steps Hotel
Where? Mawgan Porth, Cornwall.
Why? Serious about food, comfort, relaxation and childcare, Bedruthan is a north Cornish gem with spectacular views, an idyllic beach and five Ofsted-registered clubs catering for children up to 12.
How much? From £80 per person, per day, including dinner, bed and breakfast.
Contact bedruthan.com.

Southland Camping Park
Where? Newchurch, Sandown, Isle of Wight.
Why? This five-star park has top eco-credentials, with a conservation meadow and recycling schemes. Set in 4 ha of the island's rural heartland with generous sized-pitches, the site is only 5 km from the sandy beaches of Shanklin and Sandown.
How much? Seven-night, ferry-inclusive breaks from £189 for four people and a car.
Contact southland.co.uk.

The Citadines
Where? London.
Why? A fantastic location for families, these home-from-home serviced apartments are just a few steps from Nelson's column in Trafalgar Square, as well as being close to the National Gallery, Westminster Abbey, St James's Park and the West End shops.
How much? From around £120 per night.
Contact citadines.com.

Kelly's Resort Hotel
Where? Rosslare, Co Wexford, Ireland.
Why? Situated on Rosslare's 8-km-long sandy beach, this four-star hotel has won numerous awards, including best family-friendly hotel in Ireland 2006.
How much? A week in the summer season starts from around €940 per person, with reduced rates for children.
Contact kellys.ie.

Polmaily Country Hotel
Where? Near Loch Ness, Scotland.
Why? Set in 8 ha of woodland and gardens, Polmaily has a relaxed atmosphere, with supervised playroom and activities including horse riding and cycling. Nessie-spotting is available at nearby Drumnadrochit, only 5 km away.
How much? Prices from £55 per person per night, bed and breakfast, with reduced rates for children.
Contact polmaily.co.uk.

White House Hotel
Where? Herm, Channel Islands.
Why? Step back in time to a world of high teas, beachcombing, croquet on the lawn and no TV. Choose from family rooms or the delightful Harbour Cottage with its separate children's bedrooms.
How much? Prices from £76 per adult per day, with special rates for children.
Contact herm-island.com.

Bovey Castle
Where? Dartmoor, Devon.
Why? Indulge your children's fairy-tale fantasies with a stay at this luxurious castle in Dartmoor National Park. Activities include lessons in archery, tennis and golf.
How much? From around £350 per room (maximum of four people) per night including breakfast for a weekend in the high season.
Contact boveycastle.com.

Top: Knoll House Hotel.
Above: Kelly's Resort Hotel.
Right: Bedruthan Steps Hotel.
Below: Southland Camping Park.
Bottom: White House Hotel.

Farmstays

Sherbourne House Farm
(sherbournelodgecottages.co.uk) in Suffolk is mostly devoted to wheat and barley, but there are also sheep, ponies, chickens, rabbits and a lone cow available for grooming, feeding and mucking out. As dusk falls, stake out the hide for glimpses of badgers and foxes. Prices from £300 per week per cottage.

Glyn Arthur Farm (ruralretreats.co.uk), a 162-ha Welsh sheep farm, has a comfortable cottage with views over the Vale of Clywd. Help out with shearing and bottle-feeding; take a bumpy Land Rover ride over the hills and search for wildlife, from buzzards to badgers. From around £620 per week for a cottage sleeping six.

Feather Down Farm Days (featherdown.co.uk) offers a choice of eight UK locations staying in stylish wooden-floored canvas tents, with activities such as feeding goats, collecting eggs and exploring by bike. Prices from

Center Parcs: the verdict

66 99 I think Center Parcs was brilliant. It has the best pool.

David, age 8

66 99 There's loads of activities, so you haven't got time to get bored.

Robert, age 11

66 99 I thought I might not have as much to do as my younger siblings but I didn't have time to fit everything in.

Kerrina, age 14

France

Natural cycle – France is full of family-friendly biking opportunities, including the Loire shown here.

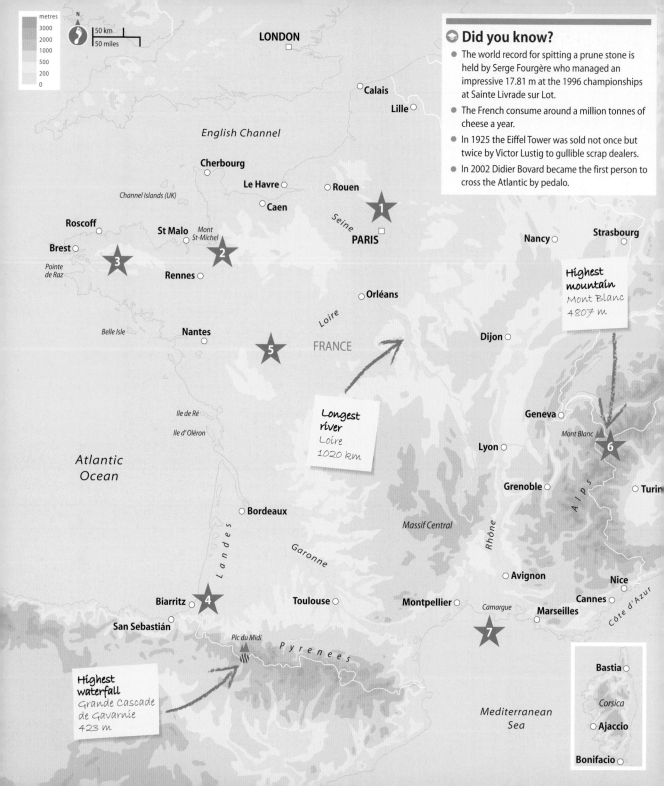

metres
3000
2000
1000
500
200
0

N

50 km
50 miles

LONDON

English Channel

Calais

Lille

Cherbourg

Le Havre

Rouen

Caen

Seine

1

Roscoff

St Malo

Mont
St-Michel

2

PARIS

Nancy

Strasbourg

Brest

3

Pointe
de Raz

Rennes

**Highest
mountain**
Mont Blanc
4807 m

Belle Isle

Nantes

Orléans

Loire

FRANCE

5

Dijon

Channel Islands (UK)

Ile de Ré

Ile d'Oléron

**Longest
river**
Loire
1020 km

Geneva

Mont Blanc

6

Atlantic
Ocean

Lyon

Grenoble

Turin

Alps

Bordeaux

Landes

Garonne

Massif Central

Rhône

Avignon

Nice

Biarritz

4

Toulouse

Montpellier

Camargue

Cannes

Marseilles

Côte d'Azur

San Sebastián

Pic du Midi

Pyrenees

7

**Highest
waterfall**
Grande Cascade
de Gavarnie
423 m

Mediterranean
Sea

Bastia

Corsica

Ajaccio

Bonifacio

★ Climb the Eiffel Tower
➤ Paris, page 94

★ Conquer Mont St Michel
➤ Brittany, page 96

★ Become a crêpe connoisseur
➤ Anywhere in France

★ Learn to surf
➤ Atlantic coast, page 98

★ Cycle to a chateau
➤ Loire Valley, page 100

★ Ski in the French Alps
➤ French Alps, page 101

★ Spot a flamingo
➤ The Camargue, page 104

Introduction

France is one of the world's most popular holiday destinations. Even the French choose overwhelmingly to stay put *en vacance* and, for that reason, you'll find most places have an intrinsic child-friendliness. The biggest problem you'll face is deciding where to go and what to do. A big city like Paris, for example, might be the last thing on your mind, but even in a world without Disney, you'd still find a city brimming with child-friendly attractions, from scaling the Eiffel Tower to getting down to some serious fun in the interactive science museum at Parc de la Villette. The real boon for families, though, is the ease with which you can combine two or three regions. Sandwiched by a few days on the Normandy coast and an interlude in the Loire, that Paris city break begins to look even more enticing. Likewise, you could make a tasty combo of walking and rafting in the Pyrenees with beach fun on either the Atlantic or Mediterranean coasts. You may decide that some regions deserve your undivided attention: Provence and Brittany spring to mind. Both have idyllic coastlines, loads of activities, medieval castles and Roman ruins. Not forgetting the fine cuisine and cheap wine. France is *tres bon* for parents too.

> ❝❞ *One of my best holidays was at Côte de Vermeille in the South of France. I love the way it's still very preserved and rustic, unlike many other French coastal areas. My favourite part was being able to swim in the sea and see the snow-topped mountains at the same time.*
>
> India Seely, age 14

France rating

Wow factor
★★★★

Worry factor
★

Value for money
★★★★

Keeping teacher happy
★★★

Family accommodation
★★★★★

Babies & toddlers
★★★★★

Teenagers
★★★★

Books to read

Katie Meets the Impressionists, Scholastic, 2007
Find out what happens when Katie visits an art gallery with her grandmother and five famous Impressionist paintings come to life. A lively and accessible way of introducing art to young children. Ages 4-6

Degas and the Little Dancer, Frances Lincoln, 2003
The fascinating story behind Degas' renowned clay model of Marie the ballet dancer is brought to life in this beautifully presented book. Budding ballerinas will be entranced. Ages 5+

Perrault's Fairy Tales, Houghton Mifflin, 1993
This classic collection of fairy tales from the French founder of the fairy-tale genre includes favourites such as 'Cinderella', 'Little Red Riding Hood' and 'Sleeping Beauty'. All ages

Young Chef's French Cookbook,
Crabtree Publishing Co, 2001
Have fun with 15 easy-to-prepare French traditional dishes with step-by-step instructions. Bon appetit! Ages 4-8

The Three Musketeers, Sterling Juvenile, 2007
Alexandre Dumas' world-famous tale has been portrayed in films, television series and all manner of books. But have you actually read it yet? This version is accessible and well illustrated. Ages 7+

The Mystery of the Mona Lisa, Red Fox, 2006
The Mona Lisa, the most famous painting in the world, has been stolen from the Louvre museum in Paris. Can Secret Agent Jack Stalwart find it before an evil thief takes it out of the country, never to be seen again? Ages 7+

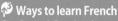

Ways to learn French

First Fun with French, Usborne
This DVD and book proves that it's never too early to start learning a language.

French for Children, McGraw-Hill Education Comprises two audio CDs for kids, colour activity book and parents' CD. Ages 3-9

Essential French for Kids, AA Publishing
Covers making friends, joining in games, ordering food, looking good and hanging out. Ages 9-12

One to watch: *Astérix and the Vikings* (2007)
DVD version of the latest adventure of Astérix, the loveable cartoon Gaul warrior created by René Goscinny and Albert Uderzo in 1959 and now translated into 107 languages with over 320 million copies sold worldwide.

Taste of France: perfect crêpes

Deliciously light and thin, crêpes are tasty with a little sugar, but douse them in chocolate and ice cream and we're talking seriously scrumptious. Here's how to do it at home.

What you need
- 150g plain flour
- ¼ pint milk
- ¼ tsp salt
- oil for cooking
- 2 eggs
- ¼ pint water
- 2 tbsp butter, melted

What to do
- Whisk together the flour and eggs; slowly add the milk and water, stirring to combine.
- Add the salt and butter; beat until smooth.
- Heat a lightly oiled griddle or frying pan over medium-high heat; pour on the batter using around ¼ cup for each crêpe.
- Tilt the pan with a circular motion so that the batter coats the surface evenly.
- Cook for about two minutes, until the bottom is light brown; loosen with a spatula, turn and cook the other side.
- Slide on to a plate, add topping and fold into a handy-sized snack.

🔍 How to play Petanque (boules)

What you need
- A coin
- 12 metal boules
- 1 cochonnet (small wooden marker ball)
- An area of open ground
- A measure and scoring cards, paper and pens

What to do
- Form two teams of up to three players each. Share out the boules.
- Toss a coin to decide which team goes first.
- Choose a starting point and draw a circle on the ground in which to stand; both feet must remain in the circle until the boule lands.
- The first player throws the cochonnet between six and 10 m away and then throws the first boule, trying to get it as near as possible to the cochonnet.
- A player from the other team tries to throw his or her boule closer to the cochonnet (or to knock away the leading boule).
- The team that is farthest from the cochonnet continues to throw.
- When a team has no more boules left the players of the other team take turns to throw theirs and place them as close as possible to the cochonnet.
- The winning team scores a point for each of its boules that has landed nearer to the cochonnet than the closest boule of the other team.
- A member of the winning team throws the cochonnet in the opposite direction from the previous 'end' and play continues until one team reaches 13 points.

❓ Where can I visit a royal palace?

Built in the mid-17th century, the enormous **Château de Versailles** (chateauversaille.fr) provides a glimpse into the opulent tastes of the French monarchy during the reign of Louis XIV. Located 21 km southwest of Paris, the chateau has no fewer than 700 rooms and 6300 paintings. Don't miss the Galerie des Glaces, 73 m long and containing 34 huge mirrors.

Tots to teens

To the uninitiated, France might appear rather too sophisticated and aloof for carefree family holidays. But once you see beyond the manicured image of *nouvelle cuisine*, chic boutiques and immaculate vineyards you'll soon encounter a more down-to-earth, *laissez faire* approach to life. The French understand the needs of families probably better than any other country in Europe. Children's facilities and attractions abound, while the opportunities for camping and self-catering – the two most popular forms of family accommodation in France – are almost endless. For holidaymakers from the UK, it's also straightforward and cheap to nip across the Channel, with or without your car.

Babies (0-18 months)

With lots going on around them, buggy-bound babies can be wheeled happily around Paris for hours while their parents soak up the sights, take in a museum or two and indulge in a spot of pavement café culture. As yet unaware of Disneyland, babies will get their kicks from a crawl about in one of the city's parks. Although public transport between Paris and its suburbs is good, you can avoid the hassle of a daily commute by staying in a centrally located self-catering apartment or hotel with babysitting services.

With babies there's a lot to be said for piling everything you need into a car (from bottle sterilizers to bales of nappies) and setting off on your own *tour de France*. Travelling outside school holidays means you can get better deals on accommodation and explore the Mediterranean either side of the fiercely hot months of July and August.

Toddlers/pre-school (18 months-4 years)

Long car journeys across France don't have quite the same appeal when you've got fractious toddlers strapped in the back who have just discovered the liberating joys of walking. Fortunately, France has an extensive network of holiday *parcs* and campsites that you can link together in a kind of self-drive dot-to-dot. Many have wonderful waterparks and ample activities for kids, including supervised clubs. You can even find *parcs* within easy striking range of cities, including Paris. As for Disneyland, Europe's number one tourist attraction, many parents claim toddlers are too young to get much out of it. Certainly, the big rides, with their height restrictions, will continue to elude them until they are five or six, but that's not to say you won't be able to keep a one- or two-year-old happy for a calmer, more gently paced day with Mickey and his pals.

Kids/school age (4-12 years)

Adventure beckons for this age range. They'll be up for anything, whether it's a maiden ride on the Goudurix loop-the-loop coaster at Parc Astérix, a cycle through the backroads of the Loire Valley or a race to conquer the Eiffel Tower *sans élévateur*. As with younger children, holiday *parcs* make an ideal base. However, now that they've reached an age when they can begin to appreciate local culture, you might also want to consider a self-catering *gîte* or villa that's more in touch with rural life. A visit to the local shops or market is a great way to get kids speaking French. If it's food for thought you're after, then France will stimulate even the most inquiring young minds. In fact, you may decide to sidestep certain aspects of the country's tumultuous history (such as the terrible legacy of the Second World War in Normandy) until your children have studied it at school. Less harrowing historical hotspots include Mont St-Michel, the Loire chateaux, Lascaux's prehistoric cave paintings and, of course, the wonderful museums and landmarks of Paris. For education with a wild twist, you can't beat Brittany with its teeming rock pools or the Alps with their flower- and insect-filled summer meadows.

Teenagers (13 years+)

Paris is cool. So is the French Riviera. Fashion-conscious teenage girls will enjoy browsing the shops, and might even tolerate mum and dad tagging along – as long as they bring their credit cards. The appeal of camping in France might be

Above right: France has an extensive network of holiday parcs and campsites. Below: The Atlantic Coast offers superb surfing.

ebbing for this age group (although many *parcs* hold special activities for teenagers like discos). A villa is a good alternative – plenty of space for independent-minded, occasionally moody, teenagers. You could even consider renting one that had enough space for them to bring along a friend. All-inclusive resorts should also meet with approval. For adrenaline-fired adventure, France has numerous possibilities, from surfing on the Atlantic coast to parapenting in the Alps. However, the Côte d'Azure/Provence region scores highest from a teenage perspective – nowhere else combines such an impeccably stylish coastline with a rugged hinterland of gorges and mountains bristling with adventure activities. Explore Worldwide (explore.co.uk) and Exodus (exodus.co.uk) offer teenage departures on their trips to France.

Special needs

The French ministry of tourism has initiated a campaign to improve access for disabled people travelling in France. Reliable and up-to-date information can be obtained from L'Association des Paralysés de France (www.apf.asso.fr), while *Access in Paris*, available from RADAR (radar.org.uk), provides excellent advice for wheelchair users visiting the city.

> 6699 We've been to Antibes in the South of France by train which was a really exciting experience. It's great to wake up to blue skies and blue seas, and if you're willing to lug your suitcases along endless platforms it's a good way to travel. It's quite expensive, but as long as you think of the journey as being part of the holiday it's OK.
>
> *Caroline Mewes*

Single parents

Acorn Adventure (families.acornadventure.co.uk) provides an infrastructure for supporting single parents on their trips to the Ardeche, the Mediterranean and Normandy. Eurocamp (eurocamp.co.uk) offers discounts for lone-parent families and will even help with unpacking on arrival. Crystal Ski (crystalski.co.uk) offers a discount scheme called One Parent Savers on some of its chalets in France, including Chamonix and La Plagne.

Take a walk on the wild side

Corsica can be a real treat for the senses – and a thrill for any young nature detective. You only have to stroll through its wonderful *maquis* (the ubiquitous scrubland of the Mediterranean) to smell the heady pot-pourri of herbs crushed underfoot. Can you identify white and pink rock rose, yellow broom, wild rosemary and lavender? You'll probably hear the staccato beat of woodpeckers hammering holes in ancient cork oaks and the electro-whirring of cicadas filling the warm sultry air. See if you can track down one of these acoustic insects – the trunks of olive trees are a good place to start. Then try your luck at catching the grasshoppers that flicker around your feet like green sparks or spotting the redstarts and green-speckled Tyrrhenian lizards that chase flies along the ancient dry-stone walls. If you're really lucky you may find a Hermann's tortoise, now extinct on the European mainland. There are no vipers on Corsica, but you might stumble upon a harmless Aesculapian snake basking in the sunshine. Remember to cast the odd glance skyward – Corsica has several birds of prey, including red kites and Bonelli's eagles.

🐾 Corsica for kids

Beaches Corsica has plenty, including sandy gems at Propriano, Campomoro, Calvi, L'Ile Rousse, and Aléria.

Les Calanques de Piana Weird granite formations on the west coast where kids will enjoy spotting faces and shapes in the rocks.

Bonifacio Medieval town perched on dramatic limestone cliffs. Explore the old town, have lunch by the marina, then take a boat trip to gaze up at the lofty citadel.

Paris

The Mouse and the Mona Lisa

From Disney to Da Vinci, Paris bridges a cultural chasm that will leave you and your kids reeling. Imagine one day staring at the world's most famous painting and the next coming face to face with a tall mouse dressed in a dinner jacket and bow tie. Whether you're looking to stimulate a spot of art appreciation or simply opting to escape into a land of make-believe, Paris makes a supremely child-friendly city break. In another life (*sans famille*), you may remember Paris as a stylish, romantic place where you wafted between cafés, delved in designer boutiques and lingered in the Louvre. With kids in tow, it's going to be different. Once you accept that fact, you'll begin to see the French capital in a whole new light – and enjoy it no less.

City highlights

⊗ ◐ ◑ ⏳ ✿

» If your kids have got Disney on their minds, spend a day there first (see opposite).
» Visit anytime, although it can be hot during Aug. Christmas lights give the Champs Elysées and Eiffel Tower extra sparkle.
» Crêperies make great energy-boosting stops – or, for a real treat, take your pick of 70 ice cream flavours from Berthillon (across the bridge from Notre Dame).
» The Métro is a good way to get around, but backpack babies rather than buggy them as there are few lifts. Alternatively, use the River Seine's hop-on, hop-off Batobus boats.

Two essentials

Tour Eiffel (Trocadéro Métro) A riveting romp up this Parisian landmark has to be top of your must-do list. You can take the lift or climb 1665 steps to the second level, from where another elevator is the only way to reach the viewing gallery at 274 m. Just 50 m shy of the tower's flagpole, this often-crowded platform provides superhero views reaching 80 km on a clear day. Apart from giving their parents palpitations (don't worry, it's like an iron cage up there), kids will love gazing down on the ant-like columns of traffic and trying to spot other city landmarks. If they start to tire on the climb up (or down), arm yourself with a few inspiring and diversionary facts about Gustave Eiffel's engineering wonder (see box).
Musée du Louvre (Palais Royal Musée du Louvre Métro) You've got to see it,

but where do you begin in a gallery displaying over 35,000 works of art? There are several ways families can crack this mighty treasure chest. If you want to remain independent, focus on just four or five major exhibits, such as the *Mona Lisa*, *Venus de Milo*, Winged Victory and Grand Sphinx. Alternatively, book one of the museum's workshops for children (available for four- to 13-year-olds and lasting up to 2½ hours), or sign up for a guided family tour with Paris Muse Clues – an educational and interactive treasure hunt that takes kids (aged six to 12) from Ancient Egypt to Renaissance Italy, testing their detective skills to lead them ultimately to a prize hidden somewhere beneath the Louvre's glass pyramid.

Top to bottom: Sailing boats in Jardin des Tuileries; an artist in Montmartre; gargoyle on Notre Dame; Catacombes de Paris.

Towering achievement

The Eiffel Tower:
» Has over 18,000 metal parts.
» Has 2.5 million rivets.
» Expands up to 15 cm on hot days.
» Took more than two years to build.
» Has clocked up over 220 million visitors since it opened in 1889.
» Weighs 10,100 tonnes (that's like 2020 elephants standing on top of each other).

Above: Le Tour Effeil.

Best of the rest

Catacombes de Paris Macabre museum piled with the bones of six million Parisians exhumed from the city's overcrowded cemeteries during the late 1700s.

Centre Georges Pompidou Wacky arts centre with visual and performance art. Don't miss the buskers, 'living statues' and surreal Stravinsky Fountain. Then ride the external escalator to the children's gallery.

Jardin d'Acclimatation Amusement park with roller coasters, pony rides etc.

Jardin du Luxembourg Puppet shows, donkey rides and boating pond.

Musée de la Curiosité de la Magie Dingy 16th-century cellars provide a creepy setting for magic shows, optical illusions and other tricks of the mind.

Musée d'Orsay One for older children. Includes Monet's *Blue Waterlilies* and Renoir's *Ball at the Moulin de la Galette*.

Notre Dame Famed Gothic cathedral. Climb to the Galerie des Chimères to see gruesome gargoyles lurking between the towers to ward off evil.

Parc de la Villete Enormous park containing the Cité des Sciences et de l'Industrie, a high-tech science museum where kids can tinker with physics and biology. Cité des Enfants has hundreds of interactive challenges for enquiring young minds.

Parc Astérix (parcasterix.com) Some 30 km north of Paris. Includes an authentic Gaulish Village (where you can meet the characters from the comic strip), a Roman Arena and numerous adrenaline-charged rides. Don't miss the Tonnerre de Zeus, Europe's biggest wooden roller coaster.

How to do Disney in a day (or three)

Disneyland Resort Paris (disneylandparis.com) is Europe's most popular family attraction. If you're thinking of taking the kids to Paris and not spending at least one day here, forget it. At best, they'll never speak to you again; at worst they'll do something spiteful in the Louvre when you drag them there instead. In any case, Disneyland, for all its zigzag queues and rictus smiles, is great fun – whether you're a Cinderella-doting five-year-old, an adrenaline-hungry teenager or the 40-something paying for it all.

When to go Well, it sure isn't Florida (that's Walt Disney World Resort, see page 344), so be prepared for an invigorating range of unpredictable European weather. The upside of visiting in winter, of course, is that queues are shorter and you can get special deals.

How to get there The train is the easiest, most relaxed and child-friendly option. If you're staying in Paris take the RER (40 minutes from the city centre) or, if you're travelling from further afield, hop on Eurostar. Either way you'll arrive at Marne-la-Vallée/Chessy station right outside the park entrance.

Where to stay It depends on whether you want to spend a day at Disney or make a long weekend (or more) out of it. If it's the latter, pick one of the hotels near Disneyland – several are run by Disney so you'll be able to 'live the magic' (breakfast with Chip 'n' Dale etc) even after the parks have closed. For a Paris holiday that simply includes a day trip to Disney you'll get better value by staying in a mid-range city hotel or a suburban holiday park, such as Camping International in Maison-Laffitte.

What to do There are two parks: Disneyland and Walt Disney Studios. You could feasibly visit both in a single day, but you'd miss loads and probably need therapy for months afterwards (see How to do Orlando, page 344). If it's your first time, focus on Disneyland where you will find five distinct zones. The entrance leads straight to Main Street USA, a nostalgic evocation of small-town America in the early 1900s, complete with horse-drawn streetcars and ice-cream parlours. Autograph hunters will find Mickey, Minnie and the Disney Princesses here. Walk through Sleeping Beauty Castle to Fantasyland where Peter Pan's Flight, 'It's a small world' and the flying Dumbos are always a hit with young children. Discoveryland features several big rides, including the revamped Space Mountain roller coaster (minimum height: 132 cm), Buzz Lightyear Laser Blast (where you score points by zapping Zurg and other nasties) and Star Tours (a simulator flight to the Moon of Endor).

Top: Fireworks at Euro Disney. **Above:** Crush's Coaster roller coaster ride.

Frontierland has the runaway roller coaster, Big Thunder Mountain (minimum height: 102 cm), the spooky Phantom Manor and live shows at the Chaparral Theatre, while Adventureland has Pirates of the Caribbean and another wayward roller coaster, Indiana Jones and the Temple of Peril (minimum height: 140 cm). Remember to intersperse the big rides with some of the smaller, queue-free attractions, such as Le Passage Enchanté d'Aladdin (with its exquisite scenes of Agrabah) and Les Mystères du Nautilus (where you can board Captain Nemo's submarine) – and be sure to stake out a good spot on Main Street to view the daily parade. Highlights at Walt Disney Studios include Crush's Coaster (minimum height: 104 cm), an indoor/outdoor spinning rollercoaster ride based on *Finding Nemo*, in which you explore real-life underwater scenes, meet Bruce the veggie great white shark and battle against the East Australian Current. Cars Race Rally takes you for a spin along Route 66, while Rock 'n' Roller Coaster (minimum height: 120 cm) inflicts Aerosmith music and high-speed loops and turns. At park closing time, nearby Disney Village continues to buzz with its plethora of shops, restaurants and cinemas.

En vacance sur la mer

A seaside holiday. That's what lures most families to Northern France. And who can blame them. From the vast sandy beaches of Normandy to the Atlantic-gnawed cliffs and sheltered coves of Brittany, this varied stretch of coastline is paradise for anyone armed with a bucket, a spade and a shrimping net. History, too, comes alive along this shore – from megalithic standing stones at Carnac to the D-Day beaches of the Second World War. And to crown it all you've got Mont St-Michel, an excuse for a Famous Five-style adventure if ever there was one.

Normandy and the northeast

⟩⟩ Self-drive touring is by far the easiest and most popular way to go.
⟩⟩ The Channel can be chilly, so consider wetsuits for the kids.
⟩⟩ For coastal diversions, try the famous lily pond at Giverny (home of Impressionist artist Claude Monet) or go walking, fishing and canoeing in Parc Naturel Régional Normandie-Maine to the south of Caen.

Beaches and battlegrounds

For many travellers arriving from the UK by cross-Channel ferry, Normandy and Pas de Calais are little more than gateways to a wider-reaching *tour de France*. However, linger a little in these regions and you'll discover a mixture of family-friendly beaches and evocative historical sites.

Best beaches The coastal strip between Calais and the Somme estuary is pretty much one long beach. Look out for resorts with 'Kid Station' status, indicating children's facilities and high standards of safety and cleanliness. They include Wissant (vast expanse of sand, good spot for land-yachting), Wimereux (gently shelving beach and shallow sea, ideal for children learning to windsurf) and Hardelot (sheltered beach backed by dunes). Le Touquet-Paris-Plage is another popular resort with everything from waterparks to carousels. Further west, near Le Havre, Trouville is one of Normandy's favourite family beaches (quieter and more relaxed than its chic neighbour, Deauville). Meanwhile, the Péninsule de Cotentin

Far right: Mont St Michel.
Right: The Normandy coast is perfect for a whole host of activities, from sandcastle building to sailing.

has some excellent beaches south of Granville, with a long promenade for walking or cycling. And if all that sand starts to drive you crazy, retreat to the Somme Estuary and spend a day birdwatching at La Parc Ornithologique du Marquenterre, a prime site for spotting seabirds and migratory species.

Battleground tour The D-Day landings endowed Normandy with one of the most poignant legacies of the Second World War. Starting at Caen drive north to Ouistreham and Pegasus Bridge where troop-laden gliders landed just after midnight on 6 June 1944, spearheading the huge allied invasion codenamed Operation Overlord. Continue to Arromanches where a museum and 360° cinema describes how an artificial port (known as the Mulberry Harbour) was built here in just 12 days to secure allied supply routes. Further along the D514, you reach Omaha Beach where American troops met fierce German resistance. On the clifftop at Colleville-sur-Mer the 9387 graves at the American Cemetery provide a stark reminder of the heroism and sacrifices of D-Day.

Bayeux If your kids are studying William the Conqueror at school, then seeing the famous 11th-century Bayeux Tapestry will bring 1066 and the Battle of Hastings into vivid relief (and just think how impressed their history teacher will be). However, very young children may find the embroidered linen boring – despite the fact it measures an impressive 70 m in length and took nuns 10 years to stitch.

66 99 The profound solemnity of a war memorial may be lost on young children, while older kids may be drawn more to hard facts relating to a school project than to the emotion-charged atmosphere pervading a field of white crosses. Nevertheless, a visit to the battlegrounds of northern France remains one of the most important and sobering travel experiences you can give your children.

Will

Kids' top 10: Brittany

1 Conquer Mont St-Michel, a 1000-year-old fortified abbey perched on a rock in the middle of a bay and guarded by lethal tides and whiffy mudflats. Climb through a steep warren of streets, hemmed in by wonky half-timbered houses to reach the Gothic abbey – a major pilgrimage site in the Middle Ages and still hugely popular.

2 Taste local delicacies, from chocolate-smeared crêpes to smoked sausages (or just stick with the crêpes), at one of Brittany's numerous markets.

3 Walk to Pointe du Raz, the Land's End of France, and strike an epic pose as you gaze across the Atlantic towards America.

4 Count (or rather lose count) of the 3000-odd menhirs and other megalithic shenanigans at Carnac, a prehistoric conundrum dating from 4500 to 1800 BC. Resist the temptation to 'do an Obélix'.

5 Cruise to the Sept-Iles, home to 20,000 pairs of seabirds (don't even attempt to count these), including a raucous gannet colony. Departures from Perros-Guirec.

6 Learn to sail a windsurfer, catamaran or sand yacht at the St-Malo Surf School.

7 Discover the secret life of a rock pool, from lightning-fast blennies to bumbling hermit crabs. Beware of tide times and those razor-sharp oyster-encrusted rocks.

8 Cycle 35 km of biking trails on La Belle Île.

9 Vote for your favourite beach, but sample lots first, including the sand sensations at Audierne, La Baule, Carnac, St Cast, Dinard, Douarnenez, Perros-Guirec, Trégastel-Plage and La Trinité-sur-Mer.

10 Explore Océanopolis, Brest's 'mega-aquarium' where you'll see everything from pipefish to penguins.

When it's raining …

Naturospace (naturospace.com) Warm and wonderful tropical garden and butterfly house on the outskirts of Honfleur.

Nausicaà (nausicaa.fr) Cutting-edge aquarium in Boulogne-sur-Mer with imaginative exhibits and thought-provoking environmental themes.

Something for everyone

There's plenty to keep families occupied in this corner of France, from surfing on the Atlantic coast and hiking in the Pyrenees to canoeing, cycling and horse riding in the Dordogne. Combine all three regions and you will probably need another holiday to recover. But you will also have experienced something of the extraordinary diversity of landscapes that France is renowned for – from serpentine rivers snug in gorges to wide sandy beaches ravaged by Atlantic breakers.

Atlantic coast

- A Mecca for surfing and boogie boarding.
- You'll find no shortage of waves to suit all ages and abilities, but choose beaches that are supervised by lifeguards.
- Take your pick of numerous campsites and holiday parks, as well as family-friendly resorts like Biscarosse, Mimizan and Moliets.

Riding waves and climbing dunes

The southwest coast of France is one long, wild, wave-swept beach – give or take a sheltered bay or two. For a surfing holiday you won't find anywhere better in Europe. There are surf schools scattered along the length of the coast with a concentration around Biarritz in the south. Families with younger children will appreciate more tranquil spots, like Basin d'Arachon – a huge bay protected from the 'Biscay bruisers' and a popular spot for gentler watersports

like sailing and kayaking. You can also visit the nearby Dune du Pyla (or Pilat), Europe's largest sand dune at 110 m high, from where there are great views and a brilliant excuse for a roly-poly. Boat trips in the bay, meanwhile, are often rewarded with sightings of dolphins and seabirds.

The Dordogne

- Horse-riding centres can be found throughout the region.
- As well as quiet backroads, cycling is possible on the car-free Piste Cyclable running southeast from Sarlat to the River Dordogne.
- For the perfect canoe trip, plot a course that takes in the main sights of La Roque-Gageac, Domme and Castelnaud, stopping at the latter for lunch.

A river runs through it

Caves, castles, clifftop villages... it's small wonder the Dordogne is such a magnet for holidaymakers – and that's before you've cajoled canoeing, horse riding and cycling into your itinerary. No visit is complete without a stroll around Domme – a fortified town (or *bastide*) with narrow streets, a market square and stomach-lurching views from a terrace perched atop a precipitous cliff. Below the village you can explore a large stalactite-filled cave. West of Domme, medieval masonry at Château de Castelnaud is brought to life through a wonderful range of workshops where kids can learn how to fire a crossbow and devise the perfect strategy for laying siege to a castle – not necessarily the

How to be a safe surfer

- You should be able to swim at least 50 m in open water.
- To begin with only use 100% soft foam boards.
- Choose a board about 30 cm taller than you.
- Make sure you have a surf leash securing the board to your ankle.
- Wear a one-piece wetsuit.
- Check with lifeguards where the best place to enter the water is.
- To avoid drifting, keep in front of a fixed point on the beach.

kinds of skills you might want your little darlings to acquire, but great fun nonetheless. Hugging the base of a steep cliff looming above the river, La Roque-Gageac is a fascinating place that's been inhabited since prehistoric times. You can climb to 'cave forts' bored in the cliffs and visit a garden of subtropical plants that thrive in the warm microclimate. The honey-stone town of Sarlat is also worth visiting, particularly during the Saturday market where you can see, and try, local delicacies such as foie gras, chestnuts, walnuts, mushrooms and truffles.

French Pyrenees

⚫⚫⚫⚫⚫⚫

» Barèges and La Mongie share one of the largest ski areas, while other winter resorts include Font Romeu and Les Angles.
» Summer activities like walking can be adapted to suit any age, while rafting, body-boarding, rock climbing and canyoning (available at several outdoor centres) are better suited to older children.
» Nearby towns worth visiting include Foix, where you can row a boat along an underground river, and the pilgrimage site of Lourdes.
» See page 121 for the Spanish Pyrenees and Andorra.

Size isn't everything

They may not be as high or as grand as the Alps, and you might struggle to name any actual peaks, but what the Pyrenees lack in size and notoriety they more than compensate for with spectacular scenery, abundant wildlife and a wide range of activities. For families, the Pyrenees also score highly for their accessibility to both the Atlantic and Mediterranean coasts, making it a cinch to combine some 'huff and puff' in the mountains with a week relaxing on the beach.

Mountain trains These are ideal if you are lugging around a baby in a papoose or have small children. Just south of Biarritz, Le Petit Train de la Rhune rattles its way to 905 m above the Basque Country, while Le Petit Train d'Artouste, accessible by cable car from Lac de Fabrèges climbs high into the central Pyrenees. Admire the views of Lurien (2826 m) and Palas (2974 m) before walking the short distance to Lac d'Artouste.

Cable car rides Another easy way up and down the mountains is to take the cable car to the top of Pic du Midi. In barely 15 minutes you'll be whisked from La Mongie at 1800 m to the summit at 2877 m, where there's an interesting observatory and museum, not to mention some breathtaking views.

Walks This is what it's all about! Pack a picnic and some warm, waterproof clothes and hit the trails. If you only have

the time (or energy) for one hike, make sure it's in the Cirque de Gavarnie – about 50 km south of Lourdes. If the children seem reluctant to walk, plonk them on a donkey (you can hire one at the village of Gavarnie), then follow the path on the right-hand side of the valley into the vast natural amphitheatre of the cirque. You can't miss the waterfall – a 400-m plume known as the Grande Cascade – but also keep an eye out for alpine flowers, such as edelweiss, and mountain birds like the chough and wallcreeper. Bonus points if you spot a golden eagle or lammergeier. Bonus points with bells on if you spot a brown bear (there's only a handful of them left around these parts).

Caves Going underground may seem like an odd thing to do with all the 'ooh-aah' scenery available topside. But the Pyrenees is a great spot for caves, and chances are you're going to get at least one rainy day anyway. When you do, make a dash for either Grottes de

Bétharram (15 km west of Lourdes) or Grotte de Lombrives (near Tarascon-sur Ariège). Both are positively dripping with stalactites and bristling with stalacmites; there are guided tours and even underground train rides.

Other activities For children around 11 and up (check with individual operators for minimum age limits), the Pyrenees offers plenty of activities guaranteed to get the pulse racing, including whitewater rafting, river boarding, potholing, rock climbing, abseiling, canyoning and via ferrata. Some might not have heard of – others you may wish you'd never heard of when you see your loved ones grappling with ropes and ladders on a precipitous mountain route that is part-hike, part-scramble (that's via ferrata) or disappearing over the lip of a waterfall wearing a wetsuit, a crash helmet and a devilish grin (just one of the thrills of canyoning).

Opposite page: Dordogne landscape; surfing southwest France.
This page: Flora and fauna of the French Pyrenees.

Bird sightings

Wallcreeper Does what it says on the label; creeps around walls, rocks and cliffs. Look out for bright red wing patches, high whistling call and long thin bill.

Lammergeier Huge vulture mostly seen circling around peaks or patrolling a mountain-side on the hunt for carcasses; look out for the long, wedge-shaped tail.

Golden eagle Smaller than the lammergeier and holds its wings in a flat V when soaring; look out for the white wing patches.

Four wheels bad, two wheels good?

Forget your traditional touring holiday. It might be time to ditch the car. The Loire Valley presents too good an opportunity for a family-friendly, eco-friendly alternative. It's called La Loire à Vélo, a signposted itinerary made up of minor roads and cycling tracks that allows you to pedal through the gently undulating, chateaux-speckled countryside of one of Europe's most beautiful river valleys. Easy to plan and easy to pedal, La Loire à Vélo forms part of a grand plan to link Nantes with Budapest via a 2400-km cycle route. But first things first – hand over the car keys and reach for your helmets …

La Loire à Vélo

⊕⊛⊛⊛♀⊛⊛⊕⊞⊛

›› Take the TGV high-speed train from Paris to Orléans, Blois, Tours or Angers.
›› Most people bring their own bikes, but there are also several hire centres along the route.
›› A baggage-forwarding service is provided by dozens of hotels and guesthouses, as well as 8 campsites.
›› Agencies offer cycling packages, including accommodation, bike hire and itineraries.
›› Cycling distances between centres can be as little as 6 km, there are literally hundreds of rest stops and even a number of sites specially labelled as being fun and educational for kids.

Exploring chateau country

Relax. No one is expecting you to cycle the entire Loire à Vélo route (800 km from Cuffy in the Cher region to St-Brévin-les-Pins in Loire-Atlantique). And, if your thighs cramp at the mere thought of two-wheel, leg-powered transport, all of the Loire highlights on the following cycle trails can easily be visited in the comfort of your car.

Chateaux Trail (Lestiou to Candé-sur-Beuvron, 51 km) Following riverbanks as far as St-Dyé this route visits the ancient port of Chambord with its long stone quayside, as well as the majestic 400-room Château de Chambord – the largest in the Loire with a famous double-turn spiral staircase and great views from the roof terrace. Small roads then lead you to the

Château Royal de Blois before continuing on tree-lined routes to the peaceful town of Candé-sur-Beuvron.

Unfaithful Trail (Tours to Langeais, 32 km) Must-see sights in Tours include the cathedral and the timber-framed buildings of the medieval quarter. Then it's off along the banks of the River Cher to Château de Villandry, one of the most family-friendly in the Loire with spectacular gardens to explore and even a maze and children's playground.

Riverbank Trail (Langeais to Chinon, 40 km) Château d'Ussé, on the willow-swept River Indre, is another favourite with kids. Charles Perrault is said to have been inspired to write the tale of *Sleeping Beauty* after visiting this fairy-tale castle of turrets and spires. Cycling through vineyards, the route continues to Chinon, overlooked by a medieval fortress.

Confluence and Caves Trail (Chinon to Saumur, 41 km) More vineyards line this route as it meanders towards the beautiful village of Candes-St-Martin and the Royal Abbey of Fontevraud, Europe's largest monastic complex. To get to Saumur and its castle, the trail follows a hillside riddled with ancient troglodyte dwellings that are now used as wine cellars or mushroom-growing beds.

Other highlights Château d'Angers is renowned for its Apocalypse Tapestries, but kids are more likely to enjoy running riot on the ramparts that link no fewer than 17 towers. Perfect for a rainy day, Château de Brézé has an incredible system of underground tunnels to

explore, while Château de Chenonceau has immaculate gardens, a 16th-century farm and a waxwork museum. Children will love paddling a boat under the chateau's arches.

🐾 Things *sans* chateaux

Canoeing You can rent a kayak at several towns, including Angers and Saumur.

Puy du Fou (puydufou.com) Theme park for wannabe time travellers where you can witness rampaging Vikings, gladiator battles and the exploits of the Three Musketeers.

Futuroscope (futuroscope.com) Maximum 'wow factor' is guaranteed at this park buzzing with 3D IMAX shows and interactive rides.

Above and top right: On the castle trail in The Loire.
Above right: On the Riverbank Trail.

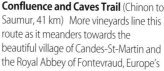

On a summer high

The snow has melted, the ski lifts are closed and the pistes are smothered in alpine flowers. Summer is coming and it's time to head to the mountains. Several alpine resorts alternate effortlessly between winter ski Mecca and action-packed summer destination, making them a perfect alternative to the traditional family seaside holiday. Just think of all that invigorating alpine air, comfortable temperatures, healthy outdoor activities and beautiful scenery. Your kids may never want to see a bucket and spade again.

Chamonix

» Stunning location beneath Europe's highest mountain, Mt Blanc (4810 m).
» Allow 90 mins to drive from Geneva or 9 hrs from Calais.
» Nip through the Mt Blanc tunnel into Italy or take the scenic route via Aiguille du Midi and Pointe Heilbronner, using 3 different cable cars.

Peak perfection

If you can't do it in Chamonix, it probably doesn't exist. From river rafting and rock climbing to parapenting and summer tobogganing, Chamonix has got to be your top choice for non-stop activities. Just don't expect a cutesy alpine village. This bustling Savoy town has 10,000 hotel and guesthouse beds, dozens of restaurants, a casino and sports centre. But what Chamonix lacks in intimacy it more than compensates for with breathtaking views of Mt Blanc, 330 km of marked footpaths and an extensive network of cable cars and mountain railways.

Kids' activities Don't miss the summer luge – a 1820-m concrete bobsleigh run that's suitable for all ages. Bikes can also be hired and then, of course, there's good old-fashioned walking. Take your pick from gentle forest ambles to high-altitude hikes. Two favourite starting points are the Aiguille du Midi cable-car station at 3842 m and Le Brévent, with its famous views across the valley towards the seven summits of the Mt Blanc massif – each one rising to over 4000 m. Rock climbing (minimum age six) and ice-climbing (minimum age 12)

are also available. Then there's whitewater rafting (for children aged 10 and up), horse riding and, if it rains, swimming and bowling in the large indoor sports complex.

Best family day out Board the rack-and-pinion railway for a spectacular mountain journey to Le Mer de Glace.

One for the grown-ups Take a leap of faith on a tandem parapente flight. Strapped to a pilot, you'll get airborne from either Brévent or the Aiguille du Midi and spend 30 minutes descending a kilometre or so to Chamonix.

66 99 Reaching over 11 km in length, the largest glacier in France snakes beneath an imposing range of saw-tooth peaks, a frozen tongue in a maw of rocky fangs. If you asked a young child to draw some mountains this is what they would look like: all pointy and improbable. Inevitably, though, it was not the scenery or hiking potential of La Mer de Glace, near Chamonix, that captivated our children so much as the little red mountain train we had taken to reach it. At Montenvers Station, a cable car whisked us down to the glacier itself where you could walk inside a man-made ice grotto, complete with frozen sculptures.

Will

Looking for something gentler?

Try the Massif Central (auvergne-tourisme.info). Gentle footpaths weave through the forested hills and you can even hire a donkey to carry your luggage or small child.

Top left: Parapenting from Mt Blanc. **Above left:** Mer de Glace. **Above:** Luge.

Tignes spirit

Built around a natural lake and surrounded by snow-capped peaks, Tignes is around three hours' drive from Geneva.

Kid's activities For maximum thrills try whitewater rafting near Centron and Gothard, or a 4WD safari on the high alpine trails in Vanoise National Park. Then there's horse riding, mountain biking, canyoning, quad biking, via ferrata and the adventure assault course in Tignes-les-Brevières. Pony riding is available for children as young as three,

while slightly older kids can learn to sail on the lake.

Best family day out From Tignes-val-Claret take the funicular and connecting cable car to reach the glacier beneath 3656 m Grand Motte. Here you will find the best summer skiing in France (with access to about 20 km of runs), not to mention stupendous views.

One for the grown-ups Europe's highest golf course can be found at Tignes-le-Lac. Be sure to book a tee-off time during high season.

How to choose the perfect family resort

1 Does it meet everyone's needs? Do you have a baby that will need crèche facilities, or teenagers who will be bored senseless without a snowboarding halfpipe to practise their eggflips and corkscrew 540s?

2 Does it have other activities available? A resort that offers extras like husky sledging, ice-skating, bowling or an indoor swimming pool can be a godsend in bad weather or if – shock, horror – you discover that your child just doesn't like skiing.

3 Does it have easy access to ski lifts and a diverse range of runs to suit everyone in the family, from infant novices to adult powder-carvers? Short legs quickly get tired when walking in ski boots, so compact resorts with well-linked slopes are a bonus.

4 Does it have ski classes for children of different ages and abilities? Do the instructors speak English?

5 Does it offer chalet or hotel accommodation that's suitable for children? Exclusive occupancy of a chalet means you don't have to worry about your kids disturbing other guests – or being kept awake after bedtime.

6 Does it involve a long journey from home? What are the options for self-drive, flying or taking the train?

7 Does it have a good reputation for being family-friendly? Saas Fee in Switzerland, for example, is a car-free resort, which instantly gives it family appeal. Other resorts, however, are exclusive and expensive.

Top 16 family ski resorts

Resort	Country	Altitude (m)	Distance to airport (km)	Nursery areas	Pistes Beginners	Intermediate	Advanced	Snowboarding parks	pipes	Lifts Funiculars	Cable cars	Gondolas	Chairs	Drags	Activities
Arinsal	AND	1500	172	2	19	18	5	1	2	0	1	1	11	13	S T SM
Obergurgl	AUS	1930	97	2	12	15	8	1	1	0	0	4	12	7	IS SS
St Anton	AUS	1300	100	3	48	71	31	2	2	1	6	3	36	36	S T IS SR
Kaprun	AUS	800	80	2	55	50	25	1	0	0	4	7	15	28	S IS B T HR
Neustift	FRA	1000	220	2	21	23	10	1	2	0	0	5	8	19	S IS T SR SS IC
Les Arcs	FRA	2000	135	6	144	66	29	5	1	1	3	12	66	58	IS SM B IC SR
Avoriaz	FRA	1800	88	3	150	110	28	10	3	0	3	11	82	110	SR B IS SS
Courcheval*	FRA	1850	128	12	183	119	33	5	3	3	3	34	69	71	IS S HS SM T
Chamonix	FRA	1035	100	4	41	25	13	1	1	0	6	6	17	12	S IS SR SS HS T
La Plagne	FRA	2100	149	6	144	66	29	5	1	1	3	12	66	58	IS B S SR HS
La Rosière	FRA	1850	170	3	32	29	12	1	0	0	1	0	17	19	SS
Tignes**	FRA	2100	165	3	80	35	16	2	1	2	4	4	45	36	HR HS B SM SS
Cervinia	ITA	2050	140	8	18	33	16	7	0	0	0	7	13	13	B IC IS S SS
La Thuile	ITA	1441	150	3	32	29	12	1	0	0	1	0	17	19	S SS
Grindelwald	SUI	1050	195	3	15	28	8	1	1	2	1	2	11	7	S IS B SS T
Saas Fee	SUI	1800	230	2	13	14	7	2	2	1	4	3	1	13	S T IS HS IC SS

* Figures cover the Three Valleys area (can also be skied from Méribel)

** Figures cover the Espace Killy area (can also be skied from Val d'Isère)

Key to activities
S (swimming) **T** (tobogganing) **IS** (ice-skating) **HS** (husky sledging), **IC** (ice-climbing) **SS** (snowshoe walks) **SR** (sleigh rides) **B** (bowling), **HR** (horse riding) **SM** (snowmobiling)

Grimentz is a beautiful Swiss village that's perfect for a skiing holiday with young children. There's a crèche at the top of the gondola (from age two) with great facilities, and only about £4.50 an hour. You can hire baby equipment (prams, sledges etc) in the village and the tourist office has a list of babysitters. The ski school has a baby slope with travelator and snowpark. You can find details at grimentz-location.ch.

Alison Williams

Checklist: keeping kids safe and happy

▸ **Two-piece ski suit** – for easy access when the need arises.

▸ **Thermals** – a cold child is a grumpy child.

▸ **Ski mittens** – easier for children to manage than gloves.

▸ **Sunblock** – psychedelic colours available for trendy teenagers.

▸ **UV goggles** – don't fall off like sunglasses, and offer better protection.

▸ **Energy-boosting snacks** – stick a bag of raisins or chocolates in their pocket.

▸ **ID tag** – write your mobile phone number on it and clip it inside your child's pocket.

▸ **Crash helmet** – an essential, whether you buy one or hire one.

Beautiful people and beautiful places

The Cannes Film Festival, Monte Carlo Grand Prix, Châteauneuf-du-Pape… the South of France is where legends are created and stars are born. It's where the world's mega-rich park their palatial launches and strut their stuff along the promenades of glitzy resorts. So not much on offer for families then? Don't you believe it! This venerated strip of Mediterranean coastline may be *trés* posh in places, but it's also irresistibly kid-friendly. Not only is the Côte d'Azure and Languedoc-Rousillon coastline star-studded with coves and beaches, but you won't have to go far inland to find action-packed gorges, wonderful wildlife and a good spattering of Roman ruins and medieval hilltop villages.

Provence-Alpes-Côte d'Azur

◐ ⬤ ⊛ ⬤ ⬤ ⬤ ⬤ ⬤ ⬤ ⬤ ⬤

» Fly to Nice or take the TGV train from Paris to Avignon.
» Jul-Aug can be stifling, beaches and roads are crammed and prices take a hike; try to visit in cooler, less crowded May-Jun or Sep-Oct.
» Accommodation ranges from hotels and apartments to campsites and rural gîtes; consider travelling with another family or two and renting out a large villa with a pool.

Worlds apart

The region of Provence-Alpes-Côte d'Azur is one of France's most popular destinations and it's easy to see why. Family holiday staples, like sandy beaches, warm sea and sunshine, come in bucket-loads along the French Riviera, but with its head in the Alps and its toes dabbling in the Camargue, adventure is never far away.

Best beaches
You're spoilt for choice. The stretch of coast between St Tropez and St Raphael has wonderful coves and beaches – just don't expect to have one all to yourself. Not only does beach towel space become a precious commodity during peak season, but parking can be a challenge too. Your best bet is to arrive early. Family favourites include Plage d'Agay, Cannes Plage, Cassis Plage and Fréjus Plage. All but Plage d'Argay have good sand for building castles. There are also several Aqualand waterparks along the Côte d'Azur, each one with a spaghetti tangle of daredevil waterslides.

Aix-en-Provence There are more than 100 fountains in this elegant town where you can visit Cézanne's studio, explore the market (Tuesday, Thursday and Saturday) and enjoy a drink in one of the cafés along tree-shaded Cours Mirabeau. The perfect place to introduce kids to a spot of Provençal culture.

Arles A Roman treasure hunt awaits children visiting this market town on the banks of the Rhône. Corinthian columns and fragments of ancient temples seem to sprout from every street corner. You can't miss the well-preserved amphitheatre (Les Arènes) or the Théâtre Antique, but will you find the remains of the Roman circus where 12 chariots once raced side by side?

Avignon The imposing fortress-like façade of the Palais des Papes dominates this walled city. Explore the maze of medieval streets, take a spin on an antique carousel in Place de l'Horloge, then visit Le Pont d'Avignon for a good ol' nursery rhyme singalong.

Monaco The tiny principality that thinks big. Teenagers will love ogling the launches gleaming in the harbour, while younger children will enjoy the aquarium at the Musée Océanographique and the glass-bottom boat trips that depart from Quai des Etats-Unis.

Le Pont du Gard Part of an ambitious Roman scheme to convey water to the city of Nîmes via a 50-km-long aqueduct, Le Pont du Gard is now a world heritage site (but kids may prefer to think of it as an early attempt to create the ultimate waterslide). The visitor centre has an interactive programme for children aged five to 12 where they can experience life as Gallo-Roman pupils, devise ways of controlling water and become archaeologists and naturalists.

Top right: Life's a beach on the south of France.
Centre right: Le Pont du Gard makes a great day out from the coast.

Languedoc-Rousillon

😀😷😾🏰😀🆑⭕🏈🏈😀

» The main centres of Carcassonne, Nîmes, Montpellier and Perpignan are all accessible by plane.

» Makes a great combination with a week in the Pyrenees (see page 99).

Castles of sand and stone

Best known for the bucket-and-spade appeal of its fine Mediterranean coastline, the Languedoc-Roussillon region has a fascinating hinterland dotted with hilltop castles and impressive abbeys. Pick of the beaches goes to Argèles-sur-Mer and Cap d'Agde, both with long sandy stretches and the added attractions of waterparks, aquaria, mini-golf and the like. Inland, you'll find the Cathar castles of Queribus, Peyrepertuse and Puilaurens – each one perched atop a seemingly unassailable cliff. Young children may find it hard to conquer these largely ruined forts (and parents will want to keep them on a

short reign when they see some of the unguarded drops). Adventurous kids, however, will love the challenge (and counting the steps). For something less crumbly, visit the restored fortress town of Carcassonne. Guarded by 52 towers and 3 km of battlements, it's an exciting place to roam, despite the crowds and inevitable rash of souvenir shops.

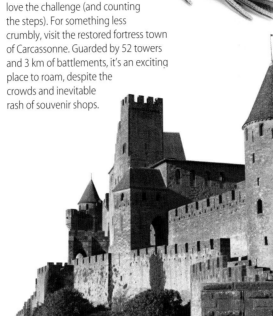

❓ What's that smell?

A walk or cycle ride on the Plateau de Valensole packs a perfumed punch between June and early September when the famous lavender fields of Provence reach their purple prime. Grasse, meanwhile, is the capital of the world's perfume industry. Join a tour around one of its many perfume houses or visit during mid-May for the Fête de la Rose.

🔅 Adventures in Provence

The Camargue Saddle up and ride a pony or bicycle into the watery wilderness where the Rhône meets the sea. Famous for its white horses, black bulls and pink flamingos, the Camargue is a like a breath of salt-laden fresh air after the flashy resorts along the Côte d'Azur. You can hire your trusty mount at Ste-Maries-de-la-Mer. Pony treks are suitable even for beginners, while the Digue à la Mer is designed for walkers and cyclists. Allow at least half a day to pedal to the lighthouse and the flamingo-nesting site at Etang du Fangassier. Remember to take a pair of binoculars – the Camargue is also home to some 400 other bird species, including ducks, egrets, herons and kingfishers.

Gorges du Verdon Don wetsuits and helmets for a splash through mainland

Europe's deepest river gorge. Canyoning (minimum age eight) in France's so-called *Grand Canyon* provides an epic perspective of sheer cliffs towering 700 m overhead as you negotiate a tortuous river by swimming, abseiling, jumping off waterfalls and sliding down natural water chutes. Other excellent spots for watersports are Gorges de l'Ardèche near Vallon Pont d'Arc and Gorges du Tarn near Parc National des Cévennes.

Parc National du Mercantour
An idyllic spot in the Alpes-Maritimes, Mercantour is a refuge for a unique

blend of alpine and Mediterranean flora and fauna. It's also prime walking country with opportunities for both short ambles and more adventurous hikes.

France essentials

When to go
Spring is an ideal time to visit **Paris** – the days are getting longer and temperatures haven't reached the muggy extremes of high summer. In fact, many Parisians flee the city during August to escape the heat. The capital has plenty of festive sparkle during December, which is also a good time to visit **Strasbourg**'s Christmas market. Skiing in the **Alps** is best from January to March, although summer is also a wonderful time to visit the mountains, with alpine meadows in full bloom, plenty of warmth and sunshine and no shortage of lakes to swim in. The **south of France** has hot, dry Mediterranean summers – too hot for some families who might prefer the milder **Atlantic coast** (albeit with its less predictable sunshine). The best time to visit **Corsica** is from May to early July and September to October. Weather forecasts for various French regions can be found at meteo.fr/meteonet.

Getting there
Through its SkyTeam Alliance network, Air France (airfrance.com) connects 199 destinations in 85 countries via its hub at Paris Charles de Gaulle (CDG) airport. Expect to pay from around £90 for a return flight between London and Paris and US$640-1100 for a return fare from New York. British Airways (britishairways.com) has flights to Ajaccio, Basel, Bordeaux, Geneva, Grenoble, Lyon, Marseille, Montpellier, Nantes, Nice, Paris CDG and Toulouse. Low-cost airlines operating between the UK and France include easyJet (easyjet.com), Ryanair (ryanair.com), Flybe (flybe.com) and BmiBaby (bmibaby.com).

Getting around
Driving in France is a pleasure thanks to its comprehensive road network, although venturing by car into Paris is not recommended. The autoroute system has service stations at approximately 40-km intervals and *aires*, rest areas with toilets and recreation areas but no food or fuel services, every 10 km. Plan your self-drive in France by using the route planner facility provided by Michelin (michelin.com). Car rental companies include Avis (avis.fr), Europcar (europcar.fr) and Hertz (hertz.fr).

France has a modern and fast **rail** system. Take Eurostar to Paris, connect with TGV (tgv.com), France's high-speed train service, and you could be in Marseille or Bordeaux just three hours later. Regional express trains, known as TER, connect smaller towns. You can book an InterRail pass, allowing three, four, six or eight days' travel in one month from Rail Europe (raileurope.co.uk).

Getting around in major cities is usually very straightforward and economical thanks to efficient Métro, bus and tram systems.

Go green: four ways to skip the flight
➡ Sail across the Channel with P&O Ferries (poferries.com) from Dover to Calais (70-90 minutes) or with Brittany Ferries (brittanyferries.com) from Portsmouth to Caen (six hours), Portsmouth to St-Malo (8½ hours), Poole to Cherbourg (four hours; Fastcraft 2¼ hours) or Plymouth to Roscoff (five hours). Speed Ferries (speedferries.com) has a 50-minute Dover-Boulogne service from just £20 one-way.
➡ Take your car through the Eurotunnel (eurotunnel.com) from Folkestone to Calais in just 35 minutes. Shuttle trains depart up to four times an hour, a standard single fare costing around £50.
➡ Hop on Eurostar (eurostar.com) from St Pancras International for high-speed train travel direct to Paris, Lille, Avignon, Disneyland and the French Alps. Standard return fares from London to Paris cost from around £60 (or £50 for children aged four to 11).
➡ Catch a bus with Eurolines (eurolines.co.uk) from London's Victoria Coach Station to Paris, via Eurotunnel or ferry.

Dover's cliffs as seen from the ferry.

Fact file

GMT
+ 1 hour

Language
French

Money
Euro € (£1=€1.50)

Code
+33

Tourist info
france .guide.com

ViaMichelin

Maps | **Driving directions** | Hotels | Tourism | Motoring

Driving directions | Guided tour

Summary

| Departure | London |
| Destination | 75000 Paris |

Date: **12/05/2007**
Vehicle type: Automobile, Hatchback
Route type: Recommended by Michelin ▼

Time and distance
Time: **05h35** including 03h21 on motorways
Distance: **421km** including 369km on motorways
et 12km on pleasant roads

Costs
Toll costs: 68.30 EUR
Petrol costs: 19.20 EUR
Road tax cost: 37.26 EUR
               11.84 EUR
Change route | Return route

🖨 Print | Send by ✉ e-mail | Add to My ViaMichelin

Display route map

Accommodation

The most popular family options are either to rent *a gîte* (a self-catering cottage or house) or to stay at a holiday park in a mobile home or pre-pitched tent. A directory of accredited *gîtes* is administered by Gîtes de France (gites-de-france.fr). Average prices per week vary from €440 in the high season to €265 in the low season. Available during the school holidays, a carefully selected range of children's *gîtes* organizes special activities for kids aged four to 15. Companies specializing in cottage and villa rental in France include Allez France (allezfrance.com), Dominique's Villas (dominiquesvillas.co.uk), Rentals France (rentalsfrance.com) and VFB Holidays (vfbholidays.co.uk).

Camping France (campingfrance.com) provides an online search and reservation system for over 10,000 campsites throughout the country. As well as searching by region, you can select various criteria, such as sites with kids' clubs, beach access or waterparks. Many of the most popular holiday parks have superb facilities, including well-equipped mobile homes, swimming pools and waterslides, children's entertainment programmes and numerous sports. Try Canvas Holidays (canvasholidays.com), Eurocamp (eurocamp.com), Keycamp (keycamp.ie) and Siblu (siblu.com).

Center Parcs (centerparcs.com) has two villages in France, one in Normandy and the other in Loire-et-Cher, while organized adventure holidays are available with Acorn Venture Holidays (acorn-venture.com) and PGL (pgl.co.uk). Esprit (esprit-holidays.co.uk) and Mark Warner (markwarner.co.uk) are the leading family specialists in winter and summer holidays in the French Alps, while Club Med (clubmed.com) has an all-inclusive resort with children's facilities in Provence.

Food and drink

The French love their food and you'll find everything from informal brasseries and family-run bistros cooking local dishes to Michelin-starred restaurants serving nouvelle cuisine. To save money, have your main meal at lunchtime when many restaurants serve a *menu du jour* for around half what it might cost in the evening. Be brave and introduce your kids to a few regional specialities. Along the **Brittany** and **Normandy** coasts, assiette de fruits de mer is a seafood platter of crayfish, oysters, prawns, mussels, crab and whelks which kids will enjoy dissecting even if they don't eat much. A sure hit from this region, though, are crêpes and galettes – pancakes with either sweet or savoury fillings. Tarte Tatin, upside-down apple tart, should also go down a treat. **Mediterranean** dishes are some of the tastiest of all. Anything 'à la provençale' promises a delicious concoction of olive oil, garlic, tomatoes, onions and herbs. Duck and geese dishes feature prominently in **Southwest France** and the **Pyrenees** – too rich for many kids, but as with anywhere in France, you'll always find standard fare like steak-frites. In the **Alps**, cheese fondues and gratin dauphinois (sliced potatoes baked in milk) are always

Fruits de mer and fruits de terre.

popular with children, while traditional lamb stew and fiadone (lemon cheesecake) should tempt them in **Corsica**.

Health and safety

The sun can be strong in France during midsummer, so pack plenty of high-factor suncream and make sure children get some shade during the middle of the day. Mosquitoes can be irritating in some areas, so it's also a good idea to take insect repellent. Tap water is safe to drink. Emergency telephone numbers are 15 (ambulance), 17 (police), 18 (fire) and 112 (general emergencies).

The €10 picnic

1 baguette €1	Packet of biscuits €0.74
270 g sliced ham €2.98	1.5 litre bottle of
200 g St Paulin cheese	Orangina €2.47
€1.18	75 g packet of crisps €0.53
4 nectarines €1.06	**TOTAL** €9.96

How much to offset your emissions?

From London to:
Paris £0.80
Brest £0.95
Bordeaux £1.40
Toulouse £1.60
Marseille £1.80

From New York to:
Paris US$25
Marseille US$27

How much for a Big Mac?
USA US$3.22
UK US$3.90
France US$3.82

Tour operators

The Adventure Company
adventurecompany.co.uk
Canvas Holidays
canvasholidays.co.uk
Center Parcs
centerparcs.com
Club Med clubmed.com
Crystal Active Holidays
crystal-active.co.uk
Esprit Holidays
esprit-holidays.co.uk
Eurocamp
eurocamp.co.uk
Exodus exodus.co.uk
Explore Worldwide
explore.co.uk
Families Worldwide
familiesworldwide.co.uk
Headwater
headwater.com
Inntravel inntravel.co.uk
Keycamp keycamp.co.uk
Mark Warner
markwarner.co.uk
Neilson Active Holidays
neilson.co.uk
PGL pgl.co.uk
Powder Byrne
powderbyrne.co.uk
Siblu siblu.com

10 family favourites

Chateau des Ormes
Where? Dol-de-Bretagne, Brittany.
Why? Large and lively holiday park set in 100 ha of chateau parkland with 18-hole golf course, waterpark with four-lane waterslide, indoor pool complex and all-weather football pitch. Children's clubs are available for toddlers through to teenagers and there is an extensive activity programme.
How much? Basic prices for seven-night, mobile-home holidays range from €225 to €1245 for two adults and all children under 18. Homes range from the three-bedroom/two-bathroom Villagrand Deluxe to four-bedroom supertents. Select accommodation that's big enough and grandparents go free.
Contact Keycamp Holidays (keycamp.co.uk).

La Baume
Where? Fréjus, French Riviera.
Why? Well-equipped parc with every amenity imaginable, from Fun Stations for kids aged four and above to a soundproof disco for over-16s. On-site activities include tennis, football, basketball, skateboarding, archery and cycling – and there are lovely beaches nearby if you can tear yourself away from the parc's two outstanding pool complexes.
How much? Basic prices for seven nights in a two-bedroom Cézanne mobile home range from €420 to €1530, including P&O ferry crossing from Dover to Calais. Upgrade to a Monaco Deluxe home (sleeps eight) from €25 extra per night.
Contact Eurocamp (eurocamp.co.uk).

Domaine de Dugny
Where? Blois, Loire Valley.
Why? Four-star parc in the heart of the Loire Valley with a pool complex, kids' adventure playground and fishing lake. Handy holiday extras include linen and towel packs, baby packs, food baskets for late arrivals and three free children's clubs for kids aged one to 14.

How much? From €325, including return Dover-Calais ferry, for two adults sharing a two-bedroom Esprit mobile home.
Contact Siblu (siblu.com).

La Haie
Where? Cléguérec, Brittany.
Why? Sleeping up to 12 (so plenty of space for two families to share), this five-bedroom farmhouse (below left) is set within its own private park, with mature oak and willow trees, lawned areas for games, a fishing lake and a covered 11-m swimming pool. Inside there's a huge farmhouse kitchen, homely living rooms and lofty bedrooms. Lac de Guerlédan, with its sandy beaches and watersports, is 12 km away.
How much? One week costs from €2200 to €3170, including return Channel crossing for one car and passengers.
Contact VFB Holidays (vfbholidays.co.uk).

Chalet Hotel Sapinière
Where? Chamonix, French Alps.
Why? Ideal for a summer or winter holiday, the Sapinière (see above) has superb views of Mt Blanc and is just a few minutes' walk from the children's ski area. A dedicated childcare programme caters for children aged from four months to 12 years. During winter there are kids' snow clubs and ski classes, while in summer, Alpies and Teen Rangers clubs offer supervised activities such as husky walking and rock-climbing.
How much? Summer rates from €425 per week per adult and €160 per child sharing parents' bedroom; winter packages (including flights from Stansted to Geneva) from €690 per adult with free child places on many weeks.
Contact Esprit Holidays (esprit-holidays.co.uk).

Opio en Provence

Where? Near Nice, Provence.

Why? Tucked into olive groves and pine forests, this spectacular all-inclusive resort (see above) boasts stylish accommodation and a wide range of facilities, including four swimming pools, a nine-hole golf course, Mini Club Med for four- to 11-year-olds, Circus School, and teen-only spaces.

How much? Expect to pay around €5880 for a family of four during August, including flights, transfers, full-board accommodation, leisure activities, drinks and snacks.

Contact Club Med (clubmed.co.uk).

Villa du Lac

Where? Cazaux, Atlantic coast.

Why? Located close to surfing beaches and the famous Dune du Pyla, this modern house makes a comfortable family base, with four bedrooms, fitted kitchen, living/dining room and 10-m swimming pool. Shops and restaurants are within easy walking distance, as is a lake offering swimming, fishing, waterskiing and cycling.

How much? One week's rental from €940 to €1750, including a return Channel crossing for one car and up to five passengers.

Contact French Affair (frenchaffair.com).

Disneyland Hotel

Where? Disneyland Paris

Why? Ultimate Disneyland hotel overlooking Disneyland Park (top right) and just a three-minute walk to Walt Disney Studios Park and Disney Village. As well as enjoying facilities like a swimming pool and Club Minnie playroom, guests receive a Fastpass and have plenty of opportunities for Meet 'n' Greet sessions with Disney characters.

How much? From €500 per adult (based on two sharing) for two nights, including accommodation, breakfast and Disneyland entrance. Check website for kids' deals.

Contact Disneyland Hotel (hotels.disneylandparis.co.uk).

Les Hauts de Bruyères

Where? Loir et Cher.

Why? Special features of this well equipped Center Parcs village include the Experience Factory (with midget golf, play areas, crêperie and electric cars), Aqua Sana spa and indoor subtropical waterpark with lagoons, waves, slides, waterfalls and jacuzzis).

How much? From €1344 for a week in August in a two-bedroom Premier Villa.

Contact Center Parcs (centerparcs.com).

Villa Pianelli

Where? Olmeto Plage, Corsica.

Why? This three-bedroom villa (see below) has a large garden leading to a sandy beach interspersed with rocks and hidden coves – a paradise for children. The spacious property has a shady terrace with sea views, while Propriano is just 6 km away.

How much? From €800 to €1230 per adult per week, including charter flights from Gatwick, car rental and a welcome hamper. Discounts of €50 for infants up to the age of two and 10-15% off adult price for children aged two to 15.

Contact Corsican Places (corsica.co.uk).

Spain and Portugal

Shell seekers on a beach in Andalucía.

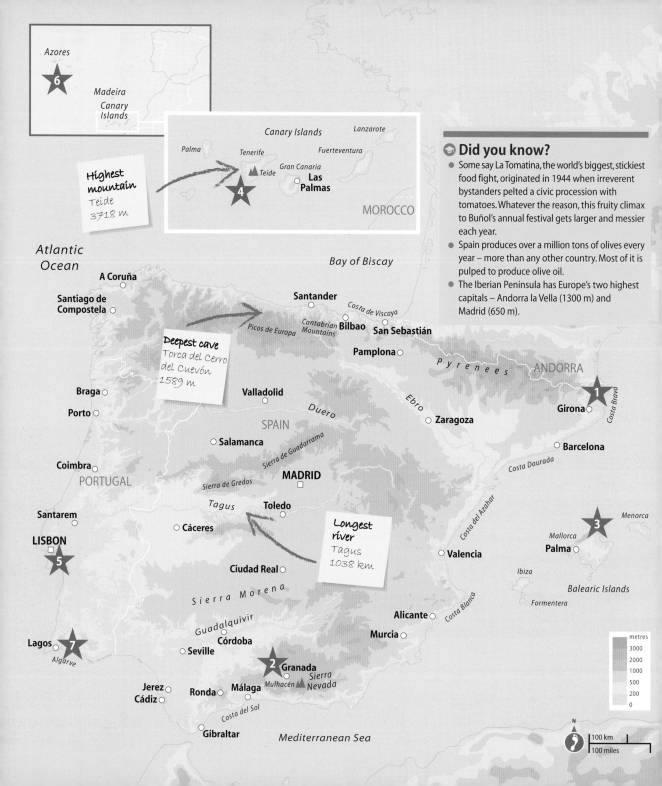

Azores

6

Madeira

Canary
Islands

Canary Islands

Palma   Tenerife   Lanzarote

Fuerteventura

Gran Canaria

▲ Teide   **Las
Palmas**

4

MOROCCO

**Highest
mountain**
Teide
3718 m

◯ Did you know?

- Some say La Tomatina, the world's biggest, stickiest food fight, originated in 1944 when irreverent bystanders pelted a civic procession with tomatoes. Whatever the reason, this fruity climax to Buñol's annual festival gets larger and messier each year.
- Spain produces over a million tons of olives every year – more than any other country. Most of it is pulped to produce olive oil.
- The Iberian Peninsula has Europe's two highest capitals – Andorra la Vella (1300 m) and Madrid (650 m).

*Atlantic
Ocean*

Bay of Biscay

A Coruña

**Santiago de
Compostela**

Santander

Costa de Viscaya

Cantabrian
Mountains   **Bilbao**

Picos de Europa   **San Sebastián**

Deepest cave
Torca del Cerro
del Cuevón
1589 m

Pamplona

P y r e n e e s   ANDORRA

Braga

Porto

Valladolid

SPAIN

Duero

Ebro

Zaragoza

1

Girona

Costa Brava

Coimbra

PORTUGAL

Salamanca

Sierra de Guadarrama

MADRID □

Sierra de Gredos

Barcelona

Costa Daurada

Santarem

LISBON □

5

Tagus

Toledo

Cáceres

**Longest
river**
Tagus
1038 km

Costa del Azahar

3

Menorca

Mallorca

Palma

Ciudad Real

Valencia

Ibiza

Balearic Islands

Formentera

S i e r r a   M o r e n a

Lagos

7

Algarve

Guadalquivir

Córdoba

Alicante

Costa Blanca

Murcia

Seville

Jerez

Cádiz

Ronda

Málaga

2

Granada

*Sierra
Nevada*

Mulhacén ▲

Costa del Sol

Gibraltar

Mediterranean Sea

N

metres
3000
2000
1000
500
200
0

100 km
100 miles

Introduction

With its stunning beaches, guaranteed sunshine and excellent value for money, it's not hard to see why Spain is such a popular family holiday destination. And while Portugal has less in the way of beach resorts and nightlife than its Iberian neighbour, it's still a friendly, fun place to take kids. Don't be put off by the reputation of certain Costas and islands for crowded beaches and rowdy nightlife. You can always find smaller, quieter resorts or travel in the low season – particularly to year-round destinations like the Canary Islands. There are also plenty of opportunities for getting off the beaten track, from roaming the Spanish steppes of Extremadura to island hopping through the Azores. And if that sounds too taxing (or too far from the beach) there is always scope for adding an adventurous twist to a traditional seaside holiday – whether you combine northern Spain's coast with some action-packed days in the Picos de Europa or head inland from the Costa del Sol on a cultural quest to Granada and Seville.

❝❞ *I was a bit nervous of going somewhere with my daughter where I didn't speak the language, so the idea of joining a group was very attractive – as was being able to combine the destination with loads of activities that we don't normally do. There were so many special moments: the beauty of the peaks, waterfalls and lakes; whizzing round hairpin bends on bikes; the kids singing at the tops of their voices all the way down the mountain, and shrieking on the narrow off-road track.*

*Rachel Hosier, Active Pyrenees tour
(The Adventure Company)*

Spain and Portugal rating

Wow factor
★★

Worry factor
★

Value for money
★★★★★

Keeping teacher happy
★★

Family accommodation
★★★★★

Babies & toddlers
★★★★★

Teenagers
★★★★

Books to read

Prince of the Birds, Frances Lincoln, 2005
In a story adapted from Washington Irving's *Tales of the Alhambra*, Ahmed, the Prince of Granada, lives in a high tower, with only birds for friends. Through his ability to communicate with them he finds true love in the form of a princess locked in a faraway tower. To win her hand he must conquer his fears before they can finally escape together on a flying carpet. Ages 5+

The Life and Work of Salvador Dali, Heinemann, 2005
Part of a series on the lives and works of great artists, this 32-page book delves into the surreal world of Spanish painter, Salvador Dali – well known for his weird and wonderful paintings, such as *The Persistence of Memory*. Ages 5+

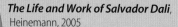

Toro! Toro!, Collins, 2002
Set in Andalucía, against the backdrop of the Spanish Civil War, this is the moving tale of Antonito and the young bull that he has hand-reared and wishes to spare from the fate of the bull ring. A delightful story, full of drama. Ages 6+

Ferdinand Magellan and the First Voyage around the World, Chelsea House Publishers, 2000
A biography of the daring Portuguese sea captain who commanded the first expedition that sailed around the world. Ages 7+

With Love from Spain, Melanie Martin, Yearling, 2005
In this diary of her family holiday in Spain, 11-year-old Melanie dances flamenco, tries Spanish food, visits museums and falls in love. Ages 8+

Asterix in Spain, Orion, 2004
When Pepe, the kidnapped son of a Spanish chief, escapes from his Roman captors, who should find him but those indomitable Gauls, Asterix and Obelix. Faced with the task of returning Pepe to his father, the gallant heroes must brave mountains, bullfights, Roman legions – and the annoying habits of young Pepe. Ages 8+

🌀 How to make a Picasso-style sculpture

▸▸ Take a look at some of Picasso's famous paintings. Notice the way that he sometimes painted pictures of faces, with lots of different views. The book *Draw with Pablo Picasso* (Frances Lincoln, 2007) is a good source of inspiration.
▸▸ Take a piece of modelling clay (that doesn't need to be kiln-dried) about the size of a tennis ball. Flatten it to make a circle, around 4 cm thick.
▸▸ Use clay tools to draw a line from the top to the bottom of the circle that shows a side view (or profile) of a face.
▸▸ On the other side of the line, draw one eye facing forward. Add raised features such as lips, eyebrows and a nose also facing forward on that side.
▸▸ Score, or make little marks, with your clay tool and then use a wet finger to help seal the features in place.
▸▸ At the top of the face make around 10 holes for adding hair later.
▸▸ Allow the clay to dry completely before painting; then insert pipe cleaners into the holes to create wacky hair.

🔍 How to be a super snorkeller

The coasts and islands of Spain are great places to learn how to snorkel, particularly sheltered rocky coves teeming with fish and other marine life. Before you take the plunge, however, follow these simple steps to happy, safe and leak-proof snorkelling.

▸▸ **Get gear that fits** Hold the mask up to your face and breath in through your nose. If it sticks to your face when you take your hands away, it fits. Choose a snorkel with a mouthpiece that isn't so big it hurts your gums. Fins should be snug, not tight.

▸▸ **A bit of spit** To stop the inside of your mask misting over, rub a little spit, a dab of toothpaste or a drop of baby shampoo over the glass, then rinse thoroughly.

▸▸ **Practise in the bath** Much more fun than plastic ducks or bubble mixture, a snorkel lesson in the bath will help you get used to breathing through a snorkel. Make sure the mask strap is high on the back of your head and not too tight. Put the snorkel mouthpiece all the way in your mouth and close your lips around it.

▸▸ **Ready for the sea** Start in a calm, shallow area. Lay face down and relax. For extra buoyancy wear a life jacket or wetsuit. Make sure you're happy with everything before you swim out of your depth.

▸▸ **Clearing water** If water seeps into your mask, tread water and pull the lower edge of the mask away from your face to allow it to drain out. A burst of air should shoot any water out of your snorkel.

▸▸ **Fin like a mermaid** Use a relaxed, 'fluttering' kick with your flippers. If you're doing it right, there should not be too much splashing.

▸▸ **Don't overdo it** Every few minutes lift your head above the surface to check that currents haven't taken you too far from the shore. Always be aware of boats in the area and stay well clear of breaking waves. Remember, it's far more rewarding to fin gently over one small area, observing the life below you, than to fin madly, see nothing and risk leg cramps.

▸▸ **Be sun smart** Wear a surf vest with built-in sun-protection, smother the back of your neck and legs with waterproof sunblock and avoid snorkelling during the middle of the day.

One to watch

Spanish Made Easy for Children: Hola Amigos Volume 1 (1997), Monterey Video. Sing songs, play games and learn about animals, colours and numbers while gently learning the Spanish language with Paco and Lupe, a pair of fun-loving Chihuahuas who have exciting adventures with their human and animal friends.

Taste of Spain: gazpacho (chilled tomato soup)

This Spanish cold tomato soup makes a great starter or a simple lunch. It's also really easy to make. Here is the Andalucían variety.

What you need

- ▸▸ 1 kg plum tomatoes
- ▸▸ 1 small green pepper
- ▸▸ 1 small cup olive oil
- ▸▸ 200 g white bread soaked in water
- ▸▸ Glass of water (optional)
- ▸▸ 1 small onion
- ▸▸ 1 small chubby cucumber
- ▸▸ 4 tsp vinegar
- ▸▸ salt and pepper
- ▸▸ Garlic cloves, peeled and crushed
- ▸▸ Bowl of diced tomatoes, red and green peppers, cucumber, onion and croutons to garnish

What to do

- ▸▸ Blend the tomatoes, onion, pepper, cucumber, vinegar, bread and oil in a food mixer.
- ▸▸ Add the water and garlic to suit your own taste; the water will make it less strong, while the garlic will make it stronger.
- ▸▸ Add salt and pepper to taste and put the mixture in a bowl. Chill for at least an hour – the colder the better (you can add ice cubes if you like).
- ▸▸ Serve in soup bowls with side dishes of the diced vegetables and croutons for people to add themselves.

Tots to teens

Planning a family holiday to Spain, Portugal or any of their islands is not only straightforward, but can also offer excellent value for money. Accommodation ranges from self-catering apartments and resort hotels to holiday villages with tents and mobile homes, while food covers everything from burgers and pizzas to tapas bars where children can try lots of small traditional dishes. Although you will usually find a friendly welcome wherever you go, the Portuguese have a special weakness for children – particularly babies and toddlers. Children in both Spain and Portugal are treated like mini-adults and it's not unusual to see them in restaurants with their parents late at night.

Babies (0-18 months)
Avoid the hot and crowded summer season – it will still be warm enough in spring and autumn to enjoy Spain's Mediterranean resorts. The main resort beaches have play areas, while babysitting is usually available in the larger hotels. High chairs are not always common, so consider bringing a travel seat that attaches to a chair.

Toddlers/pre-school (18 months-4 years)
The quietest resorts include Llafranc on the Costa Brava, San Pedro de Alcántara on the Costa del Sol and Dénia on the Costa Blanca. In the Balearics, Menorca is the most laid-back island for young families. There are some excellent beaches on the Algarve, although some are strafed by strong Atlantic currents and winds – fine for beachcombing and playing chicken with the waves, but dangerous for swimming. If you are unfazed by the longer flight, the Canary Islands are an ideal choice for toddlers. With warm, sunny weather year-round, you can travel outside the busy school-holiday season and still enjoy good beach weather. For ultimate flexibility, opt for a self-catering apartment and hire car; for onsite facilities choose a family resort.

Kids/school age (4-12 years)
Although you are restricted to busier school-holiday periods with this age group, crowded beaches at least provide guaranteed playmates for your children. They will also be able to enjoy a wide range of beach-based activities, from snorkelling to trips in glass-bottom boats. Popular tourist spots always have a waterpark (Siam Park in Tenerife being the latest and most spectacular) and there are also several excellent theme parks, such as PortAventura on the Costa Daurada. Rather than restricting yourselves entirely to the beach, however, consider a trip that combines the coast with the mountains. In northern Spain, for example, a week or so relaxing on Cantabria's lovely sandy bays can easily be followed by a multi-activity adventure in the Picos de Europa, while southern Spain's Costa del Sol combines well with

Top left: Look mum – no brakes! Exploring a backstreet in Andalucía.
Above left: The spectacular coastline of Galicia in northwest Spain.
Above: Cycling in the Picos de Europa.

walking or horse riding in the Sierra Nevada. If you just want a taster of the high ground, try Tenerife where a day or two clambering about on the volcanic slopes in Teide National Park will give kids a real sense of achievement. Educationally, Spain's premier museums and galleries are in Madrid – quite a sophisticated destination for kids until you factor the Warner Bros theme park into the equation. For an insight into the country's history and culture you could also combine the Spanish capital with Extremadura, but you'll need an itinerary that's short and sweet to keep kids interested. Valencia's super-modern City of Arts and Sciences is a guaranteed hit with children, as is Lisbon's Parque das Nações with its superb oceanarium.

Teenagers (13 years+)
If it's lively beach resorts you're after, Spain has them in bucket loads – although you should steer clear of the rowdiest fleshpots on Ibiza or along the Costa Blanca. As well as buzzing nightlife and a similarly aged, like-minded crowd to hang out with, most teenagers are up for a sporty challenge whether it's learning how to sail, windsurf or waterski. And when the beaches begin to pall, there are always the waterparks, theme parks and shops – particularly in cities like

Barcelona which teenagers will love for its trendy vibe and wacky art scene. For multi-activity breaks, The Adventure Company (adventurecompany.co.uk) has teenage trips to Andorra, while Explore Worldwide (explore.co.uk) has dedicated teenage departures to Spain, Mallorca and the Azores.

Special needs

Most tourist offices can provide information on accessible accommodation. Disabled holiday specialists Can be Done (canbedone.co.uk) lists several properties in Spain and Portugal that offer facilities such as wheel-in showers and pool hoists. Also try Accessible Travel & Leisure (accessibletravel.co.uk).

Single parents

The Adventure Company (adventurecompany.co.uk) has single-parent departures on its eight-day Active Pyrenees adventure break in Andorra. One-parent family holiday specialists Single Parents on Holiday (singleparentsonholiday.co.uk) and Mango (mangokids.co.uk) both offer group trips to rural Andalucía. Try Eurocamp (eurocamp.co.uk) for single-parent discounts on holidays to the Costa Brava, Costa del Sol, northern Spain and the Algarve.

❔ Where can I do this?
The Dolphin Connection

(dolphinconnectionexperience.com) offers holidays swimming with wild dolphins in the Azores, where it is not uncommon to meet pods of up to 200 individuals. Each 10-day trip includes six three-hour boat trips. The recommended minimum age is seven years old and all children (and adults) are given snorkel training in a pool prior to venturing into the open ocean. Professionally trained guides (with RLSS Aquatic Rescue certification) are always on hand to help children develop snorkelling confidence, while local experts provide talks on the biology and conservation of the archipelago's renowned whales and dolphins.

What the kids say:

❝❞ It was amazing looking into the ocean (very deep) and seeing the dolphins looking at me! *Jody* (age 12)

❝❞ As soon as I got in the water and put my head under, there were dolphins everywhere, making clicking noises and moving around a lot. I saw six in front of me playing. It was really good. The sea was very deep! *Henry* (age 10)

❝❞ The big ocean was a bit scary, but with the help of our guide I got in and looked down. Some dolphins swam towards us; it was very beautiful and made me very happy. *Caitlin* (age seven)

Telling tales …

The best beach I know for young families is the Praia do Barril near Tavira in Portugal's eastern Algarve. It's a great long stretch of vanilla sand, with thatched umbrellas for hire, clean showers and toilets, and a big, shady outdoor restaurant where you can always get a table. But its trump card for kids is simple and overwhelming: you reach it by taking a five-minute miniature train ride across the lagoon. Toot, toot!

Dan Linstead
Editor, Wanderlust magazine

❝❞ I love Spain because it's always hot. I love walking along the sandy beaches collecting seashells. And I also love eating swordfish.
Lottie Gales (age 6)

What? No Costas?

Central Spain may be a long way from the beach, but there is still enough in this region to keep children happy on holiday. At first glance, Madrid's reputation for fine art doesn't exactly make it an easy sell to kids. If you're desperate to see the capital's famous Prado, Thyssen or Reina Sofía galleries, you'll need to dangle a pretty tempting carrot under your children's noses – preferably in the form of the Warner Bros Park south of the city. Once you've seen some of Madrid's traditional (and not so traditional) highlights head west to Extremadura, an unspoilt region with fascinating birdlife and history (but alas, still no Costas).

Madrid

›› The Tourist Travel Pass from Madrid Card (madridcard.com) provides unlimited travel on bus, metro and suburban train routes for between 1 and 7 days.
›› If you plan to visit all of Madrid's art highlights, buy a ticket for the Art Walk (El Paseo del Arte), available at the Prado, Thyssen and Reina Sofía galleries.
›› For further information, visit esmadrid.com and turismo-en.sigimo.com.

City highlights If you have time to visit just one of Madrid's three world-class art museums, the Museo del Prado (museoprado.mcu.es) should be top of your list. Inside you'll find a wealth of paintings by Spanish masters Goya and Velázquez, as well as an impressive collection of Italian and Flemish works. Highlights for children include *Las Meninas* by Velázquez where the infant Margarita is fussed over by her ladies-in-waiting. Goya's so-called 'Black Paintings' may be too harrowing for young children – although teenagers will probably delight in the gross-factor of *Saturn Devouring his Son*. Also worth tracking down is Caravaggio's *David Victorious over Goliath*, an exquisite study in light and shadow. For more art appreciation, head to the Museo Nacional Centro de Arte Reina Sofía (museoreinasofia.es) to see Picasso's antiwar masterpiece *Guernica*, or to the Museo Thyssen-Bornemisza (museothyssen.org) to study paintings by Rembrandt, Raphael and others. A short walk from the galleries, the Parque del Retiro has plenty of space to run around, as well as boats to hire on the lake and a Sunday afternoon puppet show. On the opposite side of central Madrid, you'll find Palacio Real (patrimonionacional.es), Madrid's extravagant Royal Palace with its lavishly decorated dining hall and throne room.

Best parks A short bus or train ride south of Madrid, San Martín de la Vega's Warner Bros Park (parquewarner.com) is divided into five themed areas. Peruse the shops, cafés and cinemas along Hollywood Boulevard before witnessing a spectacular stunt show (based on *Batman*, *Lethal Weapon* or *Police Academy*) at Movie World Studios. Some of the biggest rides can be found in Superheroes World, including The Vengeance of the Enigma – a 100-m vertical tower drop (minimum height 130 cm) and the 90-kph Superman roller coaster (minimum height 132 cm). Old West Territory keeps the adrenaline pumping with a giant wooden coaster and various water rides, while Cartoon Village is where you can meet Tweety, Bugs Bunny and other Looney Tunes characters. Gentle rides for little ones include Scooby-Doo spinning cups, while the park's loudest screams are usually generated by the 106-kph Stunt Fall coaster (minimum height 137 cm).

From central Madrid, take the metro west to Batán to reach Casa de Campo, a former royal hunting ground that's home to Parque de Atracciones (parquedeatracciones.es), an amusement park with hanging roller coasters, free-fall rides and water chutes. The Tranquillity Zone offers more relaxing activities such as a jungle boat cruise, while younger children have their own special area with roller coasters, water rides, puppet theatres and an adventure playground. Also in Casa de Campo, Parque Zoológico (zoomadrid.com) has everything from koalas and tigers to dolphins and sharks, while Faunia Madrid (reached by taking the metro east to Valdebernardo) recreates various ecosystems, from polar to tropical. For waterparks, try Aquópolis de Villanueva de la Cañada or Aquópolis de San Fernando de Henares (aquopolis.es).

Top right: Museo del Prado.
Above: Flower-filled meadow in Extremadura.

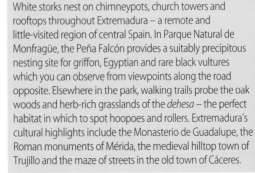

❓ Where can I see these?

White storks nest on chimneypots, church towers and rooftops throughout Extremadura – a remote and little-visited region of central Spain. In Parque Natural de Monfragüe, the Peña Falcón provides a suitably precipitous nesting site for griffon, Egyptian and rare black vultures which you can observe from viewpoints along the road opposite. Elsewhere in the park, walking trails probe the oak woods and herb-rich grasslands of the *dehesa* – the perfect habitat in which to spot hoopoes and rollers. Extremadura's cultural highlights include the Monasterio de Guadalupe, the Roman monuments of Mérida, the medieval hilltop town of Trujillo and the maze of streets in the old town of Cáceres.

A greener side of Spain

Stretching from the Pyrenean foothills to the crinkle-cut shoreline of Galicia, the Atlantic coast of northern Spain has everything from rugged cliffs to sandy bays, fishing villages and holiday resorts. What it doesn't have, though, is the almost guaranteed heat and sunshine of the Mediterranean Costas: a small price to pay, perhaps, for less crowded beaches and quieter resorts. But northern Spain appeals to families in search of more than sun, sand and sea. Lush broadleaf forests sweep up the flanks of the Cantabrian Mountains, with adventure-rich national parks like Picos de Europa just a short distance inland. There are also caves to be explored – many with prehistoric paintings – while a wonderful procession of cathedrals, churches and monuments mark the pilgrimage route to Santiago de Compostela.

❓ Where can I see this?

A living sculpture sustained by an internal irrigation system, the Puppy sits obediently outside Bilbao's extraordinary **Guggenheim Museum** (guggenheim-bilbao.es) where it contrasts with the museum's titanium-clad façade.

Regional highlights

◐ ♥ ❄ ❧ ♦ ♠ ♨ ⊞ ① ⑩ ⊛ ⊜ ○ ⊗

» Sail from Portsmouth to Bilbao with P&O Ferries (poferries.com) or from Plymouth to Santander with Brittany Ferries (brittany-ferries.com) and you stand a good chance of spotting whales, dolphins and basking sharks in the Bay of Biscay.

» Inland from Bilbao, Pamplona is renowned for its annual fiesta, Los Sanfermines (6-14 Jul), in which bulls stampede through the frenzied, crowded streets of the city.

» For further information, visit euskadi.net, infoasturias.com, turismodecantabria.com and turgalicia.es.

Vizcayan Coast Stretching east from the busy commercial port of Bilbao, the rugged Basque coastline has a long history of fishing, and at the Museo del Pescador in Bermeo you can catch the whole story, from whales to anchovies. Just beyond Bermeo the coastal road diverts inland following a scenic route along the west bank of the Oka River estuary to Gernika. It was here in 1937 that German and Italian planes unleashed a devastating bombing raid, killing over 1600 people – an outrage vividly portrayed in Picasso's powerful *Guernica* painting on display in Madrid (see page 118). A few kilometres to the north, the Cuevas de Santimamiñe are worth a visit, although the chamber with the prehistoric cave drawings of bison is closed to the public. Cantabria's caves (see below) might be more satisfying. Following the west bank of the estuary

back to the coast, you reach Mundaka, an attractive old harbour town renowned for its long surf break. Continuing east, Lekeitio has a couple of good beaches, but for the ultimate Basque holiday resort look no further than San Sebastián (sansebastian turismo.com). Surrounded by hills and overlooking the beautiful horseshoe bay of La Concha, San Sebastián has loads for kids to do – from swimming and sailing to ogling sharks in the aquarium near the town's old quarter.

Cantabria A region blessed with a heady mixture of golden-sand beaches (particularly at Laredo and Santander) and a spectacular mountainous hinterland, Cantabria not only has the best of northern Spain's scenery, but it also has the added attraction of some fascinating prehistoric caves. The most famous of these are the Cuevas de Altamira (museodealtamira.mcu.es) where charcoal-and-ochre images of bison, deer and horses festoon a rock face. In order to protect the original drawings (created by Cro-Magnon communities up to 14,000 years ago) a replica of the cave is open to visitors. For a glimpse of the real thing head to Cuevas del Castillo, a des-res for cave dwellers from as early as 130,000 years ago. Here you can see animal drawings as well as some 50 hand prints. Kids will also enjoy the nearby Cabárceno Wildlife Park where African elephants, rhinos and other exotic beasts roam a 750-ha

swathe of the Peña Cabarga Nature Reserve. For a proper taste of northern Spain's great outdoors, though, you need to set your sights on the Parque Nacional de los Picos de Europa. Easily accessed from either Santander or the Asturian town of Oviedo, this dramatic chunk of the Cordillera Cantábrica is home to vultures, eagles, chamois, wolves and bears, as well as a dazzling array of butterflies and orchids. The riverside village of Potes makes a good base. You will find several adventure operators here (offering activities ranging from mountain biking, whitewater rafting and horse riding to paragliding and 4WD tours), while nearby Fuente Dé is the setting for a dramatic cable-car ride.

Galicia The coast to the north of this westernmost province of Spain, especially the Costa da Morte, is wild and windswept – fine for a scenic drive and an invigorating picnic on a headland, but not exactly what you'd call child-friendly. Instead, head for the Rías Baixas on Galicia's southwest coast. This series of deep inlets has a milder climate and safer beaches, especially at the resort of Panxón. There are good watersports facilities at Vilagarcia de Arousa, while the tiny island of A Toxa is worth a visit to see its church which is covered in scallop shells.

Top: Langre beach, Cantabria.

Barcelona and beyond

A superb family holiday destination, Catalonia caters for all ages, whether you have 10-year-olds in search of mountain adventure, teenagers in search of city chic or toddlers in search of sand and sea. Rivalling Madrid for cultural importance, child-friendly Barcelona is the vibrant capital of this diverse region which stretches from the 3000-m peaks of the Pyrenees to the sandy bays of the Costa Daurada. One of Europe's original package-holiday destinations, Catalonia's rugged Costa Brava continues to draw the crowds, while inland attractions include the mesmerizing Monastery of Montserrat.

Barcelona

⚟ ⚶ ⚘ ⚙ ⚒ ⚕ ⚖ ⏸ ⚚ ⊗ ⚛ ⊛ ⚏ ⚓

⇥ Barcelona divides nicely into 3 family-friendly sections: La Rambla and Port Vell, Parc de Montjuïc and Tibidabo.
⇥ The Barcelona Card (available from the tourist office – see below) allows free travel on public transport as well as discounts at various museums and attractions.
⇥ For further information, visit barcelonaturisme.com.

Three-day action plan

Day 1 Start at Plaça de Catalunya, a large square at the heart of the city, and walk down La Rambla, a 1-km-long pedestrian thoroughfare adorned with colourful pavement mosaics and thronging with cafés, bird and flower stalls, buskers, street artists and spray-painted human statues. About halfway down you can detour to the left to see Barcelona's magnificent Gothic Cathedral. At the end of La Rambla, take the lift up the Monument a Colom where Christopher Columbus stands atop an 80-m column. The views are spectacular. You'll be able to see the dramatic and otherworldly spires of Gaudí's Sagrada Família (although you should schedule time for a close-up visit to this extraordinary church). From the Monument a Colom, stroll a little way along Avinguda de les Drassanes to Museu Marítim (museumaritim barcelona.com) where Barcelona's seafaring tradition is brought to life with imaginative exhibits and special effects. Nearby at Port Vell, admire the beautiful schooner, *Santa Eulàlia*, before walking across the pontoon of Rambla de Mar to visit L'Aquarium (aquariumbcn.com) – one of Europe's largest, with a walk-through shark tank. Other attractions in Port Vell include an IMAX cinema, the submarine *Ictíneo II* and the Museu d'Història de Catalunya (en.mhcat.net), a child-friendly museum which allows children to experience Catalan history through dressing up and role-play. Boat trips are available with Las Golondrines (lasgolondrinas.com) and on the catamaran *Orsom* (barcelona-orsom.com), while sandy beaches with play areas and cafés can be found at both Port Vell and Port Olímpic. For something more peaceful, make for the green oasis of Parc de la Ciutadella just to the east of Port Vell. Here you'll find a boating lake, a fountain and shady paths to explore, as well as the Parc Zoològic with its dolphin shows, pony rides, adventure playground and children's farm.

Day 2 Take the metro to Paral-lel from where a funicular connects with the cable-car station on Avinguda de Miramar. A thrilling ride up Montjuïc Hill leads to Castell de Montjuïc with its far-reaching views of the city. There's a military museum inside the castle, although most kids will be happy enough exploring the gardens which are littered with ancient cannon. On the opposite side of Parc de Montjuïc, the majestic Palau Nacional houses the Museu Nacional d'Art de Catalunya (mnac.es), renowned for its Romanesque church frescos. Admittedly, children will be more captivated by the cascades and fountains outside, but if you're determined to instil some cultural appreciation there's always the nearby Poble Espanyol (poble-espanyol.com), an open-air museum with streets, squares, buildings and monuments from around Spain. It's a bit touristy, but kids will enjoy the handicraft workshops, street entertainers and puppet shows.

Day 3 From Plaça de Catalunya take the open-topped Bus Turístic to Parc Güell, a colourful and wacky mishmash of pavilions, benches, archways and other architectural shenanigans hatched from the playful mind of Gaudí. Continue north to Avinguda del Tibidabo and take the funicular up 517-m-high Tibidabo hill where colour-coded paths and nature trails probe the woodlands of Parc de Collserola. Round off the day at the 100-year-old Parc d'Atraccions del Tibidabo (tibidabo.es) which has traditional funfair rides as well as some more modern, white-knuckle embellishments.

Top right: Rocky shore along the Costa Brava; Gaudí's Parc Güell in Barcelona.
Bottom right: More weird and wonderful designs at the Sagrada Família.

Costa Brava

The 200-km 'Wild Coast' of Catalonia is an enticing mixture of golden beaches, rocky cliffs and bustling resorts. At its northern end, Roses has sheltered beaches and makes a good base for visiting the fishing village of Cadaqués and the Dalí museum in Figueres. Further south, the small resorts of L'Escala and L'Estartit have a thriving sardine fishery and are close to the Greco-Roman ruins of Empúries. Don't miss a snorkelling or kayaking trip to the offshore Medes Isles, available through Medaqua (medaqua.com). Palafrugell has three of the Costa Brava's finest beaches (Calella de Palafrugell, Llafranc and Tamariu), while the popular resort of Platja d'Aro has a 2-km stretch of lifeguard-patrolled beach and lively nightlife. A beautiful old fortified town above the sheltered sweep of Platja Gran beach, Tossa de Mar has a watersports centre at Cala Llevadó. The busiest, liveliest and nosiest stretch of the coast, Lloret de Mar suits families with teenagers in search of watersports and a buzzing nightlife. The catamaran *Sensation* (catamaransensation.com) operates sailing trips between Blanes and Lloret de Mar, while the Jardí Botànic Mar I Murta gardens makes a pleasant retreat from the coast. Waterparks along the Costa Brava include Aquabrava (aquabrava.com) in Roses, WaterWorld (waterworld.es) in Lloret de Mar and Marineland (marineland.es) just south of Blanes.

Costa Daurada

Stretching south of Barcelona the 'Golden Coast' is renowned for its long sandy beaches. Sitges is a long-established and trendy resort, but not as popular as Salou – one of Spain's prime Mediterranean hot spots. Here you will find the gently shelving beaches of Platja de Ponent and Platja de Llevant, with smaller, less crowded coves towards Cap Salou. Beyond this lies Le Pineda with more beaches and the waterpark Aquopolis (aquopolis.com).

Valencia and Murcia

The sun-drenched beaches of the Costa del Azahar, Costa Blanca and Costa Cálida attract millions of holidaymakers each year. In the north of Valencia, the main resorts of Costa del Azahar include Benicassim, Oropesa and Peñíscola, which has a fortified old town enclosing a maze of narrow streets. There's an Aquarama (aquarama.net) waterpark in Benicassim, while inland attractions include the ruined medieval castle of Morella. Further south, boats carry visitors through the flooded subterranean passages of the Coves de Sant Joseph, while Sagunt has the remains of an ancient fortress dating back to Roman times. Aside from being a departure point for ferries to the Balearic Islands (see page 124), the regional capital of Valencia is home to the futuristic Ciutat de les Arts I de les Ciències (cac.es) which contains a hands-on science museum, IMAX cinema, planetarium and aquarium. Following the coastal road south, you reach L'Albufera, a freshwater lake that supports over 250 bird species. The Cap de la Nau marks the transition to the Costa Blanca with the resort of Denia offering a mixture of sandy and rocky beaches. The Costa Blanca's most dramatic landmark, the 332-m-high limestone bluff of Penyal d'Ifach, rises above the harbour town of Calp from where you can take a boat trip to admire the impressive coastline. A short distance inland, the mountain village of Castell de Guadalest is a popular day trip from resorts along this stretch of coast.

Top: Ciutat de les Arts I de les Ciències. **Above:** Penyal d'Ifach.

Parc Nacional d'Aigüestortes, Andorra.

Just inland, kids will be desperate to visit Costa Daurada's legendary theme park, PortAventura (portaventura.com). There are five lands to explore – China, the Far West, Polynesia, Mexico and the Mediterranean. With no less than eight loop-the-loops, the Dragon Khan roller coaster used to be the ultimate thrill ride at PortAventura, but then along came Furius Baco which accelerates its passengers from 0 to 135 kph in three seconds. More stomach-clutching moments are available on Hurakan Condor, a 42-storey free-fall tower. Families with younger children will find plenty of softer options, including the Sea Odyssey submarine ride, spinning Armadillos and South Pacific dance show. In addition to three on-site hotels, PortAventura also boasts the Caribe Aquatic waterpark, so it looks like you'll be spending at least two days here.

Spanish Pyrenees

The 464-sq-km state of Andorra (andorra.ad) is within day-trip range of most resorts along the Costa Brava but it's far more satisfying to hire a car and spend a few days roaming further afield in the Pyrenees. The Parc Nacional d'Aigüestortes, for example, is a beautiful mountain tapestry of peaks, forests, lakes and streams offering wonderful walking trails, particularly around Lake Sant Maurici. Further west lies Baquera-Beret (baqueira.es), a popular ski resort with over 40 pistes. During summer, children aged six and above can take part in an excellent activity programme including team games, horse riding, archery, handicraft workshops and picnics in the mountains. For older children and teens there's canyoning, whitewater rafting, climbing and hiking. Nearby Vall d'Aran is the perfect place to spot some of the Pyrenees' rare butterflies and perhaps even glimpse a golden eagle or bearded vulture. Further west still, in the province of Aragón, the Pyrenees reach their most dramatic in Parque Nacional de Ordesa – a rugged melange of peaks, canyons, limestone escarpments and densely wooded valleys where you need to be prepared to explore on foot.

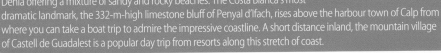

❷ Where can I see this?

Built into a mountain-side 40 km northwest of Barcelona, the *Monestir de Monserrat* is the spiritual heart of Catalonia and was built on the spot where La Moreneta – a statue of the Virgin Mary – was hidden from the Moors. Reach the monastery by car or train, then take the cable car or rack railway up the mountain. The Montserrat Visita Card (montserratvisita.com) includes tickets for the rack railway or cable car, Montserrat Museum and lunch in the café.

Spoilt for choice in sunny southern Spain

For sheer variety, Andalucía is hard to beat. Even if you opt for a beach holiday on the Costa del Sol, that still puts you within range of excursions to the lofty wilderness of the Sierra Nevada and the cultural gems of Ronda and the Alhambra. Further west, Seville and the Parque Nacional del Coto Doñana make a great city break/safari combo, while the Costa del Sol itself has several options for beach-free days, from the caves at Nerja to the Rock of Gibraltar.

Regional highlights

⛱️🐠🐢🏊🚣⛵🚴⛷️🏛️🏰🎠🏇🏟️🎭🗺️

» Stretching from Málaga to Gibraltar, the Costa del Sol receives on average around 300 days' sunshine a year.

» Avoid queues at the Alhambra by booking tickets in advance at alhambratickets.com.

» For further information, log on to andalucia.org.

Seville Andalucía's beautiful capital is rich in heritage and most of its historical highlights are within easy walking distance of each other. Just how much you see in the way of Moorish and Renaissance architecture, however, will depend on your children. You can always use Isla Mágica (islamagica.es) as a bargaining tool – an outing to this theme park with its roller coasters, waterslides and free-fall towers on Isla de la Cartuja is easily worth a day of sightseeing in return. Start with Seville Cathedral (catedraldesevilla.es), a vast Gothic creation built on the site of a great mosque. Originally built as a minaret in 1198, La Giralda now serves as the cathedral's belltower. Designed to accommodate a man on horseback, 35 ramps help smooth the climb to the top. Back at street level, explore the maze of narrow streets in Seville's historic centre (on foot or by horse-drawn carriage). Pause to admire the exotic royal palace, Real Alcázar (patronato-alcazarsevilla.es), before finding a tapas bar to sample some traditional Andalucían fare. Next, head west to Torre del Oro in the adjacent district of El Arenal. This Moorish tower contains a small maritime museum and is also the starting point for cruises on the Guadalquivir. If your kids need to burn off some energy, make instead for Parque de María Luisa.

Ronda Just half an hour's drive from the Costa del Sol (see opposite), Ronda is the most visited of Andalucía's *pueblos blancos* (white towns). However, it's worth contending with the crowds of day trippers simply to see Ronda's spectacular clifftop setting – the Puente Nuevo bridge spanning a 100-m-deep cleft to link the old town with the new.

Granada Although young children won't necessarily appreciate the Romanticism or subtle beauty of the Alhambra, this incredible medieval Arab palace – the best preserved in the world – is something you simply have to show your kids. A large complex of palaces, pools and patios with gardens at one end and a ruined fortress at the other, the Alhambra demands at least a full morning or afternoon. Your tickets will show an allocated time when you are allowed to enter the most famous section known as the Palacios Nazaríes. Highlights here include the Salón de Embajadores, a sumptuously decorated throne room, and the Patio de Arrayanes, a peaceful courtyard with a long rectangular pool reflecting the graceful arches of surrounding arcades. At the western end of the Alhambra, children will relish the chance to explore the more rugged 13th-century Alcazaba fortress where they can climb the Torre de la Vela for views of the Sierra Nevada.

Sierra Nevada Home to mainland Spain's highest mountain, Mulhacén (3482 m), and a haven for various endemic plants and rare butterflies, the Sierra Nevada has been protected as a

Top and below left: The Alhambra palace. **Above:** Costa del Sol. **Bottom left:** Skiing in the Sierra Nevada. **Below:** La Giralda, Seville.

national park since 1999. It also boasts Europe's southernmost ski resort – Solynieve (Pradollano) at 2100 m – which has a good range of pistes and a halfpipe. Las Alpujarras, a region of fertile valleys dotted with almond orchards, vineyards and olive groves on the range's southern flanks, is an ideal place to introduce children to a rural and non-commercialized part of Spain. Based in one of the region's Moorish-style villages you can explore the mountains on foot, or try a spot of horse riding or mountain biking.

Kids' top 10: Costa del Sol

1 Find the best beaches, whether you want lots of action at Torremolinos or something more low-key at Torre del Mare.

2 Escape into the mountains of the Sierra Nevada for cool air, cool views and cool mountain biking or horse riding.

3 Spot film stars and celebrities in Marbella (marbella.com). Ogle their luxury yachts in the marina, browse stylish shops in the old town and then hit the beach at Playa de Don Carlos.

4 Conquer the 450-m-tall Rock of Gibraltar (gibraltar.gi) and meet the famous Barbary apes, Europe's only wild primates. Then take to the sea on a dolphin safari (dolphinsafari.gi) in search of cetaceans in the Straits of Gibraltar.

5 Delve underground into the Cuevas de Nerja (cuevadenerja.es), a spectacular cave system where a 32-m-tall limestone column in the Hall of the Cataclysm is recognized as the world's largest.

6 Learn about sea-turtle conservation at the SeaLife Centre (sealifeeurope.com) in Benalmádena.

7 Reach new speeds on the waterslides at Aqualand (aqualand.es) in Torremolinos where highlights include the 22-m free-fall Kamikaze, an artificial surf beach and the rubber ring Boomerang ride.

8 Enjoy the fun of the fair at Benalmádena's Tivoli World (tivoli.es).

9 Discover the unspoilt beaches of Cabo de Gata, a nature reserve in Almería province that can be visited from the resort of San José.

10 Go east to find the Wild West at Almería's Mini Hollywood, a spaghetti western movie set where you can watch staged shoot-outs.

Cabo de Gata.

> 66 99 Up in the foothills of the Sierra Nevada, the tracks linking the villages and pastures provided ideal avenues of exploration for our children. We passed men leading donkeys and working threshing machines, while just 40 minutes away were the busy resorts of the Costa del Sol.
>
> *Mike Wynne, Walks Worldwide (walksworldwide.com)*

🔍 How can I see one of these?

With a great deal of luck! One of Europe's most endangered mammals, about 30 Spanish lynx have found sanctuary in the *Parque Nacional del Coto Doñana* – a 50,000-ha wilderness of marshland, sand dunes and scrub woodland located south of Seville. Other rarities include the imperial eagle and purple gallinule. An important stopover for migratory birds, including the greater flamingo, the wetlands of the Coto Doñana recede during the summer making it easier to spot mammals like deer, boar and wild cattle. Access is strictly by guided tour only, although several visitor centres on the park's outskirts provide birdwatching opportunities and nature trails. At the Centro de Visitantes El Acebuche there's an exhibition, café and shop, as well as a rehabilitation centre for injured birds.

Holiday heaven in the Med

Renowned for inexpensive package holidays, fine beaches and lively nightlife, the Balearic Islands are well-established family favourites. However, there's more to this Mediterranean archipelago than crowded beaches and wild nightclubs. The islands of Mallorca, Menorca, Ibiza and Formentera have a diversity to suit all tastes – from the cultural sights of Mallorca's capital to the quiet, unspoilt beaches of Menorca and Formentera. Accommodation ranges from boisterous resorts to rustic farmhouses, while children will find no shortage of activities both on and off the beach.

Mallorca

Best beaches Mallorca's coastline is dimpled with countless coves including those at Cala d'Or, Illetes and along the rugged west coast. The island also has several longer stretches of beach, the most desirable being on the dramatic northern peninsula where Platja de Formentor is lapped by calm turquoise water.

Best activities Snorkelling is excellent from any of the island's rocky coves, while birdwatching is rewarding during spring and autumn when migrant species use the S'Albufera wetlands as a stopover. Illa Dragonera, a tiny island off the west coast, is a lovely spot for a picnic and a walk; for more challenging hikes look to the mountains of the Serra de Tramuntana.

Best parks For wild and wacky water rides choose from Western Park (westernpark.com) in Magaluf, Aqualand (aqualand.es) in both Magaluf and El Arenal, and Hidropark (hidropark.com) at Puerto de Alcudia. Just west of Palma, Marineland (marineland.es) has dolphin and sea lion shows, while the Auto-Safari Park near Portocristo provides close encounters with giraffes, rhinos and monkeys.

Best days out Mallorca's capital, Palma, has a new aquarium (palmaaquarium.com) which combines well with a visit to the cathedral and the 14th-century Castell de Bellver. A series of spectacular caverns on the east coast, the Coves del Drac, can be explored by boat and on foot, while further north the Coves d'Artà exit dramatically on to the open sea.

Cape Formentor, Mallorca.

Menorca

Best beaches Many of the north coast beaches, like Cala Pregonda, are deserted gems, accessible only by boat or on foot. One of the most popular resorts, Cala Santa Galdana, overlooks a beautiful crescent-shaped cove on the south coast, while just to the west, Cala en Turqeta has aquamarine water, sea caves and shady pines.

Best activities Don't expect as much in the way of watersports and beach facilities as you find on Mallorca and Ibiza. Boat trips are an ideal way of exploring Menorca's beautiful and unspoilt coastline, while pony trekking along the island's rural tracks is available from horse-riding centres at Maó, Ferreries and Ciutadella.

Best parks The Los Delfines Aquapark (aquacenter-menorca.com) is located at Ciutadella.

Cala d'Hort on Ibiza's southeast coast has dramatic views of the rugged island of Es Vedrá.

Best days out Bronze Age ruins are scattered throughout the interior of Menorca. Some of the larger, more impressive ones, like Trepucó and Torre d'en Gaumes, are worth visiting with children, but not in the heat of midday. Combine them with a beach visit or a trip to Ciutadella or Maó – both of which have interesting harbours and café-lined squares.

Ibiza and Formentera
Best beaches A busy resort, with a sandy beach, safe swimming and plenty of watersports, Es Canar is a family favourite on Ibiza. With fine sand and sparklingly clear water, the sheltered bay of Cala Vadella promises excellent swimming and snorkelling, as well as boat trips. On Formentera, the large, sandy sweep of Platja de Migjorn boasts excellent facilities.

Best activities Glass-bottom boat trips operate from several beaches on Ibiza, including lively Sant Antoni where Club Náutico de Sant Antoni also offers sea kayaking and sailing tuition. For birdwatching, head to Estiny Pudent, a saltwater lagoon on Formentera where flamingos mingle with herons, stints and other waterbirds during late summer and autumn.

Best parks Waterparks on Ibiza include Aqualandia at Cap Martinet and Aguamar at Platja d'en Bossa.

Best days out Cycling is possible on both islands (leaflets describing various 'green routes' are available from tourist offices), while child-friendly horse riding is offered by Ibiza's numerous stables. Formentera is just an hour's boat ride from Ibiza's south coast.

The all-action archipelago

The Canaries have a split personality. At one extreme you could bake yourself on a beach for two weeks, eat English food and restrict your sightseeing to discos and waterparks, while at the other you could go truly wild, whale watching, climbing volcanoes, learning to scuba-dive and hiking through ancient forests. There's a huge range of things to see and do in the archipelago, but the three characteristics that all four major islands share in abundance are sun, sand and sea. Quite simply, there is nowhere better in Europe to plan a winter beach escape with the kids.

The Eastern Islands

⚓🐟🚣🏊🐚🐋🏄⛴🎣🌋🐪✈

» Flights and ferries operate between the 3 islands in the Eastern Province, while cars can be hired at airports and ferry terminals.
» Sea temperatures range from 18ºC during winter to 25ºC in summer.
» For further information, log on to grancanaria.com and turismolanzarote.com.

Gran Canaria Third largest of the Canary Islands (after Tenerife and Fuerteventura), Gran Canaria receives over three million holidaymakers each year. Most zip down the motorway on the island's east coast to resorts like Playa del Inglés, Maspalomas and Puerto Rico where apartment blocks and high-rise hotels crowd golden-sand beaches. Activities in the sunny south range from windsurfing to camel riding. Just north of Maspalomas, Aqua Sur (aqualand.es/grancanaria) is one of the biggest waterparks in the Canary Islands with no fewer than 33 waterslides. You'll find a roller coaster and other jollities at nearby Holiday World, while go-karting (for children as young as five) is available at San Agustín's Gran Karting Club. For a triple whammy of themed days out you can witness a Wild West shoot-out at Sioux City, performing parrots at Palmitos Parque and crocodile shows at Agüimes' Crocodilo Park. After that lot you'll either need a week recovering on the beach or else you will be yearning to see a more natural side to the island. If it's the latter, Spirit of the Sea (dolphin-whale.com) offers two-hour

cetacean-spotting cruises from the harbour in Puerto Rico. Alternatively, you could make tracks across the Dunas de Maspalomas, a spectacular swathe of sand dunes sandwiched between Playa del Inglés and Maspalomas. However, the two areas where Gran Canaria really shakes off its package-holiday image are along the cliff-strewn west coast and in the central highlands. Allow at least a full day to explore the rugged volcanic interior of the island. Not only are there several traditional mountain villages to visit, but there are also numerous possibilities for walks, including a moderate 6.5-km hike to the base of Roque Nublo – a dramatic basalt spire. In the north of the island, you'll find plantations of orange, mango and papaya trees in the valleys around Agaete and exotic plants at the botanical garden in Tarifa. Las Palmas, Gran Canaria's capital, is also worth a visit. In addition to Museo Elder (an interactive science museum and IMAX theatre), kids will be intrigued by the Guanches mummies on display in Museo Canario and the exploits of Christopher Columbus depicted in Casa de Colón. That's assuming, of course, you can drag them away from the city's beach – a 3-km curve of enticing sand.

Lanzarote Arid, barren and windswept, Lanzarote's volcanic interior has a stark and haunting beauty. Children probably won't notice the lack of trees on the island – they'll be too mesmerized by the volcanic carnage wrought by the Montañas del Fuego in Parque Nacional de Timanfaya. Can you

imagine their faces when your guide demonstrates how the volcano is dormant, not extinct, by shoving sticks into a crevice where they instantly ignite? And that's after you've ridden camels up the cinder-strewn slopes for spectacular views across the park's ochre-red volcanic cones. Timanfaya is an essential day trip on Lanzarote, but

🌋 Gran Canaria watersports
Windsurfing Steady breezes at Playa del Inglés and the beach of Pozo Izquierdo.
Surfing Strong breaks in the north, but the coast is rocky; try Maspalomas instead.
Diving Arguineguín's Dive Academy (diveacademy-grancanaria.com) is a PADI Gold Palm centre with its own pool for tuition.

Top right: Making tracks across Gran Canaria's Dunas de Maspalomas. **Below right:** Tenerife's Playa de las Teresitas. **Above:** Canarian bellflower.

you will spend most of your time on the coast. The majority of visitors stay in Puerto del Carmen, a sprawling resort with hotels, bars, restaurants and discos, but none of the high-rise brashness that has blighted parts of Tenerife and Gran Canaria. Another good family option is Playa Blanca at the southern tip of Lanzarote where you'll find hidden coves and gorgeous stretches of golden sand. The north of the island is also worth exploring. Visit the old capital of Teguise on Sundays to buy handicrafts at the weekly market, before continuing on to Cueva de los Verdes, a 6-km-long lava tube that you can explore on guided tours. The nearby Jameos del Agua lava caves have been cleverly landscaped to incorporate a restaurant and swimming pool.

Fuerteventura Compared with the other main islands, tourism is still in its infancy on Fuerteventura. The two most popular resorts are in the south at Península de Jandía and in the north at Corralejo. Both have spectacular beaches, although Corralejo has the added attraction of a massive belt of sand dunes. The former fishing village also boasts the Baku Water Park (bakufuerteventura.com), glass-bottom boat trips to the tiny offshore Isla de los Lobos and a 40-minute ferry service to Lanzarote. A popular day trip in the south, Oasis Park (lajitaoasispark.com) in La Lajita combines an animal park, botanical garden and camel farm.

Kids' top 10: Tenerife

1 Burrow through tunnels of *laurisilva* (ancient forests of laurel and myrtle) that festoon the slopes of the Anaga Massif in the east of Tenerife.

2 Spot pilot whales and dolphins on a boat trip out of Las Américas, but be sure to choose an operator that follows guidelines for minimizing disturbance to the whales.

3 Experience the thrill of scuba-diving at Los Gigantes Diving Centre (divingtenerife.co.uk) which offers two-hour Discover Scuba adventures (minimum age 14 if accompanied on the programme by a parent or guardian).

4 Talk to the animals at Loro Parque (loroparque.com) in Puerto de la Cruz, where you'll find the world's largest collection of parrots, as well as orcas, dolphins, gorillas, chimpanzees, tigers, jaguars and a breeding colony of penguins.

5 Track down a dragon tree at Parque del Drago in Icod de los Vinos or go bananas at the Bananera El Guanche plantation.

6 Splash out at the waterpark Aqualand Costa Adeje (aqualand.es/tenerife) or take a dip in the natural saltwater pools along the coastline of Puerto de la Cruz.

7 Ride a camel at El Tanque's Camello Centre or a pony at the Oasis del Valle in the Orotava Valley.

8 Climb Mount Teide, the highest point in the Canary Islands at 3718 m – or at least have a good scramble on its volcanic slopes. Keep an eye out for the famous Teide Eggs – magma boulders created by the same principles that make snowballs grow when rolled down a slope. Families with younger children can opt for the eight-minute cable-car ride to within 160 m of Teide's summit.

9 Sample as many beaches as possible. Some of the island's most family-friendly include Playa de las Teresitas (1.5 km of imported Sahara sand, close to Santa Cruz de Tenerife and sheltered by a breakwater), El Médano (2 km stretch of golden sand fringed by calm, shallow waters, perfect for windsurfing) and Playa Fañabé (Blue Flag beach with lots of watersports on the Costa Adeje).

10 Visit Siam Park (siampark.net), one of Europe's largest waterparks, combining thrill rides like the Dragon, Volcano and Wave Palace (boasting 3-m-high artificial waves) with a superb Thai-themed cocktail of aquariums, restaurants and even a floating market.

Top right: Mt Teide. Top left: Cueva de los Verdes. Above: Laurel Forest.

66 99 The path burrowed into a mossy tunnel of overhanging trees. It was shadowy and quiet, the air tinged with the loamy odour of decay. Occasionally sunlight penetrated the canopy, splashing colour across the forest floor, or a gap in the trees would be filled with a bright filigree of waves breaking on the coast far below.

Will

From the mild Algarve to the mid-Atlantic

Few families look further than the Algarve when it comes to holidaying in Portugal – and who can blame them? Not only is it largely sheltered from cool Atlantic winds and ocean currents, but its coastline is notched with a glorious succession of sandy coves and beaches, some of which have smugglers' den written all over them. There's also an endless variety of boat trips to choose from, as well as a good range of family-friendly accommodation. So why even consider going to Lisbon instead? Well, for starters, the Portuguese capital has plenty to appeal to youngsters, particularly at the Parque das Nações. However, it's only when you start contemplating a few days in Lisbon as the prelude to an island odyssey in Madeira or the Azores that the Algarve begins to seem less of a foregone conclusion.

Lisbon

⊗⚓🏨✕⊗🏛

» The Lisboa Card (askmelisboa.com) includes free public transport and admission to museums and monuments.
» Save money at the Parque das Nações by purchasing a Cartão do Parque which provides free entry to the Oceanarium and Knowledge Pavilion, a return ride on the cable car and a discount on bike rental.
» For further information, log on to visitlisboa.com.

City highlights There are three main areas in Lisbon worth visiting with children. The most central is the city's hilltop citadel, Castelo de São Jorge. This huge walled compound contains the tiny neighbourhood of Santa Cruz do Castelo as well as the Inner Battlements – a kind of castle-within-a-castle – where children can scamper between watchtowers and gaze across the rooftops of the city below. Originally a Moorish fort (but captured by Afonso Henriques in 1147), the castle is believed to be the site of Lisbon's earliest settlement, dating as far back as the 6th century BC. However, the period of Portuguese history that is most likely to capture the imagination of kids is the Age of Discovery. Belém, Lisbon's westernmost suburb, reached by tram 15 from the city-centre square of Praça da Figueira, is home to the 52-m-tall Pradrão dos Descobrimentos monument depicting famous Portuguese mariners, such as Vasco da Gama and Magellan.

Standing at the 'prow' of the sculpture, with a caravel in hand, is Henry the Navigator, while on the pavement nearby a huge world map is etched with the routes taken by the explorers during the 15th and 16th centuries. A monument to the wealth of the Age of Discovery, the beautiful Mosteiro dos Jerónimos, set a little way back from the waterfront at Belém, contains the tombs of Vasco da Gama and Henry the Navigator. Two museums in the monastery's west wing cover archaeology, shipbuilding and navigation – but be sure to leave time to visit the nearby Torre de Belém, a wonderful 16th-century defensive tower on the River Tagus with battlements, watchtowers and a dungeon.

Heading northeast from the city centre on the Vermelha metro line to Oriente station, you arrive at Parque das Nações (parquedasnacoes.pt), Lisbon's leisure hot spot and a guaranteed hit with children. Built on the site of the city's Expo 98 world fair, the *parque* boasts gardens, restaurants, shops, the impressive canopied Portugal Pavilion and even a cable car running along its length to the 145-m-tall Torre Vasco da Gama. The highlight, however, is Oceanário (oceanario.pt), one of the world's largest aquariums, and one of the most imaginatively designed. Based on a 'Global Ocean' theme, its central exhibit comprises a giant 7-m-deep aquarium from which four distinct zones radiate. These cover the North Atlantic,

Top: Lisbon's Pradrão dos Descobrimentos monument. **Above:** Sharks in the Oceanarium at Parque das Nações. **Left:** Belem tower.

Antarctica, temperate Pacific and tropical Indian Ocean – from both above and below the surface. One moment you are watching sea otters frolicking on a rocky shore; the next you're peering through the swaying fronds of a kelp forest. Look out for star appearances from penguins, sea dragons, wolf eels, cuttlefish, manta rays and blacktip sharks. The Pavilion of Knowledge or Ciência Viva (pavconhecimento.pt) will also captivate kids. Permanent exhibitions at this interactive science centre include the Exploratorium where you can touch a tornado, make a gigantic bubble and experiment with shadows, and the Unfinished House where three- to six-year-olds can grapple with construction tools and scamper over scaffolding.

Madeira and the Azores

⊙ ⊛ ⊜ ⊚ ⊕ ⑪

» The 9 islands of the Azores range in size from 17-sq-km Corvo to 746-sq-km São Miguel; the 5 Madeiran islands cover an area of roughly 795 sq km.

» For further information, log on to madeiratourism.org or visitazores.org.

Madeira A dot in the Atlantic, 608 km from Morocco and almost 1000 km from Lisbon, Madeira is a subtropical gem with year-round appeal. In Funchal, the island's capital, children will enjoy setting sail on a replica of Columbus's *Santa Maria*. Whale watching off the coast is also rewarding with almost guaranteed sightings of fin, sei, sperm and pilot whales during summer months. Don't miss the cable-car ride to Monte or the famous 'street toboggan' ride back down again. Swimming is possible along Funchal's Lido Promenade or you could head east to Santa Cruz where the Praia das Palmeiras has a children's play area and pedal boats for hire. Highlights on Madeira's north coast include the natural rock pools at Porto Moniz and the São Vicente Caves where you can explore 700 m of lava tunnels. At Santana there's a theme park devoted to the history, science and traditions of Madeira, while hardy walkers will find plenty of challenging trails in the island's rugged interior. For a 30-minute taster, try the

straightforward trail between Rabaçal and the Risco Waterfall. If even that sounds too much like hard work, nip over to Porto Santo, a small island lying 37 km to the northeast of Madeira and boasting a superb 9-km sandy beach along its south coast.

The Azores Scattered some 1300 km west of Lisbon, this isolated archipelago will appeal to adventurous families who enjoy walking and island hopping. Each island has its own character and special appeal. Starting in the west, Flores is one of the most beautiful, with hydrangea hedgerows lacing the island in bright cerulean each July. Graciosa is renowned for the Furnas do Enxofre, a sulphur lake located in a cave beneath the island's Caldeira. On Faial, the historic and picturesque port of Horta is worth a day of exploration, as is Capelhinos, where an eruption in 1957 added 2 sq km to the island. With its dramatic sea cliffs and deep valleys covered in lush vegetation, São Jorge is a magnet to walkers, as is Pico with its challenging ascent of Ponta do Pico. Whale watching (particularly for sperm whales) is also excellent from Pico, with three-hour boat trips from Lajes available from Espaco Talassa (espacotalassa.com). On Terceira, highlights include the World Heritage Site of Angra do Heroísmo, a town that once formed the hub of Atlantic trading routes. The twin volcanic lakes of Sete Cidades – one blue, one green – can be found on São Miguel, the largest and most diverse of the islands. However, be sure to also visit Gorreana, the site of Europe's only tea estate, and the spa town of Furnas where you can see bubbling mud pools and hissing vents. The nearby Terra Nostra Gardens is a haven of exotic flora, while a drive out to Nordeste on the east coast provides wonderful clifftop views. Dramatic scenery is also a drawcard for Santa Maria. This peaceful island has terraced vineyards at Maia and, fairly uniquely for the Azores, a white sandy beach at Praia Formosa.

Kids' top 10: The Algarve

1 Discover beach heaven at Lagos, exploring the small, sheltered bay of Praia de Dona Ana, hemmed in by cinnamon-coloured sandstone cliffs, or revel in the space of 4-km-long Meia Praia, the Algarve's longest beach. A short distance to the east of Lagos, the combination of golden beach and lively nightlife at Portimão's Praia da Rocha will appeal to teenagers.

2 Cruise through the myriad waterways of the Parque Natural da Ria Formosa (ilha-deserta.com), spotting birds and collecting shells on a deserted island. Alternatively, explore the reserve on foot by walking the 3.2-km São Lourenço nature trail across saltwater marshes and lagoons.

3 Snorkel in the shallows off Albufeira's Praia da São Rafael, a beautiful sandy bay surrounded by cliffs and rock formations riddled with caves. Located in front of the old quarter of Albufeira, Praia dos Barcos is renowned for its fleet of colourful fishing boats.

4 Surf on the Atlantic coast at Praia do Armado, Carrapateira, or seek out calmer waters in the rock pools at low tide.

5 Paddle a canoe on the Alvor Estuary (outdoor-tours.net), hauling out on a tidal sandbank for a game of beach volleyball and a swim.

6 Ride a high-speed RIB (rigid inflatable boat) out of the marina at either Lagos or Portimão in search of dolphins, orcas and sharks. Dolphin Seafaris (dolphinseafaris.com) offers daily 90-minute trips.

7 Stalk the battlements of Silves Castle, a Moorish stronghold built on the site of a Roman fort, and then visit the excellent Museu Arqueológico in the town below.

8 Sail in search of smugglers' caves aboard the *Santa Bernada* (santa-bernada.com), a replica of a 500-year-old Portuguese *caravela*.

9 Plan a day at the park, taking your pick from theme parks like Zoomarine (zoomarine.com), A Cova dos Mouros (minacovamouros.sitepac.pt) and Krazy World (krazyworld.com) or waterparks such as Aqualand Algarve (aqualand.pt) near Alcantarilha.

10 Escape the crowds by heading north to Praia de Odeceixe, a stunning Atlantic beach that's perfect for sandcastle-building or a walk at low tide. Curling behind the beach, the estuary of the River Seixe is ideal for canoeing.

Birds in the Ria Formosa

Purple gallinule Rare moorhen-like bird.

Greater flamingo Mainly an autumn visitor.

Hoopoe (left) Look out for the crest and long bill.

Spain and Portugal essentials

When to go

If possible, try to visit Spain and Portugal during May, June or September to avoid the blistering heat and tourist crush of midsummer. In the south, you can often rely on decent weather as early as April or as late as October – although the sea will be warmer, particularly around the *Balearic Islands*, during the latter period. If you have no choice but to visit southern Spain in the peak summer season, remember that you can retreat to the mountains to escape excessive heat. The Atlantic-facing Costa de la Luz in *Andalucía* receives cooling breezes, as do parts of the *Algarve*. Despite the *Canary Islands'* celebrated year-round sunshine, the islands' geography does create local variations. For example, between late autumn and early spring you can experience frost in Tenerife's El Teide National Park during the morning and be sunbathing on Playa de las Américas by the afternoon. The south of the island is sunnier than the north where trade winds bring more cloud and rain. Generally speaking, though, the archipelago has enviable weather with ample sunshine, little rain and an average annual temperature of 23°C. In the *Azores*, locals will tell you to expect all four seasons in one day. In general, expect warm temperatures (up to 27°C in summer, dropping to around 13°C in winter) and a chance of rain in any month. Visit between May and September if you are keen to go whale-watching, sailing or fishing. Walking is good year-round, but to witness the islands' famous azaleas and hydrangeas in flower, June and July are best.

Getting there

One of the most inexpensive ways of reaching Spain or Portugal is by charter flight, although departure and arrival times are not always ideal. For **scheduled flights**, Iberia (iberia.com) has the most extensive network in the region. Starting prices (including taxes) for return flights from Heathrow include Bilbao (£88), Mallorca and Ibiza (£96), Madrid and Barcelona (£98), Alicante (£103) and Granada (£125). Iberia also flies from several regional airports in the UK, as well as Dublin and the United States. British Airways (britishairways.com) serves several destinations on the Iberian

Go green: three ways to skip the flight

▶▶ Sail across the Bay of Biscay from the UK to northern Spain. Services operate between Portsmouth and Bilbao with P&O Ferries (poferries.com) and between Plymouth and Santander with Brittany Ferries (brittany-ferries.co.uk).

▶▶ Take the train from London to Madrid or Barcelona, using Eurostar (eurostar.com) to Paris and then changing to a sleeper service to Spain. Bookings can be made online at Rail Europe (raileurope.co.uk).

▶▶ Catch a ferry from mainland Spain to the Balearics with Iscomar (iscomar.com) with departures from Barcelona, Valencia and Denia. Trasmediterránea (trasmediterranea.es) operates ferries to both the Balearic and Canary Islands. High-speed catamarans are used for the shorter routes, while on longer journeys the ferries have many of the facilities you'd expect on a cruise liner, such as a swimming pool, restaurants and cinema. Online bookings can be made with Direct Ferries (directferries.co.uk).

peninsula with return flights from Heathrow to Madrid, Barcelona or Lisbon costing from around £98. Expect to pay nearer £68 if you fly from Gatwick to Madrid or Barcelona. SATA Air Açores (sata.pt) operates a direct service from London Gatwick and Dublin to São Miguel in the Azores, as well as flights from Lisbon, Madeira, Toronto, Boston and Montreal. For **budget flights** to Spain and Portugal you're spoilt for choice, with a wide range of UK regional airports covering the region. easyJet (easyjet.com) serves Madrid (from Bristol, Edinburgh, Gatwick, Liverpool and Luton), Bilbao (Stansted), Barcelona (Bristol, Gatwick, Luton, Liverpool, Newcastle and Stansted), Lisbon (Bristol, Gatwick, Liverpool and Luton), Faro (Bristol, East Midlands, Gatwick, Luton and Newcastle) and Funchal (Bristol and Stansted) in addition to various routes to Alicante, Almeria, Ibiza, Mahon, Malaga, Murcia and Palma. Ryanair (ryanair.com) has an equally comprehensive network with flights to Alicante, Almeria, Barcelona, Faro, Feurteventura, Jerez, Madrid, Malaga, Murcia, Palma, Santander, Tenerife and Valencia. Air Berlin (airberlin.com) serves Barcelona, Malaga and Ibiza, while Thomsonfly (thomsonfly.com) has many flights to the

How much for a Big Mac?
UK   US$3.90
Spain and Portugal
    US$3.92
USA US$3.22

Fact file

	Time	Language	Money	Code	Tourist info
Spain	GMT +1 (Canary Islands GMT)	Spanish, Catalan, Basque, Galician	Euro (€) £1 = €1.50	+34	spain.info
Portugal	GMT (Azores GMT -1)	Portuguese	Euro (€) £1 = €1.50	+351	visitportugal.com

Balearic and Canaries, as well as to Alicante, Barcelona, Faro, Lisbon, Malaga and Valencia. Also try Clickair (clickair.com).

Getting around

Trains operated by RENFE (renfe.es) provide a high-speed service between Madrid and other cities such as Seville and Barcelona. **Buses** also provide a relatively efficient service between major towns in both Spain and Portugal, but you'll need to hire a **car** to explore off the main routes. Major car-hire companies are represented in most cities and airports, including Avis (avis.com), Europcar (europcar.com) and Hertz (hertz.com). Unless you take organized coach trips, car hire is also essential for getting around the Balearics, Canaries and Azores. In the Balearics, regular inter-island **ferry** services are operated by Trasmediterránea (see above). Island hopping in the Canary Islands is possible with frequent connections by plane, ferry and jetfoil. All islands in the Azores are linked by the domestic airline SATA (see above) and Transmaçor ferries (transmacor.pt).

Accommodation

You can choose from a vast range of accommodation in Spain and Portugal, from family hotels, luxury resorts and villas to apartments, farmstays and holiday villages. One of the most economical options for families is to rent a **rural house** (*casa rurale*) where you can expect to pay around €400 per week

Gaudí's playful designs (seen above at Parc Güell) can be appreciated by adults and mini-travellers alike.

for a simple village property to €1000-plus for something more luxurious with a pool and gardens. Try Colours of Spain (coloursofspain.com) for an online directory, or book through regional associations such as RAAR (raar.es) in Andalucía; Ruralia (ruralia.com) in Asturias; and Ruralverd (ruralverd.com) in Catalonia. Casas Cantabricas (casa.co.uk) offers self-catering properties and small, family-run hotels in northern Spain, Pyrenees Accommodation (pyreneesaccommodation.com) has a selection of family hotels in the Spanish Pyrenees and Inns of the Canary Islands (innsofcanaryislands.com) has a portfolio of character accommodation on Tenerife and other islands in the Canaries. For **city breaks**, try Madrid B&B (madridbandb.com) for two- and three-bedroom apartments in Spain's capital, Loving Barcelona (lovingbarcelona.com) for apartments in Catalonia's trendy urban hot spot and Hotel Real Palacio (realpalaciohotel.com) for a central location and good children's facilities in Lisbon. For **seaside villas** with pools, try James Villa Holidays (jamesvillas.co.uk) which offers properties in Mallorca and the Algarve from as little as €440 per villa. Meon Villas (meonvillas.co.uk) and Simply Travel (simplytravel.co.uk) also have a good selection. To make your money go even further, book a **package** with an operator like First Choice (firstchoice.co.uk) or Thomson Holidays (thomson.co.uk).

   Camping is another excellent option for the budget-conscious. Canvas Holidays (canvasholidays.co.uk/), Camping Life (campinglife.co.uk), Eurocamp (eurocamp.com), Keycamp (keycamp.com) and Siblu (siblu.com) represent all the region's best sites.

Tour operators

In the UK

The Adventure Company adventurecompany.co.uk
Club Med clubmed.com
Eurocamp eurocamp.com
Families Worldwide familiesworldwide.co.uk
First Choice Holidays firstchoice.co.uk
Freewheel Holidays freewheelholidays.com
Headwater headwater.com
Individual Travellers individualtravellers.com
Keycamp keycamp.com
Mark Warner markwarner.co.uk
Portuguese Affair portugueseaffair.com
Powder Byrne powderbyrne.com
Siblu siblu.com
Spanish Affair spanishaffair.com
Sunvil sunvil.co.uk
Thomson Holidays thomson.co.uk

In the USA

Abercrombie and Kent abercrombiekent.com
Adventures by Disney abd.disney.go.com
Tauck Bridges family-travel.tauck.com
Thomson Family Adventures familyadventures.com

How much to offset your emissions?

From London to:
Bilbao £1.67
Barcelona £1.99
Madrid £2.15
Palma de Mallorca £2.31
Valencia £2.28
Alicante £2.49
Lisbon £2.64
Seville £2.72
Malaga £2.81
Madeira £4.07
Lanzarote £4.48
Fuerteventura £4.58
Tenerife £4.72
Gran Canaria £4.75

From New York to:
Lisbon US$23.80
Gran Canaria US$24
Madrid US$25.50
Bilbao US$25.75
Barcelona US$25.75

Eight family favourites

Torrandell

Where? Puerto Pollenca, Mallorca, Spain.

Why? Just 10 minutes' walk to a sandy beach, this four-bedroom villa (pictured below) is surrounded by beautiful gardens with olive and citrus trees, and boasts a 10-m pool with child-friendly steps. Babysitting is available on request, while older children will appreciate the Playstations.

How much? From €1160 per week, including car rental.

Contact Mallorca Farmhouses (mfh.co.uk).

Pine Cliffs Resort

Where? Albufeira, Algarve, Portugal.

Why? One of the most comprehensive resorts on the Algarve, Pine Cliffs offers a range of family-friendly accommodation options, such as two-bedroom apartments and three- to four-bedroom villas with private pools. The resort's special place for children aged six months to 12 years, Porto Pirata has two purpose-built wooden ships, a swimming pool, a separate pool for remote-control boats, a playground, bouncy castle, bicycle track, volleyball pitch and an 18-hole minigolf course.

How much? ITC Classics (itcclassics.co.uk) offers a week's B&B for two adults and one child from around €3300 during peak season.

Contact pinecliffs.com.

La Manga Club

Where? Costa Calida, Spain.

Why? One of the world's best holiday destinations for active families, La Manga runs junior sports academies in golf, tennis, football, dance, rugby, karate and cricket. Other activities include mountain biking, scuba-diving, waterskiing, horse riding, sailing, quad-biking and kayaking.

How much? A two-bedroom View Apartment in the family-friendly Hyatt Las Lomas Village costs from around €150 per apartment per night.

Contact lamangaclub.com.

Hotel Presidente

Where? Portinatx, Ibiza, Spain.

Why? Located in a quiet, family-friendly part of Ibiza, away from the nightclubs, Hotel Presidente is surrounded by pine trees and overlooks an attractive beach. Some of the hotel's 270 rooms sleep four and there's also a free kids' club for three- to 12-year-olds.

How much? From around €2180 half board for one week in August with Thomson (thomson.co.uk), based on two adults and two children sharing a room.

Contact hotelpresidenteibiza.com.

Vila Vita Parc

Where? Alporchinhos, Algarve, Portugal.

Why? This stunning resort has a range of accommodation, including 30 family suites in the Oasis Parc section. Adults can enjoy the wellness centre, while children are taken care of in the crèche or kids' clubs. Activities for children include jeep tours, surf lessons, beach volleyball and trips to the local waterpark.

How much? From €320 per night for a family suite.

Contact vilavitahotels.com.

Cambrils Park

Where? Salou, Costa Daurada, Spain.

Why? This beautifully landscaped holiday park (pictured above) has a fantastic pool complex with waterslides and squirting elephants! On-site facilities include tennis, football, minigolf and a Tiger Club for five- to 12-year-olds, while the beach (800 m away) has a range of watersports. Self-catering is a piece of cake thanks to the park's bakery and supermarket, and there's also a restaurant and takeaway for eating out.

How much? From €450, based on two adults and up to three children sharing a two-bedroom Esprit+ holiday home for seven nights.

Contact siblu.com.

Casa Villalobos

Where? Coín, Andalucía, Spain.

Why? Surrounded by gently rolling hills, Casa Villalobos suits families in search of a rural hideaway that's also within easy range of the coast (Marbella is just 25 minutes away). Sleeping up to six, the villa has a swimming pool and basketball area, while grapes, figs and oranges can be harvested, in season, from the garden.

How much? From around €1125 per week to rent.

Contact spanishaffair.com.

Finca el Almendrillo

Where? Granada, Andalucía, Spain.

Why? Set in beautiful countryside with mountain views, Finca el Almendrillo is well placed for visiting either Granada or the coast. Superbly equipped for parents with babies or toddlers, you'll find everything from high chairs, baby baths and nappy bins to stair gates and sterilizers. There's also a fenced-off pool, an enclosed courtyard for riding bikes and even some pet rabbits and chickens. Older kids will appreciate the mountain bikes, table football and horse riding.

How much? The whole *finca* (sleeps 20) is available for rent from €2250 per week. Alternatively, you can rent just the farmhouse (sleeps 16) for €1650 per week or the *casita* (sleeps eight) for €750 per week.

Contact babyfriendlyboltholes.co.uk.

Food and drink

Eating out is a family affair in Spain and Portugal and it's not unusual to see children in restaurants late at night. Some highly salted dishes are not advisable for babies and toddlers, but that still leaves plenty of choice – particularly if you pick and mix from a tapas menu with its breads, dips and other goodies. Some regional specialities to tempt adventurous children include *botifarra amb mongetes* (Catalan sausages and white beans), *gazpacho* (chilled tomato soup), *tortilla Española* (a thick potato and onion omelette), *frango assado com piri-piri* (a spicy chicken dish from the Algarve), *leitão à bairrada* (roasted suckling pig, popular in Portugal) and *empanadas* (pastry parcels stuffed with tuna or ham). Don't forget to try *paella*, Spain's famous seafood and rice dish.

Health and safety

Spain and Portugal are generally safe countries to visit. Make sure you have adequate travel and medical insurance and that your routine vaccinations are up to date. The European Health Insurance Card (EHIC) entitles you to emergency medical treatment. Drinking water is safe and standards of food hygiene are generally good. Be wary, however, of tapas dishes that may have been left out for a while or reheated.

The one that didn't get away. Catching lizards requires patience and stealth! Remember to handle them gently and put them back where you found them.

Spain's golden beaches are a major drawcard for families in search of some sun and warm seas: Fuerteventura in the Canary Islands (**top**); and Tossa de Mar on the Costa Brava (**above**).

Kids' top 10: tapas nibbles

Almendras Fried and salted almonds.
Calamares fritos Squid rings and tentacles dusted with flour and fried in olive oil.
Chorizo Sausage flavoured with paprika and garlic.
Costillas Spare ribs.
Croquetas Deep fried croquettes made with chopped ham, chicken or fish.
Diabolitos picantes Spicy mini hamburgers.
Gambas a la plancha Grilled prawns.
Soldaditos de Pavia Cod fingers fried in batter.
Patatas bravas Fried potatoes with a spicy red sauce.
Tortilla Española Potato and onion omelette.

Pollença, Puerto Pollença, Deia, Soller, Valldemossa, Cas Concos and Cala Dor

An exclusive portfolio of rustic farmhouses, cottage hideaways and elegant villas can be found in superior locations across Mallorca. From the unspoilt south east corner of Santanyi and Cas Concos to the much sought after regions of Andratx and Deia in the dramatic west as well as Pollenca in the north east and the beautiful bay of Puerto Pollenca.

Properties have been chosen to suit all tastes and requirements, from the 400 year old traditional "fincas", which have been transformed into lavish country homes, to a restored 19th century windmill, and newly built grand mansion houses with interior décor to match.

With a range of leisure interests from trekking, cycling and horse-riding to hang-gliding, wine-tasting and hot air ballooning, guests can enjoy a slower pace of life with our baby sitters, chef service and luxury hampers.

+44 (0) 845 800 8080
Book online www.mfh.co.uk

ABTA No W3809

Italy

Pigeons in the piazza – flights of fancy in St Mark's Square, Venice.

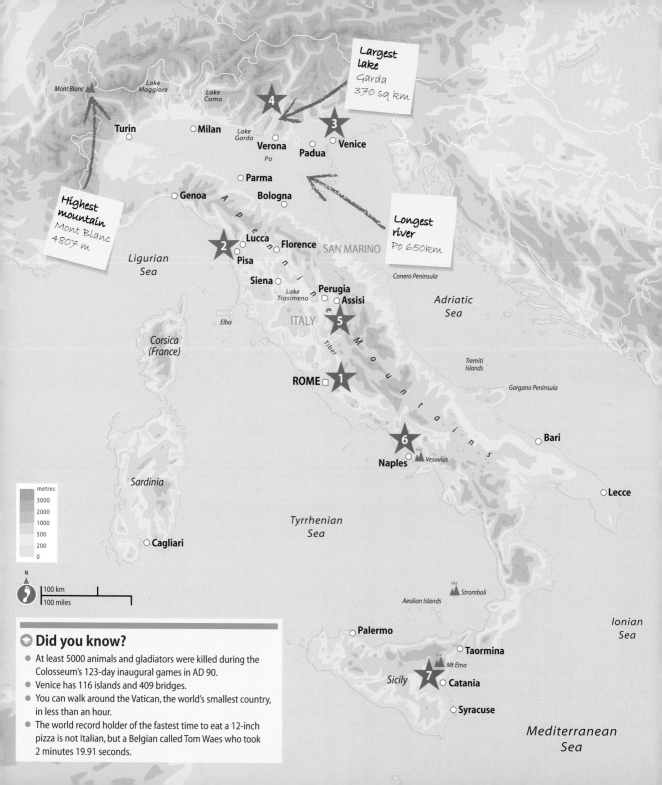

Mont Blanc ▲

Lake Maggiore

Lake Como

Turin ●

Milan ○

Lake Garda

★ 4

★ 3

Verona ●

Padua ●

Venice ○

Po

Largest lake
Garda
370 sq km

Highest mountain
Mont Blanc
4807 m

Parma ○

Genoa ●

Bologna ○

Longest river
Po 650km

Lucca ○

Florence ●

SAN MARINO

★ 2

Pisa ●

Ligurian Sea

Siena ○

A p e n n i n e

Conero Peninsula

Lake Trasimeno

Perugia ○

Assisi ○

ITALY

★ 5

Adriatic Sea

Elba

Corsica (France)

Tiber

M o u n t a i n s

Tremiti Islands

ROME □ ★ 1

Gargano Peninsula

Bari ●

★ 6

Naples ●

Vesuvius ▲

Lecce ○

Sardinia

metres
3000
2000
1000
500
200
0

Tyrrhenian Sea

Cagliari ●

N

100 km
100 miles

Stromboli ▲

Aeolian Islands

Ionian Sea

Palermo ○

Taormina ○

Mt Etna ▲

★ 7

Sicily

Catania ○

Syracuse ○

Mediterranean Sea

Did you know?

- At least 5000 animals and gladiators were killed during the Colosseum's 123-day inaugural games in AD 90.
- Venice has 116 islands and 409 bridges.
- You can walk around the Vatican, the world's smallest country, in less than an hour.
- The world record holder of the fastest time to eat a 12-inch pizza is not Italian, but a Belgian called Tom Waes who took 2 minutes 19.91 seconds.

⭐ Discover how ancient Romans lived
▸ Rome, page 144

⭐ See the Leaning Tower of Pisa
▸ Tuscany, page 146

⭐ Explore the canals of Venice
▸ Venice, page 148

⭐ Swim and sail on Lake Garda
▸ The Lakes, page 150

⭐ Go medieval in a hill town
▸ Umbria and Le Marche, page 152

⭐ Relive the days of Pompeii
▸ Naples, page 154

⭐ Stand on an active volcano
▸ Sicily, page 155

Introduction

It's one of those places you have to visit at least once in a lifetime – but should you leave Italy until the kids are older and more likely to appreciate its cultural and historical treasures? Of course not! Kids love Italy, and Italians love kids. Not only are the locals balmy about *bambinos*, but they also know a trick or two when it comes to feeding them. With a staple diet of pizza, pasta and pastries (supplemented, of course, with copious *gelato*), your children should have more than enough energy for at least a taster of Rome, Florence or Venice (Italy's triumphant trio of World Heritage cities). Don't be bamboozled into thinking you've got to see all the museums and ancient sites, and pay homage to every Michelangelo masterpiece – experiencing Italy has just as much to do with spending an afternoon in a piazza, lingering over lunch, playing around the fountain and, you guessed it, pillaging the local *gelato* parlour. Beyond the cities, Italy's beautiful countryside encompasses rolling hills, mountains and lakes – perfect for a relaxed break in a villa with a pool. There's no shortage of beaches for more traditional family holidays, while locations like Naples and Sicily add a bit of spark to sightseeing days, courtesy of Vesuvius and Mt Etna.

❝❞ *Italian piazzas are great places to go with kids. They're lined with restaurants, and a lot are car-free so the kids can run around in safety – and in view – while parents enjoy a drink or a meal. We always found waiters happy to make space for high chairs, which most restaurants had.*
Jason Hobbins

Italy rating
Wow factor
★★★
Worry factor
★
Value for money
★★★
Keeping teacher happy
★★★★★
Family accommodation
★★★★★
Babies & toddlers
★★★★
Teenagers
★★★

🔍 How to make a mosaic

‣ Study examples of Roman mosaics in books and on websites.

‣ Decide on the picture or pattern you want to create. Roman mosaics often featured animals or geometric designs.

‣ Draw your design on to card.

‣ Cut up small pieces of coloured paper, magazines or comics. Sort them into colour groups.

‣ Stick them on to your design, thinking carefully about where you place the colours to highlight the details of your design.

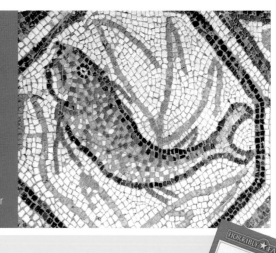

Books to read

Mr Benn – Gladiator, Andersen Press, 2005
Mr Benn's adventures always see him visiting a costume shop, choosing an outfit and then travelling to that era via a special door. This time Mr Benn turns gladiator. But can the gentle character steel himself to join in with such violent games? Ages 4+

Zoe Sophia's Scrapbook: An Adventure in Venice, Chronicle Books, 2006
Zoe Sophia and her dog, Mickey, embark on the adventure of a lifetime when they visit great aunt Dorothy in Venice. Zoe's scrapbook brings the enchantment of Venice to life, with its gondolas and glassblowers. But when Mickey gets lost in the maze of canals, the excitement really begins. Ages 6+

I Am Spartapuss, Spartapuss Tales Series, Mogzilla, 2005
This humorous series is set in Rome in AD 36, when the mighty Feline Empire ruled the world! Spartapuss, a ginger cat, becomes imprisoned by the evil emperor Catligula and is finally released into a school for gladiators. Spartapuss must fight and win his freedom in the Arena – before his opponents make dog food out of him! Ages 8+

Julius Caesar and His Foul Friends, Horribly Famous Series, Scholastic, 2006
Find out what Julius Caesar is horribly famous for in this foul fact feast – how he conquered copious countries, was once captured by pirates and who his back-stabbing chums were. Ages 8+

Pompeii – The Day a City Was Buried, DK Discoveries, 1998
A beautifully illustrated account of the life and people of Pompeii, a city in southern Italy destroyed during the eruption of Mount Vesuvius in AD 79. Information includes life in Roman Pompeii, as well as the destruction of the city and its subsequent rediscovery. Fascinating drawings and photographs of artefacts discovered at the site are featured. Ages 8-12

Leonardo da Vinci, Eyewitness Guide, Dorling Kindersley, 2006
A detailed look at the Renaissance period, revealing fascinating facts about the great artist as well as giving an in-depth view of everyday life in an Italian city state. Ages 9+

Top 30 gelato flavours

Know your *ananas* from your bananas with this guide to popular *gelato* flavours.

- *Albiocca* apricot
- *Ananas* pineapple
- *Bacio* chocolate with hazelnut pieces
- *Banana* banana
- *Caffe* coffee
- *Ciliega* cherry
- *Cioccolato* chocolate
- *Cocco* coconut
- *Cocomero* watermelon
- *Crema* egg-yolk custard
- *Fragola* strawberry
- *Frutti di bosco* wild berries
- *Lampone* raspberry
- *Limone* lemon
- *Macedonia* fruit salad
- *Malaga* raisin
- *Mandarino* tangerine
- *Mela* apple
- *Menta* mint
- *Mirtillo* blueberry
- *Nocciola* hazelnut
- *Panna* whipped cream
- *Pera* pear
- *Pesca* peach
- *Pistacchio* pistachio
- *Pompelmo* grapefruit
- *Stracciatella* chocolate chip
- *Tarocchio* blood orange
- *Tiramisu* tiramisu
- *Vaniglia* vanilla

Taste of Italy: pizza

Pizzas are plentiful throughout Italy, and making them from scratch at home is a lot simpler than you might think.

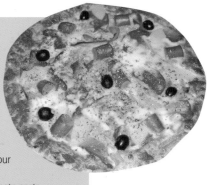

What you need

For the base:
- ➤➤ 1 tsp dried yeast
- ➤➤ 1 tsp sugar
- ➤➤ ½ cup warm water
- ➤➤ 1 cup plain flour

For the toppings:
- ➤➤ Tomato sauce such as passata or tomato paste
- ➤➤ Grated cheese
- ➤➤ Favourites toppings such as tuna, ham, mushrooms, sweetcorn, olives and pineapple

What to do

- ➤➤ Mix the yeast, sugar and water. Leave to rest in a warm place for about 10 minutes (until the yeast and sugar has dissolved).
- ➤➤ Add flour and mix to make a firm dough, adding extra flour if required.
- ➤➤ Roll out to make your pizza base.
- ➤➤ Bake for about 10 minutes at 180°C.
- ➤➤ Spread the tomato sauce over the base and then add the grated cheese and other toppings.
- ➤➤ Bake for 10-15 minutes at 180°C depending on the thickness of the base.

♠ How to play Camicia

You can play this Italian card game with a normal set of 52 cards, or use an Italian pack (often 40 cards). This is a game of pure luck for two players. The aces, twos and threes are the attack cards (suits are ignored).

- ➤➤ Deal out the cards evenly.
- ➤➤ Players take turns to place their top card face-up in a pile on the table. If the card is 'normal', no action is taken and play passes to the other player.
- ➤➤ When an 'attack' card is played by one of the players, the other player has to add to the exposed pile the number of cards corresponding to the face value of the attack card – that is one card for an ace, two cards for a two, and three cards for a three.
- ➤➤ If all the cards played in response to an attack are normal, the attacking player takes the pile of played cards and adds them to his or her hand. If one of the cards played in response to an attack is an attack card itself, the former attack is finished, and the new attack takes place.

One to watch

The Lizzie McGuire Movie (Walt Disney Home Entertainment, 2003) Lizzie McGuire and her best friends have just graduated from middle school and they're taking part in a class trip to Rome. Once there, Lizzie finds herself caught up in an Italian teen-pop idol triangle and things are made worse when her family gets wind of her new-found fame and catch the next flight to Italy.

Tots to teens

Kids are welcome everywhere in Italy. You will have no problem getting them to adapt to the local cuisine (assuming, of course, they like pizza, pasta and ice cream), while accommodation ranges across the entire family-friendly spectrum, from campsites and holiday villages to beach resorts and self-catering villas. If there's one potential 'fly in the *gelato*' it's that major tourist attractions can become very crowded and unbearably hot during the summer – so try not to overdo the sightseeing.

Babies (0-18 months)

Italy promises a well-earned rest for new parents. Most hotels offer babysitting if you arrange it in advance, but a far more relaxing alternative is to rent a villa. Self-catering might not sound like much of a rest, but it suits a lot of new parents desperate to maintain feeding and sleeping routines. If renting a car, check that the safety standards of any children's seats provided are up to scratch or, better still, consider bringing your own. Don't forget sunshades for car windows. With a baby in tow you're unlikely to want to embark on an ambitious sightseeing tour of Rome (in fact, you'd be wise to avoid all Italian cities during the fierce heat of midsummer). However, even a modest medieval town in Tuscany can reduce you to a gibbering wreck trying to cajole a pushchair along its cobbled streets and pavements. To preserve sanity, take an all-terrain three-wheeler buggy or a backpack-style baby carrier.

Toddlers/pre-school (18 months-4 years)

That villa with a pool still sounds very tempting with children of this age. However, you do need to be extra-vigilant about pool safety: holiday villages may well have fenced-off pools and lifeguards on duty; private villas may well not. For a seaside holiday, Italy has no end of lovely beaches to choose from, especially in Sicily, while the northern Lakes offer a freshwater alternative (just remember to pack jelly shoes for the kids so they can negotiate the pebbly beaches). Historical and cultural sights are always a challenge with children of this age. The concepts of queuing, keeping quiet in cathedrals and art galleries, staying behind security barriers and not mauling priceless works of art are all completely alien to them. This doesn't necessarily mean that your Italian sojourn need be culturally bereft. Car-free city *piazzas* can provide toddlers with (supervised) freedom while you admire the façades of the *duomo* (cathedral) or the *palazzo*. And you can always take it in turns to sightsee – one parent entertains the kids while the other snatches an hour or two of Bernini browsing.

Kids/school age (4-12 years)

In Italy, vast swathes of the school curriculum come to life. Few places are more synonymous with famous artists, brilliant minds and ancient cultures. The food is an education in itself; the language is fun to learn; and to top it all, Italy scores top marks on the geography front, with everything from volcanoes to vast limestone caverns. There is a downside though. Few museums and galleries have the special children's facilities or activities that you find in northern Europe. Nor is there much in the way of hands-on science centres. A few cunning museum strategies (see box right) will help keep things interesting for children. At this age they at least have the potential to enjoy a full day's sightseeing; and if

Top right: Smoothly paved piazzas are a piece of cake when it comes to pushchairs – unlike the cobbled streets that lead in and out of them. **Below right**: From Tuscan villas to Lake Garda, Italy is full of excuses for a cooling dip.

What about Sardinia?

A beautiful island with a rugged interior smothered in herb-scented *macchia* and a shoreline alternating between isolated coves and long sandy beaches, Sardinia makes a superb family-holiday destination – whether you like to hike and bike or flop on a beach.

There's plenty of family accommodation available, from country villas to coastal hotels like Forte Village where kids can be kept happily occupied without you ever needing to leave the resort. It would be a shame, however, not to track down at least one of Sardinia's quirky *nuraghe* (ancient stone structures dating from 1800 to 300 BC) that you will find dotted around the island. The Museo Archeologico Nazionale in Sardinia's capital, Cagliari, provides an insight into the people who created them.

As for the best beaches, they are not just confined to the exclusive Costa Smeralda in the northeast. Look to the northwest and to the east near Cala Gonone for equally enticing coves and aquamarine waters. At the latter don't forget to take a boat trip to the famous Grotta del Bue Marino.

not then you can always resort to bribery (a double scoop of *gelato* for the *duomo* and we'll throw in a waterpark for the Renaissance exhibition). Don't forget, though, that there is far more to Italy's heritage than shuffling around daunting museums and galleries. Most kids will leap at the challenge of climbing the steps to the top of a medieval bell tower, while sites like Pompeii and the Colosseum instantly ignite a child's imagination. And then, of course, there's all the purely fun stuff, from theme-park rides at Gardaland in northern Italy to snorkelling in the crystal-clear coves of Sicily.

Teenagers (13 years+)
Although sometimes a little too far off the beaten track for their liking, villas are still a good option for teens – particularly if they bring along a friend or two. Holiday parks and resorts, with their clubs and activities, are also a good bet. Pick a location that provides a couple of teen mainstays, such as a city for shopping and nightlife and a beach or lake for watersports and chilling out. As for sightseeing, you might find that teenagers are more in tune with their iPods than the Italian Renaissance. If it's 'wow factor' they need, concentrate on the big sights in Venice and Rome. The Adventure Company (adventurecompany.co.uk) and Explore Worldwide (explore.co.uk) offer teenage departures on their trips to Italy.

Special needs
An increasing number of hotels, restaurants, monuments and galleries are installing facilities, such as ramps and lifts, to assist wheelchair users. CO IN Sociale (coinsociale.it) provides information and assistance for disabled travellers in Rome. For excellent advice on accessible travel around Venice, try Informahandicap Venezi (comune.venezia.it) which provides several ideas for 'itineraries without barriers'.

Single parents
Eurocamp (eurocamp.co.uk), Keycamp (keycamp.ie) and Siblu (siblu.com) offer special deals for single parents at their holiday camps in Italy.

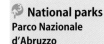

How to make art museums fun for kids
➡ Head straight for the gift shop, buy some postcards showing the exhibits and then challenge children to find the actual paintings and sculptures.
➡ Check at the ticket office whether it's okay for kids to take a sketchbook and pencil into the museum with them.
➡ Pick a couple of straightforward themes (such as horses and angels) and challenge kids to spot five or 10 of each before moving on to the next gallery.

National parks
Parco Nazionale d'Abruzzo
(parcoabruzzo.it) Rarities in this spectacular mountain sanctuary include Apennine wolf, brown bear, chamois and white-backed woodpecker. Pescasseroli is the main centre, while the forests surrounding Lake Barrea promise excellent hiking and pony trekking.

Parco Nazionale del Gran Paradiso
(granparadiso.net) Italy's foremost protected area, in the alpine region of Valle d'Aosta, provides refuge to ibex, golden eagle and marmot. The resort of Cogne is a good base from which to explore.

Parco Nazionale dei Monti Sibillini
(sibillini.net) Mountain biking, trekking, horse riding and guided tours are available in this Apennine park located in Umbria (see page 152).

Those about to sightsee, we salute you!

Touring Rome with kids requires a gladiatorial effort. It's a hot, sprawling, chaotic city packed with ancient monuments, museums, churches and galleries. Throw in the Vatican and it will feel like two city breaks rolled into one. But before you sidestep Italy's vibrant capital, just think what you will be missing: Michelangelo's Sistine Chapel ceiling, the Pantheon, the Roman Forum, the Colosseum… kids will feel like time travellers as they explore these historical icons. Just make sure you don't enslave them in a non-stop history lesson – Rome's lighter side (*gelato*, fountains, parks, shopping, etc) will help to ensure your conquest of the city is enjoyable as well as informative.

City highlights

» The 3-day Roma Pass (romapass.it) provides free admission to the first 2 museums and/or archaeological sites visited and full access to public transport.
» Bring binoculars so kids can see the details on the ceiling of the Sistine Chapel.
» For further information, visit romaturismo.it and vatican.va.

Three-day action plan

Day 1   Start with the Colosseum. It opens at 0900 and can be reached by Metro Line B to Colosseo station, as well as by bus or tram. It's not only big and impressive, but it's the one sight in Rome that children are most likely to relate to – especially teenagers who have watched Russell Crowe strut his stuff in *Gladiator*. You can join an organized tour or explore the ruins on your own. Be sure to stand centre stage where warriors, slaves and wild beasts engaged in deadly combat nearly 2000 years ago. Try to imagine the roar of the 70,000-strong crowd, and don't miss the maze of tunnels and pens where lions, tigers and other animals were held prior to the slaughter. About 200 cats still prowl the Colosseum – challenge your kids to see how many they can spot.

Now that your children are fired up about ancient Rome, take them to see the adjacent Roman Forum (Foro Romano), a patchwork of ruined triumphal arches, basilicas and temples that once formed the city's civic and ceremonial heart. You can access it from Via Dei Fori Imperiali,

but kids will grasp the layout better if you walk up the small hill behind the Colosseum and enter the Forum by the Arch of Titus on Via Sacra – the street along which victorious commanders paraded their spoils of war. Don't even attempt to see everything in the Forum. By now it will be approaching midday and you'll be getting hot and hungry. Make a beeline for the House of the Vestal Virgins and the vaulted Basilica of Constantine and Maxentius, then hop in a taxi or bus (or walk if you have the energy) to Piazza Navona. Built around three flamboyant Baroque fountains, this beautiful square is lined with palaces and pavement cafés, and is usually bustling with street performers and artists. It's a great place to boost your children's energy levels – aided, no doubt, by *tartufo*, a chocolate ice cream, fudge and cherry concoction served at Tre Scalini. From Piazza Navona, it's a short walk to the Pantheon, the best-preserved ancient building in Rome, where kids will be intrigued to discover an 8.3-m-wide hole (or *oculus*) in the dome. From the Pantheon, take bus route 116 to Villa Borghese, a large park where kids can rent bikes and boats or ride ponies – just rewards for all that sightseeing earlier in the day.

Day 2   By now, the Vatican City will seem irresistible, but you're risking cultural overload (and rebellion) by taking kids to the city state straight after a day hotfooting it around ancient Rome. Save the Vatican for your third day and keep day two relatively

laid-back. Teenagers may want to check out the big names in haute couture along Via Conditti or scour Via del Corso for anything from CDs to shoes. Nearby is the famous Trevi Fountain which is particularly beautiful when floodlit at night. Don't forget to toss a coin into the fountain, throwing it over your shoulder to ensure a safe return visit to the 'Eternal City'. A little further north, the rococo monument of the Spanish Steps (ablaze with azaleas in May) is another popular spot from which to soak up the city's atmosphere. The best *gelato* in the Trevi neighbourhood is at San Crispino on Via della Panettaria, while pick of the pizzas can be found at Pizzeria da Ricci on Via Genova. Afterwards, assuming you can stomach it, wander over to the Capuchin Crypt on Via Veneto where the bones of dead monks adorn the walls. Alternatively, for something equally macabre, head south along Via Appia Antica to visit the Catacombs (catacombe.roma.it) – a labyrinth of cemeteries where roughly hewn and dimly lit corridors are lined with tomb niches. Some, like the Catacombs of San Domitilla, still contain human bones.

Day 3   The Vatican might only cover an area of 43 ha, but what the world's smallest state lacks in size it more than makes up for with historical, cultural and

Above: The giant hand of Constantine. **Top right**: Colosseum. **Below right**: Trevi Fountain.

Bottom: Michelangelo's *Pietà*. **Left (above and below):** St Peter's; interior of the dome.
Above: St Peter's Square from the great church. **Below right:** Tivoli Gardens.

religious esteem. The quickest way to get there is by Metro Line A to Ottaviano San Pietro, from where it's a short walk to St Peter's Square. This vast papal-audience ground is flanked by the 284 columns of Bernini's Colonnade (great for hide and seek) and punctuated at its centre by an obelisk brought from Egypt in AD 37. But inevitably you will be drawn towards the massive façade of St Peter's Basilica, the world's largest church. Doors open daily at 0700, but you won't be allowed inside wearing sleeveless tops, shorts or above-knee-length skirts. Suitably attired, steer your children towards the first nave on the right where Michelangelo's exquisite marble carving, *Pietà*, depicts a grief-stricken Mary cradling the crucified body of Jesus. For children, one of the highlights of a visit to the Vatican is to climb St Peter's 136.5-m-high dome from where there are superb views across the rooftops of Rome. You can take a lift part of the way, but that still leaves you with 330 steps.

By now your kids will be developing a healthy respect for Michelangelo (St Peter's dome was his design), but if there's one 'Michelangelo masterstroke' that you've simply got to show them, it has to be the ceiling art of the Sistine Chapel. To reach it you need to

navigate the immense art treasury of the Vatican Museums. It's a 20-minute walk from the entrance of the museum complex to the Sistine Chapel without even pausing to admire the wealth of Roman antiquities and Renaissance paintings. What, if anything, you decide to linger over will depend on how your children are bearing up and how much queuing you've had to endure. Ultimately, though, those nine colourful scenes from Genesis (which took Michelangelo four painstaking years to complete, mostly while lying on his back at the top of a scaffold) are usually enough to lift the eyes and the spirits of even the most jaded child.

Best of the rest

Galleria Borghese
(galleriaborghese.it) This small museum in the Villa Borghese gardens contains an exceptional collection of Bernini sculptures, as well as paintings by Raphael and Caravaggio. Reserve tickets in advance.

Musei Capitolini Located on Capitoline Hill, these two magnificent museums contain some of Rome's greatest treasures. In Palazzo Nuovo, look out for the famous sculpture of the Dying Galatian and the original 2nd-century, bronze statue of Emperor Marcus Aurelius astride his horse (a replica is in the star-shaped *piazza* between the two museums). In the Palazzo dei Conservatori kids will be wowed by the outsize body parts from the Colossus of Constantine and intrigued by the bronze, *Lo Spinario*, which depicts a boy trying to remove a thorn from his foot.

Museo Nazionale Romano Split into two sites, the National Museum of Rome houses outstanding Classical art, including the mosaic of the *Four Charioteers*.

City escapes

Tivoli Located 28 km east of the city, this country escape for ancient Romans has temples and gardens, but is best known for nearby Hadrian's Villa, a lovely place to picnic or explore.

Acquapiper (aquapiper.it) Cool relief from city sightseeing, this waterpark is located on the road to Tivoli.

Lake Bracciano This large crater lake set in beautiful countryside to the northwest of Rome is ideal for a refreshing swim during summer.

Fancy Florence? Or leaning towards Pisa?

A beautiful Tuscan villa set amongst cypress trees and vineyards, a day or two marvelling at the art treasures of Florence and a lazy tour between historic hilltop towns like San Gimignano. No wonder Tuscany is one of Italy's best-loved destinations. But won't kids find it too sophisticated? Or just plain boring? Not if the villa has a pool and you transform your 'cultural forays' into an adventure trail of medieval streets to be explored, bell towers to be conquered and *gelato* to be sampled.

Regional highlights

» Trains are quick and efficient, but a hire car is the best way to explore Tuscany's backroads and hill towns.
» The compact city centre of Florence is easily explored on foot.
» Siena's Palio horse race takes place on 2 Jul and 16 Aug.
» For further information, log on to firenzeturismo.it, terresiena.it, pisaturismo.it. and lucca.turismo.toscana.it.

Siena At 102 m in height, the Torre del Mangia is one of the tallest medieval towers in Italy. Challenge your kids to climb the 505 steps to the top from where there are superb views across Siena's medieval maze of lanes and *piazzas*. Afterwards, relax with a picnic on the Piazza del Campo – you can get supplies from the grocery store down Via di Salicotto. One of Europe's greatest public squares, the fan-shaped Campo has been used for everything from bullfights to executions, but it is now famed for its *Palio*, a fiercely contested bareback horse race that takes place twice a year. Nearby, the Piazza del Duomo is dominated by Siena's magnificent Gothic cathedral which contains sculptures by Michelangelo.

Pisa Italy's most instantly recognizable landmark, the Leaning Tower of Pisa (opapisa.it), has immense appeal to children. The ultimate stack of building blocks teetering on the brink of collapse, there's something intrinsically childlike about the eight-storey belfry. Recent engineering work stabilized the 12th-century wonky wonder, reducing

its lean to around 5 m from the vertical. It's now safe to climb the 294 steps to the top, but only as part of a 30-minute guided tour (minimum age eight). Most people contemplate the tower (and the splendid *duomo* and baptistry) from the green lawns of the Campo dei Miracoli – a lovely spot for a picnic. If your kids are crestfallen because they're too young to climb the tower, try to placate them with the medieval alternative in the northwest corner of the Campo – it's free and there's no age limit.

Lucca Founded by the Romans in 180 BC, Lucca's crowning glory is the 11th-century cathedral of San Martino – unless, of course, you're an opera fan in which case you will want to call in at Puccini's birthplace on Via di Poggio. Children on the other hand will be drawn to Lucca's massive 16th-century ramparts which encircle the town and are wide enough for you to walk or cycle on – a popular elevated circuit shaded by overhanging chestnut trees. To the northeast of Lucca, Collodi has a Pinocchio theme park (pinocchio.it) in recognition of the fact that Carlo Lorenzini penned the story of the wooden puppet here in 1881.

Best hill towns Children will feel like they've walked into a fairy tale (or a scene from *Lord of the Rings*) in San Gimignano (sangimignano.com). No fewer than 14 weather-beaten stone towers (originally there were 72) rear above a skyline that has remained largely unchanged since the Middle Ages. For the best views, scramble up the ramparts of the Rocca, a ruined 14th-century fortress tucked into the

Above: Siena – the tower and the view of Piazza del Campo from the top.
Left: Leaning Tower of Pisa.

eastern side of the town. Torre della Diavola (She-Devil's Tower) houses the Museo della Tortura, containing enough gruesome torture instruments to make kids squirm with delight.

In the far east of the region, Cortona (cortona.net) has all the sweeping views, medieval alleyways and Renaissance art that you'd expect from a Tuscan hill town. What sets it apart from the others, though, is its rich Etruscan heritage, evident in the many ancient tombs dotting the surrounding countryside. You can see artefacts from this early civilization, including an oil lamp dating back to the 5th century BC, in the Museo dell'Accademia Etrusca. Follow Via S Margherita to the Fortezza Medicae – the views towards Lake Trasimeno make it worth the steep climb. Other hill towns worth visiting include Montepulciano, Montalcino and Monteriggioni.

Best beaches Not far from Pisa or Lucca, the sandy beach resort of Viareggio has a promenade lined with cafés and shops. There's more sand to the north at Forte dei Marmi, while the best beaches on the island of Elba – reached by ferry from Piombino – are on the west coast.

Kids' top 10: Florence

1 Rise above it all by climbing the orange-tiled dome of the *duomo* (or adjacent campanile) for stupendous views and then, back at ground level, marvel at the famous bronze doors of the baptistry and the colourful Byzantine mosaics that decorate the ceiling above the font.

2 Plan a treasure hunt in the Uffizi (uffizi.firenze.it), ticking off at least one painting by each of the following masters: Leonardo da Vinci, Michelangelo, Botticelli, Bellini, Raphael, Rembrandt, Rubens, Van Dyck and Caravaggio. An extra scoop of *gelato* afterwards if you correctly identify *The Birth of Venus* by Botticelli.

3 Grapple with science at the Museo di Storia della Scienza (imss.fi.it) which not only features two of Galileo's telescopes, but also has demonstrations of his experiments on motion. Look out, too, for early maps and globes, and a gruesome collection of 19th-century surgical instruments. An interesting excursion from Florence, the Museo Leonardiano di Vinci (leonet.it) displays wooden models of some of da Vinci's famous inventions, from a flying machine to a tank.

4 Meet Michelangelo's *David*, a 5.2-m statue of the biblical hero who slayed Goliath. The original sculpture is in the Galleria dell'Accademia (where you'll have to pay and queue), so settle instead for the copy in Piazza della Signoria.

5 Reward yourself with *gelato* for every museum, art gallery, cathedral and church that mum or dad drag you into. One of the best *gelato* parlours in the city is Vivoli's on Via Isole delle Stinche, where only a triple scoop will do.

6 Indulge in a spot of window-shopping along Ponte Vecchi – the oldest surviving bridge in Florence (built in 1345) and famous for its antiques and jewellery shops.

7 Escape to Boboli Gardens for a game of hide-and-seek amongst the statues, box hedges and cypress trees – or find a shady spot for a picnic.

8 Browse the colourful stalls at Mercato Centrale for fruit, vegetables and flowers, as well as local Tuscan fare, like wild mushrooms, truffles and *porchetta* (roast suckling pig).

9 March over to the Museo Stibbert (museostibbert.it) where a spectacular column of armour-clad knights rides on horseback through a grand hall.

10 Don't stop at *gelato* when there are all kinds of other Florentine sweets and pastries to sample, such as *ricciarelli* (chewy honey and almond cakes dusted with powdered sugar) and *zuccotto* (sponge cake stuffed with chocolate mousse, sweets and nuts).

ITALY

Piazzas, palazzos and pigeons

It's going to be busy and expensive – and oppressively hot if you go in summer. And there might be the occasional fraught moment, cajoling your buggy up and down countless bridge steps, restraining your toddler from nose-diving into yet another canal or preventing teenagers from playing havoc with your holiday budget in all the fancy boutiques. But will any of this stop you from going? Of course not. Venice is irresistible – an exciting watery maze, a fantasy city of palaces and churches slowly sinking beneath the waves. Go there soon while it manages to keep its head above water.

Above: Gliding gondola.
Far left: Towering Campanile.

City highlights

🌊😎🎭🏛️🏰🚤🏛️

▸▸ Valid for 12 hrs, 2 days or a week, the Venice Card (venicecard.com) provides unlimited use of public transport, toilets and nurseries, as well as free admission to various museums, churches and cultural sites.
▸▸ Venice is joined to the mainland by a causeway, but the best way to arrive is by *vaporetto* (actv.it), a waterbus network linking the city to Marco Polo Airport, Punta Sabbioni (Cavallino), Santa Maria Elisabetta (Lido) and other islands in the lagoon.

How to avoid that sinking feeling

You could splash out on a converted palace, or even rent an apartment in Venice, but most budget-conscious families opt to stay outside the city. Curling out from the mainland towards the east of Venice, the Cavallino Peninsula (turismocavallino.it) – also known as the *Litorale del Cavallino* – makes an ideal family base. It's packed with holiday resorts, boasts a 15-km stretch of sandy beach and has one of Italy's top waterparks – Aqualandia (aqualandia.it). While waterslides and crazy golf might seem a million miles from your dreamy-eyed vision of Venice, don't underestimate their usefulness as a negotiating tool. The kids get a day at Aqualandia, but only after you've perused the art collections in the Doge's Palace or Accademia. As for reaching Venice, Cavallino is perfectly placed, with regular boats from Punta Sabbioni taking around 30 minutes to cruise to Ca' di Dio – a 10-minute walk from St Mark's Square.

One-day action plan The moment you stroll into Piazza San Marco (St Mark's Square) your children are likely to say one of three things:
▸▸ Can we feed the pigeons? No problem. Vendors sell bags of sweetcorn for €1.
▸▸ Can we climb up there? Yes. The views from the top of the 98.5-m Campanile are exhilarating, but be prepared to queue. Help kids pass the time by challenging them to count the arches in the Palazzo Ducale (Doge's Palace).
▸▸ Can we go on a gondola? Maybe. There's a gondola mooring at the edge of Piazza San Marco, but you'll pay a premium rate. For a quicker, cheaper, but less romantic option, *traghetto* gondolas shuttle back and forth across the Grand Canal.
Once you've fed the pigeons and conquered the Campanile, explore the warren of alleyways and canals between Piazza San Marco and Ponte di Rialto (Rialto Bridge), delving into shops along the way. There's a Disney Store near Ponte di Rialto, but if it's fantasy you're after, nothing beats the views of the Grand Canal from the most graceful and famous bridge in Venice. Nearby, you can board a *vaporetto* waterbus for a cruise along the Grand Canal, passing elegant old *palazzos* and famous landmarks like the Accademia (a treasure trove of Venetian paintings) and the fine Baroque church of Santa Maria della Salute. *Vaporetto* routes 1 and 82 will take you back to Piazza San Marco. Spend some time admiring the exquisite façade of the Basilica San Marco. Five mosaics adorn each of the doorways to this Byzantine beauty, while the four Horses of St Mark (replicas of the bronze originals kept inside) prance above the main entrance. You may well feel compelled to enter this great building – kids will be entranced by the mosaic floor and the dazzling Ascension Dome – but leave time for the Palazzo Ducale where highlights include an armoury and torture chamber.

Best of the rest
Museo Storico Navale (Campo S Biagio) A shrine to ships of every kind, from Chinese junks to a replica of the Doge's ceremonial barge.

Museo di Storia Naturale (Salizzada del Fondaco dei Turchi) Contains an aquarium and a 4-m-tall dinosaur skeleton of *Ouranosauris nigeriensis* discovered in the Sahara.

Glassblowing Take a ferry to the island of Murano where skilled craftsmen have been forging fine Venetian glass for over 700 years.

66 99

It's mid-August and we're on a ferry that's more crowded than a Ganges Delta riverboat during rush hour. We're making slow progress to the world's most adult, romantic, 'couply' city. And it's hot – the kind of heat that usually makes kids whingy and clingy. But the voices around me are hushed because the Campanile is coming into view, rising like a giant exclamation mark above a sun-spangled sea.

"Is it really floating on the water?" chime Joe and Ellie, adding a touch of innocent wonder to this most magnificent of city approaches. The six-year-old twins look shocked when I tell them it's actually sinking. As soon as we disembark Joe stamps on the pavement and Ellie seems reassured.

The queues for the Campanile and Palazzo Ducale are Disneyesque. Not that it matters – all Joe and Ellie want to do is feed the pigeons, which allows their parents ample time to gawp at the head-spinning façades of Piazza San Marco. It's only when an overgenerous handful of birdfood leads to Ellie being mobbed that we tear ourselves away and search for something cooling and calming.

Unfortunately, the gondoliers are charging €150 for a 40-minute punt – €200 if you want to include Rialto Bridge. So instead we delve into the wonderful maze of narrow streets beyond St Mark's Square and feign interest in Gucci handbag shops for quick doses of air-con before the staff get wise and evict us.

The shops selling masks and little glass ornaments captivate the twins – as does the spectacle of Rialto Bridge where day trippers are scrumming down on the parapet, five or six deep, for a glimpse of the Grand Canal. There is something surreal about being wedged in this mêlée of pixel-popping humanity while below you people glide serenely past in gondolas, trailing their fingers in the water… but Joe and Ellie seem genuinely entranced by the graceful curve of palazzos and the non-stop bustle of boats.

We extract ourselves from the crowds, buy ice creams and catch a waterbus back to St Mark's Square. There's just time to feed the pigeons again (which are now so bloated they have almost lost the ability of flight) before catching our ferry.

So is it worth taking young kids to Venice? Of course! Just don't expect a romantic meal at a pavement café or a lingering look inside St Mark's Basilica. Instead, you'll experience the innocent fun of exploring a labyrinthine city floating on water. You'll also introduce your children to one of the world's cultural icons. And you'll spend a lot of money on pigeon food.

Will

Kids' souvenirs
Miniature animal Crafted from beautiful Murano glass.

Plastic model gondola Considerably cheaper than a ride in a real one.

Venetian mask Handmade in papier-mâché and brightly painted.

Northern Italy's water wonderlands

Lake Como is peaceful and relaxed, Lake Maggiore is romantic and sophisticated and Lake Garda is a bustling summer playground. That may be oversimplifying the allure of northern Italy's three major lakes (all share stunning scenery, elegant lakeside towns, a rich historic and artistic heritage and plenty of beaches and watersports), but there's no denying the obvious family appeal of Lake Garda. Largest of the trio, it has over 120 beaches and a wide range of places to stay, from villas to campsites. The medieval fortress town of Sirmione makes a great day out, but the real clincher as far as kids are concerned is Gardaland, Italy's answer to Disney World.

Bottom: Water taxi at Sirmione.
Below left: Banana boat at San Felice del Benaco.
Above: Windsurfers at Tobole.

Regional highlights

›› There are good motorway connections between Milan and all 3 major lakes.
›› Lakeside roads can become extremely busy during peak summer months, so use the network of ferries instead (gardanotizie.it/navigarda).
›› Beaches are mostly pebbly, so take jelly shoes or wetsuit boots for kids.
›› For further information, log on to milanoinfotourist.com, lagodigarda.it, lakecomo.org, distrettolaghi.it.

Lake Garda Located at the tip of a narrow peninsula protruding from the southern shore of Lake Garda, Sirmione is dominated by the 13th-century castle, Rocca Scaligera.

Children will enjoy marching across the drawbridge and storming the towers and battlements which are almost totally surrounded by water. When they've finished raining imaginary arrows on the tour boats below, lead them down the narrow lane along one side of the ramparts to a string of small beaches – all with good stone-skimming potential. Looping back into the heart of Sirmione you'll find streets and squares lined with galleries, craft shops, pizzerias and *gelato* parlours. Buy an ice cream and sit on the jetty wall, feeding the ducks and watching the ferries come and go. At the tip of the peninsula (which you can reach by following the *Passeggiata Panoramica* along the eastern shore) are the remains of a vast, sprawling Roman villa known as Grotte di Catullo – a lovely spot to contemplate the lake views.

Another child-friendly highlight in the south of Lake Garda is Gardaland (see right), but it's also worth spending a day or two exploring further north – either by ferry or by driving along the lakeside road. Heading up the west coast, you pass several towns and villages well endowed with medieval churches and castles, neoclassical mansions and idyllic waterfronts bristling with yachts and launches. Stop at Gardone Riviera to see the fine collection of alpine, Mediterranean and subtropical plants in the Giardino Botanico Hruska before pushing on up to the lake's northern tip where the approach to Riva del Garda is hemmed in by towering cliffs. With its lifeguard-patrolled swimming area and shady lakeside park, Riva is popular with families, while nearby Tobole gets the thumbs up from windsurfing and sailing aficionados. Pretty much everywhere you go, however, you'll find watersports galore – from luxury speedboat cruises to banana-boat rides. If it floats you'll find it on Lake Garda.

Romeo, Romeo: wherefore art thou?

If you base yourself on the southeast shore of Lake Garda you are around 40 km from Verona. Not to be missed are the spectacular Roman Arena and the market in Piazza Erbe which sells a mouth-watering range of local produce. Love-struck teenagers, meanwhile, will no doubt want to swoon over Casa di Giulietta where Romeo is said to have climbed to Juliet's balcony.

Where can I do this?

Italy's largest theme park, Gardaland (gardaland.it), is like Disney, SeaWorld and Universal Studios rolled into one. Located near the southeast tip of Lake Garda, the park has five themes – fantasy, adventure, energy, live shows and the Palablu dolphinarium – but anything goes at Gardaland. One moment you could be floating through the African jungle on the Tunga river cruise and the next you're witnessing a shoot-out at the Rio Bravo Wild West village. From exploring a pirate ship to delving into the myth of Atlantis, Gardaland will leave your head spinning. As well as the floorless roller coaster, Blue Tornado (*below*), big rides include Space Vertigo (a 40-m tower drop), Magic Mountain (a loop-the-loop coaster) and Sequoia Adventure (a bizarre ride where you spin round and upside down as if you were the chain on a chainsaw). For hot summer visits, there are plenty of water rides with potential for cooling splashes, like Jungle Rapids and Colorado Boat. And there is also plenty to keep little ones happy in Fantasy Kingdom with its train ride, tree house and animal farm. Don't miss 4D Adventure or the live theatre shows which include everything from Broadway spectaculars and puppet shows to Gardaland on Ice. More themed fun can be found just up the road towards Lazise, where Caneva World (canevaworld.it) pushes the boundaries of reality even further with its triple whammy of an Aqua Paradise waterpark, a Movieland Studios full of stunt rides and simulators and a Medieval Times arena complete with banquet and tournament.

Milan action plan

Start by taking the elevator up the dome of the *duomo* – the third largest in the world after St Peter's Basilica and Seville Cathedral. The Roof Terraces are bristling with spires adorned with some 3500 statues depicting saints, animals and monsters. Enjoy the views of the city and then descend to Piazza Duomo, bearing right towards the vast iron and glass-domed arcade of the Galleria Vittorio Emanuele II. Inside you'll pass shops and cafés before emerging at the other side facing Milan's famous opera house, Teatro alla Scala (teatroallascala.org). A short walk from the northwest of Milan's historic centre, Castello Sforzesco houses a large art collection, while the adjacent Sempione Park is an appealing green space with a lake.

Nearby Santa Maria delle Grazie is famous for Leonardo da Vinci's masterpiece, *The Last Supper*. Measuring 8.5 m wide and 4.6 m tall, the famous scene can be found above the doorway in what was once the convent's refectory. Reservations are required and a maximum of 25 people are admitted at a time – and only then for 15 minutes' viewing. Is it worth it? The painting is in a fragile condition, so see it while you can is one argument. But far more interesting to kids is the Museo Nazionale della Scienza e della Tecnologia (museoscienza.org) on Via San Vittore where a gallery is devoted to wooden models of inventions based on Leonardo sketches. The museum also has a wide range of interactive science exhibits covering topics as diverse as acoustics and astronomy. There's not much in the way of English interpretation, but kids will easily figure out what to do.

Other museums in Milan that kids will enjoy include the Museo di Storia Naturale and the Planetarium. Both are on Giardini Pubblici – a large city park. If the city gets too much, take the Metro Line 1 to Primaticcio, followed by bus route 64 which passes Aquatica (parcoaquatica.com), a waterpark in Milan operated by Gardaland. Teenage girls, however, will more likely want to stay central in Milan's fiendishly fashionable *quadrilatero*, where all the top Italian and international designer labels can be found, from Gucci to Prada.

Italian Riviera
The Cinque Terre
Explore by foot, boat or train the five remarkable villages that cling to this stretch of rocky coastline on the Riviera di Levante.

Aquarium of Genoa
(acquariodigenova.it) Visit one of Europe's largest aquariums where imaginative displays include an 18-m-long Caribbean coral reef and a recreation of a 15th-century wharf from the Port of Genoa.

Grotte di Toirano
(toiranogrotte.it) Venture into Italy's most beautiful caves (located in the Val Varatella) where a 90-minute tour leads you past subterranean pools and through caverns festooned with stalactites.

Cinque Terre.

Escaping the crowds in rural Italy

Unlike many of Italy's more visited regions, Umbria and Le Marche have little in the way of gold-star family attractions. There are no must-see Roman arenas, leaning towers or volcanoes – but what you will find is a gentle, rural and unspoilt part of Italy with rolling countryside dotted with medieval castles and hilltop towns, fine stretches of sandy beaches along the Adriatic coast and spectacular national parks in the Apennine mountains. It's the perfect place to relax and experience a less hectic side to Italian life with plenty of the cultural and scenic highlights you'd expect from somewhere like Tuscany, but without the crowds.

Regional highlights

>> The A1 motorway between Florence and Rome skirts the western side of Umbria, and there are also good rail and bus links.
>> The A14-E55 and a good rail service link the coastal resorts of Le Marche.
>> For further information, log on to umbria2000.it, turismo.marche.it.

The green heart of Italy

Assisi If there's one 'must-see' in Umbria, it's this medieval hill town. The magnificent Basilica di San Francesco is renowned for its frescos depicting the life of St Francis who is buried here. See if your kids can spot the beautiful *Sermon to the Birds*, one of the remarkable Giotto frescos that, like many works of art in the basilica, was carefully restored after the 1997 earthquake. From the basilica, walk to Assisi's main square, Piazza del Comune, for *gelati* on the steps of the fountain. From Assisi, a scenic route climbs the slopes of Monte Subiaso before descending to Spello where the church of Santa Maria Maggiore has frescos depicting scenes from the New Testament.

Perugia Umbria's old capital is riddled with narrow medieval streets and there's also a museum containing prehistoric, Etruscan and Roman artefacts. It won't take long, however, before your kids latch on to the fact that Perugia is home to Italy's most famous confectionary. Italian for 'kisses', *baci* are creamy dark chocolates with rich hazelnut centres, wrapped in poetic love notes. Shops along pedestrianized Corso Vannucci are laden with the stuff, but for the ultimate sweet treat you can tour the Baci factory in Perugia's San Sisto suburb. Make arrangements at the tourist information office near the Duomo. Just 2 km to the west, Città della Domenica (cittadelladomenica.com) is an animal park with various rides and attractions.

Best of the rest In the north, Gubbio is a medieval hill town with terracotta-tiled houses and pink-stone palaces set against the thickly wooded slopes of the Apennines. Lake Trasimeno in the west has small sandy beaches and clear warm water, perfect for swimming and water-sports, while lakeside towns like Castiglione del Lago offer trips to Isola Maggiore, an island known for its lace-making. Highlights in southern Umbria include the 80-m-high 14th-century aqueduct, Ponte delle Torri (Bridge of Towers), in Spoleto, and the elaborate façade of the *duomo* in Orvieto. To escape into the wilds of the Apennine mountains, head for Monti Sibillini (sibillini.net), a national park with great potential for hiking and horse riding.

Between the mountains and the sea

To the east of Umbria, Le Marche has the added attraction of almost continuous sandy beaches running the length of its Adriatic coastline. The most picturesque section is the Conero Peninsula, a dramatic seascape of limestone cliffs, sandy coves and turquoise waters. The three resorts in the area, Portonovo, Sirolo and Numana, can get busy in summer, but you can escape the crowds by taking a boat trip to one of the many small isolated coves along the coast. Head inland from Ancona (Le Marche's main town and port) and you quickly enter the foothills of the Apennines, dotted with medieval towns like Urbino and Ascoli Piceno. Highlights for children include the spectacular cave system of Grotte di Frasassi (frasassi.com), the mighty fortress at San Leo and the tiny republic of San Marino (visitsanmarino.com). In the south of Le Marche there are wonderful scenic drives through the Monti Sibillini.

Top right: Castelluccio di Norcia, Umbria.

> 66 99 We had a fantastic time in Le Marche. The beautiful undulating countryside is miraculously unspoilt and even in August it was quiet. We managed to balance our need to soak up the atmosphere in some medieval towns (aided by the customary bribe of *gelati*) with swimming, tennis and football for the children. Eating out is a joy – there's always something on the menu that children will love.
>
> *Alison Rippon*

Land of the trulli

Tucked into the heel of Italy, this little-visited province may not have the cultural clout of Rome, Florence or Venice, but what it lacks in notoriety it more than compensates for with a quirky range of monuments – from Neolithic tombs and Gothic cathedrals to the curious *trulli* houses. And even if you are not a culture vulture, Puglia has plenty of rich pickings. Natural highlights include the lovely beaches and forests of the Gargano Peninsula, the spur on Italy's heel, while 20 km offshore lie the Tremiti Islands, an unspoilt cluster of limestone islands.

Regional highlights

» The historic centres of most towns are compact and easily explored on foot.
» Buses and trains serve many destinations, but for ultimate flexibility rent a car at one of the region's airports.
» From Naples, allow 3 hrs to drive through the Apennines to Bari.
» For further information, log on to pugliaturismo.com.

Bari Most tourists arrive at this busy Adriatic port to catch a ferry to Greece or Croatia. If you find yourself with a few hours to spare in Bari, head to the old district of Città Vecchia to explore the castle. Also worth a look, Bari's Basilica di San Nicola is one of Puglia's earliest churches (begun in 1087), while further north along the coast, Trani's Norman *duomo* rises above a harbour filled with blue-hulled fishing boats. One of the most striking of Puglia's monuments can be found inland from Trani on the central limestone plateau known as Le Murge. Built around 1240, Frederick II's Castel del Monte is a perfect octagon in shape, with a hefty tower at each corner.

Alberobello A large swathe of this town is pimpled with over 1000 *trulli* – tiny, conical-roofed houses sprouting from narrow streets like stone toadstools. Constructed entirely of local limestone, each circular dwelling is no larger than a garden gazebo; most are whitewashed while a few are daubed with strange pagan symbols. Kids will love exploring this World Heritage Site, particularly since many *trulli* are now used as craft or souvenir shops.

Lecce Dubbed the Florence of the Baroque, Lecce is renowned for its elaborate architecture. The imposing façade of the 16th-century Santa Croce church is dominated by a large rose window surrounded by intricately sculpted columns and friezes where saints, dragons and gargoyles crouch in niches like seabirds on a crowded cliff. Lecce is also famed for its papier-mâché figures, often depicting nativity characters.

Otranto Pleasure boats and fishing trawlers form orderly rows across the turquoise shallows of Otranto's harbour where, 3500 years ago, Mycenaean traders beached their ships. These Bronze Age forays were a precursor to the first Greek colonies in Italy. A scenic route hugs the coast south of Otranto, weaving past medieval watchtowers, limestone caves and small seaside villages.

Best beaches Dotted with sandy coves and beaches, the rugged Gargano Peninsula (parcogargano.it) is popular with holidaymakers, as are the Tremiti Islands, accessible by boat from Termoli.

Left: Local fisherman in Trani. Top: Trulli at Alberobello. Above: Gargano Peninsula.

66 99 With its immaculate stone-flagged lanes and elegant houses, Locorotondo commands sweeping views across the Valle d'Itria – dotted with trulli and scrawled with the rich terracotta of freshly ploughed soil.

Will

In the shadow of Vesuvius

Italy's third-largest city, Naples is hot, crowded and chaotic. Not only are its pavements as congested as its roads, but scooters often fail to distinguish between the two. So why bring kids here? First and foremost, Naples is the jumping-off point for excursions to Pompeii – the most enigmatic ruins you'll find anywhere. And then there's the Amalfi Coast – a bit on the posh side, but nevertheless a fine excuse for beach hopping and a breathtaking coastal drive. But even Naples itself is worth a day or two of sightseeing. If the castles and archaeology museum don't do it for your kids, at least you can introduce them to some of Italy's most authentic pizza and ice cream.

City highlights

» Calm sanctuaries for frayed nerves include the cavernous nave of the *duomo* and the cloisters of Santa Chiara; for somewhere to let kids run around in traffic-free safety, try Piazza Plebiscito.
» The Circumvesuviana train service connects Naples with Pompeii and Sorrento.
» For further information, log on to inaples.it and guidevesuvio.it.

Action plan An ideal place to start is Castel Nuovo. Not only does this striking fortress lie at the city's heart, but its ramparts afford views towards Mt Vesuvius brooding across the Bay of Naples. Nearby, in striking contrast, is the Galleria Umberto I with its glass-domed roof built in the late 1800s. Continue walking around Piazza Trieste e Trento to Caffè Gambrinus – the city's prime spot for pastries and ice cream. Kids can

then run off their sugar high in the paved expanse of Piazza del Plebiscito while parents admire the magnificent façade of the Palazzo Reale – once one of the Mediterranean's most important royal courts. A short walk along the seafront leads to Castel dell'Ovo, the oldest castle in Naples, parts of which date from the 9th century. It now shelters a small marina and several popular restaurants. Located in the heart of central Naples, Spaccanapoli threads a 'tourist lifeline' between numerous churches, statues and historic buildings. A narrow canyon-like street, it is one of the most vibrant parts of the city. Street vendors crowd the cobbles, while shops are crammed with everything from pasta and pastries to Neapolitan masks and clay nativity scenes. Cafés overflow with locals sipping coffee, while open-air restaurants serve delicious pizza Margherita. One church definitely worth

visiting on Spaccanapoli is Santa Chiara – if only to relax in its garden-framed cloister, which is beautifully decorated with hand-painted tiles. At the end of Spaccanapoli, turn right on Via Toledo (Naples' main shopping street) and continue walking up the hill until you reach the Museo Archeologico Nazionale. Must-sees include *Hercules* and other famous statues from the Farnese Collection. Many relics from Pompeii and Herculaneum have also found sanctuary here, including some wonderfully intricate mosaics. There is also a fascinating scale model of the Pompeii excavations – a great primer before visiting the actual ruins.

Above: Pompeii victim.
Top right: Castel Nuovo.
Below right: Naples street.

Best day out: Pompeii

Set the scene for your kids: It's August in the year AD 79. For several days, small earthquakes have shaken Pompeii, but otherwise life in the thriving Roman city continues as normal. Then, on the afternoon of the 24th, Vesuvius suddenly erupts, shooting a column of ash over 30 km into the atmosphere. Fearful of Vulcan, the Roman God of Fire, the people of Pompeii cower at the sight. Then terror and blind panic seizes them as a cloud of superheated, poisonous fumes and volcanic debris sweeps down the volcano killing everything in its path. The eruption lasts 19 hours, by which time Pompeii lies buried beneath 6 m of pumice and ash, while nearby Herculaneum has vanished beneath a deep layer of mud and lava.

Such was the ferocity of the eruption that both settlements were petrified in time. At the excavated ruins of Pompeii, look for cart tracks along Via dell'Abbondanza and visit Modesto's bakery where several loaves of carbonized bread were found. Perhaps too haunting for youngsters, the Garden of the Fugitives contains over a dozen plaster casts of human victims – adults and children – frozen in anguished postures as they succumbed to the onslaught of ash and lethal fumes. There are other areas of Pompeii that you might wish to steer kids away from – particularly the brothels where frescos depict the wares of prostitutes in graphic detail. Otherwise, must-sees include the well-preserved temples, baths and theatres, as well as the House of the Vettii with its colourful friezes.

Molten lava and a melting pot of cultures

Just 3 km from the toe of Italy, Sicily is an island of contrasts where rolling wheatfields, olive groves, vineyards and citrus plantations hold sway beneath the brooding hulk of Europe's largest volcano. While Mount Etna puffs away in the east, holidaymakers seek out Sicily's sandy beaches or explore its wealth of archaeological sites – a rich legacy of the many civilizations that have left their mark on this fiery and fascinating island.

Islands highlights

» A city with a rich mixture of architecture, from Arabic to art nouveau, Palermo (palermo tourism.com) is Sicily's regional capital.

» You will find most types of accommodation on Sicily, from resorts hotels and self-catering villas to farmstays and campsites.

» For further information, log on to regione.sicilia.it/turismo and parcoetna.ct.it.

Volcanoes Constantly simmering and regularly boiling over in spectacular pyrotechnic displays of bright red sparks and molten lava, 3370-m Mt Etna is one of Italy's most impressive (and unexpected) sights. Not only is it Europe's largest volcano, but it is also one of its most active. Parents might be a little alarmed to discover that it's possible to step foot on the slopes of Etna. Few volcanoes, however, are more closely monitored and, as long as you arrange a guided tour, you should be

safe. Take the Circumetnea Train (circumetnea.it) from Catania to Nicolosi and Zafferana for walks on old lava flows. Remember to bring warm clothing, sturdy shoes and sunglasses to protect your eyes from windblown grit. Jeep tours start from the Rifugio Sapienza Etna Sud and follow the line of the cable car that was destroyed in the 2001 eruption. For a less intimidating volcanic escapade, take a boat trip from Milazzo on Sicily's north coast to the Aeolian Islands, a volcanic archipelago where you can swim and snorkel from black-sand beaches, collect fragments of pumice floating in the sea and delve back in time at the archaeological museum in Lipari. To the north of the main group of islands lies Stromboli – a feisty volcano that has been active for more than two millennia.

Temples and castles Sicily's top historical sites include the ancient Greek theatre at Taormina (Sicily's first resort),

Above: Coastline near Taormina. Below left: Etna blows her top (again). Below right: Temple ruins at Agrigento.

the Roman hunting lodge of Villa Romana del Casa, the lavish mosaics inside the Norman cathedral at Monreale and the magnificent Greek temple ruins at Agrigento and Selinunte. Among Sicily's numerous castles ripe for rampart-romping and dungeon-delving, try Castello di Eurialo, Castello di Lombardia and Castello di Venere.

Best beaches Just to the north of Palermo, Mondello has the island's most lively beaches with lots of facilities. A little further to the west, Lo Zingaro, Sicily's first nature reserve, protects 7 km of rocky coastline on the Gulfo di Castellammare. You can reach this idyllic spot (keeping an eye open for Bonelli's eagle and peregrine falcons) either by walking along the coastal path or by taking a boat trip. Don't forget masks and snorkels – there are several gorgeous coves with crystal-clear waters. At Selinunte in the southwest there's a large sandy beach just below the temples and a nearby Acquasplash waterpark. Other sandy stretches along the south coast include Eraclea Minoa, Scoglitti and Donnalucata. In the southeast corner of the island, Vendicari has beautiful sandy beaches set in a nature reserve.

66 99 We had a lovely time in Sicily when Amelia was five months old. The Sicilians just seem to adore babies. We had a young couple run halfway across the airport to say 'ciao' to Amelia and even teenage boys were happy to play peek-a-boo with her on buses. Once, on the bus to Taormina, it was so packed there was nowhere for us to sit. Amelia was gently but firmly taken from us and passed to a grinning grandmother who entertained her until we reached our destination.

Su Taylor

Italy essentials

When to go

Italy has a varied climate, based on its distinct geographical regions. In the north, expect cold Alpine winters and warm, wet summers; in the **Po Valley** the summers are hot and dry and the winters are cold and damp; the rest of Italy has a wonderful climate of long hot summers (with temperatures consistently over 25°C) and mild winters, with cooler weather and a chance of winter snow in the **Appenines**.

Italy's historic sites and cities are busy and crowded from spring to October and the heat can be oppressive during the midsummer months of July and August. Remember, though, that you can always escape into the cooler hill towns when the heat gets too much. Be aware that **Rome** and the Vatican City will be packed with pilgrims at Christmas and Easter, and that **Venice** triples its population during *Carnevale* in February. Consider visiting Venice in the winter low season (October to March) – everything stays open and gondola rides will be cheaper!

Getting there

Milan, Verona and Bologna are the key transport hubs in northern Italy; Rome and Naples in the south. The national carrier, Alitalia (alitalia.com), flies from Europe and the United States to all major cities in Italy. Check their website for special promotions, but expect to pay from around £90 for a return fare between Heathrow and Rome, or £120 for a return to Naples (via Rome). Alitalia's return fares between New York and Rome start from around £300. British Airways (britishairways.com) flies to 11 Italian destinations, including Rome, Naples, Milan, Pisa, and Bologna. Rates start at around £75 for a return flight between London Gatwick and Rome. For budget flights to Italy, BMI British Midland (flybmi.com)

Go green: three ways to skip the flight

➤➤ Get a coach pass with Eurolines (eurolines-pass.com) linking classic cities such as Venice, Florence, Milan, Rome and Naples.

➤➤ Take your car by train to Italy. Dutch company Auto Slaaptrein (autoslaaptrein.nl) operates a weekly motorail service from June to September between s'Hertogenbosch (a short drive from the Channel ports of Hoek van Holland or Rotterdam) to Bologna. The train runs overnight with couchettes and sleepers southbound on Friday nights, northbound on Saturday nights.

➤➤ Travel by train from London to Rome. Book a ticket with Eurostar (eurostar.com) to Paris. Cross Paris by Métro to the Gare de Bercy and connect with the *Palatino* sleeper train to Rome. Bookings can be made online at raileurope.co.uk.

Tour operators

In the UK

The Adventure Company adventurecompany.co.uk
Crystal Active crystal-active.co.uk
First Choice Holidays firstchoice.co.uk
Keycamp Holidays keycamp.com
Individual Italy individual-italy.co.uk
Inntravel inntravel.co.uk
Lakes and Mountains Holidays lakes-mountains.co.uk
Powder Byrne powderbyrne.com
Sunvil Discovery Italy sunvil.co.uk
Thomson Holidays thomson.co.uk

In the USA

Abercrombie and Kent abercrombiekent.com
Adventures by Disney abd.disney.go.com
Globus Family Vacations globusjourneys.com
Tauck Bridges family-travel.tauck.com

serves Naples, Rome and Venice; easyJet (easyjet.com) flies to Milan, Turin, Venice, Pisa, Rimini, Rome, Naples and Sicily; and Ryanair (ryanair.com) covers over 20 Italian destinations including cities in Puglia, Sicily and Sardinia as well as all the major hubs.

Getting around

Travelling within Italy usually poses few problems, particularly in the north of the country, where the road, bus and rail networks are modern and efficient. Alitalia (alitalia.com) operates an extensive network of internal flights as do low-cost operators such as Alpieagles (alpieagles.com) and Club Air (clubair.it).

Fly-drive deals are often the cheapest way to arrange **car hire**. Most rental agencies are located at major Italian airports. Motorways, although generally good, can become heavily congested at weekends and during peak periods. One way to avoid the congested routes is to take the **train** which provides good value and is especially useful if you want to link two or more cities (where you'd be crazy to attempt to drive yourself). Trenitalia (trenitalia.com) has an online reservation system.

How to keep a budding archaeologist happy

Bare Bones Tours (andantetravels.co.uk) takes adventurous and inquisitive people to some of the world's most exciting archaeological sites. You travel with a specialist guide who brings even the oldest, driest and dustiest ruins to life. Suitable for families with children aged nine and over, the eight-day Bare Bones Pompeii tour costs €1300 per person, with departures in the February and October half-term holidays.

How much to offset your emissions?

From London to:
Milan £1.68
Venice £2.01
Florence £2.11
Sardinia £2.38
Rome £2.45
Naples £2.74
Brindisi £3.04

From New York to:
Milan US$28.50
Florence US$30
Sardinia US$30
Venice US$30
Rome US$30.50
Naples US$31.50
Brindisi US$33

Italy also has a large and well-developed network of **ferries** that ply routes between offshore islands, as well as making international crossings. SNAV Collegamenti Marittimi (snav.it) operates ferries between Civitavecchia and Olbia (Sardinia) and Palermo, and from Naples to Palermo, Capri and Ischia. Also try Grand Navi Veloci (gnv.it).

The best way to get around Italian cities varies from place to place. For example in Venice, waterbuses or *vaporetti* are abundant; in Rome, buses are most useful; and in Milan there is an efficient metro. You will often find that walking is quicker than taking a taxi or bus through congested streets.

Accommodation

Families are spoilt for choice when it comes to places to stay in Italy – you will find everything from beachside campsites and rural farmstays to resorts, hotels and converted *palazzos*. Most **hotels** welcome children, even if they have no special facilities. Some of the cheaper hotels may not be able to supply cots, but most hotels will provide an extra child's bed if required. Many of the big international hotel chains have a presence in Italy, including Best Western (bestwestern.com) and Starwood Westin (starwoodhotels.com).

Self-catering accommodation is generally of a high standard, and is often in wonderful locations. The Associazione Nazionale per l'Agriturismo (agriturist.it) represents more than 2000 farms, villas and mountain chalets and offers reasonably priced accommodation. For something unusual, contact Apulia Bella (apuliabella.com) to arrange a stay in a converted *trullo* in the Puglia region.

For an online directory of Italian campsites and resorts, log on to camping.it. For holiday villages offering accommodation in well-equipped chalets and tents, try Eurocamp (eurocamp.co.uk), Keycamp (keycamp.com), Siblu (siblu.com) and Vacansoleil (vacansoleil.co.uk).

The €10 picnic

Four rolls €0.68
Packet of sliced ham €1.25
Packet of Maasdamer cheese €1.81
1 litre carton of fruit juice €2.55
Bar of chocolate €0.69
4 apples €0.60
Tube of Pringles €1.75
Cherry tomotoes €0.70
TOTAL €10.03

Food and drink

Food is an obsession in Italy and a quintessential part of Italian lifestyle. If your children enjoy pizza, pasta and ice cream they won't go hungry. However, encourage them to try some of the regional specialities in the table below, if only to supplement their diet of *pizza margherita*, *spaghetti bolognese* and *gelato*.

Health and safety

It is strongly recommended that you have good medical and travel insurance prior to visiting Italy. EU citizens should ensure they have a European Health Insurance Card (EHIC) which entitles the holder to emergency medical treatment . It does not cover you for medical repatriation, on-going medical treatment or treatment of a non-urgent nature.

Italy is generally a safe place to visit, with few health and safety risks. There is a small risk of contracting Leishmaniasis from an infected sand fly bite or Lyme disease from a tick bite.

Crime levels in Italy are generally low. The biggest risk to tourists is petty crime such as bag snatching – particularly in major tourist spots.

Fact file

GMT	+ 1 hour
Language	Italian
Money	Euro € (£1=€1.50)
Code	+39
Tourist info	enit.it

💰 How much for a Big Mac?

UK US$3.08
Italy US$3.82
USA US$3.22

Regional specialities

Rome	Spaghetti alla Carbonara	Spaghetti cooked with raw egg, Parmesan cheese, cracked black pepper and *pancetta* (bacon).
Tuscany	Panforte	Fruit cake made with chewy nougat, fruits and spices.
	Donzelle	Fried dough balls.
	Crostini	Rounds of bread toasted and brushed with olive oil with various toppings such as chunks of tomato.
Venice	Tiramisu	Dessert with a creamy sauce of mascarpone and eggs between layers of sponge cake drenched in coffee or liqueur.
	Pasta e fagioli	Bean soup with home-made pasta.
Umbria	Schiacciata	Similar to pizza crust, bread baked with olive oil and sometimes with cooked greens and onions.
Sicily	Cassata	Sponge cake, ricotta cream, marzipan and candied fruits.
	Granita	Fruity iced drink.

10 family favourites

Villa Pia

Where? Lippiano, Tuscany.

Why? Stylish, yet relaxed, informal and homely, Villa Pia (pictured below) is an 18th-century manor house set in stunning Tuscan scenery within easy reach of Florence and Siena for sightseeing, eating out and shopping. In addition to four family suites, with interconnecting bedrooms and private bathroom, there is a living room and kitchen with help-yourself fridge. Boasting wonderful views, the 2-ha grounds have two swimming pools, a sandpit, trampoline, adventure play areas and an all-weather tennis court.

How much? From €670 per week or €95 per day for adults; €257 per week or €37 per day for children aged 2-12 years (full board except for Thursdays, breakfast only).

Contact villapia.com.

Club Med Kamarina

Where? Ragusa, on the southwest coast of Sicily.

Why? This 96-ha beachside holiday village (pictured below) has something for all ages, from catamaran sailing, rollerblading and tennis to swimming in one of three pools. Kids' clubs include a Mini Club Med for children aged 4-10 and Club Med Passworld for youngsters up to 17. For grown-ups there's a Club Med Spa, Turkish bath and aqua fitness classes.

How much? All-inclusive weekly rates from €1027 per adult.

Contact clubmed.co.uk.

Foresteria Valdese di Venezia

Where? Central Venice.

Why? Just a short stroll from St Mark's Square, the guest lodgings of the Waldensian and Methodist Church in Venice are perfectly placed for exploring this magical city. There's a choice of private rooms sleeping up to eight people. Sheets, pillowcases and blankets are provided, but you will have to make your own beds – a small price to pay for such a central location. For a beach alternative close to Venice, see Ca'Savio below.

How much? From €110 for a four-bed room with bathroom, including breakfast.

Contact foresteriavenezia.it.

Ca'Savio Campsite

Where? Cavallino, near Venice.

Why? Venice is just a bus and boat ride away from this large holiday camp, which not only has a vast swimming pool complex, but is also located next to a sandy beach. Accommodation ranges from five-person tents to well-equipped mobile homes sleeping up to seven. Onsite facilities include a supermarket, restaurant and pizzeria, while activities range from minigolf and table tennis to cycling, canoeing and archery. Fun Station kids' clubs operate during high season.

How much? Seven nights in a two-bedroom Villanova mobile home start from around €290 per party.

Contact keycamp.co.uk.

Hermitage Hotel

Where? La Bidola Bay, Elba.

Why? With a variety of interconnecting rooms, the Hermitage (pictured below) makes a great bolt hole for families. There's plenty to keep kids occupied, with windsurfing, waterskiing, jet-skiing, banana boating and boat hire available from the private beach. In addition to three saltwater swimming pools (including a children's pool), the hotel also offers tennis, golf, mountain biking, volleyball, five-a-side football and pétanque. For adults there's a wellness centre.

How much? From around €2710 per adult, €817 for nine- to 12-year-olds and €452 for three- to eight-year-olds for seven nights half-board accommodation, UK return flights and transfers.

Contact powderbyrne.com.

Europa Silvella

Where? Lake Garda.

Why? With its own lakeside beach, this well-equipped holiday park (pictured below) is ideal for watersports. It also has its own swimming pool, along with a range of other facilities, including shop, takeaway and restaurant. Accommodation is available in six-berth tents or mobile homes – all with shade. The Gardaland theme park is just 33 km away.

How much? Seven nights in a Venezia mobile home cost from around €440 for two adults and up to four children under 18 years old, including return midweek P&O ferry crossings between Dover and Calais.

Contact eurocamp.co.uk.

Relais San Clemente

Where? Bosco, near Perugia.

Why? A former Benedictine monastery, the elegant four-star Relais San Clemente (see below) opened as a guesthouse in 1990. It's set within a beautiful 5-ha park which boasts a small railway station where guests can board the daily train to Perugia (€6 return). Some rooms have direct access to the park and there are two swimming pools – one for adults and one for children. Mountain bikes are also available for hire.

How much? €2600 for a family of four (based on two adults and two children aged two to 12), including accommodation with breakfast, UK return flights and car hire.

Contact sunvil.co.uk.

Pantheon Apartment

Where? Rome.

Why? Enjoying one of the best locations in Rome, just metres from the Pantheon, this stylish and comfortable apartment occupies the second floor of a grand 18th-century *palazzo*. A combination of home comforts and its proximity to the city's major sights make it a family-friendly haven (although you might want to move an antique or two out of reach of toddlers!). Sleeps up to five, plus baby.

How much? From €2235 per week for the property.

Contact individualtravellers.com.

Tuscan View Apartments

Where? Montaione, Tuscany.

Why? Perfect base from which to explore the nearby hill towns of San Gimignano, Certaldo and Volterra, this large working estate (see below) has loads to keep families happy, from tennis to horse riding. There is even a bar, restaurant and mini-market selling groceries and the estate's honey and olive oil. Several trails wind through the estate which you can explore either on foot or by mountain bike. Equipped with living rooms and kitchenettes, the one, two or three twin-bedroom apartments are located in a dozen or so attractively restored farmhouses with shared swimming pools.

How much? One week's rental of a two-bedroom apartment (sleeping four people) costs from around €1030, including Dover-Calais ferry crossings, or €1227 with a week's car rental.

Contact inntravel.co.uk

Chia Laguna

Where? Sardinia, 50 km from Cagliari.

Why? Sardinia is well known for its white sandy beaches and clear sparkling water and you'll find both at this family-orientated resort. Scott Dunn's childcare facilities at Chia Laguna are second to none. Qualified nannies are available to care for babies aged four-to-eight months, while children up to two can join the Starfish Club with activities such as face painting and picnics in the hotel's garden. The Dolphin Club keeps three- to five-year-olds busy with minigolf, boat races and treasure hunts; the Shark Club (six- to eight-year-olds) gets more adventurous with obstacle races, bike rides and visits to local waterparks; while the Barracuda Club involves nine- to 13-year-olds in exciting sports like mountain biking and sailing.

How much? One week in a garden cottage for a family of four costs from around €6445 half board, including UK return flights and transfers. Children's clubs are extra.

Contact scottdunn.com.

Central Europe

There's no business like snow business.

metres
3000
2000
1000
500
200
0

N

50 km
50 miles

North Sea

Baltic Sea

Rügen

Frisian Islands

○ **Hamburg**

Elbe

☆2

○ **Bremen** ☆3

NETHERLANDS

□ **AMSTERDAM**

Hanover ○

Hook of Holland

○ **Rotterdam**

GERMANY

☆ **BERLIN**

Rhine

Harz Mountains

○ **Bruges**
○ **Ghent**

Flanders

□ **BRUSSELS**

☆1

BELGIUM

○ **Cologne**
○ **Bonn**

Largest city
Berlin, population 3.39 million

Ardennes

Frankfurt ○

LUXEMBOURG

Longest river
Danube 2850 km

□ **PRAGUE**

○ **Nürnberg**

Danube

VIENNA □

☆4

Wasserfaelle Gutach

Black Forest

Munich ○

Bodensee

Salzburg ○

AUSTRIA

Zürich ○

LIECHTENSTEIN

Tyrol

▲ *Grossglockner*

Styria

BERN □

Lake Lucerne

SWITZERLAND

☆6

Granbünden

Carinthia

S

Lake Geneva

☆5

Bernese Oberland

A

I

P

Geneva ○

Valais

Matterhorn ▲ ▲ *Dufourspitze*

Lyon ○

Milan ○

Highest mountain
Dufourspitze 4634 m

○ **Did you know?**

- Amsterdam has 1281 bridges, 2000 houseboats and 600,000 bicycles.
- Belgium produces 172,000 tons of chocolate each year, which is equivalent to 1000 solid chocolate blue whales.
- The Manneken Pis in Brussels has over 700 costumes in the City Museum, including an Elvis jumpsuit.
- Liechtenstein is the world's largest exporter of false teeth.
- Mountains cover more than 70% of Switzerland.

★ **Find out where Tintin was created**
▸▸ Belgium, page 168

★ **Explore the canals of Amsterdam**
▸▸ Netherlands, page 168

★ **Tour the Castle Road**
▸▸ Germany, page 170

★ **Experience all of Europe in one park**
▸▸ Germany, page 178

★ **Stand on top of the world**
▸▸ Switzerland, page 172

★ **Get active in the Alps**
▸▸ Switzerland and Austria, page 172-175

At first glance, the problem with Central Europe is that everywhere surrounding it looks more exciting. Head north to Scandinavia, south to the Mediterranean, east to Poland and the Baltics and west to France. But keep focused, keep staring straight ahead, because the *mélange* of high and low countries wedged into the middle of Europe not only offers an excellent range of family-holiday options, but is also less crowded (and sometimes better value) than its higher-profile neighbours. Let's start with the essentials: Belgium, the Netherlands and Germany all have excellent sandy beaches along the North Sea coast, while Austria and Switzerland have countless lakes that are perfect for swimming and watersports. Accommodation throughout the region includes numerous family-friendly hotels, guesthouses, farmstays and holiday villages; public transport is super-efficient, and regional cuisine features chocolate, chips, cheese and waffles. As for adventure, you will find every kind of action sport available in the Austrian and Swiss Alps, from rock climbing to whitewater rafting, while the Low Countries promise more in the way of gentle touring and cycle routes. In Germany you can follow in the fairy-tale footsteps of the Brothers Grimm, in Austria you can take your cue from *The Sound of Music* and in Switzerland you can ride on some of the world's most spectacular mountain railways.

❝❞ *Amsterdam is like one big children's playground. We found loads to do, so don't let its red light reputation put you off.*

Will

Introduction

Central Europe rating

Wow factor
★★★★

Worry factor
★

Value for money
★★★

Keeping teacher happy
★★★

Family accommodation
★★★★

Babies & toddlers
★★★★

Teenagers
★★★

How to do a backside 360 spin

This is one of the easiest and safest advanced tricks to learn. Make sure you start the spin on the kicker before you take off. Drive your front shoulder towards your back foot and wind your arms in front of you, before unwinding them towards your back just as you approach the jump. After leaving the kicker you'll be flying backwards; keep turning your upper body, and you should still be travelling upwards, spinning blind until you're at your highest point in the jump. Keep turning those shoulders in the direction of the spin as you get ready to land. Don't forget, the board needs to travel 360 degrees, so keep that board turning. Using your arms for balance, prepare for the oncoming landing. Bring the board to the ground and meet the floor with a fully extended body, your board pointing perfectly forwards and your weight centred over the board.

Books to read

Play, Mozart, Play! Greenwillow, 2006
Artist Peter Sís introduces the child genius, Wolfgang Amadeus Mozart. Ages 3-8

The Complete Brothers Grimm Fairy Tales,
Random House, 2006
With over 700 pages, this illustrated volume contains every published story by the Brothers Grimm, including well-known classics like 'Cinderella', 'The Frog Prince', 'Hansel and Gretel', 'Little Red Riding Hood', 'Rapunzel', 'Rumpelstiltskin' and 'Snow White'. Ages 4+

The Adventures of Tintin, Egmont, 2007
Read three classic Tintin adventures – 'The Castafiore Emerald', 'Flight 714 to Sydney' and 'Tintin and the Picaros' – by Belgian cartoon-strip supremo, Hergé, in volume 8 of this latest series of compilations. Ages 6+

Heidi, Puffin, 1995
Johanna Spyri's classic tale of a little Swiss girl who is sent to live with her grandfather in a mountain hut high in the Alps – an idyllic life that's shattered one day when Heidi is brought back to Frankfurt by her aunt Dete. Ages 8-11

Diary of Anne Frank, Longman 1989
The tragic, deeply moving and inspiring story of a Jewish girl living in Amsterdam who is forced into hiding during the Holocaust. Ages 12+

One to watch

The Sound of Music, 20th Century Fox, 2005

There's no excuse for not joining in with 'Edelweiss', 'Do-Re-Mi' and other catchy tunes in this sing-along edition of one of the world's most popular films.

🍫 Toblerone facts

▸ The famous Swiss chocolate is named after creator, Theodor Tobler, and *torrone*, a type of Italian nougat.
▸ The first Toblerone was sold in 1908.
▸ Toblerone's unique shape is based on Switzerland's Matterhorn.

🔍 How to grow tulips

Did you know that over nine billion flower bulbs are produced in the Netherlands every year? Tulips are some of the easiest to grow. Just follow these simple steps:

▸ Decide on a colour scheme or pattern.
▸ Purchase your bulbs; generally the bigger the bulb, the bigger the bloom.
▸ Prepare the soil by removing rocks and adding some compost and bone meal.
▸ Plant the bulbs any time during autumn, placing them around 15-20 cm apart, and at a depth that's roughly twice the width of the bulb.
▸ After flowering, let the plant continue to grow until it dies back naturally.

Taste of Central Europe: pretzel

Hailing from southern Germany in the 12th century, the humble pretzel is now a popular snack worldwide. This recipe shows you how to make soft pretzels, traditionally served in Bavaria for breakfast and accompanied by *weisswurst* (white sausage) and sweet mustard.

What you need
▸ 3½ cups flour
▸ 4 tbsp brown sugar
▸ 2 tsp salt
▸ 1 tbsp yeast dissolved in water
▸ 2 tbsp baking soda
▸ 1 egg

What to do
▸ Mix one cup of warm water with the yeast, brown sugar and salt.
▸ Gradually add the flour and mix to form a smooth dough.
▸ Chill the dough for an hour and then divide it into six pieces.
▸ Roll out each piece until it is slightly thicker than a pencil.
▸ Arrange each dough string into an upside-down U-shape.
▸ Hold the ends of each string and twist them together.
▸ Flatten the ends with your fingers, then bring them to the top of the pretzel pressing them into the dough.
▸ Place the pretzels on a greased baking tray and leave them to rise for about 30 minutes.
▸ Boil four cups of water, add the baking soda, then dip each pretzel in the solution for about 10 seconds before placing them back on the baking tray.
▸ Beat the egg with one teaspoon of water, then brush it over the pretzels.
▸ Sprinkle the pretzels with salt, sesame seeds, cheese or cinnamon.
▸ Bake for around 15 minutes until golden brown.

🔍 How to yodel

▸ Find a remote mountain pasture with plenty of echo potential.
▸ Take a deep breath, open your mouth wide and sing, "Hodl oh-ooh-dee".
▸ Try it again, going high-pitched on the "ooh".
▸ Now practise "Hodl-ay-ee-dee", going up a note on the "ee".
▸ Put the two lines together, and you're yodelling.
▸ Optional: finish with a "heh-ee-dee-ho-ooh-dee-yo".

Travelling with kids in Central Europe is a breeze. The Dutch in particular are relaxed and friendly, but you'll find families are generally welcome wherever you go. Children receive discounts on admission to most major sights, and often travel free on the slick public transport systems that operate across the region. You'll also have no problem finding family-oriented accommodation and places to eat.

Babies (0-18 months)

Take the low ground or the high ground. Buggy-friendly Amsterdam is ideal for a relaxed city break, just as Austria or Switzerland are perfect for an alpine jaunt or two while your baby is still light enough to be lugged around in a carrier or papoose. Flying from the UK to anywhere in Central Europe is quick and simple, but with a baby in tow you might feel happier piling everything you need into your car and taking a ferry to Belgium or the Netherlands. Don't forget that several hotel brands in the region, such as Kinderhotels and KidsHotels, offer all-inclusive packages with outstanding childcare for the tiniest of tots – not to mention some pampering incentives for their parents.

Toddlers/pre-school (18 months-4 years)

Amsterdam's reputation for being family-friendly might not strike a chord with parents of hyperactive toddlers. One glance at a city map and all those canals is enough to give any parent instant palpitations. The same could be said for the Alps with its mountain paths and precipitous drops. In both cases, toddler reins are essential. The big boon with this age group, of course, is that you can sidestep the busy school-holiday periods and take advantage of cheaper travel deals and less crowded cities, beaches or ski slopes. Just watch the weather though. Central Europe's climate can be unpredictable at the best of times – stray too far either side of mid-summer and that beach holiday on the North Sea coast could be decidedly damp and chilly. Still, there's always Center Parcs where it's permanently subtropical thanks to their dome-covered water worlds. You'll find them in Belgium, the Netherlands and Germany.

Kids/school age (4-12 years)

Holiday villages, such as Center Parcs and Eurocamp, are a great option for children of this age who often have limitless energy and require constant stimulation. Active holidays in Central Europe can include anything from cycling in the Low Countries to learning how to rock climb in the Alps. You can also satisfy many a childhood passion by touring one of Germany's themed routes, such as the Castle Road or Fairy Tale Route, and spending time at world-class theme parks like Europa-Park and Legoland. From an educational point of view, Central Europe has plenty of lessons in store for children, from Van Gogh's strokes of genius to Salzburg's intriguing brush with salt.

Teenagers (13 years+)

When children begin learning about the world wars at school, Central Europe will inevitably loom large in their minds. The tragic, thought-provoking story of Anne Frank, the Jewish teenager who hid from the Germans for over two years in a tiny annexe that is now a museum in Amsterdam, will grip many teenagers. So too will the rise and fall of the Berlin Wall – again, meaty stuff, but something that teenagers can at least begin to grasp the magnitude and meaning of.

Of course, you probably won't get teenagers within a hundred miles of either Amsterdam or Berlin unless you tempt them with something slightly less bitter. Fortunately, both cities carry the sweet promise of retail heaven, as well as a suitably trendy café and arts scene. For teenagers who prefer the sound of thrills over tills, head for the mountains for year-round action sports. The Adventure Company (adventurecompany.co.uk) offers teenage departures on its trips to Switzerland.

Below: One of the seven rollercoasters at Walibi Belgium. **Bottom:** Amsterdam's Houseboat Museum. **Right:** Hiking in the Swiss Alps.

Special needs

Several organizations in Central Europe provide advice and assistance to travellers with special needs. In Belgium, Toegankelijk Reizen (toegankelijkreizen.be) has information on accommodation and transportation for people with disabilities. The Netherlands Board of Tourism (holland.com) issues a *Holland for the Handicapped* brochure, while in Germany, NatKo (natko.de) promotes 'tourism for all people'. In Austria, IBFT (ibft.at) has information on 'barrier-free tourism'. Mobility International Switzerland (mis-ch.ch) has information on wheelchair-accessible travel, accommodation and attractions in Switzerland.

Single parents

Single Parents on Holiday (singleparentsonholiday.co.uk) offers both winter and summer holidays in Austria, while Crystal (crystalski.co.uk) offers discounts for one-parent families on its Austrian skiing holidays. Special lone-parent deals are also available with Eurocamp (eurocamp.co.uk) and other camping operators.

Telling tales ...

We are not a skiing family, but we decided to give it a go this year. Our children are six and three. To our complete astonishment, our week's skiing holiday was one of the most successful ever. Why? Firstly, we skied at Easter which meant the weather was warm (warm kids equals happy kids). Secondly, both Daisy and Poppy had gone ice-skating a couple of times in the UK and developed a taste for balance and ice, which I am sure helped them stay upright on skis. Thirdly, we punctuated the skiing day with breaks for delicious, hot chocolate which both children looked forward to when they were getting tired.

Simon Calder, Senior Travel Editor, the Independent, and
Charlotte Hindle, freelance travel journalist

Big fun in Little Europe

Belgium, Netherlands and Luxembourg might not cause the biggest blips on family-holiday-planning radars, but there's more to this diminutive trio than chocolate, windmills and a dismal reputation in the Eurovision Song Contest. They tend to be the kinds of places you drive through on the way to your family holiday, but linger in Luxembourg, for example, and you will discover some beautiful countryside and one of Europe's most spectacularly situated capitals. Belgium and the Netherlands, on the other hand, not only share a long stretch of sandy coastline but possess a liberal scattering of theme parks, cycling routes and other family attractions. Amsterdam emerges as the region's most child-friendly city with its 'green light' district of museums, parks and canals.

Belgium

🚴 🏖 ♿ 🏛 🎡 🎠

» Sandy beaches, up to 500 m wide at low tide, run between Knokke-Heist and De Panne.
» Brussels has several green oases, including Parc du Cinquantenaire, Brussels Park, Egmont Park and Duden Park.
» Grand Place and Place Sainte Catherine in Brussels host a Christmas market and nightly sound-and-light show during December.

A waffley good time

Brussels Belgium's capital is nothing if not diverse. At one extreme you have the bureaucratic edifice of the European Union headquarters, at the other a statue of a little boy peeing into a fountain. An obligatory first stop on any family sightseeing tour of the city, Le Manneken Pis (manneken-pis.com) has been eliciting sniggers from children since it was unveiled in 1619 on the corner of Rue de l'Etuve and Stoofstraat. The city's most significant historical landmark, however, is the Grand Place, a beautiful square surrounded by ornate buildings dating from the 13th century. It's in complete contrast to Atomium (atomium.be) – a 'massive molecule' of nine escalator-linked spheres rearing above Bruparck in northern Brussels. Not far from the mighty atoms you'll find Mini-Europe (minieurope.com), a quirky collection of 300 pint-sized monuments, plus an IMAX cinema and waterpark. Other child-friendly attractions include the Musée des Enfants (museedesenfants.be), Musée des Sciences Naturelles de Belgique (sciencesnaturelles.be) and the interactive exhibits at Scientastic (scientastic.be). The Centre Belge de la Bande Dessinée (comicscenter.net) showcases Belgium's comic-strip heroes, including Hergé of Tintin fame. Several cartoon-adorned buildings around the city form part of an outdoor exhibition known as the Comic Strip Route.

Wallonia Occupying the southern half of Belgium, Wallonia's big crowd-puller is Walibi Belgium (walibi.be), a theme/water park combo boasting over 50 rides, including seven roller coasters and a 140-m river run through rapids and waterfalls. For more natural thrills, go underground at the Grottoes of Han (grotte-de-han.be) or kayak along the River Lesse (lessekayaks.be). To give your brain a buzz, head for the Eurospace Centre (eurospacecenter.be) or Pass (pass.be), an interactive science adventure park.

Flanders Deeply moving lessons in the mindless brutality of two world wars can be found in cemeteries and museums throughout northern Belgium, including the Memorial Museum Passchendaele 1917 (passchendaele.be) near Ypres, where, in 1917, casualties exceeded 500,000 in 100 days for a gain in territory of just 8 km. On a lighter note, the North Sea coast has sandy beaches, while Ghent and Bruges have canals to explore and chocolate shops to peruse.

Little squirt – the Mannekin Pis in Brussels.

❓ Where can I see this?

Located 20 minutes' drive south of Brussels, the site of the Battle of Waterloo (waterloo1815.be) has an excellent visitor centre, battlefield tours and a puzzle book to help children aged 7-12 decipher the strategies that led to Napoleon's defeat. Don't miss the re-enactments of cavalry and artillery manoeuvres at Lion Mound Hamlet every weekend in July and August.

The Netherlands

😊😌😊🅾️💷🎭🎒

» For value and flexibility, consider staying outside Amsterdam. Molengroet campsite (molengroet.nl) is close to beaches, but just 40 km from the city centre.

» For an insight into how the Dutch lived in times gone by, visit the Open Air Museum (openluchtmuseum.nl) on the outskirts of Arnhem.

» For theme parks, try De Efteling (efteling.com) or Linnaeushof (linnaeushof.nl). The island of Texel has the Maritime and Beachcombers Museum (texelsmaritiem.nl).

Going Dutch

Amsterdam The Dutch capital may have something of a seamy image, but it gets an emphatic green light when it comes to travelling with kids (see box, right). This is largely due to its spider's web of 13th-century canals – a great excuse to transform boring old city sightseeing into something far more exciting. You can get afloat on a pedal boat, but you'll see more on a canal tour boat (canal.nl). Keep an eye out for *De Pozenboot*, a houseboat moored on the Singel that has become a refuge for stray cats. You can also hire bikes at several locations in the city (Vondelpark has safe paths, as well as a café, paddling pool and puppet theatre). Alternatively, hop on a tram (museumtram-amsterdam.nl) at Centraal Station for the 20-minute ride to Amsterdamse Bos, a woodland park with space to run around.

Kids' top 10: Amsterdam

1 Pedal a four-seater canal bike around the waterways.

2 Ogle a Van Gogh (or revere a Rembrandt) at either the Van Gogh Museum (vangoghmuseum.nl) or Rijksmuseum (rijksmuseum.nl).

3 Climb the 85-m-tall tower of Westerkerk church for a pigeon's-eye view of the city.

4 Find out what makes your brain tick, discover how to purify water and uncover the science behind adolescence at the hands-on technology museum, NEMO (e-nemo.nl).

5 Travel back in time as you board the replica Dutch East Indiaman *Amsterdam*, moored at NEMO (above right) while the Scheepvaart Museum (scheepvaartmuseum.nl) undergoes renovation.

6 Cycle out of town to Amstelpark to see the well-preserved De Rieker windmill, built in 1636 and a favourite subject for Rembrandt.

7 Marvel at the tragic, yet inspiring, story of Anne Frank at Anne Frankhuis (annefrank.nl), the secret annexe in which the Jewish teenager and her family hid from the Nazis for 25 months during the early 1940s.

8 Discover what it was like to live on a houseboat in the old days at the Houseboat Museum (houseboatmuseum.nl).

9 Cook up a feast at KinderkookKafé (above left), where kids get to prepare, cook and serve meals.

10 Run wild at TunFun (tunfun.nl), a subway-turned-adventure playground for one- to 12-year-olds.

🚴 Cycling routes

Flower bulb route Petal power meets pedal power. This 30-km route between Haarlem and Sassenheim (near Leiden) passes through the dazzling bulb fields of southern Holland – at least, they will be when the daffodils and tulips are in bloom during April and May. Purchase a route guide at the tourist information office in Lisse.

Windmill route A 43-km spin through the Alblasserwaard area in southern Holland. Start near Kinderdijk (which has a row of 19 windmills), then it's plain sailing as you follow the signposts through a typical Dutch polder landscape of rivers and meadows.

North Sea route Stretching from Den Helder to Boulogne-sur-Mer, the Dutch part of this coastal epic is still 300 km long – so be sure to do it in a northerly direction to make the most of tailwinds. Apart from beaches, dunes and seaside resorts like Scheveningen, highlights on the ride include the Oosterschelde storm-surge barrier in Zeeland.

❷ What about Luxembourg?

The Grand Duchy may be little more than a dot on the map, but it crams in everything from a World Heritage-listed capital to the forested hills of the Ardennes and the wine region of the Moselle Valley. Perched on a rocky promontory, Luxembourg city offers fine views over the Pétrusse Valley, particularly from the Place de la Constitution. Walk along the Chemin de la Corniche up to the Bock – a cliff where Count Sigefroi laid the foundations for a fortress more than 1000 years ago. All that remains is a honeycomb of underground passages known as the Bock Casemates. These, and other highlights, can be visited on a City Safari Tour for families that leaves from the tourist office at Place Guillaume. Heading north towards the Ardennes, Bourscheid Castle is worth a detour, as is the National Military Museum in Diekirch with its displays of the 1944 Battle of the Bulge. The Ardennes is ideal for exploration by bike. Well-signed routes vary in length from 10 to 40 km and there are some specifically for kids.

Underrated and under your nose

Nice cars, good beer, fine composers – but surely not that great for family holidays? Well, actually, yes. Germany might lack the charisma of the Spanish Costas or the magnetism of Disneyland Paris, but what it lacks in big names and notoriety it more than compensates for with a veritable 'cheer-fest' of family attractions, ranging from island retreats in the Baltic Sea to roller-coaster mayhem at Europa-Park. What's more, Germany is easy to reach and a piece of (Black Forest) cake to get around, whether you're cruising the autobahn towards Berlin or dawdling along the Fairy Tale Route on the lookout for the seven dwarves.

Country highlights

➤ Several cities, including Berlin and Hamburg, have super-saver cards, offering free travel on public transport and free or discounted admission to major attractions.
➤ Satisfy sweet-tooth cravings at the Chocolate Museum in Cologne (Köln) and the Haribo factory in Bonn.
➤ Germany has an extensive cycle route network (adfc.de) and over 5000 'bike-friendly' places to stay (bettundbike.de).

Berlin Germany's happening capital doesn't exactly buzz with family appeal, but don't overlook it as drab or uninviting. There's plenty to keep families interested for a day or two – although older children will definitely get more from the city. In addition to iconic landmarks like the Brandenburg Gate, Berlin's defining moments of post-war history are best revealed at Haus am Checkpoint Charlie (mauermuseum.de), a small museum documenting the rise and fall of the Berlin Wall and the numerous, often fatal, attempts made to flee East Germany. If you visit just one other museum in Berlin, make sure it's the Pergamon Museum (smb.spk-berlin.de) – one of the collection of museums on Museum Island – where pride of place goes to the Hellenistic masterpiece, the Pergamon Altar,

a frieze of sparring gods and giants which dates from the 2nd century BC. Continue into the adjoining Ancient Near East collection and you will find other amazing artefacts collected by German archaeologists, including a truly monumental reconstruction of the Babylonian Ishtar Gate and Processional Way. Berlin may be heavy on history, but light relief for kids is available in the form of the excellent Berlin Zoo (zoo-berlin.de) with its famous sculptured Elephant Gate and extensive animal collection. Don't miss the Hippopotamus House where you can view the lumbering river horses from both above and below water. The aquarium is also worth a visit, particularly for its walk-in Crocodile Hall, black-tip reef sharks and breeding jellyfish. Take the U5 underground or M17 tram to the city's outskirts and you'll discover Tierpark (tierpark-berlin. de), a 160-ha landscape zoo with spacious open-air enclosures for everything from pachyderms to primates.

Coast and islands Germany's North Sea coast has no shortage of sandy beaches, including the 12-km-long St Peter-Ording. Avid naturalists should head to the Elbe estuary off Cuxhaven where the islands of the Hamburg Wattenmeer National Park are popular with terns and seals. Just to the north, Schleswig-Holstein Wattenmeer

Clockwise from top: dramatic cliffs on Rügen; autumn in the Black Forest; Brandenberg Gate in Berlin; cuckoo clock from Bavaria.

National Park provides a memorable, if messy, opportunity to venture into the world's largest contiguous area of mudflats – a rich wildlife habitat that, for safety reasons, should only be explored on a guided tour. On Germany's Baltic coast, the island of Rügen (ruegen.de) makes a superb family-holiday base, with everything from sea promenades and sandy beaches to steam-train rides and boat trips.

Black Forest Home of the cuckoo clock, the Black Forest in southwest Germany can easily be toured by road, but you'll feel much better walking – especially after indulging in a slice or two of ubiquitous cherry-filled chocolate cake. A guided trail lasting from one to 10 days starts at Triberg (triberg.de) where you can also take a day hike to the 160-m Wasserfaelle Gutach, the highest cascade in Germany. St Märgen also makes a good base for walks, while Furtwangen has a cuckoo clock museum.

🚍 Touring routes

Castle Road
(burgenstrasse.de)
Mannheim to Prague: 1000 km

Tales of witches, knights and dragons add zest to this long-established scenic tour of castles and palaces in Germany and the Czech Republic. In Heidelberg Castle, for example, children can discover the 'witch's bite' – a crack in an iron door ring where a witch tried to force entry to the castle using her teeth. Several castles organize costumed festivals, ghost tours and medieval banquets. You'll also encounter medieval games in towns like Bad Wimpfen, while others, such as Ansbach and Schwetzingen, run special guided tours for children. Other highlights include the impressive fortifications of Auerbach, the medieval imperial city of Nürnberg and the ancient towns of Bamberg, Coburg, Kronach, Kulmbach and Bayreuth. The Castle Road is a designated cycle route and there are also coach tours and train stations along its length. Other child-friendly highlights include Sea Life Speyer (sealifeeurope.com) near Heidelberg – a series of aquariums evoking the various habitats of the Rhine from alpine source to Rotterdam harbour – and Zirndorf's Playmobil Fun Park (playmobil.de) where the knight's castle stands alongside a pirate ship, gold mine and jungle ruins.

The Toy Road
(spielzeugstrasse.de)
Nürnberg to Waltershausen: 300 km

Site of an international toy fair (toyfair.de), Nürnberg is an appropriate place to start this short trail through a land of dolls, teddies and model railways – although don't forget that Legoland Germany (legoland.de) lies well to the south of the route near Günzberg. A short distance from Nürnberg is the Playmobil Fun Park (see left), while the town of Fürth is home to several major toy manufacturers and a puppet festival in May. Coburg dotes on dolls, Weidhausen tends towards teddies, while Neustadt not only has copious amounts of both (in the Museum of the German Toy Industry), but also has a doll and teddy bear doctor. Educational toys are on display at Friedrich Froebel's memorial museum in Oberweissbach; Lauscha is the birthplace of Christmas tree baubles, while Ohrdruf's claim to fame is the rocking horse and porcelain doll. Don't miss the massed display of gnomes at Trusetal Gnome Park (note that sledgehammers and golf clubs must be left at the entrance).

Fairy Tale Route
(deutsche-maerchenstrasse.com)
Bremen to Hanau: 600 km

The road to enchantment starts in Bremen, birthplace of the Brothers Grimm, whose timeless fairy tales come to life as you travel north. There's a chance you might meet Snow White and the Seven Dwarves in the Weserbergland hills. Schwalmstadt, meanwhile, is Little Red Riding Hood country, while Mother Goose waddled about in the Werra Valley. Sleeping Beauty nodded off in Sababurg Castle, Cinderella had a ball at Polle Castle, Rapunzel let her hair down in Trendelburg and, of course, Hamlyn is where the Pied Piper led his rats on a merry dance. In just about every town you will find fairy-tale tours, theatre shows, museums, and picture-perfect half-timbered buildings. At the heart of the Fairy Tale Route, Kassel is home to the Brothers Grimm Museum and also hosts a summer folklore festival and fairy-tale Christmas market. Don't miss the Bremen Town Musicians, on stage every Sunday between May and September.

❓ Where can I ride this?

Silver Star, the biggest rollercoaster in Europe, is at Europa-Park (europapark. de) in Rust. Reaching speeds of 130 kph and centrifugal forces of 4 G, it's just one of the 100-plus rides and attractions at this outstanding theme park. Silver Star riders must be at least 11 years old and 140 cm high. Other highlights include Fjord Rafting through Scandinavia and an interactive Atlantis Adventure where you explore a sunken citadel armed with laser harpoons. But it's the themed streetscapes of 12 European countries, from Greece to Russia, which may well leave the most lasting impression.

Holidays that run like clockwork

The great Swiss outdoors has more family-friendly attractions than you can shake a ski stick at. From nature trails and mountain railways to gold panning and whitewater rafting, boredom is easily banished in the squeaky-clean, rosy-cheeked land of Heidi and Peter the Goatherd. Public transport runs with typical Swiss precision and there are even 30-odd resorts and nearly 50 hotels that have been cited as particularly family friendly. Any downsides? Well, Switzerland can be pricey, but you'll find family travel passes (plus some Toblerone therapy) will help to sweeten the pill. See page 102 for a round-up of winter ski resorts.

Country highlights

⊙⊙⊛⊛⊛⊕⊛⊙⊙⊛⊛⊕

»» The Swiss Pass (swisstravelsystem.ch) permits unlimited free travel by train, bus and boat (including scenic routes like the Glacier Express), plus free entry to 400 museums.
»» Swiss holiday resorts that have a range of services geared specifically to the needs of children and parents are awarded a 'Families Welcome' label (swisstourfed.ch).
»» Zurich Airport (zurich-airport.com) has a children's playground with a trampoline and Alouette helicopter, as well as 75-min tours of the apron, runways and nature reserve.

Bernese Oberland   Eiger, Mönch and Jungfrau reign supreme above the Bernese Oberland (berneroberland.ch), Switzerland's ultimate outdoor playground and the setting for such classic alpine destinations as Interlaken and Gstaad. For peak perfection, set your sights on the Jungfraujoch (jungfraubahnen.ch), a breathtaking visitor centre perched on a mountaintop with giddy views of summits and glaciers. You reach the 'top of Europe' using three different rack-and-pinion trains and, once there, you can visit the Ice Palace and go hiking, dog sledging and summer skiing. Another summit that's easily bagged is 2190-m Stockhorn (stockhorn.ch), reached by cable car from Erlenbach in just 20 minutes. The views from the top take in everything from distant Mont Blanc to the lakes of Thun and Brienz. More down-to-earth adventures include Aldeboden Flower Trail (adelboden.ch),

a gentle 3-km amble from the Hahnenmoos Pass to Sillerenbühl with drawings and information to help you identify alpine flora. If you prefer something more fluffy, try the Marmot Trail on Betelberg Mountain. Kids aged four to 10 will also enjoy the Dwarf Trail (alpenregion.ch). Upping adrenaline levels slightly, the Bernese Oberland is riddled with hiking and biking opportunities, and there's also whitewater rafting on the Saane (swissraft.ch).

Graubünden   Family highlights in this eastern canton include 'luggage-free' hiking holidays in the Engadine, Val Bregalia, Val Poschiavo and Swiss National Park (engadinferien.ch), where your bags are transported from hotel to hotel leaving you to carry little more than a pack lunch and a stash of cable-car tickets. For hiking with a literary twist, skip along the Heidi Adventure Path above Maienfeld. Gold panning (gold-rush.ch) is available on the Rhine at Disentis, while those who splash about on the Inn River at Scuol will be rewarded with some gold-star whitewater rafting (engadin-adventure.ch) along a 6-km gorge – minimum age 14.

Valais   With the Matterhorn and numerous other 4000-m giants straddling the French and Italian borders, it's little wonder that Valais is a magnet to rock climbers. Children can get to grips with ropes and carabiners on the Aletsch Fixed-Rope Trail (alpincenterbelalp.ch), a four-hour

scramble around Gibidum Reservoir. Also on offer are two-day adventures, combining *via ferrata* and a glacier hike or rafting on the Rhône and canyoning through the Massa Gorge. Slightly more contrived, but no less fun, is Aquaparc (aquaparc.ch) at Le Bouveret on the shores of Lake Geneva.

Pick of the resorts: Saas Fee

Kids' activities   For those with energy, try horse riding, mountain biking and hiking some of the 350 km of marked footpaths; for those who want an easier way up and down the mountains take the cable car to the start of the Feeblitz summer toboggan run. Husky buggies (think 'mushing on wheels') are also available.

Best family day out   A 40-minute drive away, Zermatt and the Matterhorn are well worth a visit. Closer at hand, however, is the 3500-m Mittelallalin, reached by cable car and underground railway. Here, you can find out about glaciers in the Ice Pavilion and have lunch in the world's highest revolving restaurant. Summer skiing is also available.

Top right: Hydrospeeding and rafting in the Vorder Rhine Gorge. **Below top right:** The Wengernalp Railway in the Bernese Oberland.

? Where can I ride on this?
The Lake Lucerne Navigation Company (lakelucerne.ch) operates five vintage paddle steamers and 15 modern cruisers. The most interesting section of the lake is the Urnersee where you can intersperse ferry travel with walks along the 35-km lakeside Swiss Path.

Kids' top 10: Switzerland

1 Race down the Churwalden toboggan run (pradaschier.ch) at speeds of up to 40 kph.

2 Hoof up the Binn Valley on a mule trek (bergland.ch).

3 Sleep in a fairy-tale castle at Mariastein-Rotberg (youthhostel.ch).

4 Spot ibex, red deer and marmots in Swiss National Park (nationalpark.ch).

5 Strike it lucky at Grabenmühle (grabenmuehle.ch), trout fishing or panning for gold.

6 Swing like Tarzan at Pilatus Seilpark (pilatus.ch), a suspension rope park in central Switzerland suitable for kids aged eight and above.

7 Ride Switzerland's oldest steam cog railway up 1678-m Rothorn Kulm (brienz-rothorn-bahn.ch).

8 Discover sweet sensations on the Chocolate Train from Montreux to the Nestlé factory in Broc, or visit Schoggi Land in Flawil (schoggi-land.ch).

9 Ride a cool scooter-bike from Belalp to Blatten along 7 km of mountain paths and surfaced roads (brig-belalp.ch).

10 Meet Peter the Goatherd in Savognin (savognin.ch) or live like a shepherd for the day at Alpine Museum Riederalp (riederalp.ch).

Sights in Lucerne

Chapel Bridge Lucerne's 14th-century landmark, spanning the Reuss River.

The Dying Lion of Lucerne Rock sculpture described by Mark Twain as "the saddest and most moving piece of rock in the world".

Weinmarkt Old city square surrounded by buildings adorned with elaborate frescos.

Austria

Mountains, Mozart and the Sound of Music

Altogether now: "Doe, a deer, a female deer; ray, a drop of golden sun…" Welcome to the land of the family singalong. Resistance is utterly futile. If you're not singing it, you'll be humming it. And if it's not a ditty from *The Sound of Music* it will be Falco's 'Rock Me Amadeus' or, worse still, an impromptu yodelling session. Depending on their age, your children will either join in with gusto or shrink away in disgust. Salzburg, Austria's musical 'maestro-piece', is great fun for kids, while Vienna, with its Lipizzaner stallions, is somewhat more refined. But it's only out on the mountain paths, the bike trails and the sparkling lakes that you'll tune in to the some of the best 'sounds' in Austria – the rarefied silence of alpine wilderness.

Country highlights

>> The Vienna Card allows unlimited free travel by underground, bus and tram for 72 hrs, plus discounts at over 200 attractions, shops and restaurants.
>> Allow a week to pedal along the easy, level Danube Cycle Path from Passau to Vienna.
>> A drive of about 1 hr from Vienna, the Sonnentherme Lutzmannsburg (sonnentherme.com) has a baby spa and adventure waterpark.

Vienna   Horse-lovers will be enchanted by Vienna's Spanish Riding School (srs.at) where the famous Lipizzaner stallions strut their stuff. You can book tickets online for the limited performances that take place, usually on Sundays, throughout the year. However, there's a stampede to get them, so you may have to settle for the Morning Exercises (daily, except Mondays) when the white beauties are put through their paces. Rarer, but more accessible, creatures can be viewed at Schönbrunn Zoo (zoovienna.at), which not only has giant pandas, a Borneo rainforest habitat and a 'polarium', but also does its bit for the less fortunate equines of this world – namely the endangered Turkmenian donkey and Mongolia's Przewalski horse. To escape horses altogether, take a spin on the 65-m-tall Riesenrad (wienerriesenrad.com), Vienna's iconic Ferris wheel which first cranked into life in 1897. For a more hands-on view of the past, the Schönbrunn Palace (schoenbrunn.at) has a kids' museum where you can learn how to lay a royal table and dress up as a prince or princess.

Salzburg   There's something you should know before visiting Salzburg: most of the locals have never seen *The Sound of Music*. They don't wander around singing 'Edelweiss' and they haven't erected a statue of Julie Andrews in the city centre. They do, however, appreciate its tourism potential, so if you want to see movie locations, like the Mirabell Gardens where Maria and the Von Trapps sang 'Do-Re-Mi', simply sign up to one of the many Sound of Music Tours (panorama tours.com). Try to spare some time, though, for Mozart. You can see his memorial in Mozartplatz Square in the heart of the old town. Of the two Mozart museums in Salzburg, the house at Getreidegasse 9 (containing his concert violin, clavichord and other memorabilia) is probably of more interest to children.

Salzburg's baroque splendour was financed largely through sales of salt mined from the Dürrnberg. At Salzwelten Hallstatt (salzwelten.at) you can explore the ancient mines, descending into their depths on thrilling wooden slides (reaching over 60 m in length) to an underground lake where salt was dissolved from the surrounding rock. To add a pinch of creepiness to the experience, you'll also learn of the remarkable discovery in 1734 of a miner who, having died during a tunnel collapse centuries earlier, became naturally embalmed in the salt. Salzburg's 'white gold' brought

Above right: One of the famous Lipizzaner stallions. **Top far right**: Riesenrad, Vienna. **Far right**: Edeilweiss.

Pick of the resorts: Kaprun

Kids' activities   The highlight of any visit to Kaprun is a trip to the Kitzsteinhorn glacier where, year-round, you can ski, snowboard, toboggan or try your hand at snow-scooting. Down in the valley, there's easy cycling to nearby Zell am See where you can hire rowing boats on the lake. Alternatively, you can go horse riding, rock climbing, tandem paragliding or whitewater rafting on the Salzach River.

Best family day out   An hour's drive from Kaprun, the 11th-century Werfen Castle (filming location for *Where Eagles Dare*) perches dramatically on a 150-m-high rock and has an excellent falconry show. Equally impressive are the nearby ice caves – a subterranean *Narnia* world of blue-ice stalactites and frozen waterfalls.

immense wealth to its prince archbishops and one of them, Markus Sittikus, indulged in a summer palace, known as Hellbrunn (hellbrunn.at). A 20-minute cycle from the city centre or a short hop on bus 25, 17th-century Hellbrunn is always a big hit with kids – particularly for the 'water jokes' that riddle its gardens. Sittikus, who evidently loved a good laugh, designed all sorts of push-button pranks, from trick fountains and spurting grottoes to a stone dining table where all but one of the seats is rigged with a water jet. Come with a sense of humour and change of clothes.

Carinthia Austria's southernmost province has some 1270 lakes, 200 of which are suitable for swimming. Other summer activities include hiking and cycling, while winter snows create over 800 km of pistes. One of the region's most popular family attractions is Minimundus (minimundus.at) where you can see the world in miniature.

Styria Located in southeast Austria, Styria's forest-draped hills are perfect for

biking (there are over 5000 km of cycle trails), while lakes and rivers offer boating, fishing and whitewater rafting.

Tyrol This magnificent alpine region in western Austria is the country's adventure playground, with everything from horse riding and mountain biking to climbing and year-round skiing. Prepare to be dazzled at the Swarovski Crystal World (kristallwelten. swarovski.com) in Wattens, and to be spooked at Hexenwasser Hochsöll (hexenwasser.at), a land of sorcery and witchcraft in Hohe Salve.

66 99 There were the inevitable stress points when the hills seemed to be alive with the sound of whingeing children. How come none of the Von Trapp family ever seemed to get mauled by horseflies, brush against stinging nettles or scrape their knees on gravelly mountain paths?

Will

❸ Where can I see this?
Drive along the Grossglockner High Alpine Road (grossglockner.com) into the heart of the Hohe Tauern National Park for views of Austria's highest mountain, the 3798-m Grossglockner, soaring above the Pasterze glacier. There are four themed children's playgrounds along the way, as well as an Alpine Nature Show Museum.

Central Europe essentials

When to go

The most popular time is summer – unless, of course, you're going for the winter sports. Snow cover lasts from December to March in the alpine valleys of **Austria** and **Switzerland**, although in higher regions you can often eke out a skiing holiday as late as April or May (some resorts, like Kaprun, offer summer skiing). If it gets cold enough in the **Netherlands** for the canals and waterways to freeze over, it's possible to go skating on the canals and floodplains. Otherwise, April is the best month for seeing daffodils in bloom; May for tulips. In **Germany**, the forests are golden-hued and gorgeous in autumn, a time when resorts are less crowded and the weather less settled.

Getting there

Several airports in the region are major international hubs, particularly Schipol (Amsterdam) and Frankfurt. National carriers include Austrian Airlines (aua.com), KLM (klm.com), Lufthansa (lufthansa.com) and Swiss Air (swiss.com). Expect to pay from around €130 for a return flight between London and Amsterdam with KLM. The Dutch carrier operates an extensive European and global network, linking up with Northwest Airlines to serve numerous cities in the United States. Return fares from Amsterdam include Berlin (€165), Vienna (€180), Orlando (€435), New York (€500), and Los Angeles (€630). Low-cost airlines serving Central Europe from the UK and Ireland include easyJet (easyjet.com), with flights to Amsterdam, Berlin and Zurich, and Ryanair (ryanair.com), which flies to Brussels, Frankfurt, Karlsruhe-Baden and Salzburg. Air Berlin (airberlin.com) also has an extensive network with return fares between London and various German cities from as little as €70.

Getting around

Public transport is excellent throughout the region. If you arrive in **Brussels** by Eurostar your ticket includes travel to any other Belgian station within 24 hours (b-rail.be). Bus services are operated throughout Belgium by TEC (infotec.be).

In the **Netherlands**, a slick **rail** network (ns.nl) can whisk you from Schiphol Airport to Amsterdam in just 16 minutes. Once in the capital you can rent a **bicycle** from around €6 per day, or explore the city by Canal Bus (canal.nl). In Luxembourg, the Luxembourg Card (ont.lu/card-en) provides free travel on trains and buses, plus free admission to over 50 attractions in the Grand Duchy – a one-day family card costs €20.

Germany's rail network is operated by Deutsche Bahn (bahn.de), with InterCityExpress (ICE) **trains** capable of

ⓒ How much to offset your emissions?

From London to:

Amsterdam £0.80
Brussels £0.80
Geneva £1.40
Berlin £1.70
Vienna £2.20

From New York to:

Amsterdam US$25
Brussels US$25
Geneva US$27
Berlin US$27
Vienna US$30

Go green: four ways to skip the flight

» Take Eurostar (eurostar.com) from London St Pancras to Brussels, a 111-minute journey with fares from around £60 return. Onward connections are possible to Amsterdam by high-speed Thalys (thalys.com) or Germany by Deutsche Bahn (bahn.de). Switzerland is also served by fast, reliable inter-European rail services.

» Catch a bus. Eurolines (eurolines.com) has an extensive service across Central Europe.

» Take the ferry from the UK to France (see page 106), Belgium or the Netherlands. P&O Ferries (poferries.com) has 14-hour services from Hull to Zeebrugge and Rotterdam; Stena Line (stenaline.com) sails from Harwich to Hook of Holland with one-way fares starting from around £50 for a car plus driver.

» Use Eurotunnel (eurotunnel.com) to reach mainland Europe, then access the superb motorway network.

reaching speeds of 320 kph. Some ICE trains have a Kleinkindabteil (or 'toddler compartment') reserved for families with small children. Most major German cities boast an underground, bus and tram system, and in many you'll find Welcome Cards offering discounted admission to various tourist attractions, as well as unlimited travel on local public transport. A 48-hour Berlin Welcome Card (btm.de) costs €16 and provides free travel for one adult and up to three children under 14.

As you might expect, super-efficient, integrated public transport systems reach their peak in **Switzerland**. The Swiss Travel System (swisstravelsystem.com) offers a variety of travel passes for making use of the country's network of over 20,000 km of **rail**, **bus** and **boat** routes. The Swiss Pass allows unlimited free travel on the entire network, including scenic

How to see the Swiss Alps without walking

Trading hiking boots, map and compass for a public transport pass and a pair of sensible shoes places a whole new perspective on travel in Switzerland. It takes the 'puff' out of the views, makes more sense if you have very young children and puts you in touch with more of the country's cultural highlights. Take Mount Rigi's rack railway, for example. Tenacious little red locomotives (which use a cog-and-pinion system to grip the rails) have been shuttling tourists up and down the Queen of the Mountains since 1871 when the Vitznau–Rigi line became the first rack railway in Europe. They're mostly electric now, but occasionally one of the few surviving steam trains is coaxed into action.

routes like the famous Glacier Express (glacierexpress.ch), city trams and buses, a 50% discount on several mountain railways and cableways and free entry to 400 museums. A four-day pass costs from around €230 per adult, while children aged between six and 15 travel free if accompanied by a parent. **Coaches** in Switzerland are operated by PostBus (postauto.ch) and **trains** are run by Swiss Federal Railways (sbb.ch). RailAway (railaway.ch) offers winter and summer excursions combining discounted rail fares and admission to various attractions. **Austrian Federal Railways** (oebb.at) connect major towns and cities in **Austria**, while various **cruise** operators offer excursions on the Danube (ddsg-blue-danube.at).

Accommodation

There are Center Parcs (centerparcs.com) in Belgium, Netherlands and Germany, each one with its own special attractions (see box, page 178). Camping holidays are available throughout Central Europe with Canvas Holidays (canvasholidays.com), Eurocamp (eurocamp.com) and Keycamp (keycamp.ie). Also try Select Sites (select-site.com). Ski specialists offering all-inclusive family packages to Austria, Switzerland or both countries, include Esprit (esprit-holidays.co.uk), Mark Warner (markwarner.co.uk) and Powder Byrne (powderbyrne.com).

In **Belgium**, Belsud (belsud.be) offers a comprehensive range of accommodation in Brussels, Wallonia and the Ardennes, including farmstays, rural *gîtes*, horse-riding *gîtes*, apartments and holiday villages. Also try Gîtes de Wallonie (gitesdewallonie.net) and Logis de Belgique (logis.be).

Germany has more than 2500 campsites, most of which are open from April to October. There are also some 600 youth hostels (djh.de) and a huge choice of self-catering properties and B&Bs (bed-and-breakfast.de). For farm holidays, browse the selecton at landtourismus.de. Hotels that cater specifically for families include Dorfhotels (dorfhotel.eu), Familotel (familotel.de) and Kinderland (kinderland.by). Europa-Park also has some great themed hotels.

Switzerland offers a bewildering array of family-friendly accommodation, ranging from igloos (iglu-dorf.ch) and mountain huts (sas.cas.ch) to sleeping in giant barrels at Trasadingen (feste-feiern.ch). Over 40 KidsHotels (kidshotel.ch) offer quality family accommodation, with larger-than-average rooms, well-equipped play areas, children's menus and baby essentials if you need them (see page 179). Some even provide free childcare during the high season, as well as a weekly programme of activities. Another long-established family favourite, Reka (reka.ch), operates several holiday villages around Switzerland, each one with a relaxed mixture of self-catering cottages, playgrounds, swimming pools and occasionally a wellbeing centre for the grown-ups. Farm holidays from around €230 per week for four people are available from Swiss Holiday Farms (agrotourismus.ch). Hostels operated by Swiss Youth Hostels (youthhostel.ch) and Swiss Backpackers (swissbackpackers.ch) have good-value family rooms and self-catering kitchen facilities, while Bed and Breakfast Switzerland (bnb.ch) has an online directory with rates starting at around €18.

Austria's all-inclusive, full-board Kinderhotels (kinderhotels.com) are well known for their outstanding childcare. English-speaking childminders are provided free of charge (even for babies as young as seven days old) for up to 60 hours a week. Baby and toddler equipment is provided free of charge, and all food is organic, fresh and locally produced.

Fact file

	GMT	Language	Money	Code	Tourist info
Belgium	+1	French, Dutch, Flemish	Euro (£1 = €1.50)	+32	visitbelgium.com
Netherlands	+1	Dutch	Euro (£1 = €1.50)	+31	holland.com
Luxembourg	+1	French, German, Luxembourgish	Euro (£1 = €1.50)	+352	visitluxembourg.com
Germany	+2	German	Euro (£1 = €1.50)	+49	germany-tourism.de
Switzerland	+1	German, French Italian, Rumantsch	Swiss Franc (£1 = CHF2.50)	+41	myswitzerland.com
Austria	+1	German	Euro (£1 = €1.50)	+43	austria.info

Center Parcs at a glance

Belgium	Erperheide	• Aqua Mundo in an Asian fishing village setting • Indoor play world • Surrounded by forests, and lakes of the Limburg Kempen
	De Vossemeren	• Aqua Sana wellbeing centre • Discovery Bay in jungle setting with pirate treasure • Indoor skate arena
Netherlands	De Kempervennen	• Montana Snowcentre • Outdoor High Adventure Experience • Waterskiing and Dive College
	Het Meerdal	• Aqua Mundo with 101-m water slide • Mini Baluba indoor playworld
	Het Heijderbos	• Aqua Mundo with wild-water rapids • Horse-riding school • Tropical dome with Jungle Expedition
	De Eemhof	• Aqua Mundo with body-boarding Flow Rider • Magnetic climbing in Action Factory • Watersports centre
	Port Zélande	• Sail and Dive College • Adventure Factory play area • Close to Zeeland coast
Germany	Bispinger Heide	• Aqua Mundo with Dragon Rock water spout • Aqua Sana wellbeing centre
	Park Hochsauerland	• Aqua Mundo with sauna • Water play house and crazy river
	Park Heilbachsee	• Indoor play world • Bike routes along the Moezel • Watersports at nearby Eifelmaar
	Butjadinger Küste	• Aqua Mundo with crazy river • Surrounded by Waddenzee nature reserve

Food and drink

Although you will find a cosmopolitan range of restaurants, cafés and fast-food outlets everywhere you go, be sure to try one or two regional specialities. In **Belgium**, kids will love getting to grips with *gauffres* – thick waffles dripping with chocolate, strawberry or raspberry sauce and doused with whipped cream. The **Netherlands** has *poffertjes*, small pancakes dusted in sugar; **Germany** has the formidable Black Forest cake, a calorific concoction of cherry-filled chocolate sponge smothered in cream and flakes of chocolate; **Austria** has strudels and **Switzerland** and **Belgium**, of course, are magnets to chocoholics. If that lot doesn't have your children drooling nothing will. On the savoury front, **Germany** is renowned for its sausages – but be warned: they are not always your typical barbecue bangers. Try red Rotwurst from Thuringia, liver sausage from Kassel and black sausage spiced with thyme, cloves and nutmeg from Bavaria. In **Switzerland**, fondues, raclettes and rosti should all go down a treat with kids – as long as they haven't overdosed on Toblerone beforehand.

Health and safety

Apart from a small risk, during spring, of contracting illnesses from tick bites in forested parts of Germany, no special health precautions are necessary for travel in Central Europe. Remember that strong currents can affect the North Sea coast, so always check whether it's safe to go swimming. Ultraviolet radiation is more intense at high altitude which means you need to cover up, slap on some sun cream and wear sunglasses if spending a day in the mountains.

These are not just waffles … these are Belgian *gauffres* …

Top 10 Swiss family hotels

▸▸ Victoria Ritter Hotel, Kandersteg (hotel-victoria.ch)
▸▸ Muchetta Children's Hotel, Wiesen (kinderhotel.ch)
▸▸ Park Hotel Waldhaus, Flims (parkhotel-waldhaus.ch)
▸▸ Robinson Club Schweizerhof, Vulpera (robinson-schweiz.ch)
▸▸ Gasthaus Sternen, Gais (sternengais.ch)
▸▸ Santis Family Hotel, Unterwasser (hotel-saentis.ch)
▸▸ Parkhotel Delta, Ascona (parkhoteldelta.ch)
▸▸ Alphubel Panorama Hotel, Saas-fee (hotelalphubel.ch)
▸▸ Edelweiss Hotel, Engelberg (edelweissengelberg.ch)
▸▸ Style Hotel, Zermatt (stylehotel.ch)

Eastern Europe

Lightning over Piran, Slovenia.

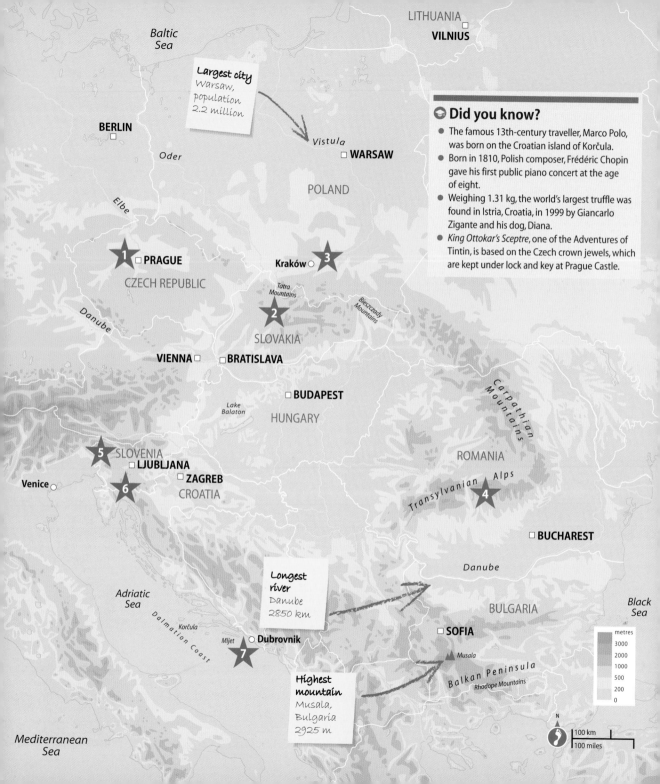

Baltic Sea

LITHUANIA
VILNIUS ☐

Largest city
Warsaw, population 2.2 million

Vistula

☐ **WARSAW**

BERLIN ☐

Oder

POLAND

Elbe

Did you know?

● The famous 13th-century traveller, Marco Polo, was born on the Croatian island of Korčula.
● Born in 1810, Polish composer, Frédéric Chopin gave his first public piano concert at the age of eight.
● Weighing 1.31 kg, the world's largest truffle was found in Istria, Croatia, in 1999 by Giancarlo Zigante and his dog, Diana.
● *King Ottokar's Sceptre*, one of the Adventures of Tintin, is based on the Czech crown jewels, which are kept under lock and key at Prague Castle.

⭐1 ☐ **PRAGUE**

Kraków ○ ⭐3

CZECH REPUBLIC

Danube

Tatra Mountains

⭐2

Bieszczady Mountains

SLOVAKIA

VIENNA ☐   ☐ **BRATISLAVA**

Carpathian Mountains

☐ **BUDAPEST**

Lake Balaton

HUNGARY

ROMANIA

⭐5 SLOVENIA
☐ **LJUBLJANA**

Venice ○   ☐ **ZAGREB**
⭐6   CROATIA

Transylvanian Alps

⭐4

☐ **BUCHAREST**

Adriatic Sea

Longest river
Danube 2850 km

Danube

BULGARIA

Black Sea

Dalmatian Coast

Korčula

Mljet ○ **Dubrovnik**

⭐7

☐ **SOFIA**

▲ Musala

Balkan Peninsula

Rhodope Mountains

Highest mountain
Musala, Bulgaria 2925 m

metres
3000
2000
1000
500
200
0

Mediterranean Sea

N

100 km
100 miles

⭐ Take a family-friendly break in Prague

▸▸ Czech Republic, page 188

② Hike or ski in the Tatra Mountains

▸▸ Slovakia, page 189

⭐ Search for dragons

▸▸ Slovenia, page 192, and Poland, page 190

⭐ Dare to step inside Count Dracula's castle

▸▸ Romania, page 191

⭐ Swim in a mountain lake

▸▸ Slovenia, page 192

⭐ Explore the world's largest underground canyon

▸▸ Slovenia, page 192

⭐ Island hop along the Dalmatian coast

▸▸ Croatia, page 193

Introduction

When it comes to carefree holidays in Europe with the kids, traditional favourites like France, Spain and Italy will always reap the most beach towels. However, an increasing number of families are looking to the east for a holiday that not only gives them excellent value for money, but also has many of the facilities offered by resorts further west. Following the turbulent 1990s, Croatia's tourism is back in top gear with excellent hotels, villas and holiday camps along the Adriatic coast. Adventurous families can paddle by sea kayak through the Dalmatian archipelago or explore inland national parks like Plitvice Lakes. Making a quieter splash, Croatia's northern neighbour, Slovenia, is slowly gaining popularity. It's small (about the size of Wales), but has everything from mountains and castles to alpine lakes and a dash of Adriatic coastline. Prague and Kraków are well established city break destinations, but families in the know will be able to find plenty to please children, from Prague Castle to the Wieliczka Salt Mine near Kraków. A cultural sojourn in either city combines well with an adventure- or wildlife-focused break in the Carpathian Mountains. There are wolves and bears to be spotted in Romania's wildwoods – and if that doesn't have enough bite, try Dracula's Castle.

❝❞ *Little Slovenia not only proved to be big on boredom-busting, but it enabled our children to experience something new, from whitewater kayaking to sipping water straight from a mountain spring. It was less crowded and better value for money than its more popular European rivals, but ultimately its main draw was that it was somewhere just that little bit different.*

Will

Eastern Europe rating

Wow factor
★★★

Worry factor
★★★★

Value for money
★★★★

Keeping teacher happy
★★★

Family accommodation
★★

Babies & toddlers
★★★

Teenagers
★★

⊘ How to be a cool kayaker

Croatia's island-spattered Adriatic coastline is crying out for some serious sea kayaking. You must wear a life jacket and be able to swim. Sea kayaks are quite stable, but try to avoid rough water. If you're a beginner it's a good idea to share a two-person kayak with an adult.

Here's how to perfect your paddling:

▶▶ Adjust your seat and foot pedals so that your knees are touching the inside of the hull. This will help your balance.

▶▶ Sit upright so that your arms are not taking all the strain of paddling.

▶▶ Space your hands on the paddle about 50 cm apart.

▶▶ Grip the paddle lightly, otherwise your forearms will quickly feel tired.

▶▶ Don't dip the paddle too deeply into the water.

▶▶ Rather than pulling the blade through the water, trying pushing with the opposite arm.

▶▶ Imagine tracing a figure-of-eight with your hands as you paddle. Keep a smooth and steady rhythm, allowing the kayak to 'run' between strokes.

▶▶ Use the rudder only when necessary – oversteering will slow the kayak and make paddling much harder work.

Books to read

Little Dracula's First Bite, Walker Books, 2001
The inhabitants of Castle Dracula are a colourful bunch – not least Little Dracula who is small, bald and green. In this story Little Dracula tries to be just like Dad and has a 'fangtastic' time! Ages 4-6

Stories of Dragons, Usborne Books, 2007
There's a dragon to match every mood in these myths and folklore tales gathered from around the world. Some are friendly, some fierce and there's even one which loves to dance. Ages 8-12

Hidden Tales from Eastern Europe, Frances Lincoln, 2002
A collection of elegantly told and beautifully illustrated folk tales from Poland, Slovakia, Russia, Croatia, Serbia, Slovenia and Romania. All ages

Dracula, Usborne Classics retold, 2007
Can eccentric Professor Van Helsing and his brave young friends take on the world's vilest vampire? A modern retelling of the classic Bram Stoker horror novel. Ages 9+

Chopin and Romantic Music, Barron's Educational Series, 2000
Discover the accomplishments of Polish-born Frédéric Chopin, including his influence on the romantic movement of music. Ages 12+

Surviving Auschwitz: Children of the Shoah, ibooks, 2005
The harrowing story of three young girls who survived Hitler's most notorious death camp. Intensely moving, these children's stories provide a remarkable insight into the Holocaust years and its implications. Ages 14+

❓ Where can I see one of these?

Bears still roam the dense forests of Eastern Europe, but they can be very elusive. One of the best spots to catch a glimpse is Kingstone Mountain National Park in Slovenia. Poland's Bieszczady Mountains are still roamed by Europe's Big Five: wolf, bison, bear, lynx and red deer, while Croatia's Plitvice Lakes National Park is home to bears and wolves.

Taste of Eastern Europe: apple baba

A popular dessert in Poland, apple baba is a light and delicious cake using tart apples and plenty of sugar.

What you need
- ⇒ 4 tart apples (such as Granny Smiths), peeled, cored, quartered and thinly sliced crosswise
- ⇒ 2¼ cups of granulated sugar
- ⇒ 1 tsp cinnamon
- ⇒ 4 large eggs
- ⇒ 1 cup vegetable oil
- ⇒ ½ cup fresh orange juice
- ⇒ 2 tsp vanilla extract
- ⇒ 4 cups plain flour
- ⇒ 1 tsp baking powder
- ⇒ confectioners' sugar for sprinkling

What to do
- ⇒ Heat oven to 175°C and grease a 25-cm loaf tin.
- ⇒ Place the apples in a bowl and sprinkle with ¼ cup sugar and the cinnamon.
- ⇒ In another bowl, beat the eggs and the rest of the sugar until pale yellow and thick.
- ⇒ Gradually beat in the oil, orange juice and vanilla extract.
- ⇒ Sift the flour and baking powder and slowly add it to the egg mixture until it is like thick honey.
- ⇒ Fold the apples evenly into the batter and pour into the tin.

- ⇒ Bake for around 1½ hours until the top is well browned and splitting.
- ⇒ Invert on to a wire rack to cool and sprinkle with confectioners' sugar just before serving.

🏰 Romanian castles

Bran Castle For the legend of Dracula (see right).

Peles Castle For its opulent interior.

Corvinesti Castle For its vaulted Knights' Hall.

🔍 How to decorate an egg

It is traditional to paint and decorate eggs in many parts of Eastern Europe. Here's how to create your own *pysanka*, or Ukranian Easter egg, using the written-wax batik method. It's fiddly but fun.

What you need
- ⇒ Smooth fresh eggs (room temperature)
- ⇒ Long straight pins stuck into corks (your writing tools) Wax (equal amounts of beeswax and paraffin)
- ⇒ Wax warmer (candle-heated container)
- ⇒ Egg dyes in containers large enough to submerge eggs
- ⇒ Paper tissues
- ⇒ Candle
- ⇒ Varnish

What to do
- ⇒ Blow your egg by using a long pin to make a tiny hole at each end (slightly larger at the bottom). Pierce and break the yolk with the pin, shake to mix the contents. Blow gently through the smaller hole to empty the contents into a bowl. Rinse carefully and leave it to dry.
- ⇒ Practise your design on paper.
- ⇒ Dip your pinhead into melted wax and use it to draw your design on the egg.
- ⇒ When you are happy with the design, place the egg in the lightest-colour dye for 10 to 30 minutes. Blot dry with tissues.
- ⇒ When completely dry add further designs with wax before submerging in the next colour of dye. Repeat with one more colour.
- ⇒ An adult can complete the design by holding the egg, a small section at a time, against the side of a candle flame for no more than five seconds to remove the wax (by blotting with a tissue).

One to watch:
Count Duckula – the Complete First Series
Freemantle, 2006
Eleven hours of animated antics about the vegetarian vampire duck who is terrified by the sight of blood.

When it comes to family holidays there's no doubt that some parts of Eastern Europe, particularly rural areas, can be more of a challenge than elsewhere on the continent. You won't, for example, find as many theme parks here as you do in Scandinavia or France. And on more remote forays in Eastern Europe you might occasionally find yourself wondering whether you've strayed too far off the beaten track. However, all of the countries covered in this chapter have not only popular resort areas and fascinating cities but also a good range of family-friendly accommodation, activities and facilities.

Babies (0-18 months)

If you've tried a Mediterranean holiday in France, Italy or Spain with tiny tots, you'll find that Croatia's Adriatic coast is just as warm, comfortable and friendly. True, it's further to fly – and there can't be many new parents willing to summon the energy required to drive 1600 km from the UK to Split. However, once you reach Croatia, there's a wide range of baby-friendly accommodation to choose from, including self-catering villas and hotels with paddling pools.

Now is also the time to snatch a weekend city break in Prague or Kraków while your little darling is still buggy-bound and hasn't yet found the voice to offer unwanted suggestions to your sightseeing plan. Avoid the crazy midsummer months, though, when you'll spend half your time apologizing for running your buggy over the feet of endless streams of other tourists.

Toddlers/pre-school (18 months-4 years)

As with babies, travelling to Croatia with pre-school children means you can avoid the blisteringly hot month of August. It's cooler and less crowded in June and September. Be aware that many beaches along this stretch of Adriatic coast are either rocky or pebbly – a godsend to parents who abhor the prospect of sand finding its way into every nook and cranny, but a tad frustrating for a budding sandcastle-building three-year-old. It's worth remembering to pack jelly shoes or wetsuit boots to help littl'uns negotiate pebbly coves.

With its shallow waters and gently shelving shores, Lake Balaton in Hungary (page 189) is another good beach option for young children – and excellent value if you're on a tight budget. So too are the Baltic states (see opposite).

Kids/school age (4-12 years)

The Czech Republic, Slovakia, Romania and Slovenia all start to have more appeal around this age. Slovenia is a doddle to travel around and its compact size means you can give youngsters a taster of all things Eastern European, from spooky castles and mysterious forests to action-packed mountain resorts.

Usually, you will find that the minimum age for things like

All-action Slovenia – **Left to right:** exploring Skocjan Caves, hiking in Triglav National Park and multi-activity at Lake Bohinj.

PARAGLIDING
HYDROSPEED
CANYONING
KAYAKING
RAFTING
BIKING

river rafting (with gentle rapids) is five or six. It's around this age (possibly earlier if they have older siblings) that kids start nurturing a fascination with all things gruesome – vampires included. Bran Castle in Romania, the legendary home of Dracula, will either titillate or terrify them. If it's likely to be the latter, opt instead for Kraków where the Royal Castle has an altogether less sinister dragon's lair.

The history of Eastern Europe doesn't feature as much on the school curriculum as other parts of the continent, but that's no reason to sidestep the beautiful Czech capital, Prague. Forget its reputation as a 'couples-only' city break destination. With a little forward planning you can easily adapt it to suit children and adults alike.

Teenagers (13 years+)

One aspect of Eastern European history that older children will encounter in their studies is the rise and fall of Nazi Germany. However, prepare yourself for some difficult questions before taking teenagers (14 and over) to Auschwitz in Poland. Reading about it in school textbooks is one thing, but to actually visit the site of this notorious death camp is a harsh lesson for young minds.

Elsewhere in the region, teenagers will love the mix of nightlife and water-based activities along the Croatian coast. Plan a sea-kayaking expedition among the Dalmatian islands or opt for a centre-based holiday in which youngsters can dabble in a range of activities, from sailing to scuba-diving.

The Adventure Company (adventurecompany.co.uk), Explore Worldwide (explore.co.uk) and Exodus (exodus.co.uk) offer teenage departures on trips to various Eastern European countries, including Croatia, the Czech Republic, Poland, Romania, Slovakia and Slovenia.

Special needs

Certain attractions in Eastern Europe, such as Slovenia's Skocjan Caves, present obvious difficulties to wheelchair users. However, although facilities for the disabled are still somewhat limited throughout the region, most countries are making strong moves to improve access for all.

Wheelchair-accessible monuments in Prague include St Vitus Cathedral, Old Royal Palace, St George's Basilica, Ballgame Hall and Prague Castle Gardens, while Wawel Royal Castle in Kraków can be reached (albeit with some effort) by its ramp-like approach road. Thanks to a million-dollar accessibility project disabled travellers can tour most parts of the Wieliczka Salt Mine.

Single parents

The Adventure Company (adventurecompany.co.uk) offers single parent family departures on its Croatian sea kayaking and multi-activity holidays, as well as trips to the Czech Republic and Slovenia. Mango (mangokids.co.uk) specialises

Bound for the Baltics

Easily overlooked, but bursting with fresh ideas for a family holiday, the Baltic states of Estonia, Latvia and Lithuania promise exceptional value for money. English is widely spoken, it's easy to get around by hire car or public transport and accommodation includes child-friendly guesthouses, farms and cottages.

Lithuania family holiday Start with two nights in a three-star hotel in Vilnius Old Town where you can explore the narrow lanes, secret courtyards and fairy-tale spires of one of Europe's architectural gems. Then head into the countryside for four nights in a family guesthouse, exploring the area by kayak or cycle. Round off the holiday with three nights in a spa hotel or at a resort on the Amber Coast.

How much? From around £365 per adult and £255 per child (excluding flights), based on a family of four staying in two en suite rooms on a bed-and-breakfast basis.

Contact Baltics and Beyond (balticsandbeyond.com).

in group holidays for single parent families and runs a Single Parent Family Ski Holiday to Romania each February half-term. For a gentle seaside break, Small Families (smallfamilies.co.uk) runs a trip to the Island of Lopud in Croatia.

You get Prague … they get the mountains

The beautiful medieval capital of the Czech Republic, Prague has become one of Europe's most trendy city-break destinations – a magnet for couples in search of café culture, a spot of shopping and a lazy trawl around the historical sights. However, before you ship your brood off to the grandparents, you might want to know that Prague is also quite child-friendly. One or two carefully planned days will mean you can still see many of the city's highlights and keep the kids happy in the process. Of course, it would help if you promise them a week of mountain fun in Slovakia's Tatra Mountains afterwards …

Prague

O 🛟 🏛

›› Pick up a travel pass for the city's trams, metro and buses at the tourist office in Old Town Square (prague-info.cz). The Prague Card can also be used as a ticket to some 40 tourist attractions, including Prague Castle and the zoo.
›› The Nostalgic Tram 91 (Nostalgická Linka 91) departs from Vozovna Strešovice every hour from 1200 to 1800 at weekends and weaves through the Old Town.
›› Certovka, a small park with a playground at the western end of Charles Bridge, and the Franciscan Garden near Wenceslas Square both offer freedom for kids to run about.

Two-day action plan

Day one Take the funicular railway up 318-m Petrín Hill where you'll find an imitation Eiffel Tower built for the Jubilee Exhibition of 1891. Although it's only a quarter the height of the Parisian version, the 299 steps lead to a viewing platform with far-reaching views of the city and distant mountains. Next, head to the nearby maze which has walls lined with distorting mirrors, so you can get lost and laugh about it at the same time. Inside this bizarre labyrinth is a huge painting depicting the 1648 battle that ended the Thirty Years War. On the way down from Petrín Hill, stop for a snack at the Nebozizek restaurant which has an outdoor patio, fine views and a varied menu.

In the afternoon, tram route 22 or 23 will take you to Prague Castle (hrad.cz). Founded in the ninth century, the city's crowning glory contains churches, palaces, towers and convents within its fortified walls. As you enter, look out for the statue of the fighting giants above the castle gates. Beyond the president's office looms Prague's richly decorated Gothic icon, St Vitus's Cathedral. See if you can spot the gargoyles on the western façade . Inside, you'll find the tomb of 'Good King' Wenceslas who founded a chapel here around AD 925, only to be murdered by his brother a few years later. A relief depicting the brutal act can be seen on the west door.

If cultural fatigue starts to take its toll on your children, give them a quick boost at the Toy Museum (barbiemuseum.cz). This quirky collection has everything from tin soldiers, model aeroplanes and wooden farm animals to clockwork robots, teddy bears and several hundred Barbie dolls. While you're at this end of Prague Castle, take a wander down Golden Lane with its quaint 16th-century artisans' cottages, then backtrack towards the cathedral for one last cultural 'biggie'. It's a difficult decision between the Royal Palace, with its massive vaulted halls and coats of arms, and St George's Convent with its national collection of Renaissance and Baroque art.

Top: The Vltava River. Above: One of the statues on Charles Bridge. Left: The astronomical clock on the Old Town Hall.

Day two Start in the Little Quarter where kids can play in the park on Kampa Island and feed the swans on Vltava River. Then cross Charles Bridge, admiring the famous statues of various saints, and walk the short distance to the Old Town Square. Traffic-free (unless you count the horse-drawn carriages) this wonderful public space, with cafés spilling out on to the cobbles, is framed by beautiful churches, palaces, town houses and arcades. The most eye-catching building is the Old Town Hall. Make sure you get a good position in front of its astronomical clock, which strikes the hour accompanied by an elaborate charade of clockwork Apostles, and other moving figures.

In the afternoon, catch a tram to the Prístaviste Parníku landing stage

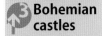
Karlstein (25 km southwest of Prague, pictured above) Rises above woodland that has changed little since Charles IV hunted there in the 14th century.

Konopište (40 km southeast of Prague) Striking for its extravagant displays of stags' heads and other hunting trophies.

Krivoklát (45 km west of Prague) Dominated by its massive Great Tower, the castle has a vaulted Gothic hall reminiscent of the one in the Royal Palace at Prague Castle.

Top left: Golden Lane within the walls of Prague Castle. **Top centre**: Hiking in the Tatras. **Below top left**: Orava Castle.

(located between Palackého and Jiráskuv bridges) for a boat ride on the Vltava. Heading north, you'll pass riverside landmarks, like the National Theatre, before reaching Stromovka Park and the Výstaviste fairgrounds – site of a dancing fountain and the Sea World aquarium (morsky-svet.cz). On the opposite bank, Prague Zoo (zoopraha.cz) is renowned for its captive breeding programmes of endangered species, such as Przewalski's horse.

Slovakia's Tatra Mountains

» Take the overnight sleeper train from Prague to the Slovakian town of Liptovský Mikuláš, which is within easy striking distance of the Tatra Mountains.
» Nestled beneath the Roháce range, the small village of Zuberec (rohace.sk) has become a thriving centre for winter and summer activities.
» Other popular resorts in the High Tatras include Štrbské Pleso, Starý Smokovec and Tatranská Lomnica.

Some gentle alpine action

Zuberec As well as being the starting point for hiking trails to nearby lakes and waterfalls, Zuberec is within cycling distance (around 18 km) of Brestova's open-air museum (museum.sk) where traditional buildings – from sawmills to churches – evoke rural Slovakian life from the late 19th century. Hands-on activities allow children to take part in crafts, games and folk dancing. In winter, Zuberec is an ideal place for learning to ski or snowboard, with easy access to around 4 km of pistes. Cross-country trails, snowshoeing and dog sledging are also available.

Malá Fatra National Park Cloaked in beech forests and home to bear, lynx and golden eagle, this beautiful mountain reserve (80 km from Zuberec) is also renowned for its whitewater rafting. Trips depart from Parnica, swooping you through grade II-III rapids in the Vratna Valley.

Oravice More gentle float trips are possible here drifting downstream on traditional wooden rafts to Orava Castle (oravamuzeum.sk), perched on a rocky bluff 100 m above the river. Oravice also has a thermal pool complex (meanderpark.com) which doubles as a ski park in winter.

What about Hungary?

Lake Balaton is the place to go. Central Europe's largest lake has an average depth of just 2-3 m. It warms quickly in the sun and has gently shelving beaches, making it ideal for young children. Sailing, windsurfing, canoeing and other water sports can be found on the southern shore, while the north has rugged scenery that will appeal to hikers, cyclists and horse riders. Thermal springs and spas, meanwhile, offer a spot of relaxation. Ryanair (ryanair.com) flies direct from London three times a week. Vacansoleil (vacansoleil.co.uk) offers a week at Camping Autós on the lake's southern shore from around £285 for a fully equipped six-berth tent, including Dover–Calais ferry crossings. The campsite offers excursions to Budapest where kids will love exploring the 10-km labyrinth of passageways beneath Buda Castle (labirintus.com). Further info: Hungarian National Tourist Office (hungary.com).

Would you like salt with your city break?

Like Prague in the Czech Republic (see page 188), Kraków in southern Poland is one of Eastern Europe's essential city-break destinations. Spared the ravages of the Second World War, its Old Town is a medieval marvel that could almost have been lifted straight from the pages of a child's storybook (there's even a dragon's den under the castle). Combine a day or two in Kraków with a visit to the nearby Wieliczka Salt Mine (not as dry and dull as you might imagine), then head south into the Carpathian Mountains.

Kraków

» Hire a horse-drawn carriage to explore the Old Town (krakow-info.com).
» For light relief, head for the IMAX cinema, puppet theatre, zoo or Park Wodny (parkwodny.pl), a waterpark on the northern outskirts.
» Auschwitz death camp (auschwitz-muzeum. oswiecim.pl) is an hour's drive from Kraków. However, even if your kids have studied the barbarism of Nazi Germany at school, Auschwitz is not suitable for anyone under 14.

The storybook city

Heart and soul of the city, Kraków's central square (Rynek Glowny) is a great place to start your sightseeing. Young children will be obsessed with feeding the pigeons, while teenagers can practise being cool at the pavement cafés. Either way, parents will be able to snatch admiring glances at the square's impressive buildings, including the Cloth Hall and the 14th-century St Mary's Church.

Kraków's Old Town is only 800 m wide by 1200 m in length, so it won't take you long to walk to the Czartoryskich Museum (muzeum-czartoryskich.krakow.pl) with its exquisite portrait, *Lady with the Ermine*, by none other than Leonardo da Vinci. Next, it's off to Wawel Hill (wawel.krakow.pl) where Kraków's greatest urban myth lurks beneath the Royal Castle. Once upon a time there was a powerful prince called Krak who built a castle on a hill above the Vistula River. He founded a town named after himself and everyone lived happily ever after – or at least they would have done had it not been for the dastardly dragon living in the cave under the castle. This monstrous beast was a perfect nuisance, gobbling up cattle, sheep and people (it was particularly partial to pretty maidens). But wise Prince Krak had a cunning plan. One day, he ordered a sheep's hide to be stuffed with sulphur and tossed into the dragon's den. Of course, the repulsive reptile swallowed it in one gulp, only then feeling the sulphur burning its stomach. Rushing down to the river, the dragon drank and drank… until it exploded. The end. Well, not quite – you can visit the Dragon's Cave for yourself by clambering down the steps inside one of the castle's towers, but be sure to explore the fine treasures in the fort beforehand.

Wieliczka Salt Mine Caves made of salt? You may well have to pinch yourself when venturing into this extraordinary subterranean labyrinth, carved entirely from salt and extending to some 300 km of passages and more than 2000 caverns. Mined since the Middle Ages, when salt was as valuable a commodity as oil is today, the Wieliczka Salt Mine (kopalnia.pl) is just 10 km from the city centre. Although excavations reach a depth of 327 m, the section accessible to visitors only goes down as far as 135 m. The 2-km tour takes you through a surreal, almost fairytale, world of vast floodlit chambers – some with underground lakes, others with salt carvings and murals left by Wieliczka's miners. There are chapels illuminated by chandeliers, great wooden stairways, displays of old

Top: Krakow Castle. **Above**: Wieliczka Salt Mine. **Below**: Wood carving.

mining equipment and even a subterranean restaurant, souvenir shop and post office.

Where can I go skiing?

Located in the Tatra Mountains about 100 km south of Kraków, Zakopane (zakopane.pl) is Poland's premier ski resort, offering access to over 50 lifts and a wide variety of runs to suit all abilities.

Walk in the woods…if you dare!

The Carpathian Mountains sweep through Romania in a broad swathe of densely forested peaks, peppered with small villages and farming communities, while the River Danube scrawls a lazy outline along the country's southern border. Rural Romania feels remote and unspoilt – locals will tell you the country has more bears than British Columbia. But despite this image of tranquil wilderness, there's always something gnawing away at your mind – or rather your neck – when you contemplate Romania. Just the mere mention of the words 'Dracula's castle' will have your kids more riveted than any amount of spiel about the adventure, wildlife and cultural highlights in this land of Transylvanian vampires!

Country highlights

» Rail travel is inexpensive, although a hire car will give you more freedom to roam.
» As well as the highlights below, try to fit in a visit to the medieval town of Sighisoara.
» Beach resorts are located along the Black Sea coast between Mangalia and Mamaia.
» Bran Castle Museum (brancastlemuseum.ro).

Fangs for the memories

Bran Castle Creepy courtyards, dingy passageways and an underground network of secret tunnels – if this austere, forbidding Gothic stronghold, perched on a rocky outcrop in the village of Bran, doesn't give you goose pimples, nothing will. After all, this was the lair of Dracula, wasn't it? Before you dash off to buy garlic cloves, wooden crosses and any other vampire repellents, let's be absolutely (and historically) clear about Bran Castle and its Dracula association. Dracula never existed. He was a character in Bram Stoker's 1897 classic novel. Vlad Tepes, on the other hand, did exist. Born in 1431, he was the son of a Transylvanian governor who happened to be a member of an anti-Turk secret society known as the Order of the Dragon. In folklore, the dragon was associated with the devil, so Vlad's father was known as Dracul ('Devil'), while Vlad himself became Dracula ('Son of the Devil'). What's this got to do with vampires? Well, that's where fact and fiction begin to blur. Tepes grew up to be a ruthless warlord, battling the hated Turks and picking up a few of their less salubrious habits, such as impaling prisoners on long stakes (earning him the jolly title of 'Vlad the Impaler'). So, more of a blood-letter than a bloodsucker, but the whole Dracula vampire myth has somehow stuck to Bran Castle where Tepes briefly sought refuge in 1462. When it comes to the crunch, though, no kid is going to let a bit of history spoil a juicy excuse for a vampire hunt.

Carpathian Mountains A three-hour drive north of Bucharest, Kingstone Mountain National Park has one of Europe's largest concentrations of brown bears, wolves and lynxes. Based in nearby Zarnesti, you can make forays into the reserve's primeval woods, tracking these elusive predators or even seeing them up-close from a hide. Elsewhere in the Carpathians there are plenty of opportunities for activities, including mountain biking and whitewater rafting in summer, and cross-country skiing and horse-sleigh rides in winter. The village of Lunca Bradului will lull you into a gentle pace of life, where you can experience rural life while indulging in a spot of hiking,

Top: Bran Castle. **Above:** Danube Delta. **Below right:** Traditionally painted eggs.

horse riding or fishing.

Painted churches Located in Bucovina, northern Romania, this extraordinary cluster of medieval 'picture book' churches are painted, inside and out, with elaborate murals depicting Biblical stories, ranging from Genesis to the Last Judgement.

Danube delta Sprawling over 5700 sq km, Europe's largest wetland is a watery wilderness of lakes, channels, reed beds, meadows and islands that's home to raucous nesting colonies of pelicans, herons and terns, plus huge flocks of overwintering wildfowl. You can feast your eyes on this avian spectacle by taking the train to Tulcea and then hopping on a tour boat.

❓ What about Bulgaria?

There's more to Bulgaria than Black Sea resorts and cheap skiing packages. Head for the Rhodope Mountains in summer for hiking, caving, rock climbing and horse riding. If a winter visit appeals, base yourself in one of the quieter resorts, like Chepelare, which offer dog sledging and snowmobiling as well as skiing.

A little bit of what you fancy

Small, but perfectly formed, Slovenia is a medley of dramatic alpine peaks, beguiling lakes and bear-filled forests tucked away at the top of the Adriatic. It is often hailed as one of Europe's last genuinely unspoilt destinations. But if that translates in your mind as 'wild and uninviting', then think again. Slovenia is not only emerging as prime adventure territory, but its compact size, extraordinary diversity and well-established infrastructure makes it ideal for family holidays. With its modest 46-km coastline, there's not much in the way of sun-soaked beaches, but at least you can paddle your toes in the Adriatic at the lovely old town of Piran.

Country highlights

🌊 🚣 🚠 🏊 ⛰ 🏰 🏛

» Head to Lake Bohinj (bohinj.si) for a no-frills, action-packed break. If you want more hotels, restaurants, nightlife (and tourists), opt for Lake Bled (bled.si) instead.

» Roads are well-maintained and uncrowded, making self-drive a breeze. A scenic train journey links Bohinj to Nova Gorica, within striking distance of the coast.

Pocket-size Europe

Ljubljana Slovenia's capital (Ljubljana-tourism.si) won't blow your mind, but it's pleasant enough for a day or two at either end of your itinerary. Climb up to the castle for views over the city's terracotta-tiled rooftops, and wander the old quarter's tangle of cobbled streets and squares. Tivoli Park has a children's playground, and there's a waterpark (atlantis-vodnomesto.si) on the city's outskirts. The nearby medieval hilltop town of Skofja Loka is a good excuse for a day trip.

Lake Bled With paved lakeside paths, picture-perfect Lake Bled is a godsend if you've got a baby or toddler in a stroller.

There are also horse-and-cart rides, boat trips to the island and an excellent swimming area with waterslide and shady trees. Treat the kids to a cream cake at the Park Hotel.

Lake Bohinj Far less manicured than Bled, Lake Bohinj is wild and woody. Pick up a map from the tourist office, pack a picnic and set off to explore Triglav National Park (sigov.si/tnp). Right on your doorstep there are easy, level trails around Lake Bohinj – or you could hire a bike, canoe or rowing boat. Mt Vogel cable car has stunning views over the lake and Julian Alps, while a 90-minute hike through beautiful beech woodland leads to the impressive 78-m-high Savica Falls. Children will love horse riding at Ranch Mrcina where the ponies are small and docile. For adrenaline addicts there is canyoning, tandem paragliding, rock climbing, quad-biking and gentle whitewater rafting on the Sava Bohinjka. Swimming is also popular – but bring something for the kids' feet because the lakeside beaches are gritty and stony.

Caves and castles A combo ticket will allow you to explore Postojna Caves (postojnska-jama.si) and lay siege to the nearby 700-year-old Predjama Castle, wedged dramatically in a 123-m-high cliff face. But if you go underground just once in Slovenia, make sure it's into the mighty Skocjan Caves (park-skocjanske-jame.si). You'll need jackets, torches and a head for heights. It's pitch black (surprise, surprise), so don't take kids who are afraid of the dark

Top: Lake Bled. **Above:** Triglav National Park. **Left:** Rafting on the Sava Bohinjka. **Top right:** Dubrovnik. **Bottom right:** Dalmatian Coast.

– or bats for that matter. After several smallish caverns that are drizzled with stalagmites and stalactites, you enter a vast chamber with plunging cliffs, a subterranean river and Indiana Jones-style bridge. The guided tour lasts 90 minutes; there are hundreds of steps (slippery in places), but kids will emerge wide-eyed with wonder.

Adriatic Sea With its cutesy harbour, Venetian architecture and restaurant-lined waterfront, Piran (piran.si) is a perfect little seaside retreat. For sandy beaches and sunloungers, though, you'll need to nip around the coast to Portoroz (portoroz.si).

Top tip

When staying in Piran, try to get Room 40A in Hotel Tartini (hotel-tartini-piran.com). It's a family apartment with lovely views over the town square and harbour. Shame about the church bells which chime not only every hour, but on the quarter-hour as well.

Croatia

Joining the dots along the Dalmatian Coast

Of all the countries in Eastern Europe, Croatia is the one that cries out 'family holiday'. Not only is its beautiful coast bathed in crystal-clear waters and warm sunshine, but it is also endowed with enough islands and cultural nuggets to turn a seaside holiday into an Adriatic adventure. Base yourself in Dubrovnik, for example, and the kids could be scaling the ramparts of the old city one day and paddling a sea kayak to a deserted cove the next. Rocked by war in the early 1990s, Croatia's tourism industry is back in top gear, whether you want to island hop along the Dalmatian coast or head inland to explore the freshwater wonder of the Plitvice Lakes National Park.

Dubrovnik

» There's a small beach next to Dubrovnik's Old Town (tzdubrovnik.hr), with additional pebbly coves around the Lapad headland.
» The Elaphite islands are connected by ferries, while 'Oldtimer' motor cruisers (maestral.hr) can be chartered for voyages lasting from a few days to a week or more.
» Local companies offering sea-kayaking trips include Adriatic Kayak Tours (adriatickayaktours.com) and Adriatic Sea Kayaking (adriatic-sea-kayak.com).

Walk the walls and hop to the islands
City highlights Built between the 13th and 16th centuries, Dubrovnik's fortified walls encircle the Old Town in a curtain of stone 6 m thick and 25 m high, punctuated by 16 towers. You can walk right around the walls – an epic 2-km amble which offers spectacular views across Dubrovnik's terracotta-tiled rooftops and the Adriatic beyond. The access point for the one-hour circuit is at

Pile Gate; head clockwise to get the uphill bits over with first. Down at street level, most of the highlights are concentrated around the Old Port, including the Dominican Monastery and Rector's Palace. There's also an aquarium, but better to don mask and snorkel and head to one of the city's offshore islands.

Best islands Just a stone's throw from the city walls, tiny Lokrum is a beauty, with its own subtropical gardens, an 11th-century monastery and a small lake linked to the open sea. You can join a half- or full-day sea-kayaking trip here, or take the less strenuous option of a boat tour. Lying further afield are the three, equally verdant isles of the Elaphite archipelago: Kolocep, Lopud and Šipan. All have small, picturesque villages with options for staying overnight, making them an excellent proposition for a multi-day, island-hopping adventure, either by kayak or ferry. If you take the former option, you should be prepared to paddle up to 14 km a day, although in a double kayak you can at least share the workload. Be sure to visit Lopud's sandy Šunj Bay and explore the sea caves on Kolocep. Further north lies the large island of Mljet (mljet.hr) – possibly the most beautiful in the Adriatic, with emerald forests, turquoise seas and saltwater lakes. That said, however, Korcula (korculainfo.com), further along the coast, is also pretty special – not to mention the hundreds of other islands dotted along the Dalmatian coast.

❓ Where can I see this?
A beautiful mosaic of 16 lakes connected by waterfalls, the densely forested Plitvice Lakes National Park (np-plitvicka-jezera.hr) lies 140 km from Zagreb. You can take boat trips on the larger lakes or explore walking trails in the woods.

Eastern Europe essentials

When to go

The climate varies widely across Eastern Europe. **Croatia**'s long hot Mediterranean summers, for example, might allow you to eke out a beach holiday in late October – a time when the Carpathian Mountains of **Poland**, **Slovakia** and **Romania** are bracing themselves for their first winter snowfalls. As you might expect, anywhere in the region away from the Adriatic coast can be bitterly cold during winter. The skiing season lasts from December to mid-April, while the peak summer months are July and August. Avoid the crowds (and the prospect of irritable, overheated children) by visiting popular cities like Prague and Kraków during spring or autumn.

Getting there

The proliferation of low-cost airlines has made Eastern Europe more accessible and forced national carriers to cut prices and improve their services. From the UK, Czech Airlines (czechairlines.com) flies from London and Manchester to Prague. There are also services from Dublin, Paris, Amsterdam and numerous other European cities. From the US, there are flights from New York, Montreal and Toronto. Allow around £240 (including taxes) for a return flight in June with British Airways (britishairways.com) between London and Prague. Low-cost airlines serving the Czech Republic include easyJet (easyjet.com), Ryanair (ryanair.com), Flybe (flybe.com), BmiBaby (bmibaby.com) and Jet2 (jet2.com). The most useful of these is probably easyJet which serves Prague from Gatwick, Stansted, Bristol, East Midlands and Newcastle. Ryanair only flies to Brno. Smartwings (smartwings.com), a Czech low-cost airline, has flights to destinations throughout Europe, but not the UK.

Direct flights from London to Bratislava and Poprad (Tatra Mountains) in Slovakia are available with SkyEurope (skyeurope.com) from as little as £40 return, including taxes. Also try Slovak Airlines (slovakairlines.sk).

LOT Polish Airlines (lot.com) has flights from London and Manchester to Warsaw, but only serves Kraków from Frankfurt, Munich, Paris and Vienna. Ryanair is a better bet for reaching Kraków from Britain and Ireland, with direct services from Dublin, Shannon, East Midlands, Glasgow, Liverpool and Stansted.

Romania's national carrier, Tarom (tarom.ro), offers return flights London–Bucharest from around £140 plus taxes. Low-cost airline, Wizz (wizzair.com), also flies this route.

In Slovenia, national airline Adria (adria-airways.com) has return flights London–Ljubljana from around £20. Also serving Ljubljana is easyJet, while Ryanair flies London–Maribor.

Croatia Airlines (croatiaairlines.hr) has return flights London–Dubrovnik from around £115 return, including taxes.

Tour operators

In the UK
The Adventure Company adventurecompany.co.uk
Bond Tours bondtours.co.uk
Croatian Affair croatianaffair.com
Crystal Active crystal-active.co.uk
Eurocamp eurocamp.co.uk
Explore explore.co.uk
Exodus exodus.co.uk
Families Worldwide familiesworldwide.co.uk
Holiday Options holidayoptions.co.uk
Just Slovenia justslovenia.co.uk
KE Adventure Travel keadventure.com
Keycamp Holidays keycamp.ie
Romanian Affair romanianaffair.com
Lakes and Mountains Holidays lakes-mountains.co.uk

In the USA
Adriatic Tours adriatictours.com
Croatia Travel croatiatravel.com
Slovenia Travel sloveniatravel.com

It also flies from London to Split and Zagreb. Budget airlines serving Croatia include Wizz, easyJet and Flybe.

Getting around

Trains and **buses** probe most corners of the **Czech Republic**, although you will find that buses have a reduced service at the weekends. For public transport timetables, visit vlak.cz.

In **Slovakia**, Lod (lod.sk) upholds the long tradition of river travel on the Danube with regular **cruises** departing from Bratislavia, while major rail routes (slovakrail.sk) connect the capital with Kúty, Zilina, Košice and Štúrovo. Slovakia also has a good road network (some 300 km of new highways were constructed in 2004).

Go green: three ways to skip the flight

➤ Skim across the Adriatic from Venice to Piran (Slovenia) aboard a high-speed catamaran operated by Venezia Lines (venezialines.com).

➤ Several river-cruise companies based in Austria ply the Danube River to Hungary. DDSG Blue Danube Shipping (ddsg-blue-danube.at) offers return trips by hydrofoil between Vienna and Budapest from around £75 (50% less for children aged 6-14). Alternatively, you can take the boat one way and return by night train for about £85.

➤ Travelling by coach to Eastern Europe inevitably means long journeys, but if you're feeling up to it Eurolines (eurolines.com) has services to Poland, Czech Republic, Hungary and Romania. Capital Express (capitalexpress.cz) has a London–Prague service.

CO₂ How much to offset your CO2 emissions?

From London to:
Prague £1.80
Ljubljana £2.20
Budapest £2.50
Warsaw £2.50
Dubrovnik £3.00
Bucharest £3.50

From New York to:
Prague US$28
Ljubljana,
Warsaw US$30
Budapest US$31
Dubrovnik US$32

Information on **rail** travel in Poland is available from PKP Intercity (intercity.com.pl), while international **coach** lines connect cities like Warsaw, Kraków and Gdansk. LOT Polish Airlines will whisk you from Warsaw to Kraków in just 55 minutes from around £75 return.

In **Romania**, domestic **flights** are operated by Tarom (see left) and Carpatair (carpatair.com). Getting around by **bus** and **train** is also straightforward and inexpensive. For details of rail services log on to infofer.ro.

Small in size, but with an excellent road network, **Slovenia** is perfect for **self-drive** and you will find all the main car-rental companies in Ljubljana. Daily charges for a Vauxhall Corsa during August with Europcar (europcar.si) are around £35 (including CDW and unlimited kilometres), while a Renault Laguna will cost nearer £80. For details of **bus** services in Slovenia, contact Avtobusna Postaja Ljubljana (ap-ljubljana.si). For **trains**, contact Slovenske zeleznice (slo-zeleznice.si).

In **Croatia**, **buses** operated by Autotrans (autotrans.hr) connect main towns and cities, while Hrvatske zeljeznice (hznet.hr) runs trains to most major centres except Dubrovnik. If you have the time, **rent a car** and drive the scenic Adriatic Highway from Rijeka to Dubrovnik. Car and passenger **ferries** are operated by Jadrolinija (jadrolinija.hr) between islands as well as ports along the mainland.

Accommodation

You can pitch a tent in one of the **Czech Republic**'s 500 or so campsites for as little as £2.50 a night. At the other end of the scale, a room in a five-star hotel in Prague will easily relieve you of £200 or more. Cloister Inn (cloister-inn.com) is a good mid-range option in Prague's Old Town, just a few minutes' walk from Charles Bridge. An increasingly popular alternative for families is to rent a self-catering apartment. Apartments.cz (apartments.cz) offers more than 80 furnished apartments in Prague, with rates starting at just £20 per person per night.

Apartments and hotels in **Slovakia**'s capital, Bratislava, are available from Bratislava Hotels (bratislavahotels.com), while

ABC Slovakia (abcslovensko.sk) has links to a wide range of rural properties, from cottages and pensions to horse ranches. For information on where to stay in the Tatra Mountains, try tatry.sk.

Fact file

	GMT	Language	Money	Code	Tourist info
Czech Republic	+1	Czech	Czech Koruna (£1 = CZK41)	+420	czechtourism.com
Slovakia	+1	Slovak	Slovak Koruna (£1 = SKK49)	+421	slovakiatourism.sk
Poland	+1	Polish	New Zloty (£1 = PLN5.50)	+48	poland-tourism.com
Romania	+2	Romanian	New Leu (£1 = RON4.90)	+40	romaniatourism.com
Slovenia	+1	Slovenian	Euro (£1 = €1.50)	+386	slovenia.info
Croatia	+1	Croatian	Croatia Kuna (£1 = HRK10.8)	+385	croatia.hr

Four family favourites in Croatia

Hotel Albatros

Where? Cavtat, 20 km south of Dubrovnik.

Why? A great choice for families with children of any age, the four-star Hotel Albatros (see below) has a seafront position in the attractive town of Cavtat with its stylish mansions,

restaurants, bars and boutiques. Hotel facilities include adult and kids' swimming pools, a play area, wellness centre and watersports.

How much? From £425 to £728 per person per week (25% discount for children), including return flights, transfers and half board.

Contact Croatian Affair (croatianaffair.com).

Lanternacamp

Where? Porec, Istrian peninsula.

Why? Good value for money and excellent facilities, including pools, supermarket, pizzeria, tennis and watersports, make this large campsite a safe bet for families. The resort of Porec is just 10 km away, while the Euphrasian Basilica of Porec and the UNESCO world heritage site of Plitvice Lakes National Park are also within easy striking distance.

How much? From £215 to £415 per person for seven nights in a two-bedroom mobile home with decking and BBQ, including flights from London Gatwick or Manchester to Pula.

Contact Keycamp Holidays (keycamp.ie).

Fisherman's Cottage

Where? Trstenik, Pelješac.

Why? Tucked away down a gravel track surrounded by vineyards overlooking an idyllic bay on the island of Pelješac, this traditional stone house (see below) is ripe for a childhood adventure. Simply furnished, with an open-plan living room, it is just 20 m away from the deserted beach. At nearby Trstenik you can rent a boat, while Prapratna (30 km away) has a ferry service to the island of Mljet and its two beautiful lakes.

How much? From £406 to £597 per person per week, based on four sharing, including London return flights and car hire.

Contact Croatian Affair (croatianaffair.com).

Camping Mareda

Where? About 4 km from the small coastal town of Novigrad.

Why? Sprawling through an oak wood and surrounded by vineyards on the Adriatic coast, Camping Mareda (top right) appeals to families in search of a peaceful location with plenty to do. Take your pick from mini golf, football and various watersports at the nearby pebbly beach. There's a café and restaurant on-site, while the ancient harbour town of Porec is just 10 km away.

How much? From around £314 for seven nights in a Venezia mobile home, including P&O ferry crossing Dover-Calais.

Contact Eurocamp (eurocamp.co.uk).

A four-person apartment in Kraków's Old Town costs from around £75 per night with Stay Poland (staypoland.com) which also offers a range of hotels in Warsaw, Kraków and Gdansk. Rural holiday accommodation (or agroturystyka) is gaining popularity in Poland. Polish Country Invites (agritourism.pl) has an online search facility for farmstays throughout the country.

In Romania, a good base for exploring Bran Castle and the Carpathian Mountains is Hotel Balada (balada.ro) in Suceava, which has doubles from around £50 and an apartment from £80 per night, including breakfast.

Accommodation in Slovenia ranges from campsites, farmstays and pensions to grand lakeside hotels. At Lake Bohinj, well-equipped campsites like Autokamp Zlatorog cost from £5 per person, while the four-star Hotel Bohinj has doubles from around £40 per person half-board. Both can be booked through Alpinum (alpinum.net). A good self-catering option is the Zdovc Apartments (bohinj.si/zdovc).

With its alluring Adriatic coastline and offshore islands, Croatia has the cream of Eastern Europe's family-friendly accommodation. Mainstream holiday-camp operators, such as Eurocamp and Keycamp, both feature northern Croatia, while villa and apartment specialists like Croatian Affair have properties throughout the country. For inspiration, see box Four family favourites in Croatia, opposite.

Food and drink
Hearty and non-spicy (though occasionally on the stodgy side), traditional Eastern European cuisine should appeal to most children. In the Czech Republic and Slovakia, expect plenty of fried or roast meat, usually pork or beef, accompanied by dumplings, potatoes or rice. Pot-roasted beef in a rich creamy sauce with cranberries and vegetables is delicious, as are fruit dumplings, strudels and pancakes. In the cities, you will find everything from pizzas to Chinese. A typical meal in Poland consists of noodle soup followed by pork cutlet with red cabbage and potatoes and rounded off with a wedge of cheesecake. Traditional dishes in Romania include *ciorba de perisoare* (meatball soup), *scrumbie la gratar* (grilled herring), *sarmale* (pickled cabbage leaves stuffed with minced meat and rice) and *papanasi* (cottage cheese doughnuts). Parents will no doubt want to sample *tuica*, a potent plum brandy, as well as a few of Romania's best wines, such as Murfatlar, Cotnari and Jidvei. In Slovenia, dishes range from Hungarian goulash, Austrian strudels and Italian risotto to more local fare, such as fresh lake trout and sweet pastries. Expect lots of cabbage and potatoes with everything and don't forget to try *potica*, a roll stuffed with walnuts, poppy seeds, raisins, herbs, cottage cheese or honey. Not surprisingly, Croatia has excellent seafood, ranging from universal favourites like scampi to Dalmatian brodet, a mixed fish stew served with rice. You'll also find no shortage of Italian-inspired food along the coast, from pizza and pasta to ice cream.

Health and safety
No special inoculations are required for Eastern Europe. However, if you plan on walking in any thickly forested areas, take precautions against tick-borne encephalitis, a potentially fatal disease that affects the central nervous system. Although a vaccination is available, it is not generally recommended for those at low risk, such as day trippers. You can prevent tick bites by avoiding tick-infested areas from May to August, using an insect repellent, tucking long trousers into socks and wearing a hat. On the whole, tap water is safe to drink. If in doubt, err on the cautious side and buy bottled water. Sunburn and dehydration can be a threat during summer, particularly along the Adriatic coast where you should also keep an eye out for black spiny sea urchins on rocky shores.

The €10 picnic

100 g chocolate bar €0.95
500 ml bottle of water €0.30
Large packet of crisps €0.50
250 g blueberries €3.10
2 cartons of fruit juice €0.76
4 freshly made cheese and ham rolls €4.20

TOTAL €9.81

🍔 How much for a Big Mac?
USA   US$3.22
UK   US$3.90
Czech Republic   US$2.41
Hungary   US$3.00
Poland   US$2.29
Slovakia   US$2.13

Cape Dastris, Corfu.

Greece & Turkey

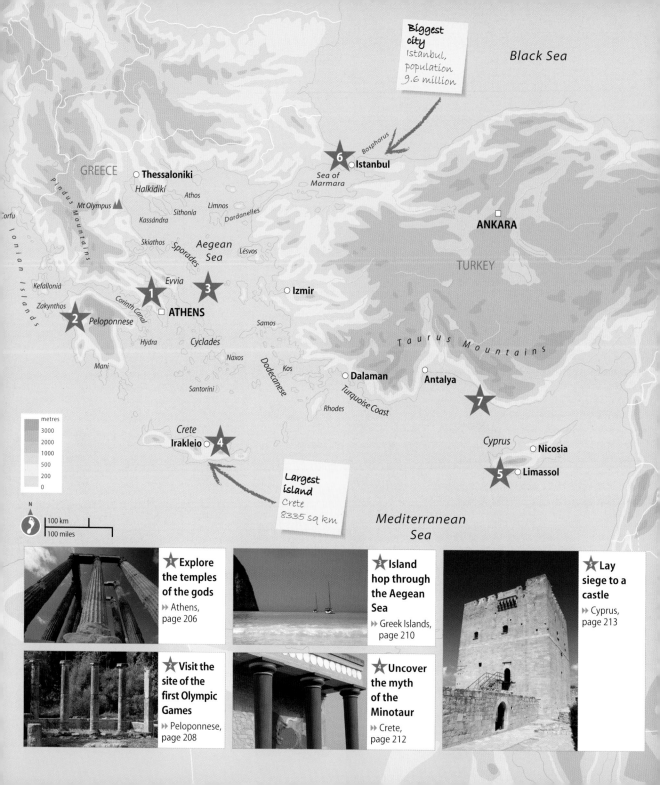

Black Sea

Biggest city
Istanbul, population 9.6 million

Sea of Marmara

⭐ 6 ○ **Istanbul**

Bosphorus

□ **ANKARA**

TURKEY

GREECE

○ **Thessaloniki**

Halkidikí   *Athos*

Mt Olympus ▲   *Sithonía*   *Limnos*

Kassándra   *Dardanelles*

Skiathos   *Sporades*

Aegean Sea

Lésvos

Corfu

Pindus Mountains

Ionian Islands

Kefalloniá

Evvia

⭐ 1   ⭐ 3

□ **ATHENS**   ○ **Izmir**

Zakynthos

⭐ 2 *Peloponnese*

Corinth Canal

Samos

Taurus Mountains

Hydra   *Cyclades*

Mani

Naxos

Dodecanese   *Kos*

○ **Dalaman**   ○ **Antalya**

Santoríni

Rhodes

Turquoise Coast

⭐ 7

Crete

Irakleio ○ ⭐ 4

Largest island
Crete 8335 sq km

Cyprus   ○ **Nicosia**

⭐ 5 ○ **Limassol**

metres
3000
2000
1000
500
200
0

N

100 km
100 miles

Mediterranean Sea

⭐ **Explore the temples of the gods**
» Athens, page 206

⭐ **Island hop through the Aegean Sea**
» Greek Islands, page 210

⭐ **Lay siege to a castle**
» Cyprus, page 213

⭐ **Visit the site of the first Olympic Games**
» Peloponnese, page 208

⭐ **Uncover the myth of the Minotaur**
» Crete, page 212

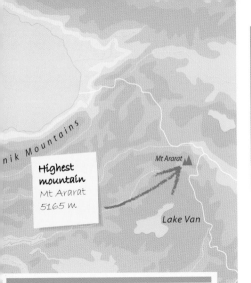

nik Mountains

Mt Ararat

Highest mountain
Mt Ararat
5165 m

Lake Van

⊘ Did you know?

- When a child loses a tooth in Greece it is thrown on the roof for good luck (the tooth not the child).
- Two of the Seven Wonders of the Ancient World stood in Turkey – the Temple of Artemis at Ephesus and the Mausoleum of Halicarnassus in Bodrum.
- The word 'astronaut' is derived from the Greek words *ástron* (star) and *nautes* (sailor).
- Glass beads are a popular talisman which Turks believe ward off the 'evil eye'.
- Pausanias, a Greek geographer who lived in the second century BC, is credited with writing the first ever travel guide, *Description of Greece*.
- The Turks introduced tulips to the Netherlands in the 1500s.

⭐ **Delve into a Turkish bazaar**
▸▸ Istanbul, page 214

⭐ **Cruise on a sailing *gület***
▸▸ Turkey, page 217

The people are friendly, the sea is warm, the sunshine is guaranteed and the food and accommodation won't upset the contents of your wallet or your children's stomachs. No wonder Greece and Turkey are such popular family holiday destinations. You probably went there as a kid yourself and know just the place with that perfect toddler-friendly beach or laid-back taverna. The Greek Islands are the undisputed stars of the region, spattering the azure Aegean with over 2000 irresistible reasons to pack your bags and go Greek. Only a few dozen islands are holiday hotspots, but such is their diversity that you could easily spend a lifetime sampling them. Well-established favourites include Corfu, Rhodes and Crete. Then there's Cyprus and the coasts of Turkey and the Peloponnese – all with enough sandy beaches, ice-cream kiosks and banana boat rides to satisfy most kids. There's also a lot to be said for combining beach bliss with a little culture. The Greeks practically invented the stuff, so it would seem rude not to spend a day or two exploring the historical wonders of Athens or strutting your stuff in Ancient Olympia. Istanbul, meanwhile, carries more 'shock' with its culture, but its hectic bazaars and flamboyant architecture will leave most children wide-eyed with wonder.

❝❞ *Youngsters love playing hide-and-seek at ancient ruins, collecting stones or chasing grasshoppers, while older children will enjoy the detective challenge of working out what's what.*

Will

Introduction

Greece & Turkey rating

Wow factor
★★★

Worry factor
★★

Value for money
★★★★

Keeping teacher happy
★★★★★

Family accommodation
★★★★★

Babies and toddlers
★★★★

Teenagers
★★★★

Books to read

Aesop's Fables, Usborne, 2007
Book/CD pack of famous tales, such as 'The Hare and the Tortoise', from the most moral-minded of Greek storytellers. Easy-reading text. Ages 5-8

Greek Myths for Young Children, Usborne, 1999
'Pandora's Box', 'Theseus and the Minotaur' and 'Jason and the Golden Fleece' are just three of the classic tales in this beautifully illustrated collection. Ages 5+

The Wooden Horse of Troy, Book House, 2004
Trojan prince, Paris, abducts Helen, the beautiful wife of King Menelaus, in a crime that unites Greek armies against Troy. Featuring cartoon-style illustrations, this book also has a 'who's who' section and pronunciation guide. Ages 7+

How Would You Survive as an Ancient Greek?, Franklin Watts, 1999
What would you wear? How would you make a living? And what would happen to you if you cheated at the Olympic Games? Ages 8+

My Family and Other Animals, Puffin, 2006
Gerald Durell's classic account of how his family moved to Corfu in the 1930s is humorous and insightful. Share Durell's passion for creatures great and small and gain an insight into Greek culture and family life. Ages 12+

How to be an archaeologist

What you need
- Large terracotta dish
- Black and white acrylic paint
- Paintbrushes
- Mallet
- Safety goggles
- Gardening gloves
- Gardening trowel

What to do
- Paint pictures that symbolize an aspect of your life on to the dish and leave to dry. Consider what the pictures would tell archaeologists if they dug up the dish.
- Ask an adult to break the dish into several pieces, using a mallet and safety goggles.
- Use gardening gloves and a trowel to bury your pottery pieces.
- Challenge a friend to discover the pieces.
- Help your friend put the pieces together. Can your friend guess what the pictures were trying to say?

Guide to the Gods
Roman names in brackets

Aphrodite (Venus) Goddess of love and mother of Eros (Cupid).
Apollo God of music, poetry and healing.
Ares (Mars) God of war.
Artemis (Diana) Goddess of hunting and Apollo's twin.
Athena (Minerva) Goddess of wisdom and guardian of Athens (below).
Demeter (Ceres) Goddess of earth and fertility.
Dionysos (Bacchus) God of wine and merriment.
Hades (Pluto) God of the Underworld and brother of Zeus.
Hephaestus (Vulcan) God of the forge.
Heracles (Hercules) God-hero famed for completing the seemingly impossible Twelve Labours set by Eurystheus, King of Mycenae.
Hermes (Mercury) Messenger of the gods.
Poseidon (Neptune) God of the seas and brother of Zeus.
Zeus (Jupiter) Father of the gods and supreme deity.

Taste of Greece and Turkey: baklava

A sticky, indulgent and irresistible pastry that's impressive to look at and easy to make.

What you need

- 400 g ground almonds
- 250 g butter
- 2 tsp cinnamon
- 1 pinch cloves
- 500 g filo pastry
- lemon juice
- 250 ml thyme honey
- 2 tsp vanilla extract
- 1½ cups water

What to do

- Mix together the almonds, cinnamon and cloves.
- Butter four sheets of pastry and place in a deep pan or dish.
- Spread a thin layer of nuts and spices on top of the pastry sheets, then add another two sheets of the pastry.
- Repeat the process until you have four sheets left, which you use for the top layer.
- Cut the baklava into squares, making sure you cut all the way through.
- Top with the remaining butter and bake in a medium-hot oven for 45 minutes.
- Mix the sugar, honey, vanilla, lemon and water and boil in a saucepan for five minutes.
- Pour over the baklava (removing any froth) and serve cold.

❷ What to buy in Greece

- Bazouki musical instrument
- costumed doll
- polished stone eggs
- miniature Greek vases and statues
- embroidered slippers
- ceramic boxes
- painted wooden donkeys
- tiny bronze helmets
- clay horses
- onyx boxes
- komboloï (worry beads)
- Athena's owl carvings
- Greek music CDs

❷ How to be an Ancient Olympic hero

The year is 708 BC and you've been training hard for 10 months, living life as a soldier. Your challenge is to win the first ever pentathlon event (discus and javelin throwing, wrestling, 180-m sprint and leaping – a kind of long jump). Try these tricks and tips to claim glory, fame and that all-important olive wreath.

Javelin Take a long run up – put all your weight on your stronger foot before you throw – Use your whole body's strength – don't cross the line.

Discus Hold a heavy object in your stronger hand – bend your knees and hold out both arms in front of you – spin slowly at first, gradually increasing speed before letting fly.

Sprint Ask two friends to hold a rope (the finish line) at chest height – Run as fast as you can to the line – when you are a couple of paces from the finish, lean forwards, flinging both your arms back and looking down at the floor in a winning 'chest dip'.

Wrestling Stand on one leg and ask a friend to do the same – practise keeping your balance when gently pushing each other.

Leaping The run up is the key – get your strongest foot planted just before the line to give yourself the best chance – spring forward and try not to lean back.

❸ Websites for Ancient Greece

thebritishmuseum.ac.uk/childrenscompass Take a virtual tour to see what it was like in the ancient Olympic Games and the Trojan War.

bbc.co.uk/schools/ancientgreece Loads of information and ideas for activities based on the life, myths and legends of Ancient Greece.

ology.amnh.org/archaeology The children's site for the American Museum of Natural History has a great interactive section on archaeology. Take a peek into the past with activities on all things ancient and buried.

One to watch: Hercules Disney, 2002

Laugh and sing along to the animated antics of the ultimate Greek superhero as he battles to outwit the hideous Hades.

Tots to teens

Turks and Greeks love children. They dote on them and are usually very forgiving of their moods. Don't be surprised, for example, if your irritable, scowling, post-tantrum toddler receives a squidge on the cheeks and some affectionate hair ruffling rather than a disapproving glance from the locals. While shopping you might find storekeepers spontaneously lavishing balloons, sweets and other freebies on your little darlings, while waiters will often go out of their way to cater for children at restaurants and cafés. Accommodation, meanwhile, covers the entire family-friendly spectrum, from activity-packed all-inclusive resorts to self-catering rural villas.

> Young children are always fascinated by the ubiquitous cats and well-fed fish at harbour-side tavernas. Just don't let them get too close to either of them!
>
> *Will*

Babies (0-18 months)

Should you really even consider Athens with a baby? What would possess you to drag him, her or, heaven forbid, *them* around one of the hottest, busiest cities in Europe? After all, most things you will want to see, like the Acropolis and Ancient Agora, are about as buggy-friendly as an SAS assault course. City pavements are either narrow, wonky or non-existent and can you imagine the havoc you'd create pushing your Mamas and Papas three-wheeler into a Pláka curio shop crammed with imitation Greek vases? Still determined to go? Well, the good news is that, during the run-up to the Athens 2004 Paralympics, access for wheelchair users in the city was greatly improved (see opposite). This doesn't mean families with prams or pushchairs can use the wheelchair lift on the north side of the Acropolis, but it does mean that they can take advantage of the fully accessible metro and other improved access facilities around the city. Of course, you could ditch the wheels altogether and carry your baby around in a papoose or sling. Just be extremely wary of doing this during summer when it becomes insanely hot. If you're determined to feast your eyes on propylaea, stoas and the like, it will be far more relaxing to base yourself at a comfortable beachside hotel or apartment in the Peloponnese and make brief forays to Corinth, Epídaurus or ancient Mycenae. Plenty of Greek Islands also have ancient ruins, so you can combine the odd day's sightseeing with a predominantly beach-based holiday. The same applies to the Turkish coast. As for Istanbul, it could well be as hot and challenging as Athens. Hygiene may be more of a concern, but one thing is certain: locals will fall over themselves to help you, your baby and your buggy.

Toddlers/pre-school (18 months-4 years)

This could possibly be an even worse age to take children to Athens or Istanbul than when they were babies. Not only are they still largely buggy-dependent (for naps or when they get tired of toddling), but they are heavier to push and more prone to accidents when you set them free. Having said that, this is a great time for taking them to the Peloponnese, Halkidikí, Greek Islands or Turkish coast. You might need to ask yourself whether these destinations are worth flying the extra distance (with a fractious, fidgety toddler) when you could have a similar Mediterranean beach holiday in Italy, France or Spain. Ultimately, of course, it all comes down to personal preference. But for sheer variety and value, Greece and Turkey are hard to beat.

Kids/school age (4-12 years)

Ancient Greece storms on to the school curriculum around the age of seven – a time when your mini Greek warrior (or goddess) will be thrilled at the prospect of a family odyssey. They are better able to cope with bewildering cities like Athens at this age, although it's still crucial to take precautions against heat and sun exposure. Don't forget to help fire their imagination when visiting ancient ruins (see page 209 for some tips). As with all ages, there are plenty of

Left: Learning to dive. **Top:** Patara Beach. **Bottom:** Greek island sailing.

kids' clubs at excellent resorts throughout Greece, but don't assume this type of accommodation is the only one that will meet with approval. A villa tucked into a forested mountainside on Corfu, for example, might be just the kind of thing to unleash the budding 'Gerald Durrell' in your child.

Teenagers (13 years+)

Mass tourism in parts of Greece and Turkey have spawned the kind of nightlife that might well appeal to your teenager, but most parents of this age group will be happier in a more controlled resort environment where there are special activities and social areas provided for teens. The Lakitira Summer Beach Resort on Kos, for example, caters superbly for teenagers. Available from Mark Warner (markwarner.co.uk) it has an Indy Activ Club where 14- to 17-year-olds can hang out at their own beachfront centre. Organized activities include water polo and pool gladiators,

while evening entertainment could be anything from floodlit volleyball to quizzes and discos. This style of resort is also an excellent opportunity for teenagers to learn a new sport, such as kitesurfing, sailing or scuba-diving – all under professional supervision. The Adventure Company (adventurecompany.co.uk) and Explore Worldwide (explore.co.uk) offer teenage departures on their trips to Greece and Turkey.

Special needs

Greece is slowly addressing access issues, helped in no small part by the 2004 Paralympics which spearheaded the need to improve facilities for the disabled. There is now a wheelchair elevator on the Acropolis, although once at the top the ground is irregular and littered with fragments of marble. Athens airport and the metro both have good access, while the larger catamarans are usually the best option for getting to islands. Athens's National Archaeological Museum is accessible, as is the main floor of Irákleio's museum on Crete. Many parts of Knosós are also wheelchair-friendly, but watch out for sudden unprotected drops. In Rhodes, many lanes of the old city are cobbled but generally negotiable. Visit greecetravel.com/handicapped for further information on accessible sites, hotels and tours – including Greek sailing tours for the disabled.

Turkey does not cater particularly well for visitors with special needs. Located in relatively flat areas, resorts like Dalyan and Fethiye are better suited to wheelchair users, but always check exactly what facilities are available before booking.

Single parents

Single Parent Holidays (singleparentsonholiday.co.uk) offers affordable quality holidays to many popular destinations including Crete, where you stay in a four-star hotel on a private sandy beach, close to the villages of Stalis and Malia with superb facilities for children and adults. Mango (mangokids.co.uk) offers group holidays for single parent families to Paphos, Cyprus.

Ancient gods and heavenly islands

You don't need to be Athena (goddess of wisdom) to fathom why Greece is such a popular holiday destination for families. Boasting fantastic beaches, warm, sheltered seas and an easy-going atmosphere, the Greek Islands are legendary. With holiday bliss scattered so liberally throughout the Aegean Sea, the Greek capital is always going to have a hard time vying for attention. But spare a thought, and a day or two in your itinerary, for Athens. It's a hot and chaotic city, but the ancient sites truly are amazing. And then there's the Peloponnese, that large, spiky peninsula clinging to the mainland like a stubborn maple leaf. There are more crumbly old wonders here (so that'll impress your history teacher), but the Peloponnese, like Halkidikí in the north, is also blessed with an enticing coastline of beaches, coves and laid-back tavernas.

Above: The Acropolis. **Left:** The Caryatids.
Below: The Tower of the Winds.

Athens

» The Acropolis and Ancient Agora are within easy walking distance of each other.
» Modern, cheap and efficient, the metro (ametro.gr) links major sites, as well as the port of Piraeus, from where ferries depart for the islands.
» Launched in 2004, the new tram service (tramsa.org) links central Athens with southern suburbs and the coast.
» Many sites and state museums (culture.gr) close early afternoon.
» Cool off by getting a day pass to the Athens Hilton pool or seeking shade in the pine forests at Moní Kaisarianí on nearby Mount Ymittós.

City highlights

To sightsee in Athens is to romp through the ages. With a little bit of planning, a modest itinerary and a healthy dose of imagination you'll be able to fire your kids' imagination with tales of gods, heroes, villains and geniuses.

The Acropolis Still rising supreme above Athens, this 90-m-high global icon is the crowning glory of ancient Greece. But as with any ruin you will need to bring it to life for kids. So, picture the scene as you walk through the grand temple gateway of the Propylaea: you are following in the footsteps of the Panathenaic Procession when, 2500 years ago, the people of Athens marched through the city to the Acropolis bearing a special robe to honour their patron goddess, Athena.

Beyond the Propylaea, towering bronze statues would have reared either side of you – one of Athena Promachos (so dazzling she could be seen by ships sailing towards Athens) and the other of a Trojan horse. But it was the Parthenon that drew the crowds on. Inside this magnificent temple, with its 46 columns and 13,400 blocks of marble, stood another statue of Athena – a 12-m beauty, clad in gold and ivory and bearing a huge shield.

The exterior of the temple was lavishly adorned with sculptures and brightly coloured friezes – most of these have succumbed to erosion, wars or theft, but you can still imagine something of the fine detail of the Acropolis temples by seeking out the Porch of the Caryatids. You'll find it on a building called the Erechtheion (a sacred site where Poseidon and Athena are said to have fought for control of the city) where, instead of columns, exquisitely carved priestesses support the roof.

Spend some time admiring the views of the surrounding city, then visit the Theatre of Herodes Atticus, added to the Acropolis by the Romans in the 2nd century AD and still used for performances during the summer Festival of Athens (greekfestival.gr). By now you'll probably need some shade and a rest, so head for the pine-clad hills to the west of the Acropolis for a picnic. Philopáppou Hill is the classic vantage from which to admire the Parthenon. Imagine the scene in 1687 when Turks ruled Athens and used the temple as a gunpowder store. You're in the Venetian army trying to wrestle control of the city; you aim your cannon towards the Parthenon, light the fuse and … kaboom! It's a wonder archaeologists were able to piece any of it together again.

Ancient Agora If anything, kids will be able to relate more to the Agora than the Acropolis. This was where the nitty-gritty of daily mortal life was carried out in ancient Athens. You'll be able to find the remains of everything from law courts and markets to schools and a prison. The most obvious building is the replica of the Stoa of Attalos – a two-storey shopping arcade. The original version, opened in 138 BC, would have housed 42 shops, but the modern one contains the Agora Museum. Inside, see if you can find the children's toys and an ancient potty.

Pláka and Monastiráki Lying to the

north of the Acropolis and Ancient Agora, these historic districts are chock-a-block with ancient ruins, as well as some more modern goodies. Among the contemporary highlights are the curio shops along the pedestrianized streets of Pandrósou and Adrianoú and the flea market at Platéia Avissynías. There are also dozens of cafés, tavernas and restaurants. If your kids are game for more 'old stuff', however, start with the Roman Agora where you can challenge them to spot all eight winds depicted on the 12-m-tall Tower of the Winds – a multi-purpose sundial, water clock, weather vane and compass devised by Andronikos around 150 BC. Nearby Anafiótika is a tangle of narrow streets hemmed in by whitewashed houses nuzzled up against the Acropolis.

Syntagma Ermoú street links Monastiráki with this city-hub district centred on Plateía Syntágmatos. However, it's more fun to ride the metro – the underground station at Syntagma is a veritable museum of Athenian history with displays of relics uncovered during its excavation. Above ground, take a minute to watch the traditionally attired soldiers high-stepping in slow motion by the Monument to the

Best museums in Athens

School-age children studying the Ancient Greeks will find more than enough inspiration at the **National Archaeological Museum**. Star exhibits include the Mask of Agamemnon (a gold death mask discovered at Ancient Mycenae – see page 208) and a collection of bronze statues (Poseidon, the Horse with the Little Jockey, and the Youth of Antikythira) salvaged from ancient shipwrecks. It's a huge collection, so prioritise or devise a treasure hunt for your children to find their favourite characters from Greek mythology. The **Benáki Museum** (benaki.gr) houses another exceptional collection of Greek treasures, but of particular interest to kids is the wonderful display of toys dating from antiquity to 1970 and ranging from costumed dolls to intriguing board games. Other museums worth an hour or two include the **Museum of Greek Popular Musical Instruments** (bouzoukis and lutes galore), the **Hellenic Children's Museum** (interactive displays and activities), the **Museum of Greek Children's Art** (paintings inspired by an annual children's competition), the **Museum of Greek Folk Art** (traditional costumes and shadow puppet theatre) and the **War Museum** (weapons and strategies from Mycenean battles to the Second World War).

Unknown Soldier, then seek refuge in the National Gardens. There are children's play areas here, as well as shady benches, a duck pond and a café. Walk through the gardens and you'll emerge opposite the Temple of Olympian Zeus. It's a whopper, although only 15 of the original 104 17-m-tall columns remain.

❷ Where can I see this view?

Departing every 10 minutes from Ploutárchou Street a funicular railway scales 277-m **Lykavitós Hill**. At the top you'll find cafés and an observation deck with Olympian views of the Acropolis and other landmarks.

🐾 Athens escape plans

▸ Catch a ferry from Piraeus to one of the islands in the Saronic Gulf. Aegina has beaches at Perdika and Agia Marina, Hydra has a beautiful harbour lined with tavernas and shops and Spétses has beaches at Agioi Anárgyri and Agia Paraskeví.

▸ Hop on a bus for the two-hour drive south to Cape Soúnion and watch the sun set behind the Temple of Poseidon.

▸ Join an organized tour or rent a car and drive three hours north to Delphi – a spectacular ruin on the flank of Mount Parnassós where ancient Greeks communed with gods through the mysterious oracle.

Top tips for city sightseeing

▸ Don't try to cram too much into a single day.
▸ Don't forget sunblock, hats and plenty of drinking water.
▸ Do intersperse city days with excursions further afield.
▸ Do get to the Acropolis (and other major sites) early to avoid the heat and the crowds.
▸ Do wear shoes with good grips – ancient marble is slippery and riddled with potential ankle-twisters.

The waterfront at Hydra.

Cape Sounion.

Where myth meets history

Cross over the Corinth Canal to the Peloponnese and watch your children's faces light up as you explain that this was the birthplace of winged wonder-horse Pegasus and the evil snake-headed Hydra. Tell them about Greek hero, Heracles (or Hercules to the Romans) who battled here to complete the daunting Twelve Labours. It's all myth, of course, but that won't stop your kids' imaginations running riot when you explore the ancient sites of this enigmatic peninsula.

Above: The Lion Gate at Ancient Mycenae.
Below: Voïdokiliá beach.

The Peloponnese

» You can visit the Peloponnese sites of Corinth, Epídaurus or Ancient Mycenae on whistle-stop tours from Athens.
» A rental car will provide freedom and flexibility to visit the sites at your own pace.
» The Epídaurus Festival, when Greek dramas are held at the ancient theatre, takes place in Jul and Aug.

Regional highlights

Ancient Mycenae Rearing from a rugged mêlée of mountains and ravines, this 3300-year-old Bronze Age citadel leapt to fame in 1867 when archaeologist, Heinrich Schliemann, discovered what he thought was the grave of a legendary king. "I have gazed upon the face of Agamemnon!" he proclaimed – moments before it crumbled to dust as he lifted the gold death mask (now on display in the National Archaeological Museum, page 207). You can still see the grave circles where Schliemann toiled, but far more exciting are Ancient Mycenae's Cyclopean walls, so called because later generations, who had lost the ability to move such massive rocks (weighing an average of six tons), believed that the giant, Cyclops, must have had a hand in it. In places they still tower 15 m above you. Even more mind-blowing is the Lion Gate at the citadel's main entrance, where a 12-ton lintel has been raised 3 m off the ground. An unsurpassable feat? Don't you believe it. The nearby Treasury of Atreus has a 9-m-long lintel weighing 120 tons – twice the weight of the heaviest rock at Stonehenge (see page 72).

Epídaurus Snug in a cluster of hills clad in pines and oleanders, Epídaurus boasts the best-preserved theatre in Greece. Try to visit before the tour buses arrive so that you can demonstrate its near-flawless acoustics. Get the kids to sit 55 rows up in the spectacular scoop of tiered seats while you stand on the stage and whisper something. They should be able to hear every word.

Ancient Olympia For sporting fans these incredible ruins are a must-see. Inhabited as early as 4000 BC, Ancient Olympia only achieved esteem as a religious and athletics centre in 776 BC when the first Olympic Games were held there. Many of its treasures are displayed in the Olympia Archaeological Museum, including fine statues, temple reliefs and various sporting artefacts. Check out the Stone of Bybon, a 144-kg rock with the inscription, "Bybon, son of Phorys, threw me above his head with one hand." An Olympian feat if ever there was one. Exploring the ruins themselves, you can almost imagine the roar of the crowd as you walk beneath the archway leading to the stadium where running races were held. You can still see the starting line, marked in stone with grooves for athletes' toes. Challenge your kids to a race and then have them in fits of giggles (or disbelief) when you explain that ancient Greek athletes competed naked. Other essentials at Olympia include the remains of the Temple of Zeus and the reconstructed colonnade of pillars surrounding the Palaestra (a training centre for boxers, wrestlers and jumpers).

Nafplio An elegant city with airy squares and narrow streets choked with bougainvillaea and geraniums spilling from wrought-iron balconies, Nafplio is perfect for a spot of curio browsing and a relaxed meal at a pavement restaurant.

Best beaches Head to the south and west coasts. You'll find sandy bays and clean, warm seas near Methoni, Pýlos and at Porto Kayio on the Mani Peninsula. Stamped like a disc of turquoise in the rocky shoreline, Voïdokiliá near Pýlos is a sheltered, shallow-water gem. Further north, top beaches include Kalogria, a 6-km stretch of sand bordered by pine trees. On the east coast, Tolon is a popular resort offering watersports as well as boat trips to Hydra and day-excursions to Athens.

Kid's top 10: Greece

1 Cruise on a caique – a traditional Greek sailing boat – island hopping through the Cyclades, dropping anchor in deserted bays to swim and snorkel.

2 Search for chameleons in the dunes near Giálova Lagoon (near Pýlos in the Peloponnese) – one of the only places in Europe where you can find African chameleons.

3 Challenge mum or dad to a running race in the 2700-year-old stadium at Ancient Olympia – and win.

4 Hunt for brilliantly tacky souvenirs, like painted wooden donkeys and miniature Greek statues, among the streets and flea markets of Pláka and Monastiráki in Athens.

5 See a Mediterranean monk seal before they become extinct. They're one of Europe's most endangered mammals (only around 500 are left), but you might be lucky enough to glimpse one in the seas around Alónissos – there are boat trips to Sporades Marine Park.

6 Ogle the gold treasures discovered at Ancient Mycenae and now on display in the National Archaeological Museum in Athens.

7 Explore the ruins of the Palace of Knosós on Crete, pretending it's the legendary labyrinth of the Minotaur – a fearsome beast, half-bull and half-man, that devoured young victims lost in the maze.

8 Learn to sail a yacht around the Greek Islands (see page 217).

9 Make lots of new friends on the beach, in the resort or at the kids' club.

10 Imagine what happened to the legendary city of Atlantis when the Santorini volcano erupted 3500 years ago.

Halkidikí coastline.

Halkidikí

⊛⊛⊛⊛⊞⊞

» Greece's second city, Thessaloníki, is the international gateway to the region.

» Although the best family holiday resorts are located in Halkidikí, there are other options further east at Alexandroúpoli.

» Halkidikí has more Blue Flag beaches than any other region in Greece.

» Take a ferry from Kavála to visit the northern Aegean islands or from Thessaloníki to reach the Sporades.

How to keep them interested in all the old stuff

What comes to mind when you look at the tumbled pillars of Ancient Olympia's Temple of Zeus? A classic example of Doric-style columns dating from the 5th-century BC? Giant slices of chocolate Swiss roll? Rocks, rocks and more rocks? Let's face it – the average parent's grasp of ancient Greek history is going to be limited to distant recollections from the 1963 movie, *Jason and the Argonauts*. That's fine for starters, but you're going to need additional tactics if you want to avoid a mutiny from the kids at every ruin you visit. Here are eight tips for keeping them inspired:

» Try to view a model reconstruction beforehand so your kids have an idea of what the site looked like in its heyday.

» Give them a leaflet with an artist's impression of the reconstruction and let them play detectives – matching the drawing to the remains.

» Swat up on a few epic tales of mythology.

» Play hide-and-seek – although make sure it's safe and that children are aware of roped-off no-go areas.

» Quiz them on what was good and what was bad about living in ancient Greek times.

» Role-play a Greek tragedy, an ancient procession or a sporting event.

» Touch the ancient marble and ask them to name anything they've touched that's older.

» Strike a deal – one ruin equals one day on the beach, a shopping trip or a boat ride.

Regional highlights

Dangling into the northern Aegean like a cow's udder, Halkidikí has three peninsulas. Two of them – Kassándra and Sithonía – have some of the best sandy beaches in Greece and a good choice of resorts to go with them, while the third – Athos – is an autonomous republic ruled by monks. You have to be male and obtain special permission to visit this hallowed ground, although boat trips from Ouranoúpoli offer views of holy Mount Athos and the monasteries that lie beneath it. Be sure to tear yourself away from the beach for at least a day or two in order to explore the northern part of Halkidikí. Here you'll find the prehistoric troglodyte dwelling of Petrálona Caves and the birdwatching haven of Lake Korónia. Further afield, there are Macedonian treasures to peruse in the Thessaloníki Archaeological Museum and walking trails to pound on the slopes of Mount Olympus.

Top 10 Greek islands

Look at a map of Greece and it's almost as if someone has shaken a pepper pot over the Aegean Sea, such is the abundance of islands and islets scattered between Turkey and mainland Greece. Some, like Corfu, attract hundreds of thousands of tourists each summer, while others remain quieter and less developed. Somewhere in this archipelagic constellation you're bound to find a particularly bright star – an island that's made in beach-holiday heaven. But how to find it, that's the trick. Start by asking yourself the questions shown opposite – although chances are you'll end up visiting the Greek Islands over and over again, sampling a different one each time.

Above: The delights of Corfu.
Far right: Kos sunset.

Corfu (Ionian Islands)

Family appeal One of the greenest and most beautiful of the Greek islands, Corfu's hilly interior is draped with forests of olive and cypress trees. Gerald Durrell based *My Family and Other Animals* here, and you can still stumble upon wild, unspoilt corners of Corfu that inspired the author. There are resorts like Benítses where nightclubs, not cicadas, reverberate through the night, but there are also plenty of bolt holes where you'll find a more sympathetic balance between traditional Greek charm and tourist facilities.

Best beaches Most of the mass-market resorts are concentrated in the southeast. For something quieter look to the southwest (for sandy Maltas backed by thickly wooded hills), the northwest (for Palaiokastrítsa with its three coves

clustered around a forested headland), the north (for long sweeping bays and interesting rock formations at Sidári) and the northeast (for sandy Almíros or the lively resort at Kassiópi).

Best days out Older children will appreciate the elegant Venetian architecture, pavement cafés and shops of Corfu Town, and even littl'uns will enjoy exploring the maze of narrow streets in the old quarter – especially if you plonk them in a horse-drawn carriage. Also worthwhile is a day (or two) of island touring. Hire a car and dawdle inland, stopping for Durrell-style nature hunts (or more strenuous jaunts on Mount Pantokrátor). Alternatively, hire a motorboat and potter along the coast in search of hidden coves. And if you're seized by wanderlust, don't forget that Albania is just a ferry ride away.

Kefalloniá (Ionian Islands)

Family appeal Kefalloniá has it in bucket loads. From mountains and caves to beach resorts and fishing villages, this large island is ideal for families seeking a bit more than just a beach holiday.

Best beaches The liveliest resorts are at Lássi and nearby stretches of coast. Elsewhere you'll find a mixture of pebbly and sandy beaches, usually with a striking backdrop of mountains. Lourdas and Skála in the far south both have long stretches of white sand with safe swimming, while the north of Kefalloniá has mainly white-pebble beaches. Myrtou Bay, south of Asos, is considered the island's most beautiful.

Best days out Bus services are limited, so it's essential to hire a car. Allow plenty of time for getting around this large, rugged island. Highlights include Asos (with its nearby Venetian fortress), Fiskárdo (Kefalloniá's prettiest village), Mount Aínos (home to wild horses and native fir trees), Drogkaráti caves (the size of a large concert hall and dripping with stalactites) and the Melissaní Cave-Lake (a mysterious subterranean azure-blue lake). The island of Ithaca – fabled as the home of Odysseus – is also worth a visit. Join a tour with a good guide who will bring to life the legends of Homer's epic, the *Odyssey*.

Kos (Dodecanese)

The sandy beaches in the southeast of Kos, as well as north-coast resorts like Tigkáki, make this a popular family destination. Inland, you'll find the remains of the Asklepieion, a fourth-century BC sanctuary dedicated to the god of healing. Kos Town, meanwhile, is the jumping off point for boat trips to Kalymnos, renowned for its sponge-fishing industry.

Lésvos (Northeast Aegean Islands)

Family appeal Once a favoured holiday haunt of the Romans, Lésvos still has what it takes to draw the crowds. A large island with a good scattering of beaches and resorts, the so-called

'Garden of the Aegean' has a rugged landscape rich in tradition.

Best beaches Skála Kallonis, a fishing village at the head of the Kallonis Gulf, has a gently shelving beach and warm shallow water that's ideal for small children. To the west, Skála Eresoú boasts one of the island's finest beaches – a 3-km stretch of dark sand.

Best days out There's a petrified forest and 12th-century monastery at Mount Ordymnous – an extinct volcano in the west of the island. Birdwatchers should stake out the reedy lagoons along the western coast, while culture vultures should descend on the atmospheric harbour town of Sykaminiá.

Límnos (Northeast Aegean Islands)

Perfect for families in search of a traditional island with few other visitors, Límnos has plenty of sandy beaches for children, although teenagers may find it a little too quiet. The west coast has the pick of the beaches – try Avlónas, just to the north of Myrina with its cobbled streets, bazaar and Ottoman houses.

Rhodes (Dodecanese)

Family appeal Deservedly popular, this large sunny island has excellent beaches, a fascinating historic town and a certain 'buzz' that will appeal to families with teenagers.

Best beaches The east coast has a string of sandy beaches: from boisterous resorts like Faliráki, with watersports and nightlife, to quieter coves further south.

Best days out Base yourself on the east coast and it's a straightforward bus ride into Rhodes town. Kids will love exploring the walled Old Town where the Palace of the Grand Masters, a medieval citadel built by the Knights of St John in the 1300s, is guaranteed to spark their imagination. Inside, challenge them to find the mosaic of the mythical Gorgon Medusa, with hair of writhing serpents. The nearby Street of the Knights, with its austere gateways and impressive coats of arms, is also worth a look. In the new town

How to pick the perfect island

What do we want to do? Relax on a beach, swim in the sea, sample a few tavernas… these are all pretty much Greek-island staples and won't help much in whittling down your shortlist. Instead, think of specifics. Do you want lots to do away from the beach? The larger islands – such as Crete, Evvia, Rhodes and Lésvos – have plenty to tempt you inland. Do you want to split your time between two or more islands? The Cyclades, for example, are well suited to island hopping by ferry, cruise ship or chartered yacht. What about activities? Do you need somewhere that offers good walking (Corfu, Crete, Lésvos, Naxos and Samos) or scuba-diving (Corfu, Kefalloniá and Zákynthos).

How do we get there? Some islands have direct international flights (ideal for younger kids who will want to hit the beach as soon as possible), while others require a ferry transfer which older children might see as part of the adventure.

What kind of accommodation do we need? You'll find something to suit most budgets, from luxury hotels and villas to self-catering apartments. Consider sharing a larger, pricier villa (which might have extra facilities like a pool) with the grandparents or another family. Lively resorts (like those on Kos and Corfu, for example) will suit families with teenagers, while anything with a kids' club and childcare facilities will appeal to parents with babies and toddlers.

you can arrange diving and boat trips at Mandráki harbour where the 40-m statue of the Colossus of Rhodes is believed to have once stood. A popular boat excursion is to Líndos where an ancient acropolis looms over a village of whitewashed houses and cobbled streets. If you want shade and tranquillity, visit Petaloúdes, a wooded valley where thousands of Jersey tiger moths gather between June and September (get there before the tour buses arrive).

Santoríni (Cyclades)

This famous island blew its top around 1450 BC, spewing clouds of molten debris over 30 km and unleashing a tsunami that devastated Minoan Crete. The volcanic eruption left a giant caldera, which subsequently flooded with seawater and inspired the legend of Atlantis. With whitewashed buildings perched on volcanic cliffs, the town of Firá is a port of call on just about every cruise ship operating in the Aegean Sea. Although there are black sand beaches on Santoríni, families will find more inviting stretches of sand on other

islands in the Cycaldes, such as Náxos and Páros (a ferry ride of three to four hours from Santoríni). For independent-minded families this beautiful archipelago is ideal for island hopping.

Skiathos (Sporades)

Just 13 km long and with more than 50 sandy beaches, it's small wonder that package tourists overrun Skiathos during July and August. This exquisite little island is buzzing with resorts, water sports and nightlife, but combines well with much quieter Alónissos to the east.

Zákynthos (Ionian Islands)

Although blighted in places by new development, Laganás Bay of Zákynthos has fine sandy beaches. Certain stretches are off-limits to tourists to enable loggerhead turtles to lay their eggs in relative peace between May and August. The resorts of Tsiliví and Alykes are further north, along with the island's most popular boat-trip destinations – Shipwreck Beach and the Blue Caves. Meanwhile, at the tip of Vasilikós peninsula, Gerakí beach has clean, white sand and is gently shelving.

> 66 99 In the crumbling walls of the sunken garden lived dozens of little black scorpions, shining and polished as if they had been made out of bakelite; in the fig- and lemon-trees just below the garden were quantities of emerald-green tree-frogs, like delicious satiny sweets among the leaves; up on the hillside lived snakes of various sorts, brilliant lizards and tortoises.
>
> *From My Family and Other Animals by Gerald Durrell*
> Puffin Books, 2006

Uncovering the mysteries of the Minoans

This gnarled island of mountains and gorges, stubbled with olive groves and orchards, and fringed with superb sandy beaches, may lack the cutesy, intimate feel of smaller Greek islands, but you'll never be bored. As well as delving into ancient Minoan ruins, there are gorges to trek through, caves to visit and rare birds and flowers to spot.

Crete

😀 😸 😩 😄 🏖 🎢 🎭 🎪 🏛 ☢

» The largest, most southerly and most spectacular of the Greek islands.
» For flexibility (and somewhere for the kids to cool down) hire a car with air-con.
» Buses ply the north-coast highway, while ferries link villages along the southwest coast.
» Crete has ferry connections with Piraeus, the Peloponnese, Rhodes and the Cyclades.

Island highlights

Irákleio Like Chaniá in the west, Irákleio's instant appeal for kids is the old harbour and Venetian fortifications. Lure them beyond the uninspiring façade of the city's archaeological museum, however, and they will discover a treasure trove of Minoan artefacts. Star exhibits include the Phaestos Disc (a clay tablet inscribed with mysterious symbols), the black-stone Bull's Head (used for pouring ritual wines) and a pair of figurines depicting snake goddesses (serpents symbolized immortality for the Minoans).

The museum provides a vivid insight into the highly sophisticated Minoan civilization that thrived on Crete some 3000 years ago – but don't overdo it; spend an hour or two checking out the highlights, then head out of town to Knosós.

Palace of Knosós Many of the exhibits displayed in the Irákleio Archaeological Museum were found at these extraordinary ruins. The first palace was levelled during an earthquake in 1700 BC, so the Minoans knocked up a swanky new one – multi-storied and with grand courtyards, over 1000 rooms and an elaborate drainage system. The Royal Apartments even had an en suite bathroom with what is believed to be the first-ever flush toilet (water was poured down by hand). The palace and some of its colourful frescoes were partially restored in the early 1900s, so they're not quite as baffling as many other Greek ruins. And, of course, Knosós has the big advantage of a really juicy myth – there

never was a labyrinth beneath the palace, but that won't stop kids pretending they're in the lair of the Minotaur.

Samariá Gorge It's a long way (18 km to the coastal village of Agía Rouméli), but older kids and teens may well be up to the challenge of hiking through this dramatic gorge in western Crete. The well-trodden route takes at least five hours; it's mostly downhill, but take plenty of water and snacks, wear good walking shoes and set off early in the morning. Keep an eye out for wild goats. You don't need to hike back up – boats depart from Agía Rouméli to Sfakiá and Palaiochóra until around 1700.

Best beaches Crete has no shortage of good family beaches, although some (particularly in the north where there is more development) tend to get very crowded at weekends and during peak summer months. The west-coast beaches are more remote and have fewer facilities. Elafonisi is a pink-sand beauty. Separated from an islet by a sheltered tidal lagoon of knee-deep water it's perfect for small children. Nearby, the laid-back resort of Paleochora also has a fine beach and is just a 90-minute bus ride to Chaniá with its old Venetian quarter, covered market and taverna-lined harbour.

🐦 Flora and fauna

Giant orchid A striking 60-cm-tall bloom, flowering in spring along with a profusion of other orchids and wild flowers.
Woodchat shrike Renowned for its habit of impaling prey (insects and small lizards) on thorns. Look out too for other summer migrants like Eleanora's falcon.
Avocet The saltpans at Eloúnta are a favoured feeding ground for these graceful waders.

Right: Elafonisi beach.
Top: Knosós.

The divided island

Fabled as the birthplace of Aphrodite, goddess of beauty and love, Cyprus has legions of holidaymakers well and truly smitten by its beaches, climate and scenery. The southern part of Cyprus is by far the more developed with the kind of all-singing, all-dancing resorts that most teenagers will rave about. However, if you prefer something quieter and more off the beaten track, then North Cyprus (occupied by Turkey since 1974) couldn't be more of a contrast to its Greek Cypriot neighbour. Here, you will find sleepy harbour towns and rural villages, castles perched in the Kyrenia Mountains and beaches where turtles still dare to nest.

Lizard on the walls of Kolossi Castle.

South Cyprus

▸▸ The antithesis to the large resorts of Limassol, consider renting a traditional Cypriot house in the countryside (agrotourism.com.cy).
▸▸ You'll bake in Jul and Aug, so try to visit Cyprus either side of this period; it often stays fine through to Oct.
▸▸ Travel between the Greek and Turkish Cypriot regions is legal and straightforward.

Beyond the pleasure coast

The fine sandy beaches along the south coast are what most families come here for. However, a few days in a rental car will put you in touch with the quieter, more authentic hinterland. It will also enable you to escape the heat by driving into the Troödos Massif (high and cold enough for skiing in winter). Walking in the mountains is superb, especially during spring when wild flowers are in bloom. A few kilometres outside Limassol, Kolossi Castle stands as testament to the rule of the Knights of St John in the 13th century, while the ancient port of Paphos in the southwest is famous both for its Roman mosaics and as the mythical birthplace of Aphrodite. If you want to find out more about the mysteries of the sea, check out the Museum of Marine Life and the Thalassa Municipal Museum of the Sea in Ayia Napa. Other favourites include the donkey sanctuary near Limassol (donkeycyprus.com) and the Mazotos Camel Park (camel-park.com). If go-karts are preferred, you'll find circuits at Erimi, Polis and Ayia Napa.

Crusader castles in North Cyprus

Although divided by the UN's Green Line, the city of Nicosia remains a friendly, laid-back place. However, kids will be far more interested in the harbour town of Kyrenia (Girne). Not only is there a great castle to explore (below), but inside you'll find the Shipwreck Museum where a 2300-year-old Greek trading vessel is on display – along with its cargo of wine amphorae and some 9000 almonds that were salvaged from the seabed. Perched on a rocky crag in the mountains behind Kyrenia, St Hilarion Castle is a fairy-tale ruin of crenellated walls and watchtowers. Take extra care exploring this castle – some of the paths are steep and slippery, and there are no safety barriers. A little further inland, Bellapais Abbey, however lovely, may be one ruin too many. If that's the case, strike out along the Karpas Peninsula where you can delve into caves, run wild on long sandy beaches and experience traditional life in a string of rural villages.

🌀 Waterparks

Fasouri Watermania (fasouri-watermania.com) Waterpark at Limassol with a kamikaze slide, wave pool and six-lane mat-racer.
Waterworld (waterworldwaterpark.com) Ayia Napa's splash zone, boasting the hair-raising waterslide, Fall of Icarus, and Poseidon's Wave Pool with its own geyser.
Aphrodite (aphroditewaterpark.com) Waterpark at Paphos with 26 rides, including a pirate ship slide and a splashing rain forest.

Where Europe meets Asia

With a foot in both Europe and Asia, Turkey is just that little bit more exciting and off the beaten track than Greece. Istanbul provides a distinctively Turkish workout for the senses, while ancient ruins like Ephesus and Aspendos are some of the finest in the Mediterranean. There are also plenty of family resorts and enticing beaches along its 8300-km coastline, and you'll find that the Turks dote on children just as much as their Greek neighbours.

City highlights

» Most of the major sites (kultur.gov.tr) are located in the small district of Sultanahmet; the Grand Bazaar is just a 15-min walk away, while the ferry dock for trips on the Bosphorus is located at the nearby Eminönü waterfront (tourist departures daily at 1035).
» Take a pair of binoculars to help children see the fine detail in the high domes.

Two-day action plan
Don't feel bewildered. Istanbul is certainly crowded and noisy, but it's also a relatively straightforward place to explore.

Day one Save the history lesson until later. Your main priority is to get to Aya Sofya early when morning light filters through the upper windows of this magnificent basilica. Any child who has ever attempted to create a design from tiny pieces of coloured paper will be enthralled by the exquisite artistry of Aya Sofya's mosaics. When Emperor Justinian opened his grand Byzantine design in AD 532, the interior was adorned with some 30 million gold mosaic tiles. But when the city fell to Islam in 1453, the great dome was converted to a mosque, four minarets were added and the iconic mosaics (unacceptable to Muslim beliefs) were plastered over – inadvertently preserving them. Now a museum, with many of the mosaics restored, Aya Sofya is regarded as one of the world's most important artistic treasure troves. Take a long, close look at the Deësis (Prayer) mosaics depicting Jesus, Mary and John the Baptist, and it's not hard to see why.

A short stroll from Aya Sofya, the Blue Mosque was constructed over 1000 years later as a rival to its Byzantine neighbour – and its colossal 43-m-high dome and six minarets still dominate the Sultanahmet district. The interior is decorated with some 20,000 exquisitely painted tiles, shimmering in the light pouring through 260 windows. Each of the 'elephant foot' pillars supporting the dome is 5 m wide.

With all the head spinning, neck craning and hushed reverence that goes on at Aya Sofya and the Blue Mosque, you'd be asking a lot of your kids to take in the Topkapi Palace in the same day. Save this historical gem for your second day and instead head for the spooky (and blissfully cool) Basilica Cistern – a vast underground chamber with pillars supported by carved Medusa heads. A few hundred metres away, you'll find the 650-year-old Grand Bazaar. A vaulted labyrinth of 4000 shops, this is the world's original shopping mall where you'll be able to buy anything from a gold trinket to a belly-dancing costume. Be prepared to haggle, to enter into friendly banter with stallholders and to get lost – it's all part of the fun. If your children are tired and fractious, however, the Grand Bazaar is almost guaranteed misery.

Day two Start with a boat trip on the Bosphorus, arriving at least an hour before departure to get a good seat. A typical four-hour tour takes you north along the famous straits that link the Sea of Marmara with the Black Sea. On your left is Europe, on your right is Asia. How cool is that! You'll pass the extravagant Dolmabahçe Palace, where

Above: The interior of Aya Sofya. **Below left:** Blue Mosque. **Bottom left:** The underground cisterns – enter if you dare.

Ottoman sultans were enthroned in rooms of gold leaf and alabaster. Then you'll sail under the Bosphorus Bridge and continue to the imposing fortress of Rumeli Hisari before returning to the Eminönü waterfront in Istanbul. From there it's a short walk to the Topkapi Palace – once the powerhouse of the sultans and now a magnificent museum. Don't miss the treasury which displays riches from the Ottoman Empire, including solid-gold thrones, the emerald-encrusted Topkapi Dagger and the 86-carat Kasikdi Diamond. The rooms in the palace are lavishly decorated with painted tiles and gold leaf, particularly in the harem, which functioned as a glorified prison for the sultan's wives, concubines, children and servants.

Aegean coast highlights

» Tourism is more established in the southern Aegean with a greater choice of resorts.
» Too packaged for some, but handy for visiting Ephesus, Kusadasi is a major cruise port, while equally boisterous Bodrum is a popular sailing and watersports centre.
» To reach the southern Aegean from Istanbul, one option is to take the overnight express train to Pamukkale, then head west to the coast.

Trojans, Romans and Crusader Knights

Northern Aegean Think hard before visiting the legendary city of Troy in the far north – it's a patchy, largely uninspiring ruin that children might struggle to marry with Homer's epic tale of the Trojan War. Having said that, the site does have a large wooden horse which children will enjoy clambering inside, just as Greek soldiers are said to have done when they besieged the city thousands of years ago. A better all-round family destination in the northern Aegean is the popular spa resort of Cesme. Explore the 14th-century Genoese fortress overlooking the harbour, and take a trip on a *gület* (traditional schooner) to Donkey Island – a sanctuary for abandoned beasts of burden.

Southern Aegean In complete contrast to Troy, above, Ephesus fires the imagination with its incredibly well preserved gateways, columns and streets. The most complete ancient city in the eastern Mediterranean, the former Roman capital of Asia Minor began life in the 11th-century BC as a centre of worship to Artemis, goddess of fertility. Ephesus only floundered in the 6th-century AD when its port silted up, effectively severing the city's lifeblood. Try to reach Ephesus early – there's little shade. The site also gets very crowded, but if anything that will help to recreate the atmosphere of this once-bustling city – especially when you stroll down Curetes Street. This colonnaded

Library of Celsus at Ephesus.

thoroughfare was the equivalent of London's Oxford Street or New York's Fifth Avenue. Get the kids to imagine they're Romans out for a morning's shopping. At the end of Curetes Street looms the grand, two-storey façade of the Library of Celsus, while the Marble Way (its surface etched with ancient cartwheel tracks) leads to a vast Roman theatre capable of seating 24,000 people. If the heat and dust begin to take their toll, retreat to the resort of Kusadasi where kids will find cool relief in the form of the Adaland Aquapark (adaland.com). The best beach, meanwhile, is Kadinlar Plaji.

Further south, Bodrum and its satellite resorts of Bitez and Gümbet are magnets to the 'bronze and booze' crowd. However, the old part of Bodrum is

definitely worth visiting for its medieval castle. When kids tire of firing imaginary arrows from the ramparts on to the yachts moored in the harbour below, entice them into the castle's fascinating Museum of Underwater Archaeology (bodrum-museum.com). As well as finding out about Roman shipwrecks and crusading knights they can venture into the dungeons and learn about ancient medicine in the Snake Tower.

> ❝❞ To put Ephesus into even greater focus, visit the museum at nearby Selçuk where a multi-breasted statue of fertility goddess Artemis will either bemuse or amuse your children, depending on their age. *Will*

❓ Where can I see this?

Limestone deposits from a mineral-rich spring have created the travertine waterfall at **Pamukkale** in the southern Aegean, 220 km east of Kusadasi. The best viewpoint of these mysterious pools is from the north gate, but beware of steep, unfenced drops.

Turquoise Coast

⊗⊗⊗⊗⊕⊕⊗⊗⊗⊗

» There are several family resorts at centres such as Kas and Olüdeniz.
» Rent a car to explore the coast and the rugged hinterland.
» Rhodes (see page 211) is an easy day trip from Marmaris.

Exploring a coastal gem

Hemmed in by pine-covered mountains and stretching from Marmaris in the west to Antalya in the east, the unspoilt Turquoise Coast offers a wide range of activities – particularly if you like boat trips.

Dalyan River One of the region's most popular excursions, tour boats depart at 1030 and return to Dalyan around 1600. At the start of the cruise you'll see some of the perplexing Lycian tombs for which the Turquoise Coast is renowned. How stonemasons from the 4th-century BC managed to chisel these elaborate graves in the middle of a cliff face is still something of a mystery. Remember to pack binoculars – you'll need them for scanning the tombs and spotting birds, terrapins and other river wildlife. After a stop at the ancient Roman trading centre of Kaunos (where you may also glimpse herons and storks in the nearby reed beds) you continue to Istuzu Beach, a 7-km sandy strip which is frequented by nesting turtles between May and July. Then it's back through the marshy waterways to Ilica for the tour's gooey highlight – a frolic in the natural mud pools.

Fethiye For a sweet treat, stop at one of Fethiye's Turkish delight stores where you can see the sticky stuff being made and sample the bewildering range of flavours.

Kekova Island Most boat trips to uninhabited Kekova leave from Andriake and involve a 40-minute boat journey across open water. A better option for families is to drive to the fishing village of Uçagiz from where it's

Sea kayaking on the Turquoise Coast.

🦎 Adventures on the Turquoise Coast

Paraglide from the 1969-m summit of Mount Baba to the beach at Olüdeniz (altitudeaction.com).
Go **canyoning** through Saklikent Gorge (bougainville-turkey.com).
Scuba-dive or **sea kayak** in the waters near Kas.

only a 15-minute crossing. That way, you get more time for swimming, snorkelling and viewing the strange Sunken City – a Lycian town off the island's northern shore that was inundated by rising sea levels.

Myra If the cliff tombs at Dalyan, above, sound intriguing, then the extraordinary Sea Necropolis at Myra will give you an opportunity to study more of these vertiginous graveyards. Get there early, though, because the site can feel like an oven by mid-morning.

Best beaches Spectacular, some say overdeveloped, the teardrop beach and azure lagoon of Olüdeniz graces almost every other postcard along the Turquoise Coast. The shallow, sheltered waters are perfect for tots, while older children will enjoy the wide range of

watersports. Further east, Patara is a complete contrast – a 19-km swathe of sand that has been spared the curse of the concrete mixer thanks to its popularity with nesting loggerhead turtles. There are no facilities here, but it's still a beach made in sandcastle-building heaven. Just inland there are some atmospheric Roman ruins, while canoe trips on the nearby Xanthos River include gentle rapids as well as wallowing in some natural mud pools.

The original Santa Claus

At Demre, near Myra, you'll find a small church containing the tomb of Nicholas I, a local 4th-century bishop who was canonized after his death for performing a number of miracles and for his generous habit of dropping bags of gold down the chimneys of the poor. In the 17th century, Dutch immigrants brought tales of St Nicholas (or *Sinterklaas*) to America where the name was eventually corrupted to Santa Claus. Because the feast day of the Turkish-born saint was celebrated in December, people naturally began to envisage him in winter attire, riding a sleigh.

Mediterranean Coast

😀😀😀😀😀😀😀😀

>> With its cafés, shops and marina, the stylish resort of Antalya would suit teenagers.
>> The popular resort of Alanya has 11 km of sandy beaches and a 13th-century citadel.
>> Side combines ancient Roman ruins with a thriving holiday centre.

Between the sea and a rocky place
With the Taurus Mountains rearing behind this stretch of coastline, adventure addicts can take to the hills in search of hiking and rafting opportunities. Beach-lovers, meanwhile, will find no shortage of long sandy bays and warm, sheltered sea.
Best ruins Crowned by a vaulted walkway, the magnificent Roman theatre at Aspendos is so well preserved that it's still used for opera, ballet and folk concerts during June and July. Perge, meanwhile, showcases more 2nd-century remains, including a stadium measuring 234 m by 34 m that could hold 12,000 spectators. Statues found at the site are on display at Antalya Archaeological Museum.
Best adventures Frothing and sloshing its way through a canyon in the Taurus Mountains, the Köprülü River is a popular rafting destination between May and October (minimum age eight). For something drier (but no less bouncy) book a 4WD safari into the mountains with any of the tour operators at Antalya, Side and Alanya.

🔍 How to get afloat
Gület cruises are available from several resorts along Turkey's Aegean and Mediterranean coasts, while **Sunvil** (sunvil.co.uk) operates sailing trips from Lefkas in the Ionian Islands. **Families Worldwide** (familiesworldwide.co.uk) offers eight-day family sailing holidays in the Greek Islands, suitable for all ages. So, what can you expect from a Greek island sailing holiday? Families Worldwide managing director and sailing enthusiast, Mark Wright and his 11-year-old daughter, Hannah share some nautical nuggets:

Is it better than a beach holiday?
Dad: Absolutely 100%.
Daughter: Yes, it's much more adventurous.

Best thing about sailing in the Aegean?
Dad: Sailing on calm seas and arriving in a port like Hydra where there are no roads and the only way to travel is by boat, donkey or on foot.
Daughter: It's very peaceful and I like having a go at steering the boat.

Top tip?
Dad: Go with a locally owned company which can introduce you to a genuine slice of local life.
Daughter: Be prepared for some very different experiences.

Greece and Turkey essentials

When to go

Spring and autumn are ideal times to visit **Athens**. The weather is not usually too hot and the city's attractions are less crowded. Summer lingers in this corner of the Mediterranean, so you might find decent weather as late as November. Temperatures in January reach an annual low of around 12°C, while summer highs soar well above 30°C.

The tourist season in the **Greek Islands** begins during April and May when you can expect few other tourists, warm sunny days and cool nights; the spring flowers are out, but not all facilities, shops and tavernas will be open. In June and early July temperatures start to reach 25°C and although resorts remain uncrowded, most facilities will be open. Mid-July to late August is peak season (with prices to match). It's hot and busy with everything up and running. Crete, the Dodecanese and the Cyclades may be windy during this period. September's weather is still good, although you can expect a few thunderstorms; tourist facilities start to close down towards the end of the month. October sees changeable weather, but it's often sunny, especially on southern islands like Crete.

In **Turkey**, the weather and tourist season follow a broadly similar pattern, with Istanbul becoming unbearably hot (35°C+) during July and August – a time when locals and holidaymakers make for the coast. Try to visit in spring or autumn when it's cooler and less busy.

flights are available with easyJet (easyjet.com), with direct services from Luton and Gatwick to Athens. Thomsonfly (thomsonfly.com) has flights from over 20 UK airports to numerous destinations in the region, including Corfu, Zákynthos, Crete, Kos, Rhodes, Santoríni, Thessaloníki, Antalya, Dalaman and Cyprus.

Cyprus Airways (cyprusairways.com) has non-stop flights from all over Europe to Lárnaka, with a return fare from London costing around £450 during August.

Charter flights serve popular resort areas along the Turkish coast. Turkish Airlines (thy.com) offer scheduled flights to Istanbul from London, Manchester and Dublin, as well as numerous European and worldwide destinations, including New York. Expect to pay around £280 for return London–Istanbul flights during August. Other airlines flying this route include British Airways, easyJet and GB Airways – the latter also flies to Dalaman on the Turquoise Coast.

Getting around

Following huge investment in the run-up to the 2004 Olympics, **Athens** is now the proud owner of a modern, fully integrated public transport system. The Athens **metro** (ametro.gr) has three main lines converging on the city centre, while the Athens **tram** system (tramsa.org) provides a

How much to offset your emissions?

From London to:

Athens	£4
Corfu	£4
Irákleio	£4.50
Istanbul	£4.50
Rhodes	£4.50
Cyprus	£5.50

From New York to:

Corfu	US$33
Athens	US$35
Istanbul	US$37
Cyprus	US$40

Getting there

The majority of holidaymakers to Greece arrive by **charter flight** arranged through a package tour company. However, there are also numerous **scheduled flights** operated by various airlines. Olympic Airlines (olympicairlines.com) flies to Athens from several European cities, as well as from Montreal, Toronto, New York, Sydney and Johannesburg. Expect to pay around £300 return for a London–Athens ticket during August. British Airways (britishairways.com) has direct flights from London to Athens (around £350 return during August) and also flies to Thessaloníki. Transatlantic flights to Athens operate from Atlanta, Los Angeles and New York with Delta (delta.com) and from Montreal and Toronto with Air Transat (airtransat.ca).

BA's low-cost subsidiary, GB Airways (gbairways.com), serves several destinations in Greece. One-way fares to Corfu, Irákleio (Crete) and Rhodes start from just £55, while flights to Mykonos cost as little as £70. GB Airways also serves Paphos on Cyprus with one-way fares starting at £75. Other low-cost

Go green: four ways to skip the flight

» Take a ferry from the Italian port of Bari to Patras in the Peloponnese with Blue Star Ferries (bluestarferries.com) or Superfast Ferries (ferries.gr/sff). Alternatively, sail from Venice to Corfu and Patras with Minoan Lines (minoan.gr).

» Join a family-friendly cruise in the eastern Mediterranean.

» Travel by train using Europe's international rail network. You can travel from London's Waterloo International station to Greece in just 48 hours, either by train and ferry via Italy or solely by train via Budapest.

» Link mainland Greece and Turkey by travelling on the air-conditioned Thessaloniki–Istanbul sleeper train.

fast link between Syntagma and the southern (coastal) suburbs. The **suburban railway** (proastiakos.gr) connects Elefthérios Venizélos International Airport to central Athens, Corinth and Piraeus. Rent a **car** from one of the numerous agencies based at the airport and you can easily drive to western Attica via the smart new Attiki Odos motorway (aodos.gr) and onwards to the Peloponnese across the Rio-Andirrio Bridge – the longest cable-stayed suspension bridge in Europe. There are also numerous tour operators in Athens, such as Hop In Sightseeing (hopin.com) offering excursions to Cape Soúnion, Corinth, the Saronic Gulf Islands and further afield.

Most major towns and cities in Greece are connected by **coach** services operated by KTEL (ktel.org), while the **Hellenic Railways Organisation** (ose.gr) offers another reasonably priced means of getting around. A one-way fare from Athens to Thessaloníki, for example, costs around £15. Companies operating **domestic flights** in Greece include Olympic Airlines and Aegean Airlines (aegeanair.com).

Not surprisingly Greece has an extensive domestic **ferry** network, with the port of Piraeus acting as the main hub. There are around 25 operators, offering everything from high-speed catamarans and hydrofoils to slower and cheaper ferries. Schedules, timetables and online bookings are available at ferries.gr. A day trip from Piraeus to Hydra on a Blue Dolphin hydrofoil operated by Hellenic Seaways (hellenicseaways.gr) costs around £15 return per person. A return voyage between Piraeus and Irákleio (lasting 6½ hours each way) with Minoan Lines (ferries.gr/minoan) costs from around £150 for two adults and two children.

Like Athens, **Istanbul** has an excellent public transport system. To save money, time and stress at ticket booths get hold of a daily Akbil travel card. You pay a deposit of around £1.50, then charge the card with as much as you like. Then it's simply a case of pressing the card into the fare machine on a bus, ferry, train or tram and the correct amount is deducted. Your Abkil card will come in useful on **ferry** trips to and from the Asian and European shores of the Bosphorus (the main docks are at Eminönü, Sirkeci and Karaköy at the mouth of the Golden Horn) and on the **Light Rail Transit** which connects Atatürk Airport with Askaray, from where it's easy to connect with a **tram** to Sultanahmet and Eminönü.

Turkish Airlines operates daily **flights** from Istanbul to Izmir, Antalya, Bodrum and Dalaman. If you have the time, a cheaper alternative is to catch a long-distance **bus**. You won't need to drive in Istanbul, but **hiring a car** is the most relaxing and flexible way of touring the coast. Allow around £400 for two weeks' rental in August for a Renault Clio or £750 for a Renault Laguna – both with that all-essential air conditioning.

Accommodation

In a country so heavily dependent on tourism, **Greece** has abundant accommodation – and much of it is good value compared to other European countries. Numerous package holiday companies and specialist tour operators offer a bewildering range of hotels, resorts, villas and self-catering apartments. The Hellenic Chamber of Hotels (grhotels.gr) has an online search facility for 9000 properties, while a directory of authorized campsites is available from the Panhellenic Camping Association (panhellenic-camping-union.gr). Agrotravel (agrotravel.gr) has a list of rural lodgings.

In **Istanbul** there are dozens of hotels to choose from, but an excellent alternative for families are the Istanbul Holiday Apartments (istanbulholidayapartments.com). Located near the tourist sights of Sultanahmet, these modern, well-equipped suites sleep up to six and cost from around £60 per night.

Like Greece, **Cyprus** and coastal parts of Turkey have a great choice of family-friendly villas, hotels and resorts. See Six family favourites, page 220, for inspiration.

Food and drink

Eating out in **Greece** is often a family affair where it's not unusual for children to stay up late in restaurants. What makes it all the more fun and relaxed, though, is the food itself. A traditional Greek meal starts with a selection of *méze* dishes. These nibbles and tidbits are a great way to introduce your kids to a range of Greek cuisine and there's bound to be one or two dishes which find favour with juvenile taste buds, whether it's bread dipped in *tzatzíki* or *taramosaláta* or a handful of olives (especially the fat, juicy *Kalamátas* ones). Other must-try *méze* snacks include *souvláki*

Fact file

	GMT	Language	Money	Code	Tourist info
Greece	+2	Greek	Euro (£1 = E1.50)	+30	gnto.gr
Cyprus	+2	Greek, Turkish	Cypriot pound (£1 = CYP0.85)	+357	visitcyprus.org.cy
Turkey	+2	Turkish	New Turkish Lira (£1 = TRY2.65)	+90	tourismturkey.org

Six family favourites

Palmiye
Where? Antalya, Turquoise Coast, Turkey.
Why? Fantastic family package with sports galore (sailing, waterskiing, wakeboarding, circus school, kayaking, football etc), two children's pools, dedicated clubs for babes to teens, plus a spa and *hammam* (Turkish bath) for the grown-ups.
How much? Expect to pay around £3500 for a family of four during August, including flights, transfers, full-board accommodation, leisure activities, drinks and snacks.
Contact Club Med (clubmed.co.uk).

Alexandrous
Where? Kassiópi, Corfu.
Why? Spacious villa sleeping up to six; superb views from quiet mountainside location – perfect for 'Durrell-style' exploration and just 15 minutes' walk to the beach and 2 km from watersports and boat hire at Kassiópi.
How much? From £415 to £720 per person per week including flights and transfers.
Contact CV Travel (cvtravel.co.uk).

Eleftheria Hotel
Where? Agia Marina, western Crete.
Why? Just a short walk from a long, sandy beach and the shops and tavernas of Agia Marina, this quiet hotel has family rooms and a large pool with children's area.
How much? From £595 to £765 per week including breakfast and car hire.
Contact Cretan Ambience (cretanambience.co.uk).

Club Tamarisk Beach
Where? Bodrum, Turkey.
Why? Windsurfing, sailing and sea kayaking are included at this family-run hotel (pictured right) which also boasts on-site childcare, a large pool and four-bed suites. PADI scuba-diving courses are also available for children aged 12 and over.
How much? From £1048 to £2338 per week for a family of four, including flights, transfers, B&B accommodation and tuition in sailing and windsurfing. Pepi Penguin Crèche for children aged six months to four years costs £150 for five days; Mini Active Club (age five to seven) and Junior Active Club (age eight to 12) costs £80 for five half-days.
Contact Crystal Active (crystal-active.co.uk).

Nautica Bay Hotel
Where? Porto Heli, Peloponnese.
Why? Inclusive tuition in dinghy sailing, windsurfing and mountain biking, plus a dive centre and on-site tennis coach make this a perfect option for active families. Hotel facilities include family rooms, children's clubs and a large pool.
How much? From £499 to £819 per adult and £399 to £655 per child per week, including flights, transfers, half-board accommodation, sporting activities and tuition.
Contact Neilson Active Holidays (neilson.co.uk).

Lithakia Beach Hotel Apartments
Where? Aghios Sostis, Zákynthos.
Why? Lovely location overlooking a sandy beach where pedalos, motor boats and bikes can be hired. Tavernas, cafés and shops are just a short stroll away, while hotel apartments include sofa beds for children and kitchenettes.
How much? From £399 to £558 per person per week (based on four sharing), including flights.
Contact Sunvil Holidays (sunvil.co.uk).

(grilled pork kebabs flavoured with lemon and herbs that kids will also enjoy as a main course), *melitzanosaláta* (grilled aubergine purée), *melitzánes* (aubergines stuffed with onions and tomatoes) and *choriátiki saláta* (the ubiquitous Greek salad made with feta cheese, tomatoes, cucumbers and onions).

The main course, if your children still have room, is usually a meat or fish dish. For visual impact, order *psária plakí*, a whole fish baked with potatoes and vegetables. Other seafood worth trying is grilled swordfish, fried calamari and, for the more adventurous, whitebait and octopus. For the carnivore in your family, order *stifádo* (braised beef and onion stew), *keftédes* (pork mince balls), *kotópoulo riganáto* (roast chicken) or *choriátiko choirinó* (pork chop marinated in olive oil and lemon juice).

When it comes to dessert, *giaoúrti kai méli* (Greek yoghurt and honey) always slips down a treat, or you could go the whole hog and order a platter of *loukoúmia* (doughnuts drenched in syrup). Parents will no doubt want to wash everything down with a bottle of local wine and a shot or two of aniseed-flavoured ouzo.

Food in **Cyprus** is a similarly daunting, yet pleasurable, affair with plenty of *méze* dishes to try, as well as lamb or fish cooked with olive oil, tomato and herbs.

In **Turkey**, the *méze* is more of a social event than merely a meal course – something to be lingered over with friends and raki (a raisin and aniseed spirit). Dishes include garlic yoghurt, mashed broad bean salad, salted fish, olives, hummus and bread. For a basic main course, few children will turn their noses up at a grilled meat kebab or *lahmacun* (Turkish pizza topped with ground meat or sausage). You'll also find many Greek-influenced foods, such as fried calamari and eggplant, while the more adventurous can grapple with local specialities like *hülüklü dügün çorbasi* (a thick soup of chopped tripe and meatballs). Those with a sweet tooth will find salvation in *lokum* (Turkish delight) and *baklava* (a layered pastry – see page 203).

Health and safety

Greece is generally a very safe country with a low crime rate compared to other European nations. Tap water is generally safe to drink in Greece and Cyprus. The most obvious precaution to take while travelling in the region is to avoid overexposure to the sun: wear a hat and sunglasses, drink plenty of water, use a high-factor sunblock, seek shade during the middle part of the day and consider taking swimsuits with built-in sun protection for young children. Other potential dangers in the region include road accidents – Greece has one of the highest crash rates in Europe. Take your time when driving anywhere and make sure that any children's seats you may have rented with your hire car are fit for the job. To avoid traveller's diarrhoea steer clear of street food (particularly

meat or fish snacks in Istanbul). However, if you are unlucky enough to suffer a bout of 'sultan's revenge' make sure you have some sachets of rehydration powder to hand. Think carefully before taking asthma-sufferers to Istanbul as Turks smoke like chimneys .

Above: Sweet Turkish delights.

Tour operators

The Adventure Company adventurecompany.co.uk
Anatolian Sky anatolian-sky.co.uk
ClubMed clubmed.com
Cretan Ambience cretanambience.co.uk
Crystal Active crystal-active.co.uk
CV Travel Greek Islands cvtravel.co.uk
Exodus exodus.co.uk
Explore explore.co.uk
Families Worldwide familiesworldwide.co.uk
Greek Islands Club greekislandsclub.com
Greek Options greekoptions.co.uk
Greek Sun Holidays, greeksun.co.uk
Inntravel Greece inntravel.co.uk/Greece
Ionian Island Holidays ionianislandholidays.com
Islands of Greece islands-of-greece.co.uk
Mark Warner markwarner.co.uk
Neilson Active Holidays neilson.co.uk
Planos Holidays planos.co.uk
Powder Byrne powderbyrne.com
Sailing Holidays sailingholidays.com
Sunvil Holidays sunvil.co.uk
Top Yacht top-yacht.com
Turkish Places turkishplaces.co.uk

How much for a Big Mac?
USA   US$3.22
UK   US$3.90
Greece   US$3.82
Turkey   US$3.20

Scandinavia

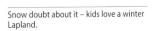

Snow doubt about it – kids love a winter Lapland.

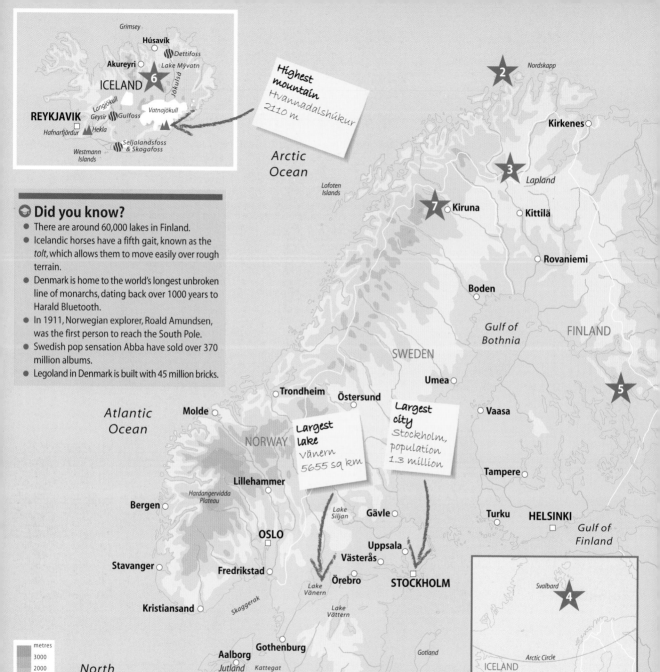

Grimsey

Húsavík

Dettifoss
Akureyri
Lake Mývatn
ICELAND 6
Jökulsá

REYKJAVIK
Langjökull
Geysir Gulfoss
Vatnajökull
Hafnarfjörður Hekla
Seljalandsfoss & Skogafoss
Westmann Islands

Highest mountain
Hvannadalshúkur
2110 m

Arctic
Ocean

Nordskapp 2

Kirkenes

3
Lapland

7
Kiruna
Kittilä

Lofoten
Islands

Rovaniemi

Boden

Did you know?

- There are around 60,000 lakes in Finland.
- Icelandic horses have a fifth gait, known as the *tolt*, which allows them to move easily over rough terrain.
- Denmark is home to the world's longest unbroken line of monarchs, dating back over 1000 years to Harald Bluetooth.
- In 1911, Norwegian explorer, Roald Amundsen, was the first person to reach the South Pole.
- Swedish pop sensation Abba have sold over 370 million albums.
- Legoland in Denmark is built with 45 million bricks.

Gulf of
Bothnia

FINLAND

Trondheim
Östersund

Umea

Molde

SWEDEN

Vaasa

Largest lake
Vänern
5655 sq km

Largest city
Stockholm, population
1.3 million

5

Atlantic
Ocean

NORWAY

Tampere

Lillehammer

Hardangervidda
Plateau

Lake
Siljan
Gävle

Turku

HELSINKI
Gulf of
Finland

Bergen

OSLO

Uppsala
Västerås

Stavanger

Fredrikstad

Lake
Vänern
Örebro

STOCKHOLM

Kristiansand

Skaggerak

Lake
Vättern

Svalbard
4

Gotland

Arctic Circle

ICELAND

metres
3000
2000
1000
500
200
0

North
Sea

Aalborg
Jutland

Gothenburg

Kattegat

Öland

Baltic Sea

DENMARK

Aarhus

Esbjerg

COPENHAGEN

Odense
1
Malmö

Bornholm

★ Board a Viking ship
» Denmark, page 230

★ See the midnight sun
» Throughout northern Scandinavia

★ Go husky sledging
» Lapland, page 232

★ Sail to the Arctic
» Svalbard, page 234

★ Learn how to cross country ski
» Finland, page 236

★ Walk on lava
» Iceland, page 238

★ Stay in an ice hotel
» Sweden, page 242

When it comes to family holidays, there's more to Scandinavia than Santa Claus and Legoland – although both will probably get a vigorous chorus of approval from your children. Cities like Copenhagen, Stockholm and Oslo may be on the pricey side, but they are also supremely kid-friendly with plenty of attractions, ranging from theme parks and gardens to museums and castles. Further afield you'll discover nature's very own theme park – a wilderness of lakes, forests and mountains where thrills and spills come in the form of rafting trips, husky sledging and a veritable *smörgåsbord* of other activities, depending on when you visit. Scandinavia is also an easily accessible place to introduce your children to some of the world's most extraordinary phenomena. Lapland has the Northern Lights and midnight sun, Iceland has volcanoes and ice caps and Finland has the Moomintrolls. If those endearing white hippo-like characters don't do it for your kids, however, Denmark's Viking legacy is sure to fire their imagination. Lapland's reindeer-herding Sami culture will also captivate most children, while the home of the big man himself, Mr S Claus, can be visited year-round.

❝ ❞ *Unlike the British salad bar, where you get one shot at loading and no chance of a refill, the thing about all Swedish buffets is that there is no stigma attached to shuttling back to the trough as many times as you fancy. For children this free-range approach to feeding comes close to heaven.*

David Wickers, journalist and director, Bridge & Wickers

Scandinavia rating
Wow factor
★★★★
Worry factor
★★
Value for money
★★
Keeping teacher happy
★★★★
Family accommodation
★★★★
Babies & toddlers
★★★★
Teenagers
★★★

🔍 How to see Santa

▶▶ Don't forget to write a letter to Santa Claus a few weeks before your journey.

▶▶ Fly to Ivalo airport in the Lapland region of northern Finland where you will be met by one of Santa's elves and a reindeer with its Sami handler.

▶▶ Get kitted out in thermal bodysuits, boots, gloves and hats.

▶▶ Make a snowman, go tobogganing and try your hand (and feet) at snowshoeing.

▶▶ Take a reindeer sleigh ride, then learn how to mush your own team of huskies.

▶▶ Receive a special certificate celebrating your crossing of the Arctic Circle and listen to traditional stories from a Sami guide.

▶▶ Ride a snowmobile through snow-clad forests, keeping an eye out for wild reindeer and a glimpse of Santa's cabin.

▶▶ Meet Santa in his secret hideaway and tell him how good you've been all year.

Books to read

Children of the Forest, Floris Books, 1987
Elsa Beskow's exquisitely illustrated story of the little folk who live deep in the roots of an old pine tree. Ages 2-6

Fairy Tales of Hans Christian Andersen,
Reader's Digest, 2005
An illustrated collection of 40 captivating stories, including 'The Little Mermaid', 'The Princess and the Pea', 'The Tinderbox' and 'The Emperor's New Clothes'. Ages 4+

Fairy Tales of Hans Christian Andersen, Reader's Digest, 2005
An illustrated collection of 40 captivating stories, including The Little Mermaid, The Princess and the Pea, The Tinderbox and The Teapot and The Goblin at the Grocer's. Ages 4+

Viking, DK Publishing, 2005
Vivid photography and at-a-glance captions transport young readers into the world of the Vikings. Ages 9-12

Pippi Longstocking, Oxford University Press, 2007
Astrid Lindgren's classic tale about the feisty, unconventional nine-year-old who lives at Villa Villekulla with a horse, a monkey and a suitcase full of gold coins. Ages 8-11

The Vicious Vikings, Scholastic Hippo, 2007
Find out how to build a longboat and why some Vikings had names like Fat Thighs and Stinking. Ages 8+

Troll Blood, HarperCollins, 2007
The action-packed conclusion to Katherine Langrish's acclaimed trilogy describes a perilous journey to Vinland (North America). Ages 12+

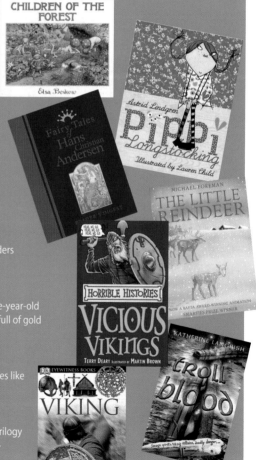

🔍 How to build an igloo

What you need
» Saw
» Spade
» Several short sticks
» Hard snow

What to do
» Use the sticks to mark out a circle measuring no more than 2 m wide.
» Cut out blocks of snow around 20 to 30 cm thick.
» Arrange the first row of blocks, making sure they are angled slightly inwards (otherwise you will end up with a tower instead of a dome shape). Don't worry about gaps between blocks at this stage.
» Use vertically placed blocks for each side of the entrance with a solid block on top to form a small 'porch'.
» Continue adding snow blocks to the igloo, removing any snow that piles up inside. You can also dig out the floor at this stage, increasing headroom.
» Slide the last few blocks through the entrance and push them up into the remaining gap in the roof to 'close' the igloo.
» Fill in any cracks with snow.
» Smooth the inside of the igloo using your gloved hand.

Taste of Scandinavia: *madekeitto*

A popular winter dish in Finland, madekeitto is a delicious creamy soup of fish and potatoes traditionally made using burbot, but salmon works just as well.

What you need
» 1 kg burbot or salmon
» 6 potatoes
» 2 onions
» ¼ tsp allspice
» 500 ml water
» 500 ml milk
» 250 ml double cream
» 2 tbsp flour
» Chopped dill and a pinch of salt

What to do
» Peel and dice the potatoes and onions; add to boiling water with salt and allspice and simmer for 10-15 minutes.
» Cut the fish into large chunks and add to the vegetables.
» Whisk the milk and flour together and pour into the soup; simmer for a further five minutes.
» Add the cream, sprinkle with chopped dill and serve with freshly baked bread.

❓ Where can I see one of these?

Up to 80% of Icelanders admit to believing in elves. In 2006, machinery failure interrupted an extension project at the Blue Lagoon when it became clear that the work was disturbing local elves. Staff lit 12 candles to make peace with the Hidden People and avoid further mishaps. Your best chance for spotting an elf is at Hafnarfjodur, near Reykjavik. Also look out for dwarfs (moodier than elves and about the size of human toddlers), light-fairies (think Tinkerbell) and trolls (who live solitary lives inside mountains and glaciers and don't like being disturbed).

Will you spot Sweden's Big Six?

Moose
Wolverine
Brown bear
Lynx
Wolf
Musk ox

Scandinavia, as you might expect, is generally a very straightforward place to take children on holiday. It's the Volvo of the family travel world – safe, reliable and efficient. Everywhere you go you will find copious and clean facilities, whether you're looking for a city park playground, family accommodation or somewhere to change a nappy. The only potential downside is that travelling *en famille* in Scandinavia can wallop your wallet. Iceland, Norway, Sweden, Finland and Denmark are some of the world's most expensive travel destinations. But when you weigh this up against a reassuring level of child-friendliness and unique attractions (Santa Claus and Hans Christian Andersen to name a couple), the extra expense is usually more than justified.

Babies (0-18 months)

Stick to the cities and you'll find supermarkets stocked with baby food and wet wipes, shady parks with playgrounds and restaurants with high chairs. Most Scandinavian cities are also compact (especially Copenhagen) with excellent public transport that is gentle on both your stroller and your nerves. Most people speak English and in summer there's a relaxed outdoor café culture that new parents will relish. If you're feeling slightly more adventurous, head for the countryside or coast where you'll find plenty of options for renting cottages or staying at a holiday park. Just be wary of the fact that the further north you go the more severe the landscape and climate become and the less you'll find in the way of facilities.

Toddlers/pre-school (18 months-4 years)

It's every child's dream to visit the home of Santa Claus high above the Arctic Circle in Finnish Lapland and it's surprisingly easy to make it come true (see page 236). Arrange a package trip through a reputable operator and you can avoid the slightly tacky, over-commercialized aspects of a Santa pilgrimage and instead experience something far more intimate and magical. Santa is at home all year (except during a certain night in December, of course) so you can pop up and see him during the long balmy days of summer if you like. However, it's much more fun when Lapland is transformed into a winter wonderland and you can ride in a reindeer-pulled sleigh – and perhaps even glimpse the Northern Lights. Remember that Jack Frost will definitely be

nipping at the toes, nose and other extremities of your toddler at this time of year (temperatures can plunge to -30°C during a Lapland winter). Be sure to pack plenty of warm clothing, including spare sets of essential items like gloves, hats and snow goggles. It's amazing how these things tend to go missing when your children are this age.

Another obsession for toddlers and pre-schoolers is Lego – and the original home of building-block heaven can be found at Legoland in Denmark. Piece together a day in the theme park with a couple of days in Copenhagen and a few more at the coast and you'll make most three- and four-year-olds very happy indeed. Denmark is also ideal for family cycling.

Kids/school age (4-12 years)

Legoland and Santa Claus still appeal to this age range, as do many Scandinavian cities. All seem to have more than their fair share of theme parks and child-friendly museums, with enough attractions to satisfy toddlers through to teenagers. Visit Santa with a three-year-old, for example, and they will probably be content with a sleigh ride; take kids aged seven or eight, however, and they'll want to ride a team of huskies to St Nick's door. Similarly, Legoland and other theme parks are more than capable of meeting the hyped-up adrenaline demands of older children. Just don't let the slick marketing of these contrived pleasurelands divert you from Scandinavia's real adventure hotspot – its wilderness. The woody, watery hinterland of countries like Sweden and Finland is prime territory for hiking, rafting and canoeing in summer, and snowmobiling, cross-country skiing, ice fishing and husky sledging in winter. Iceland, too, offers plenty in the way of outdoor activities, from scouring the north Atlantic for minke whales to riding Icelandic ponies across glacial valleys. Several family tour operators offer winter or summer multi-activity packages to Scandinavia where, in just a week or 10 days, you can sample a variety of adventure pursuits – all under expert guidance and in the company of other families. Alternatively, strike out alone on a self-drive tour. With its coastal ring road and laid-back farmstays, Iceland is particularly well suited to this form of travel.

Educationally, Scandinavia scores highly on the national curriculum. When your children start to learn about Vikings at school, plan a visit to Denmark where they will be able to

Top: Rafting in Finland.
Above: Horse riding in Iceland.

❓ Where can I see this?

Head to the northern extremes of Scandinavia to witness the midnight sun. A celebration of the longest day, midsummer in Scandinavia is as popular as Christmas. In what was originally a fertility ritual, flower-wreathed women dance around maypoles in Sweden, while in Finland and Norway bonfires are lit to ward off evil spirits.

witness this vibrant culture through restored longships, hands-on museums and even themed parks where actors role-play characters from the period. A visit to the spectacular Viking ship museum on Oslo's Bygdøynes Peninsula is also worthwhile – as are the nearby Maritime Museum and Kon-Tiki Museum. In fact, if your kids have an interest in boats there is probably no better place in the world to take them.

Another aspect of Scandinavian culture that will appeal to school-age children (and impress their teachers) is the Sami culture. You can visit these reindeer-herding people in the remote reaches of Lapland or get a taster of their lifestyle at the open-air museum of Skansen in Stockholm.

Animal lovers may find Scandinavia slightly frustrating. The prospect of seeing wolves, bears and lynx is guaranteed to prick the ears of most children, but arctic wildlife is notoriously elusive. Your best bet is to visit a wildlife park specializing in native species or focus instead on coastal critters, like puffins, whales and dolphins, which can often be seen on ferry trips and cruises in Norway and Iceland. That said, a quiet rafting or canoeing trip along a river in Sweden or Finland may well reward you with sightings of beaver and otter.

Scandinavia's strong literary tradition is a great excuse to get your kids' noses in books. Hans Christian Andersen's *Little Mermaid*, Tove Jansson's *Moominland* and Astrid Lindgren's *Pippi Longstocking* are all here – and chances are you'll also find a theme park or hands-on museum where they can see the characters brought to life.

Teenagers (13 years+)
Image-conscious teenagers will find suitably trendy shops and cafés in cities like Copenhagen, Bergen, Stockholm and Oslo, though prices may hamper their style somewhat. Big thrill rides can be found at amusement parks like Liseberg near Gothenburg and Oslo's Tusenfryd. For adventure, Iceland has challenging horse riding and whitewater rafting journeys, while Sweden and Finland offer all kinds of epic undertakings from weeklong husky-sledging expeditions to wilderness survival and multi-activity breaks. Various family adventure tour operators offer teenage departures on their Scandinavian itineraries, including The Adventure Company, Explore Worldwide, Exodus and Families Worldwide.

Special needs
Most tourist boards in Scandinavian countries can advise on hotels, restaurants and attractions that are wheelchair-friendly, while many forms of public transport have facilities for travellers with mobility, sight or hearing impairment. In Denmark, many restaurants, hotels, campsites, hostels, attractions and public toilets provide facilities for the disabled; ferries have special cabins and wide elevators for wheelchair users and intercity trains have toilets for the disabled as well as special lifts and ramps. Sweden has launched *Tourism For*

Telling tales …

Tom and eight-year-old Niko are grinning like mad things. So is their 74-year-old granny. We hurtle into the wide avenue of Sogne Fjord before the helicopter pilot presses the up button. We shoot skywards, the horizon tilts at a silly angle, the fjords seem miles below as we clear the plateau and are in a revealed new world of gashed hanging valleys, snow fields and sparkling tarns. The pilot asks if we are up for some fun – and gets a resounding affirmation from the back. He puts the chopper into a sharp left-hand bank – stomachs churn as we speed at head height over an ice field before screaming over the edge, an endless drop opens up below, Niko and granny screeching in unison.

Sanka Guha, TV presenter

All – Accessible Equality (turismforalla.se) which features an online database of accessible facilities. In Finland check out the travel4all website (travel4all.fi). In Iceland, several hotels in Reykjavík and Akureyri have rooms specially designed for guests with disabilities. The coastal ferries, *Baldur* and *Herjólfur* are also wheelchair-friendly. A list of fully accessible tourist attractions can be found at sjalfsbjorg.is. One of the best options for disabled travellers in Norway is to book a voyage on a wheelchair-friendly cruise ship. Try Accessible Travel & Leisure (accessibletravel.co.uk).

Single parents
Small Families (smallfamilies.co.uk) offers hosted group holidays for single parent families. They have a number of Lapland itineraries, including a visit to Santa in his log cabin, husky sledging and a trip to a reindeer farm. The Adventure Company (adventurecompany.co.uk) offers single parent family departures on its Winter Wonderland trip to Finland.

Iceland was fantastic; the children loved the scenery. Highlights included Gulfoss Falls which silenced them for a good 10 minutes. A visit to the Blue Lagoon is a must, although I would recommend going later in the afternoon when it's less busy. The best thing was driving into the mountains between Reykjavík and Hverageroi in the middle of the night. It was freezing, but we sat there for over an hour watching the Northern Lights and occasionally jumping into the car to run the heater. The itinerary we received from Discover the World was outstanding; it took away all the stress from the trip and allowed us to make the most of our time. Our 13-year-old wants to know when we're going back. She wants to go horse trekking next, but we would also like to explore the glaciers.

The Mason family, Discover the World

How to make a snow angel in two easy steps.

Land of the Vikings (and Lego)

Denmark might not strike you as an obvious choice for a family holiday, but few European countries can match its combination of compact size, efficient and family-friendly infrastructure and range of attractions. You've probably heard of Legoland and Tivoli Gardens – two of the country's family favourites – but there's a lot more to Denmark than rollercoasters and brightly coloured bits of plastic. Copenhagen is a laid-back city endowed with parks, museums, palaces and the rich legacy of storyteller-supreme, Hans Christian Anderson. Further afield, you will find long sandy beaches, holiday centres and a veritable treasure trail of Viking sites. Denmark's real trump card – particularly with young families – is that it just seems that little bit less remote than other parts of Scandinavia.

Copenhagen

>> A CPH Card includes entry to 60 museums and sites throughout Copenhagen, as well as unlimited transport by train, bus and metro.
>> Copenhagen is compact and pedestrian-friendly, baby-changing facilities are widespread and there are numerous parks with children's play areas.
>> Tivoli Gardens are open Apr-Sep and for a few weeks prior to Christmas when there is ice-skating on the lake and a festive market. Another popular amusement park is Bakken (bakken.dk), to the north of the city.

Top: Tivoli Gardens. **Above:** Vikings River Splash at Legoland. **Far left:** Runic stone at Jelling. **Below:** Little Mermaid statue.

City highlights

The Little Mermaid If your four- to seven-year-old daughter has any say in the matter, a pilgrimage to The Little Mermaid statue will top your sightseeing list. Hans Christian Andersen's 1837 fairy tale about the mermaid who falls in love with a prince she saves from drowning has enchanted just about every girl who has seen the feature cartoon and bought the Disney Princess merchandise. Break it to them gently, but a 165-cm tall bronze figure perched on the edge of Copenhagen's harbour might be a bit of an anticlimax.
Rosenborg Slot Ample compensation for any disappointment over The Little Mermaid, this 17th-century castle (rosenborg-slot.dk) not only has a fairy-tale moat and gardens, but holds glittering displays of the crown jewels.
Amalienborg Slot Although Queen

Margrethe II resides here, visitors can peek into one wing of her palace where apartments have been reconstructed to show what royal life was like from 1863 to 1947.
Christiansborg Slot The Royal Reception Rooms (ses.dk) in this impressive palace contain colourful tapestries depicting Denmark's history.
Rundetårn A spiral staircase leads to the top of the Round Tower (rundetaarn.dk) from where there are great views of the city's red-tiled rooftops.
Nyhavn Lined by colourful townhouses and trendy cafés and filled with wooden sailing ships, historic Nyhavn canal is an atmospheric place for a drink or ice-cream.

Strøget Thronging with street performers this mile-long pedestrianized shopping strip is an essential stomping ground for teenagers or anyone in search of retail therapy.
Tivoli Gardens Easily worth a day on its own, Tivoli Gardens (tivoli.dk) combine simple pleasures with high-octane thrills. Dating from 1843, it is a nostalgic mishmash of flower gardens, amusement park rides, open-air stage shows, restaurants, cafés and a boating lake. The rides range from a train

What are the best rides at Legoland?

Located in Billund, central Jutland, Legoland (legoland.dk) has eight main lands, including the signature Miniland – a miniature masterpiece of famous world locations constructed from over 20 million Lego bricks. Kids (and grown-ups) are always gobsmacked by this part of the park, but it won't be long before they're dragging you towards the thrill rides. In Adventure Land, you will find the X-Treme Racers rollercoaster (minimum height 120 cm) and the Robot Power Builder where you programme all the twists and turns yourself. Smaller kids will get a buzz from the Dragon Coaster (minimum height 100 cm), the Jungle Rally electric cars, the Dive to Atlantis aquarium and the Falck Fire Brigade where you race other teams to douse a burning building. Don't miss the Spellbreaker 4D movie in the Imagination Zone – a riveting romp with medieval knights where you will be clutching at the characters that appear to leap from the screen.

journey through a land of pixies to the Demon rollercoaster with its triple loop-the-loop. Not to be missed is The Flying Trunk where you are transported into puppet scenes from Hans Christian Anderson stories.

Best museums Pick of the bunch is Experimentarium (experimentarium.dk), an interactive science museum with over 260 hands-on exhibits ranging from an earthquake simulator to a special area for three- to six-year-olds. Also highly recommended are the Guinness World of Records Museum and the Louis Tussaud's Wax Museum.

Best parks Most of Copenhagen's parks have great playgrounds. From June to August there are free puppet shows in Kongens Have.

Kid's top 10: Viking Denmark

1 Dress like a Viking warlord and board a 7-m replica longboat at the Children's Museum in Copenhagen's Nationalmuseet (natmus.dk).

2 Eat like a Viking at Valhal restaurant in Tivoli Gardens (vegetarians may go hungry).

3 Sail a replica longboat (or man one of the oars) at Roskilde where five Viking ships have been reconstructed from wrecks dragged from the fiord at Vikingeskibsmuseet (vikingeskibsmuseet.dk).

4 Imagine the formidable Harold Bluetooth presiding over Trelleborg, a Viking fortress built around AD 980 and excavated near Slagelse.

5 Discover the treasures found at Ladbyskibet, the burial ground of a Viking chief unearthed near Kerteminde on the island of Funen.

6 Learn how Vikings lived at Ribe Viking Centre (ribevc.dynamicweb.dk) where costumed actors bring the period to life. Join in with activities, from baking to archery.

7 Ride the Vikings River Splash at Legoland (see opposite).

8 Marvel at Jelling's runic stones (standing stones with ancient inscriptions) – one erected more than 1000 years ago by King Gorm the Old and containing the first written mention of Denmark; the other erected by Harold Bluetooth recording the arrival of Christianity and the end of the Vikings.

9 Investigate the mysterious Viking graveyard at Lindholm Høje near Nørresundby where stone circles are arranged in the outline of longboats.

10 Celebrate the ancient feast day of St Olaf at the Viking Moot held during the last weekend in July at Moesgård Museum (moesmus.dk) near Århus. As well as traditional craft stalls and spit roasts galore, faux-Vikings stage ferocious battles on foot and horseback. While you're at the museum don't forget to gawp at Grauballe Man – a two thousand year old body found almost perfectly preserved in a peat

Where can I cycle?

Just about anywhere. Denmark has a 4000-km cycle network linking most major towns. Routes follow traffic-scarce roads, forest tracks, cycle lanes and disused railway lines. There are 11 long- distance routes, or you can simply pedal about in Copenhagen on the well-marked cycle paths.

Beaches

Copenhagen Just 5 km from the city, Amager Strandpark (amager-strand.dk) is an artificial beach park with white sand and lots of facilities.

West Jutland Long, wide sandy beaches backed by dunes, but often susceptible to surf and strong currents.

East Jutland Gentle sandy beaches and wonderful swimming can be found at Kattegat, Lolland, Falster and Bornholm.

Call of the Arctic

Parents in Sweden get some of Europe's best deals in maternity and paternity rights, so you can expect no shortage of child-friendly facilities when you head there on holiday. The two major cities, Stockholm and Gothenburg, have plenty to keep all ages entertained during a short break, but sooner or later you'll feel the lure of the Arctic Circle. Head north in winter for a fairy-tale night at the Icehotel and to learn the art of husky mushing, or enjoy long summer days in Sweden's great outdoors.

Southern Sweden

»» A Stockholm Card (available online at stockholmtown.com) entitles you to free admission to 75 museums and sites, unlimited travel on buses and trains, plus a sightseeing boat trip. Children under 7 travel free.
»» An extensive ferry network (waxholmsbolaget.se) links the Stockholm Archipelago.

A tale of two cities and 24,000 islands

Stockholm The Venice of the North, Stockholm is a beautiful city spread over 14 islands. Get your bearings by taking a boat trip through the capital's waterways, then focus your attention on the parkland island of Kungliga Djurgården. You'll find several family-friendly attractions here, including Skansen (skansen.se), the oldest open-air museum in the world. Children will love stepping back in time as they explore Skansen's 150 historic buildings, ranging from a traditional Swedish farmstead to a Sami camp – each one inhabited by staff in period costumes. There's even a zoo where you can learn about Scandinavian wildlife, such as wolves, brown bears and lynx. Djurgården is also the home of Junibacken (junibacken.se), a treat for anyone who has enjoyed Astrid Lindgren's children's books. This indoor attraction (perfect for a rainy day) brings the adventures of Pippi Longstocking to life through theatre shows, craft activities, a playhouse based on Villa Villekulla and a fantasy train ride through

some of Lindgren's best-loved stories. Other children's highlights on Djurgården include the shark tunnel at Aquaria (aquaria.se) and the Vasa – an impressive, but ill-fated, triple-masted warship that sank within minutes of being launched in 1625. You can find out why at the National Maritime Museum (vasamuseet.com).
Stockholm Archipelago A liberal scattering of 24,000 or so islands fringing the Gulf of Bothnia, the Stockholm Archipelago is a popular playground for urbanites. For a taster you can simply join a cruise from the capital, but you'll find it far more satisfying to spend a few days staying on one or more of the islands. The best ones for kids are Vaxholm with its historic fortress, Sandhamn, a popular seaside resort with lots of watersports, and Utö – a three-hour ferry ride from Stockholm, but well worth the trip for its beautiful walking trails and fine swimming. You'll find restaurants, shops and accommodation (including family-friendly cabins and camping) on many of the islands. Operators on Utö, Grinda and Sandön can arrange sailing trips with an experienced skipper or rent kayaks by the hour or longer.
Gothenburg Though not as pretty as Stockholm, Sweden's second biggest city still has plenty to offer children. Top of their list will be Liseberg (liseberg.com), Scandinavia's largest amusement park. With 35 rides there's everything from a pony carousel to the hair-raising Balder – a mighty wooden roller coaster that inflicts passengers with no less than 10 doses of negative g-force. The new Uppswinget,

meanwhile, does just that – swings you up and around at 80 kph. Replenish your children's brain cells at Gothenburg's interactive science museum, Universeum (universeum.se) before striking out north along Sweden's dramatic, rocky west coast. There are plenty of simple pleasures to be found here, such as crab-fishing from jetties or exploring the offshore islands on a boat trip. Other natural diversions include Havets Hus aquarium (havetshus.se) at Lysekil and Nordens Ark (nordensark.se), a captive breeding programme for endangered species like the snow leopard and great grey owl.

Above: A snow leopard – one of the endangered species being bred at Norden's Ark.
Top right: Husky in Lapland.
Below top right: Stockholm Archipelago.

Top tip
If you need to get from Gothenburg to Stockholm, break the journey at the Sommarland waterpark (sommarland.se) near Skara or take a longer loop via Lake Siljan (siljan.se), a popular holiday centre with everything from Santaworld to a summer toboggan track.

Swedish Lapland

» A 90-min flight from Stockholm, Kiruna makes an ideal base for exploring Lapland.
» Nearby Jukkasjärvi offers many winter activities, plus the not-to-be-missed Icehotel.
» Further south, Åre doubles as a winter skiing Mecca and summer activity centre.
» Temperatures can range from -30°C in winter to +30°C in summer.
» Want to visit Santa? See page 236.

Midnight sun or Northern Lights?

With its positively balmy temperatures and 24-hour daylight, summer might seem the obvious time to take your kids to Lapland. Unleash them on Europe's Great Outdoors and they'll be more than happy fishing, kayaking, hiking and getting away with later bedtimes thanks to the midnight sun. The big question is whether winter is even more fun. Yes, the days are ridiculously short and you'll have to wear snowsuits that feel like wrap-around duvets, but the fact remains that a week of winter activities in Lapland makes a superb break at Christmas, Easter or the February half-term. Several family adventure operators (see page 243) offer guided activity breaks to either Finnish or Swedish Lapland. Typically, they

include a mixture of dog sledging, snowmobiling, snowshoeing, cross-country skiing, ice fishing and reindeer sleigh rides. More of a polar pot-pourri than a full-blown Arctic expedition, these trips are designed to give you a gentle introduction to everything –

which means they're suitable for children as young as five. And, of course, the added bonus of a winter visit to Lapland is that you may glimpse the Northern Lights. See 'The White Stuff' on page 237 for a first-hand account of a winter activity break in Finland.

ⓦ Where can I go husky sledging?

In addition to Lapland, you can mush in Greenland, Iceland and Alaska. Arctic specialists, Discover the World (discover-the-world.co.uk) cover all four destinations.

   Don't worry if the closest you've come to dog sledging is grappling with a trolley down the frozen foods section of your local supermarket. With expert tuition you'll quickly get the hang of it and don't forget that the sledges do have brakes. Older children can join dedicated husky safaris, controlling their own sledge, looking after their team of dogs and staying overnight in cosy wilderness cabins. Young children can ride in the

sledge, but make sure they are very well wrapped up – including goggles to protect their eyes from bits of ice kicked up by the huskies. Remember that huskies are excitable, bouncy and noisy – and a lot of them look like they've stepped straight from the local wolf pack. If your children are the slightest bit nervous of dogs, take them to see Santa instead. He's a lot less frisky.

> 66 99 All morning, we sweep through a winter-gilded landscape of silent forests and frozen lakes. At times all you can hear is the panting of the dogs and the tinkle of their collar chains. Twice we spot reindeer browsing amongst the lichen-clad fir trees and the huskies' ears prick alert. But the team has settled into a steady, but exhilarating, rhythm. They have only one thing on their minds – to run.
>
> *Will*

Plain sailing for mini cruisers

A maritime theme quickly emerges when you contemplate a family holiday to Norway. The fjords are perfect for a voyage on a child-friendly cruise liner, while Oslo's trio of nautical museums showcases a wonderful array of historical ships. More adventurous families can set sail for the arctic wilderness of Svalbard, while adrenaline addicts can experience the watery thrills and spills of theme parks like Bø Sommarland.

Oslo

⛵🚢🚤🛥️🎠🎡🚠

→ The Oslo Pass (visitoslo.com) provides unlimited travel by bus, tram, underground, boat and local trains, free entry to numerous museums and discounted admission to Tusenfryd amusement park.

→ Take your pick of dozens of lakeside and coastal beaches.

→ To reach the Bygdøynes Peninsula with its popular museums, ferries operate from the city hall quayside May-Oct.

City highlights

Bygdøynes Peninsula With a coastline as famous as Norway's, it's hardly surprising that the nation has a strong seafaring tradition, and nowhere is this more vividly portrayed than in the four nautically themed museums on Oslo's Bygdøynes Peninsula. Start with Vikingskiphuset (khm.uio.no) where three Viking funerary ships are displayed, along with treasures and practical objects that accompanied the deceased into the afterlife. The *Oseberg* is the most exquisite of the trio. Built in 820 AD and measuring around 22 m in length, this richly ornamented oak vessel was exhumed from a large burial mound in 1904. Two skeletons were discovered on board, one of whom may have been a queen or priestess – study the grave goods on display and decide for yourself. The Norsk Sjøfartsmuseum or Norwegian Maritime Museum

Top: Bergen. **Above:** Thor Heyerdahl's legendary Kon-Tiki raft on display in Oslo.

(norsk-sjofartsmuseum.no) chronicles the entire history of Norwegian seafaring, from a 2200-year-old Bronze Age log boat to a panoramic film depicting a cruise through the fjords. Next door, Frammuseet (fram.museum.no) contains the famous exploration ship, *Fram*, and recounts the epic voyages of Roald Amundsen and other great polar explorers. Finally, the Kon-Tiki Museum (kon-tiki.no) houses the original 14-m-long balsa raft which Norwegian scientist Thor Heyerdahl sailed 6880 km across the Pacific in 1947 – a voyage that lasted an incredible 101 days.

🎢 Theme parks

Tusenfryd Around 20 km from Oslo, Tusenfryd (tusenfryd.no) is home to Scandinavia's most extreme ride, Speed Monster, which takes you to 90 kph in two seconds and inflicts seven bouts of weightlessness.

Hunderfossen Located 13 km from Lillehammer, Hunderfossen (hunderfossen.no) is a fairy-tale land with 50 attractions, including 4D films and an adventure ship that swings through 70 degrees to a height of 14 m.

Bø Sommarland Norway's biggest waterpark, Bø Sommarland (sommarland.no) has one of the world's largest artificial waves for surfing as well as Europe's first roller-coaster flume – an enormous water chute with tight bends and stomach churning drops.

❓ Where can I go skiing?

Open from mid-November to April, Tryvann Winter Park (tryvann.no) is just 20 minutes from downtown Oslo and boasts 14 slopes, six lifts, a snowboarding park and halfpipe, plus a special area for children and beginners.

Norwegian Fjords

>> To reach Bergen from Oslo (or vice versa) take the spectacular train journey (nsb.no) across the Hardangervidda plateau.
>> Norwegian Coastal Voyage (hurtigruten.com) operates a fleet of stylish ferries calling at 34 ports between Bergen and Kirkenes.
>> Spare time in Bergen before your cruise? Visit the aquarium (akvariet.no), ride the Fløibanen funicular railway (floibanen.no) or explore the fish market and the old wooden buildings alongside Bryggen Wharf.

Cruising to the Arctic Circle and beyond

If you thought Norwegian cruising was the kind of thing only the grandparents would be interested in, think again. Just imagine the thrill your kids would get from living on a ship bound for the Arctic! Calling at remote fishing communities to drop off cargo or to collect local passengers, the Norwegian Coastal Voyage vessels are more entwined with daily life than your average cruise ship. There will also be times when you feel you can almost stretch out your arms and touch both walls of a fjord; you'll be able to spot dolphins, orca whales, puffins and sea eagles from on deck and notch up a few geographical milestones – crossing the Arctic Circle, visiting Honingsvåg (the world's northernmost village) and witnessing the midnight sun. Not bad for a week's comfortable cruising. Other highlights include stopovers at Trondheim (Norway's first capital with its well-preserved medieval district), Geiranger (nuzzled in the head-spinning grandeur of Geirangerfjord) and the Lofoten Islands (a fascinating, weather-beaten archipelago of jagged mountains, U-shaped glacial valleys and brightly coloured fishing settlements dotted with wooden cod-drying racks). Ultimately, though, your compass is set for Honingsvåg where the Midnight Sun Road dips and turns across Nordskapp plateau to reach the 'top of Europe' and an unforgettable viewpoint over the Arctic Ocean.

Land blubbers – a walrus colony hauled out in Svalbard.

Off the beaten track: the Arctic

Despite being squashed by converging lines of longitude and barely clinging to the top of a world map, Svalbard (svalbard.net) is served by scheduled flights from Norway, making it the most accessible high arctic region in the world. Visit between June and September when retreating pack ice frees the spectacular coastline of this mountainous archipelago. Expedition ships range from ice-breakers capable of holding 100 passengers to the 20-berth, steel-hulled schooner, *Nooderlicht*. Arctic cruises are by no means a cheap family-holiday option – and the style of travel is only suitable for older children. A cheaper option is to base yourself in the capital, Longyearbyen, and arrange day trips and activities such as kayaking and hiking.

66 99 It is midnight – and broad daylight – when we drop anchor near the northern tip of Prins Karls Forland in Svalbard. Shuttled ashore in the ship's dinghies, we walk to within 20 m of the walruses. There are at least 150 of them – lounging about the pebbles, snoring, belching and breaking wind, completely oblivious to our presence. In the days that follow we have other privileged encounters with arctic wildlife. Following a hike through the crystal-maze icescape of a giant glacier, we spot a polar bear loping across distant pack ice. At Alkhornet, the skies are peppered with a blizzard of guillemots and little auks, an arctic fox tiptoeing beneath the seabird city on the lookout for eggs. And at Magdalena Fjord we hear the haunting siren calls of belugas pulsing mysteriously through the ship's hull. We never see the white whales – apparently their song can carry for miles. It is a sign of true wilderness, however, that such a subtle sound can prove so captivating. Along with the cooing of eider ducks and the creaking of ancient glaciers, it embodies the very essence of the Arctic.

Gjelder hele Svalbard

Lapping it up in the Arctic

Finland has plenty to keep kids entertained, whatever time of year you visit. Give them a choice of where and when to go, however, and they will invariably choose Lapland in winter. And who can blame them? Whether it's a sleigh ride in search of Santa or a white-knuckle ride with a team of boisterous huskies, Finland's northern extremity is the ultimate winter wonderland.

> 66 99
>
> So, you just sit on that bench and get all hot and sweaty?
>
> *A typical six-year-old's reaction to the prospect of a sauna*

Helsinki

◍◍◍◍◍◍

» Get a feel for the city by hopping on the T3 tram.

» Helsinki has several parks, while the islands are perfect for a picnic and a swim. In winter you can skate on dozens of ice rinks throughout the city.

» A Helsinki Card gives unlimited travel on public transport and free entry to major sights and over 50 museums, including Suomenlinna sea fortress and Helsinki Zoo.

Above: Sunset over a frozen lake in Finnish Lapland. Top right: Moomintroll. Bottom right: Heureka science museum.

City highlights

Suomenlinna Constructed in the 1700s and now a **UNESCO** World Heritage Site, Suomenlinna (suomenlinna.fi) is one of the world's largest maritime fortresses. Built on several islands off the coast of Helsinki, it's a fun place to explore by boat and on foot. There are several museums and cafés, plus special events during the summer.

Heureka Helsinki's interactive science centre, Heureka (heureka.fi) challenges young minds with a *smörgåsbord* of high-tech activities. The adjacent outdoor Galilei Science Park (open May to September) has lots of water-themed experiments and contraptions – a kind of waterpark for budding Einsteins.

Linnanmäki A perennial summer favourite for Finnish children, Linnanmäki (linnanmaki.fi) has been providing thrills and squeals since 1950. In addition to old favourites like the wooden rollercoaster, there are numerous modern rides, as well as a Sea Life Aquarium (sealife.fi) where you can get dizzy by walking inside a ring-shaped aquarium full of shoaling herring.

Further afield To the west of Helsinki, the cities of Tampere and Turku have no shortage of quirky family attractions. For example, there's Moominworld (muumimaailma.fi), a theme park 16 km from Turku dedicated to those loveable, white hippo-looking creatures created by Finnish author Tove Jansson. Yes, that's right – you can actually meet Moominmamma, Moominpappa, Sniff, Snufkin and the Snork Maiden. Older children – though not necessarily their parents – will prefer Tampere's Spy Museum (vakoilumuseo.fi) where aspiring secret agents can learn how to decipher hidden messages, change their voice and conceal a sword inside a walking stick.

❓ Where can I see Santa?

The best way to meet Santa is to book an all-inclusive trip with a specialist operator. Esprit (esprit-holidays.co.uk) offers packages to Finnish Lapland lasting from one to four days. Further south, near Rovaniemi, Santa's Village (santaclausvillage.info) has Santa's Post Office (where elves stamp letters) and Santa House (which describes how various nations celebrate Christmas).

🤸 Wacky sports

World Wife-Carrying Championships Sonkajarvi, July.
World Cell Phone Throwing Championships Riihisaari, August.
Swamp Football World Championships Hyrynsalmi, July.
Other eccentric Finnish contests include winter swimming, snowshoe football, cattle calling, milking stool throwing, mosquito swatting, team berry picking and sitting on an ants' nest (in any forest you choose).

The White Stuff

In Finland there's no better place for a winter activity holiday than Pielinen, a 900-sq-km lake in the province of North Koraelia. Our first morning was bright and chilly, sunlight sparking through the fresh powder snow that had fallen overnight. Due to the unusually mild winter, however, the lake hadn't frozen sufficiently to safely support the weight of seven hyperactive children (aged five to eleven). Ice fishing would have to wait. Instead, we drove to a nearby farm where wild boar and reindeer looked on bemused as our children cavorted through the snow like a pack of highly-wired wolf cubs. There were calming moments – like the wonderful views over pine-stubbled hills to the Russian border, or the traditional lunch huddled around an open fire clutching steaming bowls of salmon and potato broth.

Next up was cross-country skiing where the children were briefly reduced to penguin-shuffling mode. However, with their low centres of gravity and amply padded snowsuits, they quickly learnt not to be afraid of falling over. Inevitably, the first session deteriorated into a hysterical tangle of limbs, skis and poles – but they quickly picked up the technique over the following days. Like all the activities on this weeklong trip, it was best done in quick bursts before tiredness or cold set in.

Talking of speed, nothing could match the pace of our next icy pursuit. No sooner had we stepped from our minibus into a forest clearing 'somewhere near Russia' than we were assailed by the canine cacophony of dozens of huskies. They whipped themselves into a frenzy of leaping, slavering, wild-eyed excitement that was only unleashed when they were allowed to run. Each child sat huddled on a reindeer skin in the sledge, while a parent stood on the back runners, operating the spiky foot brake, leaning into corners and generally keeping things running smoothly. That, at least, was the theory. In fact, once the dogs

started bounding though the forest it was more a case of hang on and try not to let your shoulders become dislocated.

After the exhilaration of husky sledging, there were more high-speed thrills with a snowmobiling safari and an adrenaline-charged tobogganing session in the mountains of Koli National Park. The lake never did freeze sufficiently for ice fishing. But it hardly mattered. Besides, the children would probably have been far too busy making snow angels, cross-country skiing or pelting each other with snowballs …

❓ How do I plan a winter activity break in Finland?

Pielinen can be reached via Joensuu, a 45-minute flight from Helsinki. Accommodation around the lake is mainly in rustic farmhouses or country inns. If you plan to squeeze several activities into a week you're better off booking a guided tour with a specialist family operator like the Adventure Company (adventurecompany.co.uk) who can take care of all the logistics.

Iceland

Nature's own theme park

Iceland puts the 'wild' in 'wilderness'. It's an austere land riddled with suppurating mud pits, sulphurous steam vents and lava flows that resemble vast swathes of burned apple crumble. Waterfalls bloated with glacial silt retch into canyons, while fully grown trees cower inches above ground to shelter from scything Arctic winds. It's hardly your typical image of a family holiday paradise – and yet Iceland, for all its austerity, is a superb destination for kids who have a sense of adventure. More 'back of beyond' than 'back to the beach', the Land of Ice and Fire is Europe's ultimate – though admittedly quite pricey – adventure playground, where you can search for whales one day and skidoo across an ice cap the next.

Southwest Iceland

» Ideal for a week-long break based in or near the capital, Reykjavík .

» Car hire is available, but you're better off joining an organized 4WD jeep tour if you want to venture into the interior. Flying tours with Air Iceland (airiceland.is) will get you even further afield.

» Several companies offer organized excursions from Reykjavík , including Activity Group (activity.is), Mountain Taxi (mountaintaxi.is) and Tourls (tour.is).

» Warning! Iceland's waterfalls and geothermal attractions have few safety fences – keep small children strapped in strollers or firmly tethered on reins.

Right: Thrilling and chilling – activities in Iceland range from whitewater rafting and horseriding to soaking in the Blue Lagoon. **Above**: in the year 1000, Leifur Eiríksson (son of Eric the Red) became the first European to land in America. See his statue outside Reykjavík cathedral.

An introduction to Iceland's hot stuff

Reykjavík Chances are you'll be out and about most of the time, but Reykjavík (visitreykjavik.is) has enough to keep you occupied for any spare mornings or afternoons. Littl'uns will enjoy feeding the ducks and swans at the city's central lake, while the Reykjavík Zoo (husdyragardur.is) makes a fun outing to see reindeer, seals and farmyard animals. There's also a North Atlantic aquarium here, plus a park for pony rides. For a spot of history and culture, head to the Saga Museum (sagamuseum.is) where your kids can go Viking, or the open-air Reykjavík City Museum (reykjavikmuseum.is) with its nostalgic village and farm recreations.

Blue Lagoon Located on the road between the airport and Reykjavík, the Blue Lagoon (bluelagoon.com) is about as weird and wonderful as swimming pools get. Surrounded by a barren lava landscape, the milky-blue, geothermal waters of this open-air pool steam away at 35-40°C. Wading into the waist-deep water your toes squidge into a layer of silica sludge that you can slap on your face for a therapeutic mud mask. Gently poaching yourself in the Blue Lagoon is without doubt Iceland's balmiest – and most barmy – pastime. Other thermal pools in Reykjavík include the Laugar Spa (laugarspa.is) which has the added attraction of a water slide.

The Golden Circle Iceland's definitive day trip, this geologically supercharged tour visits Thingvellir (a UNESCO World Heritage Site of lava flows, deep ravines and the site of Iceland's original parliament), Geysir (a hotspot of geothermal vents, including the Stokkur geyser which erupts 20 m every five minutes) and Gullfoss or Golden Falls (a beautiful waterfall plunging around 33 m into a 2.5-km-long gorge).

Seljalandsfoss and Skogafoss These spectacular waterfalls are accessible from Road 1. Be prepared for a good soaking from the spray – and watch your step on the slippery, uneven terrain.

Mt Hekla You can take a jeep tour to the foot of Iceland's most active volcano. It's a long and bumpy journey, but the scenery is amazing.

Westman Islands Unless it's dead calm (in which case the three-hour ferry trip is just about bearable), hop on a flight to this cluster of 15 volcanic islands off the south coast – made famous in 1973 when a volcano on Heimaey erupted and destroyed much of the main town. From May to early August you'll see thousands of nesting puffins.

Horse riding Located near the town of Hafnarfjörður, about 10 minutes' drive from Reykjavík, Íshestar Riding Tours (ishestar.is) offers plenty of riding options (for first-timers to experts) using sure-footed Icelandic ponies.

Whale watching Available from March to October, three-hour boat trips off the Reykjavík coast are often rewarded with sightings of white- beaked dolphins, minke whales and, if you're lucky, humpback whales and orcas.

Whitewater rafting For gentle to moderate rapids, paddle on the Hvítá River, about an hour from Reykjavík.

A ring around Iceland

With at least a couple of weeks to spare, you could easily tour Iceland's ring road, either in a rental car or by using the long-distance bus network (bsi.is).

Left: Close encounter with a minke whale.
Below left: Dettifoss.

Where can I ride one of these?

With their giant tyres, four-wheel drive and raised suspension, superjeeps are, quite simply, unstoppable. Join a safari from Reykjavík or the Lake Mývatn region to explore Iceland's interior in one of these monster machines and you'll spend the day driving up and down mountains, pummelling snowdrifts and treating glacial rivers like car washes. From Reykjavík it's possible to drive to the Langjökull Icecap where you can trade superjeep for an equally exhilarating snowmobile.

North Iceland

▸▸ It's a 45-min flight from Reykjavík to Akureyri, followed by a scenic drive to Lake Mývatn.
▸▸ Mývatn is named after the midges that can swarm during midsummer. Local shops sell repellents and head nets.
▸▸ In Húsavík don't miss the Whale Museum (icewhale.is), open May-Sep.

Elemental Iceland: earth, water and fire

Lake Mývatn Nowhere is Iceland's volatile character more evident than near Lake Mývatn. At Hverarönd, for example, kids will be captivated by (and no doubt keen to impersonate) the belching, foul-smelling mud pits, while at Krafla they can scurry across lava fields contorted into swirls, coils and honeycombs. Hverfjall, meanwhile, is a squat, kilometre-wide crater with a rough path stamped in its flank of loose rock. The scramble to the rim at 312 m provides dramatic views of Lake Mývatn. At Dimmuborgir a walking trail probes a bizarre maze of tortured basalt, sculptured into spires, caves, arches and a disconcerting number of trolls. Driving (or cycling) around the lake, you will also encounter pseudocraters (mini-volcanoes created by steam exploding from water trapped beneath lava) and lava pillars (formed during a fissure eruption). Don't worry if the technical interpretations are beyond you or your kids – the 'gawp factor' of the scenery far outweighs the need to grapple with too much in the way of geophysics.

Dettifoss The central highlands of Iceland are smothered in ice caps. Thousands of years ago, volcanic activity under one of the largest, Vatnajökull, unleashed a catastrophic flood that chiselled out the Jökulsá Canyon, an hour's drive east of Lake Mývatn, and laid the foundation for a series of impressive waterfalls. Dettifoss is one of Europe's most powerful – a bloated cataract spewing between terraced cliffs of lava. Every second, 200 cubic metres of dirty water is hurled 45 m to the canyon floor where it roars and froths like a gigantic cappuccino machine.

Húsavík Setting out several times a day into Skjátfandi Bay from the fishing

town of Húsavík, a small fleet of beautifully restored, oak-hulled herring trawlers (northsailing.is) have found a new lease of life as whale-watching boats. Fulmars and arctic terns swirling above the surface are often your best clues as to the cetaceans' whereabouts. Minke whales are seen on well over 90% of outings, while harbour porpoises and pods of leaping white-beaked dolphins are also fairly common. Humpback whales and orcas are regular visitors and there have even been close encounters with blue whales.

Scandinavia essentials

When to go

Milder than other parts of Scandinavia, **Denmark** has a climate more like that of London or Amsterdam. July and August are the busiest months for heading to the beach or countryside, while Copenhagen receives a burst of visitors in the run-up to Christmas when Tivoli Gardens has a festive fair and ice rink. Expect snow in the Lapland region of **Sweden** and **Finland** from November to April, with temperatures plunging to -30°C and no proper sunrise during December and January. This is the best time of year to witness the Aurora borealis, usually seen at least one night in three. Further south, cities like Stockholm and Helsinki don't get so cold or dark – and everywhere warms and brightens up in summer. Bring mozzie repellent if venturing into the wilds between June and August. The lowest temperature recorded in **Norway** is -51°C in Kárášjohka-Karasjok in the far north. However, average annual temperatures along the western coast are around 8°C with the warmest month being July. Norway's mountains protect much of the eastern part of the country from precipitation, with as little as 300 mm falling annually in some areas. Expect up to ten times this along parts of the coast. Despite its lofty latitude, **Iceland** benefits from the Gulf Stream to enjoy a temperate climate with cool summers and fairly mild winters. Average January temperatures in Reykjavík are actually higher than those in New York. Come prepared, however, for changeable weather. During mid-June you can see the midnight sun from the island of Grímsey.

Getting there

The most extensive **flight** network in the region is offered by Scandinavian Airlines (flysas.com) which serves Copenhagen daily from London Heathrow, Aberdeen, Birmingham, Dublin, and Manchester. SAS also flies daily to Stockholm and Gothenburg from Heathrow, with less frequent flights to Stockholm from Birmingham, Dublin, Edinburgh and Manchester. Oslo, Bergen and Stavanger have daily direct flights from London, with Stavanger also being served by Aberdeen and Newcastle. A non-stop service from Newark and Chicago to Stockholm is operated by SAS in partnership with United Airlines and other members of Star Alliance, while flights via Copenhagen depart from Seattle and Washington.

Finnair (finnair.com) flies from Heathrow, Bangor, Dublin and Manchester to Helsinki, as well as from Heathrow to Stockholm. Long-haul routes include New York and several Asian destinations.

Icelandair (icelandair.net) has regular scheduled flights to Iceland all year from London, Glasgow, Manchester, Amsterdam, Copenhagen, Frankfurt, Oslo, Paris, Stockholm, Boston, New York, Orlando and Washington. Additional destinations during

summer, include Barcelona, Berlin, Helsinki and Milan.

British Airways (britishairways.com) has regular flights to Copenhagen, Billund, Stockholm, Oslo, Keflavík and Helsinki. Ryanair (ryanair.com) flies daily from London Stansted to Stockholm, Gothenburg and Malmö, from where there is a connecting coach service to Copenhagen. Additional routes include Dublin to Malmö and Billund and Stansted to Oslo and Tampere. Other low-cost airlines with flights to the region

Go green: five ways to skip the flight

▸▸ Drive or take the train across the 16-km Öresund Bridge linking Denmark's capital, Copenhagen, with Malmö in Sweden.

▸▸ Catch a ferry with DFDS Seaways (dfds.co.uk) from Harwich to Esbjerg in Denmark. The crossing time is 17 hours and the service operates every other day.

▸▸ Cruise with Smyril Line (smyril-line.com) which operates a weekly passenger/car-ferry service between Bergen (Norway), Hanstholm (Denmark), Lerwick (Shetland Islands), the Faroe Islands and Seyðisfjörður (Iceland).

▸▸ Hop on a Eurolines (eurolines.com) coach bound for Denmark, Sweden or Norway.

▸▸ Travel by Eurostar (eurostar.com) from London St Pancras International to Brussels, with connecting trains to major cities in Denmark via Cologne and Hamburg.

are Bmi (flybmi.com), easyJet (easyjet.com), Iceland Express (icelandexpress.com) and Norwegian (norwegian.no).

During August, expect to pay around £85-100 for a return London-Copenhagen flight with SAS (children aged 2-15 receive a 33% discount); £180 for a return London-Helsinki flight with Finnair; and £170 for a return London-Keflavík flight with Icelandair. A return flight with Ryanair between London and Stockholm during August costs from as little as £20, plus taxes.

Getting around

All countries in the region boast an efficient transport system. In **Denmark**, the national **train** network is operated by Danish Rail (dsb.dk), **coach** services are offered by Abildskous Busser (abildskou.dk) and ferries are run by Scandlines (scandlines.dk). **Car rental** outlets are widespread – expect to pay from around £50 per day. Internal **flights** in **Sweden** are served by SAS (see above) and Flynordic (flynordic.com), both of which fly from Stockholm to Kiruna in the far north. Travel on the country's sophisticated **rail** network can be booked through Sweden Booking (swedenbooking.com). The X-2000 train travels at up to 200 kph on all major routes, including Stockholm-Malmö-Copenhagen (via the Öresund bridge) and Stockholm-Gothenburg. Some train services in Sweden offer family carriages with children's play corners. Express **coach** service is provided by Swebus (swebusexpress.se). In **Norway**, internal **flights** are available from SAS Braathens (sasbraathens.no) and Widerøe (wideroe.no). The **Norwegian State Railway** (nsb.no) has a well-developed network stretching from the southwest coast to **Nordland. Norway Buss Express** (nor-way.no) also covers most of the country, while **car rental** is offered by Rent a Wreck (rent-a-wreck.no), Hertz (hertz.no) and Avis (avis.no). Numerous **ferries** ply the fjords, including the long-established Norwegian Coastal Voyage (hurtigruten.com) which sails between Bergen and Kirkenes. The trip takes around 11 days with frequent stops along the coast. There are daily departures and the ships can accommodate cars.

HERAJÄRVEN KIERROS

Covering over 90% of public roads and with more than 40,000 daily **bus** departures, **Finland** has one of Europe's most comprehensive coach networks (matkahuolto.fi). You can also get around using high-speed **trains** (vr.fi) and internal **flights** (blue1.com). Finland's maze of interconnected lakes can be navigated on **ferries** operated by companies such as Silverline (finnishsilverline.com) and Karelia Lines (karelialines.fi). Silja Line (silja.com) and Viking Line (vikingline.fi) offer luxury cruises between Helsinki and Stockholm with activities and entertainment laid on for kids and teenagers. In **Iceland**, Air Iceland (airiceland.is) runs scheduled **flights** between Reykjavík and domestic airports throughout the country. **Buses** are operated by Trex (trex.is), Austurleid (austurleid.is) and SBK (sbk.is). **Cars** and campervans can be rented through several agencies, including Budget (budget.is). Expect to pay around £1500 for two weeks' rental of a 4WD Suzuki Vitara in August (including collision damage waiver and unlimited mileage). A more modest family saloon (without 4WD) will cost nearer £1000.

⊙ How much to offset your emissions?

From London to:
Copenhagen £1.75
Oslo £2
Stockhom £2.50
Helsinki £3
Reykjavík £3

From New York to:
Reykjavík US$18
Copenhagen US$27
Oslo US$27
Stockholm US$27
Helsinki US$29

⊙ How to save cash

A good way to save money on public transport, **travel cards** also provide free or discounted admission to various attractions. They are available online or from tourist offices and mainline train stations in major cities like Copenhagen, Stockholm, Oslo and Helsinki. See individual country entries for details.

Tour operators

Arctic Experience
arctic-experience.co.uk
Specialised Tours
specialisedtours.com

Fact file

	GMT	Language *	Money	Code	Tourist info
Denmark	+1	Danish	Danish Kroner (UK£1 = DKK11)	+45	visitdenmark.com
Sweden	+1	Swedish	Swedish Krona (UK£1 = SEK13)	+46	visitsweden.com
Norway	+1	Norweigian & Sami	Norwegian Kroner (UK£1 = NOK12)	+47	visitnorway.com
Finland	+2	Finnish & Swedish	Euro (UK£1 = €1.50)	+358	visitfinland.com
Iceland	0	Icelandic	Icelandic Krona (UK£1 = ISK130)	+354	visiticeland.com

* English is widely spoken in each of the listed countries

Accommodation

Check out tourist board websites for online booking facilities. In **Denmark**, popular family choices include rental cottages, holiday villages, farmstays, campsites and hostels. Novasol Cottages (novasol.co.uk) offer weekly rentals throughout the country. Standard cottages (modern homes with accommodation for up to six people) cost from around £300 per week during peak season, while top-end properties (sleeping up to 12 people and with luxury touches like swimming pools) start at around £1000 per week. Also try Dansommer (dansommer.com). Denmark's holiday villages are well equipped for self-catering holidays. Weekly peak-season rates range from £350 to £900, depending on the type of accommodation. Try Lalandia (lalandia.com) near Rødby which has its own waterpark; Strandhotellerne (strandhotellerne.dk) which has four beachside resorts around Denmark; Skallerup Klit (skallerup.dk) with its indoor Atlantis Waterland; and Silkeborg (danparcs.com) which boasts an artificial ski slope. You can book farmstays in Denmark at bondegaardsferie.dk and ecoholiday.dk, while family hostels are available through Danhostels (danhostel.dk). Denmark's campsites have excellent facilities and are very popular with Danish families. To stay at an approved campsite you must have a valid Camping Card Scandinavia, available for around £7.

In **Sweden**, camping is the most popular form of accommodation during summer months. SCR (camping.se) publishes an extensive directory of campsites, as well as some 12,000 rental cottages. Also offering excellent facilities for inexpensive self-catering holidays, the Swedish Tourist Association (svenskaturistforeningen.se) has a network of about 300 youth hostels (known as vandrarhem). Hotel accommodation in Stockholm is expensive, but you can save money by staying in a holiday cottage on the coast, 30-minutes' drive from the city. Destination Stockholms Skärgård (dess.se) lists properties throughout the region (including the Stockholm Archipelago) with peak-season rates from around £350 per week. Two hours north of Gothenburg, TanumStrand (tanumstrand.se) is a popular family-friendly resort with waterslides and a mini-zoo, while Isaberg (isaberg.com), 120 km east of Gothenburg, has 70 chalets in a holiday village setting, plus a plethora of year-round activities, from canoeing to skiing.

Norway's Fjord Pass (fjord-pass.com) offers discounts on accommodation at 150 hotels, guesthouses and cabins throughout the country. It costs around £10 and is valid for two adults and any children under the age of 15. With the pass, you will find cabins and apartments from as little as £40 per night. Also good value, Hostelling International Norway (vandrerhjem.no) operates 110 youth and family hostels. For family-friendly cruise lines operating in the Norwegian fjords, see page 235.

In **Finland** you will find a wide range of cottages and farmstays at Lomarengas (lomarengas.fi), while Destination Lapland (yllas-travel-service.fi) specializes in log cabins in Lapland. Camping in Finland (camping.fi) provides access to 330 campsites across the country. Expect to pay between £10 and £20 per family pitch. Located mainly in the central lakeland area, Finland has about 200 holiday villages, with prices from £100 to £350 per week per cottage.

Iceland has a wide range of hotels and guesthouses, many of which offer children's discounts. Expect to pay anything from £35 to £120 for a double room with breakfast. For hands-on rural stays, try Icelandic Farm Holidays (farmholidays.is). There are also 26 hostels around Iceland which can be booked through Hostelling International (hostel.is). Campsites in Iceland are usually open from the beginning of June until the end of August and are free of charge for children under 16.

Icehotel

Expect a frosty reception at the Icehotel (icehotel.com) in Swedish Lapland. The thermometer behind the check-in counter usually reads around -6°C. The counter is, naturally, made of ice, along with everything else in this fairy-tale hotel located in Jukkasjärvi, a small village 200 km north of the Arctic Circle. From the outside, the hotel resembles a giant, featureless igloo. But inside there are ice chandeliers sparkling with fibre optics, candles burning in carved recesses and intricately chiselled pillars. It feels like you've arrived on Planet Krypton. Each room has its own ice bed strewn with reindeer furs, but guests are also given Arctic-grade sleeping bags. Hotel staff provide a full briefing on what to wear (thermal everything) and how to breathe (preferably through your nose). In the morning you're awoken with a hot cup of lingonberry juice. Family rooms cost from around £80 per person per night.

meat and potatoes. The *smörgåsbord* buffet-style of dining will appeal to picky children, while fast-food outlets and pizzerias are widespread. In **Denmark** try herring in various guises (from raw and pickled to cooked in a rich cream sauce). *Smørrebrød*, the Danish open sandwich, is available in umpteen varieties. Expect to pay around £0.75 for a loaf of bread and £0.70 for a litre of milk. Fresh, pickled and smoked seafood (particularly herring, crayfish, salmon and eel) are popular dishes in **Sweden**, but you should also try game dishes such as stir-fried reindeer. *Dagens rätt* (dish of the day), consisting of a main course with salad, bread and a drink, is available from many restaurants for around £6. Expect to pay anything from £20 upwards for a three-course meal in a mid-priced restaurant, £0.70 for a *varmkorv* hotdog from a street stand, £1.10 for a loaf of bread and £0.60 for a litre of milk. In northern **Norway** there is a long tradition of drying cod on wooden racks. To eat this local delicacy, first beat the dried fillets with a wooden mallet, soak them in water and douse in mustard or butter. Other specialities include roast pork ribs, cured mutton and sheep's heads, with ears, eyes and all. *Fårikål*, a stew of lamb, cabbage and whole peppercorns is a traditional autumn dish. **Finland**'s traditional cuisine is closely tied to the seasons. In summer new potatoes, fresh vegetables, salmon, whitefish and Baltic herring dominate menus, with crayfish in season from late July to September. Game meats, mushrooms, cloudberries, blueberries and lingonberries figure prominently in the autumn, while fish, such as burbot, are hauled from ice-covered lakes during winter. The seafood in **Iceland** is of outstanding quality. Try Icelandic fish and chips in the old harbour area of Reykjavík, where plaice, cod and haddock are served with organic vegetables and homemade lemonade.

Health and safety
Scandinavia is generally very safe and clean and there is no need to take any special vaccination precautions. Mosquitoes can be a nuisance during summer months, particularly in Sweden and Finland. Potentially more dangerous are severe winter temperatures in the far north. Be sure to take warm clothing and be especially alert to the threat of frostbite or hyperthermia in very young children. Other safety issues to be aware of include unfenced natural hazards, like waterfalls and volcanic areas in Iceland and frozen lakes in Finland and Sweden. The emergency telephone number for all countries in the region is 112.

How much for a Big Mac?
USA US$3.22
UK US$3.90
Denmark US$4.84
Sweden US$4.59
Norway US$6.63
Iceland US$7.44

Above: Something fishy? Take your pick of raw, smoked, pickled, boiled…
Below: Iceland's hotspots – a sign warns of superheated geothermal water.

Food and drink
Seafood features predominantly in Scandinavian cuisine. Local specialities like pickled fish and black bread may demand an acquired taste, but you will also find basics like

Top of the world, Ma!
Lapland specialist, *Arctic Experience* (arctic-experience.co.uk) offers several unusual winter breaks in Lapland suitable for families. The three-night Sami Experience (available November to April, from around £420 per person based on a family of four) promises a fascinating insight into the lives of the indigenous Sami of Swedish Lapland, including a stay in a wooden *lavvu*. Three nights at Kakslauttanen Cabins in Finnish Lapland, where you have a chance to spend a night in an igloo (made of ice or glass) and explore the surrounding forest by reindeer sleigh, husky sledge or snowmobile, costs from £695 per person. Alternatively, stay at Finland's Lainio Snow Village with its ice rooms and gentle ski slopes.

Orkuveita Reykjavíkur
Varúð! Mjög heitt vatn
Danger! Very hot water

Africa

The ripple effect – Joseph Gray runs wild in the Namib Desert.

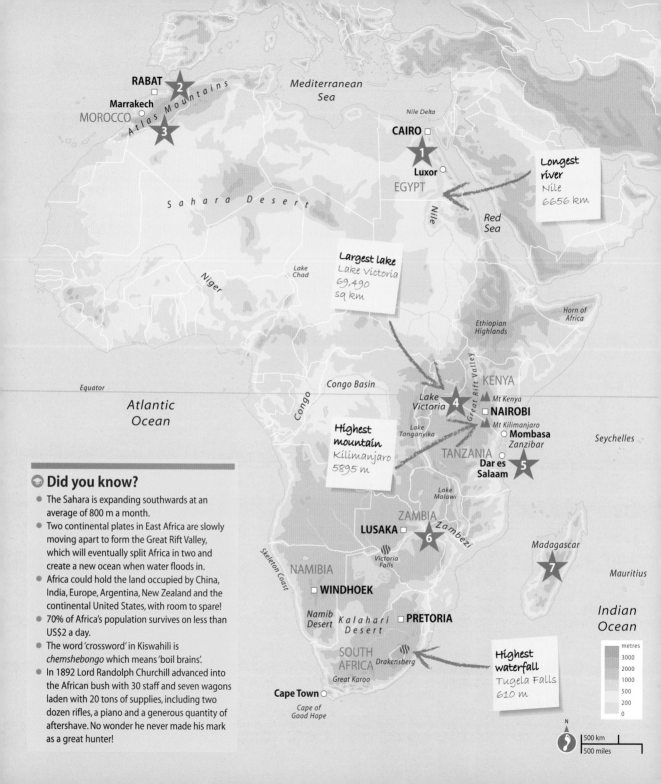

Did you know?

- The Sahara is expanding southwards at an average of 800 m a month.
- Two continental plates in East Africa are slowly moving apart to form the Great Rift Valley, which will eventually split Africa in two and create a new ocean when water floods in.
- Africa could hold the land occupied by China, India, Europe, Argentina, New Zealand and the continental United States, with room to spare!
- 70% of Africa's population survives on less than US$2 a day.
- The word 'crossword' in Kiswahili is *chemshebongo* which means 'boil brains'.
- In 1892 Lord Randolph Churchill advanced into the African bush with 30 staff and seven wagons laden with 20 tons of supplies, including two dozen rifles, a piano and a generous quantity of aftershave. No wonder he never made his mark as a great hunter!

Longest river
Nile
6656 km

Largest lake
Lake Victoria
69,490 sq km

Highest mountain
Kilimanjaro
5895 m

Highest waterfall
Tugela Falls
610 m

☆ Sail through the land of the Pharaohs
▸▸ Egypt, page 252

☆ Ride a camel through the desert
▸▸ Egypt and Morocco, pages 252 and 254

☆ Trek in the Atlas Mountains
▸▸ Morocco, page 254

☆ Track the big five
▸▸ Kenya, page 256

☆ Snorkel on a coral reef
▸▸ Tanzania, page 258

☆ Canoe on the Zambezi
▸▸ Zambia, page 260

☆ Discover rare wildlife
▸▸ Madagascar, page 261

If there's one thing guaranteed to get the grandparents tutting and clucking it's the mere mention of the words 'kids', 'holiday' and 'Africa' in the same sentence. "Is it safe? What about malaria? The local zoo has lions – why don't you go there instead?" You can't blame them for being concerned. Africa has its fair share of challenges when it comes to travel. But, equally, it has plenty of destinations that are ideal for families. South Africa's Cape region, for example, has everything from wonderful beaches to malaria-free game reserves, while East Africa is perfect for a safari/beach combo. There's more to Africa, though, than these well-established family favourites. Ever wondered what it would be like to do a roly-poly down one of the world's highest sand dunes? Or paddle in the wake of famous explorers like Dr David Livingstone? These and countless other adventures are up for grabs in Namibia and Zambia. And let's not forget North Africa. In Morocco, mule-supported treks can transport your tribe into the heart of the Atlas Mountains, while you might opt for camels or sailing feluccas to introduce your kids to the wonders of ancient Egypt.

> 66 99 *There were the inevitable scuffed knees and odd blister during our four-day hike in the Atlas Mountains, but none of the interminable whingeing that I'd feared. We settled into a gentle daily routine, supported by Ali and his friendly team of muleteers. Not only did the mules carry our luggage and food, but they also served as welcome transport whenever the children tired of walking.*
> *Will*

Africa rating	
Wow factor	★★★★★
Worry factor	★★★
Value for money	★★★
Keeping teacher happy	★★★★
Family accommodation	★★★
Babies & toddlers	★★
Teenagers	★★★

🔍 How to make a traditional snare

▶▶ Extract the fibres of Kalahari sisal by dragging your digging stick across the leaves.

▶▶ Twine the fibres together across your thigh.

▶▶ Tie one end to a 'bendy' sapling and anchor the other end in the ground with a half-buried twig.

▶▶ Attach a loop to the free end of twine and stake it in a circle using sticks.

▶▶ Attach a trigger stick baited with wild raisins.

▶▶ Scatter leaves around snare, then wait for a quail or guinea fowl to peck at the raisins …

❓ Where can I ride an ostrich?

Oudtshoorn, a small town in South Africa's Little Karoo, has been an ostrich-farming centre since 1864. Depending on their age and attitude, children will either love the ostriches at Cango Ostrich Farm (cangoostrich.co.za) or take one look at the 2-m tall pecking machines and stick their heads in the sand, so to speak. Kids as young as four or five can ride the birds (which are 'controlled' by two handlers). Just remember that these feathered giants can reach 60 kph and kill a man with a single kick!

❓ Will you spot the small five?

Elephant shrew
Rhinoceros beetle
Buffalo weaverbird
Leopard tortoise
Ant lion

Books to read

Crafty Chameleon, Hodder Headline, 2004
Beautifully illustrated, this is the story of how clever little Chameleon got the better of Leopard and Crocodile. Ages 3-8

Ebele's Favourite: A Book of African Games, Frances Lincoln, 1999
Ebele loves games. But when her friend comes to stay she finds herself wondering which is her favourite. Ten traditional Nigerian games are described. Ages 4-8

Fly, Eagle, Fly: An African Tale, Frances Lincoln, 2002
An engaging parable of an eagle chick raised amongst chickens. Despite being assured by the farmer that the eagle will never fly, a man teaches it how to soar. Ages 6-11

The Girl who Married a Lion, Cannongate, 2005
A collection of folktales from Botswana by Alexander McCall Smith. Includes the stories *Sister of Bones* and *Hare Fools the Baboons*. Ages 6-11

The Awesome Egyptians, Scholastic Hippo, 1994
History with all the nasty bits left in. Funny and gruesome, it covers everything from making a mummy to revolting recipes for 3000-year-old sweets. Ages 8+

Chain of Fire, Puffin, 2004
The apartheid government is forcibly removing black South African people from their villages. Schoolchildren, Naledi and Tiro decide to get involved in a student protest march. Ages 12+

🔍 How to play mancala

There are lots of variations on how to play this ancient board game. All you need are 36 stones, a mancala board with two rows of six holes (an empty egg carton will do) and a 'store', such as a small bowl, for each player.

▸ Place three stones in each hole.

▸ One player starts by picking up all of the pieces in any one of the holes on his side of the board.

▸ Moving anti-clockwise, the player places one of the stones in each hole until they run out.

▸ If you reach your own store, deposit a stone in it – but skip your opponent's store.

▸ If the last stone you drop is in your own store, take another turn. If it lands in an empty hole on your side, you capture any stones in the hole directly opposite and place them in your store.

▸ The game is over when all six spaces on one side of the board are empty. The winner is the player with the most pieces in his or her store.

How to read tombs

Use the hieroglyphic alphabet below to unravel the mysteries of ancient Egypt

🦅	**a**	a eagle
	a	arm
	b	foot
	c/k	basket
	d	hand
	e/i	2 strokes
	f/v	viper
	g	jar
	h	flax
	h	courtyard
	i/y/e	reed
	j	cobra
	l	lion
	m	owl
	m	bar
	n	water
	o/u/w	lasso
	p	door
	q	slope
	r	mouth
	s/z	cloth
	sh/ch	pool
	t	loaf
	th	rope
	w	quail chick
	x	basket/cloth
	y	reed
	z/s	bolt

Weirdlife: the naked mole rat that feels no pain

Also known as: Sand puppy.

Vital statistics: 8-10 cm long, 30-35 g in weight.

Found in: Kenya.

What's so weird? The lack of fur is one thing. But naked mole rats are also virtually cold-blooded – which is pretty weird for a mammal. They can only survive underground where there's a constant temperature. They use their front teeth to excavate burrows that can reach over 3 km long. And, perhaps most weird of all, they don't feel pain. Naked mole rats lack a neurotransmitter called Substance P that is responsible in mammals for sending pain signals to the central nervous system.

Taste of Africa: Moroccan tagine

A delicious slow-cooked Moroccan stew, tagine is also the name given to the clay pot that it is cooked in. Tagines can be meat, fish or vegetarian dishes, cooked with aromatic spices, vegetables and dried fruits.

What you need

▸ 1 tbsp olive oil
▸ 1 kg lean lamb, chopped into 4 cm cubes
▸ 4 pears, peeled and cubed
▸ 2 large onions, peeled and sliced
▸ 500 g sultanas
▸ 500 g flaked almonds
▸ 1 tbsp each of cumin, fresh chopped coriander, ground ginger, cinnamon and black pepper

What to do

▸ Fry the onion in the oil and transfer to the tagine.
▸ Add the meat. When browned, add the spices.
▸ Add enough water to cover the meat.
▸ Cover and simmer on a low heat for around 2 hrs until the meat is tender and infused with the spices.
▸ In the last five minutes, add the pears, almonds and sultanas.

One to watch: *Wild Africa*

BBC, 2004
Definitive DVD set, showcasing the amazing wildlife of Africa's mountains, grasslands, deserts, coasts, jungles, and lakes

Fashion statement: kikoy

Wear it as a skirt, scarf or shawl; use it as a beach towel, picnic rug or bird hide – Africa's traditional wrap has an infinite number of uses.

Whatever age your children, health risks are likely to be the main factor in deciding where you go in Africa – or even whether to go at all. Malaria, of course, is the single biggest worry (see page 271). Force-feed your children with Malarone, douse them with insect repellent and insist they wear long clothes and you may still find yourself lashing out at every winged insect that passes within a few feet of them. Paranoid? Perhaps. But it's small wonder that South Africa's Cape has become the 'default' choice for family travel in Africa. Not only is it malaria-free, but it has gold-star attractions like Table Mountain and the Garden Route. Malaria-free North Africa, on the other hand, is not such a clear-cut case. Here, the dangers of upset stomachs and overheating rear their ugly heads. Having said all that, however, there are numerous parents who are quite happy to take even young children paddling down the Zambezi, riding camels through the Sahara or spotting big game on an East African safari. Ultimately, it all boils down to your individual assessment of the risks, the precautions you are prepared to take and the age limits imposed by tour operators, camps and lodges.

Babies (0-18 months)

Think very hard before taking children aged four and under to malarious parts of Africa. If they have older siblings who are desperate to go on safari, remember that parts of South Africa have malaria-free game reserves where you can spot big game. The safest, most relaxing and affordable way to visit South Africa with babies is to split your time between Cape Town and the Garden Route, staying in comfortable hotels or guesthouses with babysitting services. If you are set on something more adventurous, consider a guided, mule-supported trek in Morocco. A pre-crawling-stage baby in a papoose is a wonderfully portable thing, while breast-fed babies have a safe and readily available food source, even in remote places like the Atlas Mountains. However, be sure to take every precaution to protect your infant from the sun, and visit during autumn or spring to avoid the worst of the heat.

Toddlers/pre-school (18 months-4 years)

Sub-Saharan Africa is one of the world's highest-risk areas for malaria (see above), so most families restrict their travels to South Africa's Cape provinces and parts of North Africa. As babies evolve from nappy-bound blob to mobile mini-explorer they inevitably encounter more in the way of germs and accidents. With hygiene and safety coming to the fore you may be further put off from visiting Africa. Don't be. In addition to the Cape and Morocco, other non-malarial places you should consider are Namibia and the Seychelles. Following the initial shock and stress of early parenthood, a self-drive campervan tour of Namibia is a great holiday choice

Top: Kenya safari. **Above:** Trekking in Atlas Mountains.

for families with toddlers. Not only does your campervan function as a self-contained bedroom, playroom and kitchen, but the Namib Desert will seem like one giant sandpit. For something a little more indulgent, the Seychelles and Mauritius boast numerous resorts with supervised kids' clubs, allowing adults some much-needed 'me-time'.

Kids/school age (4-12 years)

At this age, Africa starts to sound really exciting. Most four-year-olds will have seen *The Lion King* and you may already have taken them to see Timon and Pumba at Disneyland. Now is the time to bring the wilds of Africa to life – warthogs and all! You have two main options when it comes to family safaris – lodge-based or camping. For safety reasons, children usually need to be near the upper end of this age category for camping safaris, while many of the more exclusive lodges also have strict minimum age limits (some as high as 12 years). That's not to say you won't find family-friendly safari accommodation. Far from it. Both East and southern Africa have several excellent camps and lodges where children are specially catered for, with activities ranging from guided bush tracking to poo identification (always a hit with youngsters). Egypt is another excellent family destination for children who have reached school age. Ancient Egypt usually features on the curriculum around the age of seven or eight, so this is an ideal time for a tour of the Nile Valley using a combination of traditional sailing felucca, sleeper train and camel. Other cultural hotspots to aim for include Zanzibar and Lamu on the East African coast. These ancient Swahili settlements make perfect add-ons to safaris in Tanzania or Kenya.

Teenagers (13 years+)

Seen one lion, seen 'em all. Looks like a pile of rocks (yawn). If these are the kinds of reaction you get when trying to convince your teenager of the merits of a safari or Egyptian tour, perhaps you need to think about upping the pace (and pulse) a little. Africa has several adventure 'capitals' with more than enough adrenaline-charged activities to lure teenagers from their iPods, Nintendos and mobile phones. Top of the list has to be Victoria Falls, where you can bungee jump, ride elephants, fly in a microlight and raft some of the world's wildest water. Don't be put off by the political turmoil affecting Zimbabwe. Livingstone, on the Zambian side of the Falls, now has an excellent range of accommodation and tour operators. Other adventure hotspots include Swakopmund in Namibia (for desert sandboarding, kayaking with seals and 4WD tours along the Skeleton Coast), Cape Town (for great white shark encounters, surfing and abseiling off Table Mountain) and South Africa's Drakensburg Mountains (for hiking, horse riding, rafting and paragliding). Alternatively, why not set your teenager a single, big challenge, such as learning how to scuba dive in the Red Sea, catch a tiger fish on Lake Malawi or joining a Young Rangers' Club in Kenya. There are also plenty of opportunities for getting off the beaten track in places like Madagascar or Zambia's South Luangwa Valley. If your teenagers, however, are embarrassed simply by the mere presence of their parents, consider an overland expedition where they bring along a friend or two. These long-distance journeys are a great way to get under the skin of Africa, see lots of different countries and pick up some lessons in independence along the way. The Adventure Company (adventurecompany.co.uk) has teenage trips to Egypt, Kenya, Morocco, South Africa and Tanzania; Explore Worldwide (explore.co.uk) has dedicated teenage departures to Botswana, Egypt, Morocco, Namibia, South Africa, Tanzania and Tunisia; Exodus (exodus.co.uk) has teenage trips to Botswana, Egypt, Morocco, Namibia, South Africa, Tunisia and Zambia, while Families Worldwide (familiesworldwide.co.uk) offers teenage departures to Egypt, Morocco and Tanzania.

Special needs

Mobility impairment needn't rule out an African adventure. Specialist tour operators in South Africa and Kenya offer family-friendly, wheelchair-accessible holidays where everything from vehicles and accommodation to the pace of the itinerary are designed to suit physically disabled travellers. One or two also offer trips for people reliant on oxygen or kidney dialysis. Try Epic Enabled (epic-enabled.com), Endeavour Safaris (endeavour-safaris.com) and Able Travel (able-travel.com).

Single parents

Group safaris, Nile cruises and treks in the Atlas Mountains lend themselves particularly well to single parents. Your children will quickly bond with others in the group, while the tour leader will remove all the logistical headaches you might otherwise encounter if travelling alone. However, if you do crave independence, try a self-drive tour in South Africa, pre-booking each night's accommodation in guesthouses where you'll get to know locals faster than by staying in big, impersonal hotels.

Telling tales …

We've always wanted to do a safari. With Zak being seven, Sophie 11 and Natalie 14 it was a really good time, age-wise, with the family. When you mix this with Cape Town it's a fantastic balance. I convinced them they weren't going to see much, that the wildlife would be a long way away and that they would be extremely lucky to see a leopard. As it turned out we saw so many leopards they began saying "Big deal, Dad". We also went kayaking at Simon's Town. At first the children weren't keen. Natalie was absolutely paranoid that she was going to get attacked by a shark. By the time we got round into Boulders they thought it was brilliant. They didn't want to come in.

Children's favourite animal All Sophie wanted to see was elephants. To be stuck in the middle of a herd was absolutely unbelievable, especially with a five-day old calf. That made her trip.

Biggest disappointment We did too much. On paper it sounded great – a couple of days here, a couple of days there – but in hindsight we should have stayed another night in the Cape Town area and probably an extra night on safari as well.

Sir Steve Redgrave CBE
British rower and five-times Olympic gold medallist

② Where can I do this?
Dragoman Overland (dragoman.com) offers overland expeditions specially designed for families with children aged 7-18. Their rugged 4WD trucks carry all expedition essentials, from water tanks to camping equipment. Routes include 16- or 18-night trips in Kenya and Uganda, Kenya and Tanzania or Namibia, Botswana and Zimbabwe.

66 99 It's little wonder that safaris are such an instant hit with children. I always imagined it had something to do with the magic of seeing their first wild elephant or lion. But when we took our four-year-old twins to South Africa it suddenly struck me that it was the guide, not the wildlife, which was the focus of their fascination. Turn your nose up if you like, but the simple, blatant truth is that the vast majority of young children and safari guides share a fascination with poo. Our ranger commanded instant awe in Joe and Ellie simply by probing the contents of a hyena pellet and scooping up a handful of giraffe faeces as if they were raisins. And when he proceeded to break open and sniff an elephantine offering as if it was a freshly baked loaf of bread, our children's respect for the man immediately transcended anything I'd managed to drum into them since they were born. *Will*

Fun with dung – can you spot the tiny hooves of a puku fawn in this leopard dropping?

Unlocking the treasure chest

Got yourself an infant Indiana Jones or little Lara Croft? If your kids are into adventure and hidden treasure, Egypt makes an exciting and educational destination where you can combine the mysteries of the Pharaohs with some beach time on the Red Sea coast. Many parents get DDS (Disney Dithering Syndrome) when it comes to Egypt, constantly asking themselves: "Are our kids too young? Will they get much out of it?" Obviously, school-age children who have covered ancient Egypt in the classroom will be blown away by seeing the real thing, but that doesn't mean younger travellers will find it boring. The secret is to combine fact with fun. Don't make your trip an endless procession of museums and adult-focussed tours – instead, build itineraries around mini-adventures, like sailing on a felucca or riding a camel.

Above: Resting place of the Pharaohs – enter if you dare. Below: One hump or two?

The Nile Valley

○ △ ⋒ ♀ ⊙ ☢

» Avoid excessive heat by travelling during autumn and spring.
» At historic sites, keep children interested for longer by setting them challenges like hieroglyphic code-busting.
» Top kids' foods include *shish tawouq* kebabs, *fiteer pizzas* and *kushari* noodles. Let fussy feeders choose from a range of mezze dishes.
» Take rehydration sachets with you in case of outbreaks of diarrhoea.

Time travel down the Nile

Many families avoid the summer meltdown by visiting Egypt over Christmas or during half-term breaks in spring and autumn. However, without the luxury of long summer holidays you do have to pack a lot in and follow a fairly well-established route.

Cairo Divide your time between the Pyramids of Giza and the Egyptian Museum (egyptianmuseum.gov.eg). At the latter, don't expect much in the way of interactive exhibits or even English interpretation. However, what you do get are the dazzling treasures of teenage Pharaoh, Tutankhamun, including his famous gold funerary mask. Another must-see is the grizzly and engrossing Royal Mummy Room, displaying the remains of 11 Egyptian queens and rulers. Talking above a 'hushed whisper' is forbidden – good luck with that!

The last surviving Ancient Wonder of the World, the Pyramids of Giza, are often bemoaned by adult visitors as being 'swamped by Cairo's suburbs' or 'spoilt by over-zealous touts'. Most children, however, will simply be struck by innocent wonder at the sheer size of these extraordinary monuments – especially the Great Pyramid of Khufu (Cheops) which rises to 137 m and is thought to have been constructed using more than two million limestone blocks, each one weighing over two tonnes. Most kids' initial impulse is to climb the thing. However, this is a definite 'no-no', so quash any disappointment by exploring the pyramid's long, cramped 'secret' passages that lead to mysterious subterranean chambers.

Aswan An exciting way to reach Egypt's southernmost city is to take the overnight sleeper train from Cairo. After the hustle of the capital, Aswan appears positively tranquil, so take time to relax by strolling through the Nubian villages of Koti and Siou on Elephantine Island where you can learn about local culture (older girls, and possibly their mums, will no doubt want a henna tattoo). Later, catch a ferry to the west bank of the Nile where you can arrange a camel ride through the desert to the seventh-century Monastery of St Simeon. Aswan is also the starting point for trips to Abu Simbel and the Great Temple of Ramses II. However, it's a 560- km roundtrip and you'll be stuck in a minibus for much of

the day (unless you have the budget to fly). Instead, set your sights on Luxor and the Valley of the Kings (see *Going with the flow*, opposite, for some plain sailing between Aswan and Luxor).

Luxor With Karnak a short distance north of the city and the Valley of the Kings just across the Nile, Luxor has the potential to both amaze and daze. Don't be tempted to try and squeeze in dynasty after dynasty of tomb sightseeing, but focus instead on a few of the most enigmatic sites. Highlights of the West Bank include the elegantly colonnaded Temple of Hatshepsut and the tombs of Ramses I and Ramses VI – both of which have burial chambers with elaborately painted scenes of animal-headed gods. Older children may enjoy the challenge of reaching the tomb of Tuthmosis III with its steep shafts and challenging passageways designed in an (unsuccessful) attempt to thwart tomb robbers.

You'll find that a series of early morning excursions to the West Bank has less 'whinge potential' than a single, long, hot day trip. Spend the afternoons relaxing by a pool and then set off again when it's cooler to visit local Luxor beauties like the Great Hypostyle Hall – a forest of 134 towering pillars that forms part of the Amun Temple enclosure at Karnak. A great way to reach this spectacular complex is to take one of the local horse-drawn carriages.

How to learn scuba-diving

Imagine swooping like an aquatic Peter Pan through surreal citadels of corals and giant anemones, gazing with goggle-eyed wonder at shoals of fish flickering around you like pulses of electricity and maybe even glimpsing a shark or a turtle. Learning to scuba dive opens your eyes to a whole new world and there are few better places to learn than the Red Sea. Look out for operators that are accredited to PADI (padi.com). PADI Gold Palm Resorts (located worldwide) put as much emphasis on diver safety and environmental awareness as quality accommodation. In Egypt, you'll find several at Dahab, El Gouna, El Quseir and Hurghada. The minimum age for learning to dive is 10 – although children as young as eight can take the plunge with a PADI Bubblemaker try-dive (but only in a swimming pool and to a maximum depth of 2 m). Children aged 10+ can enrol in the Discover Scuba Diving program where they'll experience the thrill of diving – but, again, only in a pool. In order to dive in the sea, kids aged 10-14 must take a Junior Open Water Diver course (or Open Water Diver course if they're 15 and over). This typically lasts four days, during which you will learn the fundamentals of scuba-diving in a safe pool environment before putting your newfound skills to the test with four open water dives.

Red Sea resorts

El Gouna Resort town, fine for lazing on the beach or snorkelling.

Hurghada Large, sprawling resort with facilities and hotels galore.

Dahab Popular resort on Sinai Peninsula, with snorkelling, diving, kayaking, horse riding and jeep safaris on offer. A good multi-activity option for teenagers.

Going with the flow: cruiser or felucca?

A sailing trip on the Nile is a quintessential part of experiencing Egypt, but what is the best way for families to get afloat? There are two main options: small, traditional sailing feluccas or large, modern motor cruisers.

Feluccas offer a more intimate experience, a flexible itinerary that might include a visit to the captain's village and an opportunity to spend nights camping on the banks of the Nile. A felucca cruise is the cheaper of the two options, but remember to bring life jackets for the children (very rarely are they provided) and plenty of things for them to do on deck. Other essentials include bottled water and sleeping bags (it can get bitterly cold at night).

Cruisers are usually prebooked as packages where meals and shore excursions are included. Most have splash pools and some, like *Sun Boat III*, have kids' extras like cookery classes. However, cruisers are also bigger, noisier and more expensive than feluccas; they operate on fixed itineraries and you inevitably end up visiting sites en masse.

Where to go One of the most popular voyages is to sail north from Aswan (going with the current) taking three days to reach Edfu by felucca. If you are short on time, take a three-hour sunset felucca cruise from Luxor to Banana Island.

Morocco

A tonic for the senses

If you want a family trip that's big on adventure, culture and scenery, but only feel like dipping a toe outside the 'comfort zone' of Europe, then Morocco is the place for you. Nip across the 13-km wide Straits of Gibraltar and you'll find yourself transported into a world of exotic new sights, sounds, smells and tastes. Don't feel intimidated, though: the souks of Marrakech and Fès may well leave you reeling, but Morocco has plenty of other less frantic highlights – from mule-supported trekking in the Atlas Mountains to surfing on the Atlantic coast.

Pick up a peacock – or anything else you fancy in a Moroccan souk.

Marrakech

» Hone in on the medina's main square, Djemaa el-Fna, and the nearby labyrinth of souks.
» Hold hands – this is not a place you want to lose someone.
» When kids start to tire, flag down a horse-drawn *calèche* or retreat to a rooftop terrace.
» For something similar on a smaller, less bewildering scale, visit Taroudant, a walled city in southern Morocco that resembles a 'mini Marrakech'. Fès also has a wonderfully chaotic medina.

Not your average shopping centre
Brace yourself. It's going to be crowded, noisy and intense. You're going to run a gauntlet of hard-sell tactics the likes of which you've probably never experienced before. You may feel bewildered – nervous even. But you'll emerge from the medina of Marrakech with a tingling sense of having felt the very pulse of Morocco. Delving into crowded souks you might expect children to recoil with culture shock. If anything, however, it is their enthusiasm and lack of inhibition that helps the parents adjust. Youngsters will spontaneously attract the cheek-squidging attention of stallholders, drawing grown-ups into contact with locals far more swiftly than if they were lone adult tourists.

Djemaa el-Fna This huge square is the setting for one of the world's greatest cultural spectacles – a seething mêlée of musicians, snake-charmers, storytellers, water sellers, jugglers, acrobats, henna artists, fortune-tellers, market traders, potion mixers and food vendors (selling everything from cinnamon tea to stewed sheep heads). This truly bizarre bazaar (which gets particularly lively and crowded from around dusk) will hold your kids spellbound.

The souks Glistening pyramids of olives, smooth mounds of saffron, racks of multicoloured slippers… the souks (located on the north side of Djemaa el-Fna) are like a giant marketplace and maze rolled into one. You'll witness artisans at work, from blacksmiths and carpenters to tailors and jewellers. Hire an official guide at the tourist office or stick to main streets and follow the flow of people. Be prepared to bargain hard and enter protracted negotiations. Alternatively, just keep walking and soak up the atmosphere.

Beaches
Essaouira A 10-km sandy shoreline and the steady *alizée* breeze lure windsurfers in their droves. Morrocco's Atlantic hotspot (with its fortified old town and bustling harbour) is also big on surfing and you can ride camels on the beach.
Agadir Better suited to families with young children, Agadir has a good range of seafront hotels with pools and kids' activities.
Larache This relaxed and popular resort, 85 km south of Tangier, has a clean, sandy beach. Take care when swimming, though. Lifeguards are kept busy due to the strong currents.

Where can I ride a camel in the Sahara?
Erg Chebbi, Morocco's only genuine Saharan *erg* (a large expanse of sand dunes) can be found near the village of Merzouga, about 50 km south of Erfoud. Camel treks, ranging from sunset strolls to overnight expeditions, can be booked through local hotels. Auberge Kasbah Derkaoua (aubergederkaoua.com) also offers desert escapades by horseback and 4WD.

> **❝❞** Trekking in a small group with other families provided an added incentive to our own five-year-old twins. They quickly elevated older kids to hero status and were happy to scurry along beside them for much of the time. I seriously doubt whether my wife and I would have been as successful in cajoling them to walk for several hours each day. As a group the children also invented games and other ways of entertaining themselves along the way – from playing I-spy and fossil hunting to carving walking sticks and watching dung beetles trundle perfect poo-balls across the path. But remember that no matter how moved you are by all those dramatic mountain vistas, most young children are not that bothered about scenery. If you ask our twins what they remember most about the trek they will begin by telling you the names of the other children, followed by the names of the mules. They will then recount the milestone event of when 10 year-old Sam showed them how to climb their first tree – a gnarled old olive with bark like wrinkled elephant hide.
>
> *Will*

🔍 How to plan a family trek in the High Atlas

Don't try and go it alone. Not only will a good local guide smooth out logistics (such as hiring mule teams), but you'll also glean fascinating insights into the region's geology, wildlife and Berber culture, as well as contributing directly to the local economy. Several Moroccan and foreign operators offer guided treks in the Atlas Mountains, but one of the most experienced family specialists is UK-based Families Worldwide (familiesworldwide.co.uk). By arranging things through a company that understands the importance of issues like child-friendly meals, mule support and high altitude you will not only get peace of mind, but a well-thought-out itinerary that's not too demanding for children.

Two family-friendly treks:

▸▸ From Imlil, walk two days to the shrine at Sidi Chamharouch (2310 m) in the High Atlas.

▸▸ From Taroudant, drive to Afensou for a circular day walk to Imoulas, then spend two days hiking to Tazoudat, crossing the spectacular Tizi-n-al-Cadi col.

Land of the Lion King

Safari. If ever there was a word to inspire wanderlust in a child this is the one. Not only does it conjure images of lions, elephants, zebras and all the other childhood animal favourites, but it simply oozes with the promise of adventure. Safaris are the ultimate I-Spy. Yes, there will be dust, heat, pre-dawn wake-up calls and even the occasional frustrating game drive when all you see is the retreating posterior of a lone warthog, its tail held aloft like a defiant flag of victory. But Kenyans have been refining the safari for long enough to ensure that the needs of families are well catered for – this was, after all, where safaris were invented (the word means 'journey' in Swahili). Combine animal magic with beach bliss by dividing your holiday between a safari and a sojourn on Kenya's reef-fringed coastline.

Above: Big cats are a Kenyan speciality.
Below: Flamingos at Lake Nakuru. **Below left:** A sailing dhow plies the East African coast.

Great Rift Valley

❍ ❍ ❍ ❍ ❍ ❍ ❍ ❍ ❍ ❍

»» Choose from budget camping safaris to more upmarket trips staying in lodges and luxury tented camps.
»» Some lodges impose a minimum age limit of around 8.
»» Allow at least a week for a circuit which includes Mt Kenya, Lakes Nakuru and Naivasha and the Masai Mara (kws.org).

Safari so good

Choosing a Kenyan safari can leave you wallowing in logistics. Operators offer everything from specialist birdwatching tours to budget camping expeditions to Lake Turkana. When it comes to family safaris, however, there is one circuit that's hard to beat. It combines the country's best wildlife-watching areas with child-friendly lodges and as few long days on the road as possible.

Nairobi Few capitals have national parks right on their doorstep, but Nairobi is one of them. Check into your hotel, dump your luggage and, 10 minutes later, you could be watching lions or black rhinos in the wonderful, underrated Nairobi National Park. Be sure to visit the David Sheldrick Wildlife Sanctuary (sheldrickwildlifetrust.org) where orphaned elephants and rhinos are cared for.

Mt Kenya Nestled in bird-filled forest on the western slopes of 5200-m Mt Kenya, Naro Moru makes a relaxing base for nature walks, horse riding and fishing. Nearby Ol Pejeta Conservancy (olpejetaconservancy.org) is unique in being the only place in Africa where you can see the big five as well as chimps. Although not indigenous to Kenya (orphans are brought here from other countries), Ol Pejeta's Sweetwaters Chimpanzee Sanctuary offers an insight into the plight of these endearing primates.

Nakuru From Mt Kenya it's a five-hour drive to this alkaline lake renowned for its flamingos. Changes in water levels mean you're unlikely to see the concentrations of up to two million birds that were common in past decades. However, this is still a world-class spectacle – and when you tire of gawking at the flamingos there are lions, leopards and rhinos to be spotted in the woodland surrounding the lake.

Naivasha This beautiful lake to the south of Nakuru is an altogether different kettle of fish – and birds. Freshwater Naivasha is fringed with papyrus bursting with over 350 species of birds, including herons, kingfishers and ducks – but not a single flamingo. Find out about the lake's ecology at the Elsamere Conservation Centre (elsatrust. org), once the home of the late Joy Adamson of *Born Free* fame. Older children who need to burn off energy might be tempted by the two-hour hike up nearby Mt Longonot.

Masai Mara Time your trip right (July-October) and your arrival in Kenya's finest wildlife reserve may coincide with the Great Migration when over a million wildebeest and several hundred thousand zebra and Thompson's gazelle head north from their breeding grounds in Tanzania's Serengeti. Even without the migration, however, the Mara offers superb game viewing, excellent accommodation and a chance to mingle with the Maasai.

❝❞ One flamingo is a head-turner. But just imagine hundreds of thousands of them strutting their stuff. Lake Nakuru is often flushed 'Barbie pink' as lesser and greater flamingos tiptoe through the shallows, sifting blue-green algae from the water with their downturned bills.

Will

How to get more out of a safari

With their special children's clubs, Heritage properties at Lake Naivasha, Samburu, Tsavo and the Masai Mara stand out as particularly family-friendly options in Kenya. Enrol your kids in the Adventurers' Club (4-12 year-olds) and they'll learn how to brush their teeth with a twig from the Salvadora tree, make casts of big cat tracks, build their own miniature Maasai homestead and identify countless birds and butterflies. For 12-17 year-olds the Young Rangers' Club offers three-four day courses covering bush orienteering (using sun, stars and GPS), first aid (including how to treat snakebites), bird and tree identification, mammal behaviour studies, guided bush walks, animal tracking and overnight stays in Maasai *manyattas* (villages).

The Coast

⚌ ⚌ ⚌ ⚌ ⚌ ⚌ ⚌ ⚌

>> The overnight train from Nairobi to Mombasa is a fun way to reach the coast.
>> You will find accommodation and activities to suit every budget.
>> Seaweed can affect beaches Mar-Dec.
>> Think twice about dragging kids around Mombasa's old town. It's going to be hot, sticky and dusty. If you want to experience Swahili culture head instead to infinitely more chilled Lamu.

A shore thing

The perfect place to unwind after a safari and wash the dust from your ears, Kenya's Indian Ocean shoreline is a beguiling blend of coral sand beaches and turquoise lagoons. It's also within easy striking distance of some excellent wildlife reserves which means that families short on time can base themselves at the coast and still get a safari fix.

South of Mombasa Diani and Tiwi beaches have every imaginable watersport available, from scuba-diving and snorkelling to kitesurfing and banana boat rides. There's also no shortage of accommodation. With their swimming pools and children's facilities, the large seafront resorts are an obvious choice for families, but also consider the wide range of more intimate beach cottages. Just inland is Shimba Hills National Reserve – a protected fragment of coastal forest that is home to sable antelope and colobus monkey. Adjoining the reserve is the community-run Mwalugange Elephant Sanctuary where you can not only see jumbos, but also buy postcards made from their recycled dung!

North of Mombasa Head to Watamu where the Local Ocean Trust (watamuturles.com) has set up a turtle conservation project. Several species lay their eggs on the beaches here between January and April. Malindi is the most popular resort along this stretch of coast and offers snorkelling and glass-bottom boat tours in Malindi Marine National Park. Inland, you can take a guided walk to spot some of the several hundred bird and butterfly species in Arabuko Sokoke Forest Reserve and visit Gedi – the remains of a 13th-century Swahili trading centre. It is well worth making the effort to continue north to the charming and friendly Lamu archipelago. Lose yourself in the winding alleyways that riddle the World Heritage Site of Lamu Town, spend a day cruising the islands on a traditional sailing dhow, then kick back on Shela Beach.

Above: Gedi Ruins near Malindi.

❓ Where can I eyeball a giraffe?

Langata Giraffe Centre (giraffecentre.org) is your best bet for getting on level terms with these lofty creatures. Located 20 km from downtown Nairobi, the centre has rescued, hand-reared and released back into the wild about 500 orphaned giraffes. A raised wooden platform provides an excellent vantage for either watching or feeding the residents – but watch out for those tongues! They can reach up to 50 cm in length and are blue-black in colour!

Tanzania

Where the wild things are

In many ways Tanzania is like a bigger version of Kenya (see page 256). It has perhaps slightly less in the way of family-friendly accommodation (particularly for children under eight), but you can still easily combine a safari with a beach holiday. Three places that are likely to spring to mind when contemplating a trip to Tanzania are Kilimanjaro, the Serengeti and Zanzibar. Although trekking on Africa's highest peak is a considerable undertaking for adults and children alike (see *High ideals* box opposite), a guided safari to see the big game of the Serengeti and Ngorongoro Crater, followed by some snorkelling on Zanzibar's coral reefs, has all the ingredients for Africa's ultimate wildlife experience.

The Northern Circuit

○○◑▮🜚⊕🜚

» Wildlife concentrations in the Serengeti and Ngorongoro are highest from Dec-Jun; wildebeest migrate north May-Jul.
» Some lodges have a minimum age limit of 8.
» Visit your (very) distant cousins at the Olduvai Gorge human fossil site.
» Don't forget binoculars, field guides and a tick list.

Game on

From Arusha, a typical safari includes Lake Manyara National Park, the Serengeti and Ngorongoro Crater. Distances are great (for example, it's a full day's drive between the Serengeti and Arusha), so allow at least a week to do the region justice. Lake Manyara National Park encapsulates everything that is wild and wonderful about this corner of Africa. Not only does it have a magnificent setting, cowering beneath the western escarpment of the Great Rift Valley, but it's also home to an intriguing cast of wildlife, from tiptoeing flamingos to tree-climbing lions. Some safaris also loop through Tarangire National Park, which has high concentrations of elephant, zebra and wildebeest between August and October. But it's Serengeti National Park that really gets the pulse racing. Nowhere else in Africa is more synonymous with big horizons, big skies and big game. The great migration between the Serengeti and Kenya's Masai Mara (see page 256) is one of the world's greatest natural spectacles, involving over a million wildebeest, plus several hundred thousand zebras and Thompson's gazelles. Keeping a keen eye on proceedings are lions, cheetahs, leopards and other predators. The great animal-watching bonanza climaxes at Ngorongoro Crater, an 8300-sq-km caldera containing Africa's largest permanent concentrations of wildlife.

Alternatively, head south from Dar es Salaam. The vast Selous Game Reserve is not as well trodden as the Serengeti and offers less choice when it comes to accommodation, but it's an exciting option for a camping safari with older children.

Top: Zebra. **Above**: Wildlife ticklist. **Below**: The trek to the summit of Kilimanjaro is a tough slog and not to be undertaken lightly.

Zanzibar in a nutmeg shell

Get lost Explore Stone Town where a maze of streets threads between buildings like paths in a narrow, twisting canyon.

Sniff spices Join a tour to a spice plantation for a noseful of nutmeg, cinnamon, vanilla, cardamom, turmeric and cloves.

Take the plunge Snorkel off any of the east-coast beaches, which are all protected by coral reefs.

High ideals

It might look tempting, rising serenely above the tawny savannah, but the 5895-m summit of Mt Kilimanjaro is not something to set your sights on with young children in tow. Although non-technical, the return trek to the summit is a five- to seven-day slog, fraught with the possibilities of fatigue, dehydration and acute mountain sickness. Fair enough if teenagers feel up to the challenge, but parents with determined younger children should stick to a two-day taster – hiking the first day of the Marangu Trail, spending a night at Mandara camp, and scrambling up to Maundi Crater for panoramic views before heading back down again. A gentler alternative to Kili is to walk in the Crater Highlands with a Maasai guide.

Go Green in Africa

Five ways to tread lightly and support local communities

1 Choose minimal impact accommodation. Look for camps and lodges that use sustainable building materials and energy-saving devices, employ local people and reinvest profits in education and conservation schemes.

2 Support tours that have negligible environmental impact and are least intrusive to wildlife, such as canoeing safaris on the Zambezi.

3 Put something directly back into local communities by, for example, joining a township tour in Cape Town (grassroutetours.co.za).

4 Support organizations actively involved in conservation, like Namibia's AfriCat Foundation (see page 263).

5 Join tours that directly benefit local people and respect their traditions, such as a Samburu-led hike in Kenya (www.samburutrails.com).

Chumbe Island (chumbeisland.com), located off Zanzibar's west coast, has seven thatched bungalows constructed entirely of sustainably-harvested mangrove poles and thatch. There are solar-powered lamps, composting toilets and a rain catchment device that provides all freshwater needs. Used water is filtered through a special garden stocked with nutrient-absorbing plants to ensure that no waste reaches the surrounding marine reserve which is teeming with corals, fish and turtles. Chumbe's rare coral rag forest is home to the highly endangered Ader's duiker and a thriving population of giant coconut crabs. Kids will learn a great deal about coral reefs and conservation from Chumbe's outstanding local rangers.

Wildlife, waterfalls and the 'Wow!' factor

Zambia might not immediately strike you as being particularly family-friendly. However, don't let its reputation for posh lodges, private air charters and pricey five-star pampering put you off. There are some great options for family safaris in South Luangwa National Park ranging from reasonably priced self-catering camps to seriously expensive private safari houses. And then, of course, there's Victoria Falls. Over 100 m high, 1700 m wide and disgorging up to 550 million litres of water every minute, this World Heritage Site has become Africa's undisputed adventure capital.

Top: The thundering cataracts of Victoria Falls.
Above: The tranquil pool at the Zambezi Sun.

> 66 99 First, I heard the rapid, a steady thunder, like ocean surf. Ahead, the river appeared to abruptly end – just a fine mist hanging in the air, occasionally pierced by a spurt of leaping water. Suddenly the raft 50 m in front slid from view, its crew paddling furiously, the guide barking orders. A second later, it was tossed high on the first wave of the rapid, bodies and paddles spinning away like wayward fireworks.
>
> *Will*

Victoria Falls

» Knife Edge Bridge leads to a spectacular viewpoint of the Eastern Cataracts, but be prepared to get soaked by spray. *Warning!* There are no fences between you and the gorge. Victoria Falls National Park on the Zimbabwean side has more viewpoints, including Danger Point and Devil's Cataract.
» The Falls are impressive year-round, however spray during the peak flood period (Mar-Apr) can obscure views.
» Choose from accommodation in Livingstone or along the banks of the Zambezi upstream from the Falls.
» Most hotels and guesthouses can book any of the plethora of activities.

Thrills and spills

Don't worry if bungee jumping and whitewater rafting seem a tad extreme – there are activities at Victoria Falls to suit most ages and degrees of bravery.

Flight of the angels Getting airborne is the only way to fully appreciate the immense scale of this natural wonder. Choose from helicopters and fixed-wing Cessnas for flights with all the family, or microlights, ultralights and a vintage Tiger Moth biplane for one lucky passenger (batokasky.com).

Whitewater rafting Downstream of the Falls, Terminator, Devil's Toilet Bowl, Gnashing Jaws of Death and other grade V rapids conspire to form the world's wildest one-day whitewater rafting experience. You get life jackets, helmets, wetsuits and the reassurance that safety kayakers shoot the rapids first – so they're always waiting to help rafters who inadvertently find themselves

taking a swim. Be prepared for the steep trek in and out of the gorge to the put-in and take-out points. The minimum age is 15. Operators include Adrift (adrift.co.uk), Bundu Adventures (bunduadventures.com) and Touch Adventure (touchadventure.com).

Bungee jumping Take a 111-m leap of faith from Victoria Falls bridge for the ultimate adrenaline rush (shearwateradventures.com). If it's any comfort, the cord tied around your ankles has a breaking strain of 2000 kg. Minimum age is 14. Abseiling, and the world's first Gorge Swing, reaching speeds of up to 80 kph (thezambezi swing.com) are also available.

Canoeing Gliding silently past herds of drinking elephants, pausing to study a colony of rainbow-hued bee-eaters and hauling out on uninhabited islands for a well-earned picnic – paddling a canoe along the Upper Zambezi (safpar.com) is one of those classic African adventures that perfectly combines the thrill of exploration with unrivalled wildlife viewing. Two-person, Canadian-style canoes or inflatable 'crocodile' canoes are stable and easy to manoeuvre, and you can choose either day trips or overnight camping tours. The minimum age is 12.

Train rides The Victoria Falls Safari Express trundles back and forth between Livingstone and the bridge – a mini steam adventure for all ages.

Safaris Game drives (wildsidesafaris. com) in Mosi oa Tunya National Park often lead to close encounters with white rhino and other game, while

one-hour elephant-back safaris from Thorntree River Lodge (minimum age 10) provide a unique perspective of the bush and a chance to learn about elephant behaviour and conservation. Horse riding (children under seven must have had at least one year of riding lessons) and quad biking (for 16-year-olds and over) are also available.

Walk on the wild side

One of the best ways to experience untamed Africa is on a walking safari. These were pioneered in Zambia's South Luangwa National Park where both the wildlife and standard of guiding are legendary (minimum age is usually 12.) Apart from Flatdogs Camps (flatdogscamp.com) which offers camping and self-catering in a three-bedroom family house, most accommodation is in luxury lodges and tented camps.

Above: The irresistible palm-fringed beaches of the Seychelles.

Now that's what I call a beach!

In a toddler's mind the difference, say, between the beach at Lyme Regis in the UK and Beau Vallon in the Seychelles is probably minimal – both have sea to splash in and all the basic ingredients for building sandcastles. So, why bother hauling them all the way to the Indian Ocean? Well, for starters, the beaches of the Seychelles and Mauritius are some of the most idyllic and desirable in the world – something only parents might appreciate (but, hey, it's their holiday too). Beach bliss aside, though, these islands offer plenty in the way of gentle activities, from forest ambles to island hopping. And, if you have older kids with adventure on their minds, why not go lemur spotting in the national parks of Madagascar?

Seychelles

⊛⊛⊛⊛⊕⊕⊛

›› Jul and Aug are the driest, busiest and most expensive months. Consider Mar-Apr and Oct-Nov when it's not only quieter but also less windy.
›› Accommodation ranges from top-end resorts to self-catering guesthouses.
›› The Seychelles are pricey, but you can save money by using the ferry, instead of private charters, to island hop between Mahé, Praslin and La Digue.

Island hopping
With over 100 irresistible islands to choose from, the Seychelles are almost too much of a good thing. However, unless you have serious cash to splash, focus on Mahé, Praslin and La Digue, with an excursion to either Aride or Cousin Island.
Mahé The best family beach is Beau Vallon, a long curving scimitar of sand that's sheltered from the May-September trade winds and has no

Madagascar – essential viewing for all lovers of lemurs.

strong currents. Spend a day in the Baie Ternay Marine National Park where even toddlers can get a glimpse of the corals and fish on a glass-bottom boat trip. Away from the coast, hike the Trois Frères trail through cool montane forest in Morne Seychellois National Park.
Praslin For beach perfection head to Anse Lazio. Then go nuts at Vallée de Mai, famed for its rare coco de mer palms that can produce nuts weighing over 30 kg. Keep an eye out for black parrots, unique to Praslin. For the ultimate avian encounter, join a tour to either Aride (arideisland.net) or Cousin Island. Hundreds of thousands of seabirds nest on these specks of land, along with rare endemic species like the Seychelles warbler and magpie robin. Neither island has a jetty, so be prepared to carry youngsters ashore.
La Digue Backed by rounded pink boulders and lapped by emerald waters, Anse Source d'Argent consistently ranks in the world's top 10 beaches. But tear yourself away for at least one afternoon of exploring La Digue by bicycle (hire them at the pier when you arrive) or ox cart – perfect for babies or toddlers who are too small to cycle.

Madagascar

⊛⊛⊛⊕⊕

›› Your best chance of spotting lemurs is on foot – walking trails can take 2-3 hrs.
›› Avoid Jan-Mar when heavy rain makes travel difficult; May-Oct is coolest.
›› Unlike the Seychelles and Mauritius, Madagascar is a high-risk malaria area.

Land of the lemurs
For a typical two-week trip, your best bet is to focus on the north of the island where you can combine some of the most accessible wildlife reserves with time on the beach. From the capital, Antananarivo (or Tana), it's a three-hour drive to Andasibe where it's eyes (and ears) open for the indri. The eerie wailing call of this large black and white lemur with its teddy bear face can carry for over 3 km – so you'll probably hear one before you see it. From Tana, fly north to Diego Suarez from where it's a short drive to Ankarana reserve – home to no fewer than 10 species of lemur, including the shy, nocturnal aye-aye. Nearby Nosy Be is Madagascar's most popular beach destination and the starting point for boat trips to Nosy Tanikely (sheltered snorkelling) and Nosy Komba (inquisitive black lemurs).

Beach babes in Mauritius
If you want nothing more than a comfortable resort (complete with kids' club), a sandy beach and safe, shallow seas, then Mauritius is hard to beat – especially if you're travelling with tots. However, if all-inclusive resort packages sound too pricey, there are plenty of guesthouses and apartments for independent-minded families.

Desert, coast, safari … action!

When it comes to family holidays in southern Africa, the Cape will always have the lion's share. It's got everything from charismatic Cape Town to malaria-free game reserves in the Eastern Cape. So why take your kids to Namibia instead? Well, for starters it has lots in common with its southern neighbour – direct flights, guaranteed sunshine, good infrastructure and loads to do for all ages. But add to the equation Namibia's haunting emptiness, fantasy landscapes and a sandpit the size of a desert and you have a family adventure that leaves the Cape looking rather tame. What's more, planning a family trip to Namibia is a piece of cake – just slice your itinerary into three chunks: desert, coast and safari.

The Namib Desert

» No malaria risk, but it can get hot (30°C+).
» Drive yourself, join a tour or book a fly-in safari (12 kg luggage allowance per person).
» Namib lodges are pricey, but you can camp at Sesriem or stay at good-value guesthouses.
» Deserts don't get any more fun than this one.

Getting sand between your toes

Windhoek is pleasant enough, but there's nothing in Namibia's capital that's going to rivet your kids – unless, that is, they have a leaning towards German colonial architecture. And besides, you've come this far, so why not make straight for the desert.

Fly or drive Namibia is perfect for self-drive – distances are great, but roads are well maintained and traffic is light. You don't need a 4WD, but always think twice about passing a petrol station without stopping to fill up. It may be some time before you pass another! Allow five hours to drive from Windhoek to Sesriem, the gateway to the classic desert scenery of Sossusvlei. If you're short on time (but not cash) hop straight on to a chartered six-seater Cessna bound for the Namib Rand Nature Reserve (namidrand.com) – a 1800-sq-km swathe of mountains, dunes and grass-gilded plains to the south of Sesriem. The spectacular flight from Windhoek takes just over an hour.

Pick of the lodges Of the four lodges in the Namib Rand, Sossusvlei Mountain Lodge (ccafrica.com) may be a pricey option for families, but it's great for kids. Inside the chic, stone and glass suites you'll find telescopes, painting sets and wildlife tick lists. Stargazing skylights provide a mesmerising alternative to bedtime stories, while a small pool offers welcome respite from the heat.

Desert activities Guides can tailor outings to suit children aged five and up. Bring 16-year-olds here and they'll be off on the quad bikes before you can blink the sand from your eyes. Hot-air balloon flights (namibsky.com) are also a guaranteed hit with older children (minimum height 130 cm).

Even with much younger kids, you can explore springbok-dotted plains and study porcupine droppings and the S-bend tracks of horned adders. There are skittish beetles and 'sand-swimming' lizards to chase, strange outcrops (or kopjes) of granite boulders to conquer and, best of all, the sheer, unabashed exhilaration of running barefoot through the Namib Desert with a kite in tow.

Don't miss a day trip to Sossusvlei for quintessential desert scenery in the heart of the vast Namib Naukluft National Park. Youngsters probably won't stand in awe of the record-breaking 380-m-high dunes for long. Or appreciate the subtle play of light and shadow across their scalloped flanks. To your average kid (grown-up or otherwise), Sossusvlei means one thing: roly-poly heaven. It might take them a good half-hour to walk, crawl and stagger to the crest of one of the giant dunes –

Above: Sossusvlei – the world's ultimate roly-poly. Left: Traditional Himba doll.

but barely 30 seconds to somersault, slide and tumble down again. For days afterwards they'll be picking sand from their pockets, ears, hair, noses …

Teenage kicks

Damaraland Rugged scenery and a great location for overland camping trips. Track rhinos, visit Bushman rock art sites, hunt for gems and visit a fossilized forest.

Fish River Canyon Are you up for the challenge of a five-day trek through the world's second largest canyon? Arrange a guide with a satphone, and book permits for May to September.

Swakopmund

😊 🏛 🚣 😊 😊 🚲

» Namibia's adventure capital has loads to do.
» There are great value guesthouses in town.
» Be wary of strong currents and heavy surf – best leave swimming to the seals.
» How can you resist fish 'n' chips or an ice cream on the Skeleton Coast?

Fish 'n' chips on the Skeleton Coast

Namibia's surf-ravaged Skeleton Coast calms down at Swakopmund (a two-hour flight from the Namib Rand). Instead of rusting shipwrecks, whale carcasses and the kind of desolate wilderness that nearly forced British explorer, Benedict Allen to eat his camels, you'll find a quirky seaside resort with everything from sandcastles to fish 'n' chips. True, it's not as pretty as Plettenberg Bay on South Africa's Garden Route, and the water definitely feels like it's come straight from Antarctica, courtesy of the Benguela Current. But that won't stop your children shrieking with joy for an afternoon or two as they play chicken with the waves.

Namibia safari

😊 🏛 😊 😊

» Etosha has great wildlife and family-friendly camps, and you can drive yourself around, but you will need to consider malaria protection.
» Some game reserves have age restrictions.

How to pick a safari

Etosha National Park Home to large numbers of big game (including lion, leopard, elephant, black and white rhino, giraffe and zebra), Etosha is designed for visitors to drive themselves around. Independent-minded families will find simple, inexpensive rest camps with good facilities, such as bungalows with small kitchens, a shop for basic supplies and a swimming pool.

Caprivi Strip This is the least travelled and involves the greatest distance – not ideal if your kids get fractious on long car journeys. However, by striking out east

Things to do in town Swakopmund Museum may well be your best chance in Namibia to see, albeit stuffed, examples of nocturnal critters like the porcupine and aardvark, while Kristall Galerie has some whopping great quartz clusters and a scratch pit where you can search for semi-precious stones.

Adventure activities Once you've relaxed in Swakopmund for a day or two, you'll be wanting to hit the adventure trail again. Try NamibFun at the tourist office for a one-stop shop to everything from sky diving and paragliding to sandboarding and kayaking. If you book just one activity in Swakopmund, however, make sure it's a 4WD outing to Sandwich Harbour with Turnstone Tours (turnstonetours.com). Their guides not only know the ecology

towards the Caprivi Strip, you not only experience a green and verdant side to Namibia that's a wonderful contrast to the desert, but you can also round off your trip with a few days at Victoria Falls. Be aware, though, that malaria is present in northern and eastern parts of Namibia, particularly from November to June. Some lodges, like Lianshulu in Mundulu National Park, have a minimum age limit of 12.

Waterberg Plateau About halfway between Windhoek and Etosha, the Waterberg has malaria-free game reserves. Safaris here are gentle, subtle affairs. Don't expect edge-of-seat encounters with lions or elephants (head to Etosha for that). Instead you might stake out a floodlit waterhole waiting for the resident rhinos to appear or join a game drive to spot regional rarities, such as sable antelope.

Okonjima An option for families with

and history of the Skeleton Coast intimately (and are great at engaging children of all ages), but their driving skills will transform your daytrip into one long thrill ride. Hemmed in by towering dunes on one side and ocean breakers on the other, you'll find yourself racing the incoming tide along a beach riddled with quicksand and the occasional corpse of a turtle or seabird. As well as tracking jackals and spotting seals, the indisputed highlight of the trip is the 'singing dunes'. Riding the rollercoaster of the desert, your guide will cut the engine and let the Land Rover slide down the scarp slope of a particularly huge dune. As sand starts to avalanche and resonate beneath its wheels the desert hums. It's a magical, surreal experience. Don't forget to get out and try it on your bottom!

children aged 12 or over, Okonjima guest farm (okonjima.com) is home to the AfriCat Foundation – renowned for its work to safeguard Namibia's cheetahs, leopards, lions and caracals. As well as its main camp, Okonjima has a new and luxurious family villa with its own chef, guide, 4WD vehicle and pool. Activities range from cheetah tracking to learning about Bushmen traditions in this malaria-free area.

Mundulea Nature Reserve For more adventurous families, this 120-sq-km private reserve in the Otavi Mountains offers wonderful three-night walking trails, spending nights in tented camps with bucket showers. It's a superb opportunity to gain an intimate insight into Namibian wildlife and bushlore with Bruno Nebe – one of the most knowledgeable and enthusiastic guides in the business.

Above: Sossusvlei.
Below left: Sandy sandwiches at Sandwich Harbour, Skeleton Coast.
Below: Meerkat.

🐾 **Animal sightings**

Cheetah Namibia has 40% of Africa's feline Ferraris (max speed 110 kph).
Brown hyena Can sometimes be seen scavenging among seal colonies on the coast.
Meerkat Made famous by *The Lion King*'s Timon, these endearing little critters live in mobs up to 40 strong.

Following the rainbow

Give Africa a good shake, leave to stand a while and let all the best bits settle at the bottom. It's almost as if South Africa has distilled everything that is thrilling and remarkable about the continent. You might find wilder national parks in Zambia, the wildebeest migration in Tanzania or emptier roads in Namibia, but the Rainbow Nation's irresistible lure lies in its sheer diversity. You've got Cape Town – right up there with other urban beauties like Sydney and Vancouver. You've got vast swathes of wilderness, stunning wildlife, superb food, great places to stay, and, best of all for families, you've got plenty to keep you busy. Boredom simply is not an option – not in a country where, in the same day, you can stand on top of Table Mountain, swim with wild penguins and then tuck into a plate of good old-fashioned fish and chips.

Cape Town

⊙ 🌊 ⊛ 🐾 🐘 🛏 ⛵ 🎭 ⊛ ☢

» Flights from European cities to Cape Town take around 10-11 hrs, but most are direct and you only have to adjust to GMT+2.
» Collect a rental car at the airport and drive yourself around or book organized tours.
» South Africa's national parks (sanparks.org).
» The best beaches are at Clifton and Camp's Bay – but be warned: the water's chilly!

Three-day action plan

Day one First, take a peek at Table Mountain. If you can see the top, go for it. A frothy layer of cloud (known locally as the 'tablecloth') can obscure the 1073-m high icon for days on end, so you should aim to get up there at the first clear opportunity. The Cableway features a revolving floor – ensuring everyone can enjoy the spectacular views of Cape Town and Table Bay. At the top, allow two hours to walk to all 11 viewpoints (the paths are stroller-friendly) and keep an eye out for dassies.

Day two Head for the Victoria & Alfred Waterfront (waterfront.co.za) where you can explore a restored historic dockland and spot fur seals on the boardwalks. Next, take a ferry to Robben Island (robben-island.org-za). The three-hour trip includes a fascinating tour of the prison by past inmates. You'll be able to peek into Nelson Mandela's cell and see the lime quarry where the prisoners toiled during their incarceration at the hands of South Africa's brutal apartheid regime. It's all hard-hitting stuff, so if you have young children, stick to the Waterfront and visit the Two Oceans Aquarium (aquarium.co.za) instead. Here you can get nose-to-nose with ragged-tooth sharks in the 2 million-litre predator tank and stroke crabs in the touch pool. In the afternoon, take your pick of Cape Town's excellent beaches and museums. Children aged four or more will enjoy the interactive exhibits at the Telkom Exploratorium (exploratorium.co.za), while the SA Museum and Planetarium (museums. org.za), with its whale hall and dinosaur displays, will appeal to all ages.

Day three Get an early start for a spectacular tour of the Cape Peninsula. First, drive south to Simon's Town where the African penguins at Boulders (cpnp.co.za) will keep you spellbound for hours. A boardwalk leads to the heart of the 3000-strong colony at Foxy Beach – a wonderful spectacle, but a beach that is strictly for the birds. You'll find a less frustrating option for children at adjacent Boulders Beach where they can build sandcastles and, if they're lucky, swim with a penguin or two. Continue south to Cape Point and the Cape of Good Hope where, from August to December, you can spot southern right whales in the sea 200 m below. Head north back towards Cape Town along Chapman's Peak Drive (a breathtaking 10-km route etched into sea cliffs). Detour to Kirstenbosch Botanical Gardens (nbi.ac.za) where children can burn energy in the ample open spaces, then dawdle back to the city, stopping for fish and chips at Camps Bay.

Top right: The Waterfront; Chapman's Peak Drive. **Above:** The Cableway. **Bottom right:** Two Oceans Aquarium.

Garden Route

⚫◗☀☺☻☺⚠☀⛱☺♨☺☢☺

» Few stretches of coastline pack in such a variety of scenery, wildlife and outdoor activities.
» South Africa's well-maintained roads make independent touring a breeze.
» Book well ahead during the South African school holidays.
» Consider one-way car rental, with pick-up in Cape Town and drop-off in Port Elizabeth.
» Seek local advice before swimming – several beaches have strong riptides or heavy surf.

Pick of the bunch

With its sandy beaches, family resorts and countless tourist attractions, the Garden Route is unashamedly the Cape's holiday hotspot. From west to east, these are the highlights:

Mossel Bay If you've driven straight from Cape Town along the N2 you will be more than ready for a break at this gateway town to the Garden Route. Head to Santos Beach for swimming or take a one-hour boat trip to Seal Island to view the whales, dolphins, seals and seabirds that inhabit Mossel Bay. The Bartolomeu Dias Maritime Museum contains a replica of the ship used by the Portuguese navigator when he stopped here in 1488 to take on fresh water.

Wilderness National Park A network of rivers, lakes and estuaries, Wilderness supports 79 of South Africa's 95 species of waterbird. Hire a canoe at Ebb & Flow South Camp and paddle through this watery maze for a spot of twitching. Easy ticks include yellow-billed ducks and red-knobbed coots cruising open water, weaverbirds fussing about in reed beds and the neat 'plop' as a pied kingfisher dives for fish. Extra points if you see a fish eagle or the dazzling, but diminutive, malachite kingfisher.

Knysna Protected by pincer headlands, the large lagoon around which Knysna stands was originally developed as a shipbuilding and timber port. Today, it is the epicentre of Garden Route tourism, offering everything from scuba-diving to oyster-slurping. The Outeniqua Choo-Tjoe steam train (see box right) runs between here and George and there are also cruises on the lagoon and good family dining at Knysna Quays.

However, two of the most popular kids' attractions lie between Knysna and Plettenberg Bay. At Monkeyland (monkeyland.co.za) you can explore a 23-ha sanctuary and cross a 120-m-long rope bridge in search of no less than 14 species of free-swinging primates. Almost as much fun are the squirty water bottles provided at the open-air restaurant to deter mischievous marmosets from making off with your lunch. Nearby, the Elephant Sanctuary (elephantsanctuary. co.za) and Knysna Elephant Park (knysaelephantpark.co.za) offer walking tours with jumbos and a chance to learn about Africa's most southerly pachyderm population. The thickly wooded hinterland of the Garden Route was once a stronghold for elephants, but now only a few survive in the wild.

Plettenberg Bay Plett's marine life is legendary and although you can catch tantalizing glimpses from headlands and beaches, you need to get afloat to really appreciate it. Cleaving the surf in a dramatic beach launching, a boat trip (oceanadventures.co.za) will get you up-close and personal with seals lolling around Robberg Peninsula and pods of 150-plus bottlenose dolphins leaping through the curling, turquoise walls of huge rollers. Horse riding, sea kayaking and skydiving are also available, while a surf school caters to all abilities.

Nature's Valley Heaven for shell-seekers, this quiet hamlet nestles behind a beach strewn with all sorts of tidal goodies. Pink and mauve urchins stud rock pools like designer pincushions, while a dense forest dripping with old man's beard runs riot behind the beach. Pack a picnic and go exploring.

Tsitsikamma National Park Watch surf bloom four storeys high before hiking the easy 1-km boardwalk to the suspension bridge over Storms River Mouth. Learn about the native plants from interpretation boards along the way.

Jeffrey's Bay Legendary J-Bay is South Africa's surfing Mecca. Teenagers, in particular, will love its 'happening' vibe and there's no better place in the country to hone your surf style (infojeffreysbay.com).

Top: Bottlenose dolphins in Plettenberg Bay. **Above:** She sells sea shells … at Nature's Valley.

❷ Where can I ride on a train like this?

The Outeniqua Choo-Tjoe (onlinesources. co.za) chuffs its way back and forth between Knysna and George. It's a long return journey, even for the most devout *Thomas the Tank Engine* fans, so consider changing trains at Sedgefield to making it a two-hour return trip from Knysna.

South African safari

» For malaria-free safaris, stick to the game reserves of Madikwe, Pilanesberg and the Eastern Cape; for nature on a grander scale head to Kruger – but be prepared to take precautions against malaria.
» Several camps and lodges offer special activities and facilities for families.
» You can drive yourself around Kruger and stay at self-catering restcamps – or you can blow the family holiday budget on a luxury lodge in a private game reserve.

Where can I see a whale?

Africa's most family-friendly whale watching can be found at Hermanus just over an hour's drive east from Cape Town. You don't even need to get in a boat to view southern right whales which come close inshore between November and March. However, three-hour boat trips from Kleinbaai with Dyer Island Cruises (dyer-island-cruises. co.za) have the added advantage of potential great white shark sightings and the wonderfully smelly spectacle of 60,000 fur seals at Dyer Island.

In search of the big five

To put it bluntly, money and malaria are the main deciding factors when it comes to choosing a family safari in South Africa. Stick to malaria-free zones and your choice is limited mainly to the Eastern Cape and a handful of game reserves northwest of Johannesburg, such as Madikwe. Feels a bit like drawing the short straw? Don't believe it. Kruger National Park may be big and famous, but that doesn't mean you'll see less or have a 'tamer' experience in smaller, malaria-free reserves like Shamwari and Kwandwe. These, and other Eastern Cape reserves, not only boast the big five – elephant, rhino, lion, buffalo and leopard – but a wide range of other large mammals, such as giraffe, cheetah and zebra.

Best beaches

KwaZulu Natal has mile after mile of glorious, sandy beaches, but take time to pick one that suits the age of your children. South of Durban, Marina Beach is excellent for younger children since the surf is usually restrained and there are plenty of tidal pools. North of Durban, Willard Beach is also popular with families. For surfing your best bet is shark-netted Umhlanga Rocks where you can also go whale watching and kite surfing. If you want lots to do off the beach, base yourself in Durban itself, which has Sea World and the Ushaka Marine Amusement Park.

Above: On safari. **Below right:** Drakensbergs.

However, don't get too obsessed with ticking off the cast of *The Lion King*. A safari has as much to do with small wonders. A good guide will have a knack for intriguing and informing children – drip-feeding them nuggets of bushlore, like the reason woodpeckers don't get headaches, why warthogs run with their tails in the air and how termites protect themselves from sunburn. You'll study the graffiti of animal tracks around shrinking waterholes, decipher the calls of myriad birds and discover weird treasures like a shed cobra skin turned inside out or the egg cocoon of a praying mantis which the female fashions from her spit. The secret to a successful family safari is to take your time and encourage children to tune into the subtleties of the bush.

Addo Elephant National Park Just 72 km north of Port Elizabeth, this is an excellent option for families on a budget (and makes a great extension to the Garden Route). You can drive yourself around the 120,000-ha reserve, but for added value, pick up a 'hop-on ranger' at the gate. He'll be able to show you

River deep …

You can abseil off Table Mountain and ride an ostrich in the Karoo, but for South Africa's greatest concentration of adventure activities head for the Drakensberg. Merely sighting the 700-m-high rampart of the Amphitheatre in Royal Natal National Park is enough to get the adrenaline pumping. Start by hiking the Sentinel Trail, a two-hour jaunt that climaxes with a short climb using chain ladders. The views are spectacular, particularly of the 3282-m Mont-aux- Sources. Next, raft the Tugela River as it pounds its way along a 22-km stretch of grade II-IV rapids with enticing names like Horrible Horace and Whiplash Smile. Tubing (drifting downstream in large inflatable rings) is also available on calmer stretches, while the Tugela gorge is a good spot for climbing and abseiling. Mountain biking and horse riding will enable you to probe hidden corners of the Drakensberg and, for a vulture's eye view, nothing beats a spot of tandem paragliding. Get airborne at Arthur's Seat in the Central Berg.

the best spots and advise on 'ele-etiquette' in the likely event of a close encounter with one of Addo's 300 or so jumbos. Walking is prohibited except at designated points.

Kwandwe Game Reserve A 20,000-ha wilderness just north of Grahamstown, Kwandwe's Uplands Homestead offers private family accommodation with a dedicated chef, safari vehicle and guide. Just as decadent is the reserve's Ecca Lodge with its contemporary and minimalist styling – perfect for parents who might be stressed-out by more traditional safari lodges with their baskets of ostrich egg shells and vases of porcupine quills.

Shamwari Game Reserve Another top-end reserve, Shamwari is famous for its work with the Born Free Foundation to rehabilitate big cats. Long Lee Manor, with its family suites, is your best option for somewhere to stay.

Madikwe Game Reserve A three-hour drive northwest of Johannesburg, malaria-free Madikwe is home to the supremely family-friendly Jaci's Safari Lodge. Not only do Jaci's welcome kids of all ages, but they also organize special children's safaris for 3-12 year-olds with activities such as detective trails, animal tracking, touch tables and river safaris. Infants under two even get taken on their own 'jungle drives' – shorter than your typical game drive and specially tailored to suit their interest levels.

Kruger National Park There are several magnificent, all-inclusive camps in game reserves along Kruger's western boundary, but many won't accept children under 12. Those that do, such as Sabi Sabi, restrict game drives to children over six unless the family can arrange exclusive use of a safari vehicle. Many families find a more free-spirited (and cheaper) option is to drive themselves around Kruger, staying at self-catering rest camps. Many, like Olifants, have a restaurant, swimming pool, mountain bike trail and guided game-viewing excursions.

❝❞ Whereas the elephant path had been relatively easy walking, trying to negotiate untrammeled bushveld, riddled with ankle-twisting rodent burrows, razor-edged grasses and barbed shrubs was challenging – even for adults. Why our children never pleaded to be carried will always be a mystery. Perhaps it was down to the sheer, uncontrived novelty of it all – to be walking with real Bushman hunters in a wild corner of Africa. I doubt that they felt the instinctive thrill or anticipation of the hunt, but they were certainly enraptured whenever one of the hunters showed them how to pluck Kalahari raisins for a snack or excavate a Kambro tuber from which to squeeze a mouthful of water. N!ani and the others made the bushveld seem less threatening. I began to relax; let my attention drift from the children … The puff adder was several feet long, thicker than my thigh and when we saw it, it was almost too late. A warning hiss scattered the Bushman hunters like grasshoppers on hot coals. Spears lowered, they formed a wary semi-circle around the vexed viper, gently encouraging it to find an alternative resting place.

Will

❓ Where can I walk with Bushmen?

Tsumke Lodge (tsumkwel.iway.na) in northeastern Namibia operates a basic tented camp near the Ju/'hoansi Bushman village of N//qoma with proceeds going directly to the local community. You can join in with daily activities, such as setting traps, gathering wild honey and making ostrich shell jewellery. It's a unique and humbling experience – but it's not for everyone.

Top right: Ju/'hoansi trackers lead the way on a porcupine hunt. **Far left**: Archery practise using Bushmen arrows crafted from stems of elephant grass. **Left**: A Ju/'hoansi hunter with his tools of the trade.

Africa essentials

When to go

The most comfortable periods to visit **North Africa** are March to May and September to November. In mid-summer it can be unbearably hot, even for flopping at a Red Sea resort. Don't be tempted by cheap deals in July and August – your kids will fry – and remember that during Ramadan many restaurants and cafés close.

In **East Africa** there's no bad time to visit Kenya or Tanzania, although if possible try to avoid the rainy season from late March to June when some camps and lodges close. It gets busy between December and February, so consider a trip in the quieter and cooler shoulder season, July to October. To catch the wildebeest migration, visit the Serengeti from May to July or the Masai Mara from July to October. The biggest concentrations of flamingos at Lake Nakuru are generally in July, while prime time for scuba-diving is from November to April.

Most people visit **Zambia** during the dry season from May to November – although both the Zambezi and Luangwa Valley can become swelteringly hot towards the end of this period. Victoria Falls are impressive year-round, although thick spray can obscure views during peak flood months, March to April.

Apart from avoiding the cyclone season (December to March), the **Indian Ocean** islands are pleasant to visit anytime. Likewise, **Namibia** has an idyllic climate – warm and dry with some 300 days of sunshine per year. You may want to avoid the summer months (December to March), when temperatures can rocket to over 40°C. The best time to enjoy the Cape beaches of **South Africa** is during the warm summer months, December to April, while the drier winter period (June to September) offers the best wildlife viewing and lowest malaria risk in Kruger National Park.

Getting there

With international airline hubs at cities like Cairo, Nairobi, Johannesburg and Cape Town, reaching Africa is straightforward. From America, flights are usually routed through Europe, while Australian flights have connections in the Middle East. Charter flights operate between Europe and popular African destinations during peak seasons. African airlines include, Egyptair (egyptair.com), Royal Air Maroc (royalairmaroc.com), Kenya Airways (kenya-airways.com), Air Tanzania (airtanzania.com), Zambian Airways (zambianairways.com), Air Madagascar (airmadagascar.com), Air Seychelles (airseychelles.net), Air Mauritius (airmauritius.com), Air Namibia (airnamibia.com.na) and South African Airways (flysaa.com). See page 45 for other international carriers.

Getting around

With such huge distances involved in many African trips, a large chunk of your budget is likely to go on transport. If your time is limited (and cash isn't) book an all-inclusive itinerary, with flights between centres. Otherwise, hire a car or use local transport and stay in mid-range accommodation.

Alternatively, choose a one-centre base that offers a broad flavour of a country. Kenya's Diani Beach, for example, is within day-trip range of Shimba Hills National Park which will provide a 'safari taster' – even if it's not quite the Masai Mara.

Internal transport in Africa varies from the reliable and decadent to the run down and downright dangerous. You'll find everything from charter flights, private 4WD vehicles and luxury trains to horse-drawn carts, camels and overcrowded, accident-prone minibuses.

For independence in southern Africa a **self-drive** is the way to go. Major car and campervan rental companies (see page 51) can be found in cities like Cape Town and Windhoek. Be sure to factor in the additional costs of a one-way rental, plus other extras like child seats. Roads in South Africa and Namibia are uncrowded and well maintained – note that your insurance may not cover you on gravel tracks. Long-distance bus touring is a more economical, but less flexible, way of covering a lot of ground. Reputable operators include Intercape Mainliner and Greyhound in South Africa or Superjet and Delta buses in Egypt.

In East and North Africa, you are more likely to rely on a mixture of guided tours and public transport. If travelling by rail choose first class or tourist trains only – they will usually have comfortable cabins and air-conditioning, though toilet facilities may be basic. Internal flights are a convenient, if expensive, option for families keen to avoid long overland journeys. If scheduled carriers can't get you there, any of Africa's plethora of charter companies will almost certainly be able to.

Organized tours and **safaris** fall into two main categories: package and tailor-made. The latter are obviously more expensive, but they do allow you full control of your plans. If you opt for a package, be sure to find out what's

Go green: six ways to skip the flight

▸ Take a ferry from southern Spain to Morocco (trasmediterranea.es).
▸ Ride a bus from South Africa to Namibia or Zambia (intercape.co.za).
▸ Drive yourself in South Africa or Namibia.
▸ Hop on a ferry from Dar es Salaam to Zanzibar (zanzibar.net).
▸ Sail in a felucca from Aswan to Luxor.
▸ Board the overnight sleeper train from Nairobi to Mombasa or Cairo to Luxor.

included. A 'bargain' may conceal hidden extras, such as national park fees. On cheap tours you could also be fighting for window seats in a crowded vehicle or be frustrated by a driver-guide who is more 'driver' than 'guide'.

Accommodation

Roughing it in Africa, using cheap public transport and accommodation, is fine if you're a backpacker, but could become miserable and potentially dangerous with children in tow. That doesn't mean you have to splurge your life savings on a succession of all-inclusive luxury resorts and lodges. More modestly priced options, such as national park rest camps, mid-range hotels and self-catering apartments, do exist. A guesthouse in South Africa, for example, can cost from as little as US$30 per person per night, including breakfast (children sharing a room with parents usually stay free). Meanwhile, a night at an all-inclusive private game reserve can easily cost ten times this – but as well as activities, fine cuisine and lavish accommodation, you will get dedicated children's activities, excellent guides and exclusive access to areas that are otherwise impossible to visit.

You will find Hiltons, Sheratons, Oberois and all the other international hotel chains popping up in **Egypt's** main tourist centres. As you'd expect, all offer high quality accommodation and that all-important swimming pool. Look out, too, for smaller, more characterful properties like Aswan's Old Cataract (sofitel.com) or budget options such as Flats in Luxor (flatsinluxor.com) – self-catering apartments with a pool and views of the Theban Hills and Nile. On the Red Sea coast there

is no shortage of resorts and hotels geared towards families. The Hilton Dahab Resort (hilton.com), for example, has a kids' club for 3-17 year-olds, a crèche and activities ranging from camel treks with Bedouin guides to learning to dive at the PADI Gold Palm Centre.

In **Morocco**, try to spend at least one night in a riad – a traditional house surrounding a central courtyard. Some are more like palaces (with rates to match), but others offer excellent value. In Marrakech, for example, Les Jardins de la Medina (lesjardinsdelamedina.com) is just a 20-minute walk from Djemmaa el-Fna and has a swimming pool and gardens – a welcome bolthole after a morning in the souks.

Tanzania's best family-friendly accommodation is on Zanzibar where you'll find everything from the resort-style Breezes Beach Club (breezes-zanzibar.com) to the educational, eco-sensitive Chumbe Island (see page 259). A

(see page 259)

CO₂ How much to offset your emissions

From London to:
Marrakech £5
Cairo £5
Nairobi £15
Dar es Salaam £15
Windhoek £17
Mahé £17
Lusaka £17
Cape Town £20

From New York to:
Marrakech US$25
Cairo US$40
Nairobi US$55
Windhoek US$55
Lusaka US$55
Cape Town US$60
Dar es Salaam US$60
Mahé US$65

Fact file

	GMT	Language	Money	Code	Tourist info
Egypt	+2	Arabic	Egyptian pound (US$1 = £6)	+20	touregypt.net
Morocco	+0	Arabic	Dirham (US$1 = Dh9)	+212	visitmorocco.org
Kenya	+3	English, Swahili	Kenyan shillings (US$1 = Ksh70)	+254	magicalkenya.com
Tanzania	+2	English, Swahili	Tanzanian shilling (US$1 = Tsh1290)	+255	tanzaniatouristboard.com
Zambia	+2	English	Kwacha (US$1 = Kw4190)	+260	zambiatourism.com
Madagascar	+3	Malagasy, French	Madagascar ariary (US$1 = Mga2020)	+261	
Seychelles	+4	English, French	Seychelles rupee (US$1 = Rs6)	+248	seychelles.travel
Mauritius	+4	English, French	Mauritius rupee (US$1 = MRU33)	+230	mauritius.net
Namibia	+1	English	Namibian dollar (US$1 = N$7)	+264	namibiatourism.com.na
South Africa	+2	English, Afrikaans, Ndebele	South African Rand (US$1 = R7)	+27	southafrica.net

Tour operators

In the UK

Aardvark Safaris
aardvarksafaris.com

Beachcomber Tours
beachcombertours.co.uk

Bushbaby Travel
bushbabytravel.com

Discover Egypt
discoveregypt.co.uk

Expert Africa
expertafrica.com

Rainbow Tours
rainbowtours.co.uk

Safari Consultants
safari-consultants.co.uk

Safari Drive
safaridrive.com

The Gambia Experience
Gambia.co.uk

Visions of Africa
visionsofafrica.co.uk

Wild about Africa
wildaboutafrica.com

In the USA

South African Journeys
sajourneys.com

The Tanganyika Safari Company tangsafari.com

In Africa

CC Africa ccafrica.com

Cedarberg Travel
cedarberg-travel.com

Heritage Group
heritage-eastafrica.com

Wilderness Safaris
wilderness-safaris.com

Top: Jelly beans in an ostrich egg at Kwande Game Reserve. **Above:** Cape Grace Hotel in Cape Town.

few safari camps, such as Sand Rivers (sand-rivers-selous.com) in Tanzania's Selous Game Reserve, welcome children over eight.

Wilderness Safaris (wilderness-safaris.com) has a range of camps in southern Africa with interlinking family rooms and tents. Generally, the minimum age is eight, although there are no age restrictions at Kulala Tented Camp and Kulala Desert Lodge in Namibia, and Rocktail Bay Lodge in South Africa.

CC Africa (ccafrica.com) may be renowned for luxurious safari camps and lodges, but that doesn't mean kids are taboo. In fact, several of their properties, including Madikwe Safari Lodge in South Africa and Kichwa Tembo in Kenya, offer special environmental programmes for children. Activities can range from 'poo walks' and bug collecting to fishing and bark rubbing. Best of all, kids receive an eco-guide packed with quizzes and activities. Complete all the challenges and your ranger and tracker will sign a special certificate stating that you've graduated as a Planet Manager. Other family-friendly CC Africa properties include Grumeti River Camp and Ngorongoro Crater Lodge in Tanzania, Sossusvlei Mountain Lodge in Namibia and Bongani Mountain Lodge, Kwandwe Ecca Lodge, Ngala Lodge and Phinda Lodge in South Africa.

Kenya's Heritage camps and lodges (heritage-eastafrica.com) are also renowned for their children's programmes (see page 257). Another name to look out for is Cheli & Peacock (chelipeacock.com). Their portfolio of properties includes Elsa's Kopje (of *Born Free* fame), which has not only a family cottage and swimming pool, but also babysitting, special early meals and guided walks with the Maasai. Nestled in the rugged Laikipia Plateau, Loisaba (loisaba.com) also has a family cottage, but its real claim to fame are its Starbeds which can be rolled out into the open for a night under the cosmos – there's one specially for families. The classic and luxurious Governors' range of camps (governorscamp.com) in the Masai Mara welcome families. Children under two stay free, and the only age restrictions are at Il Moran (minimum age nine) and Bush Camp (minimum age 12).

On the Kenyan coast you will find numerous resorts, including Turtle Bay Beach Club (turtlebay.co.ke) and Sarova Whitesands (sarovahotels.com). On Lamu island, Manda Bay (mandabay.com) has two cottages for families and offers safe swimming and snorkelling off a gently sloping beach.

For beach bliss in the **Seychelles** and **Mauritius**, just about every resort has a kids' club, swimming pool and copious watersports. Two that should receive emphatic thumbs up are Iles des Palmes (beachbungalow.sc) on Praslin and the impeccable Le Saint Géran (saintgeran.com) on the east coast of Mauritius. For ultimate style, however, the incomparable North Island (north-island.com) in the Seychelles offers tailor-made family activities, such as private picnics, treasure hunts, and fishing trips. The two-bedroom villas on this private island are sensational.

Victoria Falls has always offered a great range of family accommodation – and it's now just as comprehensive on the Zambian side of the Zambezi as it is on the Zimbabwean side. The three-star Zambezi Sun (suninternational.co.za) is within earshot of the Falls and has a superb family pool, plus loads to keep kids entertained. Elsewhere in **Zambia**, relatively few safari camps and lodges are genuinely child-friendly. One of the, albeit expensive, exceptions is Safari Houses (safarihouses.com), a portfolio of sensational private properties with their own safari vehicle, guide and chef. You can choose between Tangala House (on the banks of the Zambezi near Livingstone), Chongwe River House (Lower Zambezi National Park), Shiwa N'gandu (an amazing old manor house in western Zambia) and two houses in South Luangwa National Park.

In **Namibia**, most lodges and guest farms, like Okonjima (see page 263), welcome children. There is also a good selection of guesthouses at Swakopmund, such as Sam's Giardino (giardino.com).

With its thriving domestic tourism, **South Africa** has a huge range of accommodation options. For an overview, check out the Portfolio Collection (portfoliocollection.co.za) which lists everything from city hotels to guesthouses. For a malaria-free safari, CC Africa's Ecca Lodge (see above) in Kwandwe Private Game Reserve offers kids Planet Manager packs, special meals, an 'interactive' kitchen, game drives, fishing, bush walks and rock painting supervised by exceptional guides. Other excellent options include Shamwari Game Reserve (shamwari.com), Mark's Camp at Lalibela Game Reserve (lalibela.co.za), Kariega Lodge (kariega.co.za) and Jaci's Safari Lodge in Madikwe Game Reserve (madikwe.com). See page 267 for details. For a do-it-yourself safari in Kruger National Park, Olifants and Lower Sabie rest camps (sanparks.org) make good bases, while Little Bush Camp at Sabi Sabi Private Game Reserve (sabisabi.com) offers an organized, more upmarket alternative for families. Slightly more off the beaten track, **Mozambique's** Bazaruto Archipelago will appeal to families looking for an unusual beach escape, while **Malawi's** Chelinda Camp (nyika.com) is heaven for confident horse riding families. In **Botswana**, Kwando Safaris (kwando.com) have a dedicated children's guide at their Lebala and Kwara Camps in the Okavango Delta.

Food and drink

If you're staying at a major hotel, resort or safari lodge there should be enough familiar foods available to satisfy even fussy feeders (top-end places will have children's menus). And, of course, fast-food outlets can be found in all major centres. But no visit to Africa is complete without sampling some local delicacies. Browse any North African market, for example, and you'll find plenty of nuts, dried fruits and other high-energy snacks. Hearty traditional dishes range from South African *potjiekos* to Moroccan tagines (both variations on a meat and vegetable stew).

Then there's the wonderful seafood, from fish and chips in Cape Town to prawn coconut curry on the East African coast. Meat-eaters meanwhile can munch their way through half the mammal kingdom in East and southern Africa – try biltong (chewy strips of spicy, cured game meat), ostrich steaks and Kenya's *nyama choma* (roast goat or chicken). Fresh fruits, including countless varieties of banana, are commonplace, as is the African staple mash made from maize meal, water and salt. If you get the chance, try some termites – the large winged ones are tasty sautéed with a pinch of salt.

Health and safety

Malaria is endemic to most of sub-Saharan Africa and it is crucial that you take precautions against this potentially fatal disease. In South Africa, malaria only occurs in the lowveld of Mpumalanga and Limpopo and on the Maputaland coast of KwaZulu-Natal. Malaria affects the northern third of Namibia (particularly between November and June), and along the Kavango and Kunene Rivers year round. Discuss malaria prevention with your doctor well before you travel. You should also plan an appropriate course of vaccinations, which may include hepatitis A, typhoid, meningococcal meningitis and yellow fever. See page 54 for information on malaria prevention and routine inoculations that should be up to date regardless of travel.

In Africa, safe **water** is another major health consideration. Tap water is generally not safe for drinking except in South Africa, Namibia and Tunisia. It's heavily chlorinated in Egypt, but if in doubt always assume the worst and take appropriate measures (see page 56). Lakes and Rivers can also harbour health risks from schistosomiasis (bilharzia). Avoid contact with this parasite (responsible for the second most common tropical disease after malaria) by not bathing or paddling in rivers or lakes – stick to swimming pools and the sea.

Wildlife is often perceived as the most obvious threat to travellers in Africa. Few safari camps and lodges have fences, which means potentially dangerous animals are free to come and go. Stay calm and keep a respectful distance and you should be perfectly safe. Young children, however, who can be unpredictable and easily excitable, might alarm some animals (or arouse the predatory instinct in others) and that is when danger can arise. For this reason, camps generally have a minimum age limit.

In terms of personal **safety**, most visits to wildlife reserves and other tourist areas are trouble-free, but as with anywhere in the world, you should be particularly vigilant in cities. Rarely will you feel vulnerable or uneasy while travelling. In addition to taking normal security precautions to deter opportunistic criminals, you should check with your hotel or local consulate if you are in any doubt as to the safety of an area.

Five special places to stay

Keeping calm in Cairo

Four Seasons Hotel Cairo, fourseasons.com. Nile-side location with views of the Pyramids – a pampered refuge from chaotic Cairo, but it's very posh and very pricey. Children get their own pool, kids' club and restaurant menus, plus bathrobes, welcome packs and video games.

Also consider: *Semiramis Intercontinental* (ichotelsgroup.com) near the Egyptian Museum, and *Hotel Longchamps* (hotellongchamps.com), a three-star hotel in the quiet suburb of Zamalek with a lovely balcony, but no pool.

Nile cruising for nippers

Sun Boat IV, abercrombiekent.com. Owned by Abercrombie & Kent, it goes without saying that this luxury cruiser has a pool, but other family-friendly touches include private, uncrowded docks at Luxor and Aswan, Egyptian cookery lessons and an onboard children's activities coordinator.

Also consider: *Explore Worldwide* (exploreworldwide.com) has a three-night motor cruise (on a more modest vessel) as part of its Land of the Pharaohs family itinerary, while *Exodus* (exodus.co.uk) includes an overnight felucca trip as part of its eight-night Egyptian adventure for families.

On safari in the Masai Mara

Mara Intrepids, heritage-eastafrica.com. Thirty tents (each with four-poster beds, en suite bathrooms and hot showers) overlooking the Talek River. Plenty of other safari camps in Kenya's premier wildlife reserve boast similar standards of accommodation, but few can rival Mara Intrepids' superb children's programme.

Also consider: *Kicheche Mara Camp* (kicheche.com) for a more rustic, but no less luxurious, bush experience with superb guides.

City chic in Cape Town

Cape Grace (capegrace.com) is a small, elegant hotel with great location and views on West Quay, Victoria & Alfred Waterfront. For the kids there are welcome baskets stuffed with goodies, story telling in the library (followed by bedtime milk and gingerbread men), children's menu, DVDs and games. Parents, meanwhile, will appreciate the two or three bedroom apartments with fully equipped kitchens, babysitting service, spa, complimentary wine tasting and excellent restaurant.

Also consider: *De Waterkant Village* (dewaterkant.com), *Bantry Bay* (bantrybeach.co.za) and *British Hotel Apartments* (britishhotelapartments.co.za) for two- and three-bedroom apartments in Cape Town, Clifton and Simon's Town respectively.

Pick of the Garden Route

Kurland Hotel (kurland.co.za), near Plettenberg Bay, is a gorgeous Cape Dutch-style hotel set in its own polo estate. Kids are spoilt rotten with free access to the kitchen for cookies and ice-creams, a walled play area with jungle gym and swimming pool, a huge playroom with pool table and home cinema, plus activities such as horse riding, cycling and tennis. Private cottages have kid-friendly loft rooms.

Also consider: *Hunters Country House* (hunterhotels.com) for more five-star pampering with excellent kids' facilities, and **Protea Knysna Quays** (proteahotels.com) for a more affordable option with a great location on Knysna's waterfont.

Asia

Going ape in Borneo – an orphaned orang-utan at Sepilok, Sabah.

★ Float in the dead sea
↳ Jordan, page 280

★ Track a wild tiger
↳ India & Nepal, pages 282 & 286

★ Walk the Great Wall of China
↳ China, page 290

★ Be transfixed by the Taj Mahal
↳ India, page 282

★ Trek in the Himalaya
↳ Nepal, page 286

★ See the big city lights
↳ Hong Kong, page 293

Highest mountain
Mt Everest
8850 m

MONGOLIA

Caucasus

Aral Sea

Caspian Sea

Tigris

Euphrates

★1 □ **AMMAN**
JORDAN

Red Sea

The Gulf

Dubai ○

□ **MUSCAT**
OMAN

Indus

H i m a l a y a

Plateau of Tibet

★3 **DELHI** □

Agra ○ ★2

★4
KATHMANDU NEPAL

Mt Everest

Ganga

Brahmaputra

Kolkata ○

CHINA

Yang

Xi'an

Yangt

HA

Arabian Sea

Mumbai ○

INDIA

Bay of Bengal

Chiang Mai

THAILAND

BANGKOK □

PHN
PE

CAMBO

Gobi Desert

○ Did you know?

- Ice cream was invented in China around 2000 BC.
- Arulanantham Suresh Joachim from Sri Lanka holds the world record for standing on one foot – 76 hours 40 minutes.
- Contrary to popular myth the Great Wall of China is not visible from space, according to Chinese astronaut, Yang Liwei, who checked it out in 2003.
- With no fewer than 170 letters, Bangkok's full ceremonial title is the world's longest place name.
- The world's largest underground chamber, the Sarawak Chamber in Gunung Mulu National Park, Borneo, could easily hold 40 jumbo jets.
- Hong Kong boasts the world's longest covered escalator system, measuring 792 m.

Malabar Coast

○ **Chennai**

COLOMBO □ SRI LANKA

Indian Ocean

Equator

SINGAPOR

KUA
LUMP
□

Sumat

JA

metres	
	3000
	2000
	1000
	500
	200
	0

N

500 km
500 miles

⭐ Explore the heart of Borneo
» Malaysia, page 296

Largest city
Shanghai, population 15.5 million

Longest river
Yangtze 6299 km

Hokkaido

JAPAN

Sea of Japan

Honshu

Mt Fuji ▲ □ **TOKYO**

Kyoto ○ ○ **Osaka**

Kyushu

○ **Shanghai**

⑥
○ **Hong Kong**

Pacific Ocean

uth China Sea

AM

Minh City

Mt Kinabalu
Sabah ▲

Sarawak ⑦
'SIA
Borneo
Sulawesi

Kalimantan

ESIA

Java *Bali*

ING

gzhou

Asia can send you reeling. Even the most travel-hardened adult is not immune to the multi-sensory onslaught of its hot, overcrowded cities and chaotic transport systems. From fervent religious festivals to encounters with abject poverty, Asia is a cultural body blow – so why even contemplate taking your kids? Perhaps it's the continent's very exuberance, its colours, tastes, smells and experiences that appeals. But there's a great deal more to the place than swarming bazaars, relentless touts and traffic-clogged streets. Cities like Dubai, Kuala Lumpur, Hong Kong and Singapore are some of the most modern and sophisticated in the world, while child-friendly beach resorts can be found everywhere from Jordan's Red Sea coast to the islands of Malaysia. And even when you venture beyond these pampered enclaves you'll usually find a spontaneous warmth and affection. Ultimately, though, Asia's allure boils down to one simple truth: your kids will never forget it. Whether it's trekking in the Himalayas or riding elephants in Thailand; exploring caves in Borneo or riding a ferry beneath Hong Kong's skyscrapers, Asia makes a big impression on little travellers.

❝❞ *I'd never been to Thailand before but I will definitely go again. Our tour leader was really friendly and helpful. He showed us how to send a plant to sleep, blow bubbles out of the stem and make a helicopter from the leaves. My favourite parts of the holiday were snorkelling, meeting Thai children and riding elephants.*
Bethany, age 12, Land of Smiles tour, The Adventure Company

Introduction

Asia rating
Wow factor
★★★★★
Worry factor
★★★★
Value for money
★★★★
Keeping teacher happy
★★★★★
Family accommodation
★★★
Babies & toddlers
★★
Teenagers
★★★★

Taste of Asia: *yuebing* (moon cakes)

Traditionally eaten during the Chinese Moon Festival, these round fruity pastries are good for feasting on at any time of the year.

What you need
- 500 g self-raising flour
- 3 tbsp vegetable oil
- 500 g dried figs
- 1 egg yolk
- 3 eggs
- 100 g sugar
- 20 dried apricots

What to do
- Pre-heat the oven to 200°C.
- Mix the flour, oil, eggs, sugar and water together in a bowl to make pastry.
- Let the pastry rest in a refrigerator for about 30 minutes.
- Cut the figs into small pieces, then purée them in a food processor.
- Roll the apricots in the fig purée to make small balls.
- Divide the pastry into 20 equal portions and flatten them into 10-cm-wide discs.
- Wrap each pastry disc around a ball of fig and apricot and press the edges of the pastry together to make a muffin shape.
- Turn the cakes over so that the sealed sides are underneath, prick them with a fork and place them on a greased baking tray.
- Brush the cakes with beaten egg yolk and bake for around 30 minutes or until golden brown.

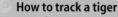

How to track a tiger

Prime time for tiger spotting in India and Nepal is from February to April when vegetation withers and trees lose their leaves at the end of the dry season. Boost your chances of a tiger encounter by following these five tips:

- Set off in the early morning or late afternoon when tigers are more likely to be active.
- Their camouflaged coats can make them almost invisible, so look and listen for telltale clues, such as fresh tracks or alarm calls from nearby wildlife.
- Try to blend in with your surroundings by wearing clothes that are dull in colour.
- Tigers are very wary of human voices. Instead of talking, use hand signals that you have practised before setting off on safari.
- Tigers have an exceptional sense of smell so, if possible, stay downwind of them or you may give yourself away.

In Corbett National Park elephants are used to track tigers.

Books to read

The Great Race: the Story of the Chinese Zodiac, Barefoot Books, 2006
Find out how the Jade Emperor sets up a race to decide the order of years in the Chinese calendar in this well-paced retelling of an ancient oriental legend. Ages 4-8

The Tiger and the Wise Man, Child's Play, 2004
How will the wise man escape being eaten by the tiger when it seems that all the other animals are against him too? The jackal appears to help, but is it simply another trick? Ages 5-8

Malaysian Children's Favourite Stories, Tuttle Publishing, 2004
The traditional culture and rich tropical environment of Malaysia are revealed in this collection of beautifully illustrated legends, including 'How the Tapir Got its Colours' and 'The Dragon of Kinabalu'. Ages 5-12

The Jungle Book, Templar Publishing, 2006
Wonderful artwork accompanies this edition of Kipling's enduring classic. Few other tales evoke the atmosphere of the Indian jungle quite like this one. Ages 6+

Panda in the Park, Hodder Children's Books, 2004
Mandy and James visit China in the school holidays to help with a wildlife conservation project. Can they help to reunite a panda cub with its mother before it's too late? Ages 6-10

Yeti Boy, Collins, 2000
A moving and magical adventure story set in a remote mountainous region inhabited by the Yeti. Ages 8+

Chinese Brush Painting: a Complete Painting Kit for Beginners, Walter Foster, 2002
Learn the oriental art of Chinese brush painting with this introductory kit that contains everything you need to get started, including a full-colour project book filled with inspiration and ideas. Ages 9+

🦜 Ways to paint a brighter future for wildlife

▸▸ Become a Young Friend of the David Shepherd Wildlife Foundation (davidshepherd.org). Since the 1960s, international wildlife artist, David Shepherd, has been campaigning and raising funds to help save tigers, elephants, rhinos and other critically endangered mammals in the wild. The annual membership fee for children under 16 is £10, so why not join forces with four friends – £50 would be enough to train and equip a forest officer in India or cover the fuel costs of an anti-poaching unit for 10 days. In return for your support, you will receive all sorts of goodies, including a wildlife poster and twice-yearly magazine, as well as online access to the DSWF Kids' Zone where you will find everything from animal facts to fundraising ideas.

▸▸ Adopt an animal. The DSWF offers adoption schemes for African and Asian mammals. Lyuti, an Amur tiger, was found, severely injured, deep in the Siberian forest after poachers had killed his mother. Unable to survive alone in the wild he was taken to the Utyos Rehabilitation Centre. Now fully recovered he lives in a protected area of natural forest where he will remain safely for the rest of his life. When you adopt Lyuti you will help fund anti-poaching operations to protect this region of the Russian Far East, where fewer than 500 of Lyuti's wild cousins survive. Annual adoptions cost £18.

▸▸ Paint a picture. Each year, the DSWF runs the Global Canvas art competition for young people aged between eight and 16. David Shepherd judges the entries, and the top 250 artworks are unveiled at London's Natural History Museum.

One to watch: *Shaolin Kung Fu*
YMAA, 2005
Drawing on his extensive knowledge of China's ancient Shaolin martial arts, Dr Yang demonstrates essential stretching, stances, punches, movements and kicking techniques.

David Shepherd's tips for budding wildlife artists
▸▸ Study the animal you are painting very carefully.
▸▸ If you can't see animals in the wild, then a safari park is the best alternative.
▸▸ The landscape around the animal or bird is just as important – there are huge numbers of books and television programmes which will provide you with reference material.

🔍 How to make a Chinese lantern

A traditional part of Chinese New Year celebrations, paper lanterns are simple to make. According to Chinese astrology, 2008 is the year of the rat, followed by cow (2009), tiger (2010), rabbit (2011), dragon (2012), snake (2013), horse (2014), sheep (2015), monkey (2016), chicken (2017), dog (2018), pig (2019 and rat (2020).

What you need
▸▸ Coloured paper or gift-wrap
▸▸ Scissors
▸▸ Glue, tape or stapler

What to do
▸▸ Fold a rectangular piece of paper in half, making a long, thin rectangle.
▸▸ Make at least 12 cuts along the fold line.
▸▸ Unfold the paper and glue or staple the short edges together.
▸▸ Cut out a thin strip of paper and attach to the lantern for a handle.
▸▸ Make lots more, string them together and hang them up.

How to survive on a desert island

▸▸ The most important thing you will need is a coconut tree.
▸▸ Use the coconut and fruit for food, drink and storage containers.
▸▸ Use fronds to make bed matting, roof thatching, clothing, baskets and canoe decking.
▸▸ Use the trunk for housing material, boat building, crafts and tools.
▸▸ Use fibre for making rope and fishing nets.

Upset tummy, Delhi belly, the trots, the squits, exploding poo… no matter what delightful terminology you or your children use to refer to it, the one aspect of travelling in Asia that's likely to be foremost in your minds is the threat of diarrhoea. Basic hygiene issues become paramount, especially when travelling with babies and young children who are more susceptible to dehydration following a bout of gastrointestinal illness (see page 56). Malaria prevention also needs to be given serious consideration – see page 54 for areas of Asia affected by the disease, as well as information on other important health matters. Now the good news: travelling with kids of any age in Asia will bring out the best of local hospitality, while getting around will almost certainly be easier than when you backpacked there 15 or 20 years ago. You will also find that Asia is generally very affordable – the exceptions, of course, being cities like Singapore and Hong Kong where even a few days of high living can haemorrhage your bank balance.

Asia's highlights range from sea kayaking around Hong Kong's Sai Kung Peninsula (**above**) to discovering ruins in Rajasthan (**right**); from wildlife-spotting in Thailand to shopping for local handicrafts in China (**below left**).

Babies (0-18 months)

Give high-risk malaria zones a wide berth. For parents with babies, two of the best malaria-free options are Dubai and Singapore – modern, squeaky-clean cities that will not only give you a taste of traditional Asian culture when you step beyond the air-con, but will also provide quick access to baby supplies and medical care should you need them. Singapore has even launched a system of 'Pro-Family Business' branding (mbp.org.sg), so you know which shops and companies will pay extra attention to your needs. In Thailand and Malaysia the risk of malaria is mainly confined to remote rural areas, so you might feel tempted by a stint on a tropical island paradise, complete with childcare facilities and parent-pampering spa. If you're travelling from Europe or North America, however, you may need to ask yourself whether a resort in the Caribbean or Mediterranean might make more sense. Jordan's Red Sea coast, or even the Maldives, would also make good 'shorter haul' alternatives, particularly for parents who are keen divers. Just be sure to avoid the blisteringly hot summer months.

Toddlers/pre-school (18 months-4 years)

They are still too young at this age to appreciate much in the way of Asia's cultural kaleidoscope, but that doesn't mean you can't have fun with a toddler at a beach resort or in the zoos and theme parks of cities like Dubai, Hong Kong and Singapore. The deciding factor with this age group is more likely to revolve around the journey than the destination. Are you really sure you want to spend 13 hours with a fidgety four-year-old on a flight from London to Singapore? On the other hand, children in this age category are still compact and highly portable which means you could contemplate something really quite adventurous – such as

a gentle, fully-supported trek in the Himalayas, staying in comfortable lodges and carrying your child (or hiring a porter to do so). A few adventure operators offer this kind of trip for families with children as young as two, but generally the minimum age for any organized Asian itinerary is five or six.

Kids/school age (4-12 years)

This is a wonderful age range to take kids to Asia. Not only are they more robust when it comes to health and safety, but they are also both physically and intellectually more equipped to cope with adventure activities and cultural issues. Jordan and Sri Lanka both make excellent introductions to Asia. They are not as far-flung as eastern China or Southeast Asia, so flying there is usually cheaper and you can also justify going for a shorter period of time. This is just as well with Jordan since it's best to visit in the cooler spring and autumn over half-term or Easter holiday periods. Both countries are also quite compact which means you can see and do lots without having to endure long overland journeys or internal flights.

From an educational point of view, most Asian destinations rate highly. Two of the most culturally and historically saturated itineraries, however, are India's Golden Triangle (Delhi, Agra and Jaipur) and China's northeast (Beijing, Great Wall and Xi'an). Both would require a minimum of 12 days.

For adventure, Nepal and Thailand offer non-stop thrills, including trekking, rafting and riding elephants. Again, 12 days, or preferably two weeks, is the minimum time you should consider – particularly if you are heading to Nepal and need to factor in acclimatization days to a trekking schedule.

Teenagers (13 years+)

Asia is an ideal destination for teens. In particular, Southeast Asian destinations like Thailand and Malaysia offer a perfect 'teen combo' of cool modern cities, chilled beach resorts and full-on adventure activities. If your teenagers are more into retail therapy than adrenaline abuse, take them to Dubai, Singapore or Hong Kong. If adventure rules, get their pulses racing on a multi-activity break in Nepal where you can combine whitewater rafting and mountain biking with a Himalayan trek and a jungle safari. The Adventure Company (adventurecompany.co.uk) has teenage trips to Bali, India,

Offbeat Asia at a glance
Oman

Explore the dunes and canyons of Wahiba Sands by jeep and camel and then visit a Bedouin camp and the 17th-century stronghold of Jabrin Fort. Ras Al Hadd is renowned for its nesting green turtles, while humpback whales and dolphins can be spotted offshore. Elsewhere along the coast, you can visit dhow-building yards and fishing villages or peruse the mosques, forts and palaces of Muscat.

When? Anytime except summer when it's too hot.
How long? Allow at least a week.
Minimum age Five.

Japan

Scale skyscrapers in modern Tokyo, visit temples in ancient Kyoto and explore the incredible marine life of the Pacific Rim at Osaka's aquarium – linking all three cities by high-speed Bullet Train. Away from the urban centres, you can climb to the 3776-m summit of sacred Mount Fuji, visit the mountain Buddhist retreat at Nikko or relax on the beaches of the Izu Peninsula.

When? May to September.
How long? Allow two weeks.
Minimum age Five.

Indonesia

Combine beach days on Bali with exciting adventures in the island's interior, climbing the volcano of Mount Batur, canoeing on Lake Bratan and exploring the Monkey Forest and Hindu temples at Ubud. Alternatively, combine Bali with a Javan odyssey, witnessing sunrise from the crater rim of Mount Bromo and visiting the coastal rainforest and turtle-nesting beaches of Meru Beriti National Park.

When? April to October is the driest period.
How long? Allow at least two weeks.
Minimum age Five.

Jordan, Malaysia, Nepal, Oman, Sri Lanka, Thailand and Vietnam; Explore Worldwide (explore.co.uk) has dedicated teenage departures to Jordan, Sri Lanka and Thailand; Exodus (exodus.co.uk) has teenage trips to Borneo, Jordan, India, Nepal, Sri Lanka, Thailand and Vietnam, while Families Worldwide (familiesworldwide.co.uk) offers teenage departures to Jordan, India, Nepal, Sri Lanka and Thailand.

Special needs

Singapore is probably Asia's most accessible destination for the physically challenged. The MaxiCab airport shuttle, all MRT train stations and several SBS Transit buses are wheelchair-friendly. Published by the Disabled People's Association of Singapore (dpa.org.sg), Access Singapore is a comprehensive guide to accessible places. Hong Kong also provides excellent facilities for disabled travellers. An access guide is available from the Hong Kong Council of Social Services (hkcss.org.hk), while Easy Access Travel (easyaccesstravelhk.com) can arrange tours. In Indonesia, Rollover Bali (rolloverbali.tripod.com) offers wheelchair-accessible holidays.

Single parents

The prospect of a family trip to Asia can be especially daunting to single parents. However, some family operators, such as The Adventure Company (adventurecompany.co.uk), offer special departure dates for single-parent families on their trips to Sri Lanka and Thailand.

66 99 Petra by night is just breathtaking and our stay at the Dead Sea was wonderful. But the best bits as far as our boys are concerned were the camels, 4WD expeditions and sleeping out in the desert.

*The Stockwell family
Journey to the Lost City
tour, The Adventure
Company*

A desert adventure

It won't be the magical desert city of Petra that first springs to mind when you contemplate a family holiday to Jordan. Nor will it be the hypnotic spattering of stars that fills a desert night in Wadi Rum. Nor even the perplexing and titillating sensation of bobbing like a cork in the Dead Sea. Inevitably, all these highlights are likely to be overshadowed by one nagging doubt: "Is Jordan safe?" Nowadays, it makes sense to seriously consider the security situation in any country you're planning to visit, but don't let Jordan's Middle East location overly prejudice your decision of whether or not to go.

Country highlights

😊😊😊🚗😊😊😊

» Allow at least a week to see and experience the essentials.
» With good roads, short distances and comfortable hotels, Jordan is an easy place to visit.
» If travelling with infants, base yourself at Petra and the Dead Sea rather than touring.
» Don't forget to take something to read while floating in the Dead Sea!

Gladiators, Indiana Jones and a pinch of salt

Jerash An hour's drive north of Amman, the well-preserved ruins of Jerash evoke the glory days of the Roman Empire. You'll discover paved streets and plazas, imposing temples and all the other trimmings of a 2000-year-old Roman city. Head for the Hippodrome at 1100 or 1500 when the Jerash Heritage Company (jerashchariots.com) stages a fantastic display of battle manoeuvres and chariot racing. You can also cheer on your favourite gladiator as four pairs of warriors slog it out using traditional weapons, the ancient arena ringing with their cries of "*Ave, imperator, morituri te salutant!*" – "We who are about to die salute you!"

Dead Sea After the gratuitous violence at Jerash, there's nothing better than a calming dip in the ever-so-salty Dead Sea. Kids love the sensation of floating in the super-buoyant water ("Look Mum, no armbands!"). Good luck trying to explain to them that this is the lowest place on earth and that they've just swum at more than 400 m below sea level. Parents and their teenage daughters will no doubt appreciate the pampering treatments available at the various luxury resorts and hotels.

King's Highway Heading south from Amman, you pass several attractions, including Mt Nebo (the holy summit where Moses is believed to have been buried), Madaba (famed for its sixth-century Byzantine mosaic map) and Karak (a crusader castle with enough corridors and dungeons to keep your medieval-minded little monsters happy for hours).

Petra You know this place, even if you've never been to it. Harrison Ford seared Petra on to our minds when he galloped through a canyon to emerge in front of the rock-hewn Treasury in the finale to *Indiana Jones and the Last Crusade*. Such is the 'wow' factor of Jordan's premier attraction that you could be forgiven for thinking it was all Hollywood hype. In fact, this Nabataean city dates from 400 BC and is riddled with elaborately carved tombs, as well as temples, shrines and a fort. For centuries, it was lost to all but a few Bedouin families – only to be 'rediscovered' by Swiss explorer Burckhardt in 1812. Nowadays, despite its popularity, it's still a thrill to walk through the narrow Siq canyon, stealing yourself for the first glimpse of the Treasury. Get the Indiana Jones theme tune out of your head by experiencing the all-absorbing sound-and-light show (Mondays, Wednesdays and Thursdays at 2030) or joining a traditional cookery lesson at the Petra Kitchen (petramoon.com).

Wadi Rum "Vast, echoing and God-like." TE Lawrence wasn't exaggerating when he used these words to describe the glorious desolation of Wadi Rum's heat-shattered mountains, canyons and sand dunes. Venturing into such a hostile environment might seem an epic undertaking, but relax in the knowledge that you'll travel by 4WD vehicle and spend the nights in comfortable camps. In addition to striking Lawrence of Arabia poses at every opportunity, activities at Wadi Rum include walks, camel rides and some of the best stargazing in the world.

Top right: Wadi Rum. **Below:** Jerash. **Above right:** Petra.

❓ Where can I see this?

Take a glass-bottom boat ride or snorkel over the reefs at Aqaba for a colourful 'window' on the psychedelic coral reefs of the Red Sea.

City highlights

>> Temperatures frequently soar to over 40°C between Apr and Oct, so aim to visit during winter when the weather is sunny but not searing.

>> Forget about hiring a car – it's only a 30-min transfer from the airport to most hotels.

>> Explore the souks on foot, and cruise the Creek by *abra* (water taxi).

>> Jumeirah's Burj al-Arab (burj-al-arab.com) is Dubai's iconic hotel of choice, but there are plenty of other high quality (and cheaper) alternatives.

Top six things to do

See the sights Explore the atmospheric old quarter of Bastakia, then visit the nearby Dubai Museum which has a series of realistic dioramas evoking the city's past. Continue walking along the Creek to the Waterfront Heritage Area. Don't miss the beautifully restored Sheikh Saeed Al Maktoum House with its wind towers (an early and ingenious form of air conditioning). Backtrack to the Bur Dubai *abra* station for a ride across the Creek before delving into the spice, gold and perfume souks.

Make a splash Wild Wadi (wildwadi.com), Dubai's famous waterpark, is awash with no fewer than 23 attractions, including Breakers Bay with its non-stop surf and the 33-m-high

66 99 Walking from the Creek, you burrow into an alleyway where sack-loads of herbs and spices pack a heady blow in the sultry heat. Shopkeepers proffering open boxes of plump dates lure you into Dubai's spice souk like a stray puppy. Nibbling the sweet fruits, you peruse mounds of cardamom, cloves and crushed rose petals, while chewing free samples of frankincense-flavoured chewing gum and sniffing pots of precious saffron.
Will

A desert fantasy

Barely a century ago Dubai was little more than a pearl-fishing village where camels outnumbered people. Now it's Arabia's premier playground and one of the most child-friendly destinations on earth. Through a number of audacious development projects, Dubai has taken the sting out of the Arabian desert and created a sensational, some say contrived, holiday destination. As well as beaches, watersports and modern hotels, you'll find theme parks, a ski dome and – due to open in 2010 – the ultimate 'super-resort' of Dubailand.

Jumeirah Sceirah slide – the ultimate slippery slope which will accelerate you to speeds approaching 80 kph. Young children that prefer their water more horizontal will find no shortage of swimming holes and tidal pools.

Explore the desert Take a 4WD safari (arabian-adventures.com) into the meringue-whip of dunes beyond Dubai City, hurtling up and down their slopes like something out of a *Mad Max* movie. Dune bashing (as well as sandboarding) is restricted to an approved area of desert, but if it still strikes you as environmentally dubious, take to the dunes on a camel instead. Afterwards, you'll retire to a Bedouin-style camp for a barbecue feast. When the evening entertainment begins you will no doubt embarrass your children with some impromptu belly dancing and they probably won't speak to you again until you give in to their pleas for a henna tattoo.

Go skiing Using 6000 tons of snow to create five different runs measuring up to 400 m in length, Ski Dubai (skidbx.com) is the world's third largest indoor ski centre. There are beginner slopes, a black run, a snowboarder's stunt zone and a snow park where kids can mess about on toboggans.

Have fun learning Children's City (childrencity.ae) takes youngsters on a hands-on educational journey through themed zones covering computers and communication, space and flight exploration, the human body, nature and international culture.

Have fun shopping Dubai is retail heaven, and Wafi City (waficity.com) has found the answer to a whinge-free shopping expedition. Simply dump the kids at its Encounter Zone (there's even a babysitting 'Drop 'n' Shop' service) and they'll be happy for hours. It's just one of Dubai's many malls where shopping and entertainment have been fused. The Mall of the Emirates is linked to Ski Dubai (see above), while Ibn Battuta Mall is themed on the six destinations (Andalucía, China, Egypt, India, Persia and Tunisia) that the 14th-century Arab traveller visited. The Mall of Arabia, meanwhile, has a Space and Science World where you can relive the first landing on the moon.

Top left: Dubai-style road-block. **Top right:** The Creek. **Above:** Dubai old and new.

Prepare for sensory overload

A cow wandering through a traffic jam; a fresh dollop of elephant poo in the road; a bullock hauling a cart; an exhilarating ride in a cycle rickshaw; people staring; people spitting … Children have an insatiable curiosity, and everything about India's chaotic street life will hold them rapt. And that's before they've seen the country's romantic palaces, explored its rugged deserts or encountered its 'Jungle Book' wildlife. Of course, India can also be hot, dusty and crowded. And you might find that your kids refuse to eat anything except boiled rice and chapattis. But with careful planning, an adventurous spirit and the odd day at the pool or beach, a family trip to India can be incredibly rewarding.

Northern India

>> One of the sub-continent's most popular circuits links Delhi with Agra, Bharatpur, Ranthambore National Park and Jaipur; allow a minimum of 10 days.
>> Join an organized tour, or travel independently using a combination of sleeper train, car with driver/guide, jeep and camel.
>> Visit between late Nov and early Feb when it is relatively cool.
>> Useful websites on Indian heritage include indiaheritage.org and cultureofindia.net.

The Golden Triangle
Delhi Venturing with kids into the hurly burly of Delhi may fill you with trepidation, but take a deep breath, hail an auto rickshaw or taxi and get stuck in. New Delhi has tree-lined avenues, swanky embassies and imposing monuments like India Gate, while Old Delhi has the labyrinthine bazaar of Chandni Chowk where you can buy anything from chess sets and silver jewellery to handmade paper and toy rickshaws. You can explore a mighty relic of the Mughal Empire at the Red Fort, while the nearby Jama Masjid (or Friday Mosque) offers eye-popping views of Old Delhi from its soaring minarets. The Rail Transport Museum (Chanakyapuri) has mighty steam engines like the 1855 Fairy Queen, plush saloon carriages used by royalty and even the skull of an elephant that charged a mail train in 1894 and lost. Shankar's International Dolls Museum (Bahadur Shah Zafar

Marg) showcases 6000 costumed dolls from over 85 countries, while the National Children's Museum (Kotla Road) has craft workshops. If your kids need some space to burn off energy, take them to the park next to India Gate or to the stone observatory of Jantar Mantar which has several intriguing stairways to explore.

Agra A symbol of undying love crafted in white marble, Agra's Taj Mahal was commissioned in 1641 by grieving Mughal emperor, Shah Jahan, in memory of his favourite wife, Mumtaz Mahal. Adults and children alike cannot fail to be overwhelmed by the exquisite beauty of this lavish mausoleum, which took 20,000 labourers 22 years to complete. Be sure to show your kids the intricate detail in the walls, which are inlaid with malachite, turquoise, lapis lazuli, coral, jasper and other precious stones. Just 40 km from Agra lies another Mughal masterpiece – Fatehpur Sikri, an ancient royal city guarded by massive gates. Around 15 km further to the west is Bharatpur, the eastern gateway town to Rajasthan, where you'll find Keoladeo Ghana Bird Sanctuary. A former royal hunting reserve, this small park is now a haven for 300 species of birds, including migratory Siberian cranes (September to February) and nesting populations of painted storks, herons and pelicans (July and August).

Jaipur Located 260 km from Delhi and 240 km from Agra, the Pink City of Jaipur completes the popular 'Golden Triangle'

Where can I see a tiger?
Of the 5000-7000 remaining tigers, over half live in India. Reserves like Ranthambore, Kanha and Corbett are the best places to find them – along with a range of other 'Jungle Book' wildlife, including leopard, langur, Indian elephant and sloth bear. Covering over 1300 sq km of forest and grassland tucked into the Himalayan foothills, Corbett National Park offers elephant-back safaris and basic accommodation, while further south, 400-sq-km Ranthambore National Park has jeep safaris and a much wider choice of places to stay. Located in central India, Kanha National Park is a six-hour drive from the nearest airport at Jabalpur, and has half a dozen jungle lodges.

route of northern India. Painted pink to commemorate a visit by the Prince of Wales in 1876, Jaipur's centrepiece is the City Palace which has exhibits of regal costumes, weaponry and art, as well as private quarters for the royal family. Don't miss the Palace of the Winds with its extraordinary honeycombed façade of 953 pink sandstone windows. In the rugged hills surrounding Jaipur, you can explore several forts – none more spectacular than the Amber Fort which can be reached by elephant-back.

Other highlights Embellish your Golden Triangle tour with a tiger safari (see above) and a visit to Pushkar, a sacred lakeside town that hosts a famous camel fair each November (see page 15). Heading north of Delhi, hill stations such as Naini Tal offer tantalizing glimpses of the Indian Himalayas, cool respite from the lowlands and some excellent family-friendly walking trails. With time you could also visit the Golden Temple at

Above : Palace of the Winds, Jaipur; Taj Mahal detail. **Far right:** Corbett National Park; beach at Goa.

Rickshaw rides
Bharatpur Keoladeo Ghana Bird Sanctuary.
Old Delhi Chandni Chowk bazaar.
Agra To the entrance of the Taj Mahal.

Amritsar and Mcleod Ganj – home of the Dalai Lama. Adventurous families will be lured to remote and dramatic Ladakh where pony-supported treks in the Zanskar Range can take a week or more and reach altitudes of over 5000 m.

Southern India

» Brace yourself for general mayhem in Mumbai, particularly during the Ganesh Chaturthi festival (Aug/Sep) when images of the elephant god, Ganesh, are paraded through the streets before being dunked in the sea at Chowpatty Beach.

» The big appeal for families heading south are the sandy beaches along the Goa and Malabar coasts.

» Southern India is generally less frenetic than the north.

Beaches and backwaters

Mumbai There's no shortage of important buildings and landmarks in Mumbai, the Gateway of India being a prime example. However, you may well find your kids are more fascinated by the general swirl of life going on around them. Give them time to soak it all up by hopping on a red double-decker bus or taking a boat trip in the harbour. For broader-minded children, Reality Tours and Travel (realitytoursandtravel.com) takes guided groups into Dharavi, Asia's largest slum, for an insight into the area's enterprising industries, such as leather tanning and plastic recycling. Mumbai's museums include Chhatrapati Shivaji Maharaj Vastu Sanghralaya (also known as the Prince of Wales Museum) which houses thousands of ancient artefacts and an interesting natural history section. Interactive exhibits can be found at Nehru Science Centre. When it all gets too much, seek refuge in the Horniman Circle Garden and along the nature trails of Maharashtra Nature Park. Located opposite the Hanging Gardens,

Kamal Nehru Park has shady gardens, a giant shoe-shaped slide and views of Marine Drive. Popular at weekends with locals and tourists, Juhu Beach has fairground rides, snack vendors and pony rides, while the combined theme parks of EsselWorld and Water Kingdom (esselworld.com), reached via a short ferry ride, boast around 100 ways (dry or wet) to get your heart thumping.

Goa An almost continuous 130-km swathe of palm-fringed beaches, Goa's coastline has obvious family appeal. There are the inevitable overdeveloped spots, just as there are peaceful wildlife sanctuaries and authentic temples to be explored inland. Accommodation ranges from simple budget hotels to five-star resorts. Some of the most popular beaches include Calangute (for watersports), Anjuna (for its party atmosphere and flea market), Morjim (a turtle nesting site) and Colva (Goa's longest beach).

Kerala Like Goa, the sandy beaches of Kerala's Malabar Coast (keralatourism.org) have several resorts offering family accommodation. But it's what lies behind the palm-fringed shore that will really captivate your children. The Malabar Backwaters, a maze of canals and rivers, is easily explored on a houseboat. These converted rice barges offer both a gentle pace of travel and a superb vantage from which to watch rural life glide by. Other highlights in the region include the fishing boats and Portuguese fort at Cochin, the temple elephants at Guruvayur and the wild elephants at Periya National Park in the cool Cardamom Hills – the perfect place to discover how India's spices are grown.

66 99 A trip on the backwaters of Kerala gives children a fascinating view of how others live – from fishermen and coir makers to toddy tappers tightrope walking between palm trees.
Emma Woollacott

66 99 It was almost as if the tiger had flicked a switch in the forest. One moment it was quiet and calm – the trees swathed in webs of early morning mist – the next, it was charged with tension. Gomati had heard the distant alarm calls – the shrill snort of a spotted deer, the indignant bark of a langur monkey – and her mood suddenly changed. She blasted a trunkful of dust up between her front legs, then shook her head so vigorously that I had to clutch the padded saddle to keep my balance. Gomati's mahout, sitting astride her neck, issued a terse reprimand before urging the elephant into the tangled forest.
Will

Island of adventure

With an enticing blend of palm-fringed beaches, rich wildlife and ancient monuments, Sri Lanka is a great family destination – particularly for those with school-age children who might appreciate the island's cultural and natural highlights more than toddlers. Split your time between exploring the Cultural Triangle, visiting a national park and relaxing on the coast. Hostilities between government forces and the Tamil Tigers are very much confined to the far north and east of the country. Elsewhere there's a peaceful, friendly, laid-back atmosphere, and foreigners – particularly children – are made very welcome.

Central Sri Lanka

» For flexibility hire a car and driver, for peace of mind book an organized tour, and for a taste of adventure try the local trains.
» The best time for visiting Cultural Triangle sites is Jan-Apr; the local pilgrimage season is May-Jun.
» Visit sites during early morning or late afternoon when it is cooler and less crowded.
» Remember to dress modestly and remove footwear and headwear when entering any Buddhist or Hindu shrine.

Sri Lanka's heart and soul

Cultural Triangle Allow four hours to drive from Colombo to the extraordinary cave temples at Dambulla. You will need to climb 200 or so steps to reach the first cave where a 14-m-long reclining Buddha has been carved from the rock. If anything, the second cave is even more spectacular, containing over 150 life-size statues of gods and a ceiling fresco depicting the Buddha's life. To the north, Anuradhapura, Sri Lanka's sprawling ancient capital, has plenty to interest budding archaeologists, including the bell-shaped dagobas of Thuparama and Ruwanweli. However, Polonnaruwa is more compact and can be easily explored by bicycle. Don't miss Gal Vihara, a group of enormous Buddha carvings hewn from granite. Sri Lanka's undisputed 'rock star' is Sigiriya rock fortress, a 370-m-high monolith crowned by a palace and surrounded by an elaborate complex of water gardens, moats and ramparts. Dating from the 5th century, Sigiriya can be scaled by anyone with good stamina and a head for heights. A stone stairway leads past wall frescos to the Lion Gate where a huge head with open jaws once served as the entrance to the palace. Now all that remains is a pair of massive paws. Gone, too, is the final section of original stone steps; to continue to the summit you'll need to use a rickety-looking metal stairway.

The hill country Spread around a lake at 500 m above sea level, Kandy (the capital of Sri Lanka's hill country) is renowned for its Tooth Temple where the sacred tooth of the Lord Buddha is enshrined. Three times daily, the magnificent temple reverberates to the drumming and conch-shell blasts of ceremonial *poojas* as clouds of incense fill the air and devotees make offerings of flowers. Elsewhere in Kandy, you can watch traditional dancing and drumming performances, take a boat ride on the lake, visit the railway museum or have a picnic in nearby Peradeniya's Royal Botanical Gardens. In the Matale hills to the north of Kandy, children can sniff-test cinnamon, cloves, nutmeg, pepper and cardamom at various spice gardens. Continuing south to Nuwara Eliya there are several opportunities to visit tea estates, while the Horton Plains offers an easy 4-km hike to World's End, a sheer escarpment with a dizzying 880-m drop. There are more dramatic views at Ella Gap where an adventure centre offers activities such as canoeing, mountain biking and abseiling.

Above: Elephant carving. Below right: Dambulla cave temple. Top right: Elephant safari; Sigiriya rock fortress.

Coastal Sri Lanka

😊😊😊😊🏠🚻🏊

▸▸ Sri Lanka has plenty of family accommodation, from guesthouses to beach resorts. Check in advance whether rooms have mosquito nets – or take your own.
▸▸ Beaches with fishing villages, where you can watch the daily catch being landed, are fascinating to visit, but stick to the cleaner, safer tourist beaches for swimming.
▸▸ The sea is particularly good for swimming during Nov-Mar.

Watersports and wildlife

West coast The main tourist beaches along the stretch of coast between Colombo and Galle are at Bentota, Beruwela and Hikkaduwa. Watersports, such as scuba-diving and windsurfing, are widely available and many beaches have lifeguards on duty outside the main hotels. There are turtle hatcheries at Induruwa and Kosgoda, just south of Bentota. Visit between November and April and you might be allowed to help release the hatchlings. Inland from the coast, Sinharaja Biosphere Reserve provides a great opportunity to explore the rainforest in search of butterflies, birds and monkeys. Walking conditions are best during the largely leech-free dry season (January to March). Guides are compulsory.

South coast Founded in the 16th century by the Portuguese, the fortified city of Galle is worth a morning's exploration. Walk along the ramparts to the lighthouse and then delve into the National Maritime Museum and the Historical Mansion Museum where you can find out about everything from traditional fishing to gemstone polishing. South of Galle is Unawatuna, a beautiful curve of coral sand where you can build sandcastles under the shade of palm trees. You can also hire snorkelling equipment and arrange glass-bottomed boat trips from beachside cafés and guesthouses. Other pristine sandy beaches along this stretch of coast include Mirissa (good for shade and gentle surf) and Rekkawa, a protected beach that you can visit at night to watch turtles laying their eggs. For more wildlife, head to Bundala National Park, a wetland sanctuary where you can spot flamingos and crocodiles, or Ruhuna (Yala) National Park which is home to elephants, leopards, sloth bears, jackals, monkeys, wild buffalos and around 150 species of birds. Bus tours are available from Tissamaharama, but you'll stand more chance of seeing wildlife (especially the park's celebrated leopards) if you go in a 4WD jeep with a guide. Herds of elephants can also be seen at Uda Walawe National Park.

Above: Outrigger on beach.

🏔 Adventure activities

Whitewater rafting Kelani River near Kitulgala has grade I rapids suitable for children as young as five.

Hiking The Gampaha district (about an hour from Colombo) offers easy hiking across gently undulating farmland.

Surfing Arugam Bay on the east coast is Sri Lanka's surfing Mecca. The main break is at Arugam Point, while Pottuvil offers a ride of around 800 m in ideal conditions. On the west coast, head for Hikkaduwa.

❓ Where can I see elephants up-close?

The most famous place in Sri Lanka for petting pachyderms is Pinnawela Elephant Orphanage where you can help feed and bathe jumbos that have been abandoned or orphaned. In recent years, there were some concerns that tourism was becoming a priority over animal welfare at Pinnawela, leading to some overseas tour operators dropping the site from their itineraries and instead visiting Udawalawe National Park where the Elephant Transit Home cares for around 30 orphaned baby elephants. If you prefer your pachyderms on the wild side, however, head for Minneriya National Park during August or September when an extraordinary 'gathering of the herds' takes place around the receding shores of a lake.

🫖 How to make a perfect cuppa

▸▸ Pluck only the tender tips from Ceylon tea bushes.
▸▸ Allow the leaves to wither for a few hours.
▸▸ Roll the leaves to release their juices.
▸▸ Leave to dry in a hot air chamber.
▸▸ Sift into various grades depending on leaf-particle size.
▸▸ Warm a teapot and add two or three teaspoons of tea.
▸▸ Pour boiling water into the teapot; stir or shake the pot.
▸▸ Add cold milk (if desired) to a tea cup, then pour the tea.

Nepal

Up a bit, down a bit

The Nepalese Himalayas include eight peaks over 8000 m, but that doesn't mean you have to plan a three-week assault on Everest Base Camp to appreciate these mighty mountains (although teenagers might relish the challenge). There are several family-friendly treks that are not only shorter but also, more crucially, avoid high passes and the inherent risks of altitude sickness. Kids may well surprise you with their trekking stamina, while porters are usually happy to carry littl'uns in their baskets. Don't forget, there is a lot more to Nepal than trekking. You may come with high ideals, but remember to also set your sights lower on the steamy jungles of Chitwan National Park.

Country highlights

» With pollution, construction, traffic and tourist hustle all on the rise in Kathmandu, consider basing yourself in healthier Bhaktapur and making day trips into the capital.
» On treks, porters carry all luggage and even small children if necessary.
» Be especially vigilant over hygiene issues in mountain villages.

A city, mountain and jungle adventure

Kathmandu With its profusion of temples, palaces and shrines, Durbar Square is the heart and soul of Kathmandu. Get there early in the morning before it seethes with curio vendors and other tourists. As you enter the square from New Road, look out for two stone lions guarding the home of the Kumari – Kathmandu's living goddess. Intricately carved lattice windows and balconies enable her to look out, but not be seen. Across the square, the towering pagoda of Maju Deval is a great spot to sit

quietly and soak up the atmosphere. Nearby is the statue of Garuda – half-man, half-bird – on which the Hindu god Vishnu travels, and behind that lies Maru Tole, a small square where devotees can buy marigold garlands to lay at the shrine of Ganesh, the Hindu god of good fortune. Maru Tole is dominated by Kasthamandap, a three-storey wooden pagoda that, according to legend, was built from a single tree in the 12th century. There are viewing platforms on the first floor. Walking in to Hanuman Dhoka Square, peep through the large lattice screen set into a wall of the old royal palace. Inside is a scary visage of Shiva – a gruesome mask with huge fangs designed to ward off evil. A little further on, you may wish to divert your children's scrutiny of the erotic carvings on the wooden roof struts of Jagannath Temple. Adjacent to this, however, is the statue of Hanuman, the much-loved monkey king who rescued princess Sita from the evil Ravana and has come to symbolize devout loyalty. It is completely covered in orange paste left by worshippers. Nearby, the ornately decorated Golden Door leads inside Hanuman Dhoka, the former royal palace. As you walk inside, look out for the statue of Narsimha, half-man, half-lion, devouring the demon Haranyakashipu. Another sight that's sure to delight most

kids is Kal Bhairav, a 3-m-tall statue of the Lord of Destruction, complete with a crown of human skulls.

Kathmandu Valley Sights worth seeing beyond Kathmandu city include the Buddhist stupas of Boudhanath and Swayambhunath, the Patan Museum and the pedestrian-friendly streets of Bhaktapur – Nepal's medieval capital.

Pokhara A six-hour bus drive or 35-minute flight from Kathmandu, this lazy lakeside town may well offer your first glimpse of the Himalaya – a spectacular panorama of the Annapurnas dominated by Machhapuchare, the 6997-m 'Fish Tail Peak'. It's a great base from which to plan a trek, but before you head for the hills spend a few days enjoying Pokhara itself – browsing the handicraft stalls, boating on Phewa Lake and visiting the World Peace Pagoda with its all-seeing eyes of Buddha.

Annapurnas From Pokhara, it's a short bus ride to trailheads leading into the Annapurna Conservation Area. Not only is this one of the world's best trekking areas, but it is also a haven for plants and animals, ranging from orchids and rhododendrons to blood pheasants and snow leopards. Treks can vary from a two-day taster, walking into the foothills and camping near a spectacular lookout, to a 16-day Annapurna Circuit crossing the 5416-m Thorung La pass. See pages 288-289 for suggestions of two family-friendly options, along with guidelines on minimizing your impact on this fragile environment. There are dozens of trek outfitters in Kathmandu and Pokhara, although booking through an overseas family adventure specialist

Left: Durbar Square, Katmandu. Far left: Prayer wheel. Right: Boudhanath. Opposite page: Annapurnas; grey langur.

will ensure that your local operator is genuinely child-friendly. Accommodation can be anything from tents and teahouses to lodges.

Chitwan National Park A popular haunt of aristocratic hunters in the 19th century, Chitwan National Park is now one of Asia's premier wildlife reserves, offering jeep and elephant-back safaris in search of tiger and Asian one-horned rhinoceros. Other wildlife includes spotted deer, leopard, sloth bear, wild boar, rhesus monkey, grey langur, wild dog, marsh crocodile, gharial (or Gangetic crocodile) and freshwater dolphin. Of the 450 bird species that have been recorded in Chitwan, look out for year-round residents like woodpeckers, hornbills and redheaded trogons. Brahminy ducks and bareheaded geese flock here in winter, while summer sees Chitwan's forests all-of-a-flutter with migrant parakeets and paradise flycatchers. The park has a good range of lodges and tented camps and can be reached by air, road or river.

🌍 Activities that don't involve walking

Whitewater rafting The Trishuli is not the wildest river in Nepal, but it's close to Kathmandu and offers one- or two-day trips on mainly grade III rapids, making it the best option for families. Teenagers in search of something more awesome should consider the grade IV Bhote Kosi and Kali Gandaki rivers. Whitewater Nepal (raftnepal.com) runs family trips, minimum age seven.

Mountain biking Hire bikes in Kathmandu and drive them out to Nagarkot from where it's downhill all the way to Bhaktapur. For serious biking expeditions, contact Dawn till Dusk (nepalbiking.com).

Ultralight flights Based in Pokhara, Avia Club Nepal (avianepal.21bc.net) offers a vulture's-eye view of Machhapuchare from an ultralight. For children aged seven and over.

❓ Where can I find one of these?

Guaranteed to titillate kids, saligrams are black stones found in the upper reaches of the Kali Gandaki Valley which, when broken open, reveal the fossil remains of 130-million-year-old ammonites. You might be lucky and find a saligram yourself on the Jomson Trek – otherwise buy one from a curio trader, but remember to bargain hard. Hindus walking to pilgrimage sites in the Himalayas believe the fossils represent the god Vishnu. Palaeontologists, however, revere the stones for adding weight to an incredible tectonic revelation – that the rocks forming the Himalayas once formed the seabed of a prehistoric ocean. How else, could the remains of an extinct sea creature find their way 4000 m above sea level?

How to trek gently

There are moments on every Himalayan trek when you'll have difficulty convincing yourself, let alone your children, that the white flecks hovering above the horizon are not clouds but mountains. White and pristine, like tall ships under full sail, the snow-capped peaks of the Himalaya seem to float – aloof and unassailable – on a sea of haze rising from the lowlands. But this towering wilderness is far more fragile than you might imagine. Home to unique plants and animals, the forests and meadows of the Himalaya are like a thin, easily torn, cloak. In recent decades, growing population and a boom in tourism have inflicted severe damage. Forests have been cleared to meet the cooking, lodging and heating needs of trekkers which, in turn, has resulted in erosion. Tourism, however, is a major source of foreign income and many locals are better off now as lodge owners, mountain guides and porters than they ever were as farmers or traders. In Nepal, protected areas like Sagamartha National Park and the Annapurna Conservation Area have been established not only to safeguard the mountain environment but also

Tourism in the Himalaya has brought greater economic prosperity to the locals but also increased pressure on the fragile environment.

to preserve the cultural identity of local people. There is now a move to develop a more sustainable form of tourism in the Himalaya and you can play a crucial role by learning the art of 'gentle trekking'.

▶▶ Make a 'gentle trekking' kit containing biodegradable soap, long-lasting lithium batteries, water filter and plastic rubbish-collecting bags.

▶▶ Lodges and teahouses can save fuel if trekkers order the same food at the same time.

▶▶ Instead of huddling around a campfire wear an extra sweater to keep warm.

▶▶ A hot shower is a luxury, unless water is heated by solar power or non-wood stoves.

▶▶ Toilet paper can take 30 years to decompose at 4000 m. Use toilet facilities provided or, if none are available, make sure you are at least 30 m from any water source.

▶▶ Use a water filter instead of buying bottled water.

▶▶ Take care to note the fragile plant life at your feet – it's easily destroyed by a misguided boot. Stay on trails and camp only in designated areas.

▶▶ Respect local culture by always asking permission before photographing somebody; dress modestly and make a donation to local schools rather than handing out money and sweets to children (which encourages begging and discourages independence and pride).

▶▶ Support local conservation groups, such as the Annapurna Conservation Area Project (south-asia.com/Kingmah/tonproj), Kathmandu Environmental Education Project (keepnepal.org) and the Himalayan Trust (himalayan-trust.org.np)

▶▶ Remember the green catchphrase: 'The Himalayas are here to change you, not for you to change them.'

66 99

We found ourselves climbing through a forest that could have germinated from the mind of Tolkien. Rhododendron, birch and maple loomed from the mist, monotone limbs gnarled and twisted with trailing beards of dripping mosses and lichens. Flycatchers and minivets flitted through the cloud

	Day	Route	Description	Altitude	Time
Royal Trek (Grade I)	1	Begnas Bazaar to Sundar Danda	A 30-minute drive from Pokhara leads to Begnas Bazaar from where a wide path leads between two lakes.	720 m	1 hr
	2	To Chisopani	A steep climb on stone steps leads to Chisopani from where there are amazing views of the Annapurna and Dhulagiri ranges, particularly from the hilltop temple above the village.	1080 m	5 hrs
	3	To Shaklung	The trail descends to a river valley, then climbs to the Gurung village of Shaklung.	1730 m	3 hrs
	4	To Kalikastan	A forested ridge links the villages of Naudanda, Mathi Thana and Thulokot before reaching Kalikastan where there are good views of Machhapuchhare and Annapurna.	1370 m	4 hrs
	5	To Bijayapur, drive to Pokhara	The trail descends gently through Brahman and Chhetri villages towards the Pokhara roadhead.	720 m	2 hrs
Ghorepani Trek (Grade II)	1	Birethanti to Tikhedhunga	After a two-hour drive from Pokhara to Birethanti, a wide trail follows the north bank of the Bhurungdi Khola before climbing steadily up to Hille at 1495 m. From there it's a short climb to Tikhedhunga.	1525 m	4 hrs
	2	To Ghorepani	Following a descent to the river, a stone stairway of 3767 steps leads to the Magar village of Ulleri (2070 m). It's the toughest section of the trek, but your efforts are rewarded with fine views of Annapurna South and Hiunchuli. The trail continues to ascend more gently, through forests of oak and rhododendron towards Banthanti (2250 m) and Nangethanti (2460 m) before reaching Ghorepani at 2775 m.	2775 m	6 hrs
	3	To Poon Hill and Tadapani	An early morning climb leads to Poon Hill (3210 m) from where there are stunning views of Machhapuchhare and both the Annapurna and Dhaulagiri massifs. After returning to Ghorepani for breakfast, the trail descends to Deurali, crosses a stream and then climbs to Tadapani (2590 m).	3210 m	8 hrs
	4	To Ghandruk	Leaving Tadapani, the trail winds through forests to Ghandruk (1950 m) where there is a visitor centre of the Annapurna Area Conservation Project.	1950 m	4 hrs
	5	To Nayapul, drive to Pokhara	Gentle walking alongside the Modi Khola river.	1000 m	5 hrs

Keeping safe in the mountains

▸▸ Be alert to the signs of Acute Mountain Sickness (AMS). In children this includes excessive sleepiness, reduced appetite, irritable or clingy behaviour and more obvious symptoms like vomiting and drowsiness. If you have any concerns about AMS affecting your child immediate descent is not only effective, it can also be life saving.

▸▸ Do not take a sick child to altitude. Children with coughs or colds are more prone to suffer High Altitude Pulmonary Oedema (HAPE) than otherwise healthy children.

▸▸ A slow ascent is essential for acclimatization. Avoid flying to the start of your trek and do not give your child Diamox.

▸▸ Be alert to the threat of hyperthermia. Children get cold more quickly than adults and they do not generate heat if being carried.

▸▸ Stress to children the importance of never approaching dogs or straying near the edge of paths with steep drops. Always keep to the uphill side of a path when passing oncoming trekkers, porters or mule trains.

In the emperors' footsteps

Everything about China makes your head spin. Not only is it the world's third largest country (covering an area of 9.5 million sq km), but it is also home to over 1.3 billion people. There are a baffling number of native tongues and around 56,000 characters in its written language. Development is proceeding at breakneck speed. The Maglev train, for example, shifts travellers from Shangai's airport to the city at 430 kph, while Shanghai itself is actually subsiding under the weight of its skyscrapers. China is nothing, if not daunting, which is why many holidaymakers stick to a fairly well-trodden circuit in the northeast, combining the imperial highlights of Beijing and Xi'an with a visit to the Great Wall. If you have time, however, make a detour south to Yangshuo where you'll catch a glimpse of traditional rural life. From there, it's just a short flight back to the future with touchdown in Hong Kong (see page 293).

Country highlights

» The best time to visit Beijing is autumn (Sep to early Nov) after the summer heat has subsided and before the often bitterly cold winter sets in.
» Take the sleeper train from Beijing to Luoyang and Xi'an, or from Guangzhou to Guilin.
» Many attractions offer children's discounts, usually for kids under 130 cm in height.

China on a plate – the essentials

Beijing The world's largest public square, Tiananmen Square, has more than enough space for children to burn off excess energy, either by flying a kite or stomping across acres of paving stones. It shouldn't, however, be too difficult to lure them through the Gate of Heavenly Peace. Located on the northern side of the square, this symbolic portal leads to the entrance of the Forbidden City – home to 24 emperors between 1420 and 1923. Cross a wide moat and walk beneath the massive Meridien Gate and you face yet another threshold – the Supreme Harmony Gate. Beyond lies a vast courtyard that once held imperial audiences of up to 100,000 people. The large building rearing before you on marbled terraces is the first of three great halls where the emperor ruled from his Dragon Throne. The inner court,

Above: Cormorant fisherman, Yangshuo.
Above right: Great Wall.

meanwhile, contains three palaces – forbidden to all but the imperial family and the emperor's concubines and eunuchs. At its rear is a remarkable garden of ancient conifers, rockeries, walkways and pavilions, while to the east of the palace complex are various exhibitions of bronzes, ceramics and jewellery. See if you can track down the Well of the Pearl Concubine – a narrow cleft into which a 25-year-old favourite was dispatched for daring to defy the emperor.

Great Wall of China Get an early start for a day exploring the Great Wall. Just 70 km to the northwest of Beijing, Badaling is one of the most popular sections, particularly during summer weekends when it can be swarming with tourists. Families with young children will appreciate the cable car that whisks you up to a wooded mountain ridge where the Great Wall, punctuated by watchtowers every 70 m, snakes off into the distance. Along its outer edge, crenellated battlements provide plenty of opportunities for your kids to fire imaginary arrows at advancing Mongol hordes – while at the same time preventing them from toppling off the 6-m-wide, 9-m-tall ramparts. At Badaling you will also find a museum, film theatre and souvenir stalls. Slightly further afield, the 19-km Simatai section of the Great Wall

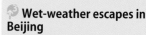

🐾 **Wet-weather escapes in Beijing**
Natural History Museum Little in the way of English captions, but the Chinese dinosaur exhibits on the ground floor will appeal to kids.
Le Cool Ice Rink Indoor skating fun at the China World Trade Centre.
ExploraScience Hands-on journey into a world of gadgets and technology.

undulates along a ridge with much steeper drops than those at Badaling. Older children may relish the challenge of a scramble, but there's also a cable car for the less stout of heart. An added attraction at Simatai is the 3-km downhill toboggan ride. If your children feel up to the challenge, head to Jinshanling from where you can hike along the Wall to Simatai. The 10-km trek takes around four hours, but be warned – there are several ruined sections of Wall to negotiate.

Zhengzhou Around 520 km south of Beijing, the modern capital of Henan province is the jumping-off point for visits to Shaolin Temple, the birthplace of Kung Fu. Your kids will be bowled over by the regular martial arts performances where young monks spar

Above: Terracotta Warriors.
Left: Forbidden City.

with one another, delivering karate chops and side kicks that look as if they could bring an elephant to its knees. Also worth seeing are the Buddha carvings adorning the Longmen Caves, 13 km south of Luoyang.

Xi'an Arrayed like massed ranks of life-size toy soldiers, the 2000-year-old Army of Terracotta Warriors is, from a child's point of view, probably the most arresting sight in China. Some 6000 stony-faced warriors, along with their horses, face east in battle formation – ready to march into the afterworld at the eternal service of emperor Qin Shi Huang. Their weapons, which include crossbows, axes and swords, are now in storage, but you can see an impressive pair of bronze war chariots in the museum. Creepy, but captivating, no two warriors' faces are exactly alike – and archaeologists believe there may be thousands more awaiting excavation at this extraordinary burial site.

Yangshuo Located 65 km south of Guilin, Yangshuo is well known to the backpacker fraternity and makes a laid-back base from which to explore the surreal karst landscape of limestone peaks that characterize this part of south China. Hire bikes and set off along tracks that lead through rice fields to nearby villages and caves. From Yangshuo you can also take a boat trip on the Li River – or paddle yourself in a canoe or raft. Don't miss the nightly cormorant-fishing tours where the birds' fetch-and-return hunting skills are demonstrated by floodlight. If you have time, head north of Guilin to the Dragon's Backbone where dramatic rice terraces scale a series of 800-m hills.

> "In Guilin we cycled along a rough track that meandered through a mêlée of conical fairy-tale hills. The sky was milky-white; fishponds flecked the rice paddies like squares of foil, and thickets of giant bamboo unfurled towering green plumes above our heads.
>
> *Will*

Off the beaten track: Mongolia

Take the kids to Mongolia? Yeah, right – might as well fly them to the moon! Actually, a family holiday to Mongolia is not as daft as it might sound. The capital, Ulaan Baatar, not only has plenty to interest kids, such as the Natural History Museum with its stunning collection of dinosaur fossils, but it is also a perfect base for exciting and safe forays into two of Asia's last great wilderness areas.

Jalman Meadows A three- to four-hour bus drive to the northeast of Ulaan Baatar takes you across treeless steppes and through larch and birch forests to reach the upper Tuul river valley. The autumn and winter pastures for nomadic herders, Jalman Meadows is also the summer location of a camp for just 20 tourists. Based on traditional gers, the camp has composting toilets, solar-powered electricity and leaves little trace when it's packed away at the end of each season. Activities include hiking, horse riding and yak-cart rafting where an inflatable raft is towed upstream by bovine power. Although rarely seen, local wildlife to keep an eye out for include wolf, lynx, brown bear, red deer, gazelle, moose and wild boar.

Arburd Sands Another low-impact ger camp has been established on the Gobi steppes, a four-hour drive from Ulaan Baatar. Arburd Sands is just 35 km from the Zorgol Hairhan Uul, a gigantic rock formation that's home to Argali sheep and Siberian ibex. You can camp out in the sands, stake out a wolf hide and ride horses or camels.

When to go July and August.
Getting there Fly to Ulaan Baatar via Berlin, Moscow or Beijing.

Singapore versus Hong Kong

They are two of Asia's most exciting and vibrant cities. Both are popular stopovers en route to and from Australia and New Zealand, and both are supremely child-friendly. So which do you choose? Hong Kong has Disneyland, but will that be enough to swing it in your favour? Don't forget Singapore's much-hyped Night Safari and the Sentosa 'island of fun'. Use the three-day action plans, below, to help you decide which Asian metropolis gets your vote.

	Day 1 FUN	Day 2 ADVENTURE	Day 3 EDUCATION
Breakfast	Try yam cakes and porridge served with *you tiao* (Chinese fried fritters) at the Tiong Bahru Market.	Pop into Ya Kun Kaya Toast at Raffles City for toast with anything from cheese and ice cream to coconut-and-egg.	Explore Chinatown Heritage Centre on a motorized trishaw (singaporeexplorer.com.sg), pausing to sample local food.
Morning	Head to Suntec City Mall to begin a 60-minute Duck Tour (ducktours.com.sg) – a light-hearted city tour and harbour cruise combo in a converted Vietnam War amphibious craft.	Go west on the MRT to Snow City (snowcity.com.sg) which is not only a great place to chill out if the heat is proving too much, but you can also ski, snowboard and build snowmen.	Get to grips with over 1000 interactive exhibits, an IMAX cinema and a huge outdoor Waterworks park at the Singapore Science Centre (science.edu.sg).
Lunch	Grab a quick snack at any of the plethora of food outlets at Suntec City.	Backtrack to Harbour-Front Tower 2 (have lunch on the go) for the cable-car ride to Sentosa Island (sentosa.com.sg). Ask for the glass-bottomed cabin and then get an even better view	Sample *char kway teow* (Singapore noodles) at any central food centre.
Afternoon	Allow 30 minutes by taxi or 75 minutes by MRT and bus to reach Singapore Zoo (zoo.com.sg). Spot free-roaming orang-utans from the Rainforest Walk before finding out about a day in the life of a working Asian elephant. Visit the walk-through Fragile Forest with its mouse deers and tree kangaroos, learn about big cat conservation at the interactive Tiger Trek exhibit and see the Hamadryas baboons in their spectacular Rift Valley setting.	of Singapore and the Southern Islands from the 110-m-high Sky Tower – just one of the attractions at Imbriah Lookout. Brace yourself for the multi-sensory 4D Magix show where special effects ensure you get a lot more than just a movie. Visit the Merlion, a larger-than-life recreation of Singapore's famous icon, then ride the 650-m luge run.	Learn about ancient traditions at the Asian Civilisations Museum (acm.org.sg) at Empress Place. Don't miss the Singapore River Gallery which traces the city's fascinating story of colonization and trade. Bring the exhibit to life by viewing the modern-day metropolis on a bumboat ride (rivercruise.com.sg) along the Singapore River. Round off the day with some souvenir hunting along the streets of Chinatown or Little India.
Dinner	Enjoy an Asian buffet at the Safari Restaurant before taking a 3-km tram ride to spot nocturnal wildlife on the Night Safari (nightsafari.com.sg).	Unwind at Coastes, a relaxed beach bar and grill overlooking Silosa Beach, then take the Sentosa Express light rail back to HarbourFront Singapore.	Dine at Lau Pa Sat Festival Market, the oldest Victorian filigree cast-iron building in Asia or enjoy a seafood feast at Clarke Quay.

Above: Singapore skyline; Sentosa Island beach.

	Day 1 FUN	Day 2 ADVENTURE	Day 3 EDUCATION
Breakfast	Not particularly adventurous, but Uncle Willie's Deli (Wyndham Street, Central) will keep you going for the day.	Try authentic *dim sum* at City Hall Maxim's Palace.	Grab a snack on the go, but remember that food and drink are not allowed on the MTR.
Morning	If you've let slip that there is a Disneyland in Hong Kong you might as well take the kids there on day one to get it out of their systems. Actually, HK Disneyland (disney.com.hk) is excellent. It may be smaller than its sister parks, but it's friendly, immaculate and the food verges on the nutritious. As well as all the regular rides, like Space Mountain, Buzz Lightyear and Autopia, there's an arboreal adventure in Tarzan's treehouse and the jungle cruise has been spiced up with geysers and erupting volcanoes. Mickey opens the doors at 1000 and it's a piece of cheese to get there on the slick Mass Transit Railway (MTR) to Sunny Bay, followed by a ride on the Disney train. If Disney doesn't appeal, then hop on a fast ferry bound for Cheung Chau island – gawking at Hong Kong's towering skyline as you slip out of the harbour.	Today, you've got two options. With children aged 10 and over, head out of town on a full-day jolly with Fast Pursuit Craft Adventures (kayak-and-hike.com). Barely 20 km from Kowloon the rugged Sai Kung Peninsula is fringed by a maze of islands and inlets that are inaccessible to all but the smallest craft. You'll spend the day careering through the archipelago in a speedboat and sea kayaking along a dramatic coast of sea caves, arches and deserted beaches. Hikes on nearby peaks are also possible. With younger children, take a three-hour boat trip off the coast of Lantau Island in search of bubble gum-pink Indo-Pacific humpback dolphins. Hong Kong Dolphinwatch (hkdolphinwatch.com) operates trips every Wednesday, Friday and Sunday, with pick-ups in Hong Kong Central and Kowloon.	Take the MTR to Tung Chung on Lantau Island, from where the Ngong Ping 360 Skyrail (np360.com.hk) whisks you 5.7 km up to the giant Tian Tan Buddha statue on Lantau Peak. At 34 m high, it is the world's largest seated, outdoor, bronze statue of its kind. Climb the flight of 260 steps that leads to the great Buddha, then visit the nearby Po Lin monastery. The touristy Ngong Ping Village has several attractions, including 'Walking with Buddha', a multimedia exhibition where you can follow the path to enlightenment of Siddhartha Gautama – the man who became Buddha. Kids will love the shows at The Monkey's Tale Theatre, based on traditional Buddhist Jataka tales like 'The jackal who saved the lion'. The streets of Ngong Ping, meanwhile, are patrolled by jugglers, Kung Fu experts and other entertainers.
Lunch	Pick and mix from live seafood tanks at restaurants along Cheung Chau's waterfront, then enjoy a meal overlooking the tangle of junks in the harbour.	Try Tasty Congee (near the Happy Valley Racecourse) for Wanton noodles.	The Ngong Ping Tea House offers traditional Chinese tea ceremonies and copious cakes, while the Po Lin monastery has vegetarian meals.
Afternoon	Back in Hong Kong, ride the Central-Mid-Levels Escalator, a 792-m conveyor belt that moves around 40,000 people through the city each day. For another 'moving' experience ride the tram up to the Peak (thepeak.com.hk) for spectacular views across the city. The Peak Tower has viewing platforms, shops, restaurants and even a Madame Tussaud's waxworks.	On Lamma Island, allow up to five hours to make the most of the island's walking opportunities. There are two easily combined routes – Yung Shue Wan to Sok Kwu Wan and a circuit taking in the sandy beach at Shek Pai Wan. Teenagers, of course, may well prefer a retail adventure in Kowloon, browsing Nathan Road's 'Golden Mile' of shops, shops and more shops.	Visit the Wetland Park (wetlandpark.com), a 64-ha nature reserve where you can learn about conservation at the huge visitor centre, with its interactive computers, wildlife models and wetland simulations. Alternatively, head to Ocean Park (oceanpark.com.hk) which has everything from sharks, orcas and giant pandas to a Dragon Rollercoaster.
Dinner	Catch the Star Ferry across the harbour to Kowloon and haggle for knick-knacks at Temple Street Night Market, while snacking at *dai pai dongs* (street stalls).	Excellent seafood is served at the Rainbow Restaurant, Sok Kwu Wan, Lamma Island.	Watch the Symphony of Lights – a sound and light spectacular put on by skyscrapers on both sides of the harbour – then tuck into good-value Cantonese food at The Jade Garden.

Above: The Peak; Tian Tan Buddha. **Above left**: Riding the escalators in Hong Kong.

Welcome to the land of fun

According to the Thai psyche, anything worth doing should involve an element of *sànùk* or 'fun' – something that fraught parents might question when cajoling overheated kids around manic Bangkok. Overwhelmingly, though, Thailand is bursting with excuses for having fun. You could start with some jetlag-recovery time on the tropical island of Koh Samet or take a sleeper train to the hill country around Chiang Mai – ideal if *sànùk* equates to some cool relief from the hot and humid lowlands. Elsewhere, children will be all-smiles riding elephants, paddling sea kayaks and snorkelling on coral reefs.

Bangkok

>> Most of the famous sights in the royal district of Ko Ratanakosin are within walking distance of each other, but get there early in the morning before temperatures soar.
>> Jump in a túk-túk (motorized three-wheeler) to get around or catch the cool river breezes on a Chao Phraya River Express boat.
>> Warn children not to approach dogs as rabies is relatively common in Thailand.

Wats it all about?

One-day action plan Prepare to be dazzled by Bangkok's temple monasteries or wats. These architectural gems with their gleaming orange-and- green roof tiles, mosaic-clad stupas and gilded ornamentation are a must-see. Head first to Wat Phra Kaew where the diminutive 66-cm-tall Emerald Buddha resides in a lavishly decorated bòt (chapel) guarded by statues of mythical giants. Adjoining Wat Phra Kaew is the Grand Palace, another impressive monument, but only worth a quick look with kids in tow. Before they get 'templed out' or frazzled by the heat, you need to stroll along to nearby Wat Pho to show them the reclining Buddha. Measuring 46 m in length and 15 m in height, it is completely clad in gold leaf and mother-of-pearl. Next, hop on a long-tail boat for a refreshing zip around Bangkok's canals and river tributaries – a veritable 'Venice of the East'. If the kids are up for another temple, squeeze in a stop at Wat Arun with its impressive 82-m-tall central spire. That's the essential sightseeing stuff over with. So, how do you keep children entertained for the rest of the day? Older children may want to mingle with trendy Thai teens in MBK, a shopping centre crammed with shops and stalls selling cheap 'designer' clothing and just about everything else. For somewhere green and clean, Lumphini Park has lawns to

Left top: Mother-of-pearl inlaid in the soles of the feet of the Reclining Buddha. **Left bottom:** Wat Pho. **Above:** Grand Palace. **Bottom:** Thailand's coast.

run about on, a lake to boat on and even a kite-flying season from February to April. For cooling down, slide over to Central World Ice Skating in the World Trade Centre. There's a Children's Discovery Museum at Chatuchak Park, a collection of rare indigenous wildlife at Dusit Zoo and a nest of vipers at the Queen Saovabha Memorial Institute where lethal snakes are milked in order to produce anti-venoms.

Out of town A 69-ha wildlife park located 45 km east of Bangkok, Safari World (safariworld.com) has rare white pandas and a drive-through safari experience, while Muang Boran (ancientcity.com), 33 km from the city, is an open-air museum with scaled

Kids' top 10: Thailand

1 Float on a bamboo raft down the Mai Pae River (and pray that it doesn't sink).

2 Explore the ancient tropical rainforest of Khao Sok National Park by elephant-back, then discover the jungle's strange nocturnal wildlife during a night safari.

3 Ride the sleeper train from Bangkok to Chiang Mai, scale the Dragon Staircase to Doi Suthep Temple and visit the elephant sanctuary at nearby Lampang.

4 Learn to scuba-dive on Ko Tao, see psychedelic coral reefs and (fingers crossed) spot a whale shark.

5 Taste delicious Thai food, like *kaeng phèt kài nàw mái* (chicken and bamboo shoot curry) and *kuaytiaw plaa* (rice noodles with fish balls) – but steer

clear of the really spicy stuff like *yam phrík chíi fáa*.

6 Trek in the hill-tribe region, sleeping in local villages and finding out how people live in this remote corner of northern Thailand.

7 Paddle a kayak into the sea caves of Ao Phang-Nga Marine National Park.

8 Discover beach bliss, lazing under coconut palms and snorkelling over coral reefs at islands like Ko Samet, Ko Samui, Ko Pha-Ngan, Ko Phi-Phi, Ko Lanta and Ko Hai.

9 Listen out for the haunting cry of a gibbon during a dawn walk in the rainforest.

10 Shop in markets for traditional souvenirs like hill-tribe embroidery, Thai silk and shadow puppets.

replicas of Thailand's famous monuments. Further afield, you can catch a train or bus to Kanchanaburi and visit the famous 'Bridge over the River Kwai' and take a dip in the natural pools

fed by the seven-tiered waterfalls of Erawan National Park. To the south, meanwhile, the beachside resort of Hua Hin has calm waters, plenty of restaurants and pony rides on the beach.

Angkor Wat.

Rainforest, reefs and really tall buildings

It may well start as just a vague idea for adding a few days to a stopover in Kuala Lumpur en route to or from Australia. Then it becomes a week once you realize that Peninsular Malaysia actually has a lot going for it in terms of family appeal – whether it's tropical islands like Langkawi or the rainforest reserve of Taman Negara. And then Malaysia plays its trump card – your mind wanders across the South China Sea to the East Malaysian states of Sarawak and Sabah and suddenly you're plotting a full-blown family adventure into the heart of Borneo. And who can blame you? With its headhunting legacy, giant bat-filled caves and endangered orang-utans, northern Borneo ranks as one of the world's most exciting destinations for children and adults alike.

Country highlights

🌊 🐚 🐠 🐢 🐒 🏝 🛶 🐘 🦜

» Allow around 3 hrs to reach Taman Negara or the Cameron Highlands by road from KL.
» In Peninsular Malaysia the risk of malaria is confined to Taman Negara National Park, however malaria is widespread in Sabah and Sarawak on the island of Borneo.

Peninsular perks

Kuala Lumpur One of the world's tallest buildings, the 88 storey, 452-m-high Petronas Twin Towers has a Skybridge with stomach-lurching views of the city. The adjacent KLCC Park has shops, a science centre, children's playground, musical fountain and aquarium. More vertigo moments are available at the top of the KL Tower and from the 60-m-tall Eye on Malaysia big wheel. Back on street level, head to the peaceful Lake Gardens, a 92-ha green oasis with a lake, butterfly park and orchid garden. Upping the tempo, Central Market is a bustling hub for traditional arts and craft – the riverside amphitheatre has regular cultural shows, batik-painting demonstrations and shadow-puppet plays. Nearby is Chinatown where, on Petaling Street, you can browse the stalls and visit the elaborate Chan See Shu Yuen Temple. By far the most popular city excursion, Batu Caves, 15 km north of KL, is a subterranean wonder of ornate Hindu shrines. You'll need to scale 272 steps to reach the main temple cave.

Jungle jollies Over 130 million years in the making, the ancient rainforest of Taman Negara (wildlife.gov.my) is teeming with life. See how many of the national park's 250 bird species you can spot from the canopy walkway, then take a river cruise in search of tapir, elephant and, if you're extremely lucky, leopard and tiger. Other activities available include jungle trekking and caving. South of Taman Negara, the Kuala Gandah Elephant Orphanage (myelephants.org) is a refuge for jumbos that have run out of space elsewhere in Peninsular Malaysia – you can ride them and give them a bath. In the northern state of Kedah, the 950-m-long Tree Top Walk in the Sedim River Recreation Park is the longest in the world, while northern Perak's Kuala Gula Bird Sanctuary is full of feathered friends between September and March when 200,000 migrant birds descend on its mudflats and mangroves. If you have time for only a brief rainforest foray, make your way to the Forest Research Institute of Malaysia. Located just 16 km northwest of KL, the centre has four walking trails and a canopy walk.

Cool retreats Escape the muggy lowlands with a visit to the Cameron Highlands where tea plantations mingle with honey farms. Trekking and birdwatching are popular activities – and useful for building up an appetite for the local ever-so-colonial tradition of tea and scones. Around 90 minutes'

Top: Petronas Towers, Kuala Lumpur. **Above:** Tioman Island. **Below left:** Orchid.

drive to the south of KL, A'Famosa Water World (afamosa.com) has a children's adventure pool, a seven-storey high-speed waterslide, a wave pool and reputedly the longest lazy river ride in the world.

Island idyll Peninsular Malaysia has tropical islands off both its east and west coasts. Langkawi, in the northwest, has arguably the country's most stunning beach – Tanjung Rhu – although there are dozens more in this cluster of 99 islands that will feel like sand made in heaven. Langkawi also has an international airport, modern resorts and plenty of activities and attractions to make family holidays a piece of cake. Don't miss out on a snorkelling excursion to the nearby Pulau Payar Marine Park. The most popular east-coast alternative to Langkawi is Tioman Island which, like lesser-developed Pulau Redang in the far north, is a paradise for scuba-diving and jungle trekking.

Best of Borneo

Visit a longhouse
Where? Skrang River or Batang Ai National Park, Sarawak.
Why? This is the best way to learn about the customs of the Iban, Sarawak's largest indigenous group. You'll find out how a typical community lives under one roof, how rice cultivation underpins their culture and – most intriguing of all – how they once gained a reputation as head-hunters. Spend a night or more in a longhouse and you may be invited to take part in fast-and-furious drumming competitions, adorn feather headdresses for traditional dancing and purchase local handicrafts, such as wooden carvings of hornbills, the sacred bird of the Iban. Just remember to go easy on the *tuak*, the locally brewed and potent rice wine.
How? Leaving Kuching by 4WD, you transfer to motorized longboat for a thrilling ride on the Skrang River. You may need to get out and help push the boat through shallow rapids.

Going underground
Where? Gunung Mulu National Park, Sarawak.
Why? Deer Cave is the world's largest cave passage, 1600 m long by 120 m high (five St Paul's Cathedrals can fit inside) – a fitting backdrop for the nightly exodus of two million wrinkle-lipped bats whose frenzied wingbeats sound like distant surf. Walking inside the cave you crunch over vast domes of bat guano, seething with cockroaches, centipedes and other minibeasts. Lovely.
How? You can fly to Mulu from Miri or take a boat from Kuala Baram via Marudi. Try to get to the viewing platform in front of Deer Cave by 1800 to witness the bat exodus.
Also consider Gomantong Caves in Sabah are famous for their colonies of swiftlets. These tiny birds use saliva to construct their nests – the prized

ingredient for bird's nest soup that is harvested between February and April by locals using a gravity-defying system of rattan ladders, ropes and poles.

Climb a mountain
Where? Mt Kinabalu, Sabah.
Why? At 4101 m, Mt Kinabalu is the tallest mountain between the Himalayas and New Guinea. Kinabalu is also a treat for naturalists. Mist-wrapped and shaggy with moss and lichen, its forests seem other-worldly. This is a place where worms grow to the length of your leg, frogs are as tiny as your fingernail and carnivorous pitcher plants feast on insects. The mountain's slopes run riot with 1200 different orchids, numerous indigenous rhododendrons and the rare, but unforgettable, Rafflesia which produces a single, whiffy bloom measuring nearly a metre across.
How? It's a knee-busting two-day slog to the summit and back. Allow at least five hours after setting out from the national park headquarters to reach Laban Rata, a hut at 3272 m where trekkers spend the night before tackling the summit. Well before dawn the following morning you steal outside and grope your way upwards by torchlight. The forest soon succumbs to the altitude as you scramble across bare slopes of granite using fixed ropes and ladders to scale the steepest sections. The effort is more than worthwhile, however, when you reach the summit in time to witness the remarkable spectacle of Sabah spread beneath you. Having conquered Kinabalu, most trekkers hobble to nearby Poring Hot Springs for a long, revitalizing soak.

Meet the Wild Man of Borneo
Where? Kabili-Sepilok Forest Reserve, Sabah.
Why? Although orang-utans are sometimes glimpsed during boat trips along the Kinabatangan River, the best place to see them is this 5666-ha sanctuary near Sandakan. Sepilok is

renowned for its rehabilitation centre – a kind of hospital and training camp for orang-utans orphaned by hunting or deforestation. Once nursed to health, young orphans literally have to be taught all the skills essential to life in the jungle – everything from swinging to eating. A tedious diet of milk and fruit encourages them to forage in the wild and gradually gain independence.
How? The best time to visit is at 1000 or 1430 when the apes emerge from the forest for their daily ration of bananas and milk placed at feeding platforms.
Also consider Turtle Islands Park, a cluster of islands lying 40 km off the coast near Sandakan, puts the conservation focus not on apes but turtles. The marine reptiles come ashore to nest year-round on Pulau Selingan where it is possible to join rangers in their efforts to safeguard the vulnerable clutches from predators.

Probe the interior
Where? Kinabatangan River, Sabah.
Why? River travel is the classic (and easiest) way to travel into the heart of Borneo (which has largely been cleared for oil-palm plantations). Sabah's longest river flows east from the Crocker Range to spill into the mangrove-fringed Sulu Sea. Its lower reaches pulse through one of Southeast Asia's richest rainforests – a haven for elephants, monkeys, otters and other rare species.
How? You will need to join an organized tour from Sandankan. Some operators, like Uncle Tan Wildlife Adventures (uncletan.com), offer overnight trips, combining boat rides with treks in the forest.
Also consider Some 83 km southwest of Lahad Datu, the 440-sq-km Danum Valley Conservation Area is home to such rarities as the Sumatran rhino, orang-utan and clouded leopard. You can stay at the Borneo Rainforest Lodge, a comfortable eco-resort offering jungle treks, river swimming, night safaris and excursions to nearby logging sites.

Top to bottom: Iban dancer; riverboat; orang-utan; Mt Kinabalu; Gunung Mulu.

Asia essentials

When to go

The best time to visit **Jordan** is during spring or autumn. You'll bake in summer, while winter brings cold winds, rain and even snow. In **Dubai**, blue skies and sunshine are the norm. Not surprisingly, summer's sizzling highs of 45-48°C coincide with the best hotel deals, so be prepared to spend more on accommodation during cooler months. **India**'s climate varies dramatically from north to south, but generally there are three seasons: hot and dry, hot and wet (monsoon) and cool and dry – the latter, most popular, period lasting from November to mid-February. Escape the brutal heat and humidity of May and June by heading for the cooler hill stations (but book well in advance because everyone else will have the same idea). The main monsoon sweeps in from the southwest during June and July, while the northwest monsoon douses the southeast coast during October and November. Peak season in south India is Christmas and New Year. Dodge the monsoons by visiting **Sri Lanka** either between December and late April or during August. The ideal months to visit **Nepal** are October and November when the air has been washed clean by the monsoon, the countryside is green and the weather is balmy. December and January are also good, but be prepared for snow and frigid temperatures on treks in the Himalayas. **China** is best visited during spring or autumn. Winters can be bitter in the northeast, while summers in the south are hot and humid. In **Hong Kong**, most rain falls between May and September. **Thailand**, **Malaysia** and **Singapore** are hot and humid all year, with fairly constant annual temperatures of around 24-31°C. Thailand's beaches are at their best during February and March, with the monsoon hitting between May and October. Try to avoid peninsular Malaysia's east coast in November and December when the monsoon brings winds and tropical downpours. The rainy season occurs on the west coast during April and May and again from October to November.

Getting there

Asia's major airline hubs at Dubai, Mumbai, Colombo, Bangkok, Kuala Lumpur, Singapore, Jakarta and Hong Kong are like giant stepping stones across the continent. National carriers serve numerous destinations throughout Europe, Africa, Australasia and North America, either as direct flights or through codeshare agreements with partner airlines. For example, Emirates (emirates.com) has flights from Dubai to Houston, New York, London, Paris, Sydney, Auckland and over 80 other destinations worldwide, while Singapore Airlines (singaporeair.com) serves 64 cities, including New York, Los Angeles and London. Other national carriers include Air China (air-china.co.uk), Air India (airindia.com), Gulf Air (gulfair.com), Malaysia Airlines (malaysiaairlines.com), Royal Jordanian (rja.com.jo), Sri Lankan Airlines (srilankan.aero) and Thai Airways (thaiairways.com). For a list of other international carriers serving the region, see page 45. Fares vary enormously, so it's always worth shopping around for the best online deals. As a rough guide to good-value, internet-based fares, expect to pay from around £250 for a return London-Dubai flight, £350 London-Hong Kong, £400 London-Beijing and £450 London-Bangkok.

Fact file

	GMT	Language	Money	Code	Tourist info
Jordan	+2	Arabic	Jordanian Dinar (£1 = JD1.4)	+962	visitjordan.com
Dubai	+4	Arabic	UAE dirham (£1 = AED7.3)	+971	dubaitourism.ae
India	+5½	Hindi	Indian rupee (£1 = R45.3)	+91	incredibleindia.org
Sri Lanka	+6	Sinhala and Tamil	Sri Lankan rupee (£1 = R109.85)	+94	srilankatourism.org
Nepal	+6	Nepali	Nepalese rupee (£1 = R128)	+977	welcomenepal.com
China	+8	Mandarin	Chinese yuan renminbi (£1 = Y15)	+86	cnto.org
Hong Kong	+8	Cantonese and English	Hong Kong dollar (£1 = HK$15.5)	+852	discoverhongkong.com
Singapore	+8	Malay, Chinese, Tamil and English	Singapore dollar (£1 = S$3)	+65	visitsingapore.com
Thailand	+7	Thai	Thai baht (£1 = B65)	+66	tourismthailand.org
Malaysia	+8	Malay	Malaysian ringgit (£1 = R7)	+60	tourism.gov.my

How much for a Big Mac?

USA US$3.22
UK US$3.90
Hong Kong US$1.54
Malaysia US$1.57
Sri Lanka US$1.75
Thailand US$1.78
Singapore US$2.34
Dubai US$2.72

Above: Outside a palace in Rajasthan. **Right:** Borneo rainforest lodge.

Getting around

Jordan has a good road network plied by modern, air-conditioned coaches, but you might also want to consider renting a car. All the international names are present, along with independent companies like Reliable (reliable.com.jo) which has weekly rates starting from around £110, including unlimited mileage.

Taxis are the easiest way of getting around in **Dubai**. Look out for the cream-coloured metered cabs from the Dubai Transport Corporation which charge around £0.40 for pick-up, plus £0.15 per kilometre. You can also hire a taxi for a 12-hour period for a fixed fee of around £70.

In **India**, the safest, least stressful way to travel independently is to hire a car with a driver/guide and use sleeper trains for longer journeys. Indian Railways (indianrail.gov.in) offers an extensive and efficient service throughout the country. For a six-hour trip from Delhi to Jaipur, allow around £12 for a ticket in a first-class carriage with air conditioning. Trains are far more preferable to buses in India, but if you need to keep internal travel times to a minimum, there are several domestic airlines, including Indian Airlines (indian-airlines.nic.in), Jagson Airways (jagsonairline.com) and Jet Airways (jetairways.com). India's growing bevy of budget airlines includes Air Deccan (flyairdeccan.net) and Spice Jet (spicejet.com).

Although some of the main routes are busy and occasionally hair-raising, road travel is still the best way to get around in **Sri Lanka**. Hiring a vehicle with a driver is also excellent value.

Domestic flights in **Nepal** are operated by several airlines, including Buddha Air (buddhaair.com), Royal Nepal Airlines (royalnepal-airlines.com) and Yeti Airlines (yetiairlines.com). Expect to pay from around £70 return for the 30-minute flight between Kathmandu and Pokhara – compared to just £8 return for the six-hour bus ride.

To meet growing numbers of tourists, **China** has modernized its domestic air and rail systems. Allow around £100 for a one-way airfare from Xi'an to Guilin in July. China Train Ticket (china-train-ticket.com) provides an online rail reservation system with popular routes such as Beijing to Xi'an costing around £65 for a four-berth sleeper.

Travelling around **Hong Kong** is a cinch with a choice of trains, buses, trams, taxis and ferries. The MTR (mtr.com.hk) shifts 2.5 million people every weekday. It costs just HK$26 for a 32-minute, one-way journey from Central to Disneyland Hong Kong. A ride on the Star Ferry (starferry.com.hk) from Central to Tsim Sha Tsui costs HK$2.20. For services to the Outlying Islands, try First Ferry (nwff.com.hk). On most public transport in Hong Kong children aged 12 and under receive a 50% discount.

's transport infrastructure is similarly efficient, thanks to taxis, buses and the MRT (smrt.com.sg). The SIA Hop-on Bus (siahopon.asiaone.com.sg) offers an air-conditioned tourist service to several of the city's most popular areas, including Orchard Road, Chinatown and Sentosa.

In **Thailand**, local airlines include Bangkok Airways (bangkokair.com). The State Railway of Thailand (railway.co.th) has first-class fares from Bangkok to Chiang Mai from around £10. In the capital, you can get around using the Bangkok Metro (bangkokmetro.co.th), metered taxis, river taxis or *tuk-tuks* (where you need to settle the fare before getting in).

Malaysia has an excellent transport system, with air-conditioned coaches and trains connecting Kuala Lumpur with all main towns. Driving in Malaysia is easy and safe as long as you steer clear of the capital. Car rental starts from around £25-30 per day.

Accommodation

A good starting point for finding accommodation in Asia is to browse the tourist boards' online directories (see Fact file). In **Jordan**, Petra has dozens of hotels, including the Mövenpick (movenpick-petra.com) with doubles from around £75. You

Tour operators

In the UK

Abercrombie & Kent
abercrombiekent.com

The Adventure Company
adventurecompany.co.uk

Cox & Kings
coxandkings.co.uk

Exodus exodus.co.uk

Explore Worldwide
explore.co.uk

Families Worldwide
familiesworldwide.co.uk

Himalayan Kingdoms
himalayankingdoms.com

The Imaginative Traveller
imaginative-traveller.com

Jetlife Asia World
jetlife.co.uk

KE Adventure Travel
keadventure.com

Kumuka kumuka.com

Kuoni kuoni.co.uk

On the Go Tours
onthegotours.com

Peregrine Adventures
peregrineadventures.com

Powder Byrne
powderbyrne.co.uk

Reef & Rainforest Tours
familytours.co.uk

Somak somak.co.uk

TransIndus
transindus.co.uk

Tribes Travel tribes.co.uk

Wildlife Worldwide
wildlifeworldwide.com

In the USA

Journeys International
journeys-intl.com

The Backroads
backroads.com

Thomson Family Adventures
familyadventures.com

treks can be anything from fully supported camping to local teahouses and more upmarket lodges. Temple Tiger Lodge (catmando.com) in Chitwan National Park has 33 en suite villas, each one raised on stilts with views across the grasslands. **China**'s main tourist centres offer a wide range of accommodation to suit all budgets. For a spot of indulgence, check out the Peninsula Beijing (beijing.peninsula.com) which has rooms from around £180 and is ideally located near the Forbidden City. Also consider the Kerry Centre Hotel (shangri-la.com). A good mid-range bet in **Hong Kong**'s Kowloon district, the BP International (bpih.com.hk) has family rooms from around £80. Family suites at Salisbury YMCA (ymcahk.org.hk) are also excellent value. Top family picks in **Singapore** include Costa Sands Resort Downtown East (costasands.com.sg) which kids will be thrilled to discover is located next to the Escape Theme Park and Wild Wild Wet. Rasa Sentosa Resort (shangri-la.com) is Singapore's only beachfront hotel, while serviced apartments in the Orchard Road area include Lotus (lotus-sanctuary.com.sg) and Somerset Compass (somersetcompass.com). **Thailand** and **Malaysia** have a plethora of international city hotels and beach resorts, as well as apartments and guesthouses. In Bangkok, the Bel-Aire Princess (bel-aireprincess.com) is less pricey than other city hotels, yet has a central location, swimming pool and Thai cookery school. In Kuala Lumpur, try the Hotel Equatorial (equatorial.com); in Langkawi, splash out on the Sheraton Beach Resort (sheraton.com) which has family rooms and a kids' club.

Food and drink

For a traditional meal in **Jordan**, expect appetizers like hummous, followed by *mansaf* (stewed lamb, rice and yoghurt) and a selection of syrup-drenched pastries. **Dubai** offers a cosmopolitan range of cuisine, from Indian and Thai to Filipino, Lebanese and Persian. Fast-food chains are also popular, but if you want to sample truly authentic Emirati cuisine head to the souks where you will find everything from dates to camel meat. Concocted from stir-fried *masalas* of onion, garlic and freshly ground spices, authentic **Indian** curries (with meat or vegetables) are usually served with rice and flat breads. Yoghurt-based *lassi* drinks are a good way to cool the taste buds of adventurous kids, but most young children will find curries too spicy. There are usually blander alternatives on the menu and, of course, in popular tourist locations you will find a choice of eateries. Rice and curry (often made with fish and coconut milk) feature predominantly in **Sri Lanka**, but beach hotels will usually offer a range of other dishes as well. The staple meal in **Nepal** is *dal-bhat* (steamed rice with lentil soup), accompanied by curried vegetables and pickles. *Momos* (stuffed dumplings) and *rotis* (flat breads) are also popular, however in places like Kathmandu and Pokhara you will also find everything from

can stay at a Bedouin camp in Wadi Rum from around £40 per night including transport, dinner and breakfast. **Dubai**'s outlandish accommodation is legendary, with pop stars and Premier League footballers snatching up villas on the offshore Palm and World developments. For the rest of us there are excellent city hotels and beach resorts, many with kids' clubs, such as Le Royal Meridien (leroyalmeridien-dubai.com) and the Jumeirah Beach Hotel (jumeirahbeachhotel.com). Out of town, try the Bab Al Shams Desert Resort (jumeirahbabalshams.com). In **India**, accommodation ranges from international city hotels to national park rest camps. Delhi's InterContinental The Grand (thegrandhotels.net) has a swimming pool and is conveniently located on Connaught Square. The Jaypee Palace (jaypeehotels.com) is a comfortable hotel in Agra with doubles from around £100, while in Bharatpur, Laxmi Vilas Palace Hotel (laxmivilas.com) provides a wonderful opportunity for sleeping in a converted palace. For a spot of luxury on the Goa coast, the Park Hyatt Resort (goa.park.hyatt.com) has an Ayurvedic spa for the grown-ups and a huge pool with waterslides for the kids. **Sri Lanka** has an excellent range of family-friendly accommodation. In Kandy, try the Chaaya Citadel (chaayahotels.com) which has interconnecting rooms and a children's pool. A good base for exploring the Cultural Triangle, Hotel Sigiriya (serendibleisure.com) organizes children's activities, such as birdwatchinwg walks and visits to local villages. Its sister property, Club Hotel Dolphin, is located on the coast at Waikkal and boasts the largest swimming pool in Sri Lanka. In **Nepal**, four- or five-star hotels in Kathmandu and Pokhara usually have pools, while accommodation on

Above: Houseboat on the Kerala Backwaters. **Left and below:** Don't be shy of sampling the region's delicious food and drink.

burgers to pizzas. **China** has more than enough variety in its cuisine to satisfy even the most pernickety feeder – from fried rice and steamed chicken to soups and sweet-and-sour dishes. In **Thailand** and **Malaysia**, meanwhile, traditional food consists of delicious seafood, satays, coconut-based curries, noodles and boiled rice in banana leaves. Kids will love coconut milk straight from the nut or sugarcane juice squeezed fresh from the cane.

Health and safety

Malaria affects large areas of Asia, so you need to discuss malaria prevention with your doctor well before you travel. Malaria-free areas include Jordan, Dubai, Singapore and Hong Kong. In India, malaria precautions are essential anywhere below 2000 m. Malaria exists throughout Sri Lanka except in the districts of Colombo, Galle, Kalutra, Matar and Nuwara Eliya in the southwest of the country. In Nepal, most malaria occurs in the low-lying plains of 'terai' districts. Urban and densely populated areas of China are normally malaria-free with the risk of serious malaria confined mainly to Hainan, Yunnan province and occasionally Guangxi province. Malaria may also occur in isolated areas near the Yangtze and Yellow rivers. In Thailand, malaria is a threat year-round, but is largely restricted to rural and forested areas near the borders with Myanmar, Laos and Cambodia. The risk is minimal in cities such as Bangkok and Chiang Mai, or in coastal resorts like Phuket. In peninsular Malaysia, malaria is only a significant threat in Taman Negara National Park. However, it affects all of Sabah and Sarawak in East Malaysia.

Before visiting Asia you should plan an appropriate course of vaccinations, which may include hepatitis A, typhoid and yellow fever. See page 54 for information on malaria prevention and routine inoculations.

Be extremely wary of drinking tap water anywhere in Asia, with the exception of modern cities like Dubai, Hong Kong and Singapore. Either boil it beforehand or buy bottled water from a reputable source. To avoid diarrhoea maintain strict hygiene by always having a pack of antibacterial wet wipes to clean hands before eating etc. It's also a good idea to bring along some oral rehydration salts should you or your children suffer a bout of gastrointestinal illness.

One of the biggest concerns with taking babies or toddlers to crowded, traffic-congested cities in Asia (or anywhere in the world for that matter) is that their buggy puts them at exhaust-pipe level – a backpack-style child carrier or papoose is a good way to get them above the fumes. The traffic itself can be chaotic and random, so take particular care when crossing streets. Getting separated is another potential worry, so make sure that your kids wear wristbands with the address and phone number of your hotel written in the local language. Finally, never let your children approach street dogs – a bite may carry a very high risk of rabies in some countries.

Other health precautions you need to take in Asia include avoiding overexposure to sun and heat and taking a sensible approach to trekking at high altitude with children. See pages 54-57 for further information.

Easy riders – learning to surf on the
Coromandel Peninsula, North Island.

Australia and New Zealand

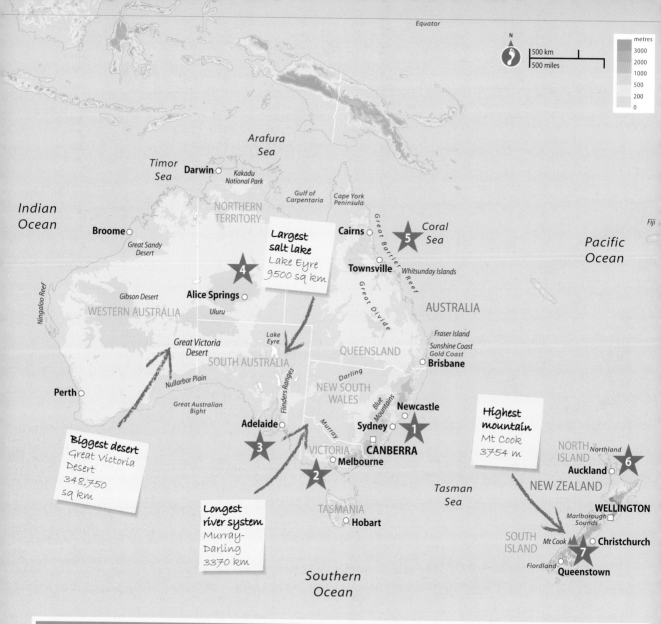

Equator

N

500 km
500 miles

metres
3000
2000
1000
500
200
0

Indian Ocean

Arafura Sea

Timor Sea

Darwin ○ *Kakadu National Park*

Gulf of Carpentaria

Cape York Peninsula

NORTHERN TERRITORY

Broome ○

Great Sandy Desert

Largest salt lake
Lake Eyre
9500 sq km

Cairns ○

5

Coral Sea

Fiji

Pacific Ocean

Townsville ●

Whitsunday Islands

4

Gibson Desert

Alice Springs ○

Uluru

WESTERN AUSTRALIA

Ningaloo Reef

Great Victoria Desert

Lake Eyre

SOUTH AUSTRALIA

AUSTRALIA

QUEENSLAND

Great Divide

Fraser Island
Sunshine Coast
Gold Coast
Brisbane ●

Darling

NEW SOUTH WALES

Perth ○

Nullarbor Plain

Great Australian Bight

Flinders Ranges

Murray

Blue Mountains

Newcastle ●

1

Sydney ○

Highest mountain
Mt Cook
3754 m

NORTH ISLAND *Northland*

6

Adelaide ○

3

CANBERRA □

Auckland ○

Biggest desert
Great Victoria Desert
348,750 sq km

2

VICTORIA

Melbourne ○

NEW ZEALAND

Tasman Sea

WELLINGTON □

Marlborough Sounds

Longest river system
Murray-Darling
3370 km

TASMANIA

Hobart ○

SOUTH ISLAND

Mt Cook

7

○ Christchurch

Fiordland

Queenstown ●

Southern Ocean

○ Did you know?

- The Maori name for Hawkes Bay, *Taumatawhakatangihangakoauauotamateaturipukakapimaungahoronukupokaiwhenuaakitanarahu*, reputedly translates as "the place where Tamatea, the man with big knees, who slid, climbed and swallowed mountains, played his flute to his loved one".
- Anna Creek Station in South Australia is the world's largest cattle station, which at around 34,000 sq km covers an area roughly the size of Belgium.
- The fact that kangaroos break wind considerably less than cows or sheep has intrigued scientists studying the effects of methane gas on global warming.
- According to Maori lore, when the goddess of the underworld, Tuhinenuitepo, saw how beautiful Fiordland was she became so concerned that people would want to live there forever that she introduced the sandfly to remind them of their mortality.

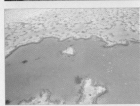

Introduction

It's a long, long way to go, but don't ever let distance or jet lag stand in the way of two of the world's best family holiday destinations. The beaches alone more than justify the long haul to Australia and New Zealand – not that you're going to fly down under just to build sandcastles and splash in the sea. This is a region ripe for adventure, whether you take tots on a motorhome odyssey around South Island or tempt teens with a taste of Aussie surf culture. From camping in the outback and snorkelling on the Great Barrier Reef to swimming with dolphins and searching for Mordor, kids will relish the non-stop action. Along the way, they'll pick up nuggets of Aboriginal and Maori lore, encounter some of the world's most endearing and fascinating wildlife and witness scenery ranging from glaciated peaks to tropical rainforest. Going hand in hand with this big bundle of fun is the constant reassurance that everything is supremely family-friendly, easy-going and affordable. But first, you just need to get there.

❝❞ *Simply grappling with the sheer distance involved in travelling to New Zealand and Australia fired the imagination of our five-year-old twins. Judging by the looks on their faces it was almost as if they had become privy to some great secret when we explained that when they're awake people in Australia are asleep.*

Will

Australia & New Zealand rating

Wow factor
★★★★★

Worry factor
★★

Value for money
★★★

Keeping teacher happy
★★★★★

Family accommodation
★★★★★

Babies & toddlers
★★★

Teenagers
★★★★★

Kids' top 10: *Lord of the Rings* film locations

1 Hobbiton Sam and Frodo's home, the Shire, was filmed near Matamata. Take a guided tour to Bag End with Hobbiton Tours (hobbitontours.com).

2 Mordor The volcano Mt Ruapehu in Tongariro National Park was just the place for Sauron to plot his domination over Middle Earth.

3 Dimholt Road Closed to all but the Army of the Dead and the heir of Isildur, this haunted passageway was filmed at the Putangirua Pinnacles near Martinborough.

4 Pelennor Fields All the wide shots for the epic Battle of Pelennor Fields were filmed near Twizel. Guided tours with local Orcs and Rohirrim are available.

5 Rivendell A popular spot for picnics, walking and swimming, Kaitoke Regional Park in the Tararua Ranges was the site of Elrond's tranquil forest refuge.

6 Ford of Bruinen The shallow river where Arwen narrowly escaped the Nazgûl is 200 m upstream from Arrowtown.

7 Rohan The rolling hills of the Ida Valley near remote Poolburn Reservoir in Central Otago were used to portray the realm of the Riddermark.

8 Lothlórien Queenstown's Dart River Safaris and Dart Stables (see box opposite) can transport you into Galadriel's enchanted forest.

9 Dimrill Dale When the Fellowship escaped from the Mines of Moria they emerged on the surreal lunar-like slopes of Mt Owen in Kahurangi National Park.

10 Fanghorn Forest Look carefully and you may spot an Ent in the dense forests around Marova Lakes, near Te Anau.

Deadliest animals

Box jellyfish 80-cm long tentacles; sting can kill a human within minutes.

Saltwater crocodile World's largest reptile, up to 7 m in length.

Blue ring octopus Only the size of a golf ball, but venom is lethal.

Books to read

One Woolly Wombat, Kane/Miller, 1987
A superbly illustrated first counting book using zany Australian animal characters, from one woolly wombat to 14 slick seals. Ages 0-5

Land of the Long White Cloud, Chrysalis Children's Books, 1997
Opera singer Kiri Te Kanawa retells the intriguing folk-histories of her people, the Maori of New Zealand, in this collection of 19 short stories. Beautiful watercolour illustrations add to the vibrancy of the tales. Ages 6+

Coral Reef Puzzletastics, Top That Publishing, 2005
A great two-in-one book and travel toy – a beginner's guide to life on a coral reef and a challenging nine-piece puzzle that's much harder than it looks and will keep children (and adults) bemused for hours. Ages 7+

The Drovers Road Collection, Bethlehem Budget Books, 2003
Three adventure stories seen through the eyes of a child as she grows up on a sheep station in New Zealand during the 1920s and 1930s paint a vivid portrait of Maori culture and rural life. Ages 7+

Jack Stalwart: The Search for the Sunken Treasure, Red Fox, 2006
Off the coast of Australia, a diver has vanished along with treasure from the wreck of HMS Pandora. Can Secret Agent Jack Stalwart find the diver and defeat a band of pirates before they escape with the treasure? Ages 7+

Australia, the People, Crabtree Publishing, 2002
Discover all things Australian from the Aboriginal Dreamtime to Aussie rules football and from surfing to the Flying Doctor Service. Ages 8+

Down Under, Down Under: Diving Adventures on the Great Barrier Reef, Prentice Hall, 1989
A 12-year-old girl recounts her experiences on the Great Barrier Reef, exploring the wreck of a ghost ship and encountering sharks, sea snakes and giant clams. Ages 8+

🔍 How to throw a boomerang

➤ Find a large grassy area, clear of trees, lamp posts and crystal vases.

➤ Hold the end of your boomerang between thumb and forefinger, making sure the curved side faces towards you.

➤ Scatter some leaves, noting which way the wind blows them. Face directly into the wind, then turn about 60 degrees to your right. This is the direction you should throw your boomerang.

➤ Always throw overhand, never side-arm. Snap your wrist at the end of the throw to create spin.

➤ Practise varying the degree of spin and the strength and direction of throw until your boomerang returns.

➤ Catch a returning boomerang by 'clapping' it between your hands.

➤ Remember, a miss-thrown boomerang can be dangerous. Always be ready to shout a warning to others – or to duck.

Taste of Australia: bush tucker

Honey ants Sweet, sugar-packed treats, these insects store honeydew in their swollen abdomens. But you need to know where to look for their underground nests.

Witchetty grubs These large beetle larvae are found in the stems and trunks of certain wattle bushes. They can be eaten raw, made into soup or barbecued with or without their heads. Delicious with peanut sauce – just like chicken satay.

Macadamia nuts These native Australian nuts are scrummy on their own, but taste even better chopped into pieces and smothered with freshly made hot toffee. Allow to cool and harden, then smash into pieces with a hammer.

Warning! Many wild foods are unsafe to eat. If in doubt, leave well alone.

Kids' top 20: adventures in Queenstown

12 Mile Delta Canyoning (xiimile.co.nz) Abseil down waterfalls, jump into rock pools and slide down natural waterchutes (min age 10).

Dart River Safaris (dartriver.co.nz) Jet-boat ride along the Dart River deep into the heart of Mt Aspiring National Park (min age 3).

Dart Stables (dartstables.com) 1½-hour horse ride through the golden woods of Lothlórien, with views over Isengard (min age depends on riding experience).

Family Adventures (familyadventures.co.nz) Grade II whitewater rafting on the Shotover River using either rafts or kayaks (min age 3-9).

Fly by Wire (flybywire-queenstown.co.nz) High-speed flight in a 'tethered' plane reaching speeds of more than 170 kph (min age 12).

Frogz (frogz.co.nz) Bodyboarding on Grade III+ rapids on the Kawarau River (min age 12).

Goldfields Mining Centre (goldfieldsmining.co.nz) Visit a gold-mining ghost town and try your hand at panning for gold in Kawarau Gorge.

Kawarau Bridge Bungy (bungy.co.nz) The original 43-m bungy (min age 10).

Kawarau Jet (kjet.co.nz) Jet-boat ride from Queenstown across Lake Wakatipu and along the Shotover River.

Kingston Flyer (kingstonflyer.co.nz) Steam-train journey along 14 km of countryside between Kingston and Fairlight.

Nevis Snowmobile Adventures (snowmobilenz.com) 12-minute helicopter flight, followed by 20-km snowmobile ride in Old Woman Ranges (min age 6).

Nomad Safaris 4WD Tours (nomadsafaris.co.nz) Backcountry adventure to gold-mining ghost towns.

Off-Road Adventures (offroad.co.nz) Quad-bike tours tailored to suit children of different ages, plus 4WD *Lord of the Rings* tours (min age 7).

Paraflights (paraflights.co.nz) Parasailing trips above Lake Wakatipu reaching heights of over 180 m (min age 2).

Sail Queenstown (sailqueenstown.co.nz) Exhilarating cruises on Lake Wakatipu aboard an America's Cup racing yacht (min age 5).

Serious Fun Riversurfing (riversurfing.co.nz) Whitewater bodyboarding on the Kawarau River (min age 8).

Shotover Stables (shotoverstables.net) Gentle horseriding along the banks of the Shotover River (min age 4).

Shotover Jet (shotoverjet.com) Thrilling jet-boat ride through the narrow canyons of the Shotover River (min age 3).

Skyline Gondola & Luge (skyline.co.nz) Take the gondola up Bob's Peak and ride either the Scenic or Advanced luge tracks (min age 3).

TSS Earnslaw (realjourneys.co.nz) Cruise on a vintage steamship to Walter Peak Farm.

Flying the family to Australia or New Zealand will be expensive. And there may well be moments on that long haul across Asia or the Pacific when boredom and jet lag transform your children into something quite unpleasant. And there may even be times when you gaze wistfully out of the aircraft window and yearn to be back in the 1980s – a footloose and child-free backpacker on your first global odyssey. But get a grip. This could well be the start of the most exciting, bonding, eye-opening family adventure you've ever had.

Babies (0-18 months)

They might bawl occasionally, but eventually they'll sleep – and at least they can't move around. It's when babies develop an insatiable desire to crawl that those flights down under are going to seem like the longest 20 hours of your life. Should you consider a stopover in somewhere like Singapore or Tahiti? You may well be desperate to escape the confines of the plane and the mutterings from fellow passengers. However, do you really want to go through the rigmarole of immigration and check-in twice before reaching Australia or New Zealand? And is it worth subjecting your infant to a double dose of jet lag, moving on to a new time zone just as he or she is starting to adapt to Asia or South Pacific time? A lot will depend on the stopovers themselves – and let's face it, they are all pretty irresistible destinations. But whatever route you take to reach Australia or New Zealand, and however gruelling the journey may be, you can be confident that once down under travel with babies is about as stress-free as it gets. You'll find all the gear, food and supplies you need are readily available (so you can travel light and buy stuff out there). The locals are friendly and laid-back, getting around with a buggy is generally hassle-free, and the beaches are clean and safe – although you do need to be extra-vigilant about sun protection.

Toddlers/pre-school (18 months-4 years)

A flight to the Antipodes with children of this age requires a deep breath, infinite patience and a daypack stuffed with toys, colouring books and anything else likely to help pass the time. It also makes a difference if you choose an airline that's as toddler-friendly as possible (see page 23) and try to go for a minimum of three weeks (you'll probably need a few days just to recover from the flight). A motorhome touring holiday suits this age group perfectly. You can get them used to one bed (rather than hopping between a succession of hotels) and you can prepare meals they like, when they like. Another great option is a city-based holiday, staying in aparthotels with fully equipped kitchens. Just about every major city in Australia and New Zealand is close to a spectacular coastline, so when you're not visiting the aquariums, museums, zoos, parks and other city attractions you can easily escape for a day on the

Above right: Enjoying the beaches of New Zealand's North Island.
Above left: Leave only footprints on Queensland's Whitsunday Islands; slip on some fins for a snorkel on the Great Barrier Reef.

beach. If your idea of a holiday is to have everything laid on for you, choose a child-friendly resort, like Hamilton Island in Queensland.

Kids/school age (4-12 years)

Whereas tots and toddlers are too young for many of the more exciting adventures down under, by the time kids reach school age they'll be chafing at the bit to try everything from jet-boating to bodyboarding. In New Zealand, those four magic words – *Lord of the Rings* – will have them double-taking every gnarled tree and snowy peak, while Aboriginal and Maori-led tours will open their eyes to fascinating indigenous cultures. Everywhere you go, the guides are outstanding – whether you're learning to pinpoint the Southern Cross, track wildlife in the outback, decipher Aboriginal art or surf on Bondi Beach. The get-up-and-go mentality of the Aussies and Kiwis is infectious, so fill your itinerary with as much as possible, from cuddling koalas to paddling kayaks. After all, you can always relax on the long flight home.

Teenagers (13 years+)

Bring it on! Australia and New Zealand are 'ripa' (Australian slang for 'great' or 'fantastic') for teenagers. The outdoor life, the sporting culture, the adrenaline activities, the trendy cities… it all adds up to one seriously cool holiday. Although pretty much anywhere will meet with their approval, a two- or three-centre trip is often the best way to go. If your mind is set on New Zealand, consider splitting your time between Auckland (for city buzz), the Coromandel Peninsula (for

Below: Meet friendly wildlife like the crimson rosella.
Bottom: Try your hand at Aboriginal rock art painting.
Far right: A flying fox, sea kayaking in Fiji and a koala.

Telling tales...

When I'm in Australia for the Ashes, whatever happens with the cricket the best part for me is when the family get on the plane and come and join me. It might only be for three or four weeks, but there is a lot you can cram into your time down under – once you've got over the jet lag. Alex (13) and Sammi (10) loved Bondi – particularly the surf, the buzzy restaurants and the shops. Next we headed for Melbourne with its great restaurants and yet more shops! Imagine the contest: it's a hot Saturday prior to New Year and I'm thinking, let's go to Black Rock Beach, half an hour out of town, and enjoy the sun. But I'm outnumbered by three girls who want to check out the sales on Chapel Street. Sorry, did I say contest? We got to the beach at about 4.30 that afternoon. Back in Sydney we stayed in the city close to the harbour and the Botanical Gardens which are full of the most gorgeous cockatoos and enormous fruit bats. Time ran out all too quickly and the girls were making notes of the things they would have to do next time. One day we might take them on the train from east to west, a trip I once made from Adelaide to Kalgoorlie. It is just mind-boggling how much red earth one can see in one day …

David Gower, former England cricket captain

surfing) and Queenstown (for just about every daredevil pursuit teens could imagine – no matter how warped their minds). In Australia, combine Sydney with the coast of northern New South Wales or Queensland for the best of city chic and beach bliss.

Special needs
Several operators in Australia offer tours for travellers with special needs, including Wheelie Easy (wheelieeasy.com.au), Wheelchairs To Go (wheelchairs.sydney.net) and Wheelchair Tours Australia (wheeltours.com.au). In New Zealand, try Accessible Kiwi Tours (toursnz.com), Rest New Zealand Tours (restnztours.co.nz) and Ucan Tours (ucantours.com). Based in Auckland, Accessible Motorhomes (accessiblemotorhomes. co.nz) provides vehicles with wheelchair lifts, while Weka (weka.net.nz) offers general information and advice for people with disabilities.

Single parents
Holidays with Kids (holidayswithkids.com.au) has an excellent section on single-parent travel in Australia and beyond – you can even subscribe to a special newsletter for single parents. Also try Australian Camp Connect (campconnect.org.au), Dads 'n' Kids (nor.com.au), Kids Holidays Online (kidsholidaysonline.com.au) and Travel with Kidz (mostravel.com.au/kidz).

❓ What about the South Pacific?
Perfect for a few days' stopover en route to New Zealand and Australia, **Fiji** (bulafiji.com) has no shortage of all-inclusive resorts and many, like Castaway Island (castawayisland.com), have kids' clubs. For exclusive pampering, splash out on Dolphin Island (dolphinislandfiji.co.nz). For something more adventurous, sign up for a week's sea kayaking with Tamarillo (tamarillo.co.nz) which offers special family departures featuring school visits and snorkelling tuition. Another great slice of jet-lag purging, family-friendly paradise can be found in **French Polynesia** (tahiti-tourisme.com), courtesy of sensational resorts like Beachcomber InterContinental

(ichotelsgroup.com) and Le Méridien Bora Bora (starwoodhotels.com). The best way to dovetail the South Pacific into your itinerary down under is to arrange everything through a specialist operator like Bridge & Wickers (bridgeandwickers.co.uk).

🐨 Places to cuddle a koala
Sydney Koala Park Sanctuary (koalapark sanctuary.com.au) **Brisbane** Lone Pine Koala Sanctuary (koala.net) **Cairns** Kuranda Koala Gardens (koala gardens.com)

❝❞ The koala was very cuddly and a little bit scratchy and her name was Phoebe.
Joe Gray (age six)

A perfect state to find

Lots of cities claim to be great for kids – and Sydney is no exception. In fact, it could well come out on top of the pile. Not only does it have that instant 'wow' factor, courtesy of its stunning harbour, but it also boasts a bewildering range of attractions, from bridge climbs to walk-through aquariums. Bright, clean, sunny and fun, Sydney doesn't simply have suburbs it has suburbs with surfing beaches. Hop on a train and within a couple of hours you could be gazing across the Blue Mountains. Head north or south and the coast unfurls in a dreamy-eyed succession of bays, coves and World-Heritage listed national parks – each one oozing with the promise of adventure.

Top: The Opera House and Coathanger, with the historic Rocks district in the foreground.
Above: See the sights from waterlevel on a ferry.

Sydney

🎢 🐨 ⛴ 👥 🎭 🏛 🚁

→ The Sydney Pass (sydneypass.info) provides unlimited travel on the hop-on, hop-off Sydney and Bondi Explorer buses, the Sydney Ferries network and CityRail trains.
→ Harbour tours are offered by Captain Cook Cruises (captaincook.com.au) and (for added adrenaline) Oz Jet Boating (ozjetboating.com).
→ For further information, log on to sydney.com.au.

Two-day action plan

Day 1 Start with a cruise. It's the best introduction to one of the world's most spectacular natural harbours. Tour boats depart regularly from Circular Quay, passing classic sights like the Sydney Opera House and Harbour Bridge. Disembark at Darling Harbour (darlingharbour.com) – home to dozens of shops, eating places and an IMAX cinema, as well as several leading family attractions. Pick of the bunch is the Sydney Aquarium (sydneyaquarium. com.au) where kids' favourites include the fairy penguins and duck-billed platypus. Tunnels get you on intimate terms with large sharks and rays and also delve beneath a wonderful seal sanctuary where you can watch fur seals and sea lions whizzing past. For a double whammy of Aussie wildlife, buy a combo ticket that includes entry to both the aquarium and Sydney Wildlife World (sydneywildlifeworld.com.au), a breathtaking biome inhabited by wallabies, parrots, koalas, frilled lizards and other native species. If, however,

you prefer warships to wombats, head for the Australian National Maritime Museum (anmm.gov.au), an indoor/outdoor nautical feast that includes a replica of Captain Cook's *Endeavour* and the destroyer, *HMAS Vampire*. Hands-on science fun at the Powerhouse Museum (powerhousemuseum.com) is another option.

Day 2 Time to raise the stakes. If your kids are aged 10 or over, test their steel (and yours) on a Harbour Bridge Climb (bridgeclimb.com) where a clamber on the Coathanger will get you 134 m above the harbour for the ultimate Sydney photo opportunity. Back at ground level, bag some local souvenirs in the weekend craft market at The Rocks (a good spot for lunch) before hopping on a ferry from Circular Quay for the 12-minute ride to Taronga Zoo (zoo.nsw.gov.au). Star species include the orang-utan, snow leopard, komodo dragon and leopard seal. If, however, you've peaked on wildlife from day one, head instead to Luna Park (lunapark sydney.com) for some traditional fairground fun. For a different twist to day two, start by getting your city views from the 305-m AMP Centrepoint Tower before taking a virtual journey across Australia with Oztrek (sydneytower oztrek.com.au). Next, stroll through Hyde Park to the Australian Museum (austmus.gov.au) – the nation's showcase for natural history where under-fives can explore their own mini-museum while older kids grapple with bugs and bones in the Search and

Discover section. Round off the day spotting fruit bats in the Royal Botanic Gardens (rbgsyd.nsw.gov.au).

Best days out The beach has got to be top of your list. Sydney has 37 of them, but Manly (manlytourism.com.au) is the most popular. Easily reached by ferry from Circular Quay, it has all the tourist trappings of a seaside holiday resort, including a lively waterfront fringed with cafés, restaurants, souvenir and surf shops and, of course, some gorgeous sandy beaches. If you didn't get a chance to visit Sydney Aquarium, catch the rays at Manly's Oceanworld (oceanworld.com.au) where you can also dive with sharks if you're over 14. For an equally active day out, Sydney Olympic Park (sydneyolympicpark. com.au) has loads to keep kids happy. Hire a bike and cycle one of three circuits, develop your archery skills, swing out on the flying trapeze, doggy paddle in the pool of Olympic champions, spot wildlife from the Badu Mangroves boardwalk and tour the famous Telstra Stadium. Superb transport links make it easy to get there.

Take a spin on the big wheel at Luna Park.

Main picture: Blue Mountains. Top: Byron Bay.
Above: Jervis Bay.

Kids' Top 10: New South Wales (beyond Sydney)

1 Ride the world's steepest incline railway at Scenic World (scenicworld.com.au) before hiking in the Blue Mountains with Auswalk (auswalk.com.au). Trek through lush rainforest, listening out for lyrebirds (which can impersonate anything from chainsaws to car alarms) and then conquer the 800 steps of the Giant Stairway next to the famous Three Sisters.

2 Slip and slide at the Big Banana (bigbanana.com), Coffs Harbour, where a day pass gets you two rides on the 600-m Wild Banana toboggan ride, entry to the ice-skating rink and a free banana split. Alternatively, swim with dolphins (minimum age six) at the nearby Pet Porpoise Pool (petporpoisepool.com). For thrills and spills south of Sydney, splash out on Jamberoo Action Park (jamberoo.net) near Kiama which has waterslides, race tracks and toboggan runs.

3 Dare to stroll the Skywalk at Dorrigo National Park (nationalparks.nsw.gov.au) where you'll feel like an eagle soaring above the rainforest.

4 Spot dolphins on a boat trip, zooming through a network of coastal waterways with Port Macquarie's Cruise Adventures (cruiseadventures.com.au).

5 Experience the past at Timbertown (timbertown.com.au) near Wauchope where steam trains and horse-drawn carriages take you back to the pioneer days.

6 See humpback whales (June to November) from the whale-watching platform at Iluka (ilukansw.com.au), reached by walking the World Heritage Rainforest Walk. Alternatively, take a boat trip with one of the many operators along the New South Wales coast, such as Whale Watching Byron Bay (whalewatchingbyronbay.com.au).

7 Learn to surf with the Byron Bay Surf School (byronbaysurfschool.com). A one-day course teaches you basic surf awareness, paddling, catching waves and, all importantly, how to stand up and ride them.

8 Check out the capital, Canberra, where a '3 in Fun' ticket provides entry to the miniature village of Cockington Green (cockingtongreen.com.au), the Australian Institute of Sport (ausport.gov.au/tours) and Questacon – The National Science & Technology Centre (questacon.edu.au).

9 Strike out south of Sydney to Jervis Bay where activities range from sea kayaking with the Jervis Bay Kayak Co (jervisbaykayaks.com) to learning about Aboriginal traditions with Barry's Bush Tucker Tours.

10 Wander west of Sydney, crossing the Great Dividing Range to Dubbo where the Western Plains Zoo (zoo.nsw.gov.au) operates Roar and Snore (minimum age five) – an exciting opportunity to spend the night at this free-roaming wildlife park.

➨ Further information: coffscoast.com.au, jervisbaytourism.com.au, portmacquarieinfo.com.au, visitcanberra.com.au and visitnsw.com.au.

> ❝❞ On the first night of our motorhome holiday in New South Wales I remember lying awake thinking, 'What have we done? Why aren't we in a lovely beachside house somewhere?' But after that it was a great success. Not only did the motorhome give us the freedom to explore the coast (we managed to fit in everything from sand-boarding to dolphin watching), but our three kids loved the challenge of turning the seats into beds every evening. Just remember that they are long vehicles and your turning circle needs to be much bigger than usual.
>
> *Mark Pougatch, BBC Sports Presenter*

Magic Melbourne and penguins on parade

Be warned. Victoria will almost certainly throw a spanner in the works when you plan a trip down under. Just when you've cajoled Sydney, the Red Centre and the Great Barrier Reef into a comfortable three-week itinerary, Melbourne catches your eye and suddenly your plans start unravelling in a tempest of fresh possibilities. Not only are Melbourne's family attractions on a par with those in Sydney, but the coastline either side is also nothing short of irresistible: the Mornington Peninsula and Phillip Island to the east and the Great Ocean Road to the west. Inland, Victoria unfurls in a panoply of fertile valleys, eucalypt forests and rugged mountains – a green and palatable land dotted with vineyards and historic gold-rush towns. By the time you start contemplating the natural wonders of Tasmania, New South Wales might, just might, have become a distant memory.

Above: Melbourne's residents flock to the nearby beaches in summer.

Melbourne and surrounds

⊙ ⊛ ⊛ ⊛ ⊛ ⊛ ⊕ ⊕ ⊕ ⊕ ⊛

➠ Getting around is straightforward thanks to Melbourne's integrated network of trains, trams and buses (metlinkmelbourne.com.au).
➠ The Royal Botanic Gardens (rbg.vic.gov.au) has a wonderfully imaginative play area for kids, featuring everything from a tree tower to a kitchen garden.
➠ For further information, log on to visitmelbourne.com and visitvictoria.com.au.

Below: Little penguin near Melbourne.

City highlights Rated one of the world's most liveable cities, Melbourne has fine Victorian architecture (best appreciated from one of the burgundy and gold City Circle trams), child-friendly restaurants and some excellent parks and beaches. To see it all from a heady height, the Melbourne Observation Deck (melbourne360rialto.com.au) offers far-reaching views from the Rialto Towers. A superb introduction to Australian natural history and culture, the Melbourne Museum (melbourne.museum.vic.gov.au) explores everything from dinosaurs to the traditions of the Aborigines and Pacific islanders. Its trump cards for families, however, are the Children's Gallery for three- to eight-year-olds, the 3D IMAX theatre and the Forest Gallery which contains living trees up to 20 m tall. Equally captivating is Melbourne Aquarium (melbourne aquarium.com.au) where you can take a behind-the-scenes, glass-bottom boat

trip over the vast Oceanarium – home to sharks, stingrays, turtles and over 3000 fish from the Southern Ocean. Kids will also enjoy getting face to face with giant spider crabs, bloodsucking leeches and other delightful critters at the Creepy Creatures exhibit. For more wild encounters, hop on tram 55 to the zoo (zoo.org.au) which has a treetop boardwalk at its new Orang-utan Sanctuary. Scienceworks (scienceworks. museum. vic.gov.au) incorporates the Melbourne Planetarium and the Lightning Room – a vivid demonstration of the power of lightning. If you have three- to eight-year-olds, unleash them at Nitty Gritty Super City where they can construct a building, steer a ship and record their own weather reports.

Best days out A 25-minute tram ride south takes you to the seaside suburb of St Kilda, a great place to enjoy the beach or walk, cycle and skate along the palm-fringed waterfront. It's also where you will find Luna Park (lunapark.com.au) with its roller coaster, ghost train, carousel and other thrill rides. Steaming through the fern gullies and mountain-ash forests of the Dandenong Ranges (east of Melbourne), the *Puffing Billy* (puffingbilly. com.au) makes a fun outing for kids – especially when you combine the steam train with a visit to Healesville Sanctuary (zoo.org.au), one of Australia's premier native wildlife parks and probably your best chance of seeing a platypus. Children

will also be enthralled by the birds of prey flight show and a tour of the animal hospital. Just an hour's drive from Melbourne, the Mornington Peninsula has sheltered sandy beaches and every kind of water activity, from sailing and surfing to fishing and dolphin swims. One of the most popular family beaches, Rosebud is protected by offshore sandbars and has picnic, BBQ and play facilities. Polperro Dolphin Swims (polperro.com.au) operates from Sorrento between October and April.

Further east, Phillip Island (penguins. org.au) hosts one of Australia's most endearing wildlife spectacles when, each dusk, a steady parade of little penguins (the world's smallest at just 33 cm in height) bumbles ashore. There are several viewing options, although some have rather stringent age restrictions. Best for families is Penguins Plus (minimum age four) where you can view the penguins from a platform and boardwalk. On the Private Penguin Parade Experience (minimum age 12) you stake out the beach with your own personal ranger, while the Ultimate Penguin Tour takes groups of just 10 people to a secluded bay far from the tourist masses (and any children under 16). Other highlights on Phillip Island include the seals and rockpools at the Nobbies, the koalas and birds at the

Where can I see this?

The Great Ocean Road (greatoceanrd.org.au) in southwest Victoria hugs one of the world's most dramatic coastlines where waves have sculpted 45-m-high limestone cliffs into a gallery of mighty sea stacks, arches and caves. Nowhere are these features more striking than at the Twelve Apostles in Port Campbell National Park. Other highlights of the notorious Shipwreck Coast (shipwreckcoast.com) include spotting southern right whales at Warrnambool between June and late September, discovering the region's seafaring past at Flagstaff Hill Maritime Village (flagstaffhill.com) and surfing, swimming or simply jumping waves at the many superb beaches. Anglesea is one of the region's most family-friendly beach towns.

treetops boardwalk and the farm animals and heritage buildings at Churchill Island.

Further afield Popular for fishing, camping and hiking, the wild and spectacular coastline of Gippsland in Eastern Victoria encompasses Wilsons Promontory National Park and Ninety Mile Beach. Two to three hours' drive north of Melbourne, the historic Port of Echuca (portofechuca.org.au) offers paddle-steamer cruises on the Murray River. A 90-minute drive west of Melbourne, Sovereign Hill (sovereignhill.com.au), on the outskirts of Ballarat, keeps alive the gold-rush days of the 1850s. Stroll down Main Street and you'll rub shoulders with prospectors, blacksmiths and other characters in period dress.

How to find a devil (and other Tasmanian wildlife)

Tasmanian devils have attitude, but don't expect the slavering, tree-felling whirlwind of fur and gnashing teeth that Warner Bros would have you believe. In fact, this carnivorous marsupial inhabits a rather peaceful wilderness of mountains, forests and deserted beaches where numerous other native Australian species have found sanctuary. At Hobart's Tasmanian Museum, you can learn about one that didn't make it – the thylacine or Tasmanian tiger. But just an hour's drive southeast to Taranna, you can eyeball devils, along with quolls and golden possums, at the Tasmanian Devil Conservation Park. Continue south to the Tinderbox Marine Reserve and a sheltered snorkelling trail trains your gaze on pipefish and leafy sea dragons. More marine marvels await at Bruny Island where albatrosses, gannets, sea eagles, dolphins, penguins and fur seals guarantee a riveting boat trip.

No trip to Tasmania is complete without a visit to Cradle Mountain-Lake St Clair National Park where the Enchanted Forest Walk, suitable for all ages, probes a magical old-growth rainforest and even turns up the odd wombat burrow. Bennett's wallabies and pademelons can be seen during the day around the visitor centre, while Tasmanian devils, quolls and eastern pygmy possums emerge at dusk. ▶▶ Further information: discovertasmania.com.au

Amble in Adelaide, hop to Kangaroo Island

South Australia has two very contrasting faces. To the north and west lies a stark expanse of the outback where huge salt lakes shimmer beneath ancient, heat-shattered mountains and the Great Victoria Desert merges relentlessly with the flat, arid Nullarbor Plain. And then there's Adelaide and the southeast, a verdant blend of manicured city parks and vineyards, gentle rivers, sandy bays and islands teeming with wildlife. No prizes for guessing where you'll be taking the kids. Notwithstanding South Australia's outback attractions (such as the opal-mining community of Coober Pedy), the Adelaide area makes for a varied and manageable family holiday.

Top: **Adelaide.** **Above:** Kangaroo Bay.
Below: Sea lion at Seal Bay.

Adelaide and the southeast

⊙⊙⊙⊙⊙⊙⊙⊙

» The Adelaide Metro (adelaidemetro.com.au) serves the greater metropolitan region with trains, buses and the Glenelg tram; look out for the bright yellow Adelaide Free buses – the 99B and 99C – which go to the main attractions in the city.
» Kangaroo Island tour operators include Adventure Charters (adventurecharters.com.au) and Wilderness Tours (wildernesstours.com.au).
» For Murray River houseboat rental, try houseboat-centre.com.au or houseboats.com.au.
» For further information, log on to southaustralia.com.

City highlights A good way to see Adelaide is by hiring a paddle boat on the River Torrens that flows through the heart of the city. You will find Riverside Bike and Paddle Boat Hire by the Festival Centre (adelaidefestivalcentre.com.au) – a great place to take kids, either for a picnic or to browse the arts and crafts at the Sunday market. On North Terrace, the South Australia Museum (samuseum.sa.gov.au) has permanent exhibits on local natural history, deep-sea life, Ancient Egypt, the cultures of Pacific islanders and Aboriginal people, the exploits of Antarctic explorer Douglas Mawson and the extraordinary opal fossils discovered at Coober Pedy. A short walk to the east lie the riverside Botanic Gardens and Adelaide Zoo (adelaidezoo.com.au), which offers a range of exciting behind-the-scenes encounters with orang-utans, sun bears and Sumatran tigers.
Best beaches Easily reached on the

City-to-Bay tram, Glenelg is Adelaide's most popular beach destination. Its waterfront is buzzing with shops and cafés, while the Town Hall contains the Bay Discovery Centre and the Rodney Fox Shark Experience. The Beachouse (thebeachouse.com.au) has waterslides, dodgems, minigolf and other amusements, while nearby Holdfast Shores Marina is the departure point for joyrides with Hel-a-Va-Jet Boat (helava.com.au) and dolphin cruises with Temptation Sailing (dolphinboat.com.au). About 5 km south along the Esplanade, Brighton is another favourite beach playground. Continue on towards the Fleurieu Peninsula to reach the popular seaside towns of Victor Harbour and Goolwa or strike out north of Adelaide to explore the Yorke Peninsula where watersports include surfing, kayaking, beach fishing and sailing.
Best days out One of the highlights of a family visit to the Adelaide region is a trip to Kangaroo Island (tourkangaroo island.com.au) – although you really need more than a single day to fully appreciate this wildlife haven. Children will love sharing the beach with a large colony of sea lions at Seal Bay and watching the nightly procession of little penguins at Kingscote and Penneshaw. Be sure to also arrange a guided nocturnal tour since many species are only active at night. In addition to wildlife, Kangaroo Island offers safe swimming at Penneshaw Beach and sandboarding in the giant dunes at Little Sahara. For messing about on the

Murray River, head east of Adelaide to Renmark where cruises are available on historic paddle steamers. You can also waterski, canoe and fish at several riverside towns, while a houseboat holiday is sure to get a thumbs-up from the kids.

❓ Where can I see these Kangaroo Island critters?

Fur seal Over 7000 breed around Cape du Couedic.
Heath goanna Basking on sunny days.
Kangaroo Flinders Chase National Park Visitor Centre.
Koala Large gum trees.
Platypus Flinders Chase Platypus Waterholes Walk.
Sea lion Sandy beach at Seal Bay.
Short-beaked echidna Digging for ants and termites.
Tammar wallaby Roadsides at night.

Above: Go-slow trams in Adelaide.

Big beaches, big skies, big fish

With over 12,000 km of pristine coastline, Western Australia shouldn't pose any problems when it comes to finding a beach – whether your kids are into surfing, snorkelling or building sandcastles. Perth, a compact, modern city with skyscrapers rising like giant crystals above the Swan River, makes an easy-going base for exploring highlights in the southwest like Fremantle and Rottnest Island. Venture further afield and you'll quickly appreciate the vast size of Western Australia, but those long drives will be more than compensated by some truly inspiring natural wonders – from the surreal Wave Rock to Monkey Mia's dolphins and the whale sharks of Ningaloo Reef.

Perth and surrounds

» Perth is way out west – a 3-hr flight from Adelaide, the nearest big city.
» Ferries to Rottnest Island are operated by Rottnest Fast Ferries (hillarysfastferries.com.au) and Rottnest Express (rottnestexpress.com.au).
» For further information, log on to perthtourism.com.au, perthtouristcentre.com.au and westernaustralia.com.

City highlights Base yourself north of Perth on the 30-km swathe of the Sunset Coast and you get the best of everything: superb beaches (see below), top attractions and easy access to the city when you need it. Located at Hillarys Boat Harbour, the Aquarium of Western Australia (aqwa.com.au) transports you through the state's major marine habitats. Children over 15 can join a guided snorkelling adventure with 4-m-long sharks in the huge Indian Ocean tank, while Ocean Safaris, in search of dolphins and humpback whales, are organized by the aquarium between October and December. A short distance inland from Hillarys, the bushland reserve of Whiteman Park (whitemanpark.com.au) makes a great family outing, offering everything from camel and steam train rides to sheep-shearing demonstrations and native wildlife displays. You'll find more Aussie critters at Perth Zoo (perthzoo.wa.gov.au) just five minutes from the city centre, while Adventure World (adventure world.net.au) is the place to go for roller coasters and other wild rides.

Best days out Founded in 1829 at the mouth of the Swan River, Fremantle (fremantlewesternaustralia.com) can be easily reached by boat from Perth. Spend some time soaking up the atmosphere of the busy harbour and marketplace, then focus on the Western Australian Maritime Museum (museum.wa.gov.au/maritime) which provides an overview of all things nautical and also houses impressive vessels such as the America's Cup racing yacht *Australia II*. On Cliff Street, the Shipwreck Galleries contain the haunting remains of the VOC ship *Batavia*, wrecked off Western Australia's coast in 1629. However, it's the submarine, *HMAS Ovens*, high and dry on Victoria Quay that will enthral kids most. Fremantle is also a departure point for boats to Rottnest Island (rottnest island.com) – perfect for exploring by bike. Keep an eye out for quokkas (cute little wallabies) and don't forget your cossies – the beaches here are stunning.

Best beaches Whether you want to swim, surf or snorkel, Cottesloe Beach is perfect for all ages. The sheltered turquoise lagoon of The Basin on Rottnest Island is a prime spot for ogling colourful fish, while Scarborough Beach with its surf breaks and trendy vibe is teen heaven. Experienced surfies will want to ride the more challenging waves at Trigg. If you've got toddlers take them for a paddle at Mettams Pool.

South and east of Perth A three-hour drive south of the city, Margaret River is not only one of Australia's premium wine-growing regions, it also has some sensational beaches. Hamelin Bay is a great family all-rounder, while Ocean Beach further along the coast at Denmark is big on surf. Whale watching is possible from Dunsborough and Albany, while the Valley of the Giants Treetops Walk (valleyofthegiants.com.au) at Walpole elevates you into the canopy of a tingle forest.

Kids' top 5: North of Perth
1 **Wade** with dolphins at Monkey Mia.
2 **Ride** a camel along Cable Beach, Broome.
3 **Spot** a dugong in Shark Bay.
4 **Peer** at the Pinnacles in Nambung National Park.
5 **Snorkel** with a whale shark off Ningaloo Reef.

Top: Perth skyline. **Above:** Ningaloo Beach. **Left:** Camel riding on Cable Beach.

From Top End to middle Outback

The Northern Territory is textbook Australia. It's home to some of the country's most enigmatic landmarks and wildlife, from the mesmerizing monolith of Uluru to the bustling billabongs of Kakadu. Underlying everything is the Dreamtime – the cultural bedrock of Aboriginal belief that children will be able to grasp by visiting the region's museums and rock art sites or by joining bush walks and workshops led by local guides. Darwin makes a great base from which to explore the tropical Top End where a trio of national parks offers everything from crocodile safaris to canoeing trips. Uluru-Kata Tjuta National Park, meanwhile, is the heart and soul of Australia's Red Centre where activities include bush-tucker walks and camel riding.

Darwin and the Top End

»» The Tour Tub (tourtub.com.au) provides a hop-on, hop-off service to Darwin's tourist sights.
»» For souvenir hunting, head to Mindil Beach Sunset Markets (mindil.com.au) where you can also sample delicious food from the Asia-Pacific region.
»» For camping tours to the Top End's national parks, contact Billy Can Tours (billycan.com.au).
»» For further information, log on to travelnt.com.au, environment.gov.au/parks/kakadu and nt.gov.au/nreta/parks.

Darwin highlights Always a winner with children, Aquascene (aquascene.com.au) at Doctor's Gully (a short walk from the city centre) allows them to feed thousands of milkfish, mullet, catfish, bream and other slithery scroungers as they gather in the shallows at high tide. At Stokes Hill Wharf you'll find more fish – battered and served with chips at the excellent harbourside restaurants or swirling in technicolour splendour at the Indo-Pacific Marine coral reef aquarium. While you're there, take the plunge into Darwin's pearling heritage at the Australian Pearling Exhibition. More historical jewels can be found at the Museum and Art Gallery of the Northern Territory (nt.gov.au/nreta/museums) which contains some of the world's finest Aboriginal paintings. Don't miss the Cyclone Tracy Gallery – a chilling display on the tropical storm than flattened Darwin in 1974. To see

saltwater crocodile (salties), head to Crocodylus Park (wmi.com.au/crocpark) on Darwin's outskirts or join a Crocodile Jumping Cruise (jumpingcrocodile.com.au) on the Adelaide River (about an hour's drive from Darwin) where crocs are teased with hunks of suspended bait. A 45-minute drive south of the city, Territory Wildlife Park (territorywildlifepark.com.au) provides a wonderful introduction to the diverse habitats of Australia's Top End, from billabongs squirming with long neck turtles and monitor lizards to monsoon forests dripping with birds and bats. Special features, such as the walk-through aviary, aquarium tunnel and nocturnal house get you up-close and personal to wildlife that is often hard to spot in the wild. More wet wonders can be found at the Window on the Wetlands Visitor Centre (nt.gov.au/nreta/parks).

Litchfield National Park Located 100 km southwest of Darwin, this beautiful park encompasses a sandstone plateau riven with forest-edged creeks and waterfalls that lead to idyllic (and safe) swimming holes. One of the most popular spots is at Florence Falls where you will also find a shady picnic site and a couple of easy walking trails. The 1-km Shady Creek Walk weaves through monsoon forest and open woodland, while the 3-km Florence Creek Walk leads to Buley Rockhole. Keep your eyes peeled for wallabies, sugar gliders and northern brushtail possums.

Kakadu National Park Around 250

km east of Darwin, Kakadu is one of Australia's best sites for wildlife and indigenous culture. Don't visit for less than three days. Arrive at Jabiru, where the Bowali visitor centre gives an overview of Kakadu's heritage and habitats; then join a ranger-guided walk at Ubirr admiring the Aboriginal art, some of which is over 20,000 years old. The following morning, explore Nourlangie Rock, another famous rock art site, before taking an afternoon cruise on Yellow Waters Billabong in search of magpie geese, jabiru and other bird species, then a nocturnal croc-spotting boat trip. Next day, join a cultural cruise on the East Alligator River with local Aboriginal guides. In the dry season (May to September), try to squeeze in a 4WD trip to Jim Jim and Twin Falls.

Nitmiluk (Katherine) Gorge National Park The town of Katherine, 300 km south of Darwin, is the gateway to a spectacular series of gorges where adventurous families can paddle beneath looming cliffs of red sandstone, pausing for a refreshing swim or a picnic on a sandbank. Canoes can be hired from Nitmiluk Tours (nitmiluktours.com.au) which also organizes boat trips – a better option for families with young children. Pack a hat, sunscreen and plenty of water.

Top: Yellow Waters Billabong, Kakadu National Park. **Above right:** Estuarine crocodile in the Top End.

Kids' top 10: The Red Centre

1 Learn about life in the outback, past and present, by visiting the Telegraph Station (nt.gov.au/nreta/parks), the School of the Air (assoa.nt.edu.au) and the Royal Flying Doctor Service (flyingdoctor.net) in Alice Springs.

2 Ride a camel along the dry riverbed of the Todd River in Alice Springs, spotting cockatoos and galahs in the gum trees before enjoying breakfast in the bush. Take a Camel to Breakfast tours are run by Anangu Waai! (ananguwaai.com.au).

3 See rock wallabies, bilbies, lizards and other outback wildlife at the brilliant Alice Springs Desert Park (alicespringsdesertpark.com.au), witness free-flying birds of prey in the nature theatre and discover how Aboriginal people use the region's plants and animals for food and medicine.

4 Hear amazing didgeridoo music at Sounds of Starlight (soundsofstarlight.com), a spectacular evening show held in Alice Springs on Tuesdays, Fridays and Saturdays, April to November (recommended for children over five).

5 Explore the MacDonnell Ranges west of Alice Springs, visiting scenic hot spots like Simpsons Gap, Standley Chasm, Serpentine Gorge and Ormiston Gorge. Spot rock wallabies and parrots, and take a cooling dip in one of the freshwater pools.

6 Experience life on a working cattle and camel farm at Kings Creek Station (kingscreekstation.com.au) 36 km from the magnificent Kings Canyon. Explore the outback by quad bike, camel or helicopter, camp in the bush and try a camel burger.

7 Visit the magnificent monolith of Uluru, starting with the Uluru-Kata Tjuta Cultural Centre (environment.gov.au/parks/uluru) to learn about the national park from its traditional Aboriginal owners, the Anangu. Delve into the display of indigenous paintings and carvings at Maruku Arts (maruku.com.au) – a great place to buy an authentic boomerang – and then join a Dot Painting Workshop (ananguwaai.com.au) with local artists. Don't miss the spectacle of Uluru glowing red at sunset, then stay up late for some stargazing at the observatory.

8 Hike around the base of Uluru, an easy 10-km loop that takes around four hours, pausing to read the interpretive signs that tell the Dreamtime stories of Kuniya and Liru. Guided tours can be booked at the Cultural Centre (see above).

9 Discover the weird and wonderful landscape of Kata Tjuta, a cluster of 36 giant domes rising from the desert to the west of Uluru. For a magical walk, set off into Walpa Gorge (the mythical home of the corkwood-tree women) which weaves between two of the rocky outcrops.

10 Fossick for gold at Moonlight Rockhole near Tennant Creek (500 km north of Alice Springs). You'll need a permit first – go to nt.gov.au/dpifm/Minerals_Energy and click on 'Fossicking'.

➤ Further information: alicesprings.nt.gov.au

Top to bottom: Uluru; Honey ant design on an Aboriginal painting; MacDonnell Ranges all of a glow at dusk.

Australia's tropical playground

'Beautiful one day, perfect the next', Australia's Sunshine State is heaven on earth for kids. Its beaches will blow their minds, whether they're clutching a surfboard, a mask and snorkel or a bucket and spade. There are riveting resorts along the Gold Coast where children of all ages will get a thrill from Australia's best theme parks. The Sunshine Coast is more relaxed, while a liberal scattering of tropical islands provides a mixture of pampered paradise and Aussie adventure. Several resorts in Queensland organize special activities for kids, whether it's exploring World Heritage rainforest in Lamington National Park or searching for Nemo on the Great Barrier Reef. Nowhere does the three Rs – reef, rainforest and recreation – better than Queensland.

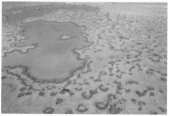

Brisbane and the Queensland coast

⊙❀❀❀❀❀❀❀❀❀❀❀❀❀❀❀

≫ Tours from Brisbane to Fraser Island or Moreton Island can be arranged through Sunrover Expeditions (sunrover.com.au) and Coastal Island Safaris (coastalislandsafaris.com).
≫ Manly Harbour Village, Brisbane's gateway to Moreton Bay Marine Park, has restaurants, shops, playgrounds, cycle tracks and walking paths.
≫ For further information, log on to queenslandholidays.com.au, goldcoasttourism.com.au, tourismsunshinecoast.com.au and whitsundaytourism.com.

Top right: Whitehaven Beach (Whitsunday Islands); ariel view of the Great Barrier Reef. Above: Surfers Paradise on the Gold Coast; Rainbow lorikeet.

Brisbane Chances are you'll be staying on the coast north or south of Brisbane, but if you have a day or two to spare in the city you'll find plenty to do. The South Bank Parklands is the place to go. Not only does it have a leisurely mix of cafés, play areas, riverside walks, open-air markets and even a swimming lagoon, but it's also close to several child-friendly attractions. At the north-western end of the park, the Queensland Museum (qm.qld.gov.au) has impressive prehistoric exhibits and interactive science stuff, while the Queensland Maritime Museum (maritimemuseum.com.au) has various historic vessels including the Second World War frigate *HMAS Diamantina*. Nearby, you can nip across the Brisbane River on the Goodwill Bridge and explore the Botanical Gardens or browse the shops along Queen Street.

Gold Coast With its irresistible blend of sand, sea and 300 sunny days a year, the Gold Coast is one of Australia's most popular holiday destinations. Around two hours' drive south of Brisbane, it boasts a huge range of accommodation, from motels and apartments to luxury resorts. Although dining out and shopping are major tourist activities (particularly at Surfers Paradise), the theme parks are more likely to wow kids. Wet 'n' Wild Water World (wetnwild.com.au) has something for all ages, from the Extreme H2O Zone to an eight-lane racing slide and special play area for children aged 10 and under. Dreamworld (dreamworld.com.au) is actually several worlds in one – a kind of 'theme park chocolate box' of daredevil rides, wildlife encounters, waterslides and cartoon characters. Sea World (seaworld.com.au) has animal shows, thrill rides, dolphin encounters and an impressive new Shark Bay lagoon. Known as 'Hollywood on the Coast', Movie World (movieworld.com.au) has a cast of Warner Bros characters, as well as some serious white-knuckle rides like the 85-kph Lethal Weapon roller coaster. If it all gets too much, escape the Gold Coast crowds by staying on the nearby, unspoiled island of South Stradbroke.

Sunshine Coast North of Brisbane, the Sunshine Coast is more restrained than the Gold Coast – not that children will find it dull. The beaches are just as spectacular and there are also plenty of non-beach attractions, such as the late

Steve Irwin's Australia Zoo (australiazoo.com.au) and the theme park Aussie World (aussieworld.com.au). The southern gateway to the region, Caloundra (caloundratourism.com.au), makes an excellent family-friendly base.

Hervey Bay and Fraser Island Renowned as one of the country's best centres for whale watching, Hervey Bay is a resting site for humpbacks migrating south towards Antarctica between August and October. The largest sand island in the world, Fraser Island has shipwreck-strewn beaches, dense rainforest and idyllic lakes, all explored by 4WD.

Whitsunday Islands For pampered holiday bliss, look no further than the Whitsundays, a tropical playground of over 74 islands scattered off the coast near Airlie Beach. Hamilton Island (hamiltonisland.com.au) is Australia's best-loved family beach resort. As well as a wide choice of accommodation, there's an airport, marina, restaurants and shops. Kids love whizzing around on the island's golf buggies, visiting the koala sanctuary, snorkelling, kayaking, fishing or taking part in activities at the Clownfish Club (for six- to 14-year-olds). Popular excursions include boat trips to Whitehaven Beach or ReefWorld (fantasea.com.au) on the Great Barrier Reef (see opposite).

Kids' top 10: Reef and Rainforest

1 Feel the sand squeak between your toes on the dazzling 9-km stretch of Whitehaven Beach, on Whitsunday Island.

2 Ride the Skyrail Rainforest Cableway (skyrail.com.au), skimming over treetops to Kuranda where you can explore the rainforest on an amphibious Duck tour before returning to Cairns on the Kuranda Scenic Railway (ksr.com.au).

3 Wade through the shallows of the coral lagoon at Heron Island (heronisland.com), where the Junior Ranger Programme helps seven- to 12-year-olds uncover the secrets of the Great Barrier Reef.

4 Shoot the grade II-III rapids on the Barron River, near Cairns, with Raging Thunder (ragingthunder.com.au) or up the adrenaline levels with a whitewater frenzy on the Tully (grade III-IV rapids) near Mission Beach. Minimum age 13.

5 Swoop through the trees like a sugar glider on the 25-m-high flying fox at O'Reilly's Rainforest Retreat (oreillys.com.au) in Lamington National Park.

6 Discover a tropical adventure paradise on Dunk Island (dunk-island.com) where you can learn how to snorkel, de-husk a coconut and throw a boomerang.

7 Explore the tropical rainforest of the Cape York Peninsula on a 4WD safari – only serious adventurers need apply.

8 Choose from 17 white-sand beaches and a host of activities (from bush walks to banana-boat rides) on Great Keppel Island (greatkeppelresort.com.au) near Rockhampton.

9 Spot saltwater crocodiles on a river cruise in Daintree National Park and then discover where the rainforest meets the sea at Cape Tribulation.

10 Learn to scuba-dive (minimum age 12) at one of the many dive centres in Cairns and Townsville.

❝❞ ReefWorld, a pontoon moored on Hardy Reef off the Queensland coast, is quite possibly the most exciting undersea adventure any six-year-old could dream of having. Just getting there was a thrill: a helicopter whisking us from Hamilton Island in the Whitsundays, swooping low over squeaky clean Whitehaven Beach, then 15 minutes of dark forbidding sea before abruptly crossing the turquoise threshold of the Great Barrier Reef. Circling above tiny Heart Reef (which really is a perfect heart shape), we spotted manta rays and turtles cruising above cerulean-coloured reef flats. Then it was touchdown – crested terns and black noddies scattering as the helicopter alighted on a raft no bigger than a tennis court. A short boat ride and we reached ReefWorld itself.

It was late afternoon and the day trippers who had visited by boat had already left. ReefWorld was deserted, except for the small team of permanent staff who began kitting us out in garish stinger suits (think Spiderman meets the Teletubbies), life jackets and snorkelling gear. Although Joe and Ellie are good swimmers, we thought it was crucial to make them wear life jackets since there were bound to be occasional mini-panics when water seeped in through their masks or a wave slopped over the tops of their snorkels.

First to take the plunge, Joe took one peek underwater, squealed and shot back on to the pontoon quicker than a flying fish. It didn't bode well. But I could see what had caused the consternation. A huge Napoleon wrasse (or "double-decker fish" as Joe later described it) had come to check us out. It took a bit of persuasion to reassure both Joe and Ellie that it wasn't going to eat them and soon we were happily bobbing over the reef holding hands, pointing at corals and giant clams and watching the technicoloured procession of fish. Lots of fish. By sunset we were back on the pontoon and being introduced to George, a 3-m-long Queensland grouper that has adopted ReefWorld and lurks under the pontoon. Joe and Ellie were fascinated by him, particularly when they got to feed chunks of mackerel to the 280-kg 'monster'. They spent the entire evening running back and forth between the open hatch where George hung out and the underwater observation chamber where you could watch mean-looking jacks patrolling the floodlit waters. After a dinner of fresh grilled fish the twins fell into a deep sleep lulled by the slosh of waves against the pontoon. Disturbing images of sleepwalking children did little to ease their parents sleep, but in the morning it was straight back into action – more snorkelling, breakfast for George and a ride in ReefWorld's semi-sub before the helicopter returned to collect us. "Not a bad way to see the Reef" said our pilot in a perfect example of Aussie understatement as he whizzed us back to Hamilton Island. *Will*

❝❞ We went snorkelling and we saw lots of stripy fish and bright blue fish and yellow fish and very big black fish and we saw a blue starfish. It was good fun. There was lots of fish.

Ellie Gray (age six)

Far left: A sugar glider in Lamington National Park.
Top: Zip-wire rider at O'Reilly's Rainforest Retreat.
Above: Napolean wrasse.
Left: Shovel-nosed shark

Craters, coast, culture and kiwis

Northland protrudes from the top of New Zealand's North Island like a giant thumbs up – and that's precisely the reaction you'll get from your kids when they discover this far-flung adventure paradise, offering everything from sandboarding and kayaking to swimming with dolphins and spotting kiwis in a forest of giant kauri trees. Endowed with excellent museums, Auckland and Wellington provide fascinating introductions to North Island's wildlife, culture and history, while Rotorua and Tongariro are the ultimate New Zealand hot spots for turbocharged adventure, Maori traditions and volcanic shenanigans. Basically, North Island has it all – whether you're a *Lord of the Rings* location-spotter or a surf dude catching the waves on the Coromandel Peninsula.

Auckland

🏄 🐚 🐋 ⛰ 🎢 🏊 ⛵ 🚣 🏕 🎡 🚂

›› The Discover New Zealand Centre at 180 Quay St can arrange transport, tours and accommodation in Auckland and further afield.
›› Ferries to Waiheke Island and other destinations in Hauraki Gulf are operated by Fullers (fullers.co.nz) and SeaLink (sealink.co.nz).
›› For further information, log on to aucklandnz.com.

Clockwise from top right: Auckland skyline; Maori carving at Te Puia, Rotorua; Bay of Islands; Dune boarding in Northland.

City highlights At 328 m high, the Sky Tower (skytower.co.nz) not only provides buttock-clenching views of New Zealand's largest city, but also gives you the option of taking the quick route down – by jumping. With a minimum age of just 11, Sky Jump (skyjump.co.nz) provides elastic-cord-assisted descents where you reach speeds of 85 kph for 11 seconds before slowing in the last few metres for a gentle landing. Unlike bungee jumping, there is no hanging upside down or bouncing around. So, no worries there then. More teeth-clattering moments are available at Rainbow's End (rainbowsend.co.nz), a theme park boasting New Zealand's only corkscrew roller coaster, and Snowplanet (snowplanet.co.nz), an indoor winter resort with three lifts and a snowboarding park. Of course, there's much more to Auckland than adrenaline abuse. The sea features prominently in some of the city's top

family attractions, such as the New Zealand National Maritime Museum (nzmaritime.org) with its seafaring exhibits and harbour cruises, and Kelly Tarlton's Antarctic Encounter and Underwater World (kellytarltons.co.nz) where you can see penguins, sharks and stingrays and explore a life-size replica of Captain Scott's hut. Native and exotic wildlife, from kiwis and tuataras to orang-utans and zebras, are always a big hit with kids at Auckland Zoo (aucklandzoo.co.nz), while the Museum of Transport and Technology (motat.org.nz) provides endless opportunities for fiddling, twiddling and experimenting. For shopping, head to Champions of the World (champions.co.nz) for authentic All Blacks merchandise, The Fairy Shop (thefairyshop.co.nz) for wands, wings and things, and Aotea Square Markets (the-edge.co.nz) for Pacific arts and crafts, traditional Maori carvings and contemporary jewellery.

Best city escapes A short drive across Harbour Bridge, or a 10-minute ferry ride from downtown Auckland, the suburbs of North Shore (northshorenz.com) have more than 20 beaches, including the 1-km stretch of Takapuna (takapuna beach.co.nz), Auckland's best urban beach with safe swimming, cracking harbour views and lots to do. Both Auckland and North Shore are perfectly placed for boat trips in the Hauraki Gulf – whether you opt for a yacht or a sea

kayak. Just 40 minutes by ferry from downtown Auckland, Waiheke Island (waiheke.co.nz) has gorgeous beaches, bush walks and plenty of family restaurants and cafés.

🔍 How to get to the top
The easiest and most exciting way to reach Cape Reinga at the tip of North Island is on a flying safari with Salt Air (saltair.co.nz). Leaving Pahia, you climb above the jade waters of the Bay of Islands before tracking north across Doubtless Bay and the dazzling silica sands of Rarawa Beach. Landing near the cape, a minibus takes you to a lighthouse presiding over the white-water hurly-burly between the Tasman Sea and Pacific. There's time for a paddle in the surf at nearby Tapotupotu Bay before sandboarding in an area of giant dunes. Then it's back in the plane, skimming low over the west coast's Ninety Mile Beach.

Wellington

⊕ 🅿 🅾 🅰 🅴 🎫

» The compact city centre is easily explored on foot.
» The Wellington cable car operates between Lambton Quay and the Lookout where you'll find the Carter Observatory (carterobservatory.org).
» For further information, log on to wellingtonnz.com.

City highlights Unusually for New Zealand, the capital's top family attraction is not a wilderness excursion, *Lord of the Rings* tour or daredevil activity – but a museum. Te Papa (tepapa.govt.nz), the country's national museum, is easily worth a full morning or afternoon. You'll find all kinds of bold and imaginative exhibits on geography, wildlife and culture, but it's the Discovery Centres and StoryPlace that captivate children. StoryPlace offers 45-minute storytelling, song and art sessions for youngsters aged 18 months to five years, while the Discovery Centres are split into four themes for older children. In NatureSpace, they can step inside a dinosaur footprint, inspect an insect under a microscope and find a fossil; Inspiration Station encourages them to get creative with cartoons and puppets; PlaNet Pasifika celebrates Pacific Island cultures, while Te Huka â Tai brings Maori traditions to life. Children will also love Te Papa's Bush City, a living exhibit with a rainforest rope-bridge and a crawl-through glow-worm cave. Having given their brains such a workout at Te Papa, your kids may well need to release some physical energy. Waitangi Park on Wellington's waterfront has a fantastic playground and skateboard park, while Ferg's Kayaks (fergskayaks.co.nz) offers kayaking trips, inline skating and New Zealand's largest indoor rock-climbing wall. For wildlife, catch the number 10 or 23 bus to Wellington Zoo (wellingtonzoo.com) or spend the evening at the Karori Wildlife Sanctuary (sanctuary.org.nz) where you can experience the dusk chorus, see native birds and try your luck at spotting a nocturnal kiwi.

Best city escapes Explore the South Coast and visit a fur seal colony on an exciting 4WD adventure with Seal Coast

ⓘ Where can I do this?

Head for Whangamata on the Coromandel Peninsula and ask for Ricky Parker who runs the Whangamata Surf School. He's great with kids and can provide an hour's one-to-one introductory lesson – 20 minutes on the beach and 40 minutes in the sea. You'll learn everything from how to position your feet correctly to how to fall off safely. Early in the summer, you will need a shortie wetsuit, while later in the season a rash shirt will do.

Safari (sealcoast.com). For gentle walks and a chance to feed animals, visit Staglands Wildlife Reserve (staglands.co.nz) in the Akatarawa Valley.

Kids' top 10: North Island

1 Learn all about New Zealand's icon at Kiwi Encounter (kiwiencounter.co.nz), a working hatchery and nursery where you can see eggs being incubated and chicks being weighed and fed.

2 Feel the heat on a White Island Tours (whiteisland.co.nz) to New Zealand's only active volcano, cruising to White Island in the Bay of Plenty before venturing to the crater's edge.

3 Zorb like you've never zorbed before. It's bouncy, it's barmy – it's a big inflatable ball bounding down a hill with you strapped inside. Try it wet or dry with Zorb (zorb.co.nz) in Rotorua. There's even a kids' zorb for the under six.

4 Paddle over the edge of a 9-m-high dam with Taranaki Outdoor Adventures (toa.co.nz). Well, why not? You're in New Zealand after all.

5 Glimpse glow-worms by night on a Lake McLaren Glow Worm Kayak Tour (kayaks.co.nz), paddling stable two-person sea kayaks into a twinkling canyon.

6 Watch a traditional Maori *haka* at Te Puia (nzmaori.co.nz), practise posturing, feet stamping and sticking your tongue out at your parents and then experience some of Rotorua's other highlights, like the Skylines Luge (skylineskyrides.co.nz/rotorua) and Agrodome (agrodome.co.nz).

7 Experience the magic of the Waipoua Forest at night, when the cries of kiwis echo amongst the world's tallest kauri trees. Feel a tingle along your spine as Maori guides from Footprints Waipoua (footprintswaipoua.com) recount ancient legends and sing spiritual songs as you venture deep into the forest.

8 Discover the legacy of pioneer mining days on a tour with Kiwi Dundee (kiwidundee.co.nz) where guides will show you how prospectors toiled for gold and silver in the hills of the Coromandel Peninsula during the late 1890s.

9 Snorkel or kayak around Goat Island Marine Reserve (goatislanddive.co.nz) where snapper, blue cod, red moki and other fish swim right up to you.

10 Poach yourself at Hot Water Beach on the Coromandel Peninsula where, at low tide, geothermal water bubbles up through the sand. Bring a shovel, dig a hole, check the temperature (there are some seriously hot areas), then lie back and relax.

ⓘ How to be a surf dude

» Lie flat on the board, your toes just touching the end.
» Look over your shoulder, ready for a suitable wave.
» When it's a few metres behind you, start paddling.
» As you begin to surf, grip the sides of your board.
» Spring up into a low crouching position.
» Spread your arms for balance; space feet well apart.
» Your front foot should point forwards, your back foot at right angles.

Top: Dam dropping.
Above: Maori *haka* and fuming fumaroles.

Where fantasy becomes reality

Have you ever wondered why Gandalf never spurred his white charger across a deserted beach? Or why Frodo was never confronted by a wild, surf-gnawed headland on his way to Mt Doom? It's a pity Tolkein never sought inspiration in New Zealand because its coast is every bit as dramatic as the mountains, plains and forests popularized in *Lord of the Rings*. South Island's epic shore ranges from brooding fiords in the southwest to turquoise coves in the north; from sandy bays on the Catlins Coast to wildlife honeypots at Kaikoura and the Otago Peninsula. Combine with inland highlights like adrenaline-pumping Queenstown and the saw-tooth peaks of the Southern Alps and you have something quite irresistible. Just don't tell Gollum.

Christchurch

😊 ✈ 🏛

» The Christchurch Tramway (tram.co.nz) links key attractions such as Cathedral Square, the Arts Centre, Botanic Gardens and Canterbury Museum.
» Punts operate from various landings along the river, including Worcester Bridge.
» For further information, log on to christchurchnz.net or christchurch.org.nz.

City highlights Ensnared by a loop of the River Avon, the Christchurch Botanic Gardens (ccc.govt.nz/parks) has sweeping lawns, trees, a rose garden, children's play area and paddling pool – the perfect place to shrug off jet lag if you have just arrived in New Zealand. On the edge of the gardens, the Canterbury Museum (canterbury museum.com) features a 'Discovery' natural history centre where children can dig for fossils and learn about wildlife. From there, it's a short stroll along Worcester Boulevard to the Arts Centre (artscentre.org.nz) where there are craft workshops, stalls and cafés. Continue to Cathedral Square and you will find the Southern Encounter

Aquarium (southernencounter.co.nz) with its touch pool and kiwi encounter. South of the city centre, The Circuit (thecircuit.co.nz) includes six entertainment venues: Supa Kart Raceway, Laserstrike, Garden City Bowl, Aimtru's Indoor Archery, Alpine Ice Sport Centre and Science Alive! The one Christchurch attraction you shouldn't miss, however, is the International Antarctic Centre (iceberg.co.nz) on the city's outskirts. The base for the New Zealand, US and Italian Antarctic programmes, this is where people are kitted out before being flown to the great white continent in huge Hercules aircraft fitted with skis. But it's also a fascinating interactive museum where kids (large and small) can discover what life is like in Antarctica. The Hagglund ride, in which an all-terrain vehicle hurls you around an assault course sculpted with crevasses and precipices, is positively genteel compared to the Antarctic storm simulation in which you are shut in a giant freezer and pummelled with gale-force winds. Other highlights 15-20 minutes' drive from downtown Christchurch include the Air

Force Museum (airforcemuseum.co.nz), Ferrymead Heritage Park (ferrymead.org.nz) and Willowbank Wildlife Reserve (willowbank.co.nz). To get above it all, the Christchurch Gondola (gondola.co.nz) provides panoramic views of the city, Lyttelton Harbour, Banks Peninsula, Canterbury Plains and the distant peaks of the Southern Alps.

❓ Where can I see this?

At the southern tip of South Island, Bluff is the departure point for Stewart Island (stewartislandexperience.co.nz) where you can visit tiny Ulva Island to glimpse kakas, wekas, tuis and other avian rarities in the moss-clad splendour of one of New Zealand's most pristine forests. Night trips in search of kiwis on surf-pummelled Ocean Beach are also possible.

Above right (top to bottom): Rocky Catlins coast; Hagglund Ride all-terrain vehicle outside International Antarctic Centre; watching dusky dolphins at Kaikoura. **Below right:** Watch out! It's a weka (notorious picnic predators). **Below:** Dusky dolphin doing a backflip.

❝❞ There's something vaguely surreal about flying direct from London to Christchurch. You sit on a plane for at least 24 hours, travel 19,000 km to the other side of the world and then find yourself in Stratford-upon-Avon, England. At least, that's what it feels like. It's mildly comforting to enter this parallel universe where another River Avon exists, complete with weeping willows, punts and ducks. When it comes to culture shock, Christchurch delivers nothing more than a gentle tingle.
Will

The ultimate South Island tour

Days 1-2 Wellington Wellington in North Island (see page 321) makes the ideal start to this epic journey and cuts out a lot of potential backtracking in South Island. And, of course, it also makes it easy to add on a North Island extension should you have the luxury of a four- or five-week holiday.

Days 3-5 Marlborough Sounds Sauvignon Blanc heaven to parents, this enticing region of inlets, coves and vineyards is reached by ferry across Cook Strait. Spend your days walking, kayaking and boating. Cruises are operated by the Maori-owned Myths and Legends Eco Tours (eco-tours.co.nz) and Beachcomber Fun Cruises (mailboat.co.nz) where you help deliver mail and groceries to families living in remote bays. The Malborough Adventure Company (marlborough sounds.co.nz) offers half-day guided kayaking trips for families with children aged 13 and over, or you could go horse riding with High Country Horse Trek (high-horse.co.nz). Don't forget Abel Tasman National Park where sandy beaches, turquoise waters and lush native forest conspire to form one of New Zealand's most luxuriant adventure playgrounds. Getting around is easy – just hop on the Abel Tasman Aqua Taxi (aquataxis.co.nz) which shuttles back and forth to all the park's main beaches and walking trail-heads. Kaiteriteri Kayak (seakayak.co.nz) can kit you out for paddling excursions.

Days 6-7 Kaikoura Kaikoura is one of the world's best marine wildlife destinations. The traditional sperm whale tour with Whale Watch Kaikoura (whalewatch.co.nz) is exciting enough, but children may well find the smaller, more intimate Albatross Encounter (oceanwings.co.nz) more enthralling. With Dolphin Encounter (dolphin.co.nz), children aged eight and over can don wetsuits and swim with the dolphins. On dry land, Maori Tours (maoritours.co.nz) offers one of South Island's most enlightening cultural tours, visiting fortified villages and learning about bush medicines. Continuing south from Kaikoura, a diversion inland leads to Hanmer Springs (hanmersprings. co.nz) with thermal spa and children's pool complete with waterslides.

Days 8-9 Aoraki/Mt Cook Bypassing Christchurch, continue towards Geraldine where 4x4 New Zealand (4x4newzealand.co.nz) offers a *Lord of the Rings* tour. Nowhere in New Zealand does the scenery reach more epic proportions than in Mt Cook National Park where kids can hike beneath snow-capped peaks. Glacier Sea Kayaking (www.mtcook.com) organizes trips in iceberg-strewn lakes, while Mt Cook Ski Planes (mtcookskiplanes.com) whisks you past Aoraki's 3764-m summit for a landing on the Tasman Glacier.

Days 10-11 Wanaka A fine spot to spend a couple of days experiencing farm life at a hill station (see page 327), Wanaka is also within easy range of the Cardrona Valley where Backcountry Saddle Expeditions (www.ridenz.com/ backcountry) offers horse treks through gold-rush country. Nearby Arrowtown is the area's best-preserved gold-mining settlement where you can visit the Lakes District Museum and try your hand at gold panning. To up the pace, take a jet-boat ride with Clutha River Jet (lakeland adventures.co.nz) on Lake Wanaka.

Days 12-14 Queenstown From its humble beginnings as a gold-rush town, Queenstown has grown to become the adventure capital of the world. The lakeside town offers everything from skydiving to underground rafting. More mellow activities include cruises aboard the *TSS Earnslaw* (a 1912 paddle steamer) and riding the Skyline Gondola up Bob's Peak, from where there are eye-popping views of Lake Wakatipu. See page 307 for 20 of the best child-friendly activities.

Days 15-17 Te Anau Gateway to the majestic wilderness of the 21,000-sq-km Fiordland National Park, Te Anau's essential excursions include the glow-worm caves and a cruise on either Milford Sound or Doubtful Sound (realjourneys.co.nz).

Days 18-20 Southeast coast Keep an eye out for Hector's dolphins cavorting in the surf at Curio Bay on the beautiful Catlins Coast between Balclutha and Invercargill. Further north, the Royal Albatross Centre (albatross.org.nz) on the Otago Peninsula provides more close encounters with rare wildlife as well as wild and beautiful beaches. Don't miss Penguin Place (penguinplace.co.nz), home of the Yellow-Eyed Penguin Conservation Reserve, or the chance to kayak in sheltered Otago Harbour with Wild Earth Adventures (wildearth.co.nz). In Dunedin, stop for a sweet treat at Cadbury World (cadbury.co.nz) before heading north to Christchurch, via the intriguing Moeraki Boulders.

Day 21 Christchurch See opposite.

Clockwise from top: Sleepy seal, Otago Peninsula; angry albatrosses, Kaikoura; ski planes on Mt Cook's Tasman Glacier; kayaks in Abel Tasman National Park.

66 99 Part of the fun of driving across South Island is planning your route. With little more than a map and a pencil you can indulge in the ultimate dot-to-dot.

Will

Australia and New Zealand essentials

When to go

Australia can be visited year-round. The southern half of the country is best from October to April, while the more tropical north is less humid and wet from May to September. The coolest months for exploring the outback are from April to September, while Queensland's Gold Coast and Sunshine Coast have pleasant temperatures and reliable sunshine all year. The peak season for visiting Australia is mid-December to the end of January when it is essential to book accommodation, tours and transport well in advance. The best months to visit *New Zealand* are from September to April. During midsummer (December to February) temperatures average 22-26°C, but this is also the peak tourist season when accommodation is at a premium. For less crowds and better deals, travel in spring and autumn when the weather is still generally fine, particularly in North Island. May to August can be wet and cold, although don't forget that some destinations, like Queenstown, switch to skiing during the winter.

Getting there

Several airlines serve Australia and New Zealand. Flying time is generally around 24 hours, but you can easily break the long trek down under with a stopover in a US or Asian city or on a South Pacific island. Expect to pay around £650-750 for an off-season return rising to around £900 at Christmas. Stick to the most popular routes and you may find that a round-the-world ticket is as cheap, if not cheaper, than a standard return. The national carriers, Qantas (qantas.com.au) and Air New Zealand (airnewzealand.com), have extensive global networks. Qantas flies to Sydney from London, Frankfurt, Johannesburg, New York, Los Angeles, San Francisco and Vancouver, as well as from several Asian cities. There is also a service to Melbourne from London, Los Angeles and Singapore; to Brisbane from Los Angeles; and to Adelaide and Perth from Singapore. Air New Zealand (airnewzealand.com) flies daily from London to Auckland via Los Angeles, and also has frequent connections from Los Angeles to Christchurch. Asian routes go via Hong Kong. Other airlines serving the region include Emirates (emirates.com) which flies via Dubai to Melbourne from several UK airports, including Birmingham, Glasgow, London and Manchester. Virgin Atlantic (virgin-atlantic.com) has direct flights from Heathrow to Sydney.

Getting around

Distances are huge in Australia – and even in New Zealand you shouldn't underestimate travel times or petrol costs if planning a major road trip. All the major **car hire** companies are represented in airports and cities. A popular option for families, motorhomes can be rented from numerous companies, including Britz (britz.com), Maui (maui-rentals.com) and United Campervans (campervan.co.nz). A six-berth United Campervan in New Zealand costs from around £90 per day over a 7-20 day hire period, including unlimited kilometres. Compulsory third-party insurance is an additional amount per day payable locally. Although main roads and tourist routes are generally of a very high standard in Australia and New Zealand, some remote areas have gravel roads which you may not be insured to drive on. Check the small print on your rental agreement.

Australia has an excellent **coach** network with operators like Greyhound Australia (greyhound.com.au) offering a range of excellent value passes. However, bear in mind that journeys can be unbearably long for children, with few stops. **Internal flights** may well be your best bet for covering large distances. There are several regional airlines servicing Australia and some international ticket deals include free internal flights. Try Jetstar Airways (jetstar.com), Virgin Blue (virginblue.com.au) and Skywest (skywest.com.au), as well as Qantas and Air New Zealand.

Getting between North Island and South Island in New Zealand is straightforward with Interislander (interislander.co.nz) which offers three-hour **ferry** crossings (for vehicles and passengers) between Wellington and Picton. Cook Strait ferry crossings are also operated by Blue Bridge (bluebridge.co.nz).

Accommodation

Wherever you stay in Australia and New Zealand you can expect good value for money and a great range of options. Accommodation includes everything from campsites, hostels and farmstays to luxury resorts, eco-lodges and yacht charters. In Australia, apartment-style hotels, consisting of a couple of

---

How much to offset your emissions?

From London to:
Perth £34
Brisbane £41
Melbourne £42
Sydney £42
Auckland £46
Christchurch £49

From New York to:
Auckland US$71
Christchurch US$73
Brisbane US$79
Sydney US$82
Melbourne $US86
Perth US$100

Go green: three ways to skip the internal flight

➤➤ If your children *really* like trains, hop aboard the Great Southern Railway (gsr.com.au) which operates the weekly Ghan service between Darwin and Adelaide, as well as the 4352-km, three-night Indian Pacific epic from Sydney to Perth, stopping in Adelaide en route.

➤➤ Hop on the Sealink ferry (sealink.com.au) to Kangaroo Island, which runs several times daily between Cape Jervis and Penneshaw.

➤➤ Get around New Zealand with a three-in-one Intercity Travelpass (travelpass.co.nz) that combines national coach travel, one ferry crossing (Wellington-Picton) and one train journey (choose from the spectacular TranzAlpine, TranzCoastal or Overlander routes).

Tour operators

In the UK

Bridge & Wickers (bridgeandwickers.co.uk)
Discover The World (discover-the-world.co.uk)
Freedom Australia and New Zealand (freedomaustralia.co.uk)
Intrepid Travel (intrepidtravel.com)

bedrooms and a kitchen, offer a practical solution for families, although motorhomes (see Getting around) will generally work out cheaper. A campsite with power hook-up and waste disposal costs around A$25 or NZ$30 per night. Try to make room in your itinerary for a family farmstay (see page 327). You'll appreciate the occasional break from your campervan and kids love helping out on the farm. In New Zealand, self-catering seaside holiday homes, or bachs, are as popular with locals as they are with tourists. Rental is usually for a minimum of three nights and rates vary from around NZ$200-350 during peak season. Kiwi Bach and Holiday Homes (kiwibachandholidayhomes.co.nz) has a selection of properties at Ohope Beach on North Island's Bay of Plenty; Holiday Houses (holidayhouses.co.nz) rents out bachs on the popular Coromandel Peninsula, while Book a Bach (bookabach.co.nz) provides a letting service for hundreds of bachs throughout New Zealand. For a spot of luxury, Australia and New Zealand have no shortage of special places to stay. UK-based Bridge & Wickers (bridgeandwickers.co.uk) offers a range of largely upmarket family accommodation, including mouthwatering properties in Australia like Chocolate Gannets (stylish two-bedroom villas overlooking the Great Ocean Road, Victoria), Dunk Island (tropical paradise in North Queensland with a World Heritage listed rainforest, boat trips to the Reef and a kids' club) and Quay West Suites (spectacular apartments overlooking Sydney Harbour). Whatever type of accommodation you go for, book well in advance during school holidays. Try regional tourist office websites for online directories.

Food and drink

Whether you believe in the Aussie or Kiwi version of the origins of pavlova, kids will be pleased to discover that it is readily available in both countries, along with other sweet treats like Hokey Pokey ice-cream (a calorific concoction of ice cream, strawberries, golden syrup and sugar) and Rocky Road (a chocolate, marshmallow, biscuit and nut extravaganza). Parents, meanwhile, will be happy to learn that Australia and New Zealand have a bountiful cuisine with plenty of less tooth-rotting options. In New Zealand, national specialities range from kiwi fruit to lamb – both juicy and delicious in their own way. Expect to eat pumpkin and kumara (sweet potatoes) with a traditional roast. During a Maori cultural tour

Top to bottom: Luxury apartment on Hamilton Island; O'Reilly's Rainforest Retreat; typical Kiwi bach, Coromandel.

you may be invited to try food cooked in an earth oven, or *hangi*. As you'd expect, New Zealand's seafood is excellent, while grown-ups will no doubt be keen to sample the fine chardonnays and sauvignon blancs from prime wine regions like Marlborough and Hawkes Bay. Australian food and drink is equally palatable. Children with big appetites will enjoy getting to grips with authentic Aussie barbecues of chicken, steak and seafood. Fresh fruits and vegetables are abundant, particularly in subtropical and tropical regions, while coastal areas are renowned for their varied seafood. Cities offer a rich blend of flavours, with influences from Europe, Asia and the Pacific. From pies and pizza to Chinese yum cha and Thai green curry, kids can be as adventurous as they like.

Health and safety

Australia and New Zealand are generally very safe countries to visit. As with travel anywhere, it's wise to be up to date with regular vaccinations, especially tetanus. Take extra care when driving long distances or trying out adrenaline-charged adventure activities. Be especially wary of exposure to heat and sun, particularly in desert and coastal regions of Australia. Wear hats and sunblock and drink plenty of water. In New Zealand, be prepared for sudden changes in the weather, especially if you are planning outdoor activities in remote

Aussie lingo

Ankle biter Small child
Bush telly Campfire
Corker Excellent
Don't spit the dummy Don't get upset
Fair dinkum True, real, genuine
Holy dooley! Good heavens!
It's gone walkabout It's lost
Rip snorter Something fantastic
Shark biscuit Someone new to surfing
Tell a porky Lie

regions like Fiordland. Sandflies can be a nuisance in some areas, so remember to take repellent. There are several potentially dangerous animals in Australia, ranging from snakes and spiders to saltwater crocodiles, but as long as you take precautions and follow the advice of your guide in national parks and other wild areas, you're unlikely to be troubled. Box jellyfish and the Irukandji jellyfish (collectively known as marine stingers) affect beaches in northern Australia between October and June. Always seek advice from local lifeguards before swimming and wear wetsuits or lycra swimsuits. Stinger nets protect certain beaches at Port Douglas, Cairns, Mission Beach and Townsville.

Below: Lifeguards patrol many surfing beaches; stinger suits help protect against jellyfish.

Fact file

	Time	Language	Money	Code	Tourist info
Australia	GMT +8 West GMT +10 East	English	Australian Dollar (A$) £1 = A$2.50	+61	australia.com
New Zealand	GMT	English and Maori	New Zealand Dollar (NZ$) £1 = NZ$2.90	+64	newzealand.com

New Zealand farmstays

Farmstays are becoming an increasingly popular way of experiencing the 'real' New Zealand. They are located amidst some of the country's most spectacular scenery, and hosts can provide fascinating insights into farming history and rural life. You can expect few other guests, a relaxed atmosphere and genuine hospitality from people who are proud of their country and want to share it with you. Some operate year-round, while others open only for the summer tourist season, October to March. The main sheep-shearing period is June to August (with lambs sheared March to May); lambing and calving can start as early as September, while livestock numbers reach their peak between December and February.

Lake Hawea Station

Where? Wanaka, Central Otago, South Island.
Why? Farmstay accommodation is in two converted musterer's huts that, despite having been refurbished with comfortable lounges and modern kitchens, still retain a rustic air. You'll find patchwork quilts, woodburning stoves and piles of old farming magazines. The cottages sleep between five and eight, so are a good bet for families. Decks provide wonderful views of Lake Hawea and surrounding mountains. Walking, fishing and horseriding are available either on or near the farm, while Queenstown's adventure activities are all within an hour's drive.
How much? From NZ$160 per night for two people and NZ$15 per night for children under 12.
Contact lakehaweastation.co.nz.

The Farm

Where? Tutaematai, near the Bay of Islands, Northland, North Island.
Why? There's loads to do at this 400-ha dairy farm which stretches from Russell Forest to Whangaruru harbour and combines traditional farming activities (like milking cows and feeding pigs) with more adventurous pursuits such as kayaking through mangrove estuaries, horse riding in the surrounding hills and forests and even learning to ride a motorbike using special kids' mini bikes. You can stay in the farmhouse, have a party in the woolshed or build your own wilderness camp beside a swimming hole complete with cooking fire and long drop toilet. Meanwhile, some of North Island's best beaches, fishing and diving sites are just a short distance away.
How much? From NZ$24 per en suite double or NZ$12 to camp. Breakfast NZ$6 and dinner NZ$12 per person. Introductory horse riding lesson NZ$45, motorbike riding lesson NZ$50, kayak hire NZ$15 per day.
Contact Contact thefarm.co.nz

Tasman Downs Station

Where? Lake Pukaki, near Mt Cook, South Island.
Why? A peaceful and remote Angus cattle station with two guest bedrooms reminiscent of a comfortable, old-fashioned B&B with floral bedspreads and dressing tables adorned with lace mats. A farm tour is not to be missed. Not only are there incredible views of Lake Pukaki and Mt Cook from the farm's high country, but the farm sheds reek of settler ingenuity and memorabilia – from a blacksmith's forge and 1944 tractor to a handmade watermill. You can also take a ride in a 1926 Model T Ford or drive an original Hamilton jet-boat on the lake.
How much? B&B from NZ$120 per double. Dinner NZ$45 per person.
Contact bnb.co.nz.

Above: Feeding the lambs (that's not really New Zealand Chardonnay in the bottle). **Bottom left:** View from the high ground at Lake Hawea Station. **Bottom right:** Mind how 'ewe' go.

Beach on the Bay – building sandcastles in San Francisco.

North America

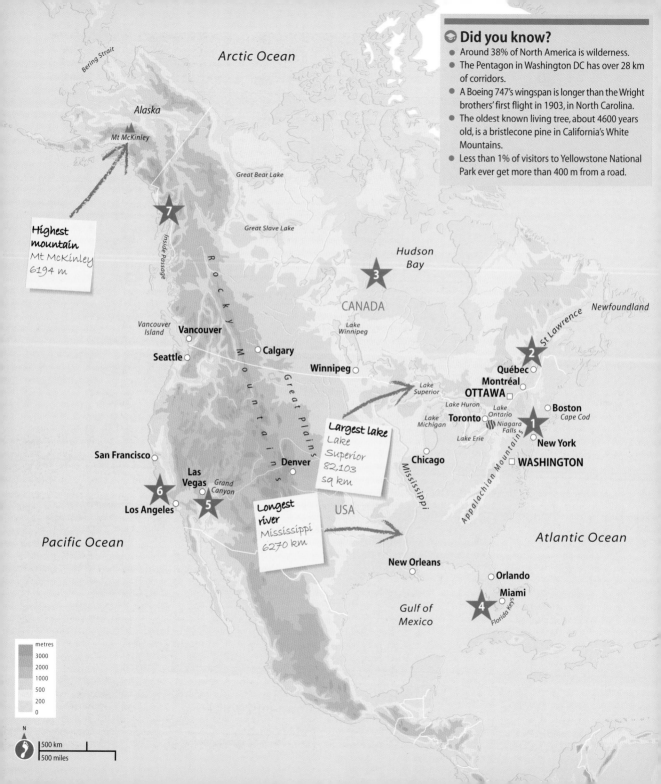

Arctic Ocean

Bering Strait

Alaska

Mt McKinley

Great Bear Lake

Great Slave Lake

Hudson
Bay

3

CANADA

Newfoundland

*Lake
Winnipeg*

St Lawrence

2

Québec

Montréal

OTTAWA

Lake Superior

Lake Huron

*Lake
Ontario*

*Lake
Michigan*

Toronto

*Niagara
Falls*

Lake Erie

1

Boston
Cape Cod

New York

□ **WASHINGTON**

Inside Passage

Rocky Mountains

Great Plains

Vancouver
Island

Vancouver

Seattle

Calgary

Winnipeg

Chicago

Mississippi

Appalachian Mountains

San Francisco

Denver

**Las
Vegas**

*Grand
Canyon*

6

5

Los Angeles

USA

Pacific Ocean

Atlantic Ocean

New Orleans

Orlando

Miami

4

Gulf of
Mexico

Florida Keys

7

Highest
mountain
Mt McKinley
6194 m

Largest lake
Lake
Superior
82,103
sq km

Longest
river
Mississippi
6270 km

metres
3000
2000
1000
500
200
0

N

500 km

500 miles

Introduction

Let's face it – given half a chance, most kids would happily trade a sibling or possibly even a parent for the chance to go on holiday to North America! And the reason can be summed up in three simple letters: 'wow'. It's not simply the fact that Canada and the United States offer spectacular wilderness, epic adventures, engaging cities, cutting-edge theme parks and idyllic beaches – lots of places in the world have those. Rather, it's the continent's flare for combining these attributes into an irresistible family-friendly package, where you know that everything from transport and food to the park ranger talk and the waitress saying "Have a nice day" will make you feel welcome and relaxed. In a child's mind, North America's 'wow' factor is also borne from the sheer scale of everything, from California's redwoods to Orlando's roller coasters. But somehow, it never seems overwhelming – there's almost always an option for any age, whether you're searching for orcas off Vancouver Island, delving into the Everglades or getting a taste of the Big Apple. North America's stringent (and inevitably protracted) airport security might put some parents off, but once you're through immigration there's no denying that this is a supremely family-friendly destination.

❝ ❞ *When our twins were 18 months old, we spent several hours trying to transport them in a buggy across Québec's Bonaventure Island to show them North America's largest colony of gannets. After the buggy collapsed into a tangle of buckled metal, I vowed never to do anything remotely adventurous again until they were at least 18. Then a park ranger appeared from nowhere and casually attached our buggy to the back of his quad bike. Within minutes we were motoring on our way towards an unforgettable encounter with 110,000 noisy, smelly gannets.*

Will

North America rating

Wow factor
★★★★★

Worry factor
★★

Value for money
★★★★

Keeping teacher happy
★★★★

Family accommodation
★★★★★

Babies & toddlers
★★★★

Teenagers
★★★★★

Books to read

Bear and Turtle and the Great Lake Race, Child's Play, 2005
Based on a traditional Native American trickster tale, turtle attempts to outsmart a grumpy old bear. Ages 4-7

A Tree for All Seasons, National Geographic, 2001
See how a maple tree changes through the year; discover the wildlife of America's maple forests and find out where maple syrup comes from. Ages 4-8

M is for Majestic, Sleeping Bear Press, 2007
"A is for Acadia, where the mountains meet the shore, and the forest stands silent beside the ocean's roar." Explore the national parks of the United States from A to Z in this evocative picture book. Ages 4-8

Gold Fever! , National Geographic, 1999
Well researched and illustrated, this absorbing book uses journals and letters from the forty-niners themselves, to evoke a colourful chapter in American history. Ages 6+

The Escape of the Deadly Dinosaur, Random House, 2007
An Allosaurus is on the rampage through the streets of New York. Can Secret Agent Jack Stalwart save the day? Over 100 pages of non-stop action. Ages 7+

Little House on the Prairie, HarperTrophy, 2007
Laura Ingalls Wilder's classic 1935 tale, based on her family's life in the 19th-century American west. Ages 9-12

Golden Gate Bridge factoids
Length 1900 m.
Rivets per tower 600,000.
Flexibility 8 m of 'bend' during an earthquake.

🔍 How to pan for gold

Panning is easy – it's finding the gold that's the hard part! First, find a pan – anything with sloping sides will do, but don't use a Teflon-coated one. Next, find a likely location. The best places are along creeks, particularly behind boulders where eddies form. Black sand containing magnetite is also a good indicator that you're in the right spot. Scoop up some sand and gravel from the creek. Fill the rest of the pan with water and start shaking it gently from side to side. After a couple of minutes (adding more water when necessary), pick out and discard the bigger stones that are becoming separated – but make sure you don't throw away any nuggets! Now start adding a circular motion to your panning, swirling the soupy mixture of water and grit around so that gravel starts to slop over the side. Always keep the rim of the pan higher than the base, otherwise you may lose the gold that naturally settles to the bottom. Take care and slow down when you get to the last traces of sediment in your pan. See any gold? "Bonanza!" is the traditional declaration of success.

How to make a dreamcatcher

Traditionally made of willow and hide, Native American dreamcatchers are hung above sleeping children (or grown-ups) to trap bad dreams and let the good ones filter through.

What you need
- A bendy twig about 30 cm long
- Thin wire
- String
- Beads
- Feathers

What to do
- Carefully bend the twig into a circle and tie the two ends together using wire.
- Take a long piece of string and tie one end to the twig hoop.
- Thread a few of the beads on to the string.
- Wrap the string around the opposite side of the hoop.
- Thread some more beads and repeat the process, creating a web design.
- Tie some smaller pieces of string to the bottom of the hoop and attach the feathers.
- Hang the dream-catcher above your bed and sleep well.

Where can I see this?

Giant redwoods, or sequoias, can be found in several national parks in California.

Measuring 274 ft 9 in (83.8 m) tall, and with a trunk circumference of 102 ft 6in (31.1 m), General Sherman is the world's biggest tree and largest living thing. You can see this champion giant sequoia in Sequoia National Park.

Ways to survive in the wilderness

It's a jungle out there (or a desert, canyon, mountain range…). You've packed the essentials: sunblock, sun hat, insect repellent, water bottle, first-aid kit, map, compass and snacks. Here are three essential extras should you become lost in the wilderness.

Whistle One of the best ways to attract attention when lost.

Identification/medical alert bracelet Vital if you're unconscious when found.

Large garbage bag Makes an excellent survival bag. Cut a slit for your face and pull it over your head to conserve body heat.

Taste of North America: Pecan pie

A popular holiday dessert, particularly in the southern states of the USA, pecan pie is delicious and easy to make.

What you need
- 23-cm pie case
- 3 eggs
- 110 g sugar
- 4 tbsp golden syrup
- 50 g butter
- Pinch of salt
- Vanilla extract
- 175 g pecan halves

What to do
- Preheat oven to 200°C and place the pastry case in a baking tin.
- Beat the eggs in a large mixing bowl.
- Add the remaining ingredients and mix well.
- Pour the mixture into the pastry case, bake for 10 minutes and then reduce the oven temperature to 180°C and bake for another 30 minutes.
- Remove from tin, allow to cool slightly, and then serve with vanilla ice cream.

Top 10 zoos
Bronx Zoo, New York
bronxzoo.com
Brookfield Zoo, Illinois
brookfieldzoo.org
Calgary Zoo, Alberta
calgaryzoo.org
Cincinnati Zoo, Ohio
cincyzoo.org
Maryland Zoo, Baltimore
marylandzoo.org
National Zoo, Washington DC
nationalzoo.si.edu
San Antonio Zoo, Texas
sazoo-aq.org
San Diego Zoo, California
sandiegozoo.org
Toronto Zoo, Ontario
torontozoo.com
Zoo Atlanta, Georgia
zooatlanta.org

Top 10 aquariums
Aquarium of the Pacific, California
aquariumofpacific.org
Georgia Aquarium, Atlanta
georgiaaquarium.org
Monterey Bay Aquarium, California mbayaq.org
Mystic Aquarium, Connecticut
mysticaquarium.org
National Aquarium, Baltimore aqua.org
New England Aquarium, Boston
newenglandaquarium.org
SeaWorld, California
seaworld.com
Shedd Aquarium, Chicago
sheddaquarium.org
Tennessee Aquarium, Tennessee tnaqua.org
Vancouver Aquarium, BC
vanaqua.org

Tots to teens

From a family travel perspective, North America is rather like an inside-out sandwich – all the tasty, interesting bits seem to be on the outside (the east and west coasts) rather than in the middle. Florida is bound to be the first place kids set their hungry eyes on, followed by California. The vast space in between becomes a blur as they bounce back and forth between Orlando and San Francisco, New York and Vancouver. However, while there's no denying the immense appeal of North America's coastal states and provinces, don't overlook Yellowstone, the Grand Canyon and other inland natural wonders.

Babies (0-18 months)

Logistically, once you're there, travelling with a baby in North America presents no major headaches. Shops selling baby supplies are open 24/7, baby-changing facilities are widespread and there's rarely a problem finding a hotel or restaurant with a cot or highchair. One of the big issues for parents travelling from Europe is going to be the transatlantic flight. It takes at least nine hours to fly from London to Orlando and around eight to reach New York or Toronto. And that's before you've factored in airport time and the gruelling queues that go hand in hand with increased security measures. Journey (and jet lag) aside, you also need to consider North America's 'baby appeal'. Tiny tots will love Florida's beaches, but will get very little from its theme parks. Similarly, they might enjoy a good crawl in Central Park, but will be oblivious to the other delights of New York. There are some amazing things to see and do in North America but can you wait until your kids are old enough to appreciate them?

Toddlers/pre-school (18 months-4 years)

With everything from Disney to Wet 'n Wild, Florida is one giant playground. However, many parents are wary of taking toddlers, claiming that "they won't appreciate the magic" or "they'll be too small for the rides". While it's true that kids will get more from Orlando's attractions when they're five-plus (see page 344), remember that it's not compulsory to spend a week trailblazing every roller coaster and waterslide in the state. A good option with young children is to pick a couple of parks (Magic Kingdom and SeaWorld, for example, have plenty to interest even toddlers) and combine these with the fantastic beaches. You might want to give the Everglades a miss with toddlers – or at the very least restrain them with reins to prevent them from nosediving into all those alligator-infested creeks. Stressful moments could also be envisaged at precipitous attractions, like Niagara Falls or the Grand Canyon. That's not to say kids of this age group are barred from anything adventurous in the USA or Canada. Far from it. There are family-friendly guest ranches in the Rockies where you can give them a taster of the Wild West and even plonk them on a horse for a gentle ride. You could also go

whale watching, skiing or base yourself in a family-friendly city like San Francisco or Vancouver from where you can make brief forays into the Great Outdoors.

Kids/school age (4-12 years)

At this age, most kids will be boggle-eyed over the prospect of a holiday in North America. Take them to Florida and they'll be able to live the magic, feel the adrenaline rush and get the autographs of all their favourite characters. You'll also get 'added value' from the state in the form of educational excursions to the Kennedy Space Center and the Everglades. If you're looking to expand your kids' minds, you won't find anywhere in North America more 'brainy' than Washington DC with its superb museum complex showcasing everything from dinosaurs to space shuttles. British Columbia's First Nation heritage also offers great scope for an educational odyssey, as does Quebec and New England with their vivid tales of early settler life. When it comes to stimulating young minds, however, the real jewel in the crown is the US National Park Service. Parks like Yosemite, Acadia and Zion not only offer access to landscapes oozing with the 'wow' factor but also provide outstanding interpretation for children – whether it's a ranger-led walk or the highly acclaimed Junior Ranger Program (see page 339). Of course, national parks are also some of the best places for embarking on adventures, from paddling a canoe in Banff to riding a mule into the Grand Canyon.

Teenagers (13 years+)

New York has immense appeal to teenagers, as do other cool cities like San Francisco, Las Vegas and Miami. If your teen is less of an urban beast and more of an adrenaline monster, let them loose on the big rides in Florida and California, or challenge them to a backcountry expedition, horse riding

The great outdoors and the great indoors – taking in the views at the Grand Canyon, counting gannets in Quebec and zapping aliens at Universal Orlando Resort

through the Rockies, trekking in the Appalachians or kayaking in Alaska. Classic road journeys, like the Pacific Coast Highway and Route 66, will also appeal to older children, particularly if you let them help plan the journey and choose the cruising music. Various family adventure tour operators offer teenage departures on their North American itineraries, including Explore Worldwide, Exodus and Families Worldwide.

Special needs

Easter Seals (easterseals.com) runs 140 accessible camping and recreation facilities for children and adults, Alpenglow Adventures (alpenglowadventures.org) offers challenging trips for people with physical disabilities, including expeditions into the Grand Canyon, and Accessible Journeys (disabilitytravel.com) offers wheelchair-accessible tours in Wyoming, South Dakota and the Canadian Rockies. Also try Adaptive Adventures (adaptiveadventures.org) and World on Wheelz (worldonwheelz.com). For regional information, contact Accessible Alaska Adventures (accessiblealaska.com), Accessible San Diego (accessandiego.com), Access Utah Network (accessut.state.ut.us), Access Victoria (access victoria.com), Disabled Accommodation Miami (disabled apartments.com) and the Colorado-based Access Anything (accessanything.net). For travellers from the UK, Virgin Holidays (virginholidays.co.uk) has a dedicated team to help plan holiday arrangements for people with special needs.

Single parents

The most comprehensive resource, Single Parent Tours (singleparenttravel.net) offers advice and tips for single parents, as well as a selection of tours. Neilson (neilson.co.uk) offers discounts for single parents on skiing trips to the Rockies.

Hawaiian hot stuff

Hawaii is a five-hour flight from San Francisco and has a time difference of GMT-10. That might seem like a long way to go for a beach holiday, but there's a lot more to this far-flung Pacific archipelago than the sun, sand and surf of Waikiki. The tips of huge volcanoes rising from the floor of the Pacific, the islands of Hawaii are one of the best places in the world to see molten lava, steam vents and other volcanic bedlam. In contrast to the smouldering desolation of calderas like Kilauea, other parts of Hawaii run riot with verdant tropical forests. There are towering sea cliffs and waterfalls, while on Kauai you'll even find a kilometre-deep 'Grand Canyon of the Pacific'. The surrounding seas teem with life, whether you want to watch humpback whales breaching off Maui or peer into the aquarium-like tidal pools of Hulopoe Bay on Lanai. Hawaii's Polynesian culture is just as exuberant and fascinating, while the Second World War monuments in Pearl Harbour provide a more sobering insight into the islands' history.

⏩ Get an eyeful of one of the world's most active volcanoes at the Kilauea Visitor Center in Hawai'i, Volcanoes National Park. If it's spewing lava, take a sightseeing flight to watch the bright ribbons of molten rock flowing into the sea amid great clouds of steam.

⏩ Watch the sunrise over Haleakala – a dormant volcano on Maui that's big enough to swallow Manhattan.

Getting there Over 20 domestic airlines and 16 international carriers serve Honolulu International Airport on Oahu. There are also direct flights from the US mainland to Maui, Kauai and Big Island.

Getting around Bus tours, taxis, public transport and hire cars are available on most islands.

Capital attractions and the Big Apple

Visiting the world's largest museum complex might seem like anathema to kids, but don't let that put you off going to Washington DC. Far from being dusty, dingy and dull, the Smithsonian Institution Museums are utterly riveting and could easily consume three or more days of your holiday with barely a yawn or a shuffle of feet. Combine the US capital with some free-spirited roaming in Virginia's Blue Ridge Mountains and then head north for a good drenching at mighty Niagara Falls. From there, either loop south to New York for a head-spinning finale of shopping and sightseeing, or strike east towards New England where the beaches of Cape Cod and Maine beckon.

Above: The Boeing Aviation Hangar at the National Air and Space Museum's Udvar-Hazy Center.

Washington DC

» Children's Concierge (childrensconcierge.com) offers city tours that are tailor-made to the ages and interests of your children.
» If you don't fancy walking, Bike the Sites (bikethesites.com), Segs in the City (segsinthecity.net) and DC Ducks (dcducks.com) offer interesting alternatives.
» Published each Friday, the *Washington Post* weekend section has a listing of child-friendly events. Further tourist information is available at washington.org.

City highlights

Above: The Apollo 11 Command Module Columbia in the National Air and Space Museum. **Below right**: Shenandoah National Park. **Far Right**: Maid of the Mist cruise at Niagara.

Lying at the heart of Washington DC, the National Mall is the epicentre for sightseeing in the capital. At one end, you've got the US Capitol (aoc.gov) and at the other, the Washington Monument and White House. All three are worth at least a walk past, but it's the treasure trove of museums lining each side of the Mall that will fascinate children. Pick two or three that particularly appeal and intersperse them with less brain-curdling stuff, like a visit to the National

Zoological Park (nationalzoo.si.edu) with its giant pandas, gorillas and tigers, an outing to the National Theatre (nationaltheatre.org) which holds free shows on Saturday mornings, or a day trip to Rock Creek Park and Nature Center (nps.gov) which has trails for walking, cycling and horse riding.

Best Museums No visit to Washington DC is complete without experiencing at least one of the Smithsonian Institution's 14 museums (open daily, 1000-1730, admission free). The National Air and Space Museum (nasm.si.edu) is a shrine to flying. Exhibits range from the original 1903 *Wright Flyer* to the command module of *Apollo 11*. You can handle a lump of moon rock, take a virtual journey through space and race paper darts. If your kids want more, a separate branch of the museum, the Udvar-Hazy Center near Washington Dulles International Airport, has a vast hangar where pride of place goes to the Space Shuttle *Enterprise*. More winged wonders can be seen in the butterfly garden outside the National Museum of Natural History (mnh.si.edu). Inside you'll

find an imposing array of creatures, including an African elephant and 15-m-long northern right whale. In the Hall of Mammals, you can experience a thunderstorm and crawl through an arctic snow tunnel. Dinosaur nuts won't be disappointed either. As well as allosaurus, diplodocus and a digitally restored triceratops, you'll find a life-size model of a pterosaur with a 12-m wingspan and the jaws of a prehistoric shark, with 15-cm-long teeth. Have a peep at the palaeontologists at work in the glass-enclosed FossilLab, then do a spot of detective work yourself in the hands-on Discovery Room. Not for the squeamish, the Insect Zoo holds tarantula-feeding demonstrations and a chance to handle live insects. If you prefer bugs of the electronic variety, slink over to the International Spy Museum (spymuseum.org) where the KidSpy programme of workshops, demonstrations, and action-packed missions will hone the skills of every 003½. Other worthwhile museums include the National Museum of the American Indian (nmai.si.edu), the Hirshhorn Museum and Sculpture Garden (hirshhorn.si.edu) and the National Gallery of Art (nga.gov).

How to escape the big city

From Washington DC, head 120 km westbound on I-66 and you'll reach Front Royal – starting point for the spectacular Skyline Drive. This 170-km route undulates across the forested ridges of the Appalachian Mountains in Shenandoah National Park. Be sure to take a walk in the woods, even if it's just on the Limberlost Trail (milepost 43), a gentle 2-km stroll that's accessible to all. At Waynesboro, the road continues south on the 755-km Blue Ridge Parkway through the Great Smoky Mountains.

Niagara Falls

Tourism is in free-flow at Niagara Falls, where both Canada and the United States have splashed out on added attractions ranging from fireworks shows to a wax museum and haunted house. However, the 800-m-wide, 50-m-high Horseshoe Falls, together with its smaller sibling, the 30-m-wide American Falls, still manage to steal the thunder. The Canadian shore has panoramic views of both cataracts, while the US side has lookouts over American Falls from Prospect Point, and Horseshoe Falls from Terrapin Point. But don't stop there. You can also look down on the Falls from the 160-m-tall Skylon Tower (skylontower.com); circle them in a chopper with Niagara Helicopters (niagarahelicopters.com); skim over rapids beneath them with Whirlpool Jet Boat Tours (whirlpooljet.com) – minimum age six; and rise serenely above it all with the Great American Balloon Company (flightofangels.net). However, the best way to guarantee that Niagara Falls leaves an indelible impression on your children is for them to get well and truly soaked. The classic way to do this, of course, is with Maid of the Mist (maidofthemist.com), a plucky little fleet of sightseeing boats that conveys its passengers (clad in blue rain ponchos) to the base of the Falls. If you prefer something firmer under your feet, the Cave of Winds Tour (niagarafallsstatepark.com) takes you down into Niagara Gorge by elevator where (after donning yet more souvenir rain capes) you follow a guide on boardwalks to the Hurricane Deck, within 6 m of American Falls. The cave was obliterated by a rockfall in 1954, but you can still experience winds of over 100 kph – not to mention lashings of spray. Perhaps the most unique perspective of Niagara, however, is from the Journey Behind the Falls (niagaraparks.com) where tunnels take you to portals that look out through the plumes of water flowing over Horseshoe Falls. As you peer through the blur of water, try to imagine 3 million litres of the stuff passing before your eyes every second.

Kids' top 10: New York

1 See the classic sights of Manhattan. The best view is from the top of the Empire State Building (esbnyc.com) where elevators whisk you up to an observation deck on the 80th floor. Be prepared for queues and crowds. The neon razzmatazz of Times Square is another must-see, as is the Rockefeller Center (rockefellercenter.com) where there are dizzying views from the 70th floor and tours of NBC Studios.

2 Shop at mega toy stores like Fifth Avenue's FAO Schwarz (fao.com) and Toys 'R' Us in Times Square. The American Girl Place is heaven on earth for anyone dotty about dollies.

3 Run free in Central Park, NYC's 340-ha green oasis where you can cycle, fly kites, throw Frisbees, ride on a vintage carousel or visit the Wildlife Center.

4 Cower beneath dinosaurs at the American Museum of Natural History (amnh.org) where you'll find T Rex, Apatosaurus and Stegosaurus. Don't miss the superb dioramas of African and North American mammals.

5 Cruise to the Statue of Liberty (nps.gov/stli) and gaze in awe at the 225-ton icon with the 140-cm-long nose, before continuing to Ellis Island (ellisisland.org) where the Immigration Museum brings history to life.

6 Catch a show on Broadway. Long-running children's favourites include *The Lion King* and *Mary Poppins*, while the New Victory Theatre (newvictory.org) stages shows and dance performances exclusively for family audiences.

7 Kayak from Pier 64 with the Manhattan Kayak Company (manhattankayak.com). Or, if you prefer something zippier, board the Beast (circleline42.com) for a 70-kph speedboat ride around the harbour (minimum height 102 cm).

8 Board the *USS Intrepid*, a Second World War aircraft carrier moored at Pier 86. Closed for refurbishment until autumn 2008, the Intrepid Sea, Air and Space Museum (intrepidmuseum.org) also features the nuclear submarine, *Growler* and the supersonic jet, *Concorde*.

9 Learn how to make a movie or animate a cartoon at the American Museum of the Moving Image (ammi.org), where interactive exhibits mingle with special effects props, such as a Yoda puppet from *The Empire Strikes Back*. For more star worship, check out Britney Spears, Brandon Routh, Johnny Depp and other waxwork wonders at Madame Tussauds (nycwax.com).

10 Ride in style on a stretch limo over Brooklyn Bridge or flit over the Big Apple with New York Helicopters (newyorkhelicopter.com) which offers 15-minute flights for around US$190 per person.

❓ What about Ground Zero?

If you have older children, consider joining a walking tour and visiting the Ground Zero Museum (groundzeromuseum workshop.com) which contains a deeply moving display of images and remnants from 9/11.

❝❞ In New York, kids love hailing cabs since it gives them a good reason to jump up and down and yell.

Will

🌎 Big Apple tips

Big Apple Greeters (bigapplegreeter.org) Free tours by locals who love NYC.

City Pass (citypass.com) A great way to save money on sightseeing and eating out.

Unlimited MetroCards (mta.info) Use subways and buses as often as you like.

Top left: *USS Constitution*. **Above:** Beach at Nantucket, Cape Cod. **Below left:** West Quoddy Lighthouse.

New England

⚑ ⚐ ⚑ ⊕ ⊍ ⊘ ⊗ ⊞

» The Boston City Pass (citypass.com) includes admission to the Harvard Museum of Natural History, the New England Aquarium and 4 other attractions.
» Regional tourist office websites include mass-vacation.com, visitrhodeisland.com, vermontvacation.com and mainetourism.com.

Boston A fun way to introduce kids to the major sights, Boston Duck Tours (bostonducktours.com) operates a fleet of amphibious landing craft. As well as splashing into the Charles River for a duck's-eye view of the city, you'll visit Boston Common (the oldest public park in the United States, established in 1634), the Public Garden (a more manicured landscape, famous for its Swan Boats) and the USS Constitution (ussconstitution.navy.mil) – a magnificent 18th-century frigate that earned the nickname 'Old Ironsides' after it shrugged off a broadside from British warships during the War of 1812.

Cape Cod The spectacular Cape Cod National Seashore (nps.gov/caco) preserves a 50-km stretch of sandy coastline, pimpled here and there with historic lighthouses and easily explored by bike along the Cape Cod Rail Trail. The walking trails at Salt Pond Visitor Center are also worth exploring, but take care if you're tempted to take a dip in the ocean – it's cold and prone to surf and strong currents. It was on this dune-backed shore, in 1620, that the Pilgrims first set foot on American soil having voyaged from England aboard the *Mayflower* – a full-scale replica of which can be seen at Plimoth Plantation (plimoth.org).

Rhode Island There's no shortage of sandy beaches along Rhode Island's 650-km coastline, but don't forget to coax the kids away from their sandcastles for a boat trip in search of humpback, fin and minke whales. Providence has a children's museum and a pleasant park, while Newport County is renowned for its decadent mansions (newportmansions.org). The grandest is Breakers – a 70-room, Italian Renaissance-style palazzo built in the late 1890s – but the best one to visit with kids is Beechwood where costumed actors evoke the refined atmosphere of Victorian high society. Other Rhode Island highlights include the International Tennis Hall of Fame (tennisfame.org) and the Flying Horse Carousel in Watch Hill that's believed to date from around 1867.

Vermont The Green Mountain State is best seen from on high, but that doesn't mean you have to be a serious trekker to reach great viewpoints. Mounts Olga, Elmore and Independence all have easy trails of less than 5 km, culminating in panoramic views across mountains, lakes and forests. Reward your efforts with a visit to either the Ben & Jerry's Ice Cream Factory (benjerry.com) in Waterbury or the Vermont Teddy Bear Factory (vermontteddybears.com) in Shelburne.

❓ Where can I see this?

More than 60 lighthouses rear above Maine's convoluted coastline, from Nubble Light in York to West Quoddy Head, the easternmost lighthouse in the United States. Check out lighthouse.cc/me for flashes of inspiration.

❓ Where can I do this?

Acadia National Park on Maine's Atlantic coast is rugged enough to appeal to adventurous children, but not too wild or remote to give parents the jitters. One of the best ways to explore this wave-gnawed outpost is in a stable two-person sea kayak, with a child up front and a parent steering in the back. Based in Bar Harbour on Mount Desert Island, Coastal Kayaking Tours (acadiafun.com) offers four-hour outings for families with children as young as eight. As well as learning the basics of sea kayaking, you will get to paddle along a dramatic coastline dotted with coves and villages. And if you're really lucky, a harbour seal or porpoise may join you for part of the way.

North American dreams for kids

Dinosaur hunter

North America is big on dinosaurs. Chicago's Field Museum (fieldmuseum.org) has Sue – the world's largest, most complete and best-preserved Tyrannosaurus rex skeleton, named after the palaeontologist who discovered it in 1990 in South Dakota. Sue's 58 teeth measure a knee-trembling 19 to 30 cm in length. For other great dinosaur exhibits, check out the National Museum of Natural History in Washington DC and New York's American Museum of Natural History (see pages 336-337). However, you can't call yourself a real dinosaur hunter unless you get out in the field. The most famous site is Dinosaur National Monument (nps.gov/dino) in Colorado where allosaurus, apatosaurus, diplodocus, stegosaurus and other Jurassic giants once roamed. Their bones lie exposed in a fossil-filled cliff in the Dinosaur Quarry Visitor Center. Sadly, this was closed in 2006 due to structural problems, but you can still see and touch replica fossils in the nearby Outdoor Visitor Center and watch a film

about the fossil wall. Just to the south lies the town of Dinosaur which has street names like Brontosaurus Boulevard, Triceratops Terrace and Diplodocus Drive. At Dinosaur Ridge (dinoridge.org) in Morrison, near Denver, you can explore the very spot where, in 1877, some of the world's first large dinosaur bones were discovered. A well-interpreted trail reveals iguanodon footprints and other prehistoric pointers. Dinosaur Valley State Park (tpwd.state.tx.us) near Glen Rose in Texas has more tantalizing tracks – this time showing how, 110 million years ago, a flesh-eating acrocanthosaurus stalked and attacked a long-necked pleurocoelus. In Canada, Dinosaur Provincial Park (tprc.alberta.ca/parks/dinosaur) in Alberta is the place to prowl. Not only can you see skeletons of Cretaceous beasts like albertosaurus and triceratops in the Royal Tyrrell Museum of Palaeontology (tyrrellmuseum.com), but you can also take guided hikes through the Alberta Badlands where discoveries are still being made. Keep your eyes peeled!

Cowboy (or girl)

There are numerous dude ranches – or guest ranches to use the preferred term – throughout the western states and provinces of North America (see pages 350-351). Riding along well-marked trails through the foothills of the Rocky Mountains is just part of the experience. You'll also toast marshmallows around the campfire, sleep in cosy log cabins and take part in other activities, from fly-fishing and float trips to roping lessons and square dancing. Many ranches cater for horse-riding novices, while others have a separate programme for children.

Junior Ranger

A fun way to learn about history, culture and the environment, the Junior Ranger Program operates in about 286 US national parks (nps.gov). To qualify as Junior Rangers, children aged 5-14 must complete a series of activities, games and puzzles during their park visit. Different parks offer different activities, so in the Everglades, for example, wannabee 'JRs' might investigate bird diversity or the importance of water conservation, while in Yellowstone they might tackle the basics of geothermal geology. Simply pick up a Junior Ranger activity pack at the park visitor centre, complete it at your own pace and then share your findings with a ranger to receive an official Junior Ranger badge and certificate. There's also an online programme called Web Rangers (nps.gov/webrangers) that contains puzzles, games and stories based on America's natural and cultural heritage.

The French Connection

A more enticing river would be hard to imagine. The mouth of the St Lawrence seems to gulp at the North Atlantic, its 1200-km gullet framed in the wolf-head profile of Québec. There's even a tongue, the Gaspé Peninsula, drooping above the dimpled chin of New Brunswick. The St Lawrence River is a hungry invitation to the heart of a continent. Along its length you'll encounter everything from whale sanctuaries to historic cities. Further west, Montréal, Toronto, Ottawa and the Great Lakes beckon, while to the north, vast swathes of forest-clad wilderness promise the ultimate initiation to Canada's Great Outdoors.

Québec

⬤ ⬤ ⬤ ⬤ ⬤ ⬤ ⬤ ⬤

» Although cities are well geared up for winter tourism, with all kinds of snowy capers, it's best to avoid the annual big freeze (Dec-Feb) if you want to venture further afield.

» Rue de Petit Champlain in Québec City is a popular hunting ground for souvenirs, but if you're serious about taking home wood carvings, model boats or traditional art try Saint-Jean-Port-Joli.

» Regional tourist office websites include bonjourquebec.com, ottawatourism.ca and ontariotravel.net.

Top: Québec City. Above: The gannet colony on Bonaventure Island, Gaspé Peninsula.

Montréal Founded in 1642 as a fur-trading centre, Québec's largest city has a fascinating historical district. You can easily explore Vieux-Montréal and its adjacent port on foot or by bike. Star sights in the old town include the richly adorned interior of the Basilique Notre-Dame (one of North America's finest churches) and the collection of early-settler artefacts in Château Ramezay. Keep these attractions short and sweet, however, since it's the old port (quaysoftheoldport.com) that really appeals to families. As well as cycling, skating or simply strolling through the riverside recreational park, you can take to the water on anything from an amphibious vehicle (amphitours.ca) to a jet boat (jetboatingmontreal.com). Don't miss the Montréal Science Centre (centredessciencesdemontreal.com) with its IMAX theatre and interactive exhibits on computers, robotics and physical phenomena. Almost as

perplexing is Montréal's Underground City – a vast subterranean maze of passageways and plazas lined with 1500 shops, 200 restaurants and 30 cinemas. Probing this parallel universe is the city's Métro, which can also whisk you to Olympic Park, site of the 1976 Olympic Games. Attractions here include the Olympic Stadium (used today for concerts, exhibitions and major-league baseball matches) and the 175-m-tall Montreal Tower. Nearby, the Biodome (biodome.qc.ca) recreates four ecosystems (tropical rainforest, polar, Laurentian Mountains and St Lawrence river) with superb attention to detail.

Québec City Overlooking the St Lawrence River, Terrasse Dufferin, a wide boardwalk beneath the copper-roofed landmark of the 1893 Château Frontenac, could almost have been purpose-built for families. Not only is the vast expanse of decking supremely buggy-friendly, but it is also riddled with street performers and ice-cream vendors. A long flight of steps (or a short funicular railway) leads to the Lower Town, or Basse-Ville, where you can wander among 18th- and 19th-century houses, browse in curio shops, watch street performers or relax in cafés. Just outside the old city walls, the historic battlefield of the Plains of Abraham is now a beautiful urban park with lots of space for picnics and hyperactive kids. Alternatively, drive 20 minutes out of town to Village Vacances Valcartier (valcartier.com) – Canada's largest waterpark with 35 slides, a Pirates'

Hideout and two themed river rides, as well as whitewater rafting and hydrospeed tours on the Jacques-Cartier River.

Tadoussac A relaxed holiday village at the confluence of the Saguenay and St Lawrence rivers, Tadoussac is steeped in history. Inside the reconstruction of the 1600 Chauvin Trading Post (tadoussac.com), kids (especially those who have seen Disney's *Pocahontas*) will be intrigued by the displays of Montagnais peace pipes, pelt scrapers and birch-frame snowshoes alongside European trade goods like rifles, metal knives and blankets – a time capsule that reflects some of the earliest meetings between settlers and Native Americans. The big reason for visiting Tadoussac, however, is what lurks beneath the St Lawrence. At the Sea Mammals Interpretation Center (baleinesendirect.net) you can learn about the 11 species of whales – from diminutive minkes to mighty blues – that migrate each summer into the river's estuary to feed on krill. A resident pod of white belugas is also present, and you have an excellent chance of spotting them on a three-hour whale-watching cruise with Croisieres 2001 (croisieres2001.com), available May to October.

Gaspé Peninsula The Appalachian Mountains fizzle out on this rugged peninsula of sea cliffs, brooding forests and 18th-century fishing villages. Highlights include the unexpectedly exotic Reford Gardens (jardinsmetis.com) and the exuberant (and whiffy) gannet colony on Bonaventure Island – reached by boat from the holiday centre of Percé. At Parc National Forillon (pc.gc.ca), the Grand-Grave National Historic Site bears witness to the hardships faced by early cod-fishing communities. Watch your kids' faces when they learn of the traditional recipe for soap: "Take water and mix with beef or pork suet, cod liver oil and sifted ashes from the woodstove."

Ontario

🅰 🅱 🅲 🅳 🅴 🅵 🅶 🅷 🅸 🅹

» Toronto, Ottowa and Niagara Falls are connected by bus and rail.
» The Toronto City Pass (citypass.com) includes admission to the CN Tower, Hockey Hall of Fame, Royal Ontario Museum, Ontario Science Center and Toronto Zoo.
» During Aug, nightly 'howls' are organized in Algonquin Provincial Park in an attempt to elicit a response from native wolf packs.

Toronto At 553 m in height, the CN Tower (cntower.ca) is the world's tallest free-standing structure. Rising like a colossal exclamation mark above Toronto's Harborfront, it offers views of up to 160 km on a clear day. With 1769 steps, the internal staircase is the longest in the world, but don't worry – the exterior, glass-fronted elevators will whisk you up the tower at ear-popping speed. The main lookout (that's the bulgy bit two-thirds of the way up) has a glass floor offering heart-in-mouth views of the city 342 m below, while above this there's an open viewing area with steel safety grills. But that's not the highest point for visitors. Just when you think you've controlled your vertigo, the kids will be dragging you towards another elevator bound for the Sky Pod at a dizzying 447 m. Back on ground level, height becomes an issue again at the Tower's Himalamazon motion theatre where you need to be at least 107 cm tall to ride. After the CN Tower, Toronto's other big family attraction requires a subway ride to the northeastern suburbs where Toronto Zoo (torontozoo.com) sprawls across a mighty 287-ha chunk of recreated African savannah, tropical rainforest, Canadian wilderness and Australian outback. Other more central highlights include the Royal Ontario Museum (rom.on.ca) which

has 18 complete dinosaur skeletons on display in the Michael Lee Chin Crystal Galleries, as well as a walk-through bat cave and a hands-on discovery centre.

Ottawa It's probably fair to say that Canada's capital has less to interest kids than Toronto, but you could easily spend a pleasant few hours in Ottawa exploring the cycling and walking paths along the banks of the Rideau Canal while ogling the Gothic pile of the Parliament Buildings. Nearby, you can pet livestock at the Central Experimental Farm or get to grips with exhibits at the National Museum of Science and Technology (sciencetech.technomuses.ca). South of the city, at Kingston, boat tours weave through the maze of The Thousand Islands. Boldt Castle, a millionaire's folly on one of the islands, has a quirky claim to fame as the birthplace of Thousand Island salad dressing.

Algonquin Provincial Park
Quintessentially Canadian, this 7725-sq-km patchwork of forests and lakes stretches to the west of Ottawa. Take your pick from some 1500 km of canoe trails, ranging from child-friendly paddles of just 6 km to epic 70-km camping expeditions. Keep your eyes peeled for beaver, moose and bear, and your ears open for the haunting cry of the loon. Find out more at the Algonquin Visitor Center

Top: Toronto skyline. **Above:** Loon on Lake Eerie.

(algonquinpark.on.ca).

The Great Lakes In addition to Niagara Falls (page 337) other highlights of the Great Lakes that lie within easy striking distance of Toronto include Point Pelee National Park (pc.gc.ca) on Lake Eerie where you can rent bikes or canoes and spot birds from the Marsh Boardwalk. North of Toronto, Georgian Bay (georgianbaytourism.com) on Lake Huron is a popular holiday spot with attractions ranging from the world's longest freshwater beach – a 14-km stretch of sand at Wasaga Beach (wasagabeach.com) – to Discovery Harbour (discoveryharbour.on.ca), a reconstruction of a 19th-century British naval base. Also in a historical vein, Sainte-Marie among the Hurons (saintemarieamongthehurons.on.ca) recreates a 17th-century French Jesuit mission. Don't miss the Bruce Peninsula – a great excuse for a day out with its sandy beaches, fishing villages and bizarre sea stacks.

❓ Where can I see one of these?
Polar bears can weigh 600 kg and sprint at over 40 kph. They are fearless, powerful hunters that can smell you coming from over 30 km away. That's why you're in a tundra buggy – a giant-wheeled 'snow bus' that provides a safe vantage from which to observe these magnificent beasts. Timing is crucial for a polar bear encounter. The peak period is October to early November when they congregate near Churchill on the west coast of Hudson Bay.

Wow! Wow! Triple Wow! With bells on

Florida is the number-one family destination in the United States – if not the entire universe. And it's small wonder. Not only is it home to Disney, Universal, SeaWorld and other dream parks, but Florida also has around 3000 km of sun-kissed coastline, and natural wonders ranging from the 'gator-filled Everglades to the coral reefs of the Florida Keys. Where else can you get face to face with Mickey Mouse, Cinderella and a real-life astronaut all within a few days? Or swim with gentle manatees one morning, and plunge down a death-defying waterslide the next. Whether your idea of fun is to paddle a canoe to a deserted island or take a simulated mission to Mars, Florida will always leave you wanting more. And more is exactly what you get – more waterparks, more theme parks, more wildlife encounters, more quirky attractions. So be warned: one visit to the Sunshine State will rarely be enough.

Top: Brown pelican on the pier at Naples. Above right: Young alligator in Corkscrew Swamp Sanctuary. Above: A handful of shells collected from the Gulf coast.

Regional highlights

» Shop around for special deals, such as free kids' places, rental car upgrades, twin-centre discounts and multi-theme-park passes.
» Rent a car at the airport – it will give you flexibility to roam at your own pace.
» Accommodation ranges from camping and self-catering apartments to resorts.
» For further tourist information visit flausa.com.

Miami Perfect if you don't want to rent a car, many of Miami's attractions are within easy walking or cycling distance. With its Latin American vibe, this is a particularly cool city for teenagers who will appreciate its art-deco buildings, buzzing nightlife and serious shopping potential, particularly at Aventura Mall, Dolphin Mall and the boutiques along Ocean Drive. As well as great beaches, Miami has numerous family attractions, including animal antics at Parrot Jungle Island (parrotjungle.com), Seaquarium (miamiseaquarium.com) and Metrozoo (miamimetrozoo.com), where there is an excellent zookeeper programme for children. The Miami Children's Museum (miamichildrensmuseum.org) has interactive exhibits ranging from a television studio to a mini cruise ship, while Gator Park (gatorpark.com) offers airboat rides into the Everglades National Park (see below). To the north

of Miami, chic Fort Lauderdale has beaches, pavement cafés and the vast Sawgrass Mills, one of America's largest outlet malls.

Florida Keys A 260-km chain of stepping stones extending into the Gulf of Mexico, Florida Keys consists of around 800 islands, 42 of which are linked by bridges. The entire archipelago lies within the Florida Keys National Marine Sanctuary (floridakeys.noaa.gov), while Key Largo provides access to the John Pennekamp Coral Reef State Park (pennekamppark.com) and Biscayne National Park (nps.gov/bisc), both of which offer snorkelling, diving and glass-bottom-boat tours. Heading west along the Keys, Islamorada's Theatre of the Sea (theaterofthesea.com) provides opportunities for swimming with dolphins, sea lions and stingrays. At Marathon, in the heart of the Keys, you can hike through a tropical hardwood grove and visit the home of an early settler family before crossing Seven Mile Bridge to Bahia Honda – a great spot for kayaking or simply lazing about on some of the Keys' best beaches. Next is Big Pine Key with its National Key Deer Refuge, while at the end of the chain lies Key West, renowned for its watersports and sunsets – the latter of which are celebrated by street performers in Mallory Square.

Everglades National Park A refuge to

endangered species like the American crocodile, Florida panther and West Indian manatee, this vast subtropical wetland sprawls over 600,000 ha of southern Florida. Stop at one of the park's four visitor centres (nps.gov/ever) for an introduction to the area's fascinating ecology and for details of independent and ranger-led activities. A short distance from the Ernest F Coe Visitor Center (the nearest to Miami), the 800-m Anhinga Trail offers one of the best opportunities for close-up views of birds and alligators. Continuing south towards Flamingo there are several short, well-interpreted trails (many of which are buggy-friendly) leading from parking areas along the 61-km Park Road. At Flamingo Visitor Center, boat tours explore Florida Bay and the backcountry. There are also several canoe and walking trails nearby (canoes can be rented from the marina). At Shark Valley Visitor Centre, off the Tamiami Trail, a tram tour leads to an observation tower providing superb views across the

❝❞ Walking through Corkscrew Swamp is like entering a movie-set for *Jurassic Park* – a lost world of giant trees and ferns rioting through a primordial swamp where alligators and turtles lurk beneath the surface.

Will

sawgrass prairie. The Gulf Coast Visitor Center at Everglades City is the jumping-off point for canoe trips along the Wilderness Waterway or Ten Thousand Islands. North American Canoe Tours (evergladesadventures.com) offer guided trips or, if you're up for a wilderness challenge, rent a canoe and set off on your own. It takes about three hours of gentle paddling to reach Kingston Key, where you can pitch a tent on a *chickee* (a wooden platform on stilts) and spend the night with nothing but manatees, ospreys and raccoons for company.

Naples Style-central for western Florida, Naples goes to town with boutique shops and gourmet restaurants. At the pier, kids will enjoy watching pelicans bellyflop on scraps tossed by fishermen. The Gulf Coast entrance to the Everglades is nearby (see above), and so too is Corkscrew Swamp Sanctuary (audubon.org) where a 3.6-km boardwalk weaves through pinewoods, prairie and an ancient stand of 40-m-tall bald cypress. As well as alligators, the 4455-ha reserve is renowned for its birdlife, including a large colony of endangered wood storks. To the south of Naples, Marco Island has gorgeous Gulf Coast beaches, like Sand Dollar Bay, where children will while away hours shelling, kayaking, snorkelling and building sandcastles. To the north of Naples are the equally laid-back islands of Sanibel and Captiva and the more lively mainland resort of Fort Myers.

Tampa Bay Two of the best-known Gulf Coast beach resorts in this area are Clearwater Beach and St Pete Beach, the latter claiming the world record for the longest string of consecutive sunny days (768). Apart from the weather, there's plenty to keep families happy here, from long sandy beaches to fishing trips and dolphin encounters. To the south lies Sarasota – another beach beauty. The big attraction in the Tampa Bay area, however, is Busch Gardens (buschgardens.com), a heady mix of exotic wildlife and pulse-pounding rides. One moment you'll be hand-feeding giraffes on the Serengeti Safari, the next you'll be clutching your stomach on SheiKra, North America's first dive coaster that sends riders on a 60-m vertical drop at speeds of over 110 kph. Other highlights include the Pirates 4D show and KaTonga, a musical celebration of African folklore. Just across the street, Busch Gardens' waterpark, Adventure Island, is awash with slippery slides, wave pools and adventure lagoons, but it's Riptide – Florida's only four-lane mat slide – that kids (over 106 cm tall) will be drooling over.

Orlando Home to Walt Disney World Resort, Universal Studios and SeaWorld, Orlando is theme-park heaven. See pages 344-345 for tips on how to plan the ultimate fantasy escape in Florida's number-one holiday destination. From Orlando, it's also possible to arrange excursions to east-coast highlights,

Fort Myers Beach.

❓ Where can I see this?

Crystal River National Wildlife Refuge (fws.gov/crystalriver) provides a unique opportunity to snorkel with manatees from November to March.

> **❝❞** I found myself face to face with a podgy mermaid figure hanging upright in the water, flippers clasping a beer-barrel body and tiny eyes lost in the wrinkled maze of its face.
>
> *Will*

including Kennedy Space Center (kennedyspacecenter.com) – see box – and Daytona USA (daytonausa.com), with its NASCAR motion simulator rides, live pit-stop races and IMAX movies.

❓ Where can I meet an astronaut?

It's just one of the 'other-worldly' experiences on offer at the superb Kennedy Space Center (kennedyspacecenter.com). Start with a tour of the LC-39 observation gantry for a bird's-eye view of the shuttle launch pads, then gawk at the huge *Saturn V* moon rocket and explore a mock-up of the International Space Station. You can then experience lift-off yourself with the Shuttle Launch Experience, a motion simulator that brings to life the sights, sounds and sensations of an actual launch. Equally riveting is the Space Station 3D IMAX presentation and the Astronaut Hall of Fame with its hands-on exhibits and collection of astronaut memorabilia. As for meeting a real-life astronaut, there are daily Astronaut Encounters where you can question a member of NASA's Astronaut Corps. Alternatively, sign up for Lunch with an Astronaut. If that inspires you to greater things, you can always enrol for Family ATX – an Astronaut Training Experience where families (with children aged 8-14) spend two days immersed in a special programme, riding simulators, building and launching rockets and performing a shuttle mission to the International Space Station in a full-scale orbiter mock-up.

🏖 Beaches

Siesta Beach Sarasota.

Caladesi Island Clearwater.

Lighthouse Point Park Daytona.

How to do Orlando

Top: Meeting Cinderella at the Magic Kingdom. **Above:** The Mummies at Universal Studios

How to fit everything in

It's not going to be easy. Your six-year-old daughter is desperate to meet Cinderella, your 10-year-old son wants to see a stunt show and your teenager is obsessed with roller coasters. To make the most of a family holiday in Orlando you need to plan each day with military precision. Once you've made a list of everyone's top five priorities you can start to shortlist which parks and attractions are 'must-dos' and which are 'maybes'. Then look critically at your itinerary and, if it's wall-to-wall theme parks, try to free up at least one day for a waterpark, one for Daytona Beach and another for Kennedy Space Center (see page 343). It's also useful to have a 'free' day where you can return to a favourite theme park to do the things you didn't have time for first time around.

How to pick the right park

There's something for all ages at every park. That said, however, certain parks appeal more to specific age groups, and many rides have height restrictions. If you have young children start by looking at Magic Kingdom and Animal Kingdom. With older children set your sights on Epcot and Disney-MGM. If you have children of widely mixed ages, SeaWorld and Universal's Islands of Adventure have a good range of attractions.

How to save money

Available for pre-purchase in the UK only, Disney's Ultimate Tickets provide unlimited admission to all Disney attractions for either two- or three-week periods. Better suited for shorter visits, five- or seven-day Premium Tickets allow unlimited entry to all four Disney theme parks and either four or six admissions to waterparks and other attractions depending on which version you purchase. The Orlando Flexticket (orlandoflexticket.co.uk) gives you 14 consecutive days of unlimited admission to four or five theme parks, including Universal Studios, Universal's Islands of Adventure, SeaWorld, Wet 'n Wild and Busch Gardens. You can also pre-book one- or two-week Universal Holiday Tickets for unlimited entry to Universal Studios, Universal's Islands of Adventure and Universal CityWalk venues.

How to save time

Personalized maps of any of Disney's four parks can be created online at disneyworld.disney.go.com. Simply select your favourite attractions, dining options and special events, and a customized map is generated which you can print out and take with you. Several of your must-dos are bound to have a FastPass facility. This is essentially a polite way of queue jumping – just insert your entrance ticket into a FastPass machine and you'll receive a designated time when you can board the ride by a special, often queue-free, entrance. The catch, of course, is that you can only FastPass one ride at a time. Still, it's worth doing as often as you can – as is Parent Switch, which allows parents with young children to take turns on adult rides, without having to queue a second time.

Walt Disney World Resort

Magic Kingdom features seven lands radiating out from Sleeping Beauty's Castle. As well as thrill rides like Space Mountain (see right), popular attractions include Mickey's PhilharMagic (spectacular 3D animation), Buzz Lightyear's Space Ranger Spin (zap aliens with a laser cannon), Cinderellabration (princess coronation pageant), Mickey's Toontown Fair (gentle coaster and a chance to meet characters), Pirates of the Caribbean (action-packed voyage with rowdy pirates) and the Laugh Floor Comedy Club (interactive adventure inspired by Disney-Pixar's *Monsters, Inc*).

Animal Kingdom's centrepiece is a huge, exquisitely carved Tree of Life, from which six themed lands spread out. The attention to detail in the African and Asian villages is remarkable. Must-see attractions include Kilimanjaro Safaris (open-air vehicle ride through an African savannah with elephants, rhinos and lions), Maharajah Jungle Trek (walk through a ruined palace inhabited by tigers, tapirs and fruit bats), It's Tough to be a Bug! (3D animation inspired by *A Bug's Life*), Finding Nemo (musical puppet show) and Festival of the Lion King (Broadway-style song and dance).

Epcot is probably the one park you'll want to return to more than any other. There is simply so much to see and do. World Showcase transports you to 11 nations, each one depicted by an authentic pavilion. Future World focuses on science and discovery with big rides and interactive exhibits. Don't miss Soarin' – a virtual hang-gliding adventure over California's natural wonders and The Seas with Nemo & Friends – a gentle undersea ramble in a clam shell.

Disney-MGM Studios brings movie-making to life with special effects shows like Lights, Motors, Action! and Indiana Jones Epic Stunt Spectacular. New for 2008 is the 3D Toy Story Mania ride and Jedi Training Academy where you can learn the art of light-saber fighting. You can also learn about animation and see live performances of Playhouse Disney and *Beauty and the Beast*. Thrill rides include the Star Tours flight simulator, the Rock 'n' Roller Coaster Starring Aerosmith and the Twilight Zone Tower of Terror.

Blizzard Beach waterpark boasts one of the world's tallest, fastest, free-fall speed slides – Summit Plummet. Open year-round, other highlights include the Downhill Double Dipper (inner-tube speed slide on parallel flumes), Teamboat Springs (family raft ride) and Tike's Peak ('snow-covered' play area.

20 hair-raising reasons to have a growth spurt

Park	Ride	Thrills and spills	Wow factor	Min height
Magic Kingdom	*Space Mountain*	High-speed coaster through the blackness of space	●●●●	112
	Big Thunder Mountain Railroad	Runaway train through the Old West, mild but wild	●●	102
Epcot	*Mission: SPACE*	Extreme-motion simulator; don't forget your sick bag	●●●●●	113
	Test Track	100-kph test drive through hairpins and banked turns	●●●●	102
MGM Studios	*Tower of Terror*	Elevator from hell, random drops of up to 13 storeys	●●●●●	102
	Rock 'n' Roller Coaster	Twists, turns and loops to the beat of Aerosmith	●●●●●	122
Animal Kingdom	*DINOSAUR*	Mad dash back in time, plenty of dino-surprises	●●	102
	Expedition Everest	High-speed train, forwards and backwards; scary yeti	●●●●●	113
Blizzard Beach	*Summit Plummet*	90-kph, 110-m-long freefall waterslide from 37 m up	●●●●●	122
	Slush Gusher	27-m-high waterslide with bumps and a big splash	●●●	122
Typhoon Lagoon	*Crush 'n' Gusher*	Water coaster with gravity-defying ups and downs	●●●	122
	Humunga Kowabunga	Choice of three 65-m enclosed speed slides	●●●	122
Universal Studios	*Men in Black Alien Attack*	Zap aliens in mad dash through New York's streets	●●●	107
	Revenge of the Mummy	Psychological thrill ride at 70-kph – and it's dark	●●●●	122
Islands of Adventure	*Duelling Dragons Coaster*	Two coasters in 90-kph aerial combat	●●●●●	137
	The Incredible Hulk Coaster	0-60 in 2 seconds, 108 kph max, 7 inversions	●●●●●	137
SeaWorld	*Kraken*	Dangling feet on floorless, 105-kph monster coaster	●●●●●	137
	Journey to Atlantis	High speed, spooky ride with 18-m splash drop finale	●●	107
Busch Gardens	*SheiKra*	Floorless dive coaster, 90-degree drop to 110 kph	●●●●●	137
	Kumba Coaster	33-m drop, 3 seconds of weightlessness	●●●●●	137

Typhoon Lagoon waterpark has roaring rapids, relaxing rivers and even a wave pool where you can hone your body-surfing skills.

Universal Orlando Resort

Universal Studios Florida takes you beyond the screen and puts you in the thick of the movie action. Brave the storm in Twister… Ride it Out; trot along with your favourite ogre and donkey in Shrek 4-D and battle the supernatural in Revenge of the Mummy. New for 2008 is a riotous motion-simulator ride through the cartoon world of The Simpsons. Long-established kids' favourites include ET Adventure (take to the skies on flying bikes) and Earthquake (an authentic simulation of a 'quake registering 8.3 on the Richter scale). Younger children will enjoy Jimmy Neutron's Nicktoon Blast where you meet SpongeBob SquarePants and the Rugrats, and Woody Woodpecker's KidZone which has a gentle coaster

and a singalong Barney show.
Islands of Adventure gives myths, legends and comic-book heroes a high-tech spin with attractions like the Amazing Adventures of Spider-Man, the Incredible Hulk coaster and the High in the Sky Seuss Trolley Train Ride.
Wet 'n Wild Experience a rush of adrenaline and a surge of water on rides like Brain Wash (16-m drop into a giant funnel) and Der Stuka (six-storey speed slide). There are also numerous water-play areas for younger children.
Universal's City Walk hosts nightly music and comedy shows by the highly-acclaimed Blue Man Group.

Anheuser-Busch Adventure Parks

SeaWorld Orlando (seaworld.com) is famous for its live mammal shows starring Shamu the orca. You can also see beluga whales, penguins, manatees, dolphins, sharks, turtles and rays. The Pacific Point Preserve is a clever recreation of a rocky cove, complete with Californian sea lions, harbour seals and herons. Thrill rides

range from the floorless Kraken roller coaster to kiddie's stuff at Shamu's Happy Harbour play area. Don't miss Mistify – a spectacular fountain and firework show where images are projected on to 18-m mist screens. For details of Busch Gardens and Adventure Island Tampa Bay, see page 343.
Aquatica, SeaWorld's stunning new water park, features sandy beaches, a surf pool and no less than 36 slides and tube rides, including Dolphin Plunge where a pair of clear perspex tubes whisks you through a lagoon inhabited by Commerson's dolphins.

Other attractions

Cypress Gardens Adventure Park
cypressgardens.com
Discovery Cove
discoverycove.com
Ripley's believe it or not!
ripleysorlando.com

Below left: the Kraken coaster at SeaWorld.
Below: Duelling Dragons at Universal Studios Islands of Adventure.

Rounding up the big sights of the Wild West

Two weeks to explore the highlights of Southwest USA? It's going be fast and furious, just like the Wild West ought to be. But what a ride! In just a fortnight you can combine a tour of some of North America's most famous natural wonders, including the Grand Canyon, Monument Valley and Bryce Canyon, with three of its cultural icons – Las Vegas, Route 66 and the Navajo Reservation. Casting a huge lasso across Nevada, Arizona and Utah, your grand circuit will inevitably involve some long driving days, but there are also plenty of opportunities for hiking and even inner-tube floats and helicopter flights. And it wouldn't be the Wild West without saddling up for a spot of horse riding. *Yee-ha!*

Two-week Wild West tour

» Join an organized tour or rent a car in Las Vegas and drive yourself.
» Make sure your kids have plenty to do on the long car journeys (see page 47).
» With another week or more, why not add on California (page 348) to create the ultimate Wild West tour? Allow around 8 hrs to drive from Zion to Yosemite.
» For further tourist information visit travelnevada.com, arizonaguide.com and utah.com.

Above: Mule train in the Grand Canyon. **Top right**: Bighorn sheep. **Below**: Dusk in Monument Valley.

Days 1-2: Las Vegas It's brash, bewildering and brilliant fun. Las Vegas (visitlasvegas.com) has a 'Sin City' image, but there's still plenty to appeal to kids in this outrageous desert metropolis. Nowhere in the world will you find a more imaginative, bizarre and neon-clad array of themed hotels than along Las Vegas Boulevard South (the Strip). Watch a volcano explode at the Mirage and pirates battle at Treasure Island; ride a roller coaster through the faux-Manhattan façade of New York-New York and drift in a gondola through 'virtual Venice' at the Venetian.

Day 3: Drive to Grand Canyon Allow five to six hours for the drive from Las Vegas to the Grand Canyon – or make a full day of it by stopping en route at Hoover Dam (usbr.gov/lc/hooverdam) where the Discovery Tour takes you 150 m down into the Black Canyon to see eight colossal power generators. Back on the road, take Route 66 (historic66.com) at Kingman to get a taste of the Mother Road (and Disney-Pixar's *Cars* movie). You'll pass historic stores with rusty old trucks, wagons and other Wild West kitsch parked outside. Rejoin I40 East at Ash Fork from where it's another two hours to the Grand Canyon.

Days 4-5: Grand Canyon Get up early to watch sunrise over this mighty chasm – 445 km long, up to 24 km wide and plunging to more than 1800 m at its deepest point. The visitor infrastructure in Grand Canyon Village on the South Rim is excellent. Orientate yourself at the Canyon View Information Plaza and see opposite for child-friendly activities in Grand Canyon National Park (nps.gov/grca).

Day 6: Drive to Lake Powell Continuing north on Highway 89, you enter the 70,000-sq-km Navajo Reservation (discovernavajo.com). Stop at the Cameron Visitor Center for an insight into the history and culture of the Navajo nation and a chance to shop for Native American arts and crafts, before continuing on to Lake Powell.

Day 7: Lake Powell Swimming, canoeing and other watersports are available at this dazzling man-made lake, but try to squeeze in a visit to nearby Antelope Canyon (navajonationparks.org). Known to the Navajo as *Tse' bighanilini* (the place where water runs through rocks), this narrow cleft is only 37 m deep, but has been sculpted by flash floods into a surreal masterpiece of curvaceous amber-hued sandstone.

Day 8: Monument Valley Few landscapes are as iconic of the Wild West as the huge sandstone towers and spires that soar from the desert of

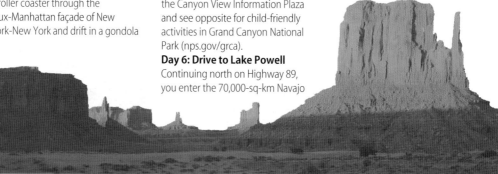

Monument Valley Navajo Tribal Park. A favourite location for moviemakers, the best way to get your own take on the Mittens, Three Sisters, Camel Butte and other famous landmarks is to join a jeep tour with a local Navajo guide. On the way to Monument Valley, stop at Navajo National Monument (nps.gov/nava) where you can see the remains of lofty cliff dwellings once inhabited by the Ancestral Puebloan people.

Day 9: To Capitol Reef Another long drive north brings you to Capitol Reef (nps.gov/care), a spectacular, 160-km-long wrinkle in the earth's crust where kids can learn about geology as part of the park's Junior Ranger activities.

Days 10-11: Bryce Canyon Named after Mormon settler, Ebenezer Bryce (who declared it "a hell of a place to lose a cow"), Bryce Canyon National Park (nps.gov/brca) is yet another weird and wonderful landscape – this time an amphitheatre riddled with a giant maze of rocky pillars known as *hoodoos*. You can walk to four viewpoints along the 8-km Rim Trail (an incredible spectacle at dawn or dusk when the *hoodoos* seem to glow like embers), but be sure to hike (or ride a pony) into the canyon itself. Although you need to take similar precautions against overexposure to sun and heat, it's nothing like as epic an undertaking as venturing on foot into the Grand Canyon. Try the Navajo Loop and Queen's Garden Trail (5 km in total) or, if your kids are good walkers, take them on the 13-km Fairyland Loop Trail.

Days 12-13: Zion National Park Around 140 km to the south, Zion National Park (nps.gov/zion), with its cathedral-like canyon of sandstone cliffs, waterfalls and hanging gardens, is a fitting finale to your two-week tour. As well as several family-friendly hikes, such as the Emerald Pool Trails, activities include horse rides alongside the Virgin River (for children as young as seven) and an excellent Junior Ranger Program.

Day 14: To Las Vegas Zion is around 250 km from Las Vegas.

66 99 When I asked our guide which was the best viewpoint over the Grand Canyon she didn't hesitate by answering, "Wherever there aren't a million people".
Will

66 99 I had to hand it to Dora, our guide from the Grand Canyon Field Institute – she knew how to make rocks sound cool. Instead of droning on about 1.7 billion years of geological shenanigans, she got the children to act it out. Imagine a game of Twister where, rather than spinning an arrow pointer, you have thrusting mountains, invading seas and eroding rivers as cues. It ended up as an excuse for an all-out scrum, but Dora still succeeded in getting across the basic principles of Grand Canyon tectonics to children aged six to 11. She then produced several small pouches containing ten different rock samples and challenged everyone to match them to the correct strata in the canyon walls.

You may be wondering if all this is really necessary when you take your kids to somewhere as iconic as the Grand Canyon. Surely the views are enough? Well, I'm not so sure. "I wasn't expecting it to be so big," was about as profound a reaction as I heard from children in our group. You won't find many 10-year-olds staking out a South Rim viewpoint to appreciate the subtle interplay of light and shadow as afternoon advances towards sunset.
Will

🔍 How to make the Grand Canyon rock for kids

There are plenty of ways to make the Grand Canyon more child-friendly. The big-screen production of *Grand Canyon* at the National Geographic IMAX Theater (explorethecanyon.com) in nearby Tusayan is both thrilling and informative. And a sightseeing flight over the Canyon (grandcanyonairlines.com or papillon.com) is another adrenaline-charged, if pricey, way to experience the world wonder.

Essentially, though, to get the most from the Grand Canyon you need to walk. Obviously, age and ability play a crucial role in what you can do. Some parents reach the brink of nervous breakdowns as they struggle to restrain high-energy offspring from climbing on viewpoint railings along the popular South Rim. That's not to say the Canyon is a no-go zone for young children – just make sure you've got a firm harness-hold at the very least.

Older children can join hikes into the Canyon, even if it's just for a day walk on either the South Kaibab or Bright Angel Trail. For overnight trips to Phantom Ranch, consider joining a mule-assisted hike. Kids aged 4-14 who make it to this cluster of cabins at the Canyon's base can qualify as Phantom Rattler Junior Rangers with the National Park Service (see page 339). Further details on the Grand Canyon Field Institute can be found at grandcanyon.org/fieldinstitute. Or try a Colorado River rafting expedition through the Canyon. Eight-day trips are offered by Grand Canyon Expeditions (gcex.com), minimum age eight.

For something different, head to the Grand Canyon Skywalk

(grandcanyonskywalk.com), a glass walkway suspended 1200 m above the Colorado River at Grand Canyon West.

From seaside cities to the high sierras

The fun begins the moment you board a cable car in San Francisco, whirring and clanking its way up and down the city's slow-motion roller coaster of streets; the two-man teams working the brakes, traffic weaving around you as skyscrapers frame tantalizing views of the Bay. 'Frisco is a great place to spend a few days with kids, but sooner or later you'll feel the need for some good old California cruisin'. Two of the most exciting options are the Pacific Coast Highway – an ocean odyssey that will transform your kids into beach connoisseurs – and the inland Sierra Nevada route, which reaches its peak, both spiritually and physically, at Yosemite National Park.

San Francisco

>> A free shuttle links the international airport with the car-rental centre or BART station, from where trains take you downtown for around US$5.
>> The San Francisco City Pass (citypass.com) includes admission to the Aquarium of the Bay and Exploratorium.
>> For further tourist information visit onlyinsanfrancisco.com and visitcalifornia.com.

City highlights
A ride on a cable car (sfcablecar.com) is an essential San Francisco experience. The best route is Powell-Hyde, which begins at the Powell/Market turntable and ends near Fisherman's Wharf. On the way you can hop off at Union Square (where you'll find shops ranging from Macy's to Disney) and Lombard Street – America's most bendy, with eight hairpin turns. Try to allow a full day at Fisherman's Wharf. Fortunately, the Powell-Hyde cable car stops at the opposite end to Pier 39 so you'll be able to enjoy the waterfront's many and varied attractions before your kids are lured like zombies into the vast Riptide Arcade. The first must-see is the San Francisco Maritime Historic Park (nps.gov/safr) where you can stand at the helm of the 1886 three-masted square-rigger, *Balclutha*, and board a variety of other old-timer boats ranging from schooners to tugboats. Servicing a 300-strong fishing fleet, Pier 45 is dominated by seafood-processing plants, but it's also the mooring for two

Second World War vessels – the *SS Jeremiah O'Brien* Liberty ship and the *USS Pampanito* submarine. Have a quick peep at the busy bakers in Boudin Sourdough Bakery, grab a lunchtime snack of freshly steamed Dungeness crab from a curbside stand, then book a sightseeing cruise with Blue & Gold Fleet (blueandgoldfleet.com) at the kiosk near Pier 39. The one-hour trip features both of San Francisco Bay's classic landmarks. First you'll cruise right under Golden Gate Bridge (with on-board commentary from Captain Nemo recounting yarns about everything from bolt riveters and humpback whales to the devastating earthquake and firestorm of 1906). Then you'll circle Alcatraz Island (nps.gov/alcatraz). If you want to go ashore and tour the infamous federal penitentiary, you need to book with Alcatraz Cruises (alcatrazcruises.com). The Walk-in Prison Experience, suitable for ages eight and above, takes you behind bars to where prisoners ate, slept, exercised, or did solitary time in the notorious Hole. Alcatraz Kidz Tourz (parksconservancy.org) offers special family-oriented programmes. Back at Fisherman's Wharf, the Californian sea lions at Pier 39 (pier39.com) are free to come and go as they please – numbers reach a winter high of around 900. In addition to 110 shops and 13 restaurants, Pier 39 is home to the excellent Aquarium of the Bay (aquariumofthebay.com) where you can see medium-sized sharks in a 92-m-long walk-through tunnel, stroke small ones in a touch pool and see what a very

large one (a great white) can do to a surfboard. On the subject of marine hazards, do not be tempted to swim or wade at Ocean Beach on the west side of San Francisco – the surf and currents are too dangerous. You're far safer at Crissy Field, on the Bay side of Golden Gate Bridge with a sheltered beach and great views. The nearby Exploratorium (exploratorium.edu) invites hands-on science investigation.

Kids' top 10: Fisherman's Wharf

1 **Scoff** freshly made chocolates at Ghirardelli Square.
2 **Count** the sea lions hauled out at Pier 39.
3 **Explore** the Second World War submarine, *USS Pampanito*.
4 **Watch** the fishing fleet come in along Jefferson Street.
5 **Dunk** warm sourdough in a bowl of seafood chowder.
6 **Cruise** under Golden Gate Bridge.
7 **Feel** what it's like to be locked up on Alcatraz.
8 **Touch** sharks at the Aquarium of the Bay.
9 **Meet** Hollywood celebrities at the wax museum.
10 **Shop** for souvenirs at Pier 39.

Top Right: Golden Gate Bridge. **Above top:** Tour boat passing Alcatraz. **Above:** Fresh-caught Dungeness crab at Fisherman's Wharf.

❷ Where can I see this?

Half Dome is one of the most celebrated icons of America's Great Outdoors. A glacier-scalped mountain in the Sierra Nevada of Yosemite National Park (nps.gov/yose), it can be climbed by anyone prepared to hike for 27 km and use cables to haul themselves up the final very steep section. Needless to say, most families will set their sights lower. Sentinel Bridge, a short stroll from Valley Visitor Center, offers a classic view of Half Dome, while paved trails to Mirror Lake, Lower Yosemite Falls and Bridalveil Falls are also easy – although remember that waterfalls in Yosemite usually run dry by August. Keep your eyes and ears open for mule deer, squirrels and blue jays and try to visit one of the park's giant redwood groves.

❾ How to disguise an American history lesson

Wooden sidewalks, horse-drawn carriages and Mississippi-style riverboats offer a hands-on introduction to American pioneer days in Old Sacramento (discovergold.org), an 11-ha historic district in California's state capital. At the California State Railroad Museum, kids can clamber aboard enormous steam locos, like the 500-ton Southern Pacific 4929. The Discovery Museum's Gold Rush History Center has dressing-up and role-play areas, while the Schoolhouse Museum has costumed 'schoolmarms' teaching lessons. As a reward for good behaviour, you'll also find shops selling everything from traditional candy to movie memorabilia.

❸ Theme parks

Legoland features the Pirate Shores water-play area, a miniature Lego-brick version of the Strip in Las Vegas and the Lego Technic roller coaster (minimum height 107 cm). **Disneyland Park** has all the regulars (Space Mountain, Splash Mountain etc), plus a Finding Nemo submarine voyage where you meet Bruce the Shark. **Universal Studios Hollywood** (universalstudioshollywood.com) is packed with movie-themed attractions, including Shrek-4D and Jurassic Park – The Ride.

❝❞ Legoland hasn't really hit mainstream USA, so the park wasn't too busy and the queues were reasonable – whereas our visit to Disneyland that same week was pure hell because the park was packed, and the lines for various rides were so long.

John Oestreich

The Pacific Coast Highway

Long road journeys and family travel are not always easy partners, but if there's one drive guaranteed to banish boredom, this is it. It doesn't matter which direction you drive California State Route 1, you will have a spectacular ocean view most of the way. Hugging the Pacific coastline from Leggett in the north to San Juan Capistrano in the south, the entire route covers nearly 900 km. However, unless you plan to tag on visits to Legoland (legoland.com) in Carlsbad and Disneyland (disney.com) in Anaheim, you would be wise to skip the southernmost part of the drive, avoiding LA's congestion, and start or finish at Santa Monica (which has the added incentive of a glorious beach). Allow at least three days to complete the drive,

stopping wherever a beach or viewpoint takes your fancy. Don't pass Monterey without visiting the mesmerizing Monterey Bay Aquarium (montereybayaquarium.org) with its towering three-storey kelp forest display, sea otter habitat, jellyfish exhibit and gargantuan 3.8-million-litre Outer Bay tank – home to sharks, turtles, giant tuna and barracuda. Another must-do, Monterey Bay Whale Watch (gowhales.com) offers three- to five-hour boat trips in search of the region's outstanding marine life. Orcas, sea lions, sea otters, harbour seals and several species of dolphins are seen year-round; grey whales are present from mid-December to April, while humpback and blue whales arrive to feed during the summer and autumn.

A shore thing – highlights of the Pacific Coast Highway include the Big Sur Coast and watching blue whales in Monterey Bay.

There's fun in them thar hills

Extending some 4800 km from New Mexico to British Columbia, the Rockies are the great backbone of North America. The tallest peak, Mt Elbert, soars to 4399 m, while the range varies in width from 120 to 650 km. A towering wilderness of ice fields, alpine meadows and forests, the Rockies are a stronghold for all of America's big critters, from elk, moose and bighorn sheep to grizzly bear and mountain lion. Your best chance of seeing them is in one of the national parks established to protect this fragile high ground. Popular activities in the Rockies include hiking, biking, whitewater rafting and horse riding.

US Rockies

» The Yellowstone Association (yellowstoneassociation.org) offers summer or winter 'ed-ventures' in Yellowstone National Park where families can learn about anything from wolves to volcanoes.
» Don't forget sun hats, sunblock and sunglasses for time spent at high elevations.
» For further tourist information try colorado.com, wyomingtourism.org and visitmt.com.

Highlights

Denver Colorado's big city has plenty to keep families occupied for a day or two. Pick of the museums goes to Wings over the Rockies (wingsmuseum.org) which has aviation exhibits ranging from a B-52 Stratofortress to a Star Wars X-Wing fighter. Also worth a look are the Denver Museum of Natural History (dmns.org), The Children's Museum of Denver (cmdenver.org) and the Colorado Railroad Museum (crrm.org). Ultimately, though, Denver is all about the Great Outdoors and you'll be chafing at the bit to get stuck into an adventure or two. Start by swinging yourself into the saddle at a horse-riding ranch in the Rocky Mountain foothills. There are several family-friendly options to choose from, including the American Safari Ranch (americansafariranch.com) near Fairplay, Triple B Ranch (triplebranch.com) near Colorado Springs and North Fork Ranch (northforkranch.com), about a 90-minute drive south of Denver. Next, swap reins for paddles. Based near Buena Vista, Wilderness Aware (inaraft.com) offers whitewater rafting trips on the Upper Colorado River and Upper Bighorn Sheep Canyon for families with children as young as four.

National parks Just 105 km from Denver, Rocky Mountain National Park (nps.gov/romo) gets very busy in July and August. The best way to escape the summer crowds is to take a hike. Child-friendly options range from paved paths around Bear and Sprague Lakes to more ambitious hikes across alpine tundra starting from various points along Trail Ridge Road. Families with children aged at least 10 can pedal in the park with Colorado Bicycling Adventures (coloradobicycling.com), while horse riding is available at Moraine Park for children as young as six. Rocky Mountain's Junior Ranger programme is considered one of the best in the park system.

Tucked into a corner of Wyoming, Grand Teton and Yellowstone National parks (nps.gov) make a truly spectacular combination – the former an awesome jumble of jagged peaks, the latter a vast mountain plateau roamed by bison and wolves and pockmarked by geysers. As well as hiking, horse riding and biking, Grand Teton offers canoeing on Jackson Lake and gentle rafting on the Snake River (the rougher whitewater sections are south of the park). In Yellowstone, brave the crowds to watch Old Faithful perform (the famous geyser spurts water 55 m into the air roughly every 90 minutes), and then get a taste for the backcountry on the nearby 8-km Lone Star Geyser Trail. Other highlights include the multihued limestone terraces of Mammoth Hot Springs and the 10-km round-trip hike up Mt Washburn. Horse riding (eight plus) is available through Yellowstone National Park Lodges (travelyellowstone.com) at Canyon Village, Mammoth Hot Springs and Roosevelt Lodge.

Snug against the Canadian border where it merges with Waterton Lakes National Park, Montana's Glacier National Park is a rugged *mélange* of jutting granite peaks, U-shaped valleys and azure lakes. As well as sightseeing from the Going-to-the-Sun Road, which traverses the heart of the park, you can hike, ride horses and cruise on lakes.

Above: Old Faithful in Yellowstone National Park.
Below: Rocky Mountain National Park.

Top eight North American family winter resorts

RESORT	Apex Mountain	Northstar-at Tahoe	Copper Mountain	Snowmass	Steamboat	Bretton Woods	Okema	Smugglers Notch
AREA	British Colombia	California	Colorado	Colorado	Colorado	New Hampshire	Vermont	Vermont
DISTANCE FROM AIRPORT	Penticton 33 km	Tahoe 65 km	Denver 121 km	Aspen 19 km	Denver 252 km	Boston 265 km	Rutland 40 km	Berlington 48 km
ALTITUDE	1629 m	1929 m	2926 m	2470 m	2103 m	500 m	1019 m	1108 m
NURSERY AREAS	0	0	1	0	1	0	0	1
RUNS	11/32/24	20/39/20	26/31/45	5/44/2	21/92/51	31/41/28	36/44/36	15/39/24
SNOWBOARD	1/1	2/1	3/2	3/1	4/0	3/0	6/2	5/0
LIFTS	0/4/1	1/13/2	0/20/2	1/13/8	1/18/2	0/7/2	0/12/6	0/6/2
ACTIVITIES	SR/IS/SM	SM/IS/SS/HS	SM/T/IS/SR/SS/HS	HS/IC/IS/SM/S	IS/SR/HS/SM/T/IC	IS/SS/T/HS/SR/SM	SS	IS/S/SR
WEBSITE	apexresort.com	northstarattahoe.com	coppercolorado.com	snowmassvillage.com	steamboat.com	Mtwashington.com/brettonwoods	okemo.com	smuggs.com

Key: *Runs:* Beginners/Intermediate/Advanced. *Snowboard*: Parks/Pipes. *Lifts*: Gondolas/Chairs/Drags
Activities: S Swimming; T Toboganning; IS Ice skating; HS Husky sledding; IC Ice-climbing; SS Snowshoe walks; SR Sleigh rides; SM Snowmobiling

Canadian Rockies

»» If you have time to spare in Calgary, visit Glenbow Museum (glenbow.org), a multicultural showcase with a discovery centre for kids.

»» The stylish Rocky Mountaineer (rockymountaineer.com) offers 2-day train journeys between Vancouver and Banff or Jasper.

»» For further tourist information visit discoveralberta.com and hellobc.com.

Highlights Driving west from Calgary on the Trans-Canada Highway, you should reach Banff National Park (pc.gc.ca/pn-np/ab/banff) in around two hours. The town of Banff (banfflakelouise.com) makes a comfortable base, whether you're there for winter skiing or summer hiking. Don't miss the Banff Gondola (banffgondola.com) which transports you to 2281 m on Mt Sulphur where an elevated boardwalk leads to an old weather observatory. Back down in the valley, Lake Minnewanka Boat Tours (minnewankaboattours.com) offers 90-minute cruises between May and October, but most kids will get more of a buzz from paddling a canoe. You can rent Canadian-style canoes (with middle seats for young children) from Blue Canoe Rentals (banfftours.com). The highlight of any visit to the Canadian Rockies, however, is a journey along the Icefields Parkway (icefieldsparkway.ca), a 288-km scenic route linking Banff, Lake Louise and Jasper that twists and turns through a crystal kingdom of ice-fluted peaks, sparkling glaciers and turquoise lakes. On the way, stop at the Columbia Icefield (columbiaicefield.com) which, at 325 sq km, is the world's largest non-polar icecap. This vast dome of snow and ice feeds eight major glaciers.

Where can I see this?

Held annually in July, the Calgary Stampede (calgarystampede.com) has events ranging from chuck-wagon racing (see right) to steer wrestling and wild cow milking. It's best to book well in advance if you want to stay at one of the popular ranches in the area. These include

Kananaskis Guest Ranch (brewsteradventures.com), which has a prime spot on the Bow River between Banff and Calgary and offers overnight horse trips and 'ride and raft' packages. The Lazy M Guest Ranch (lazymcanada.com) in Caroline is a working ranch specializing in horsemanship, while the Homeplace Guest Ranch (homeplaceranch.com) in Priddis offers riding lessons and horseback trips into the Rockies.

You can walk on one of them – the 6-km-long Athabasca – after scaling its frozen snout in a 56-seater all-terrain Ice Explorer bus on Brewster's Ice Age Adventure (brewster.ca).

Bear essentials

For sheer 'cute-and-cuddly' appeal, bears are unrivalled. Stories abound of tourists in US national parks offering adult bears a slurp of ice cream or even urging their children to pose for photos alongside them. Needless to say, bears demand the same high levels of respect and space as any wild animal you might encounter on holiday. The most dangerous bear is a surprised bear. If you do encounter one make plenty of noise to let it know you're there. Don't approach it and never offer food. Avoid attracting bears by placing rubbish in bear-proof boxes. In the rare event of an attack, don't run. If it's a grizzly bear, fall to the ground, curl into a ball with your hands behind your neck and play dead. If it's a black bear, fight back.

Moraine Lake, Banff National Park.

Where the mountains meet the sea

It's quite possibly the ultimate fusion of America's Great Outdoors – the rainforest-cloaked Pacific Coast Ranges and the spectacular crinkle-cut Pacific shore. Base yourself in either Vancouver or Seattle and you'll find wilderness right on your doorstep, whether you plan to hike, kayak or simply admire it from the deck of a ferry. Both cities have loads to keep kids occupied, from sandy beaches and sprawling parks to learning about totem poles and the fascinating culture of the First Nations. Not to be missed is a visit to Vancouver Island where picture-perfect Victoria is the jumping-off point for whale-watching adventures and some of the world's wildest and most exciting beaches.

Top: Kayaking in Johnstone Strait.
Above: Beluga whale at Vancouver Aquarium.

Regional highlights

⊙⊙⊙⊙⊕⊙⊙⊗⊙⑩

›› The Victoria Clipper Ferry (victoriaclipper.com) from Seattle takes just under 3 hrs to reach Vancouver Island.
›› In Vancouver, pick up a free copy of *Kids Guide Vancouver* at tourist information centres.
›› For further tourist information visit experiencewashington.com, seattle.gov, hellobc.com, tourismvancouver.com and tourismvictoria.com.

Seattle For a rainy day, top of your list should be the Pacific Science Center (pacsci.org) which has everything from animatronic dinosaurs to a Puget Sound tide pool. There's also The Children's Museum (thechildrensmuseum.org) and Woodland Park Zoo (zoo.org). If the sun is shining, head south to Long Beach – 18 km of sandcastle-building, kite-flying and birdwatching heaven. Alternatively, nip across to the Olympic Peninsula where Olympic National Park (nps.gov/olym) transports you into a mysterious forest of giant, moss-strewn hemlock and spruce.

Vancouver It's hard to imagine a more family-friendly city park than Vancouver's Stanley Park – a 400-ha peninsula with walking trails, cycle tracks, a miniature train, horse-drawn carriage rides, a children's farm, totem poles, a water park and fantastic views of big ships coming and going. But it's the Vancouver Aquarium (vanaqua.org) that is the park's real crowd-puller. In addition to habitat-themed displays

ranging from the walk-through Amazon gallery (with piranhas, crocs and sloths) to rocky coves inhabited by sea lions, sea otters and beluga whales, you can learn about Marine Mammal Rescue and other conservation programmes. Two of the best museums for children in Vancouver are Science World (scienceworld.bc.ca) and the Vancouver Museum (vanmuseum.bc.ca). Located about 10 minutes from downtown Vancouver, Kitsilano Beach is a favourite with locals, while Grouse Mountain (accessible by cable car) has great views and hiking potential.

Victoria and Vancouver Island

Situated at the southern tip of Vancouver Island, Victoria is renowned for its historic buildings and formal gardens. It's worth spending a few hours soaking up the atmosphere around the Inner Harbour and seeing the natural history and First Nations exhibits in the Royal British Columbia Museum (royalbcmuseum.bc.ca). However, you could easily spend a week or more exploring the natural wonders of this beautiful island. Start by heading north to Qualicum Beach, a laid-back east-coast village with safe, sandy beaches and lots of child-friendly activities, including easy walking trails to waterfalls and old-growth forest. Next, strike across the island to the more invigorating Pacific coast settlement of Tofino – gateway to a spectacular wilderness of surf-swept beaches, teeming rockpools and ancient cedar

forest. Activities here include whale watching, surfing, kayaking and beachcombing. Families with younger children will enjoy exploring the boardwalks at the Tofino Royal Botanical Gardens. Backtracking to the east coast, continue north to Telegraph Cove. This popular ecotourism destination is well known for its whale-watching tours – either by boat or sea kayak – in search of Johnstone Strait's famous orcas which come in search of salmon during the summer months. You can also visit Alert Bay on Cormorant Island where ceremonial masks, totem poles and other artefacts provide a vivid insight into Namgis First Nation culture. Near the tip of Vancouver Island, Port Hardy is the embarkation point for ferries bound for the Inside Passage and Alaska (see opposite). For a taster of this epic maritime journey, take a 15-hour cruise from Port Hardy to Prince Rupert with BC Ferries (bcferries.com). From there, you can take a fabulous two-day, 1160-km rail trip on the *Skeena* (viarail.ca) to Jasper National Park in the heart of the Canadian Rockies (see page 351). Then, either return to Vancouver or push on towards Calgary.

❝❞ An exuberant humpback whale greeted the ferry as we entered Fitz Hugh Sound – breaching repeatedly before wallowing on its back, clapping flippers as we passed. I wondered if it was applauding the scenery.
Will

Top: Alaska Marine Highway ferry. **Above left**: Totem pole at Saxman Village, Ketchikan. **Above right**: Bald eagle at the Raptor Rehabilitation Center in Sitka.

Heeding the call of the wild

They called it the last grand adventure. In July 1897, the streets of Seattle echoed with the wild cries of "Gold!" and over 100,000 people surged north. The Klondike Gold Rush promised escape and quick wealth during a time of depression and poverty. But to reach the gold fields of the interior the prospectors had to haul their supplies over mountain passes and along rapid-strewn rivers. And all this was only possible once they had voyaged in crowded steamers along North America's vast marine highway – the 1600-km Inside Passage. Today, the lure of the north is as strong as ever. Each summer, luxury cruise ships slip sedately through a maze of forested islands, probing inlets, straits and sounds to reach the old Alaskan gold-rush town of Skagway. They share these convoluted waters with fishing boats, timber barges, floatplanes and, best of all for independent travellers, a fleet of public ferries.

Alaska

Southeast Alaska

›› Bellingham, 140 km north of Seattle, is the southernmost terminal for Alaska Marine Highway Ferries.
›› Route maps, ferry schedules and online reservations can be made through the Alaska Marine Highway System (akferry.org).
›› Keep watch on deck for sightings of orcas and humpback whales.
›› For further tourist information visit travelalaska.com.

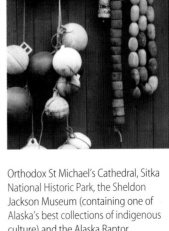

Kids' top 10: Alaskan adventures

1 See tidewater glaciers and whales in Kenai Fjords.
2 Raft the Class II-IV rapids of the Nenana River.
3 Speed along in a jetboat on the Susitna River.
4 Travel on the legendary Alaska Railroad.
5 Spot a grizzly bear in Denali National Park.
6 Paddle a sea kayak on Prince William Sound.
7 Pan for gold or fish for salmon in an Alaskan creek.
8 Fly in a floatplane to a lakeside wilderness cabin.
9 Ride a horse or bike in Chugach National Forest.
10 Hike or husky sledge across a glacier.

Inside Passage highlights

The Southeast Alaska Discovery Center in Ketchikan (visit-ketchikan.com) provides an excellent introduction to the region, while nearby Saxman Village boasts the world's largest collection of standing totem poles and a chance to watch modern-day carvers at work. Ketchikan is a gateway to the Misty Fjords National Monument, a rugged, brooding wilderness that's perfect for hiking, kayaking or fishing. At Wrangell (wrangell.com) you can search for ancient petroglyph rock carvings on the beach or venture by kayak into the mouth of the Stikine River. Petersburg (petersburg.org) offers the chance to appreciate the workings of a busy Alaskan fishing port. Facing the open Pacific and built in the shadow of an extinct volcano, Sitka (sitka.org) has several attractions, including the Russian Orthodox St Michael's Cathedral, Sitka National Historic Park, the Sheldon Jackson Museum (containing one of Alaska's best collections of indigenous culture) and the Alaska Raptor Rehabilitation Centre. At Juneau (juneau.com), stretch your legs by hiking to the Mendenhall Glacier, take a boat trip to Tracy Arm Fjord and visit Admiralty Island (the 'Fortress of the Bears'). Juneau is also the starting point for cruises into Glacier Bay National Park (nps.gov/glba), while Skagway (skagway.com) offers a nostalgic and captivating glimpse into the gold-rush days. The more adventurous can hike the five-day Chilkoot Trail in the prospectors' footsteps or ride the White Pass and Yukon scenic railway.

North America essentials

When to go

North America's climate covers every extreme. Some parts offer year-round sunshine, while others become inaccessible during winter. Although Québec City is geared up as a year-round destination with a spectacular carnival of snow slides, parades and ice-sculpting during early February, it is best to avoid winter if you want to venture further afield. With over 3 m of snowfall and temperatures plunging as low as -25°C, many tourist attractions outside the city close down during winter months. By contrast, summers are warm, with temperatures up to 30°C. Autumn is crisp and favoured by those in search of flamboyant fall colours. If you want to see a polar bear, visit Churchill from October to early November – but wrap up warm. June to October is best for sightings of humpback, minke and fin whales along the Atlantic Coast, while May to September is prime time for spotting orcas off Vancouver Island. It is no coincidence that the Pacific Coast of **British Columbia** and **Southeast Alaska** is cloaked in lush forest – the region's climate is generally mild and wet. Temperatures average 20°C in summer, the driest and most popular time to travel. Ferries and accommodation can become heavily booked from June to August, so it's worth considering a visit in May or early September. Spring and autumn are also the best seasons for visiting **Southwest USA**. Summer can be insanely hot in the desert canyons – take plenty of water if you are planning to hike or bike. Many of the big national parks such as Yellowstone and Yosemite become crowded in the height of summer– another good reason for travelling in the shoulder seasons. The best period to visit **Florida** is from late November to the end of April when it is drier and cooler with daytime temperatures reaching 29°C. Avoid the hurricane season, officially 1 June to 30 November.

Getting there

There is no shortage of scheduled non-stop and direct flights from the UK to various cities throughout the USA and Canada, with onward connections to hundreds of other destinations. See page 45 for a list of airlines. There are also a number of charter flights from the UK to destinations such as Orlando and Las Vegas. American Airlines (aa.com) has return flights from London to New York and Miami starting from around US$800 and US$1340 respectively. British Airways (britishairways.com) has direct flights to San Francisco from US$1045 return, and to Denver from US$1075 return. Check airline websites for the latest online offers, as well as flight brokers like Expedia (expedia.co.uk). Try Travel 4 Holidays (travel4.com) and Virgin Holidays (virginholidays.co.uk) for package deals combining flights with car hire, hotel accommodation and attractions.

Getting around

Despite the American love affair with the car, there are plenty of alternatives for getting around. Due to competition on domestic routes, **internal flights** in the USA are a relatively cheap way to cover large distances. Try JetBlue (jetblue.com) or Ted (flyted.com). In Canada, internal flights are a little more expensive, but you can get good deals on budget carriers like WestJet (westjet.com).

For **rail travel**, Amtrak (amtrak.com) covers most major US destinations, while *The Canadian* (viarail.ca) can whisk you, in 1950s style, from Toronto to Vancouver, with stopovers along the way.

Canada's east and west coasts are well served by fast, frequent and reasonably priced **ferries**. The St Lawrence Seaway provides passage from the Atlantic Ocean to the Great Lakes, while BC Ferries (bcferries.com) operates services linking British Columbia's mainland with Vancouver Island and the Inside Passage.

Major international **car-hire** companies have offices at all gateway airports and in most cities. You can often save

CO₂ How much to offset your emissions?

From London yo:

New York £12
Toronto £12
Orlando £14
Vancouver £16
San Francisco £18

From New York to:

Toronto US$2
Orlando US$5
Las Vegas US$12
Los Angeles US$16
Vancouver US$16
Anchorage US$23

Go green: four ways to skip the flight

➤ Amtrak (amtrak.com), the USA's national railroad network, serves over 500 destinations in 46 states, on 33,800 km of routes. Amtrak Vacations can tailor-make rail journeys that include accommodation and tours.
➤ The Rocky Mountaineer (rockymountaineer.com) train links Vancouver with Banff, Jasper and Lake Louise in the Canadian Rockies.
➤ The Great Lakes Cruising Company (greatlakescruising.com) offers dozens of cruising options on the Great Lakes or along the St Lawrence River.
➤ Greyhound (greyhound.com) has great deals on transcontinental bus travel, such as their range of Discovery Passes, valid from four to 60 days in the USA and/or Canada.

money by arranging a fly-drive deal or by booking a car in advance. The American Automobile Association (aaa.com) and Canadian Automobile Association (caa.ca) offer touring services and travel advice to affiliate auto club members. Hiring a motorhome, or 'recreational vehicle' (RV), is a supremely family-friendly option for getting around. Cruise America (cruiseamerica.com) is one of the best-known **RV-hire** specialists.

Food and drink

Your family will certainly not go hungry on a trip to North America. Your biggest problem will probably be finding that you keep ordering too much food, as portions tend to be larger than you're used to back home. You can order any type of coffee, any size of pizza or steak and any style of eggs. That's before you've even had a chance to ponder the fries, burgers, shakes, ice creams and doughnuts. But it's not all junk food: there's a mouthwatering spread of nutritious regional specialities, such as key lime pie (Florida), clam chowder (New England), fresh Florida orange juice, Winnipeg goldeye trout and juicy steaks from Alberta's cattle ranches. And no trip to Canada would be complete without sampling buttermilk pancakes doused in maple syrup.

Health and safety

Health care in the USA and Canada is not cheap. Be well insured with medical cover up to US$1 million, which includes

Fact file

	USA	**Canada**
GMT	Eastern -5 hrs	Newfoundland -3½ hrs
	Central -6 hrs	Altlantic – 4 hrs
	Mountain -7 hrs	Eastern -5 hrs
	Pacific -8 hrs	Central -6 hrs
	Alaska -9 hrs	Mountain -7 hrs
	Hawaii -10 hrs	Pacific -8 hrs
Language	English	English, French
Money	US Dollar (£1=US$2)	Canadian dollar (£1=Can$2.1)
Code	+1	+1
Tourist info	visitusa.org.uk	canada.travel.ca

hospital treatment and medical evacuation. Always check that your travel insurance covers you for any activities that you plan to do. As with travel anywhere in the world, it's wise to be up to date with your regular vaccinations, especially tetanus. Some summer camps require proof of innoculation. Accidents pose the greatest risk to your health and safety when holidaying in North America, so take care when driving or trying out new adventure activities. Potentially dangerous animals include bears (see page 351), scorpions and bats – the latter may transmit rabies. There is also a small risk of contracting the tick-borne Lyme disease when walking in forested areas. Be sure to apply insect repellent and check your body for ticks, removing them gently with tweezers.

Crime rates are high in some of the major cities, so take sensible precautions such as not leaving valuables visible in your car. For the latest advice on potential terrorist activity, visit the website of the Department of Homeland Security (dhs.gov).

Accommodation

It is possible to find family-friendly accommodation in every region you visit – some hotels lavish cookies and goodie bags on your children or provide kids' programmes and babysitting, while others have games consoles in children's rooms or fantastic locations in wonderful natural playgrounds.

From camping to five-star luxury, there is something for every budget and taste. Kampgrounds of America (koa.com) has sites across the USA and Canada with tent pitches, RV hook-ups and cabins. For the ultimate camping adventure, Canadian Adventure Rentals (canadian-adventure-rentals.com) in Vancouver will kit you out with everything you need, from car hire to tent, cooking equipment and bedding

Tour operators

In the UK
Abercrombie and Kent abercrombiekent.com
The Adventure Company adventurecompany.co.uk
American Round-Up americanroundup.com
Discover the World discover-the-world.co.uk
Exodus Family Adventures exodus.co.uk
Explore Family Adventures explore.co.uk
Families Worldwide familiesworldwide.co.uk
Hayes and Jarvis hayesandjarvis.co.uk
Kuoni kuoni.co.uk
Neilson neilson.co.uk
Skiworld skiworldltd.ukk
Trek America trekamerica.co.uk
Virgin Holidays virgin.com/holidays

In the USA/Canada
Alaskan Tour alaskantour.com
Austin Lehman austinlehman.com
The Backroads backroads.com
Cruise America RV rentals cruiseamerica.com
Fresh Tracks freshtracks.ca
Thomson Family Adventures familyadventures.com

😋 **How much for a Big Mac?**
USA US$3.22
Canada US$3.62
UK US$3.90

– they'll even throw in some bikes or kayaks on request.

If you are planning to stay in one of the more popular national parks during peak season, you will need to book well in advance (up to a year for some parks). Log on to recreation.gov for information and reservations. Bookings in Yellowstone, Zion and Grand Canyon are covered by Xanterra Parks and Resorts (xanterra.com). Yosemite has a collection of affordable and family-friendly resorts and lodges that can be booked through Yosemite Resorts (yosemiteresorts.us). Located a few kilometres from the El Portal entrance to the park, Yosemite View Lodge, for example, has kitchenettes, restaurant and shop. In Banff, The Sunshine Inn (skibanff.com) is well placed for adventure activities and is the resort's only ski-in, ski-out hotel.

For playing at cowboys and cowgirls, search for the ranch that suits your family's needs through the Dude Rancher's Association (duderanch.org). For the all-out Disney experience, stay at a Disney Resort like Animal Kingdom Lodge (disney.com) where you will be surrounded by an African savannah roamed by giraffes, zebras and kudus. Other Orlando family favourites include Disney's All Star Movies Resort, the Nickelodeon Family Suites (nickhotel.com), Universal's Hard Rock Hotel (universalorlando.com) and the Hyatt Regency Grand Cypress Resort (grandcypress.hyatt.com) which features 'dive-in' movies over the pool area. For a budget, family-friendly option, pitch a tent in one of Florida's State Parks (floridastateparks.org). Many, like St Andrews, have well-equipped campsites. Flamingo Lodge (flamingolodge. com) makes an excellent base for exploring the Everglades.

Six family big city favourites

Washington DC
Where? The Embassy Suites Downtown.
Why? Close to the museums and zoo. Great complimentary breakfast. Kitchen facilities.
Contact embassysuites.com.

New York
Where? Novotel New York, Times Square.
Why? Less than 1 km to Central Park. Two kids go free in parents' room and eat free in the café. Indoor playground and babysitting on request.
Contact novotel.com.

Montreal
Where? Delta Montréal.
Why? Video games available in the room. Kids sharing parents' room stay free. Craft activity centre, pool and playgrounds.
Contact deltamontreal.com.

Toronto
Where? Four Seasons Hotel.
Why? Children receive a gift, milk and cookies on arrival. Helpful concierge service, including suggestions for family outings. Indoor-outdoor pool.
Contact fourseasons.com/toronto.

Las Vegas
Where? New York-New York Hotel and Casino.
Why? Older children can ride The Roller Coaster with its famous heartline twist, which simulates a jet fighter's barrel roll.
Contact nynyhotelcasino.com.

San Francisco
Where? Stanyan Park Hotel.
Why? Half a block to Golden Gate Park. Self-catering suites.
Contact stanyanpark.com.

Ways to blow the budget

Cheeca Lodge and Spa (cheeca.com)
Islamadora, Florida Keys
The place to go if your children are water babes. Children's activities include kayaking, fishing, snorkelling and sailing.

Sadie Cove Wilderness Lodge (sadiecove.com)
Kachemak State Park, Alaska
The ultimate wilderness family adventure, Sadie Cove is accessible only by seaplane, helicopter or boat. Stay in handcrafted eco-cabins with delicious home-cooked Alaskan fare – often caught by yourselves. Activities include bear watching and glacier kayaking.

Fairmont Le Chateau Frontenac
(fairmont.com/Frontenac) Québec City
In the heart of Old Québec, this fairy-tale castle will have little princes and princesses swooning. But it will probably be the canine ambassador that meets and greets guests and can be taken for walks that will stay in your children's memories the longest.

Opposite: New York-New York Hotel, Las Vegas. **Left**: Universal's Hard Rock Hotel, Florida. **Top**: Sadie Cove Wilderness Lodge, Alaska.

Latin America

On a mountain high – Machu Picchu, the
Lost City of the Incas

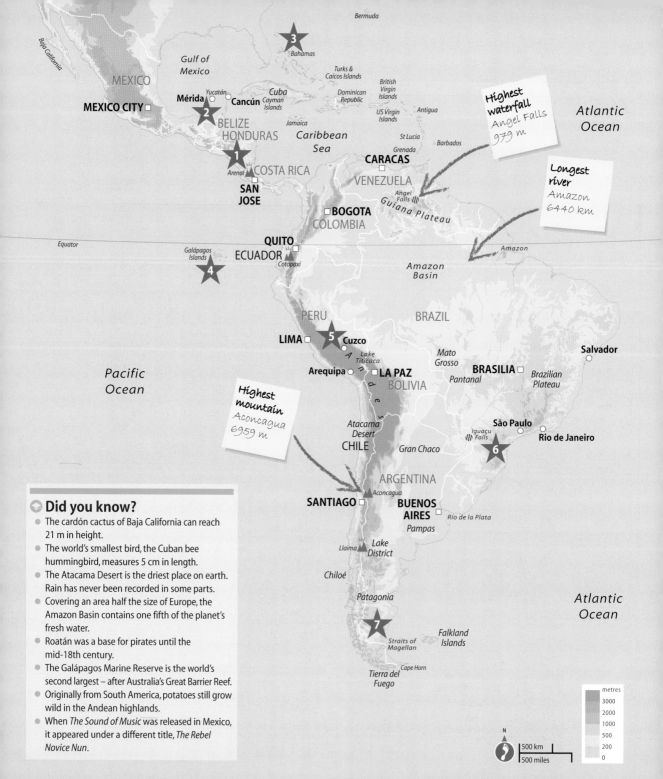

Bermuda

Baja California

MEXICO

Gulf of
Mexico

Bahamas

3

Turks &
Caicos Islands

British
Virgin
Islands

Atlantic
Ocean

MEXICO CITY □

Mérida ○

Yucatán

○ Cancún

Cuba

*Cayman
Islands*

Dominican
Republic

US Virgin
Islands

Antigua

Highest
waterfall
Angel Falls
979 m

2

BELIZE
HONDURAS

1

Arenal

COSTA RICA

SAN
JOSE

Jamaica

St Lucia

Caribbean
Sea

CARACAS

Grenada

Barbados

VENEZUELA

Longest
river
Amazon
6440 km

□ BOGOTA

COLOMBIA

*Angel
Falls*

Guiana plateau

Equator

QUITO

ECUADOR

*Galápagos
Islands*

4

□

Cotopaxi

Amazon

Amazon
Basin

PERU

BRAZIL

Pacific
Ocean

LIMA □

5

Cuzco

*A
n
d
e
s*

*Lake
Titicaca*

Arequipa ○

□ LA PAZ

BOLIVIA

Mato
Grosso

Salvador

BRASILIA □

Pantanal

Brazilian
Plateau

Highest
mountain
Aconcagua
6959 m

*Atacama
Desert*

CHILE

Gran Chaco

São Paulo ○

*Iguaçu
Falls*

6

Rio de Janeiro

ARGENTINA

SANTIAGO □

Aconcagua

BUENOS
AIRES

Río de la Plata

Pampas

Llaima

*Lake
District*

Chiloé

Patagonia

Atlantic
Ocean

7

*Straits of
Magellan*

Falkland
Islands

Cape Horn

*Tierra del
Fuego*

◯ Did you know?

- The cardón cactus of Baja California can reach 21 m in height.
- The world's smallest bird, the Cuban bee hummingbird, measures 5 cm in length.
- The Atacama Desert is the driest place on earth. Rain has never been recorded in some parts.
- Covering an area half the size of Europe, the Amazon Basin contains one fifth of the planet's fresh water.
- Roatán was a base for pirates until the mid-18th century.
- The Galápagos Marine Reserve is the world's second largest – after Australia's Great Barrier Reef.
- Originally from South America, potatoes still grow wild in the Andean highlands.
- When *The Sound of Music* was released in Mexico, it appeared under a different title, *The Rebel Novice Nun*.

N

500 km

500 miles

metres
3000
2000
1000
500
200
0

⭐ **Climb into the rainforest canopy**
▸▸ Costa Rica, page 368

⭐ **Explore a Maya temple**
▸▸ Central America, page 368

⭐ **Swim with wild dolphins**
▸▸ The Bahamas, page 372

⭐ **Gaze at an iguana**
▸▸ Galápagos Islands, page 374

⭐ **Hike to Machu Picchu**
▸▸ Peru page 376

⭐ **Get soaked by Iguaçu Falls**
▸▸ Brazil, page 378

⭐ **Discover the wilderness of Patagonia**
▸▸ Argentina and Chile, pages 380 and 381

Introduction

Latin America might strike you as a rather exotic and impractical place to take children, but it's easier than you think. Not only have basics, like transport and accommodation, been greatly improved in recent years, but many of the key sites – from Maya ruins to Patagonian glaciers – are surprisingly accessible. If you don't feel you're quite ready for an Amazonian adventure, focus instead on the family-friendly Brazilian coast or the Caribbean, where you can combine a beach holiday with day trips to the forested interior. But if it's all-out action you're after, Latin America is unrivalled. From sea kayaking in Mexico and horse riding in Argentina to trekking in Peru and snorkelling in the Galápagos Islands, you'll find professionally organized activities to suit all levels. Your children's minds will be equally stimulated as they learn about ancient civilizations and vibrant cultures. And don't forget that Latin Americans adore children, so your kids can expect a friendly welcome and plenty of cheek-squidging and hair-ruffling wherever you go.

&& The trip to Costa Rica was the best holiday ever and our tour guide, Vinny, and bus driver, Raffa, were great. I met so many really nice people and made some new friends. We saw loads and we learned new things every day.

Olivia Titmuss (11 years old),
Natural Magic tour, The Adventure Company

Latin America rating

Wow factor
★★★★★

Worry factor
★★★

Value for money
★★★

Keeping teacher happy
★★★★

Family accommodation
★★★

Babies & toddlers
★★★

Teenagers
★★★★

Books to read

Caribbean Animals, Tamarind, 2004
From his tree house, Ned spots animals ranging from an agouti to a zandoli. Exquisite illustrations linked by rhyming text, plus extra facts on each creature. Ages 3-8.

From Beans to Batteries, Child's Play, 1999
In Peru, Aldomero and Amerita go to the market and try to sell the beans they have picked, hoping to make enough money to buy batteries for their radio. Ages 4-8.

The Shaman's Apprentice: A Tale of the Amazon Rain Forest, Harcourt Brace International, 2001
A richly illustrated and vividly told story of a child's belief in the medicinal properties of plants and his aspiration to become a healer for his people. Ages 5-14.

Butter-finger, Frances Lincoln Publishers, 2006
Riccardo Small lives on a Caribbean island. He loves cricket and can tell you the averages of every West Indian Test match player in history and more besides. But when he is dropped from the cricket team after missing a vital catch, Riccardo wanders the island, taking refuge in his poems. Ages 6+

The Incredible Incas, Scholastic Hippo, 2000
A 'Horrible History' of the Incan Empire with gory details, such as how to predict your future with inflated llama lungs and how to make a shaker bracelet using llama toenails. Ages 8+

Aztec, Inca & Maya, DK Eyewitness Books, 2005
Engaging photographs and detailed captions draw you into the worlds of the three great Latin American civilizations, with topics covering everything from religious masks to food and drink. Ages 9-12

Football crazy

If you want to strike a rapport with Latin locals, there's no better subject than football. The 'beautiful game' is a national obsession just about everywhere you go, so arm yourself with the following facts and kick off a conversation.

All-time superstars
• Pelé: born 1940, 92 appearances for Brazil, 77 goals .
• Garrincha: 1933-1983, 50 appearances for Brazil, 12 goals.
• Mario Kempes: born 1954, 43 appearances for Argentina, 20 goals.
• Maradona: born 1960, 91 appearances for Argentina, 34 goals.

🔍 How to make a piñata

A centrepiece of traditional Hispanic celebrations, a piñata is a bright container that is filled with sweets and toys and suspended from a tree or ceiling. Children, blindfolded and wielding a stick, take turns to break it open.

What you need
→ Old newspapers
→ Flour and water paste
→ Mixing bowl
→ Large balloon
→ Coloured crêpe paper, paints, stickers and decorations
→ Glue, pin, coat hanger, thick string
→ Sweets and small toys

What to do
→ Tear newspaper into strips.
→ Mix flour and water in bowl to make a sticky paste.
→ Inflate balloon and smear a little cooking oil over it.
→ Dip the strips of paper into the paste and stick them in layers around the balloon.
→ Allow to dry.
→ Burst the balloon at the top and pull it out.
→ Paint and decorate your piñata.
→ Make a small hole in the top of the piñata and fill with sweets and toys.
→ Make a hook in the top using the coat hanger. Suspend the piñata using string, tied firmly to the hanger.

❓ Where can I see lots of penguins if we can't afford an Antarctic cruise?

Rising from the Straits of Magellan, a short boat ride from Punta Arenas, Magdalena Island hosts around 60,000 pairs of Magellanic penguins – over 95% of the world population. Sit quietly and these endearing little creatures will hobble right up to you. Their behaviour is endlessly fascinating – from excavating nesting burrows to braying like donkeys.

Taste of Latin America: Mexican quesadilla

Quesadilla (pronounced 'kay-suh-dee-uh') literally means 'little cheesy thing' and, traditionally, that's exactly what you get – a tortilla or dough wrap stuffed with melted cheese. However, they work just as well filled with potato, sausage, chicken, mushrooms, onions and anything else you fancy adding!

What you need
- 4 cups of harina flour (to make your own masa dough) or 4 ready-made flour tortillas
- 2 large potatoes
- Chorizo sausage
- Can of refried beans
- Butter and cooking oil
- Salt and pepper
- Guacamole, salsa and sour cream

What to do
- Boil and mash the potatoes with salt, pepper and butter .
- Heat the beans; slice the chorizo and gently fry.
- Mix the mashed potatoes, beans and chorizo together; set aside and keep warm.
- To make masa dough, mix the flour with warm water, kneading until dough is firm.
- Make small balls of dough about 5 cm in diameter and roll them out into flat tortillas.
- Add the filling, carefully fold in half and seal edges with your fingers.
- Fry over a medium heat until both sides are golden brown.
- Cut into triangles and serve with guacamole, salsa and sour cream.

Scary sightings

Tarantula
What? Common name for a group of about 800 hairy, sometimes very large, spiders.
Where? Asia, Africa and the Americas.
Fright factor Low. They look scary, but you'd be lucky (or unlucky) to see one unless you go poking sticks in their burrows at night. Recently discovered in Peru, the chicken-eating tarantula measures up to 25 cm across and has a fowl reputation.

Anaconda
What? Super-size snake that can reach 10 m in length.
Where? Tropical wetlands, like Brazil's Pantanal.
Fright factor Medium. These mighty constrictors squeeze their prey to death and then swallow it whole, head first. Animals as big as deer and sheep are on the menu, but human fatalities are almost unheard of.

Vampire bat
What? Pesky bat with 20-cm wingspan and razor-sharp nippers.
Where? Mexico, south to the Amazon.
Fright factor Off the scale. These bloodsuckers hunt at night, honing in on sleeping mammals (usually cattle). Their saliva contains draculin, a special substance that keeps the blood flowing. They do not attack humans, but accidental bites can transmit the disease, rabies.

Weirdlife: the 'stink bird' that can swim before it can fly

Also known as: Hoatzin.
Vital statistics: About the size and weight of a chicken.
Found in: Swamps and flooded forests of the Amazon.
What's so weird? The spiky head crest and blue eye shadow are pretty wacky, but what really elevates this feathered freak into the realms of the super-weird is that the chicks have a prehistoric-like claw on each wing. When danger threatens (in the form of a hungry capuchin monkey) the chick clambers to safety using its claws to grip branches. If that fails, it dives underwater (hoatzins always nest in trees overhanging lakes or rivers) until the danger has passed. Local people call hoatzins 'stink birds' because the aromatic oils in their diet of leaves gives them a distinctive whiff.

How to catch a piranha

- Find a quiet backwater with overhanging branches where piranhas like to lurk.
- Make yourself a fishing rod from a wooden stick.
- Tie some fishing line and a hook to one end; bait with chunk of raw chicken.
- Toss your hook into the water and splash your rod on the surface – these feisty nippers are often attracted to anything that sounds like a floundering animal.
- Keep feet, hands and other body parts inside the boat!
- Yank hard and sideways as soon as you feel a bite (wait too long and they'll eat your bait and be gone).
- Haul your catch aboard and let your guide remove the hook. Warning! A piranha out of water is still dangerous enough to inflict a powerful bite, as your guide will no doubt demonstrate by holding a stick to its mouth.
- Traditionally, piranha teeth are used to make tools and weapons. Grilled, they taste rather like trout.

One to watch: *Evita* (1997)

Madonna stars in the title role of Argentina's first lady, Eva Perón, in this big-screen adaptation of the Andrew Lloyd Webber/ Tim Rice musical. The film follows the rise of Perón to supreme social and political celebrity in the 1940s.

The Caribbean is a well-established family destination, but would you consider taking your kids to Peru? Or Patagonia? What's the minimum age you should contemplate a cruise in the Galápagos Islands or a trip to the Amazon? And what about more fundamental issues, like health and safety?

Babies (0-18 months)

You've endured months of sleepless nights, the kitchen has been doused in baby vomit more times than you can remember and you've strained your back lifting the stroller out of the car. There had better be a good reason for hauling the little monster half away around the world on holiday – particularly if it means potentially undoing what little feeding and sleeping routine you've managed to install. In the Caribbean and Bahamas, of course, there are plenty of excellent reasons for a holiday with babies, and they all have one thing in common: parent pampering. Your baby will no doubt love splashing in the warm sheltered sea, shovelling clean white sand into his mouth and making friends at the resort's crèche, but ultimately a Caribbean holiday with tiny tots has as much, if not more, to do with parents' facilities than those for children. This is the ideal time and place to snatch a couple of weeks of well-earned rest at an all-inclusive, no-effort-required, family-friendly resort where you can nurse that bad back at the on-site wellbeing centre. Don't forget – with a baby on your lap during the flight and sharing your hotel room – it might also be the only time you can afford a family holiday in the Caribbean! To ease the journey time, choose an island with direct international flights and as short a transfer to your hotel as possible. You will need to be extra-vigilant to prevent sunburn and heat exposure, but (apart from the Dominican Republic) there is no risk from malaria.

Toddlers/pre-school (18 months-4 years)

The Caribbean also scores highly for this age range. As well as toddler-friendly beaches, guaranteed sunshine and a wide choice of food, you'll find a friendly and laid-back atmosphere on just about any island you choose. Try to avoid the more exclusive resorts, though. There's nothing worse than having to hush your hyperactive three-year-old every five minutes for fear of disturbing other guests. In any case, there's a great choice of family resorts with kids' clubs, children's pools and toddler-tempting food.

Another option for a beach holiday is to head for the Brazilian coast. Bahia is renowned for its string of family-friendly eco-resorts, while the stretch of coast south of Rio de Janeiro has some wonderful family villas. It's all malaria-free and has the added bonus of some great city-sightseeing potential. Kids will love riding the cable car in Rio or exploring the old town of Salvador.

Latin America's other top beach destination is Mexico,

where you will find no shortage of resorts. Don't underestimate the toddler appeal of the country's ancient Maya temples. The technical stuff, of course, will be way over their heads, but they'll see it as one of life's great new challenges to clamber up the steps of a pyramid or two. Before you decide to roam too far in Mexico with children of this age range, just be aware that malaria does affect some parts of the country.

Other malaria-free options in Latin America include Chile and (most of) Argentina. There's no denying that Buenos Aires has some of the best ice cream anywhere on the continent, and that Chile has an agreeable climate, but pre-school-age children will generally be too young to make the most of the superb adventure opportunities in these countries.

Kids/school age (4-12 years)

If you still have a yearning for the Caribbean, boost the excitement levels by visiting Cuba or the Dominican Republic where there's a greater choice of adventure and sightseeing opportunities. By the time your children reach the age of five, however, you may be feeling more comfortable with the idea of giving them anti-malarial pills. If that's the case, skip the Caribbean and head instead to Costa Rica. It's one of the safest and friendliest countries in Latin America; the transport system is excellent and, best of all, there are enough national parks in this little green nation to satisfy all budding creepy-crawly experts. Belize and Honduras are also excellent choices, particularly if you combine jungle escapades with time-out on the offshore coral islands. If your children are near the upper end of this age category, you might like to consider a Central American tour, linking several countries.

Ecuador, Peru and Chile are equally well suited to overland adventures. Family operators offer various organized tours (usually for ages six and above), with all kinds of enticing combinations. In Peru, for example, you can travel from the coast high into the Andes before taking a dip in the Amazon basin. In Ecuador, perhaps the ultimate Latin American feast is served up in the form of the Andes, Amazon and Galápagos Islands, while in Chile you can head north to south, taking in the wonderfully diverse Atacama Desert, Lakes District, Patagonia and Tierra del Fuego.

Which option you choose depends on a range of factors – not least your budget. Galápagos cruises don't come cheap, but you can save money by staying on the main island and taking day excursions. Similarly, a visit to the more accessible cloudforest regions of the Andes will work out cheaper than a full-blown Amazon adventure. You may also have safety concerns over young children climbing in and out of boats in the Galápagos – or being bitten by mosquitoes in the Amazon (don't forget this is a malarial region). Other health factors to be aware of include high altitude and sun exposure in the Andes.

Above: Beach activity – and inactivity – in the Caribbean.

Telling tales ...

Chile is, in my view, particularly suited to children's activity holidays. It is developed and safe, yet not at the theme-park stage of its evolution. We were there for three weeks and I felt that Wilf (my eight-year-old son) had a genuine wilderness experience within a totally safe framework.

Highlights of our trip included explora in the Atacama Desert. This was one of the best activity centres I have ever visited. The cycling in the desert, culminating in a swim in the salt lakes, was top of Wilf's list. The explora staff are well trained and, crucially, can speak good English. I particularly appreciated the care they took to teach Wilf how to 'work' in the stables, hosing down the horses etc. He loved hanging out with the gauchos.

What would you do different next time? I would take further advantage of the new scheme whereby tourists lodge in the homes of local people. We stayed on two farms on Chiloé Island and Wilf was able to participate in everything from milking cows to riding on tractors.

Top two adventures A three-day horse trek up an old Andean trading route from Cochamó and a sea kayaking trip off Chiloé Island. The guide went in a two-man kayak with Wilf -- and took honey sandwiches to keep little arms padding – and I went solo.

Sara Wheeler Author, Chile: Travels in a Thin Country (Abacus)

" " The marine life of the Galápagos Islands was incredible. The highlight for Amy (age 11) was when she saw a Galápagos shark. Ellie (age eight) put her face in the water and was immediately hooked on snorkelling. Dry ground was just as good – the animals were so friendly it was easy to tread on them. In fact, I think we may have created a new species – the purple-footed booby!

The Williams Family Enchanted Islands tour, The Adventure Company

Ultimately, though, with a few sensible precautions and (in the case of the Galápagos) a healthy bank balance, any of these countries promises a superb family adventure. Educationally, they will have your kids' eyes popping, while adventure hotspots, like Cusco in Peru or Pucón in Chile, offer numerous activities, such as cycling, whitewater rafting and horse riding.

Teenagers (13 years+)

Latin America has huge appeal for teens. Several of its cities are super-cool – tango in Buenos Aires, beach life in Rio, shopping in Nassau, classic cars in Havana – while the whole continent is pervaded by lively rhythms, sassy fashion and a love of sport.

You can also take adventure to new levels. So, instead of a sea kayaking day trip in Baja California (suitable for younger children), you can set off on a week-long paddling odyssey. There are also dozens of trekking opportunities in the Andes, including the classic Inca Trail to Machu Picchu and camping trips in Patagonia. If that sounds too much like hard work (for your teenagers that is) there's always the Caribbean. A laid-back resort with watersports, a bit of nightlife and other teens to mix with could well be the ultimate place to chill.

Special needs

Latin America may not have the level of accessibility you're used to at home, but don't write it off as a no-go zone for anyone with special needs. Several resorts and villas in the Caribbean and Bahamas are wheelchair accessible, while the cruise ships of Royal Caribbean International

(royalcaribbean.com), for example, were designed with spacious corridors and gradual inclines to public rooms. México Accesíble (accesiblemexico.com) offers trips to Puerto Vallarta with special facilities, such as roll-in showers. Go with Wheelchairs (gowithwheelchairs.com) offers wheelchair travellers a safe and reliable means of visiting Costa Rica, while Experience Belize Tours (experiencebelizetours.com) offers wheelchair-friendly tours to the Mayan site of Altun-Ha. Decthird (decthird.com) offers an excellent range of tours throughout Argentina for people with special needs. Apumayo Expeditions (apumayo.com) can arrange trips to Peruvian highlights, such as Machu Picchu, Pisac and the Amazon. In Chile, try Amapi Accessible Tours (amapiexpeditions.com).

Single parents

With their small size and well-equipped resorts, the Caribbean Islands are the best bet for single-parent families who want minimal logistical fuss. Generally, though, most of the information in this chapter applies equally to single-parent families as two-parent ones. The most important thing to remember is not to venture too far off the beaten track where, if an emergency did arise, you would be stuck on your own. Either join a group tour or hire a guide. In some Latin America countries there may also be an issue on arrival if you're a single parent with a child, so it's worth checking with the embassy beforehand whether you need the consent of the other parent.

Top: Atlantis resort, Bahamas. **Above:** Havana.

Pick of the peninsulas

Mexico can be as adventurous as you want it to be. You can play it safe at fly 'n' flop mega-resorts like Cancún and Acapulco, or you can play at being Indiana Jones by exploring the jungles and Maya ruins of the Yucatán Peninsula. Mexico City can be overwhelming for children, but nearby archaeological ruins are well worth visiting. Further north, the vast Copper Canyon is the setting for a dramatic rail journey, while Baja California – Mexico's desert peninsula – is a prime spot for whale watching and sea kayaking.

Mexico City

›› Mexico's capital has the world's largest taxi fleet of 60,000 cars, but only use ones from marked taxi stands. The subway is fast and modern; some stations have bits of Aztec ruins.
›› Explore the historical centre on a traditional tram or, if you have older children, take a tour using Segways (upright electronic scooters).
›› Chapultepec Park (where you can hire bikes and ride ponies) is a popular bolt hole for local families, while Aguas Salvajes is a water park with pools and slides.

City highlights

Built on the site of the Aztec capital of Tenochtitlán, Mexico City is a somewhat manic metropolis that's home to over 20 million people. But take a deep breath and focus on one or two highlights and you will discover a city rich in heritage.

Plaza de la Constitucion Also known as the Zócalo, Mexico City's historical square is dominated by the Catedral Metropolitana, a baroque giant that took 250 years to complete. Like much of the city, it is built on an ancient lake bed and needs frequent reinforcement to prevent it from sinking. For a quick visual guide to Mexico's history, take a look inside the Palacio Nacional where the Diego Rivera murals recount scenes ranging from the Aztec empire to the revolutionary hero of Francisco Villa. On most days in the Zócalo, indigenous dancers dressed in flamboyant costumes and feathered headdresses re-enact Aztec ceremonies, while a short walk away you can see the excavated ruins of Templo Mayor – the Great Temple that was once the sacred centre of the Aztec universe.

Museums The Museo Nacional de Anthropologia houses an enormous collection of pre-Hispanic artefacts, including all the best bits excavated from the ruins of ancient civilizations, such as the Aztec, Maya, Olmec, Toltec and Zapotec. You would need at least two days to see everything, so instead set your sights on the Aztec calendar, the Maya Chacmool from Chichén Itzá and the jade mask from Palenque. Another museum worth visiting is the Papalote Museo del Niño, a children's museum with hands-on science and cultural exhibits and an IMAX cinema.

City getaways Escape the smog and mayhem by taking a day trip to the mysterious ceremonial site of Teotihuacán (pronounced 'teh-oh-tee-wa-*khan*'). While parents contemplate the ghost of a once great city (abandoned around AD 700), children will be eager to climb all 248 steps to the top of the Pyramid of the Sun – the third largest in the world.

Further afield you can reach Oaxaca by luxury inter-city coach or a short flight. This handsome colonial city has a tree-shaded central plaza surrounded by cafés and a cathedral. Peruse the local market for colourful textiles and handicrafts, sample the traditional *mole* dishes (meat smothered in a chocolate and chilli sauce) and visit the ancient Zapotec capital of Monte Albán.

Yucatán Peninsula

›› Mérida, with its cobbled streets, colonial buildings and street salsa, is an attractive and relaxed gateway to the region; take a horse-drawn carriage ride to soak up the atmosphere of the place.
›› Avoid the crowds and midday heat by aiming to reach Chichén Itzá early in the morning – or better still spend the night and enjoy the sound and light show.
›› If you can't face the resorts at Cancún head south towards Tulum where you'll find great beaches but more basic accommodation.

My oh Maya!

On the Yucatán you're never that far from an idyllic Caribbean beach, so there's no excuse for not making those hot and sweaty archaeological jaunts into the interior.

Chichén Itzá Kids may always

Above right: Chitchén Itzá.
Below: Maya calendar.

remember it as Chicken Pizza, but the fact remains that this magnificent Mayan site (pronounced 'chee-*chen* eet-*zah*') is a must-see for anyone visiting Mexico. The imposing El Castillo pyramid is always a magnet to children, but once they tire of counting the 91 steps in its four stairways and romping across the ruined city's wide-open plazas they will begin to discover some fascinating, often gory, clues to Chichén Itzá's past. The Juego de Pelota, for example, was where the Maya played a killer ballgame (see Copán, page 369) in which contestants sometimes received a fate far worse than a red card. See if you can spot the carving on the ball court wall depicting a beheaded player, blood spurting from his neck, while an opponent holds the severed head aloft – an early form of 'sudden death' perhaps?

In the Temple of the Skulls, meanwhile, youngsters will go pop-eyed over scenes of eagles ripping hearts from human victims.

Tulum Within day-trip range of Cancún and perched right on the edge of the Caribbean, the cliff-top ruins of Tulum can become clogged with visitors, so stay nearby and visit in the early morning when sunlight rakes the walls of this coastal Mayan city. Tulum is smaller than Chichén Itzá and the carvings aren't as gruesome, so it is probably a better bet for younger children.

Xel-Ha Just 13 km from Tulum, Xel-Ha (xel-ha.com) is a Mayan-themed water park. Based around natural creeks, lagoons, caves and forests, it offers everything from swimming with dolphins and snorkelling to jungle walks and a 5-m cliff jump.

Above: Xhela. **Below**: Kayaking in Baja.

Baja California

😎 🐋 🚣 ⛰ 🍴

» Boat trips to see grey whales in Baja's Pacific lagoons (Dec-Apr) operate from Guerrero Negro and Lopez Mateos.

» Sea-kayaking trips range from week-long wilderness expeditions suitable for families with adventurous teenagers to shorter excursions based at Espíritu Santo island in the Sea of Cortez for children as young as 6 (sharing a double kayak with a parent).

Blazing paddles

A gnarled peninsula of desert mountains and cactus-stubbled plains, Baja probes the Pacific like a skeletal finger. But where barren land meets cobalt sea, this 1300-km-long Mexican frontier teems with life. Each winter, over 20,000 grey whales visit Magdalena Bay and other sheltered lagoons along the Pacific coast to give birth and mate before resuming their epic 8000-km migration to the Bering Sea. Travelling through a mosaic of waterways and camping on uninhabited islands, a sea-kayaking expedition is a wonderful way to explore the whales' nursery grounds and, if you're lucky, to paddle alongside them. Grey whales are naturally inquisitive and you may find yourself getting eye-to-eye with one of these gentle giants. The Sea of Cortez, meanwhile, is a cetacean hotspot where you can encounter anything from the mighty blue, humpback and fin whale to more diminutive species such as minke, Bryde's and orca. Dolphins can be found in pods occasionally numbering a thousand strong, while sea lions, turtles and manta rays add to the marine bonanza. As with the Pacific coast, you can either kayak here or take a boat trip. For another, possibly even greater thrill visit Los Islotes where you can snorkel with playful sea lions.

The Grander Canyon

For adventurous families, Baja combines well with one of the world's great train rides. Simply take the ferry from La Paz to Topolobampo and on to Los Mochis, from where the Chihuahua-Pacific Railway rattles inland for 655 km, stopping at several points in the Copper Canyon – a vast axe-stroke through the Sierra Madre that could swallow four Grand Canyons. It's a straight-through 14-hour ride to Chihuahua, but spread this epic journey over three or four days to take advantage of the hiking, biking and horse-riding opportunities en route.

🐳 Spouts in Baja

Blue whale (maximum length: 34 m) Produces a tall column of spray rising to 9 m or more.

Grey whale (maximum length: 15 m) Blow is often heart shaped, reaching a height of 4.5 m.

Humpback whale (maximum length: 19 m) A dense and bushy blow that can rise to 3 m.

Grey whale

> 66 99 We paddled all morning in the lee of the island, pausing to glide silently towards herons taut with concentration as they stalked fish. Every hour seemed to herald a different species. From the brazen snowy egret to the skulking green-backed heron, Magdalena Bay was festooned with birds. Pacific loons and surf scoters bobbed in our wake, while turkey vultures, frigatebirds and ospreys pirouetted overhead.
>
> At midday, we beached the kayaks and walked across to the ocean side of the island where Pacific breakers misted the air with spray and drove sea spume across a beach littered with sand dollars and shells. Half-digested by sand lay the twisted wreck of a small fishing boat, bearded with seaweed.

Will

Welcome to Jurassic Park

It's not surprising that Costa Rica was chosen as one of the filming locations for Spielberg's epic dinosaur fantasy. Trekking deep in one of the country's cloudforests or canoeing through one of its mangrove swamps you can almost sense the velociraptors skulking in the shadows, ready to execute their deadly pincer movement. Perfect for the nature-loving family, this Central American beauty has jungles, active volcanoes, Pacific and Caribbean beaches, plus lots of opportunities for adventure. But probably no dinosaurs (sorry kids).

Costa Rica

😊 ✿ ⚘ 😊 😊 ⏸ 🔟 😊 ⛴

» Join a guided tour or plan an independent self-drive – a 4WD is recommended. Distances are short and there are plenty of guesthouses, eco-lodges and beach retreats.
» Make sure your itinerary includes a mixture of Caribbean and Pacific coasts, a volcano or two, plus a visit to the cloudforest. Allow at least 2 weeks.
» There's something for all ages, although you need to take malaria precautions.

Coast to coast

No less than 25% of Costa Rica is protected as national parks and reserves. A fifth the size of the UK it boasts 1200 species of orchids, 850 varieties of birds and more types of butterfly than Africa. Binoculars ready? Then let's begin…

San José and the Central Highlands Costa Rica's capital has a few interesting museums, but you haven't come all this way to be stuck inside. Instead, spend a day or two exploring the Central Highlands. The Lankester Botanical Gardens (jardinbotanicolankester.org) provide a gentle and informative introduction to Costa Rica's dazzling flora (and you'll probably spy your first hummingbird here). With spectacular lake-filled craters that you can drive to within a few hundred metres of, Poás and Irazú are the two volcanoes closest to San José. For peak perfection, however, aim for Arenal, a classic cone rising above the town of La Fultuna. One of the world's most active volcanoes, it erupts almost daily and on clear nights you can see

(from a safe distance) the incandescent lava spewing from the crater.

Monteverde Cloudforest Reserve This misty, high-altitude, moss-drizzled forest looks like it's sprouted straight from the pages of *The Lord of the Rings*. Top tick is the resplendent quetzel, a secretive bird that was sacred to the Maya. The male has an iridescent green head and back, scarlet belly and long tail streamers. Get on level-beak terms by strolling the Sky Walk (skywalk.co.cr) – a series of suspended walkways in the canopy (all with strong wire mesh from floor to handrail) – or for something a little more exhilarating take a canopy zip-line ride.

Pacific coast Manuel Antonio National Park has an easy 1-km forest trail leading to a pristine sandy beach. Take your time and you may spot squirrel monkeys, coatis, racoons, sloths, iguanas, toucans and parrots. Reached by boat from Sierpe, the more remote Corcovado National Park offers sea kayaking, snorkelling and whale watching.

Caribbean coast For a country rich in wildlife Tortuguero National Park is Costa Rica's biodiversity honeypot. Most of the excursions here are by boat, allowing you to cruise beneath trees festooned with everything from howler monkeys and sloths to parrots and poison-dart frogs. Don't forget to keep an eye on the water's edge where you may spot herons, otters or an emerald-coloured basilisk – also known as the Jesus Christ lizard (see if you can find out why).

Best beaches If you're a turtle it has to

be Tortuguero; if you're a surfer Jacó on the central Pacific coast is where the action is (but beware of rip tides). The Nicoya Peninsula has quiet coves sheltered from the Pacific surf by reefs and forested headlands. There are also fine beaches at Manuel Antonio and Gandoca-Manzanillo. For something more off-the-beaten-track, nip into Panama for a few days of desert-island living on the coral cays of Bocas del Toro.

Best action Spice up your wildlife watching with a whitewater rafting trip (adventurecostarica.com). Costa Rica has three wild and wonderful rivers: the Pacuare (Grade III-IV rapids, minimum age 12), Sarapiquí (Grade III rapids, minimum age 10) and Corobicí (Grade II rapids, minimum age eight).

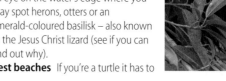

Belize

⊙⊙⊙⊙⊙🍴⊕⊗

» Exotic combination of tropical rainforests, coral reefs and Maya ruins.
» Belize's compact size and good tourist infrastructure means you can squeeze in a lot in.
» Accommodation ranges from eco-lodges in the jungle to beach resorts on popular Ambergris Caye.

Left: Treefrog. **Below left**: Sloth. **Above and right**: Copán.

Reef to rainforest

Wildlife sanctuaries A great introduction to the country's wildlife, the Belize Zoo (belizezoo.org) is home to a wide range of native species. Located on a 34-ha swathe of tropical savannah, the adjacent Tropical Education Centre offers walking trails and a half-day canoe trip on the Sibun River. Stay at one of the centre's forest cabanas and you'll be able to join a nocturnal tour of the zoo. Once you've honed your wildlife-watching skills, put them to practice at some of Belize's renowned wildlife reserves (belizeaudubon.org). Crooked Tree Wildlife Sanctuary is a good spot for birds, crocodiles and howler monkeys, while Cockscomb Basin Wildlife Sanctuary is a vast area of rugged, forest-clad mountains where you may be lucky enough to spot the elusive tapir or jaguar.

Belize Barrier Reef Measuring nearly 300 km in length, the world's second-longest barrier reef is scattered with thousands of coral islands, ranging from desert-island specks to Ambergris Caye (ambergriscaye.com) – a large island in the north with a wide choice of places to stay and things to do.

Maya ruins Altun Ha is the most easily accessible site from Belize City. However, if you're in the mood for some Maya ruins, they don't get more impressive than Tikal – a day trip across the border into Guatemala. One of the great Maya cities, Tikal flourished between 600 BC and AD 900. Today, its pyramids rise majestically above the rainforest, providing amazing views across the canopy and the bonus of

spotting monkeys and toucans. The Temple of the Double-Headed Serpent is the tallest – an exquisitely forged pyramid looming 65 m above the city's plazas.

Adventure activities In addition to canoeing, biking, hiking and snorkelling, one of the more daredevil pursuits in Belize is tubing along the subterranean rivers of the Caves Branch system (cavesbranch.com). Sitting in an inflated inner tube with just your headlamp to light the way, it's not for the faint-hearted.

Honduras

⊙⊙⊙⊙🍴⊕⊗

» The small colonial town of Copán Ruinas makes an attractive and peaceful base from which to visit the nearby Maya ruins.
» Roatán in the Bay Islands offers a wide range of accommodation and is an excellent place to learn how to scuba-dive.

More of the three Rs

Like Belize, Honduras is endowed with that exotic, irresistible cocktail of reefs, rainforests and ruins. Not only does it boast the region's largest tract of virgin jungle (La Mosquitia), but it also has the coral-fringed Bay Islands and the ruined city of Copán – the crowning glory of Maya achievement.

Copán Sprouting from a forest clearing, tall stone pillars (or stellae) depicting great Maya rulers like 18-Rabbit are the trademarks of these enigmatic ruins. There are also temples beneath temples – the compressed 400-year dynasty of 16

kings through which archaeologists have burrowed to reveal intricate hieroglyphs and elaborate facades. Look out for the Ballcourt, a narrow alley hemmed in by sloping walls on which six upright macaw heads were mounted – the equivalent of goalposts. Over one thousand years ago, this was where Copán's sporting heroes refined the art of ball control. The game was called *pok-a-tok*, the rubber ball weighed the equivalent of a human head and full-time usually resulted in a sacrifice or two. In the Great Plaza you'll find an intriguing ball-shaped sculpture that has been identified as the plinth for bloodletting.

Rainforest reserves Take your pick from the mangrove channels of Punta Izopo (perfect for canoeing), Punta Sal (for spotting howler monkeys) and Pico Bonito (for birdwatching, hiking and whitewater rafting).

Bay Islands For the perfect way to round off a tour of mainland Honduras, rent a beach house in the laid-back settlement of West End on the island of Roatán. The snorkelling is superb and you can also rent sea kayaks, go horse riding, glass-bottom boating, learn how to scuba-dive or simply chill out on the beach.

❓ Where can I see one of these?

Five varieties of sea turtle nest on Costa Rica's beaches, ranging from modest olive ridleys to mammoth leatherbacks (weighing a hefty 550 kg). Head to Tortuguero and Santa Rosa national parks where, at night, it's possible to observe these marine reptiles hauling themselves on to beaches to lay their eggs. Leatherbacks nest from February to July and green turtles from October to October.

Top 12 islands

Antigua
Family appeal Very laid-back with safe reef-fringed waters and beaches galore – one for each day of the year.
Best days out Take a boat trip to Barbuda to visit the frigatebird sanctuary.
Find out more antigua-barbuda.com.

Bahamas (see page 372)
Find out more bahamas.com.

Barbados
Family appeal Something for everyone, from lively to totally chilled, plus a great choice of accommodation, from all-inclusive resorts to self-catering.
Best days out Spend a day exploring colonial Bridgetown then strike out on an island safari in search of some of the old plantation houses hidden in the hills.
Find out more visitbarbados.org.

British Virgin Islands
Family appeal Islands made in heaven for families keen on sailing. Peaceful, relaxed and unspoilt with a good range of accommodation.
Best days out Take a boat trip to find your own deserted cove. Visit the more lively US Virgin Islands (see below).
Find out more bvitourism.com.

Cayman Islands
Family appeal A Holy Grail to divers, the Caymans also offer plenty for families. There's a wide choice of accommodation, from self-catering to five-star luxury, while watersports, from snorkelling to submersible rides, will appeal to most ages.
Best days out Spot a prehistoric-looking blue iguana in the Botanic Park, interact with stingrays at Stingray City (a shallow sandbank off the coast of Grand Cayman) or hone your skills at the Black Pearl Skate and Surf Park.
Find out more caymanislands.co.uk.

Cuba
Family appeal All the sun, sea, sand and laid-back vibe of the Caribbean, but with a unique cultural twist.
Best days out Admire the faded grandeur of Havana's Spanish colonial architecture and classic 1950s American cars, learn how to dance the salsa and visit the Museum of the Revolution. Other historical hotspots include the Bay of Pigs and the Mausoleum of Ché Guevara at Santa Clara. For adventure head to Vinales for biking trips into a

How to pick the perfect island

Now here's a pleasant dilemma: there are thousands of islands in the Caribbean, ranging from chunky Cuba to the sandy slivers of the Exuma Cays. Take it as granted that most, if not all, will have idyllic beaches and warm sea, so how do you begin to zone in on your perfect piece of family paradise? Start by asking yourself the following five questions:

1 What do we want to do? If you're looking for an island adventure with lots to see and do, try Cuba, Jamaica or the Dominican Republic where you can hike in mountains one day and flop on a beach the next. If island hopping is more your thing, think about joining a cruise (see page 49) or visiting the Bahamas where you can easily combine two or three islands. Some Caribbean islands are renowned for particular activities, such as diving (Grand Cayman) or sailing (British Virgin Islands), while others tend to attract couples seeking luxury and privacy (such as St Martin and St Kitts).

2 What flights can we get? Several islands, like Barbados, Jamaica, the Cayman Islands and St Lucia, have non-stop flights from Europe or the United States (a real boon if you have a fractious toddler on your lap). Remember to factor in the transfer time to your hotel. Caribbean islands are GMT-4 or -5 hours.

3 What kind of accommodation do we need? Teenagers will appreciate full-on resorts where they can hang out with other teens and do stuff as and when they feel like it. For older teenagers a villa within a resort is ideal since it gives them the option to slob around like they do at home without irritating other guests or embarrassing their parents. You'll find good options in the British Virgin Islands and Antigua. For younger children look for a dedicated pool and kids' club, plus a gently shelving sandy beach that's sheltered from the wind. Tots, of course, will need childcare facilities like babysitting and crèches if you want any adult time for watersports or a romantic meal. At the other extreme, a self-catering beach house will give you independence and put you more in touch with local Caribbean culture.

4 When should we go? The hurricane season typically runs from early June to late November, but patterns vary from year to year and island to island. Temperatures average between 27 and 31°C, although the Bahamas and Bermuda will be cooler during winter. Some upmarket resorts don't allow children during the high season.

5 What is the local language? English is the official language of most Caribbean islands, with the exception of Aruba, Bonaire and Curaçao (Dutch); Cuba, Dominican Republic and Puerto Rico (Spanish); Guadeloupe, Haiti, Martinique and St Barth (French).

dramatic landscape of limestone peaks, to Trinidad for snorkelling on the reef at Cayo Blanco and to Topes de Collantes National Park for hiking and birdwatching. **Find out more** cubatravel.cu.

Dominican Republic
Family appeal Superb beaches, a good range of accommodation and endless adventure opportunities.

Best days out Take a 4WD safari into the mountains to visit rural villages and to witness coffee and sugar cane farming in action. The mountain town of Jarabacoa is a base for whitewater rafting, parasailing, hiking and horse riding, while Ocean World is a large marine park with dolphin and shark encounters.

Find out more godominicanrepublic.com.

Grenada
Family appeal Low key and eco-friendly, with a mixture of sandy beaches and jungle interior; accommodation options range from luxury resorts to self-catering cottages.

Best days out St Georges has the most beautiful harbour in the Caribbean where you can browse market stalls piled with nutmeg, cinnamon and other locally grown spices. Take a family walk in Grand Etang National Park to spot monkeys and cool off under waterfalls. Keen snorkellers should take a boat ride to nearby Carriacou island.

Find out more grenadagrenadines.com.

Jamaica
Family appeal Beautiful beaches, vibrant towns, spectacular mountain scenery and legendary reggae beat.

Best days out For the ultimate induction to Jamaican culture, visit the Bob Marley Museum in Port Royal, take in a reggae session and then visit the beach shacks at Blue Lagoon or Boston Bay for the island's famous jerked chicken. Adventure activities include walking and biking in the Blue Mountans, exploring the caves and waterfalls near Port Antonio and floating on a bamboo raft down the Rio Grande.

Find out more visitjamaica.com

St Lucia
Family appeal A stunning island ripe for exploration; good range of accommodation.

Best days out See flatulent mud pits and jets of steam at the 'drive-in' volcano; explore the lush interior by horseback or mountain bike, visit the famous Pitons, explore the ruins at Pigeon Island National Park and go humpback whale watching.

Find out more stlucia.org.

Turks & Caicos
Family appeal Miles of deserted beaches, impressive coral reef system, perfect for a Robinson Crusoe experience.

Best days out Pack a picnic and find yourself a desert island. Humpback whale watching is possible between January and March.

Find out more turksandcaicostourism.com.

US Virgin Islands
Family appeal The ultimate Caribbean playground, rivalling even the Bahamas for its choice of accommodation and activities.

Best days out Children who don't feel confident snorkelling will enjoy Coral World Marine Park with its underwater observatory and touch pool, while fashion-conscious teenagers will no doubt want to browse the duty-free shops in Charlotte Amalie. Adventure activities include everything from sailing and scuba-diving to hiking and horse riding.

Find out more usvitourism.vi.

❓ What about Bermuda?

Family appeal Just six-and-a-half hours from London and less than two hours from New York, Bermuda boasts fine beaches and accommodation ranging from luxury resorts to intimate cottages.

Best days out Walk part of the gentle, tree-lined Bermuda Railway Trail, explore Crystal Caves (an enormous cavern and underground lake with easy walkways) and visit the Bermuda Maritime Museum where you can board historic vessels. Children aged eight and above can experience Bermuda bell diving, using an underwater helmet to walk along the ocean floor.

Find out more bermudatourism.com

Bermuda boasts some fine accommodation options.

Islands in the sun

In the Bahamas you don't simply have sandcastles – you have pink sandcastles. And the sea is so warm, clear and shallow you can spend hours bobbing around in a rubber ring, occasionally reaching down to pluck a starfish off the sandy bottom. The Bahamas have long held that exotic, rather exclusive lure for discerning couples and cruiseship travellers, but the appeal is just as strong for young families.

Nassau/Paradise Island and Grand Bahama

>> Nassau is located just 90 km east of Miami.
>> Accommodation ranges from self-catering apartments to all-inclusive resorts.
>> A great way to meet locals, the tourist board's People to People Programme arranges for you to share a day with a Bahamian family.

Pirates in paradise

Nassau's Bay Street is renowned for duty-free shopping, but you will also find handicraft markets, historic buildings and museums. For swashbuckling fun head to Pirates of Nassau (pirates-of-nassau.com) which features a replica pirate ship and a simulated attack from Blackbeard and his cut-throats. Most of Nassau's family hotels are on Cable Beach, whereas the resorts on Paradise Island (linked to Nassau by two bridges spanning the harbour) are concentrated around Cabbage Beach – the best spot for swimming. Numerous excursions operate from hotels and harbour quays, including the Blue Lagoon Dolphin Encounter (dolphinencounters.com) and day trips to Blackbeard's Cay (stingrayadventure.com). If you're staying at the Atlantis, however, you probably won't want to go anywhere else. For most children this sensational mega-resort is paradise well and truly found (see page 384). On Grand Bahama, more dolphin encounters are available at Sanctuary Bay through UNEXSO, (unexso.com) which also offers scuba-diving trips. Grand Bahama has superb sandy beaches

(some deserted, some with watersports galore), but tear yourself away for at least a morning to explore the forests of Lucayan National Park.

The Out Islands

>> Each group has its unique appeal, from fishing in Bimini to sailing in Abaco.
>> Island hopping is simple thanks to regular flights and high-speed ferries.
>> Powerboat Adventures (powerboatadventures.com) from Nassau offer an exciting taster of the Exuma Cays, stopping at uninhabited islands where you can snorkel and feed the native iguanas.

Pick of the bunch

When pirates ran amok in the Bahamas during the 18th century, marooning (or being made 'governor of your own island') was a fate worse than walking the plank. Nowadays, however, people would pay handsomely for a stint on one of the 700-odd Out Islands. But which ones to choose? Here are three of the most interesting.

Andros Largest of the Bahamian islands, Andros is dotted with inland blue holes. Track down one of these mysterious pools of water (fantastic for swimming) by cycling through the island's forested interior. Keep an eye out for lizards, butterflies and hummingbirds. The chickcharnee, half-man, half-bird, is also said to inhabit these woods – think bad thoughts about Andros and he will fix your head backwards. Scuba and snorkelling fans will rave about the 225-km-long Andros Barrier Reef, a spectacular coral wall that plunges 1800 m into an underwater canyon known as the Tongue of the Ocean. Dive sites range from shallow-water coral groves at the Aquarium to the vertiginous drop-off at Hanging Gardens where the reef is festooned with sponges and sea fans.

Eleuthera A peaceful, barefoot retreat for families, Harbour Island is a short water-taxi ride from Eleuthera's northeast coast. Old clapboard houses draped in bougainvillaea and hibiscus line the narrow streets of Dunmore Town where the only form of transport is the golf cart.

Abaco Another traffic-free hideaway, Hope Town on Elbow Cay hugs a sheltered bay peppered with yachts and fishing boats and overlooked by a red-and white-striped lighthouse. Hire a boat for some snorkelling or fishing.

Top: Starfish on sea floor. **Above:** Blue hole on the island of Andros. **Right:** Atlantis mega-resort.

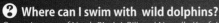

❓ Where can I swim with wild dolphins?

Operating out of North Bimini, Bill and Nowdla Keefe's Wild Dolphin Adventures (wilddolphins.com) are based entirely on the dolphin's terms. It's up to them if they want to interact with you, but if you're patient and lucky a pod of spotted dolphins will accompany you on the swim of a lifetime.

❝❞ Two hours out of Alice Town, with Bimini just a sandy whisker above the horizon, our launch is beset by spotted dolphins, their silver bodies flashing through the shallow waters of the Great Bahama Bank. Donning masks and snorkels, we slip over the side. Like a long-wave radio struggling to tune, the sea reverberates with clicks, whirrs, squeaks and all manner of dolphin gossip. A pale streamlined shape cruises past, and then suddenly we're confronted by spotty, smiling faces. The dolphins seem intrigued. When we free-dive towards the sandy seabed they follow us, belly to belly, so close that (if it were allowed) you could reach out and embrace them. A mother and calf join us. The youngster seems as excited as we are, racing around us like a faulty torpedo while its mother swims sedately nearby keeping a watchful eye.

Will

❝❞ We discovered a track that petered out in dunes on the east coast of Harbour Island. For Ellie, the endless stretch of pinkish sand that lay beyond was a beach made in Barbie heaven. For Joe it was the crowning glory of his castle-building career.

Will

Small but perfectly formed

Size isn't everything. Although dwarfed by neighbouring Peru and Colombia, Ecuador (about the size of New Zealand) is neatly sliced into Amazon rainforest, Andean mountains and Pacific coast – with an irresistible side order in the form of the Galápagos Islands lying 1000 km to the west. In just a couple of weeks, you could sample all of these South American icons. It's not a cheap option for a family holiday (particularly once you've splashed out on a Galápagos cruise), but if you're looking for that once-in-a-lifetime experience, few countries can match Ecuador for jaw-dropping scenery, vibrant culture and unforgettable wildlife encounters.

Ecuador

⊙ ⊙ ⊙ ⊛ ⊛ ⊛ ⊞ ⊛ ⊕

»» Quito makes a convenient base for exploring Ecuador's key highlights.
»» Self-drive is possible, although most people arrange tours. A colourful 'bus on tracks', the Chiva (chivaexpress.com) is a quirky way to get around.
»» Accommodation ranges from city hotels to highland haciendas (countryside ranches).
»» Allow a minimum of three nights to visit a jungle lodge in the Amazon.

From the Andes to the Amazon

Quito Ecuador's capital lies at an altitude of 2800 m so it's worth taking it easy for the first few days while you adapt to the thin air. Spend an afternoon wandering the cobbled streets of Quito's old town, a UNESCO World Heritage site containing several impressive colonial buildings, such as the Jesuit church of La Compañía with its elaborately carved and gilded altar. For fantastic views of the city and surrounding peaks take the Teleferiqo cablecar (teleferiqo.com) up Pichincha or a taxi to Cerro Panecillo, site of a 45-m-tall statue of the Winged Virgin.

Mitad del Mundo About 25 km north of Quito, Mitad del Mundo marks the spot where, in 1736, Charles Marie de la Condamine pinpointed zero degrees of latitude. Children will enjoy straddling the equator and jumping from one hemisphere to the other. The Inti-Ñan museum explores the astronomical knowledge of the region's pre-Hispanic people who used solar observatories and temples to determine Quito's

The perfect cone of Cotpaxi.

position at the 'centre of the earth' long before Europeans arrived.

Cotopaxi National Park At 5897 m, Cotopaxi is the world's highest continuously active volcano, and most alluring of the peaks lining Ecuador's fabled Avenue of the Volcanoes. On a day trip from Quito it's possible to drive as high as 4500 m on Cotopaxi's lava-scoured flanks, then walk about 45 minutes to the *refugio* at 4723 m. Be warned though that the air is very thin at this altitude; you should not attempt this unless you've spent a couple of days acclimatizing in Quito. Older children will no doubt want to forge ahead for another hour to the snout of Cotopaxi's glacier. Make sure they've got warm clothes and good hiking shoes – the terrain is rough and the wind can be bitter. If you're feeling the effects of the altitude, set your sights lower – there's great cycling and horse-riding country at various haciendas near the base of the mountain. A couple of nights at one of these traditional ranches, helping out with daily chores like collecting eggs, milking cows and feeding guinea pigs, is a great option for all ages.

Mindo cloudforests Just two hours'

drive from Quito the seaward slopes of the western mountains are draped with cloudforest. If you're short on time, this rich habitat, teeming with over 350 species of birds, makes a good alternative to an Amazon excursion. Bring your binoculars and see how many kinds of hummingbird you can spot.

Otavalo Another two-hour drive from Quito, this time to the north, Otavalo is a shopper's paradise. The town's market (held every day, but biggest and most colourful on Saturday) is crammed with textiles, handicrafts, musical instruments, jewellery and clothing.

Ecuadorian Amazon The most popular region is centred on the Río Napo where the small town of Coca (reached by road or air) is the starting point for jungle jollies. There are several lodges downstream of Coca, including Napo Wildlife Centre, La Selva and Sacha Lodge. All provide comfortable accommodation, excellent guides and various means of watching wildlife, from forest trails and dugout canoes to canopy towers. You'll also get a chance to go fishing for piranhas at night.

Best beaches Many of Ecuador's beaches have white sand, good surf and excellent seafood. Two of the finest are at Canoa and Bahía de Caráquez. If you find the Galápagos Islands simply too expensive, stick to the mainland where you'll see albatrosses, boobies, frigate-birds and sea lions at Isla de la Plata and humpback whales on boat trips from Puerto López (June to October).

A nose for heights

Riobamba is the embarkation point for one of the world's most dramatic train journeys. Descending from the mountains to the coast, the Trans Andean Railroad reaches a 45-degree climax at the Devil's Nose where the track zigzags across a steep slope. And if that wasn't exciting enough, many passengers ride on the carriage roof. Take a coat, a hat, sunblock, water and a head for heights.

Galápagos Islands

Left: Slumbering seals.
Below: Blue-footed booby.

⟩⟩ Several boats in the Galápagos offer family departures featuring special lectures, activities and children's meals; cruises from 3 to 10 days are available.

⟩⟩ As an alternative to a cruise, stay in a hotel on Santa Cruz and take day trips to surrounding islands – a better option for children aged 5 and under.

⟩⟩ Visit year-round, although the water is warmer for snorkelling Jan-Apr. Boat landings are a mixture of wet (wading to a sandy beach) and dry (stepping on to a rocky shore).

In Darwin's footsteps

Can you imagine how thrilled your children would be to get up-close and personal with prehistoric-looking iguanas that snort salt water from their nostrils? Or to watch the wacky courtship dance of the blue-footed booby? Or to swim with playful sea lions? The wildlife on these volcanic islands has not only evolved along peculiar lines, but it is also largely unfazed by humans, making this a unique and exciting opportunity for children to learn about ecology, evolution and conservation.

Santa Cruz The most populated of the islands, around 6000 people live in Puerto Ayora. Not to be missed is the Charles Darwin Research Station (darwin foundation.org) where you can gen up on the islands' geology, natural history and conservation. There is also a breeding centre for giant tortoises – including poor old Lonesome George, last of the Pinta Island subspecies. Other highlights on Santa Cruz include a pair of large volcanic craters known as Los Gemelos (the Twins) and several lava tubes, some of which are big enough to walk through.

Seymour An easy day trip from Santa Cruz, this tiny island offers a perfect introduction to Galápagos wildlife. The moment you step from your *panga* on to the rocky shore you'll notice marine iguanas, sea lions and a variety of birds, including blue-footed boobies, lava gulls, swallow-tailed gulls, noddy terns and pelicans.

Española Special even by Galápagos' standards, Española hosts the entire world population of waved albatrosses between March and December when these great ocean wanderers arrive to nest. You may also see the Hood mocking bird and the Española lava lizard – both endemic to the island. Blue-footed boobies, tropicbirds and marine iguanas are also much in evidence, while the sandy strip of Gardner Bay is a favourite haunt of sea lions and nesting turtles.

Fernandina Westernmost and youngest of the islands, Fernandina is also the most volcanically active. The contorted lava flows and large colony of marine iguanas make a primeval combination. Brightly coloured Sally-lightfoot crabs are everywhere and you can also see flightless cormorants and sea lions.

Floreana Interesting for its history as much as its natural history, Floreana was one of the first islands to be inhabited. In the late 18th century, whaling ships called by to stock up on water and giant tortoises (for food). At Post Office Bay the sailors left letters in a barrel for homeward-bound ships to collect and deliver – a tradition that continues to this day, only now it's tourists leaving postcards. Check to see if there are any you can post once you get home. A short walk inland from Punta Cormorant, a brackish lagoon is home to a large population of flamingos.

Genovesa Also known as the Tower, Genovesa is renowned for its seabird colonies.

Isabela The largest of the islands in the archipelago, Isabela has several sites of interest, including the Mariela Islands (penguins), Tagus Cove (marine iguanas) and Urvina Bay (flightless cormorants).

San Cristóbal Home to Puerto Baquerizo, the capital of the Galápagos, San Cristóbal also has a naval base and airport. Head to Frigatebird Hill for nesting colonies of both great and magnificent frigatebirds, to Punta Pitt for three species of boobies (red-footed, blue-footed and masked) and to Isla Lobos for sea lions.

Santa Fe You may well find yourself weaving between dozing sea lions when you wade ashore to Barrington Bay on the northeast side of Santa Fe. The island is also renowned for its endemic land iguana – paler and with more pronounced spines than the other species found in the archipelago.

Santiago Tidal pools at Puerto Egas are squirming with fur seals, while overhead you should spot the Galápagos hawk. Buccaneer Cove has a large sea lion population, while a trail leading from Espumilla Beach should reward you with sightings of several species of Darwin's finches.

🐦 Galápagos residents

Giant tortoise Can weigh up to 250 kg and live for more than 100 years. Three of the 14 subspecies are thought to be extinct.

Marine iguana Up to 300,000 inhabit the Galápagos. Feeds mainly on algae in tidal pools and excretes excess salt through a special gland connected to the nostrils.

Booby Derived from the Spanish word 'bobo' meaning clown, a reference to their striking plumage and comical mating dance.

Adventures in the Andes

Peru makes an exciting and unusual destination for adventurous families – and your children will no doubt have always wondered what Paddington Bear's home was like. The Inca ruins of Machu Picchu are a must, whether you take the train from Cuzco to Aguas Calientes and hike for a day, or embark on the four-day Inca Trail. Children will also be enthralled by the mysterious Nazca Lines, giant desert etchings best viewed from a light aircraft. Other highlights include searching for condors at Colca Canyon, taking a boat trip to the famous floating reed islands on Lake Titicaca and exploring the steamy jungles of the Peruvian Amazon.

Peru

⚫ ⚫ ⚫ ⚫ ⚫ ⚫ ⚫ ⚫ ⚫ ⚫ ⚫

›› Peru is a big country, so don't plan an overambitious itinerary. The most family-friendly highlights are in the southern half of the country, but if you have time include 3-4 days in the Amazon, a 30-min flight and a 2-hr boat ride from Cuzco.
›› Domestic flights and buses link main towns, but for maximum flexibility join an organized tour.
›› Base yourselves for a few days in Cuzco – Peru's adventure capital and the jumping-off point for the Inca Trail and Machu Picchu.
›› Cuzco lies at 3310 m, so don't overdo things until you've adapted to the altitude. You'll find accommodation to suit all budgets, plus a wide range of restaurants.

Above: Handicraft is an intrinsic part of life in the Peruvan Andes and makes for some wonderful souvenirs. **Right:** Reed boat on Lake Titicaca.

Country highlights

Nazca Get airborne in a light aircraft to gaze down on these huge and mysterious designs, which include a 100-m-wide monkey and a 50-m-long spider, as well as a killer whale, a hummingbird and various geometrical shapes, etched into the stony desert about 22 km north of Nazca. There's even one of a humanlike figure, its hand raised in greeting, which has been dubbed 'the Astronaut'. For decades scientists have pondered the meaning of these spectacular desert doodles. Some believe that the Nazca Lines were an astronomical calendar, while other theories point to giant running tracks, weaving designs, fertility rights, the map of a vanished empire or the spiritual journey of ancient shamans. It's still open to debate, so hop on a plane, take a peek and see if you can crack the Nazca code.

Arequipa Located in a valley at the foot of El Misti volcano (a perfect snow-capped cone, 5822 m high), Arequipa is a beautiful colonial city adorned with fine churches and mansions. The jewel in the crown is the Santa Catalina convent (santacatalina. org.pe), a colourful contrast to the 'White City's' predominantly pale, volcanic stonework. Join a 90-minute tour to explore the convent's maze of cobbled streets, cloisters, flower-speckled plazas and brightly painted houses. The nearby Plaza de Armas has peaceful gardens, attractive buildings and a good selection of handicraft shops and restaurants.
Colca Canyon Twice as deep as the Grand Canyon (and only 163 m shy of being the deepest canyon in the world), the Colca Canyon offers spectacular views of pre-Inca

terracing, precipitous rock faces, traditional Andean villages – and condors. In fact, these giant vultures (with a wingspan up to 320 cm) steal the show at Cruz del Cóndor, a mirador located at the deepest point in the canyon, where people flock to watch them swooping past. Get there by 0900 when the condors are riding the morning thermals. They spend the middle part of the day scouring the upper slopes for carrion before returning to the canyon late afternoon.
Lake Titicaca Like a sliver of lapis lazuli slipped into the high Andes, the startlingly blue waters of Lake Titicaca are awash with intrigue. For starters, Titicaca is the highest navigable lake in the world – a breathless 3856 m above sea level. But it's the floating Uros Islands (reached by boat tours from Puno) that will really fire the imagination of your children. The Uros people have lived on these islets (fashioned entirely from totora reeds) since Inca times. Tourists regularly visit around 15 of the 32 islands. You can walk on their springy, spongy surfaces and buy straw handicrafts from local women and children – a supplement to the more traditional fishing and hunting lifestyle of the Uros.
Cuzco A lively and comfortable city in which to spend a few days, Cuzco stands at the head of the Sacred Valley of the Incas. Its popularity stems mainly from the fact that Machu Picchu lies only a train ride or four-day hike away. However, it's well worth scheduling some extra time in and around Cuzco to visit other key sites and to take advantage of the wide range of activities on offer. A 30-minute walk or short taxi ride from the city centre, the ruined ceremonial site of Sacsayhuaman is an impressive introduction to the Inca's mastery of masonry. Some of the rocks in the perfectly sutured walls weigh over 120 tons. There are more outstanding Inca ruins at Pisac, 30 km north of Cuzco, although it's the famous local market here that draws the crowds. In Cuzco there are dozens of tour operators offering rafting, mountain biking, walking and horse-riding trips. The gentlest rafting option for children is the Huambutio-Pisac.

Magical Machu Picchu

The easiest way to reach the fabled Lost City of the Incas is to take a four-hour train ride from Cuzco to Aguas Calientes and a bus from there to the ruins. However, you should really use your feet if you want to sense some of the magic and majesty surrounding Machu Picchu. That doesn't mean you have to slog it out on the four-day, 43-km Inca Trail (see box on right). From Kilometre 104 (on the railway line from Cuzco) it's a short, one- or two-day trek to Machu Picchu via the beautiful ruins of Wiñay-Wayna (Forever Young). The first part is a steady, three-hour ascent and the trail is narrow and exposed in parts, but otherwise this option is ideal for families. For those up to the challenge, however, there's no denying that the Inca Trail is a superb and immensely satisfying adventure.

What to see when you're there   Don't miss the view from the **Watchman's Hut** (the one you've seen on all the postcards), or, if you're feeling energetic and haven't hiked the trail, head up to the **Intipunku** (Sun Gate) to see the ancient citadel in its glorious setting, surrounded by green jungle peaks with the Río Urubamba snaking its hairpin course far below. Also check out the **Temple of the Sun** (with its windows aligned to catch the sun's rays at the winter solstice), **Intihuatana** (a carved rock known as the 'hitching-post of the sun' that may have functioned as a sundial) and the **Sacred Rock** (a carved slab that echoes the outline of nearby mountains).

Let's go to... Manu Biosphere Reserve

Why? Wildlife. Lots of it. This vast chunk of Peruvian Amazon probably has more species of plants and animals than anywhere else on earth, including 1000 different birds and 13 varieties of monkey. You will literally be surrounded by thousands of yet-to-be-discovered species.

How? Fly in or take the three-day overland journey from Cuzco, crossing the Andes and delving into cloudforest en route. Once in Manu explore the jungle on foot and by canoe, staying in simple but comfortable lodges.

When? Year-round, although heavy rains, November to January, can cause transport problems.

Nine things you need to know about the Inca Trail

1 You can only trek with a registered agency which will arrange permits, guide, porters, camping gear, food and transport to and from trailheads.

2 Dry season is from May to October.

3 It's camping all the way, except at Wiñay-Wayna where you can stay in a hostel.

4 Take trekking poles with rubber tips or buy bamboo ones – your knees will be eternally gratefully.

5 Don't take short cuts – the vegetation at high altitude may take years to recover from careless trampling.

6 Bring clothing to cope with everything from rain-drenched subtropical forest to freezing mountain passes.

7 Help keep the Inca Trail litter-free by packing out your rubbish and using boiled/treated water instead of buying bottled water.

8 Remember that porters usually run downhill. If you hear them coming step to the side furthest from the edge.

9 Drink plenty of fluids to help you acclimatize to the altitude.

Top: Classic view of Machu Picchu. Above: Inca staircase. Left: Scarlet macaw.

Not for the squeamish

There's not a great deal to interest kids in Lima, but since you'll probably have a bit of spare time in Peru's capital head to the San Francisco Monastery where the catacombs are piled with thousands of skulls. And if that doesn't satisfy your morbid curiosity, try Arequipa's Museo Santuarios Andinos which displays the frozen mummies of Inca child sacrifices found on Ampato volcano.

The ubiquitous llama can be a comical beast at times (don't say it to their face though).

The heartbeat of Latin America

Brazil is vast. Only four countries – Canada, China, Russia and the United States – are larger. And it's not all Amazon jungle. There are iconic cities, like Rio de Janeiro, São Paulo and Salvador; there's the watery wilderness of the Pantanal, the ground-shaking Iguaçu Falls, a spectacular coastline, carnival, samba, football… Clearly you are going to have to make a few hard choices when it comes to taking the kids to Brazil. Few families will have the time, energy or money to see it all in one go. The good news is that local air passes link many of the main attractions, making it possible to visit two or three in a single holiday. A great option is to combine a few active days in the Amazon, the Pantanal or Iguaçu Falls, followed by time out in Rio or at one of the family-friendly resorts along the Atlantic coast near Salvador.

Rio de Janeiro

>> Rio is a year-round destination, but it's hot Jan-Mar, wet during Dec and chaotic in the build-up to the Carnival (usually in Feb).
>> Locals take their kids everywhere, including restaurants and dances, so you won't feel out of place doing the same.

City highlights

Sugar Loaf (Pão de Açúcar) The cable-car ride to the 396-m summit of Sugar Loaf Mountain (bondinho.com.br) is Rio's essential attraction. Spread out in panoramic perfection you'll see Copacabana and Ipanema beaches, the Christ statue, the Bay of Guanabara, Tijuca Forest and other city highlights. The cable car leaves every half hour from 0800. It's a two-stage journey, stopping at Morro de Urca where there is a café and children's play area.
Corcovado For more heavenly views of

Above: Christ the Redeemer statue. **Top right**: Cable car to Sugar Loaf Mountain. **Above right**: Copacabana beach, Rio.

🌀 Local tips
Take a jeep trip to Tijuca Forest, the world's largest urban rainforest.
Witness a classic 'Fla-Flu' showdown between Flamengo and Fluminense at Maracanã football stadium.
Sample the ice creams at Mil Frutas (Ipanema) – cinnamon and ginger flavour is highly recommended.

Rio, a narrow-gauge railway winds its way up 710-m Corcovado (corcovado.com.br) to the foot (or feet) of the huge Christ the Redeemer statue. For the best views sit on the right-hand side of the train.
Best beaches On Sundays, the waterfronts at Copacabana, Flamengo, Ipanema and Leblon beaches are closed to traffic and instead you'll find all kinds of street performers, from musicians to fire-eaters. Leblon also has a play area for toddlers, while Copacabana has plenty of kiosks selling snacks and drinks.

Iguaçu Falls

>> Try to allow at least 3 days at the falls so that you can view them from both the Brazilian and Argentinian sides, take a river safari and explore the surrounding forest.
>> There's plenty of accommodation available, including hotels with pools.
>> You can walk to within a few metres of some of the cataracts, close enough to give you a good soaking and loud enough to terrify young children.

The Great Water
Straddling the border between Brazil and Argentina, Iguaçu Falls are about 4 km wide and consist of 275 cascades ranging from 62 to 84 m in height.
The falls The Guaraní people weren't exaggerating when they named these falls *Iguaçu* (Great Water). At the peak of the wet season (January to February), some 12 million litres of water surge over the cataracts every second. Niagara can manage a relatively paltry peak flow of just eight million litres per second (upon seeing Iguaçu, First Lady Eleanor Roosevelt reportedly exclaimed, "Poor Niagara!"). The most spectacular cataract is Garganta del Diablo (Devil's Throat), a narrow horseshoe canyon. Helicopter flights provide a wonderful perspective of the falls, but for pure exhilaration take a boat ride to the very base of the cataracts. You'll battle upstream through rapids in a large inflatable dinghy until you are surrounded on all sides by curtains of water. Be warned, however, that the boat drivers like to nose the

66 99 As sunrise enflamed the forest canopy and sent tendrils of mist squirming across the water surface, we noticed something odd about the trees. Several of them were bare, and what we'd originally mistaken for leaves were actually parrots – hundreds of blue-headed and orange-cheeked parrots. Like a stained-glass window exploding, they simultaneously took flight and streamed overhead, their whirring wings and high-pitched squawks shattering the predawn calm.

Will

dinghies under one or two of the smaller cascades. Older kids will love the pummeling. Younger kids might not.

The forest A guided walk along one of the trails in the subtropical rainforest that surrounds Iguaçu Falls is a real treat. You might hear howler monkeys or glimpse an agouti, but it's the 250 species of butterflies that will enchant children. Look out for the metallic blue morphos flitting about on hand-sized wings. Keep your eyes peeled, too, for some of Iguaçu's 448 bird species. Toucans, parrots and tanagers are the most conspicuous.

Bahia Atlantic Coast

😎 😎 😎 🅰 🚻 🚺 🚲 🅰

» The Bahia region is malaria-free and just GMT-3.
» Trade winds bring rain mainly Dec-Apr.
» There are several excellent beach resorts in the area.
» Humpback whale watching is possible Jul-Oct.

Sand, Salvador and sea turtles
For a beach holiday with a twist, Brazil's Bahia region mixes family essentials, like soft sand and safe swimming, with some unusual excursions. Praia do Forte EcoResort (one of the most popular along this stretch of coast) is next to the Tamar sea-turtle conservation project (tamar.org.br). No less than five turtle species nest along Brazil's coast and Praia do Forte is one of the most important egg-laying sites. You can see various turtles, from adults to hatchlings, at the visitor centre, while guided

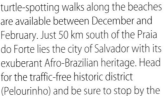

turtle-spotting walks along the beaches are available between December and February. Just 50 km south of the Praia do Forte lies the city of Salvador with its exuberant Afro-Brazilian heritage. Head for the traffic-free historic district (Pelourinho) and be sure to stop by the main square where *capoeira* dancers

Top left: Iguaçu Falls. **Above:** Bahia beach scene; Leatherback sea turtle. **Right:** Caiman in the Pantanal.

demonstrate their acrobatic and martial-arts skills. For something less frenetic visit Igreja de São Francisco, a baroque church adorned with some 100 kg of gold.

Lets go to … the Pantanal

Why? It's a huge wetland (about half the size of France) where you have a better chance of seeing wildlife than in the rainforest. Top ticks include anaconda, caiman, giant anteater, hyacinth macaw, jabiru stork and jaguar.

How? Stay at an eco-lodge, like the Refúgio Ecológico Caiman which offers activities ranging from caiman-feeding and canoeing to horse riding and night-time safaris.

When? Any time, although the land dries out between May and September, concentrating wildlife around pools and making it easier to see. Temperatures are also cooler during this period.

From tango to Tierra del Fuego

Most kids will feel right at home in Argentina. There's plenty they can relate to, from football and dance-hall fever in Buenos Aires to a day on the farm rounding up sheep. But don't imagine for one minute that Argentina is dull or predictable. Far from it. Stretching from the subtropical rainforest at Iguazú/Iguaçu Falls in the north to the ice-scoured wilderness of Patagonia in the south, this huge country can put you in touch with some extraordinary landscapes. Brace yourself for towering glaciers, jagged peaks, vast windswept plains and ancient brooding forests.

Above: Tierra del Fuego. **Left:** Maye Marie penguin. **Below:** Recoleta Cemetery in Buenos Aires.

Argentina

» Buenos Aires can be visited year-round, although temperatures are more pleasant during spring (Sep-Nov) and autumn (Mar-May).
» Patagonia is big – it takes 4 hrs, for example, to fly from Buenos Aires to Tierra del Fuego. Aim to spend at least 3 nights in any one location.
» Iguazú Falls (see page 378) is accessible from Puerto Iguazú.

Country highlights

Buenos Aires Argentina's capital makes a great launch pad for kids visiting South America. The locals love them (children are welcome everywhere except nightclubs), while the city itself has plenty of attractions. A good way to spend a day is to combine a visit to the central Plaza de Mayo area and the converted docks at Puerto Madero with a trip 32 km north to El Tigre where you can take a boat trip on the Paraná Delta – perfect if you need to escape the city heat. Other Buenos Aires highlights include Recoleta Cemetery. Not many cities can boast a graveyard as a tourist trap, but Recoleta's macabre maze of extravagant tombs is worth a visit. Challenge your kids to find the grave of Eva Perón. For security reasons, La Boca (a lively neighbourhood renowned for its colourful houses and street artists) should only be visited during the day and with a local driver and guide to show you around. It's also probably wise to avoid the area on match days when Boca Juniors are playing at

home in their famous Bombonera stadium – unless you're a football fan and going to the game of course.

Patagonia Covering almost a third of Argentina, this vast, empty and hauntingly beautiful region is ripe for adventure. If you only have time for visiting one part of Argentinian Patagonia (don't forget, there's more of it in Chile) set your sights on Los Glaciares National Park, a rugged melange of Andean peaks and giant glaciers that oozes wilderness yet has enough tourist infrastructure to keep families happy. The lakeside resort of El Calafate makes an ideal base for icy escapades to the creaking, groaning snout of the 60-m-tall Perito Moreno Glacier. You can also go hiking, horse riding and fishing. Although rather far-flung, Tierra del Fuego is also an excellent place to travel with kids. You arrive at the small city of Ushuaia where, each Austral summer, a steady trickle of tourists join cruise ships bound for the Antarctic Peninsula – just two days' voyage across Drake's Passage. But there's plenty to do in and around Ushuaia itself. Excellent museums trace the city's history, from the hardships faced by shipwreck survivors and the

indigenous Yámana people to the settlement's early role as a prison. You can also hike in the ancient and mysterious beech forests of Tierra del Fuego National Park and take boat trips on the Beagle Channel to spot rare wildlife, such as the flightless steamer duck which propels itself across the surface on stubby wings. Finally, there's Península Valdés, a spectacular wildlife haven jutting from the Patagonian mainland near the town of Puerto Madryn. Southern right whales gather here between June and mid-December to mate and give birth, while Magellanic penguins congregate in one of the largest colonies in South America. The beaches are positively squirming with elephant seals, sea lions and fur seals. Pups born between August and November add to the beach hullabaloo, but things reach fever pitch in March when orca whales surf on to the beach to seize unsuspecting youngsters.

National obsessions

Meat Argentineans love their steaks. They eat more meat than any other nation in the world. Try a succulent *bife de chorizo* at a *parrilla* (grill restaurant).

Football It's more than simply a beautiful game in Argentina. Feel the passion for *futbol* during a match at River Plate stadium.

Tango Don't miss out on a tango show in Buenos Aries where this exotic dance was invented.

Fat rewards in a skinny land

For a thin slip of a country, Chile certainly packs a lot in. From the lofty Atacama Desert in the north it's like one long thrill ride all the way to wave-scoured Tierra del Fuego in the south. Along the way you'll find everything from coastal resorts and vineyards to sheltered fiords and austere Andean wilderness. Travel in Chile can be as pampered or as hardcore as you like. Families with young children may want to plump for the country's gentle midriff where the Lakes District has none of the extreme altitude or climate often associated with Patagonia or the Atacama Desert. Wherever you go, however, you'll find travel reassuringly straightforward. And yes, even though it's Chile you'll still get a warm welcome.

Above: Torres del Paine. **Below right:** Cape Horn.

Chile

⚫🌙❄️🦐🐚🏔️🎭🏛️⛵☀️

▸▸ Chile may be thin (less than 180-km wide), but it's long (4270 km), so you'll find it easiest and quickest to use internal flights to get around. However, also consider renting a car or using the efficient long-distance buses.

▸▸ High season is Dec-Mar (Chile's summertime).

▸▸ Don't forget Easter Island. It's full of big heads and can be reached by flights from Santiago.

Country highlights

Santiago Chile's capital has enough to keep children occupied for a day or two. The walk up Cerro Santa Lucia, for example, provides great views of the city and – if it's clear – the Andes, while the Museo de Santiago portrays local history through some imaginative displays. If you're not in the mood for cities, however, Cascades de las Animas (cascada.net), just 60 km southeast of Santiago, offers easy walking, horse riding and whitewater rafting (minimum age eight) on an old horse ranch in the Andean foothills. Between June and September, there's excellent skiing at several resorts to the east of Santiago. El Colorado (elcolorado.cl) and Farellones (farellones.cl) both offer a good range of facilities, including ski classes for kids.

Atacama Desert San Pedro de Atacama is the staging point for forays into the driest desert on earth – and a pretty weird and wonderful place it is too. Your kids will feel like lunar explorers when they 'touch down' in the Valley of the Moon with its otherworldly rock formations. Then there are eggs to boil in the steaming geysers at El Tatio and flamingos to spy in the giant salt flats of Salar de Atacama.

Lake District Moving south from the Atacama, Chile gets wetter but no less magical. The Lake District has smouldering volcanoes, forests of araucaria (monkey puzzle) trees and a serene patchwork of lakes and fiords. At Parque Nacional Conguillio you can take a nature trail through an araucaria forest, while just to the south, Pucón is a centre for whitewater rafting, canyoning, horse riding, cycling and walking, as well as swimming and watersports on Lago Villarrica. Further south still, Puerto Montt is the gateway to the Chilean fiords. Boat trips here range from a one-day affair to see the rainforest at Parque Nacional Alerce Andino to a four-day cruise to Puerto Natales, gliding through a truly spectacular wilderness of mountains, glaciers and forests. Alternatively, you could simply nip across to tranquil Chiloé Island, a verdant time capsule of traditional villages and ancient forests where kids can run free on deserted sandy beaches, explore hidden creeks and enjoy life on a farm. It's like something out of Arthur Ransome's *Swallows and Amazons*.

Chilean Patagonia Torres del Paine is the showcase national park on the Chilean side of Patagonia (see opposite for what Argentina can offer). The iconic, cloud-snagging towers of Torres del Paine are a magnet to walkers, while hotels like the visionary Remota (see page 385) offer a range of excursions, from horse riding and boat trips to estancia visits and exploring the Milodon Cave – the object of Bruce Chatwin's quest in his classic travelogue, *In Patagonia*.

❓ How can I get one of these?

Few passport stamps evoke that 'ends of the earth' feeling more than the one you get upon making landfall at Cape Horn. However, the southernmost point of the Americas is surprisingly easy to reach. Departing on four-day voyages between Ushuaia and Punta Arenas, the cruise ship *Mare Australis* (australis.com) makes weekly visits throughout the summer. This weather-beaten outpost, notorious for its ship-swallowing gales and distinctly unfriendly seas, has a permanently manned lighthouse, a chapel and boardwalks.

Latin America essentials

When to go

The most comfortable time to visit **Mexico** is from December to February when the Yucatán Peninsula is at its coolest and least humid. The desert heat of Baja California is often tempered by a refreshing sea breeze, while the highlands of the Sierra Madre offer cool respite from the muggy lowlands.

Affecting the **Caribbean**, the **Bahamas** and **Central America**, as well as Mexico, the hurricane season runs roughly from May/June to October/November. The National Weather Service (nws.noaa.gov) provides daily updates. Costa Rica, Belize, Honduras, Cuba and other islands are sunny and dry from December to April, although even in the wet season rain tends to be short-lived – if torrential. Another feature in common with this region is that hotels charge premium rates during the peak winter period.

Ecuador and **Peru** are year-round destinations, with climate varying more with altitude than time of year. One of the best times to visit the mountains is during the dry, sunny period between June and September. Coastal areas can be wet from January to April – although this is the driest time for the jungle. The **Galápagos Islands** are sunny, hot and humid from December to June and cooler, with the chance of mist or drizzle, between June and November.

Amazonian **Brazil** is hot and humid all year with temperatures ranging from 25 to 35°C. Visit between June and November, however, and you can expect less rain and fewer mosquitoes. Head to the coast for cooling sea breezes and book well in advance if you want to visit during the local holiday periods of July and December to February.

Argentina and **Chile** are generally best visited between October and April when the days are longer, there's more chance of sun and Patagonia is at its most accessible. However, the further south you go, the more unpredictable and volatile the weather becomes.

Getting there

Operating from Madrid, Iberia Airlines (iberia.com) offers more Latin American destinations and non-stop flights than any other European carrier. Aerolineas Argentinas (aerolineas.com.ar) has daily flights from London to Buenos Aires and onward to other major South American cities. Between them, Air France (airfrance.com) and KLM (klm.com) have more than 170 weekly departures to Latin America and the Caribbean. British Airways (britishairways.com) has direct flights from London to Antigua, the Bahamas, Barbados, Bermuda, Jamaica, Mexico City, Miami and São Paulo with numerous onward connections throughout the region. From its hubs in Houston and New York, Continental Airlines (continental.com) has an extensive route network across

The world's original – and still the best. Rio is reduced to a gridlock of gyrating bodies in dazzling costumes as the Carnival's Samba Parade struts its stuff from dusk to dawn.

Central America and the Caribbean, as well as to Lima, Quito, Buenos Aires and Rio de Janeiro. Other airlines serving the region include Lufthansa (lufthansa.com), Mexicana Airlines (mexicana.com) and Varig (varig.com). Virgin Atlantic (virgin-atlantic.com) is worth checking out for flights to the Caribbean.

A direct flight in August with BA from London to Rio, for example, typically costs around £950 per adult and £750 per child (including taxes). Flying with Iberia via Madrid can save around £50. Similarly, a direct flight with Continental from New York to Mexico City costs around US$1700 for a family of four during August, but via Houston saves up to US$300. Another way to save money is to keep an eye on website special offers. BA and Virgin Atlantic often have a bit of a price battle early in the year with discounts on flights to the Bahamas and Caribbean.

Getting around

If you want to cover large distances or combine several countries, an **airpass** is convenient and good value. The South America Airpass from LAN (lan.com), for example, allows you to purchase one-way tickets to multiple destinations in Argentina, Brazil, Chile, Ecuador and Peru. Some of the more useful internal flights include LAN's Santiago to Buenos Aires route (US$230 one-way) and Aerolineas Argentinas' flights from Buenos Aires to Iguazú Falls (US$165) and Ushuaia (US$341).

Several South American countries, including Brazil, Mexico and Peru, have good road networks served by comfortable intercity **coaches**. You could also consider **self-drive**, although car rental can be expensive and distances huge. Latin America specialists, Geodyssey (geodyssey.co.uk) can arrange self-drive itineraries in Costa Rica – ideal for adventurous families who want the freedom of independent touring, but the security of pre-booked accommodation every

Bartolomé in the Galápagos Islands.

night. Don't attempt to drive in any major South American city – book a tour or use public transport instead.

As with flights, it's always worth scouring the internet for good deals on car rental. For one week's rental of a mid-range vehicle with air-conditioning and unlimited mileage, expect to pay US$250-275, plus an extra US$30 for a child seat. Petrol costs US$0.65-0.90 per litre.

There are several tourist-orientated **train** services in South America, two of the most popular being from Cuzco to Machu Picchu and Lake Titicaca (perurail.com). **Ferries** can also be useful, particularly in southern Chile and Baja California, while there's no shortage of operators offering **cruises** around the Caribbean, the Galápagos Islands and, to a lesser extent, Patagonia and Tierra del Fuego.

Accommodation

Accommodation ranges from modestly priced haciendas to expensive all-inclusive resorts. However, generally speaking you should be able to budget on US$30-75 per night for a mid-range hotel room.

In **Mexico**, a good choice for families visiting the Yucatán Peninsula, Omni Puerto Aventuras (omnihotels.com) is a small resort with just 30 rooms on a palm-fringed beach near Playa del Carmen, and well located for visiting the Mayan ruins at Tulum and Xel-Ha water park. On the Pacific coast, Fiesta Americana Puerto Vallarta (fiestamericana.com) has a kids' club and plenty of watersports, and you can also go cycling, horse riding and birdwatching in the Sierra Madre. In La Paz, Baja California, you can find B&Bs for under US$50 per double. Try Baja Bed and Breakfast (bajabedandbreakfast.com) which has a small pool.

Five-star family operator
Journey Latin America (journeylatinamerica.co.uk)

Pick of the trips The 19-day Albatross Tour takes in the top sights of Ecuador and the Galápagos Islands. Spend two days in Quito before taking a 45-minute flight and two-hour canoe trip to La Selva Lodge in the Amazon rainforest where you can fish for piranha and go alligator-spotting at night. Fly back to Quito and drive down the Avenue of the Volcanoes to Riobamba for the spectacular train ride down the Devil's Nose. Return to Quito via the market at Otavalo, then fly to the Galápagos for a seven-day cruise. Expect to pay around £3500 per family member (minimum age 12), including flights from London, twin room accommodation (with breakfast), full board in the Galápagos Islands and Amazon, all excursions and full-time tour leader.

Tour operators

In the UK
Austral Tours
latinamerica.co.uk
Beacon South America
beaconsouthamerica.com
Cathy Matos
 Mexican Tours
cathymatosmexico.co.uk
Geodyssey
 geodyssey.co.uk
Journey Latin America
journeylatinamerica.co.uk
Last Frontiers
lastfrontiers.com
Latin America Travel
latinamericatravel.co.uk
Sunvil Latin America
sunvil.co.uk

In the USA
Amazon Adventures
amazonadventures.com
Argentina Discover
argentinadiscover.com
Serendipity Adventures
serendipityadventures.com

In Latin America
Albee Adventures
albeeadventures.com
Amazing Peru Ltd
amazingperu.com
Amazonas Explorer
amazonas-explorer.com
Chile Tours chiletours.org
Chimu Adventures
chimuadventures.com
Cuba Select Travel
cubaselecttravel.com
Enchanted Expeditions
enchantedexpeditions.com

Fact file

	GMT	Language	Money	Code	Tourist info
Mexico	-6	Spanish	Mexican peso (US$1 = PS$11)	+52	visitmexico.com
Costa Rica	-6	Spanish	Colón (US$1 = C520)	+506	visitcostarica.com
Belize	-6	English, Spanish	Belize dollar (US$1 = Bz$2)	+501	travelbelize.org
Honduras	-6	Spanish	Lempira (US$1 = L19)	+504	honduras.com
Bahamas	-5	English	Bahamian dollar (US$1 = B$1)	+1	bahamas.com
Ecuador	-5	Spanish, Quichua	US dollar	+593	vivecuador.com
Peru	-5	Spanish, Quechua	Nuevo sol (US$1 = S/3)	+51	peru.info
Brazil	-3 to -5	Portuguese	Real (US$1 = R$2)	+55	turismo.gov.br
Argentina	-3	Spanish	Argentine peso (US$1 = P$3)	+54	turismo.gov.ar
Chile	-4	Spanish	Chilean peso (US$1 = P$537)	+56	visit-chile.org

Above: Hope Town Hideaways on Abaco, Bahamas. **Right:** Caribbean Resort.

The **Bahamas** excel in family-friendly accommodation, boasting everything from private self-catering villas, such as those offered by Hope Town Hideaways on Abaco (hopetown.com) to all-inclusive resorts like the legendary Atlantis (atlantis.com), which is described in detail below. In the **Caribbean** you are also spoilt for choice, but a shortlist of the best family resorts would have to include Almond Beach Village, Barbados (almondresorts.com), Holiday Inn SunSpree Resort, Jamaica (ichotelsgroup.com), Beaches Turks & Caicos Resort (beaches.com), Club Med Punta Cana, Dominican Republic (clubmed.com), Windjammer Landing Villa Beach Resort, St Lucia (windjammer-landing.com), Four Seasons Resort Nevis (fourseasons.com), Westin St John Resort & Villas, US Virgin Islands and Westin Casuarina Resort & Spa, Grand Cayman (starwoodhotels.com).

In **Central America**, you will find a good range of beach resorts and jungle lodges. Casa Bambu (casabambu-beach-house-rentals.com) provides great value for families on Costa Rica's popular Osa Peninsula. Nearby Corcovado Camp (corcovado.com) has 20 twin-bedded tents on raised platforms overlooking the Pacific, as well as a canopy platform for wildlife watching. Further along the coast at Manuel Antonio National Park, the upmarket Tulemar Bungalows (tulemar.com) are also worth considering.

Rising above the rest

Atlantis (atlantis.com) Paradise Island, Bahamas

This vast resort has over 2300 rooms, 30 restaurants and a 75-million-litre open-air marine habitat that's home to over 50,000 sea creatures, including sharks, rays and barracuda – all of which swim above, around and under guests as they stroll around the resort's grounds. It also recreates the legend of Atlantis with The Dig, a subterranean maze through the ruined Lost City, complete with lost treasure, mysterious hieroglyphics and yet more stunning aquariums. Outside, fantasy becomes thrilling reality with a bewildering variety of water rides.

For the kids An unrivalled range of kids' clubs and attractions, including Splashers (body slides, rope bridges, cargo nets and water cannons for kids under 137-cm tall); Morning Escape (themed games and crafts for three- to five-year-olds); Discovery Kids' Adventure (mind and sport challenges for six- to 12-year-olds); Evening Escape (dancing, karaoke, computer games and the latest movie releases); an adrenaline-charged waterslide complex for children over 122-cm tall (featuring the six-storey Mayan Temple and The Abyss with its 21-m near-vertical drop); Aquaquest (with more waterslides and a 1600-m river ride with high intensity rapids); a dolphin interaction and education centre and no fewer than 11 swimming areas.

For the parents Mandara spa with water-therapy treatments; fitness centre and candlelit French restaurant for adults only.

The lodge at Pico Bonito, Honduras.

Jungle jollies in **Belize** are available at Chaa Creek (chaacreek.com), which has its own butterfly farm and spa; Lamanai Outpost Lodge (lamanai.com), a cluster of 18 thatched cottages near Maya ruins, and The Lodge at Big Falls (thelodgeatbigfalls.com) where you can go kayaking, birdwatching and cycling. Top picks for family-friendly beach properties in Belize include Xanadu Island Resort (xanaduresort-belize.com) and Captain Morgan's Retreat (belizevacation.com) on Ambergris Caye, and Jaguar Reef Lodge (jaguarreef.com) in southern Belize.

For a splash of luxury in **Honduras**, The Lodge at Pico Bonito (picobonito.com) borders a verdant national park of jungle-clad mountains and is only a 30-minute drive from La Ceiba, the jumping-off point for the Bay Islands. On Roatán, largest of the Bay Islands, Palmetto Bay Plantation (palmettobayplantation.com) has thatched villas, each with a living room and kitchen.

In **Ecuador**, Hacienda Manteles (haciendamanteles.com), near Baños, is excellent value at around US$60 for a four-bed room, Hacienda Guachalá (guachala.com) is just a half-hour drive from Otavalo, while Hacienda San Agustin de Callo (incahacienda.com) makes an ideal base from which to explore nearby Cotopaxi National Park. In the Ecuadorian Amazon, Kapawi Lodge (kapawi.com) is run in partnership with members of the local Achuar community who will lead you on hikes through the rainforest, identifying medicinal plants and some of the 400 varieties of birds. Other options include Napo Wildlife Centre (ecoecuador.org), another community-based ecotourism project and La Selva Lodge (laselvajunglelodge.com). The best liveaboard vessel for families wishing to explore the **Galápagos Islands** is the MV Santa Cruz (mvsantacruz.com) which has triple and quadruple cabins with discounts for children. One of the larger ships operating in the Galápagos, the 90-berth Santa Cruz has plenty of space and good stability, as well as child-friendly touches, such as a glass-bottom boat. For something smaller and more intimate, consider the MV Evolution, which carries just 32 passengers and offers kayaking, shorter walks, swimming and a children's guide.

In **Peru**, for a gentle introduction to the Amazon, Reserva Amazonica (reserva-amazonica.info) is just 45 minutes by boat from Puerto Maldonado. In Cuzco, meanwhile, you can choose from budget hostels to top-end hotels, like the Monasterio (monasterio.orient-express.com).

South of Rio de Janeiro, **Brazil's** Costa Verde has a Mediterranean feel with numerous villas for rent, while the Bahia coast to the north has resorts like Praia do Forte (ecoresort.com.br), a supremely child-friendly property, an hour's drive from Salvador. Another excellent option along this stretch of coast is Costa do Sauipe (superclubs.org). Heading inland, Refugio Ecologico Caiman (caiman.com.br) is located on one of Brazil's largest cattle ranches and offers exciting tours by boat, jeep or horseback in search of the Pantanal's legendary wildlife, while Amazon Village Lodge (amazon-village.com.br) has 21 thatched bungalows located on a tributary of the Amazon, three hours by motorized canoe from Manaus.

To fully appreciate the ranching lifestyle of rural **Argentina** you should spend at least one night in a traditional homestead. Just 20 km from El Calafate (gateway to the Perito Moreno Glacier), Galpón del Glaciar (estanciaalice.com.ar) will allow you to witness the daily workings of a Patagonian sheep farm, while Estancia Huechahue (huechahue.com) is just the place for wannabee gauchos.

Chile also has several farmstay opportunities. Fundo Chacaipulli (chilefarmholidays.com), in the Lakes District, offers cosy self-catering in rustic beech-wood cabins, with horse riding and fishing. If you want to experience some of Chile's more extreme environments without sacrificing creature comforts, try explora (explora.com), a pioneering company with properties in the Atacama Desert, Torres del Paine National Park and Easter Island. Be sure to also check out the equally cutting-edge Remota (remota.cl) in Patagonia.

The Petito Moreno glacier, Argentina.

Food and drink

Allow anything from US$5-15 for a reasonable meal in a decent restaurant. If your kids eat potatoes and beans at home they won't go hungry in Latin America. Along with corn, tomatoes, cocoa and vanilla, these child-friendly staples all have their origins in Latin America and still form the basis of many traditional menus. In **Mexico**, for example, children will enjoy chomping through corn *tamales* (stuffed dumplings), tortillas, beans and chilli con carne, while those with more adventurous appetites can sample *mole poblano* (meat covered in a sauce of chocolate and chillies) and *sopa de lima* – a lime soup speciality popular in the Yucatán Peninsula.

In **Central America**, a typical meal consists of beef, rice, beans, fried plantain, sour cream and a stack of tortillas on the side. Fried chicken is also common, while grilled fish and lobster (often with coconut) is available along the coast. Not surprisingly, local seafood dishes feature predominantly on menus throughout the **Caribbean**. In the **Bahamas** you have to try conch. Cracked and fried, tossed in a salad or reduced to thick, spicy chowder, this mega-mollusc is delicious. Other local specialities include peas 'n' rice and grouper fingers. Slices of guava duff make an irresistible dessert, while fresh fruit juices slip down a treat (parents will no doubt want a splash of rum to convert theirs into a Goombay Smash or Bahama Mama cocktail).

In South America, Andean food is a hearty and wholesome spread of potatoes, rice, pork, chicken and lamb. Guinea pig is a local delicacy, but you won't get many kids willing to eat something they've always regarded as Nibbles, the family pet. In the Amazon, fresh local produce is the mainstay of recipes, so expect plenty of fish, fruit and vegetables.

One of the best-known dishes in **Brazil** is a black bean and pork stew known as *feijoada*, but you'll also find everything from seafood and steak to pasta and salad. On the northeast coast you should sample the exotic African-Brazilian fusion cuisine.

In **Argentina** they like their beef, so barbecue fans will be in heaven here. Also try the savoury *empanada* pasties. **Chile**, meanwhile, is renowned for its seafood (*curanto* is a typical shellfish stew served with potato bread), rich pastries and – for the grown-ups – its wines and *pisco sour* cocktail.

Health and safety

Malaria is present in parts of Latin America. In Mexico, there is some risk in rural areas along the west coast and in the south of the country. In Belize, Honduras and Costa Rica, malaria (usually of the benign, not malignant, form) is present year-round, particularly in low-lying areas. The main risk of malaria in the Caribbean is in the Dominican Republic – particularly in the western provinces of Castanuelas, Hondo Valley and Pepilla Salcedo. Malaria is not normally present in Cuba, Jamaica, the Lesser Antilles or the Bahamas. In Ecuador, malaria is widespread throughout the year below 1500 m, mostly in rural areas to the north and east, and there is very little risk in Quito, Guayaquil or the Galápagos Islands. Malaria precautions are essential for visits to the Amazon – even if you are joining a cruise in Manaus. There is usually only minimal risk of infection at Iguaçú Falls and along the populated eastern coast of Brazil from Fortazela south to Rio de Janeiro and Sao Paulo. In Argentina, there is only a small risk of malaria in rural areas bordering Bolivia and Paraguay. Malaria does not normally affect Chile.

Before visiting Latin America you should plan an appropriate course of vaccinations, which may include hepatitis A, typhoid and yellow fever. See page 54 for information on malaria prevention and routine inoculations that should be up to date regardless of travel.

In general, you should stick to bottled or purified drinking water. Only eat properly prepared food (peeled fruit, salad washed in treated water etc.) and be strict on hygiene measures in order to minimize the chances of diarrhoea. Be also aware of the potential affects of exposure to high altitude and severe sunlight in the Andes. Rabies is widespread, so never let your children approach dogs. Similarly, leave all the poking around in the rainforest to your professional guide – those hairy caterpillars may look cute to hold, but they are loaded with noxious irritants.

Major cities, particularly Rio, have a reputation for being violent and unsafe, but this is an exaggeration. As long as you use common sense, your visit to Brazil or any of the countries covered in this chapter should be trouble-free.

Piggy on the griddle

Those of a nervous disposition may prefer to look away now. We're afraid guinea pig (or *cuy*) is a local delicacy in Ecuador, as well as other Andean countries. Spit roasted, it's actually quite crisp and tasty.

Tread your own path
Explore the world with Footprint

Footprint can be depended on for accurate travel information and for imparting a deep sense of respect for the lands and people they cover.
World News

NEW Activity titles…

Diving the World and *Body & Soul escapes* are two exciting new additions to the *Footprint* activity range. Get top tips from the experts on the planet's best locations to pursue your passions and pastimes, plus essential travel information on the countries, their people, history and culture.

Footprint
Travel guides

www.footprintbooks.com

Index

Photography credits

All images are suplied by the author, **William Gray**, except the following: **10 best holidays** p8 Crystal Active; p11 Cedarberg Travel; p11 Cheli & Peacock; p11 Earthwatch; pp11, 19 Discover the World; p13 Families Worldwide; p13 Rome Cavalieri Hilton; pp13, 19, 23 Journey Latin America; p15 Activities Abroad; p15 Blue Chip Vacations; p15 Eurocamp; p17 Esprit Holidays; p17 Real Holidays; p17 Sani Resort; p19 Cox & Kings; p19 Wildlife Worldwide; p21 PGL; p23 Powder Byrne; p23 Sandy Lane.

Essentials p30 Exodus; p38 Le Loft 1911/Shutterstock; p38 Elena Ray/Shutterstock; pp40-43 all images (except 2 and 22) supplied by th emanufacturers; p48 T-Design/Shutterstock; p50 Darren Baker/Shutterstock; p51 Alan Murphy.

Britain and Ireland p61 Joe Gough/Shutterstock; p61 Kevin Eaves/Shutterstock; p61 North East England Tourism; pp61, 66 BA London Eye; pp61, 77 Pembrokeshire County Council Tourism & Leisure Services; pp61, 80, 81 Tourism Ireland; p62 Bryan Busovicki/Shutterstock; p62 Chris Sargent/Shutterstock; pp62, 74 Gail Johnson/Shutterstock; p63 rebvt/Shutterstock; p64 Chessington World of Adventures; p65 Jersey Tourism; p67 agefotostock/Superstock; p67 British Museum; p67 Rick Thornton/Shutterstock; p68 Isle of Wight Tourism; p68 Mark Breck/Shutterstock; p68 Thorpe Park; p69 Bewilderwood; p69 Richard Bowden/Shutterstock; p70 Nick Stubbs/Shutterstock; p72 John Evans/Shutterstock; p72 Peter Brett Charlton/Shutterstock; p74 Dale Mitchell/Shutterstock; p74 Trevor Buttery/Shutterstock; p76 Mary Lane/Shutterstock; p78 Jemini Joseph/Shutterstock; p80 Alfio Ferlito/Shutterstock; p80 Joe Burns/Shutterstock; p85 Bedruthan Steps Hotel; p85 Kelly's Resort Hotel; p85 Knoll House Hotel; p85 Southland Camping Park; p85 White House Hotel.

France p89 Aga & Mike Materne/Shutterstock; p89, 102, 108 Esprit Holidays; p89 Manik Chauvin/Shutterstock; p91 Kameel/Shutterstock; p91 Vladislav Garfinkel; p92 Siblu; p93 Keycamp; p94 Franck Chazot/Shutterstock; p94 Shutterstock; p96 Crystal Kirk/Shutterstock; p96 Stephen Meese/Shutterstock; p97 C Alexis Rosenfield/Nausicaa; p99 Andy Z/Shutterstock; p100 Futurescope; p104 Eurocamp; p104 Stephen Finn/Shutterstock; p105 Cre8tive Images/Shutterstock; p105 Mikhail Lavrenov/Shutterstock; p105 Sean Nel/Shutterstock; p105 Suze Piat/Shutterstock; p105 Yanik Chauvin/Shutterstock; p108 VFB Holidays; p109 © Disney; p109 Club Med; p109 Corsican Places; p110 Pepe Ramirez/Shutterstock.

Spain and Portugal p113 Irina Korshunova/Shutterstock; p113 Oleg & Sophy Kozlova/Shutterstock; pp113, 116 Rui Vale de Sousa/Shutterstock; pp113, 124 Rafael Martin-Gaitero/Shutterstock; pp113, 125 Elena Aliaga/Shutterstock; pp113, 127 Natalia Sinjushina & Evgeniy Meyke/Shutterstock; p115 Gelpi/Shutterstock; p115 Gert Johannes Jacobus Very; p116 Exodus Travel; p116 Rui Vale de Sousa/Shutterstock; pp116, 122 Nick Stubbs/Shutterstock; p117 Ciaran Edwards; p118 Rafael Ramirez Lee/Shutterstock; p119 Arturo Limon/Shutterstock; p119 Cornel Achirei/Shutterstock; p120 Albo/Shutterstock; p120 Denis Babenko/Shutterstock; p120 rubiphoto/Shutterstock; p121 Hannu Liivaar/Shutterstock; p121 Lagui/Shutterstock; pp121, 122 Jennifer Stone/Shutterstock; p122 Francisco Javier Alcerreca Gomez/Shutterstock; p122 Philip Lange/Shutterstock; p123 Daniela Schraml/Shutterstock; p123 Ettore Emanuele Fanciulli/Shutterstock; p123 Martin Trajkovski/Shutterstock; p124 Nicky Jacobs/Shutterstock; pp124, 126 Karolina Ksiazek/Shutterstock; p126 Alex James Bradwell/Shutterstock; p126 Richard Clarke/Shutterstock; p127 Andresr/Shutterstock; p127 Andrzej Gibasiewicz/Shutterstock; p128 Francisco Amaral Leitão/Shutterstock; p128 Rui Manuel Teles Gomes/Shutterstock; p128 TAOLMOR/Shutterstock; p129 Inacio Pires/Shutterstock; p129 Shootov Igor/Shutterstock; p131 Marek Slusarczyk/Shutterstock; p132 La Manga Tennis Academy; p132 Mallorca Farmhouses; p133 Siblu; p134 Jose Antonio Sanchez/Shutterstock.

Italy p139 Fantauzzi/Shutterstock; p139 Gianni Fantauzzi/Shutterstock; p139 Martin Pohlack/Shutterstock; p139 Mikhail Nekrasov/Shutterstock; p139 Shutterstock; p139, 144 Pippa West/Shutterstock; p140 Clara Natoli/Shutterstock; p141 Kasia/Shutterstock; p141 Ricardo Miguel Silva Saraiva/Shutterstock; p141 Ternovoy Dmitry/Shutterstock; p142 Alison & Alex Rippon; p142 Jason Hobbins; p143 Bruno Pagnanelli/Shutterstock; p143 Gertjan Hooljer; p143 Lori Sparkia/Shutterstock; p144 Marek Slusarczyk/Shutterstock; p144 PaintedLens/Shutterstock; p145 Amra Pasic/Shutterstock; p145 Denis Babenko/Shutterstock; p145 Eugene Mogilnikov/Shutterstock; p145 Vinicius Tupinamba/Shutterstock; p145 Yannick Luthy/Shutterstock; p146 Jennie Gray; p146 Mauro Bighin/Shutterstock; p146 Stuart Taylor/Shutterstock; p147 Angela Jones/Shutterstock; p147 Asier Villafranca/Shutterstock; p149 Danilo Ascione/Shutterstock; p150 Peter Hansen/Shutterstock; p151 Anna Nemkovich/Shutterstock; p151 Gardaland; p151 Marc Dietrich/Shutterstock; p152 Luri/Shutterstock; p153 Nathan B Dappen/Shutterstock; p154 John Hua/Shutterstock; p155 Bart Parren/Shutterstock; p155 Govert Nieuwland/Shutterstock; p155 Willem Dijkstra/Shutterstock; p160 swiss-image.ch.

Central Europe p163 BI-TC; p163 Victor Pryymachuk/Shutterstock; pp163, 167, 172, 173 swiss-image.ch; pp163, 171 Europa Park; pp164, 165 Jeffrey Van Daele/Shutterstock; p165 Marc Dietrich/Shutterstock; p165 Sarah Johnson/Shutterstock; p165 Trout 55/Shutterstock; p166 Walibi Belgium; p168 Ronald Sumners/Shutterstock; p168 waterloo1815.be; p169 Styve Reineck/Shutterstock; p170 Iryna Shpulak/Shutterstock; p170 Xufang/Shutterstock; pp170, 175 Olga Shelego/Shutterstock; p171 Elena Schweitzer/Shutterstock; p171 Emilia Kun/Shutterstock; p171 Philip Lange/Shutterstock; p173 Margaud/Shutterstock; p174 Shutterstock; p174 Wikus Otto/Shutterstock; p175 Andrea Seemann/Shutterstock; p175 sierprionka/Shutterstock; p178 Lori Sparkia/Shutterstock; p179 ©Switzerland Tourism: ST/swiss-image.ch/Robert Boesch.

Eastern Europe p183 Ioan Nicolae/Shutterstock; p183 Krkr/Shutterstock; p183 Prism 68/Shutterstock; p183 Tomisl av Stajdushar/Shutterstock; p185 Brian M Lambert/Shutterstock; p185 Cornel Achirei/Shutterstock; p185 Richard Hoffart/Shutterstock; pp185, 191 Radu Razvan/Shutterstock; p186 Shutterstock; p187 Marc C Johnson/Shutterstock; p188 Rui Vale de Sousa/Shutterstock; p188 Vova Pomartzeff/Shutterstock; p188 WH Chow/Shutterstock; p189 Anastazzo/Shutterstock; p189 Antoni o Ovejero Diaz/Shutterstock; p189 Niserin/Shutterstock; p189 Solodovnika Elena/Shutterstock; p190 Aleksander Bochenek/Shutterstock; p190 Puchan/Shutterstock; p191 Catalin Plesa/Shutterstock; p193 Croatia National Tourist Board; p193 Elisa Locci/Shutterstock; p193 Exodus; p196 Croatian Affairs; p196 Eurocamp; p196 Keycamp; p198 Ljupco Smokovski Cape Dastris/Shutterstock.

Greece and Turkey p200 Koster/Shutterstock; p200 Michael Onisiforou/Shutterstock; p200 Tsonis/Shutterstock; p201 Can Balcioglu/Shutterstock; p201 Vladimir Melnik/Shutterstock; p202 S Dmit/Shutterstock; p203 Azmil Khazali/Shutterstock; p203 Florin Cirstoc/Shutterstock; p203 James Steidl/Shutterstock; pp204, 216, 217 Exodus; p205 Bill McKelvie/Shutterstock; pp205, 217 Mark Wright; p206 David H Seymour/Shutterstock; p209 Denis Babenko/Shutterstock; p210 Ljupco Smokovski/Shutterstock; p210 Olga Shelego/Shutterstock; p212 Irina Korshunova/Shutterstock; p212 Wojciech Jaskowski/Shutterstock; p213 Graham Bloomfield/Shutterstock; p213 polartern/Shutterstock; p214 David Romero Corral/Shutterstock; p214 Jarno Gonzalez Zarraonandia/Shutterstock; p215 Brent Wong/Shutterstock; p215 Clara Natoli/Shutterstock; p218 Rebvt/Shutterstock; p219 Emil Vasilev Iliev/Shutterstock; p220 Crystal Active; p221 Shutterstock.

Scandinavia pp225, 230, 231, 243 VisitDenmark; p226 Shutterstock; p227 alexan55/Shutterstock; p227 Jaroslaw Grudzinski/Shutterstock; p227 Roman Sigaev/Shutterstock; p227 Tishenko Irina/Shutterstock; p228 Exodus; p228 Roman Krochik/Shutterstock; pp228, 233, 238, 239 Discover the World; p232 Franzelin Franz-W/Shutterstock; p232 Holger Ehlers/Shutterstock; p234 Kon-Tiki Museum; p236 Heureka; p236 Moominworld; p240 Michael Warnock/Shutterstock.

Africa pp247, 252 The Adventure Company; p249 kikoy.com; p250 Cheli & Peacock; p251 Dragoman Overland; p251 Steve Redgrave; p252 Vova Pomartzeff/Shutterstock; p253 Konstantin Baskakov/Shutterstock; p254 Renars Jurkavskis/Shutterstock; p257 Christopher Testi/Shutterstock; p257 Heritage Group; p259 alle/Shutterstock; p261 Amazon; p270 Cape Grace Hotel; p274 Chen Wei Seng/Shutterstock; p274 NEO/Shutterstock.

Asia p274 Chen Wei Seng/Shutterstock; p276 Ronen/Shutterstock; p277 Courtesy of David Shepherd; p277 Marcus Tuerner/Shutterstock; p280 Alex Brosa/Shutterstock; p280 C J Photo/Shutterstock; p280 Elisei Shafer/Shutterstock; p280 Salem Alforaih/Shutterstock; p282 Taolmor/Shutterstock; p283 Mikhail Nekrasov/Shutterstock; p284 Charlotte Moss/Shutterstock; p284 Exodus; p284 Magdalena Bujak/Shutterstock; p284 Suzanne Bickerdike/Shutterstock; p285 James Steidl/Shutterstock; p285 Simone van den Berg/Shutterstock; p285 Timothy Passmore/Shutterstock; p286 Wojcik Jaroslaw/Shutterstock; pp286, 294 Jason Maehl/Shutterstock; p290 James Stuart Griffith/Shutterstock; p291 Ke Wang/Shutterstock; p291 Sapsiwai/Shutterstock; p292 Johnny Lye/Shutterstock; p292 Lim Yong Hian/Shutterstock; p294 Perry Correll/Shutterstock; p295 Alistair Michael Thomas/Shutterstock; p295 Vova Pomortzeff/Shutterstock; p296 Szefei/Shutterstock; p299 borneojunglelodge; p301 Anna Nemkovich/Shutterstock; p301 Dennis Albert Richardson/Shutterstock.

Australia and New Zealand p305 Amra Pasic/Shutterstock; p305 WizData, inc./Shutterstock; pp305, 313 Robyn Mackenzie/Shutterstock; pp306, 307 David Franklin/Shutterstock; p307 Suzy Bennett/Shutterstock; pp307, 321 Tourism New Zealand; p309 Eric Isselée/Shutterstock; p309 javarman/Shutterstock; pp310, 323 Holger Mette/Shutterstock; p311 Ilya Genkin/Shutterstock; p311 Ximagination/Shutterstock; p312 Nicole Paton/Shutterstock; p312 Rob Ahrens/Shutterstock; p312 Susan Flashman/Shutterstock; p313 Patsy A. Jacks/Shutterstock; pp313, 315 Colin & Linda McKie/Shutterstock; p314 David Hancock/Shutterstock; p314 kwest/Shutterstock; p314 Styve Reineck/Shutterstock; p315 Peter Chafer/Shutterstock; p316 Max Earey/Shutterstock; p316 Neale Cousland/Shutterstock; p317 Ronald Sumners/Shutterstock; p318 ee Torrens/Shutterstock; p318 Lee Torrens/Shutterstock; p318 Manuel/Shutterstock; p319 Ian Scott/Shutterstock; pp319, 325 O'Reilly's Rainforest Retreat; p320 Albert H. Teich/Shutterstock; p327 New Zealand farmstays.

North America p331 Anthony Jay D. Villalon/Shutterstock; p331 Brent Reeves/Shutterstock; p331 Keith Levit/Shutterstock; p332 Robert Gubbins/Shutterstock; p332 Steffen Foerster Photography/Shutterstock; p333 Bill Kennedy/Shutterstock; p333 Nikolay Okhitin/Shutterstock; p333 Roslen Mack/Shutterstock; p333 Terekhov Igor/Shutterstock; p335 Amy Nichole Harris/Shutterstock; p335 Dhoxax/Shutterstock; pp335, 344, 345, 357 Copyright 2007 Universal Orlando. All rights reserved.; p336 Carolyn Russo/NASM, National Air and Space Museum, Smithsonian Institution; p336 Eric Long/NASM, National Air and Space Museum, Smithsonian Institution; p336 Susan Gottberg/Shutterstock; p337 Brandon Jennings/Shutterstock; p337 Donald R. Swartz/Shutterstock; p337 Jiwoon Kim/Shutterstock; p338 Chee-Onn Leong/Shutterstock; p338 Coastal Kayaking Tours; p338 Mark Yarchoan/Shutterstock; p338 Michael Rickard/Shutterstock; p339 B. Speckart/Shutterstock; p339 Harris Shiffman/Shutterstock; p339 Marc Dietrich/Shutterstock; p341 Brad Thompson/Shutterstock; p341 FloridaStock/Shutterstock; p341 Olga Skalkina/Shutterstock; p341 Valery Potapova/Shutterstock; p342 Kirk Peart Professional Imaging/Shutterstock; p343 Scott Pehrson/Shutterstock; p343 Tim Pleasant/Shutterstock; p343 Wayne Johnson/Shutterstock; p344 © Disney; p344 © Disney; p345 © SeaWorld Orlando; p346 Oksanaperkins/Shutterstock; p347 Anton Foltin/Shutterstock; p349 copeg/Shutterstock; p349 Sebastien Burel/Shutterstock; p350 Christa DeRidder/Shutterstock; p350 Kaleb Timberlake/Shutterstock; p351 Calgary Stampede; p351 Craig Mills/Shutterstock; p351 Mike Norton/Shutterstock; p351 Vail Resorts; p352 Andre Nantel/Shutterstock; p357 Sadie Lodge.

Latin America p361 Andre Nantel/Shutterstock; p361 visitmexico.com; pp361, 375 rebut/Shutterstock; p362 Stephen Coburn/Shutterstock; p363 Peter Jochems/Shutterstock; p363 Ra'id Khalil/Shutterstock; p363 Robynrg/Shutterstock; pp364, 372, 384 Atlantis Resort; p365 Alex James Bramwell/Shutterstock; p365 Sara Wheeler; pp366, 367, 374 Vora Pomartzeff/Shutterstock; p368 7877074640/Shutterstock; p368 Tom C Amon/Shutterstock; p369 Carolina K Smith/Shutterstock; p369 TTphoto/Shutterstock; p371 Dhoxax/Shutterstock; p372 Julie Angove; p375 Adam Hewitt Smith/Shutterstock; p376 Bryan Busovicki/Shutterstock; p376 David Ranson/Shutterstock; p377 Joel Shown/Shutterstock; p378 Celso Popo/Shutterstock; p378 Marcaux/Shutterstock; p379 Tamar Project; p380 Jonathan Brizendine/Shutterstock; p382 Dr Morley Read/Shutterstock; pp382, 383 Shutterstock; p385 Maria Veras/Shutterstock; p386 Andrey Amyangor/Shutterstock; p386 Roman Sigaer/Shutterstock.

Credits

Footprint credits

Editor: Alan Murphy
Text editor: Tim Jollands
Map editor: Sarah Sorensen
Layout and production: Patrick Dawson, Angus Dawson, Emma Bryers

Managing Director: Andy Riddle
Publisher: Patrick Dawson
Editorial: Felicity Laughton, Nicola Jones, Jo Williams, Sophie Blacksell
Cartography: Robert Lunn, Kevin Feeney
Cover design: Robert Lunn
Design: Mytton Williams
Sales and marketing: Hannah Bonnell
Business Development: Zoë Jackson
Finance and administration: Elizabeth Taylor

Photography credits

Front cover: main image Terry Williams/Getty Images; girl on float, William Gray; dune running, William Gray; bodyboarding, Andre Jenny/Alamy; elephant safari, Exodus; ski tow, StockShot/Alamy; boat, William Gray.
Back cover: maasai man, Wildlife Worldwide; rock pool, William Gray; theme park ride, ©SeaWorld Orlando; viking boy, VisitDenmark; diving, Exodus.

Print

Manufactured in Italy by EuroGrafica
Pulp from sustainable forests

The colour maps are not intended to have any political significance.

Every effort has been made to ensure that the facts in this guidebook are accurate. However, travellers should note that places change, owners move on and properties close or are sold. Travellers should also obtain advice from consulates, airlines etc about travel and visa requirements before travelling. The authors and publishers cannot accept responsibility for any loss, injury or inconvenience however caused. See also page 5.

Publishing information

Travel with Kids
1st edition
© Footprint Handbooks Ltd
November 2007

ISBN 978-1-906098-03-2
CIP DATA: A catalogue record for this book is available from the British Library

® Footprint Handbooks and the Footprint mark are a registered trademark of Footprint Handbooks Ltd

Published by Footprint

6 Riverside Court
Lower Bristol Road
Bath BA2 3DZ, UK
T +44 (0)1225 469141
F +44 (0)1225 469461
discover@footprintbooks.com
www.footprintbooks.com

Footprint feedback

We try as hard as we can to make each Footprint guide as up to date as possible but, of course, things always change. If you want to let us know about your experiences – good, bad or ugly – then don't delay, go to www.footprintbooks.com and send in your comments.